JOHN, JESUS, AND HISTORY, VOLUME 2:
ASPECTS OF HISTORICITY IN THE FOURTH GOSPEL

Society of Biblical Literature

Early Christianity and Its Literature

Gail R. O'Day, General Editor

Editorial Board

Number 2

JOHN, JESUS, AND HISTORY, VOLUME 2:
ASPECTS OF HISTORICITY IN THE FOURTH GOSPEL

JOHN, JESUS, AND HISTORY, VOLUME 2:
ASPECTS OF HISTORICITY
IN THE FOURTH GOSPEL

Edited by

Paul N. Anderson,

Felix Just, S.J.,

and

Tom Thatcher

Society of Biblical Literature
Atlanta

JOHN, JESUS, AND HISTORY, VOLUME 2:
ASPECTS OF HISTORICITY IN THE FOURTH GOSPEL

Library of Congress Cataloging-in-Publication Data

John, Jesus, and history / edited by Paul N. Anderson, Felix Just, and Tom Thatcher.
    p. cm. — (Society of Biblical Literature symposium series ; 44)
  Contents: v. 1. Critical appraisals of critical views.
  Includes bibliographical references and indexes.
  ISBN: 978-1-58983-293-0 (paper binding : alk. paper)
  1. Bible. N.T. John—Criticism, interpretation, etc.—Congresses. 2. Jesus Christ—Historicity—Congresses. I. Anderson, Paul N., 1956– II. Just, Felix. III. Thatcher, Tom, 1967–.
  BS2615.52.J65 2007
  226.5'067—dc22
                                      2007035191

Volume 2: ISBN 978-1-58983-392-0 (Society of Biblical Literature Early Christianity and its literature ; 2)

Contents

Abbreviations ix

Aspects of Historicity in the Fourth Gospel: Phase Two of the John,
Jesus, and History Project
Tom Thatcher 1

PART 1: ASPECTS OF HISTORICITY IN JOHN 1–4

Introduction to Part 1: Aspects of Historicity in John 1–4
Paul N. Anderson 9

"We Beheld His Glory!" (John 1:14)
Craig S. Keener 15

Jesus' Bethsaida Disciples: A Study in Johannine Origins
Mark Appold 27

"Destroy This Temple": Issues of History in John 2:13–22
James F. McGrath 35

John as Witness and Friend
Mary Coloe 45

The Symbology of the Serpent in the Gospel of John
James H. Charlesworth 63

The Woman at the Well: John's Portrayal of the Samaritan Mission
Susan Miller 73

The Royal Official and the Historical Jesus
Peter J. Judge 83

Aspects of Historicity in John 1–4: A Response
Craig R. Koester 93

PART 2: ASPECTS OF HISTORICITY IN JOHN 5–12

Introduction to Part 2: Aspects of Historicity in John 5–12
Paul N. Anderson 107

The Jewish Feasts and Questions of Historicity in John 5–12
Brian D. Johnson 117

Feeding the Five Thousand and the Eucharist
Craig A. Evans 131

Jesus and the Galilean 'Am Ha'arets: Fact, Johannine Irony, or Both?
Sean Freyne.. 139

The Pool of Siloam: The Importance of the New Discoveries for Our
Understanding of Ritual Immersion in Late Second Temple
Judaism and the Gospel of John
Urban C. von Wahlde 155

The Overrealized Expulsion in the Gospel of John
Edward W. Klink III.. 175

The Bethany Family in John 11–12: History or Fiction?
Richard Bauckham 185

What's in a Name? Rethinking the Historical Figure of the Beloved
Disciple in the Fourth Gospel
Ben Witherington III... 203

On Not Unbinding the Lazarus Story: The Nexus of History and
Theology in John 11:1–44
Derek M. H. Tovey 213

Aspects of Historicity in John 5–12: A Response
Paul N. Anderson 225

PART 3: ASPECTS OF HISTORICITY IN JOHN 13–21

Introduction to Part 3: Aspects of Historicity in John 13–21
Paul N. Anderson 245

John 13: Of Footwashing and History
Jaime Clark-Soles... 255

John's Last Supper and the Resurrection Dialogues
Bas van Os... 271

Imitating Jesus: An Inclusive Approach to the Ethics of the
Historical Jesus and John's Gospel
Richard A. Burridge 281

The Historical Plausibility of John's Passion Dating
Mark A. Matson 291

At the Court of the High Priest: History and Theology in John 18:13–24
Helen K. Bond 313

See My Hands and Feet: Fresh Light on a Johannine Midrash
Jeffrey Paul Garcia 325

Peter's Rehabilitation (John 21:15–19) and the Adoption of Sinners:
Remembering Jesus and Relecturing John
Michael Labahn 335

John 21:24–25: The Johannine *Sphragis*
R. Alan Culpepper 349

Aspects of Historicity in John 13–21: A Response
Gail R. O'Day 365

CONCLUSION

Aspects of Historicity in the Fourth Gospel: Consensus and Convergences
Paul N. Anderson 379

Epilogue: Whence, Where, and Whither for John, Jesus, and History?
Felix Just, S.J. 387

Works Cited 393

Contributors 421

Index of Ancient Sources 427

Index of Modern Authors and Authorities 449

Abbreviations

AB	Anchor Bible
ABD	*Anchor Bible Dictionary*. Edited by David Noel Freedman. 6 vols. New York: Doubleday, 1992.
ABRL	Anchor Bible Reference Library
ACNT	Augsburg Commentary on the New Testament
Ag. Ap.	Josephus, *Against Apion*
AGJU	Arbeiten zur Geschichte des antiken Judentums und des Urchristentums
AnBib	Analecta biblica
ANF	Ante-Nicene Fathers
ANRW	*Aufstieg und Niedergang der römischen Welt: Geschichte und Kultur Roms im Spiegel der neueren Forschung*. Part 2, *Principat*. Edited by Hildegard Temporini and Wolfgang Haase. Berlin: de Gruyter, 1972–.
Ant.	Josephus, *Jewish Antiquities*
BAR	*Biblical Archaeology Review*
BBR	*Bulletin for Biblical Research*
BECNT	Baker Exegetical Commentary on the New Testament
BETL	Bibliotheca ephemeridum theologicarum lovaniensium
Bib	*Biblica*
BibInt	*Biblical Interpretation*
BIS	Biblical Interpretation Series
BJRL	*Bulletin of the John Rylands University Library of Manchester*
BNTC	Black's New Testament Commentaries
BRev	*Bible Review*
BZNW	*Beiheft zur Zeitschrift für die neutestamentliche Wissenschaft*
CBQ	*Catholic Biblical Quarterly*
CBQMS	Catholic Biblical Quarterly Monograph Series
ConBNT	Coniectanea biblica: New Testament Series
CCEL	Corpus Christianorum Ecclesiarum Latinum (Turnhout: Brepols, 1965)
CH	*Church History*
CIL	*Corpus inscriptionum latinorum*

DJD	Discoveries in the Judean Desert
ETL	*Ephemerides theologicae lovanienses*
ExpTim	*Expository Times*
FRLANT	Forschungen zur Religion und Literatur des Alten und Neuen Testaments
GBS	Guides to Biblical Scholarship
Haer.	Irenaeus of Lyons, *Contra haereses* (*Against Heresies*)
HALOT	Koehler, Ludwig, Walter Baumgartner, and Johann J. Stamm, *The Hebrew and Aramaic Lexicon of the Old Testament*. Translated and edited under the supervision of M. E. J. Richardson. 4 vols. Leiden: Brill, 1994–1999.
Hist. eccl.	Eusebius of Caesarea, *Historia ecclesiastica* (*History of the Church*)
HTR	*Harvard Theological Review*
ICC	International Critical Commentaries
IEJ	*Israel Exploration Journal*
Int	*Interpretation*
J.W.	Josephus, *Jewish War*
JBL	*Journal of Biblical Literature*
JETS	*Journal of the Evangelical Theological Society*
JJS	*Journal of Jewish Studies*
JSHJ	*Journal for the Study of the Historical Jesus*
JSNT	*Journal for the Study of the New Testament*
JSNTSup	Journal for the Study of the New Testament Supplement Series
JTS	*Journal of Theological Studies*
LCL	Loeb Classical Library
LNTS	Library of New Testament Studies
LSJ	Liddell, Henry George, Robert Scott, and Henry Stuart Jones, *A Greek-English Lexicon*. 9th ed. with revised supplement. Oxford: Clarendon, 1996.
LXX	Septuagint
NCBC	New Cambridge Bible Commentary
NIB	*The New Interpreter's Bible: General Articles and Introduction, Commentary, and Reflections for Each Book of the Bible*. 13 vols. Nashville: Abingdon, 1994–2004.
NIGTC	New International Greek Testament Commentary
NovT	*Novum Testamentum*
NovTSup	Novum Testamentum Supplements
NPNF	Nicene and Post-Nicene Fathers
NTS	*New Testament Studies*
NTTS	New Testament Tools and Studies
OTP	*Old Testament Pseudepigrapha*. Edited by James H. Charlesworth. 2 vols. New York: Doubleday, 1983–1985.
RB	*Revue biblique*

RBL	*Review of Biblical Literature*
RTL	*Revue theologique de Louvain*
SBLDS	Society of Biblical Literature Dissertation Series
SBLRBS	Society of Biblical Literature Resources for Biblical Study
SBLSBS	Society of Biblical Literature Sources for Biblical Study
SBLSymS	Society of Biblical Literature Symposium Series
SNTSMS	Society for New Testament Studies Monograph Series
SSEJC	Studies in Early Judaism and Christianity
SwJT	*Southwest Journal of Theology*
TDNT	*Theological Dictionary of the New Testament.* Edited by Gerhard Kittel and Gerhard Friedrich. Translated by Geoffrey W. Bromiley. 10 vols. Grand Rapids: Eerdmans, 1964–1976.
TSAJ	Texte und Studien zum antiken Judentum
TTS	Theologische Texte und Studien
TynBul	*Tyndale Bulletin*
TZ	*Theologische Zeitschrift*
UTB	Urban Taschenbuch
VC	*Vigiliae christianae*
WBC	Word Biblical Commentary
WUNT	Wissenschaftliche Untersuchungen zum Neuen Testament
ZNW	*Zeitschrift für die neutestamentliche Wissenschaft und die Kunde der älteren Kirche*

Aspects of Historicity in the Fourth Gospel: Phase Two of the John, Jesus, and History Project

Tom Thatcher

This book is the second in a series of volumes that have emerged from the deliberations of the John, Jesus, and History Group in the Society of Biblical Literature. Volume 1, subtitled *Critical Appraisals of Critical Views* (Anderson, Just, Thatcher 2007), featured papers from the Group's 2002–2004 meetings, which focused largely on the state of the field and problems of method. Volume 2 addresses *Aspects of Historicity* in the Fourth Gospel, the theme of the Group's 2005–2007 program. Several more books are scheduled to emerge from the project, including a third collection of essays that will reflect the deliberations of the 2008–2010 John, Jesus, and History sessions, as well as collaborative efforts with other research groups. While the number and range of these publications reflect the current renewal of interest in the Fourth Gospel as a possible source for understanding Jesus' life and ministry, the ultimate success of the John, Jesus, and History Project will be measured in terms of its impact on research into Gospel historiography and historical Jesus studies over the next several decades.

The John, Jesus, and History Project was founded in 2002 to create a venue for serious reconsideration of the historical character of the Johannine tradition and the role that the Fourth Gospel might play in future quests for the historical Jesus. While John's story was once treated as a comprehensive framework for harmonizing the Gospels, recent Jesus research has aligned itself with Bultmann's dictum that "the Gospel of John cannot be taken into account at all as a source for the teaching of Jesus" (1958, 12). Both of these approaches, however, overlook more problems than they solve. The present collection and the larger John, Jesus, and History Project are both driven by the belief that a dismissal, either casual or programmatic, of a significant body of evidence is just as inadequate for serious inquiry into the life and teachings of Jesus as an uncritical acceptance of John's presentation. As will be seen, the contributors to this book take a variety of positions on the particular historical value of the Fourth Gospel's presentation of the ministry of Jesus, yet all are agreed that the Johannine rendering cannot be dismissed categorically simply because it is Johannine. Put another way, regardless of any specific conclusions, a reconsideration of the Fourth Gospel's historical value promises to shed new light on the Johannine writings, Jesus studies, and the methodological premises underlying the study of Christian origins.

In addition to challenging prevalent historical-critical approaches to—or dismissals of—the Fourth Gospel, the John, Jesus, and History Project promises to inform the burgeoning field of Johannine studies in several important ways. First, a serious reconsideration of the Fourth Gospel's historical location and relationship to the originating events of the Christian movement provides an important balance to the swell of methodological approaches that have emerged in the past two decades in the wake of the pivotal works of Alan Culpepper, Fernando Segovia, and other literary theorists who have focused on John's story and its readers. Readings that focus on the narrative structure and real-world impact of the biblical texts have offered significant new insights into the theology, rhetorical strategies, and latent implications of the Johannine literature. Ultimately, however, the Gospel of John remains a text from the distant past, and considerations of its originative character promise to anchor contemporary readings in the historical realities of the contexts from which it emerged.

Second, even those approaches that are interested primarily in narrative dynamics and reader responses must reckon with the fact that the Gospel of John, more than any other ancient Christian document, is driven by a deeply historical consciousness. Perhaps the greatest irony of the Johannine literature lies in the fact that the Fourth Gospel offers "the most [theologically] mature" outlook on Christ in the New Testament while also making the most explicit claims to direct contact with the historical Jesus (see John 19:35; 21:24; quotation from Robinson 1985, 342). Regardless of the historical value of any portion of the text, then, any attempt to comprehend the Fourth Gospel on its own terms necessarily requires a serious consideration of this book's relation to the actual past. For that reason, we have welcomed papers that express any stance regarding John's historicity, both for and against it, but we have requested all our contributors to explain why their judgments are valid and to comment on degrees of plausibility where appropriate.

As the essays in the present volume reveal, the John, Jesus, and History Project also promises to offer substantial new insights for studies of the historical Jesus. Of course, few Jesus scholars will affirm the historicity of certain aspects of John's presentation, particularly its more exalted christological elements. At the same time, however, the Fourth Gospel promises to add important new strokes and shades to the portraits that have emerged in the course of the "third quest" for the historical Jesus, as well as some details that have been side-stepped in previous quests. John's outlook on Jesus' journeys from Galilee to Judea and possibly also Samaria, and his varying receptions in these different regions, raise important questions about the scope and duration of Jesus' career. While the Fourth Gospel says very little about Jesus' proclamation of the kingdom of God, it provides important perspectives on issues that would inform our understanding of the earliest kingdom movement:

Jesus' connection to John the Baptist; the structure of the movement, as evident from Jesus' relationships with the first disciples; aspects of Jesus' healing ministry, particularly his strategic use of healings to challenge popular beliefs about illness, blessing, and Sabbath (see esp. John 5 and 9); and the complex interface between the kingdom of God and the dominion of Caesar. The Fourth Gospel also brings to the foreground Jesus' ambivalent stance toward the Jerusalem temple and its weighty institutional apparatus, the aristocratic Jewish priesthood, the Mosaic law, and other core elements of the symbolic universe of the mainstream Judaism of his day. John's presentation of Jesus' passion, and of Jewish and Roman involvement in those events, is now widely regarded as an important supplement to the Synoptic perspective. In all these ways and many more, the Fourth Gospel promises to substantially enrich, and perhaps even to challenge, studies of Jesus' life that have been based almost exclusively on the Synoptic perspective.

Finally, the John, Jesus, and History Project has consistently called for a significant reevaluation of the goals and methods of New Testament criticism. For more than a century now, the study of the Gospels and Christian origins has been informed by methodological tools that categorically privilege the Synoptics at the expense of the Gospel of John. Form-, source-, and redaction-critical approaches have served Synoptic studies well, but they are less serviceable when applied to the Fourth Gospel. The historical criteria that have emerged from Synoptic quests for Jesus function to exclude Johannine material a priori from the mix, and images of early Christianity forged upon the anvil of the Two-Source Theory and its corollary premises programmatically treat the Fourth Gospel as a second-class citizen. The marginalization of the Johannine evidence is particularly evident in studies that privilege noncanonical Gospels while essentially ignoring the Fourth Gospel, even in cases where these other Gospels betray significant points of contact with John's thought world and mode of presentation. Any serious reconsideration of the Fourth Gospel's historical value necessarily requires a retooling of these methods and the development of new conceptual frameworks that can adequately address the special problems associated with the Johannine witness. In the process, significant new methodological insights may be gained, and new and more adequate forms of historical criticism may emerge. At the very least, John's unique witness promises to enrich understandings of primitive Christianity by preserving the memories and insights of a distinct and influential trajectory—one that interacted variously with both heterodox and the emerging orthodox streams of the developing faith.

In view of the breadth of this project and its potential implications, and especially because of the many attending challenges and obstacles, the first three meetings of the John, Jesus, and History Consultation (2002–2004) highlighted and addressed preliminary philosophical and methodological problems associated with any reevaluation of the Fourth Gospel's historicity and historical location. The papers offered in these sessions were published in the SBL Symposium Series under the title *John, Jesus, and History, Volume 1: Critical Appraisals* of *Critical Views* (Anderson, Just, Thatcher 2007). As the subtitle suggests, the essays in that book focused on the history of research, methodological considerations, potential barriers to success, and possible ways forward. Both the book and the conference discussions that it summarized were unified by the critical engagement of two closely connected themes: the *dehistoricization of John* and the *de-Johannification of Jesus*. Stated as questions: (1) How and why did John come to be viewed as "the spiritual Gospel," a theological allegory with no real connection to, or even interest in, the actual events of Jesus' career? (2) How and why did contemporary reconstructions of Jesus' life and ministry come to treat John's witness as almost categorically irrelevant to their projects, to such an extent that some of the most significant recent studies of the historical Jesus scarcely mention the Fourth Gospel at all? The various essays in volume 1, all by premier scholars representing an international collection of experts, reflect the diversity of opinions within the guild, and they underscore the need for sustained discussion of specific problems and passages. In sum, the tandem disparagement of the Fourth Gospel's historicity and potential value to Jesus research is by no means an open-and-shut case. More work is yet to be done.

After receiving extensive interest and feedback from members of the Consultation, the John, Jesus, and History steering committee sought to extend the project for at least six more years by moving beyond broad theoretical questions to case studies of specific points where the Gospel of John may or may not shed new light on Jesus' career. With the approval of the SBL program committee, the Consultation was reconfigured as an ongoing research Group, and the scope of the project was now conceived with two additional phases interacting with the dual themes of the methodological analysis laid out in the first phase: the dehistoricization of John and the de-Johannification of Jesus. Thus, phase two of the project (2005–2007) focused on *aspects of historicity in John*, while phase three (2008–2010) will feature *glimpses of Jesus through the Johannine lens* (the passion narrative, 2008; the works of Jesus, 2009; the words of Jesus, 2010). Following this outline, for phase two the Fourth Gospel was divided into three sections, with topics and events native to each segment creating a framework for discussion in the John, Jesus, and History sessions at a national SBL meeting. Thus, the 2005 meetings highlighted John 1–4, the 2006 sessions focused on John 5–12, and the 2007 meetings emphasized John 13–21. Each annual meeting included two sessions: one featuring invited papers by specialists on topics of note; and the other an "open" session representing the best offerings selected from a general call for papers. The results of the six sessions from phase two of the John, Jesus, and History Project are represented in the present volume, and their emphasis on historical issues that emerge organically from the Fourth Gospel's presentation is reflected in the subtitle, *Aspects of Historicity in the Gospel of John*. To unify the discussion and identify common threads, three leading Johannine scholars were asked to respond to each group of papers. These responses are contributed by Craig Koester, Paul Anderson, and Gail O'Day, who further the inquiry by not only evaluating the papers below but also by contributing their own judgments.

The organization of the present volume reflects both the goals and logic of the 2005–2007 discussions and the varying approaches and perspectives of the contributors. Thus, the essays in part 1, "Aspects of Historicity in John 1–4," treat issues that emerge from the Prologue and from John's accounts of the call of the disciples, the temple incident, the Samaritan mission, and the healing of the royal official's son—all of which add substantially to the Synoptic portrait of Jesus' career. Part 2, "Aspects of Historicity in John 5–12," features papers on Jesus' participation in the Jerusalem festivals, the feeding of the five thousand, the healing at Siloam, the relationship between Jesus' followers and the synagogue, Jesus' prominent female disciples Mary and Martha, the Lazarus miracle, and the identity of the mysterious Beloved Disciple whose witness is said to underlie John's presentation (see John 21:24). Part 3, "Aspects of Historicity in John 13–21," moves to the final hours of Jesus' life to cover those chapters of the Fourth Gospel that include many of the closest parallels to the Synoptic accounts. Studies here explore the events of the upper room, including the footwashing and Jesus' Farewell Discourse, the chronology of the passion, Jesus' trials and death, and possible echoes of Jesus' ministry in John 21. As a means of introducing the historical issues especially pertinent to each of these three parts, Paul Anderson has outlined seven or eight pressing issues—both for and against John's historicity—in each. He then introduces each of the essays and their authors, connecting their approaches with the larger set of issues, and provides a helpful analysis of consensus and convergences at the end. As he did for volume 1, Felix Just, a founding member of the project and co-editor of its volumes, closes the collection with an epilogue reflecting upon the advances made in volume 2 and commenting upon the next phase and future directions of the John, Jesus, and History Project.

In closing, I want to express my gratitude for being allowed to serve as chair and co-chair of the Group for the last six years, and also for the privilege of continuing to serve with co-chairs Paul Anderson and Jaime Clark-Soles as an administrative facilitator of the Project. In addition, the steering committee of the John, Jesus, and History Group—which includes Jaime Clark-Soles, Alan Culpepper, Mary Coloe, D. Moody Smith, Felix Just, Paul Anderson and myself—would like to extend our most cordial thanks to the many people who have made this project much more successful than we ever imagined it could be. First and especially, we are grateful for the many excellent papers that were offered by the contributors to this volume and for the many more very good proposals that we were not able to include on the program. The quality and quantity of this work, along with the continuing large attendance at the Group's annual sessions, indicates the relevance of the John, Jesus, and History Project. Second, we appreciate the ongoing support of Matthew Collins and the SBL office staff, who have gone out of their way to accommodate the Group's needs and to ensure that our meetings and discussions enjoy adequate resources. Finally, we are grateful to Bob Buller and the staff of SBL Publications for their vision and support of our publishing program. Bob's enthusiasm and encouragement have made these first two volumes possible, and we look forward to several more publications that will reflect our further deliberations.

PART 1
ASPECTS OF HISTORICITY IN JOHN 1–4

Introduction to Part 1:
Aspects of Historicity in John 1–4

Paul N. Anderson

John 1–4 covers the beginning of Jesus' ministry, including his being pointed out by John the Baptist in the Transjordan region and his being joined by five disciples (John 1), Jesus' first sign performed at the wedding feast in Cana of Galilee and his prophetic demonstration in the temple (John 2), Jesus' dialogue with Nicodemus and further testimony about his being the anticipated Messiah by John the Baptist (John 3), and Jesus' dialogue with the woman at the well, her effective mission to the Samaritans, and his second sign performed in Galilee, the healing of a royal official's son from afar (John 4). While space will not allow all the historical questions in the Fourth Gospel to be mentioned, let alone addressed, several major issues in each of its three parts will be introduced in service to the contributions made by the essays in each part. As such, distinctive features of the Johannine presentation of the beginning of Jesus' ministry raise questions—both for and against—aspects of historicity in John 1–4.

First, the Fourth Gospel begins with a christological hymn—a communal confession of Jesus as the divine agency of God, who as *logos*, light, and the only-begotten Son of the Father has made it possible for those who receive him to receive life and inclusion into the family of God (John 1:1–18). This, of course, is a cosmic itinerary rather than a mundane one, so historians have often dismissed the rest of the narrative as a theological construct rather than a historical one. Given its similarities to the hymnic confession in 1 John 1:1–4, however, the Johannine Prologue appears to reflect a corporate response to content of the narrative, and it was likely added to the Johannine Gospel as a later introduction, rather than being the touchstone from which the original narrative flowed. Even so, emphases upon the incarnation of the Word (John 1:14), which has been seen, touched, and heard (1 John 1:1–3), show an interest in the physical and mundane ministry of Jesus, and appeals to firsthand encounter function to substantiate the Johannine witness in the Prologue and elsewhere (John 19:35; 21:24).

Second, the calling of the disciples is considerably different from presentations in the Synoptic Gospels. Instead of featuring a programmatic singling out of twelve men to be his followers matching the symbolic number of the twelve tribes of Israel, a handful of John the Baptist's followers in the Fourth Gospel leave him and follow Jesus as a factor of John's witness and their discovery. Here, issues of theology and rhetorical interests engage Synoptic and Johannine studies alike, requiring historical inquiry in more than one direction. While the Jesus of history probably did call twelve disciples (described simply as "the twelve" in John 6:67), the programmatic feature of the twelve is portrayed as playing organizational functions within the early church (Acts 1:15–26), making the less formal presentation in John a plausible alternative to the more institutional view of the disciples in the Synoptics. On the other hand, if the Johannine Gospel were indeed written by a member of the twelve or their associates, as John 21 claims, why is there not a fuller presentation of their calling within it, and why are only half of the disciples mentioned by name?

Third, the sign performed by Jesus at the wedding feast (John 2:1–11) is presented as "the first of his signs, in Cana of Galilee," whereupon his disciples believe (2:11). While turning water into wine is found in folkloric accounts of the time (Apollonius of Tyana), this miracle is not found in the Synoptics. It shows Jesus as beginning his ministry with a "party miracle," seeming to render a portrait of Jesus as "God walking on the face of the earth" (Käsemann 1968, 73; see also 9) rather than the historical Jesus of dusty Palestine. Indeed, the declaration of the steward that the best is saved for last (2:10) heralds both the culminating sign of the raising of Lazarus and, finally, the resurrection of Jesus, so theology seems to trump history on this account. Then again, the mundane character of the details in this sign is also striking: the purification jars are made of stone, and their capacity (twenty or thirty gallons, 2:6) is explicitly emphasized. If the emphasis is upon the first of Jesus' signs—certainly a contrast to the exorcism of Mark 1:23–28—it may imply an independent source or even an alternative beginning of Jesus' ministry from a Johannine perspective.

Fourth, the temple incident is presented at the beginning of Jesus' ministry in John, whereas in the Synoptics it serves as the culminating offense of Jesus' ministry leading to his arrest, trials, and death. The primary way scholars have approached this difference in recent decades is to consign John's presentation to the canons of theology and spiritualization and the Synoptic presentation to chronology and history. This approach, however, creates new problems. Later references to the signs and things Jesus had done in Jerusalem at the feast (2:23; 3:2; 4:45) and the increasing opposition in Jerusalem (John 5; 7–10) suggest a sequential understanding of the events portrayed in John 2:13–23; further, since Matthew and Luke followed Mark's single visit to Jerusalem, the dissonance is not three-against-one but a John-versus-Mark contrast. Given the fact that Mark locates all the Jerusalem events and debates together, between Mark 11 and 16, Mark's "chronology" must be seen as a narrative construct rather than a strictly historical one. So, was John's location of the temple incident a factor of theology instead of history, or was Mark's? Harmonizing here does not work; one must choose between the Synoptics and John.

Fifth, in contrast to the Synoptics, where Jesus' ministry is presented as beginning after the Baptist's imprisonment, both John the Baptist and Jesus are presented as ministering simultaneously in John 1 and 3—perhaps even correcting the sequential reference in Mark 1:14 (John 3:24). This raises questions, of course, about the ministries of John and Jesus, particularly how their ministries should be seen as similar and/or distinctive. An intriguing contrast between the Synoptic and Johannine presentations of the prophetic typologies of Elijah and Moses is that in the Synoptics John the Baptist is presented as fulfilling the roles of Elijah and "the Prophet," whereas in John 1:20–21 he denies being either the Christ, Elijah, or the Prophet. These typologies are fulfilled instead by the Johannine Jesus; might such an interest explain this particular Synoptic-Johannine contrast? Clearly, the Baptist's role in the Fourth Gospel is to point to Jesus as the Messiah, and while that witness would have played well among the developing tradition's audience, might it also reflect a primitive traditional memory?

Sixth, Jesus' dialogues with Nicodemus and the Samaritan woman are distinctive to John, and they clearly reflect the constructive work of the Johannine narrator. Does this mean, however, that their origin was fictive rather than historical? In addition, the dialogues with Jesus in other parts of John (with the crowd, the Jews, the disciples, and Peter in John 6; with the Jewish leaders in Jerusalem in John 5 and 7–10; with the blind man and others in John 9; with Peter and other disciples in John 13–16; with Pilate in John 18–19; with Mary Magdalene and Thomas in John 20; and with Peter and the Beloved Disciple in John 21) show a distinctive Johannine pattern of construction. Misunderstanding discussants often serve a rhetorical function, whereby Jesus corrects their flawed notions and presents them (and the reader) with a more enlightened view coinciding with the perspective of the Evangelist. Like the dialogues of Plato, the historical question regarding the Johannine dialogues centers on the question as to whether the teachings of the master or the teachings of the narrator are here primarily reflected.

Seventh, several distinctive images in John show a strikingly Jewish character rather than a Hellenistic one. While the symbol of the serpent lifted up on a pole would have played well among Hellenistic audiences familiar with the healing claims of the Asclepius cult in Asia Minor and elsewhere in the Greco-Roman world, Jesus' reference to Moses' action in John 3:14–15 shows a clear connection with Num 21:8–9, suggesting a Jewish origin of the metaphor. Further, while Jesus' engagement with the Samaritans is minimal in the Synoptics (with some exceptions in Luke), John's presentation of Jesus' traveling through Samaria on his way to and from Jerusalem is a geographical likelihood, and John's presentation of the tensions between Jews and Samaritans reflects historical knowledge of socioreligious realities. Archaeologically, the site of Jacob's well at Sychar and the worship site upon Mount Gerizim also confirm the topographical realism of the events, but the fact of these narratives' omission from the Synoptics makes historical questions understandable.

Eighth, the "second sign that Jesus did after coming from Judea to Galilee" (4:46–54) involves a healing quite similar to the healing of the centurion's servant in the Q tradition (Matt 8:5–13; Luke 7:1–10). In both cases, the official is from Capernaum, the healing of his son/servant is performed from afar, and the role of faith is significant. Was this the same event presented in different ways? If so, which presentation is more a factor of historical knowledge and/or traditional development: the Synoptic account or the Johannine? Within Johannine studies, the numeration of the "second sign" has been taken as a reference to a hypothetical signs source, but what if the numeration reflects a dialogue with Mark? Rather than seeing the healing of Simon Peter's mother-in-law as the first healing performed by Jesus, might the Johannine reference to the second sign imply an earlier healing miracle so as to present the earlier ministry of Jesus before the events narrated in Mark 1:30–31? Indeed, Matthew also locates the healing from afar just prior to the healing of Peter's mother-in-law (Matt 8:14–15), so if sequential intentionality was a factor in the Johannine ordering, it was not alone.

While not all of these historical issues are addressed directly by the contributors to part 1, many of them are. Craig S. Keener launches our investigation of aspects of historicity in John 1–4 with an analysis of the Johannine Prologue. Rather than focus on the poetic and cultic features of this poetic composition, Keener notes the emphases upon firsthand encounter and connectedness to what has been seen and heard in the ministry of Jesus. Given that the first Johannine Epistle expands upon the firsthand encounters with the fleshly Jesus in whom the glory of God is beheld, Johannine rootedness in experience extends from encounters with the Jesus of history to connectedness with the Christ of faith (see Keener 2007). In that sense, the Johannine narrative intentionally bridges the gap between the historical ministry of Jesus and other audiences separated by time and space.

Mark Appold then contributes an important historical analysis of Bethsaida, the hometown of three of Jesus' followers. Not only does Bethsaida figure prominently in the Markan tradition around the feeding narratives (see Appold 2007), but even more so is it featured in the Johannine story as an important location in relation to Jesus' followers. As a result of archaeological finds over the last several decades, we see now that Bethsaida was more than a fishing village. It was the locus of a Hellenistic and Jewish nexus, explaining the outreach of Philip to the Greek visitors to Jerusalem (John 12:20–21) and later stories of his missionary outreach in Asia Minor (Eusebius, *Hist. eccl.* 3.31). Even Peter's role as a bridge between later Jewish Christians and Greek Christians would have been impacted by his having come from a culturally blended town, and personal knowledge of Andrew's, Peter's, and Philip's place of origin bears intriguing historical implications.

Taking up the issue of Johannine chronology, James F. McGrath casts valuable light on the distinctively Johannine contribution to our understanding of the temple incident in Jerusalem. Indeed, John, Mark, and tersely in Thomas

(Gos. Thom. 71) provide three independent presentations of the event, and material distinctive to John contributes valuable historical content that would otherwise be lost. In particular, because the length of time it has taken to build the temple mentioned in John 2:20 coincides with a dating of the event around 27 or 28 C.E., this gives one pause before ascribing the Johannine early rendering of the event as "rooted in theological interests" alone. While McGrath stops short of declaring either John's early presentation or Mark's later one as the more historically plausible, he sides with John's multiple-visit-to-Jerusalem itinerary of Jesus as the more plausible—suggesting the need for a critical appraisal of Mark's "chronology." Indeed, the Jerusalem crowd in Mark 14:58 and 15:29 declares that they had heard what Jesus declared, that he would raise up the destroyed temple in three days (a detail found only in John 2:19); with further assists from Paul and Thomas, the Johannine account of the temple incident deserves a second look in terms of its historicity.

Mary Coloe then plies her exegetical skills to the Johannine presentation of John the Baptist. Her analysis not only challenges the Synoptic-derived view that Jesus' ministry got going only after John's arrest, but she shows how Johannine and Synoptic presentations alike show John as the friend of the bridegroom, who came to make Jesus known. In her judgment, the Baptist's ceding the Elijah typology in favor of Jesus' fulfilling that role—as presented in the Fourth Gospel over and against the Synoptics—is a warranted move, while his plausible embracing of the role of the voice of one crying in the wilderness and preparing the way of the Lord (Isa 40:3) is most lucidly presented in the Johannine rendering. Coloe shows how the artistic presentation of John's witness to Jesus nonetheless contributes significantly to historical understandings of his work, as well as its relation to the historical ministry of Jesus.

In his essay, James H. Charlesworth brings to bear the fruit of his major treatment of the religious backdrop of the serpent typology employed in John 3 (2010) with a special focus on challenging prevalent interpretations with his own set of theses. Because this symbol occurs only in the Fourth Gospel and is highly theological, some claim that its origin lay in the theologizing interest of the Evangelist rather than a traditional Jesus memory. Because the serpent is often associated with temptation and death, some overlook its redemptive associations in John 3. Because the uplifting action refers to the cross, some deny any association with Jesus' resurrection. Finally, because the serpent motif was associated with the Asclepius cult, some assume it had a Hellenistic origin rather than a Palestinian one. In Charlesworth's argument, each of these views is flawed. The serpent typology of John 3 connects the life-giving work of Jesus with the action of Moses in Num 21 and the promise of life availed through Jesus for later audiences. Might it even have originated within the teaching of Jesus himself?

Susan Miller then walks us into the Johannine presentation of Jesus' interaction with the woman at the well and the Samaritans as a historically plausible scenario. If Jesus traveled to and from Jerusalem, as most observant Galileans would have done, he inevitably would have traveled through Samaria (see Luke 17:11). This being the case, what is surprising is not that such an engagement with Samaritans is present in John; the oddity is that such encounters are absent from Mark and Matthew (Luke does feature Samaritans more favorably: 11:30–37; 17:16). Miller also notes similarities of religious ethos between Samaritans and the Fourth Gospel, especially in their attitude toward the temple and a geography-transcending understanding of authentic worship. Regarding Synoptic parallels, if Jesus would have engaged in conversation a Syrophoenician woman in Mark 7, it is not at all unlikely that he would have engaged in conversation a Samaritan woman in John 4—even if these narratives functioned to motivate later cross-cultural outreach. Not only do the archaeological facts support John's rendering of Mount Gerizim as a place that Samaritans worshiped, and Jacob's well as a revered site in Palestinian culture, but might the accusation of Jesus' being "a Samaritan" in John 8:48 suggest a back-handed attestation to the historicity of Jesus' Samaritan mission?

In comparing and contrasting the Johannine presentation of the healing of the royal official's son in John 4:46–54 with Jesus' healing of the centurion's servant in Matthew and Luke, Peter J. Judge builds on his earlier analysis of Luke 7:1–10 (1989). Posing an alternative approach to Moody Smith's advocacy of an independent Johannine tradition (Smith 2001), Judge builds upon the platform of the Leuven school, arguing for John's dependence upon Synoptic traditions. Historical tradition in John is thus seen as a factor of Synoptic dependence and incorporation into the Johannine narrative. In making use of redaction-critical analyses, Judge seeks to distinguish between traditional and editorial features of the Johannine presentation of this scenario, building upon inferences of what the Q tradition might have looked like and how it was also used by Matthew and Luke. In so doing, Judge argues that in John we have a profound reflection upon the Jesus presented in Synoptic traditions, not simply a fabrication of a story to suit the Evangelist's interests. He also builds on the work of John Painter (in Anderson, Thatcher, Just 2007), seeking to show how the transformed memory of the Fourth Evangelist contributed to the theological way in which he performed his historical work.

The essays in part 1 are responded to by Craig R. Koester, who has long emphasized that symbolism alone does not imply ahistoricity, but he also warns us that the lack of symbolizing features does not ensure historical accuracy (Koester 2003). By analyzing connections between the Johannine post-Easter memory and pre-Easter events, Koester suggests how the Johannine narrative both preserves and interprets tradition and thus aspects of historicity. His responses to each of the seven essays in part 1 tease out the strengths and weaknesses of each of the arguments, while also suggesting degrees of plausibility along the way.

"WE BEHELD HIS GLORY!" (JOHN 1:14)

Craig S. Keener

Most scholars today concur that the Fourth Gospel includes both history and theology. Even many patristic interpreters, who often harmonized John with the Synoptics (hence apparently stressing history), recognized John as a "spiritual" Gospel, emphasizing its interpretive aspects. The Gospel clearly interprets theologically the eyewitness claim that apparently stands behind it (cf. 21:24); perhaps most conspicuously, in the Fourth Gospel as a whole the eyewitness claim of water and blood from Jesus' side (19:34–35) is made to climax a motif of water running through the narrative (1:26, 33; 2:7–9; 3:5, 23; 4:10, 13–14; 5:2; 7:37–39; 9:7; 13:5).[1]

John's Prologue supplies us with something of an interpretive grid for the Gospel, and it may also suggest both an eyewitness claim and a theological interpretation, starting from the phrase, "we beheld his glory" (1:14). Although I shall develop at greatest length the character of John's theological interpretation, I must comment first on what John professed to interpret, because this historical substance is central to his theological perspective. His theology is inseparable from his interest in historical events concerning Jesus.

"WE BEHELD"

Perhaps not surprisingly, in a variety of genres of ancient literature, the first-person plural normally implied the narrator's inclusion in the action.[2] Both historians and biographers were eager to mention their own direct knowledge of events in the (usually) few places where they possessed it.[3] Of course, bias often shaped how even eyewitnesses interpreted events (e.g., Thucydides 1.22.2–

---

1. In several of these passages, Jesus supersedes or fulfills traditional rituals associated with the water, esp. purification rituals (see Keener 2003, passim, esp. 441–48, 509–13, 542–44, 858, 903–4, 908–10; earlier Keener 1997, 139–62).

2. E.g., Philostratus, *Vit. soph.* 2.21.604 shifts to the first person because the author was now present (2.21.602).

3. See, e.g., Polybius 29.21.8; Cornelius Nepos 25 (Atticus), 13.7; 17.1.

3), and eyewitness accounts sometimes diverged even on public events that the sources all claimed to have witnessed.[4] Usually participants employed first-person language when noting their eyewitness testimony; even when employing the third person, however, writers who inserted themselves into narratives were claiming their presence and direct knowledge of events or reports (e.g., Euna-pius, *Lives* 494).

Naturally, "we" becomes fictitious in a fictitious narrative,[5] but such narra-tives were rarely tied to events surrounding a recent historical person as closely as John's narrative is (which, when the speeches are excepted, both parallels the Synoptics at points and is generally "Synoptic-like" elsewhere; see e.g., D. Moody Smith 2007; Keener 2007). "We" nearly always attests a real speaker's presence and was barely ever fictitious outside of novels (see Nock 1972, 828). Novels about historic characters (such as Pseudo-Callisthenes' *Alexander Romance* and Xenophon's *Cyropedia*) are exceptional,[6] biographies and novels generally being distinguishable genres in antiquity.[7]

Although "we" could refer to humanity in general here, the parallel with Moses beholding God's glory (developed below) suggests that "we" refers to those who witnessed and understood Jesus' ministry;[8] the first-person plural functions with an analogous authority claim elsewhere in Johannine literature.[9]

With many others, I believe that the later claim in the Gospel attesting that blood and water flowed from Jesus' side (19:34–35) indicates an eyewitness claim concerning a specific historical event with theological implications (see Keener

---

4. E.g., Arrian, *Alex.* 4.14.3; cf. the Gospels' Easter accounts.

5. E.g., Lucian, *Ver. hist.* 1.5–2.47 (entitled "A True Story"; explicitly identified as fictitious, however, in 1.2–4).

6. Philostratus's later *Life of Apollonius* might also fit this category; so also two fictitious eyewitness accounts of the Trojan War (Merkle 1994, 183–84). But novels as a whole were apparently most popular in the late second and early third centuries (Bowie 1994, 452–53; Ste-phens 1994, 414), and even then, perhaps less popular than historiographic works (Stephens 1994, 415).

7. For the Gospels, including John, as ancient biographies, see esp. Burridge 1992. Although biographers often depended on legend (as they themselves conceded for characters of the distant past; those writing about more recent persons tended to be more reliable), they were not freely composing novels (often focused on humorous and generally amorous adventures) from whole cloth (see Keener 2003, 8–11).

8. Cf. Paul's comparison of the apostolic ministry with Moses in 2 Cor 3:7–18, treated again below, although Paul's experience of Jesus was largely if not wholly "postresurrection."

9. Of greatest relevance is 1 John 1:1–2, where the author distinguishes the first-person plural who testify of what they saw and touched of Jesus from the audience that depends on this testimony (perhaps emphasizing the historic Jesus of the Johannine Gospel tradition above purely pneumatic claims to have received revelations from him; see 1 John 4:1–6).

2003, 1154–57).[10] This is a third-person claim, but third-person and first-person claims sometimes appeared together in the same documents in ancient literature; thus, for example, Polybius employs first-person claims when he was an observer (e.g., 29.21.8) but prefers third-person claims when he was an active participant in the narrative.[11] I have argued elsewhere, along with many other interpreters, that the Fourth Gospel reflects an eyewitness tradition or source, so I shall not belabor that point further here (see Keener 2003, 81–115). Such eyewitness material is congruent with John's factual accuracy, even on many points of detail increasingly noted in recent work (see, e.g., Anderson 2006a; von Wahlde 2006).

However one interprets apparent eyewitness claims in the Gospel, the claim to behold Jesus' "glory" in the events of his historical ministry is necessarily also theological. John refers not to a single, visible transfiguration such as appears in the Synoptics, but overall to Jesus' ministry (see the first and last "signs" in 2:11; 11:4) and passion (12:16, 23–24; cf. 13:31; 17:1, 5). He employs the language of theophany (as we shall argue below), but he applies it to "signs" that differ from the character of visible theophanies in Israel's Scriptures. Thus what the eyewitnesses "beheld" is not only the events themselves (since John did not believe that all who witnessed them interpreted this as his glory; cf., e.g., 11:45–46; 14:17; 17:24–25), but their meaning (e.g., the promise of a theophany recalling Jacob's to Nathanael in 1:50–51). Some of this meaning was available to them only in retrospect (2:22; 12:16).

Such a perspective does not by itself explain fully the divergences from the Synoptics. It does, however, suggest from the beginning that John is interested not only in the events but in their theological interpretation. As scholars have often argued, the content of John's narratives generally resembles those in the Synoptics; because of this character, they stand a good chance of representing an independent tradition no less historical than what we find in the Synoptics.[12] But whereas the speeches often contain ideas attested elsewhere in the Jesus tradition, even in terms of Christology (see Keener 2003, 280–320), these speeches may function the way speeches often did in ancient historiography, as interpretive events providing perspective on the history surrounding them (see Keener 2003, 53–80).

---

10. Authors or narrators could include themselves in narratives using the third person, if their ideal audience already knew their identity; e.g., Thucydides 1.1.1; 2.103.2; 5.26.1; Xenophon, *Anab.* 2.5.41; 3.1.4–6 and passim; Caesar, *Gallic War* 1.7; 2.1; 3.28; 4.13; 5.9; 6.4; 7.17 and passim; *Civil War* 1.1 and passim; Polybius passim (see below).

11. E.g., Polybius 31.23.1–31.24.12; 38.19.1; 38.21.1; 38.22.3; cf. 39.2.2. Caesar mixes occasional first-person phrases (e.g., *Gallic War* 2.9) with his general third-person usage (*Gallic War* passim).

12. See Keener 2003, 3–52; for the state of scholarship on John and the Synoptics, see esp. Smith 2001.

What does John mean by his claim in 1:14 that "we saw his glory"? In addressing this question, I shall focus especially on the theological perspectives that supplement rather than repeat what I already included in my commentary, to ensure that this essay is a distinctly new contribution.

Vision of God in John and His Milieu

We may start this discussion with one of the Fourth Gospel's earliest interpreters. Most scholars view 1 John as one of the earliest interpretations of the theology in John's Gospel; this is true whether, as most scholars hold, the authors are distinct or, as I and some other scholars have argued, the same final author is responsible for both.[13] I begin with three claims in 1 John that would be readily intelligible to John's first audience: (1) those who continue in sin have not "seen" God (1 John 3:6), a claim relating to the past vision of God; (2) those who contemplate seeing him thereby become pure like he is pure (3:3), a claim that might relate to the present vision of God (in a limited sense; cf. 4:20); (3) God's children will be fully transformed into his likeness at his coming (3:2), a claim relating to the future vision of God.

Most members of John's first audience would have heard of visions of the divine before reading his Gospel; John is distinctive not for advocating knowing or seeing God but rather for claiming that the locus of revelation is in Jesus. The theme of seeing the divine was pervasive in Greek and Hellenistic Jewish spirituality. For example, Middle Platonists such as Philo of Alexandria and later Maximus of Tyre emphasized the soul's vision of the divine, an experience of the divine that increasingly divinized the soul. In the mid-second century c.e., Maximus urged his audience to strip away the layers of sense perception to see God (Or. 11.11). He regarded this as necessary because divine beauty, while perfect in the unchanging heavens, appears much less clearly in the lower realms of the senses (Or. 21.7–8). Philo was a first-century Jewish philosopher who drew on Middle Platonism and other sources.[14] Because Philo emphasized God's absolute transcendence, he believed that one best experiences the divine ecstatically

---

13. Keener 2003, 123–26 (although after my commentary's publication I discovered that I had inadvertently omitted several pages of discussion concerning the scholarship on this question); for Johannine authorship, see 81–115. Those who do not share this assumption will at least assign both to the "Johannine community."

14. The preservation of his writings suggests that at least in Alexandria, and probably elsewhere in the Diaspora, some Jewish intellectuals shared his views; other Jewish works (such as Wisdom of Solomon and 4 Maccabees) show that many Jewish intellectuals heavily imbibed from the well of Hellenistic philosophy.

through mystical vision.[15] Only the pure soul may envision God;[16] as in Scripture, this vision is utterly dependent on God's self-revelation (*Abraham* 80).

In many Hellenistic and Roman sources, the soul was of heavenly origin and cultivated its heavenly character by meditating on the divine, on what was heavenly.[17] This prepared the soul for its heavenward ascent after death.[18] That ideas such as these were also common among Jewish readers literate in Greek is suggested by their inclusion in the Wisdom of Solomon.[19] This work claims that the body weighs down the soul with earthly cares, distracting it from heavenly matters (Wis 9:15–16).[20] It goes on to argue that the only way people can understand heavenly matters is the divine gift of wisdom and God's spirit from heaven (Wis 9:17).

John's portrayal of Jesus' heavenly revelation (John 3:11–13) resembles such themes from the Wisdom of Solomon.[21] The correspondence is not surprising in view of John's claim that God revealed his character through wisdom enfleshed, Jesus Christ (1:1–18; see the discussion below). Other early Christians also developed the divine vision theme: for example, the letter to the Colossians employs analogous imagery to invite believers to look to the exalted Christ rather than to human rituals (Col 2:16–3:3).[22]

Jewish mystics emphasized visionary ascents to heaven,[23] probably sometimes cultivated by the same means through which philosophers sought to experience the divine. Some of these "ascents" probably produced many of the apocalyptic journeys reported in the Enoch and other apocalyptic literature. One traditional model was Moses, who in some sources ascended to heaven to receive the Torah.

---

15. Isaacs 1976, 50; Dillon 1975; Hagner 1971, 89–90. On parallels to ecstatic vision, see also Kirk 1934, 23. On the impossibility of full vision of God in this life, see Philo, *Rewards* 39.

16. *Confusion* 92; for biblical examples, see *Names* 3–6; *QG.* 4.138; *Confusion* 146; *Dreams* 1.171; *Abraham* 57.

17. E.g., Porphyry (a much later Platonist), *Marc.* 6.103–108; 7.131–134; 10.180–183; 16.267–268; 26.415–416; cf. also Col 3:1–2.

18. For the soul's postmortem ascent, see, e.g., Maximus of Tyre, *Or.* 41.5; Menander Rhetor 2.9, 414.21–23; this can be portrayed as divinization (2.9, 414.25–27), which goes beyond the closest early Christian parallels to the idea (2 Cor 3:18; 2 Pet 1:4).

19. Its wide circulation is attested by its inclusion, along with other books of the Apocrypha, in some manuscripts of the Greek Bible.

20. Analogous language appears in the Greco-Roman philosophic tradition; see, e.g., Musonius Rufus (Lutz 1947) 18A, pp. 112.20, 27–28 (a first-century Stoic); Maximus of Tyre, *Or.* 1.5.

21. See Wis 9:10; 18:15; cf. Bar 3:29–32.

22. Relevant to ancient philosophic approaches, the same context invites hearers to meditate on things above (Col 3:1–2) rather than to contemplate sins, which characterize earthly appetites (3:5–11).

23. See, e.g., Chernus 1982; Himmelfarb 1988; Kirk 1934, 11–13.

John is emphatic, however, that the only one who has ascended to heaven and can fully reveal heavenly things is the one who first came down from heaven (John 3:11–13; see Keener 2003, 559–63). This affirmation need not rule out the sorts of heavenly visions reported in the book of Revelation (e.g., 4:1–2), probably circulating in the same community, but it filters claims to heavenly revelation through the Spirit who exalts Christ (e.g., John 16:13–15; Rev 4:2; 5:5–6). Jesus is the heavenly revealer, and no claims to heavenly revelations that contradict him may be admitted.

Such an approach to John's understanding of divine "vision" is not new. Both Augustine and Eastern Orthodox thinkers, familiar with the philosophic tradition, emphasized the importance of not merely knowing about but *contemplating* the divine character.

The Vision of God in Israel's Scriptures

From what we have observed so far, it may seem as if John's emphasis on spiritual vision stems purely from Greek sources about the soul's meditation on the divine (even if this emphasis was also adopted by many of his Jewish contemporaries). From this connection we might infer that John's interests are purely abstract and ahistorical. Such a conclusion would, however, be premature at best.[24]

John's discussion of the vision of God is intelligible in a Greek setting, and Greek philosophic sources significantly contribute to our understanding of his language. Yet his Gospel explicitly articulates a biblical rationale for his approach. As we shall explain more fully below, John draws a multifaceted parallel between Moses' vision of God's glory on Sinai and the disciples' vision of God's glory in the word made flesh (1:14–18). Because a prologue normally sets the tone for the work that follows, it is significant that two elements of his vision motif must be clear to his audience from the start. First, Christ is the fullest revelation of God (1:18); as in earlier Scripture, God's character is revealed in concrete history. Second, Exodus provides John's paramount interpretive grid for understanding the vision of God.

Later, in a transitional section summarizing Jesus' works and teachings just before the passion narrative, John also interprets the vision of Christ through the grid of Isaiah's call (John 12:37–41). Both Isaiah (John 12:41) and Abraham (8:56)

---

24. This would be true even if John had not provided a biblical basis for his claim. Most Jews writing in the Greek language used Greek images and categories to varying degrees. After centuries of interaction with Hellenism, Judaism had learned to articulate its ideas in forms intelligible in a Hellenistic milieu. But a distinction remains (with a few extreme exceptions) between pagan Hellenism, on the one hand, and Judaism that was to various degrees Hellenized, on the other. Purely Greek sources lack traditional Jewish language (except sometimes in magical papyri); documents that included both Greek and Jewish language (like John's Gospel) were *Jewish* (see, e.g., Claussen 2007, 36).

witnessed Christ's glory in advance.[25] John undoubtedly identifies the latter vision with Isaiah's experience of God enthroned (Isa 6:1–8) in the immediate context of the quotation he offers (Isa 6:9–10, in John 12:40).

The two texts John uses at fullest length to explain the vision of God in Christ (Exod 33:18–34:7; Isa 6:1–8) are both theophanies, and both were widely known in Jewish circles. Some used such theophanies as models for mystical ascent to secure "visions" of God's throne. For John, however, seeing God's character in Christ in history is itself the deepest vision of God. That is, John's theological vision is grounded in the historical mission of Jesus.

God's Revelation Is in Christ

Although some pagan intellectuals preferred the unmediated vision of God, even they generally allowed idols and other physical entities to provide reminders of his character (e.g., Maximus of Tyre, *Or.* 11.12). John, a Jewish-Christian monotheist, draws on a tradition closer to home.[26] For John, vision of God is never unmediated; humanity is already in darkness and must come to the light where God has offered it, in Christ (John 3:19–21). John could draw on earlier traditions to support this view. In Scripture, humanity itself was in God's image (Gen 1:26, connoting being God's children; cf. Gen 5:1–2), contrasted with idols.

But in articulating his conception of divine revelation in the historic person of Jesus, John probably draws especially on an idea that was apparently fairly widespread in contemporary Greek-speaking Judaism, namely, of Wisdom or the Logos as God's image.[27] Scholars have long noted John's Wisdom Christology, highlighted in the opening Prologue that sets the tone for his Gospel.[28] Here it is also a Torah Christology: Jesus as the "Word" is greater than Moses and reveals God more completely than the law (which is also God's "Word") did (1:17).[29] Wisdom was often identified with the law in Jewish tradition (Bar 3:29–4:1; Sir 24:23; 34:8; 39:1).[30]

---

25. For early Jewish discussion of patriarchal visions of the future era, see e.g., 4 Ezra 3:14; 2 Bar. 4:3–4; L.A.B. 23:6; 4Q544, 10–12; 4Q547, 7; Sifre Deut. 357.5.11; b. B. Bat. 16b–17a, bar.; 'Abot R. Nat. 31A; 42, §116B; further in Keener 2003, 767–68.

26. Although some philosophers' rationale for divine images could inform the later Eastern Christian tradition of icons, that tradition emphasizes its connection instead with the incarnation, drawing heavily from Johannine theology.

27. E.g., Wis 7:24–27; Philo, *Confusion* 97, 147; *Dreams* 1.239; 2.45; *Sobriety* 133; *Eternity* 15; *Flight* 101; *Heir* 230; *Planting* 18; *Spec. Laws* 1.81; *Creation* 16, 36, 146; cf. Col 1:15; Heb 1:3.

28. See, e.g., Witherington 1995b; Ringe 1999; Keener 2003, 350–55.

29. See esp. Epp 1975; Keener 2003, 354–63.

30. See further 4 Macc 1:16–17; later rabbis developed this theme more elaborately (e.g., Sifre Deut. 37.1.3; Gen. Rab. 17:5; 31:5; 44:17; see further Epp 1975, 133–36; Keener 2003, 354–55).

Like Wisdom in some early Jewish sources, Jesus appears as God's image, the one who makes God fully known (1:18; see also 5:37–38; 14:7–9). Wisdom as God's image mediated the divine image to the world (see Wis 7:22, 25–26). In Philo, the Logos as God's image imprints his image not only on people but also on all creation.[31] Thus it is not surprising that in 1 John, as we have noted, those who behold Jesus become like him, both in the past (1 John 3:6), present (3:3), and future (3:2; cf. 2:28).[32] The beatific vision of God that some ancient thinkers associated with the time of death or the end-time[33] is for John's circle of Christians (at least in 1 John) a matter of both future and realized eschatology. The defining point here for John is in fact not eschatology (i.e., *when* they see God) but Christology (i.e., *where* they see God: in Jesus who had come in the flesh; cf. 1 John 4:2).

John was not the first Christian writer to adapt such language to communicate Jesus for his milieu; at least Paul did so earlier. Because Jesus is God's "image" (2 Cor 4:4–6),[34] those who behold him are being transformed into the same image (2 Cor 3:18), as Moses was transformed by beholding God's glory (2 Cor 3:7; see Keener 2005, 169–71). Just as John compares the eyewitnesses of Jesus' glory with Moses in Exod 33–34 (see discussion of John 1:14–18 below), so Paul compared Christ's agents with Moses (2 Cor 3:6–4:4).[35]

For both Pauline and Johannine theology, therefore, transformation through vision was not simply good Greek philosophy (although it would be intelligible there); it followed the model of Moses. The glory of the earlier covenant transformed Moses (Exod 34:29–35); the greater glory of God's word made flesh also transforms its agents. For John, all people not transformed remain children of the devil, sharing his deceptive and violent character (John 8:44); those who embrace Christ, however, share the imprint of his character, born from above as children of God rather than of the devil (John 1:12–13; 3:3–6).

For John, there is no unmediated vision of God. If believers wish to experience the complete vision of God, they must do so not in a vacuum, nor merely by Platonic meditation on supreme goodness, nor by their own *merkabah* mysticism or visionary ascents to God's throne. Rather, believers experience the vision of God through the enfleshed Jesus on whom John's Gospel focuses, whom John

31. *Dreams* 2.45; cf. *Planting* 18, 20, 22.

32. Although the disciples' historical vision of Christ was not repeatable in the strictest sense (see John 20:29), even in the Gospel it presumably does offer a model for believers' continuing experience of God in Christ (cf. 14:7, 9, 17; 16:16).

33. With death, e.g., 4 Ezra 7:98; Maximus of Tyre, *Or.* 9.6; 10.3; 11.11; with the end-time, see 1 En. 90:35.

34. The Wisdom language in Col 1:15 is even more emphatic in this regard. For Wisdom language there, see, e.g., Lohse 1971, 48; Bruce 1976, 94; cf. also Glasson 1969.

35. For Paul, this glory is mediated through weak vessels (2 Cor 4:7–12); for John, too, glory is revealed in weakness (see discussion of John 1:14–18 below).

presents as the only way to come to the Father (John 14:6; cf. also 14:2–9). As divine Wisdom incarnate, Jesus is the ultimate revelation of God's character and the mediator of God's presence.

Examining his work more broadly, we see that John's focus on behold-ing Christ belongs to the related Johannine notion of the "knowledge of God," which serves almost the same purpose as his "vision of God" motif (see Keener 2003, 243–51). Certainly John regards this experience as theologically significant. Scripture already depicts Israel's covenant relationship with God as "knowing" him (Exod 6:7); often it uses the phrase to distinguish those faithful to the cov-enant from those who are not (e.g., Judg 2:10; 1 Sam 2:12; Jer 22:16; 24:7; Hos 2:20; 5:4; 6:3; 8:2; 13:4). The same experience would characterize the promised new covenant (Jer 31:34; even Gentile nations in Isa 19:21; cf. also Exod 7:5); for John, "knowing God" marks off true believers from those who merely pretend adherence to the covenant. Israel was God's flock (e.g., Pss 95:7; 100:3; Isa 40:11); for John, all those who follow Jesus are his flock, and they "know" him (John 10:3–4, 14–15).

This emphasis on the remnant having a unique covenant relationship with God comports well with John's polemical distinction between Jewish followers of Jesus (probably along with their Gentile converts), to whom he writes, and the rest of their ethnic community. The same language of "knowing God" served an analogous purpose for the Qumran community, who also viewed themselves as the authentic remnant of Israel.[36] But for John, the present experience of knowing God rests on knowledge of the Jesus who came historically, according to Johan-nine tradition (John 1:10, 26; 6:69; 8:19; 9:29; 14:17; 16:3).[37]

John thus grounds authentic religious experience in God's own gracious reve-lation in history. This is true especially of believers' experience through the Spirit, who comes to testify about Jesus (14:26; 15:26; 16:13–15; 1 John 3:24–4:6).[38]

JESUS' ENFLESHMENT AND DEATH AND THE SINAI THEOPHANY

Not only is divine vision mediated through the enfleshed Christ for John; it also focuses on the cross, the epitome of Christ's enfleshment, demonstrated in his mortality. In John's Prologue, which introduces his approach, Jesus is God's *logos*, his supreme revelation. As noted above, his wisdom imagery may also facilitate the identification of Jesus with God's law (see John 1:17–18). That is, what God

---

36. On knowledge of God in the Qumran Scrolls, see, e.g., 1QS 4:22; 10:12; 11:3; 1QM 11:15; 1Q27 1:7; for further discussion, see Flusser 1988, 57–59; Keener 2003, 239–43.

37. Perhaps even John's motif of spiritual "abiding" (John 14:17; 15:4–10) is connected by analogy with the historical experience of earlier disciples (John 1:38–39; 4:40).

38. See further discussion of this point in Dietzfelbinger 1985, 395–408; Keener 2003, 977–79.

revealed of himself by his "word" to Israel, he was now revealing in person in a more accessible way.

John fairly conspicuously compares the ultimate revelation of God's character in the flesh with God's revelation of his character on Mount Sinai.[39] This is clarified by the compounding of allusions to an account of Moses' vision of God's glory in the setting of his second receiving of the law:[40]

JOHN 1:14–18: THE WORD	EXOD 33–34: THE LAW
"Tabernacled" among us (1:14b)	Moses pleads for God to grant his continued presence (33:15–16)
"We [the eyewitnesses] beheld his glory" (1:14c)	Moses beheld God's glory (33:18–19)
The glory was "full of grace and truth" (1:14e)	The glory was "abounding in covenant love and truth" (34:6)
The law came through Moses, but "grace and truth" through Jesus Christ (1:17)	Grace and truth were present at the law-giving (34:6), but Moses' revelation was partial (33:20, 23)
No one has seen God, but God the unique Son has revealed him (1:18)	No one can see God, so Moses sees only part of God's glory (33:20, 23)

The parallel themes highlight the contrasts. Grace and truth were present in the law, but John declares that they came more fully in Christ (1:17). This is because Christ is God's word—his Torah, become flesh. Moses saw only part of God's glory; in Jesus, all of God's character is unveiled (1:18; see also 14:8–9, probably adapting Exod 33:18).

How is this glory revealed? When God revealed his "glory" to Moses, he showed him his "goodness" (Exod 33:19); he revealed his character, with an emphasis on his love and faithfulness. God's just anger extended as far as three or four generations, but his covenant love and faithfulness lasts for thousands of generations, probably a Hebrew expression for forever (Exod 34:7; cf. 20:6; Deut 5:10; esp. clear in Deut 7:9). His mercy is far greater than his anger, and Moses, knowing this, effectively pleads for God to forgive his people (Exod 33:14–17; 34:9–10).

---

39. John's allusion to Exod 33–34 might counter a charge of ditheism attached to Exod 32 (where his people violate the idolatry prohibition even when Moses is receiving the law). Countering a ditheism charge (cf. m. Sanh. 4:5; Sifre Deut. 329.1.1; b. Sanh. 38ab; Pesiq. Rab. 21:6; 3 En. 16:2), John contrasts artificially making something created into God (see John 5:18; 10:33) with God coming down and tabernacling, reflecting a contrast he may find in Exod 32–34.

40. See, e.g., Boismard 1957, 135–45, esp. 136–39; Hanson 1976; Mowvley 1984; Keener 2003, 405–26.

In John's Gospel, God reveals his character to humanity as his word becomes human and shares human existence (1:14). God reveals his glory through Jesus' ministry of compassion, explicit in his first and final "signs" (2:11; 11:4, 40),[41] but the ultimate revelation of glory in Jesus is in the cross (and consequent and inseparable exaltation; 12:16, 23–24; 13:31–32), the epitome of both the divine message's enfleshment and of God's love and faithfulness earlier revealed at Sinai. Moses saw God's glory on Sinai, and Isaiah saw it in the temple (John 12:41). Yet the Johannine witness (see 19:34–35), and through such witness later believers (see 20:31), see it in the cross (cf. 2 Cor 3:7–11). Platonists might meditate on divine transcendence and Jewish mystics on God's majestic throne, but Johannine theology meets God most climactically in the brutal suffering of an unjust Roman execution by slow and shameful torture.

CONCLUSION

The claim "we beheld his glory" in John 1:14 compares the vision of Jesus with a central biblical theophany. Connected as it is with Jesus' enfleshment (and an eyewitness claim concerning it), it claims to find theological meaning in the historical Jesus and ultimately in his passion. This passage suggests to us that John does not draw a clear line separating his history from his theology (as if some "events" he reports belong to the one and others to the other); still less does he promise us success in separating these into distinct sources or layers. Instead, he offers both (and the latter as a definitive interpretation of the former) as part of his "witness."

Johannine theology also draws on Greco-Roman and Jewish ideas of vision available in the milieu, but it insists on a historical, Christocentric locus for this vision. In contrast to the disembodied, mental encounter with the divine preferred by many Hellenistic thinkers, John emphasizes an encounter that climaxes various divine revelations in biblical history (to Abraham, Moses, and Isaiah). Like most of his contemporaries, he undoubtedly accepts biblical reports of such revelations as both historically genuine and theologically accurate. In this light, John's focus of the revelation in the Jesus who came in the flesh, evidenced and exemplified in the story he reports in his Gospel, suggests that he would make the same claim for his own narrative.

---

41. Taken together, these texts also constitute Moses allusions: Jesus turns water to wine instead of blood (the first plague) and raises the dead rather than striking the firstborn (the last plague).

Jesus' Bethsaida Disciples:
A Study in Johannine Origins

Mark Appold

Seldom do biblical scholars reach full agreement on issues of textual interpretation. That certainly has to do with the very nature of the texts themselves. One notable exception, the product of two centuries of scholarship, is the now generally accepted recognition that none of the four Gospels can be read simply as historical reportage but that each one must rather be taken as an ultimately irresolvable mix of discoverable "facts" and faith. The problem does not hang on a simple either/or but on an examination of the many points in between. Johannine scholarship has examined virtually every interpretive possibility that falls between the conclusion of Friedrich Schleiermacher (1864), that the Fourth Gospel's eyewitness author validated the most reliable presentation of the life and words of Jesus, and the conclusion of the Jesus Seminar (Funk and Hoover 1993), that none of the Johannine Jesus' words could be traced back to the historical Jesus. In between these polar opposites is the emergent recognition that, despite the thoroughly theologized character of the multilayered Fourth Gospel, significant references and structural elements betray their rootedness in the earliest levels of the historical Jesus tradition.

Granted, the Johannine words of Jesus present a unique challenge, born as they are within a prophetic community where the sheep continue to hear the voice of the shepherd through the ongoing work of the Paraclete. The *ipsissima verba* of the historical Jesus may remain irretrievable, since even the Synoptic words of Jesus are also theologically conditioned, demonstrating that the only Jesus available to us is Jesus as he was seen, heard, and experienced by those who first encountered him and formulated the traditions we now have. The Johannine trajectory of Jesus' words would spin off into later developments in the gnostic discourse traditions and the second-century Montanist experience. The Fourth Gospel, however, remained resistant to these developments because it was shaped by its tight integration with the passion narrative and controlled by a pervasive high Christology whose signature abbreviation occurs in the "oneness" of the Father and the Son, Jesus and the disciples, and the community itself in a reciprocal solidarity. A consequent dialectic of openness and closeness, exclusiveness and inclusiveness, becomes one of the trademarks of this Gospel.

No less complicated than the Johannine words of Jesus tradition is the Johannine narrative material. It too bears witness to the formative impact of theological reflection. Yet embedded in the narrative is a John the Baptist tradition as well as chronological and geographical references that not only are unique to the Fourth Gospel but also give evidence of remembered traditions that reach back to the historical Jesus period. How did all of these varying traditions ultimately come together into one document? There has been no shortage of attempted explanations. Johannine scholarship is replete with hypotheses upon hypotheses, leading to possibilities upon possibilities and plausibilities upon plausibilities. Unending authorship theories together with attempts to isolate units of original source materials—whether signs, discourse, or passion sources—have all but run into dead ends. There are no "smoking guns" in Johannine research. Still, the search continues. One of the most underdeveloped yet promising areas of investigation for historical elements in the Fourth Gospel lies with the special nature of many of John's geographical locations. Karl Kundsin (1925), followed by Rudolf Bultmann (1941) and many others, was among the first to call attention to John's unique place names: Bethany on the other side of the Jordan, Aenon by Salim, Sychar, Gerizim, Ephraim, the Pool of Siloam, Solomon's Porch, and so forth.

In this essay I propose to focus on one location: Bethsaida, on the northeast side of the Sea of Galilee. Mentioned seven times in the Gospel tradition, Bethsaida, which figures prominently in the Galilean ministry of Jesus, has to date drawn little attention in the critical literature. In addition to textual analysis, this study includes the results of the archaeological excavation at the Bethsaida site. Until recently, all that was known about Bethsaida came from scattered text references. Prominent among these were the independent attestations found in Josephus, who identifies the Tetrarch Herod Philip as the one who elevated the village of Bethsaida to the status of a πόλις and renamed it "Julias," in honor of Caesar's daughter (*Ant.* 18.2.1 §28). Josephus's statement is actually in error. Honoring a city with the name of a banished daughter is hardly likely. The renaming must have been in honor of Augustus's wife, Livia-Julia, as shown by numismatic evidence (Rousseau and Arav 1995, 20). Pliny the Elder (*Nat. Hist.* 5.15) speaks of Bethsaida as "one of the four lovely cities on the Sea of Galilee." In all four of the Gospels, Jesus' feeding miracle is located within the context of Bethsaida. Only in Mark's Gospel (8:22–26) do we find the healing of a blind man identified with Bethsaida. While some see this reference as a literary construct (Kuhn 243), others see it as intrinsic to the text and part of an independent Bethsaida tradition (Koester 1990, 284–85; Appold 2007). The well-known Q statements of Matt 11:21 and Luke 10:13 are cast as harsh words of judgment, woes against Bethsaida, Capernaum, and Chorazim, prominent locations in the ministry of Jesus.

It is striking that the Fourth Gospel, with the exception of the feeding miracle, knows none of these traditions, or at least makes no reference to them. In

John, by contrast, Bethsaida appears as the home and/or workplace of Andrew, Peter, and Philip. This information, embedded in a complex call narrative (1:35–51), includes an oblique reference to another unnamed disciple (1:40), John's well-known mystery figure who appears throughout the Gospel with intentionally multivalent meanings and applications. The earliest application, with others to follow, was John the son of Zebedee, otherwise notably absent in the naming of the disciples. If John were, in fact, originally part of this complex of Bethsaida disciples, then his brother James would be in the mix as well. These connections seem all the more likely when one considers the shared fishing enterprise with Andrew and Philip (Matt 4:21). Three explicit and two implicit references bring the number of Bethsaida disciples to five. Both John and James stand out because of their conspicuous absence in the Fourth Gospel. Neither one is ever named explicitly. Taking that silence seriously and reading between the lines, as we are intended to do, we end up with five disciples from the same small village. It is remarkable that this piece of information identifying Bethsaida as the home or work place (ἐκ can have all of these meanings) of five disciples appears in no other text, canonical or noncanonical. It is unique to the Fourth Gospel.

Before we consider the call narrative itself, four important considerations need attention. They help frame the distinctive character of the Johannine disciple tradition. First, both the Synoptic Gospels and John use the number twelve when speaking of the disciples, even though the names vary. Nathanael of Cana does not appear in the Synoptic lists. John's inclusion of Judas, son of James, coheres with the Lukan tradition but not the Markan one. Second, in the Synoptic accounts, all twelve of those whom Jesus calls are named, whereas in John only seven receive that distinction. Third, each of the seven named disciples receives a speaking part. Additionally, four of those seven (Andrew, Philip, Nathanael, and Thomas, all of whom are marginalized in the Synoptic accounts) play very prominent roles in the Johannine narrative. Fourth, it is now clear that the number of disciples in John is flexible. For example, the appendix in John 21 mentions the "sons of Zebedee" without naming them (21:2). Going with a traditional understanding of that appellation, we come to a total of nine disciples. There are other curious unexplained references, such as "two others of his disciples" (21:3), "Joseph of Arimathea, a disciple of Jesus" (19:38), or the "other disciple known to the high priest" (18:15). Whereas both designations of "disciple" and "apostle" appear in the Synoptics, John never uses the term "apostle" but always speaks of "disciples." Luke preempts the term "apostle" and uses it almost exclusively for the twelve (Paul breaks that Lukan pattern by insisting on his own apostleship). By contrast, John exclusively uses the term "disciple," with an equivalent meaning to "apostle," yet broad enough, using the language of the Samaritans (4:41), to include all who believe the word of Jesus.

All of this is important for understanding the call narrative in 1:35–51. Beneath this highly theologized portrayal of Jesus and his first disciples lie reminiscences that connect with the historical Jesus. Here I point to three. First, the cluster of three Aramaisms is striking: *Rabbi, Messiah,* and *Cephas.* All three need translation and are given such in the current text. These three words stand as markers for an earlier remembered tradition. Second, an earlier experience shimmers through this text, reminiscent of a time when Jesus leaves his home and makes the journey to the Judean wilderness where a Jewish prophet in the tradition of Elijah is baptizing. Jesus' own baptism by John, uniformly attested in the Synoptic Gospels, is not disclosed here, and there is a time when Jesus draws back from this prophet of Israel's renewal, now interpreted as the primal witness to Jesus. Along with Jesus come two former followers of John, one named Andrew—presented only in the Fourth Gospel as the first-called—and the other unnamed. Was John a mentor for Jesus? Was there a parting of the ways and a subsequent rivalry between the two groups? This potentially troublesome series of experiences proved to be a source of embarrassment for later followers of Jesus, a likely sign of its original authenticity. Third, we turn to the inclusion of Bethsaida, announced as the home of Andrew, Peter, and Philip. There is nothing in the text to support the contention that the mention of Bethsaida is simply a literary or a theological construction. Nor is it surprising that this is never suggested as a possibility in any of the critical literature.

Against this background, I shall briefly sketch the pivotal roles played by each of the Bethsaida disciples, with the exception of the "sons of Zebedee," since they are not explicitly named and a treatment of that issue would go beyond the parameters of this essay. First, it should be noted that, unlike the other named disciples, the three Bethsaida disciples have distinctly Greek names. In fact, the names Andrew and Philip are so Greek that they have no first-century C.E. Hebrew equivalents. Simon, surnamed Peter, is also native Greek but has a similar-sounding equivalent in the Hebrew for Simeon. The nature of these names alone provides a telling clue in suggesting the possible background and cultural setting formative for the Bethsaida disciples. Part of the background for Andrew has already been stated. He left his home in Bethsaida, went south to the Jordan Valley, and there joined the circle of those identified with the Baptizer. There in his encounter with Jesus he became the πρωτόκλητός (the first-called), known that way throughout all of later tradition, particularly in the Eastern Church. In the feeding event of John 6, he emerges as an interlocutor with Jesus, and in Philip's response to the Greeks looking for Jesus (12:20–22), he is sought out as a resource person or the intermediary with the Greeks. In the Fourth Gospel, Andrew is remembered as a key figure in the ministry of Jesus; in the Synoptics, he is basically ignored.

Peter, the second Bethsaida disciple, is a central figure throughout the overall Gospel tradition but is minimized in the Fourth Gospel. Apart from the call narrative (1:40–44), the indirect reference at the feeding of the five thousand (6:8), and again at the conclusion of the "bread from heaven" discourse (6:68), he is never mentioned in the first half of the Gospel, devoted to the ministry of Jesus. Only in the second half (John 13–21), the part devoted to the discourses and passion account, is Peter named often, totaling twenty-nine times. It is also only in the appendix (John 21) that one hears of Peter's fishing capabilities. Theological reflection is strongly in evidence, and one senses a tension between the Petrine and Johannine groups within the larger church. Indeed, prominent though Peter's role is, he appears in the shadow of the unnamed Beloved Disciple. Recall the Easter event and the well-known foot race where the other disciple outruns Peter to reach the tomb first. He does not go in. Peter is first to enter, but it is the other disciple who is the first to "see and to believe." If Peter's home is in Bethsaida, what about the Capernaum tradition in the Synoptic accounts? It has a long tradition on its side (Strickert 1998, 22–28). Without going into detail at this point, I would side with those who hold the pertinent Johannine verses to be an older authentic tradition that ultimately is compatible with the Synoptic versions. To unpack this issue further would go beyond the parameters of this essay.

We turn to the third Bethsaida disciple, Philip, who, in contrast to the Synoptic references, plays a pivotal role in the ministry of Jesus. His name appears twelve times, and he is mentioned more frequently than any other disciple, with the exception of the Beloved Disciple and Peter. Philip is the only disciple, according to John, *whom Jesus calls directly* (1:43). He is part of the chain reaction where Andrew, the first disciple, finds his brother Simon, whose name is changed, and where Philip, identified as the one who recognizes Jesus to be the fulfillment of Moses and the prophets, finds Nathanael, a true Israelite. Then a startling narrative begins to unfold. Philip emerges as a conversation partner with Jesus. The first exchange is set within the context of the feeding of the five thousand (6:5–7). Philip joins Andrew to question Jesus' intentions. In the next scene, at the Passover festival, Philip is again paired with Andrew as they pass on the requests of Greek-speaking inquirers to Jesus (12:21–22). Both appear as "bridge people" to the Gentiles. Finally, in Jesus' prepassion discourse with the disciples (14:8–9), Philip joins Thomas in responding to Jesus' discourse on "the way." It is important to note that all of these distinctive descriptions of Andrew, Peter, and Philip appear only in the Gospel of John. This is not simply reportage. Nonetheless, John's idealized portrayals reflect church leadership realities at the time of writing and, in addition, suggest the significance of the earlier historical relationships of those Bethsaida disciples and their real-life roles played out in the ministry of Jesus.

Up to this point, I have examined texts. Texts, as we have seen, have their limitations. Those limitations have over time led to a remarkable proliferation of methods and approaches. It is no small wonder that one increasingly hears today of the "balkanization" of biblical studies (Carson 2007, 133), the drift toward more and more specialty areas in grappling with the issues of interpretation. In his significant contribution to Johannine studies, Martin Hengel (1989a, xi) complains of "the widespread methodological confusion in the exegesis of John." On the other hand, one can hardly deny that new approaches produce fresh insights and provide new vantage points. Such is the case today with the growing importance of archaeology and its interfacing with the texts. No longer is such work simply a matter of using picks and shovels in the attempt to "prove" the accuracy of biblical texts. Archaeologists now are armed with sophisticated new technologies used to lay bare the cultural, social, and religious past. In just one generation, archaeology has had an enormous impact on Old Testament studies, and its influence is beginning to be felt in New Testament studies as well. This essay is an example of its impact on Johannine studies. It addresses the question of what archaeological exploration can add to our understanding of the text and, in particular, our understanding of the place that was home to the Bethsaida disciples.

For almost two millennia, the location of Bethsaida was a mystery. Ravaged by earthquakes and pillage, it had gradually slipped from historical view. Medieval pilgrims confused its location with sites close to the shoreline of Lake Genessaret, and nineteenth-century investigators followed suit, identifying the location with el-Araj, a few hundred meters from the mouth of the Jordan, or with el-Mesadiyeh, a small ruin to the southeast. Ground-penetrating radar and systematic geological surveys have now established that biblical Bethsaida is located a mile and half back from today's shoreline on an elevation called et-Tell. What was once lost has now been found. The four-volume Bethsaida series (Arav and Freund 1995, 1999, 2004, and 2009) tracks the discoveries that continue to contribute to a reconstruction of the story behind Bethsaida. What makes the Bethsaida excavation site so unique and sets it apart from other New Testament projects is its complete accessibility to first-century-level investigation, since no significant building took place following its demise in the early centuries of the Common Era. No other site currently can make that claim. At this point, I shall restrict my further assessment of the data to three areas: population numbers, economy, and the religious composition of the inhabitants.

In the New Testament era, Bethsaida already had a thousand-year history. It had been the capital of the Geshurites, an Aramean stronghold in alliance with the house of David (Absalom, son of David, and his wife Maacah, a Geshurite princess, 2 Sam 3:3). After the destruction of this capital city by the Assyrians in the late eighth century, significant occupation of the tell did not take hold until the Hellenistic period, followed by a resettlement effort of the Hasmoneans in the first century B.C.E. Then there was decline. Based on the available data, the current estimate puts the population of Bethsaida at the time of Jesus at approximately two hundred. Imagine the scenario. Three Bethsaida disciples alone, with their extended families, would potentially constitute from 8 to 10 percent of the total population of the village. These people had connections with one another and knew each other long before their encounter with Jesus.

Second, multiple factors shaped the economy of the area. Bethsaida traditionally was thought of primarily as a fishing village. The name itself testifies to that: beth-saida(n) means "house of the fisherman" (in some references, "hunter"). The abundance of fishing implements, lead weights, stone weights, iron fishhooks, bronze and iron needles for repairing nets, and a basalt anchor found on the site confirm this. On the other hand, recent data has underscored the central place of agriculture, a small flax industry, and a possible tannery. None of this, however, testifies to a thriving economy. On the contrary, the lack of any monumental structures and the poor quality of the Roman-era houses on the site leave the impression of an economically marginalized village. A history of constant warfare, violent reprisals, dynastic corruption, excessive taxation, peasant discontent, and an ever-expanding banditry led to economic deprivation and population decline. This corresponds with what Josephus tells us about this area (J.W. 2.95). Compared with the urbanized territory of the Galilee, Philip's area of jurisdiction was much poorer and more rural. His yearly income was half as much as that of his brother Antipas.

Third, the question of Bethsaida's cultural, ethnic, and religious composition frames a final point. For over a millennium the location of Bethsaida had been oriented to the Gentile north, the northwest and northeast. It was part of the Golan. The rabbis regarded this area as outside of the land of Israel. This is the territory that was under the jurisdiction of Philip Herod, whose tetrarchy, Josephus asserts, was of mixed population, with Greeks, Itureans, Syro-Phoenicians, and Jews (J.W. 3.57). Philip himself, although Jewish, was better known for his un-Jewish ways: minting coins with human images and tolerating varieties of Greco-Roman religious practices. Indeed, the still-uncertain remains of a small pagan temple, built during the Hellenistic period and perhaps later used by the imperial cult in connection with Bethsaida's refounding ceremonies, may be indicated by one of the site's Philip coins, which has an impression of a temple on the backside. During the time of Jesus, on other hand, Bethsaida reflects a significant Jewish presence as well, as indicated by a preponderance of locally made Galilean coarse-ware brought in from nearby Kefar Hananya. Additionally, one may point to the nine Herodian coins and pieces of limestone vessels, all signs of a Jewish presence. Clearly, Bethsaida at Jesus' time presented its inhabitants with a distinctly multicultural environment. Could this fact alone have seminally shaped the lives of the Bethsaida disciples? Does not Luke-Acts describe Peter's post-Easter encounter with the Gentile world, his stay with Simon the tanner (Acts 9:43; a ritually impure act no less problematic than the tannery at Bethsaida), his mission to the Roman centurion Cornelius? Is not Philip described as the bridge person to the Greeks (John 12:21–22) and later known as the "great luminary" of Asia (Eusebius, *Hist. eccl.* 3.31.2)? Is not Andrew, in the apocryphal texts, presented as the missionary to the Scythians?

CONCLUSION

References identifying the village of Bethsaida as the home or workplace for five of Jesus' disciples (three explicitly and two implicitly) are embedded in texts found only in the Gospel of John. These texts have all the earmarks of remembered connections preserved in an early Galilean tradition. When these texts are combined with recent material finds discovered in the archaeological excavation at Bethsaida, a descriptive picture emerges that brings us one step closer to understanding the shared background and formative setting that for a limited time shaped the early lives of these first Jesus followers, who went on to play leading roles in the early church. The archaeological picture of a destabilized area controlled by client kings matches the Synoptic setting that contextualizes the Galilean ministry of Jesus. Thus, the Johannine presentation of Bethsaida not only illumines Johannine origins, but it casts valuable light upon the historical context from which the Jesus movement developed.

"Destroy This Temple":
Issues of History in John 2:13–22

James F. McGrath

The material found in John 2:13–22, depicting Jesus' action in the temple and the saying about its being destroyed and rebuilt in three days, is a key point of intersection between the Gospel of John, the Synoptics, and the Gospel of Thomas. As such, it provides one of the relatively few places where questions of John, Jesus, and history can be discussed, as it were, "synoptically." Because of this multiple attestation, there are very few scholars who dispute that Jesus engaged in *some sort* of action in the temple, however small or symbolic, and that he spoke *in some way* about the temple being destroyed.[1] Another advantage this passage has for our interests is that, unlike the majority of the Fourth Gospel, where the words of Jesus and those of the Evangelist flow together seamlessly, here we have a distinction drawn by the Evangelist himself between Jesus' words, their interpretation with the benefit of hindsight, and the later recollection of the disciples (see Lieu 2005, 173).

A key issue in assessing the value of material in the Gospel of John is determining whether we are dealing with tradition that is independent of the Synoptic Gospels, and thus potentially of value as independent testimony. Yet the dichotomy as frequently posed (i.e., that John is based on the Synoptics or else written with no knowledge of those other Gospels) is prone to ignore the possibility that the Fourth Gospel may be *both independent and dependent*. It is entirely possible that the Fourth Evangelist may have known other Gospels in written form and yet may also have known particular stories, sayings, or traditions *prior to*, or at least *independently of*, his contact with other literary sources. Indeed, once one raises the question in these terms, it becomes clear that it is *a priori likely* that

---

1. See Funk et al. 1998, 25–26, 121–22, 373–74. Jesus' action in the temple is recounted in Mark 11:15–17, with parallels in Matt 21:12–13 and Luke 19:45–46, and Gos. Thom. 71. Various sayings about the temple's destruction are recorded in Mark 13:2 (par. Matt 24:2; Luke 21:6), Mark 14:58 (par. Matt 26:61; see also John 2:19 and Acts 6:14), and Mark 15:29 (par. Matt 27:40 but not in Luke).

the Fourth Evangelist, and indeed all early Christians, would have heard on more than one occasion at least some of the traditional sayings and stories that eventually found their way into the written Gospels, before or apart from reading them in a written text. The issue should thus be considered not simply from the angle of possible dependence on the Synoptics but in terms of the evidence (or lack thereof) for a saying or incident having been known independently of the Synoptics as well.[2]

The aforementioned considerations relieve us of the need to consider at length, without any real hope of achieving secure conclusions, whether John knew any of the Synoptic Gospels directly. Rather, the only question of absolutely essential importance for our purposes is whether John knew the story and/or saying *independently* of the Synoptics, even if he may also have encountered it in the Synoptic Gospels themselves at some point.

A number of features of the Johannine narrative of 2:13–22 are usually listed as elements that appear to be neither derived from the Synoptics nor likely added by the Gospel's author: (1) John alone mentions Jesus making a whip of cords, which serves no obvious Johannine purpose (Smith 1984, 159; Anderson 2006b, 160); (2) John is also alone in mentioning oxen and sheep (Fortna 1988, 121); and (3) John alludes to different texts from the Jewish Scriptures than the Synoptics, ones that do not connect in an obvious way with the author's own perspective on the event (Dunn 1991, 378; Dodd 1963, 160). Mark Matson points out that "if FG [the Fourth Gospel] were derivative of Mark, then we must imagine that FE [the Fourth Evangelist] has chosen to replace Mark's Isa 56 and Jer 7 citations with those from Ps 69 and Zech 14. And if so, one would expect a far clearer use of the citations to support FE's central understanding."[3] It may be further observed that, in view of the allusion to Zechariah, one might have expected John to have incorporated Mark's reference to Jesus' preventing people from carrying merchandise through the temple, had he used Mark's Gospel as a source. What similarities there are to the Synoptics in this passage do not clearly indicate John's knowledge of those sources in written form.[4]

---

2. As D. Moody Smith writes, "One cannot weigh only the positive evidence of points of similarity in parallel pericopes, but must hold them in the scales over against the wide divergences elsewhere" (1984, 160).

3. Matson 2001b, 152. See also Meyer 1979, 306 n. 65; Evans 1999, 382–84.

4. It is sometimes claimed that John's wording shows him to have been dependent on the Synoptics. The arguments used are fairly unimpressive. Using modern technology, it is easy to determine that the phrase ἐν τρισὶν ἡμέραις (2:19, "in three days") was not at all uncommon or untypical in this period. C. K. Barrett's observation (1978, 199–200) that it is not classical is very much beside the point. The Perseus database includes it in a number of Egyptian papyri, Xenophon, and elsewhere, in data that runs on for several pages. Nor does the fact that John normally prefers ἱερόν have any relevance, since this passage includes not only ναός as a variant but also οἶκος. It may be that the use of one or more of the words was simply a traditional feature of the

Most important here is the evidence that the Fourth Gospel's author had a source of information that was not the same as any of the Synoptic Gospels. Whether that source was oral or written, and whether it was there in front of him or merely remembered, is impossible to ascertain and need not concern us here. Similarly, the distinctively Johannine features (such as the form of the request for a sign and the reference to "the Jews") only tell us what we already knew: that *John* is telling the story and is doing so in his own way.[5] In at least a few of its details, in particular the question about Jesus' authority, we can confirm from the Synoptics that we are dealing with a distinctively Johannine way of retelling something that was already in the tradition. All of the evidence in this particular passage suggests that John was drawing on source material other than, or in addition to, the Synoptic Gospels. Nevertheless, these considerations can only take us so far; they may enable us to distinguish between redaction and tradition, but further examination of the evidence will be necessary if we are to ascertain whether this traditional material may in fact go back not just to the pre-Johannine church but to Jesus himself—the ultimate question of the John, Jesus, and History Project.

For the most part, studies of the temple saying have tended to ignore some intriguing evidence from Paul's letters that seems relevant to the topic. Paul twice uses the image of the "temple" in ways that echo the saying from the Gospel tradition found (among other places) in John 2:19.[6] In 1 Cor 3:17, Paul writes that if anyone destroys the temple of God, God will destroy that person, and in 2 Cor 5:1–4 Paul speaks of a tent or tabernacle being pulled down (using the same verb as in Mark 14:58) and the existence of a house not made with hands (again using the same word as in Mark).[7] The similarity is such that it demands consideration as potentially the earliest allusion to the saying we are considering.[8]

---

story but that word preference could be an element of John's oral tradition, rather than something derived from Mark. While John uses ναός here and ἱερόν elsewhere, the same is true in the case of Mark as well (Juel 1977, 127). If anything, this indicates that *both* Mark and John here knew a traditional saying that used this particular word *or* that the distinction between ἱερόν and ναός was considered important in this context (Juel 1977, 128). In short, nothing in the wording of the story or the saying requires us to regard John as dependent on the Synoptics; however, as already emphasized, the key question is not ultimately John's dependence but his independent knowledge *irrespective of whether he also knew the Synoptics in written form*.

5. Here I am, of course, using "John" as shorthand for "the author of the Fourth Gospel" and not making assumptions about the author's actual name.

6. Sweet 1991, 368–90, is the only detailed treatment I am aware of that considers Paul's allusions to this saying of Jesus. See also Young and Ford 1987, 132–33; Fuglseth 2005, 174. Crossan (1991, 437) declares the saying authentic even without considering this very early evidence.

7. See also Heb 9:11, 24; Col 2:11.

8. In connection with this, it is interesting to note Peder Borgen's observation that John's verbal agreements with the Synoptics are not closer than those of Paul to the Synoptics (Borgen 1990, 434–35).

The most obvious connections one initially notices in these passages are between Paul's language and the specifically *Markan* form of the saying, with its reference to another temple not made with hands. However, we will have difficulty making sense of what Paul wrote in relation to the Gospel tradition, unless we also bring John into the picture. It is unlikely that Paul could have known the saying in the form in which it appears in the Synoptics and Thomas, with the first-person "I" on the lips of Jesus, and still have claimed that God will destroy the one who destroys God's temple. Likewise, given his positive use of the image of one tent that will be taken down and another to replace it not made by hands, it seems clear that Paul did not simply regard the saying as inauthentic, as Mark would have his readers believe. How can this be accounted for? The most satisfactory explanation is to suggest that Paul was familiar with a transformation of the saying along the same lines as would much later be incorporated into the Gospel of John, in which the saying was applied to death and resurrection and where the agency for the destruction of the temple is attributed to others rather than to Jesus himself.[9] So, the evidence from Paul's correspondence with the Corinthians strongly suggests that the saying took on a form or forms resembling *both* the Markan *and* the Johannine versions and did so sometime before Paul wrote the letters in question.[10]

It is significant to see that Paul's allusions to this saying connect not only to the later Markan way of dealing with its more troublesome aspects but also with the Johannine take on this tradition as well. This, however, does not mean that John is equally historical as, or more historical than, any other Gospel. It still remains most likely that the form in which the saying is found in John is a secondary transformation of a saying of Jesus, applying it with hindsight (as the Fourth Gospel itself suggests) to the death and resurrection of Jesus. But what is significant is that the evidence from Paul suggests that this transformation was the act, not of the Fourth Evangelist at the time this Gospel was written, but of the Christian community sometime before Paul wrote to the church in Corinth. This is significant for the work of the John, Jesus, and History Project, but its relevance is somewhat complex. While there is strong evidence that some elements of the Johannine Gospel are indeed *early*, it also becomes clear that an early date is not the most crucial issue in assessing a tradition's value as evidence about the historical figure of Jesus.[11] If we genuinely treat these early Christian writings as literary products of an oral culture, it is necessary to realize not only that it is rarely possible to speak of the "original" form of a saying but also that sayings

---

9. One possible meaning of the saying in its Johannine form is "If you destroy this temple..." (see Lindars 1972, 142).

10. Usually dated to roughly the mid 50s C.E. (so, e.g., Brown 1997, 514–15).

11. John, it turns out, tells us not only about two levels, that of the historical Jesus and that of the Christian community in the 80s or 90s, but also about stages in between.

that appear in writing much later may have an oral antecedent, not only years, but decades and perhaps even generations earlier. In short, there appears to be independent confirmation of some of John's information at a very early date. This does not, however, demonstrate John's historicity. Rather, it indicates that the free transformation and reinterpretation of sayings of Jesus is a product not simply of the Evangelist's activity in the late first century but of the earliest Christian communities in the first decades after the crucifixion.

Let us now turn to another aspect of John's distinctive information: his placement of the saying about destroying the temple in the context of the temple action. Jesus' action in the temple is thought by many scholars to be symbolic of its imminent *destruction* (e.g., Sanders 1993, 260). It is surely not insignificant when we find that John's placement of the saying confirms a conclusion reached by historians almost entirely on the basis of the Synoptics. That Jesus spoke about the temple's destruction is rarely disputed, and it would seem intrinsically plausible that Jesus' action in the temple was in some way connected to this emphasis of his that we find elsewhere.[12] Also worth noting is that Luke also connects Jesus' action in the temple closely to a prediction of the city's destruction (19:41–46).

The request for a sign to show Jesus' authority, although worded in a typically Johannine way in the Fourth Gospel, is a traditional component of the story (Dunn 1991, 369–70; Fuglseth 2005, 149 n. 60). In Mark 11:27–28 we are merely told that, after the triumphal entry, Jesus was walking in the temple and confronted about his authority. As C. H. Dodd suggests (1963, 160–61), it seems that here we see evidence of Mark having edited his source material, which originally connected this incident more closely to Jesus' action in the temple. Mark's failure to mention the saying about destroying and rebuilding in this context is unsurprising, since Mark elsewhere presents this saying of Jesus as one that is falsely attributed to him (14:57–59). Thus, the implications of Mark's omission bear little historical weight. In short, John's connection of the action, the question about authority, and the saying about destroying and rebuilding is historically plausible.

Finally, we turn to the topic of John's placement of this event toward the beginning of Jesus' public activity. Judith Lieu has recently noted the problems with our tendency to assume that here we have but another example of John's lack of concern with chronology, with his concern for the *why* at the expense of the *what* (Lieu 2005, 172–73). In fact, we have only two contrasting independent sources regarding the chronology, Mark (followed by Matthew and Luke) and John (see Anderson 2006b, 158–59). Mark's account leaves no place for the inclusion of this event, other than the only visit by Jesus to Jerusalem that he records.

---

12. There has been some recent criticism of this interpretation of the temple action, and in particular of the views of E. P. Sanders (e.g., Bauckham 1988, 87), but the real issue in the current debate is whether Jesus' action was *only* a prediction of destruction and thus need not detain us here.

On the other hand, historians usually accept John's depiction of a multiyear public ministry and multiple trips to Jerusalem. Moreover, it is clear that moving a story for the sake of narrative convenience was practiced not only by John but also by the Synoptic Evangelists.[13] That Mark could have shifted the event to the only place it would fit in his narrative needs to be taken seriously, although John's having moved the incident remains plausible as well.

One detail that is rarely given enough attention is the saying of Jesus' opponents about how long it has taken to build the temple (John 2:20). If understood as referring to the amount of time the temple had been "under construction," this statement would place the discussion in 27 or 28 c.e., which is around the time Jesus' public activity is thought to have begun. We thus have a saying, put in writing decades later, that seems to reflect a correct calculation of when this incident occurred as recorded in the Fourth Gospel, based on a dating of Jesus' public activity that depends on information from outside of John.[14] On what grounds might one decide that this represents improbable luck rather than accurate historical information that somehow managed to be preserved in some retellings of the story?

This matter cannot be decided simply by weighing the merits of Mark or John as a whole, since both were capable of shifting events around to serve a narrative or theological purpose. The question in this regard is ultimately about where this event can be fitted into an overall reconstruction of the chronology of the life of Jesus. Unfortunately, neither Mark nor John provides information that is beyond question in this regard. However, John A. T. Robinson has highlighted a line of inquiry that is interesting, namely, the question of how this event ties into the overall relationship of Jesus and his teaching to John the Baptist (Robinson 1985, 184–86). In John's Gospel, the temple incident occurs not only toward the beginning of Jesus' public activity but even before John the Baptist is put into prison. On public activity by Jesus at this period, the Synoptics are largely (although not altogether) silent, and here once again we have in John an alternative viewpoint that many historians find plausible.[15]

---

13. Both Matthew and Luke drop out Mark's reference to Jesus' having left the temple and returned the next day for his symbolic action (Scott 1952, 21–22).

14. Barrett's comment (1978, 200) about the wording reflecting the temple being completed ignores the fact that most Jews probably did not consider the temple "unfinished" simply because additional construction projects were going on. On the construction and its relative completion, see further Sanders 1992, 57. For a grammatical parallel for the use of the aorist in reference to the temple when yet uncompleted, see lxx Ezra 5:16 (Lindars 1972, 143). See also Anderson 2006b, 160–61.

15. Robinson (1985, 168) draws attention to Acts 1:21–22, which presupposes what John alone explicitly states, namely, that a core group of disciples had contact with Jesus from the time of his baptism by John. Also note that in the Synoptics the question concerning Jesus' authority mentions the Baptist (Lindars 1972, 137).

Discussions of this specific episode need to be set in the context of a plausible reconstruction of the development of Jesus' own teaching in relation to that of his mentor. Did Jesus begin by following closely the emphases of John the Baptist, as Matthew's Gospel suggests? Was it only subsequently that Jesus moved toward different emphases, which led the imprisoned Baptist to question whether he was the one who is to come? Ultimately, this question is answerable only in speculative terms, but *if* it seems more plausible to reconstruct the development in Jesus' teaching and emphases as starting closer to his mentor's and moving away from them, *then* the most appropriate setting of the temple incident in the life of Jesus is arguably *earlier* rather than *later*.[16] Robinson argues precisely this point, and disputing it cannot be done in terms of the earliness or lateness of Mark or John, nor in terms of the propensity of one or the other to move events around. The argument must be made in terms of the overall understanding of Jesus' activity, which is itself a creative enterprise and not merely something one can derive from these sources.

Conclusion

A study of the incident and saying in John 2:13–22 suggests that earlier tradition, some of which may be historically accurate, did indeed find its way into the Fourth Gospel. A careful examination of this passage further suggests that we *might not always need the Synoptics in order to identify such earlier traditions*. Even without the Synoptics or Thomas, the evidence within the Gospel of John itself may well provide sufficient basis for scholars to recognize that an earlier saying was being reinterpreted. When John's information about this particular incident and saying is compared with the Synoptics, it retains its value. If the information about the date of the event fits so well by a mere fluke, then it is certainly an impressive one (see Robinson 1985, 130–31). John's placement of the saying on the lips of Jesus in the context of his temple action is historically plausible. Further, if the wording of the saying in John represents an alteration from its original form, the changes are not more extensive than is the case in the other works in which the saying appears. In Mark's version, the contrast about the temple being made with hands is inserted and the words are depicted as something Jesus did not in fact say (Mark 14:58). In Matthew's version, the wording is changed to "I am able" (Matt 26:61), while in Luke the saying is omitted altogether, except in some hints in the accusation brought against Stephen (Acts 6:14). In the version in Thomas, the second half of the saying is changed, either to reflect the fact that the temple was not rebuilt or simply as part of a negative view of the temple (Gos. Thom. 71). John's version resembles the most likely original form of the saying, at least as plausibly as the versions found in other written sources. And as we saw

---

16. Murphy-O'Connor (2000, 54) makes the same point, but without citing Robinson.

above, the changes reflected in John seem to have originated much earlier—at least as early as those reflected in Mark.

Let us conclude by considering the implications of our study of this pericope for the broader question of this volume. What would it mean to "alter the default setting" with respect to the Gospel of John and to take seriously the oral culture in which this Gospel was produced?[17] In most scholarship on the historical Jesus, the Synoptic portrait has been predominant, and it is certainly legitimate to ask about the extent to which that approach is fair and serviceable in its present form.[18] We constantly need to be reminded that the apparent dominance of the Synoptic portrait of Jesus in early Christianity is quite possibly an illusion, created precisely by our focus on the *literary remains* of a group whose primary contact with the Jesus material was not through this medium. Precisely because of their literary interdependence, the agreement of Mark, Matthew, and Luke is the least significant form of agreement from a historical perspective, and it may be precisely the *literary* connection that accounts for the relatively conservative use of sources by Matthew and Luke.

On the other hand, attempting to take the Fourth Gospel and its independent witness to the oral tradition seriously is unlikely to change radically our historical conclusions. This is because John's reliability is doubted in most instances, not simply because of its differences from the other Gospels, but also because of its internal consistency, showing that any and all stories are told in the author's unique language and from his personal perspective. Nevertheless, to the extent that this is true of our other sources as well, we may still find ourselves able to include *more* from John in our view of Jesus' self-understanding. Conversely, we may find ourselves asking similar questions about whether the style of Mark, Q, or Thomas might not just as clearly reflect a particular way of recalling and performing the Jesus story. At any rate, these considerations affect the *sayings* attributed to Jesus and other characters in the Fourth Gospel. They do not automatically discount the value of *narrative* details about places and events in John. In general, historians have found such material in John to be useful at times, certainly more so than the distinctive Johannine monologues placed on the lips of Jesus.

If our argument about Paul's knowledge of a version of the temple saying resembling the one found in John is persuasive, this should encourage historians of early Christianity to reflect further on the implication of the date of sources for their historicity. Our early Christian sources are the textual artifacts of a primarily oral culture. It remains a worthy principle that earlier sources tend to be more reliable, all else being equal. This needs to be counterbalanced, however, with the ability of oral cultures to keep stories and memories alive for generations, as well as the relative freedom such cultures exercise each and every time a story is

---

17. For this way of referring to our altering assumptions, see Dunn 2005, 79–125.
18. See further Meier 1991, 44–45; Theissen and Merz 1998, 36–37.

retold. It may thus at times be true that, even though the Gospel of Mark is the earlier writing, another Gospel may preserve a saying in its earliest *form*, where Mark (or the tradition he was drawing on) had elaborated, edited, or otherwise modified it.[19]

The difference of a few decades between the writing of the earliest Gospels is of only relative importance when we consider that they are all most likely closer in date to each other than any of them is to the historical figure of Jesus. John, even if written somewhat later, may stand in the same sort of relationship to the Jesus tradition as the Gospel of Mark does. It may be that Mark, John, and Thomas all represent similar reworkings and then crystallizations of the Jesus tradition. Thus, to paraphrase Martin Hengel's famous statement about the development of Christology, it may indeed be the case that more happened of significance in the Johannine (and Markan and Thomasine) traditions in the *first decade* than in the next several centuries. If this is in fact the case, then the fundamental question becomes not whether John or Mark is more reliable, but whether we can in any way, shape, or form get back behind these multiple Christian "performances" of and variations on the teaching of Jesus to the historical figure who lies behind them.

---

19. See in particular Dunn 1992b, 1349–59; Sweet 1991, 375–76. See also Lord 1978, 44, 58–89; but also the cautionary remarks of Charles H. Talbert in the same volume (1978, 100–101). The differences between the transmission and memory of *songs* and of other forms of speech should not be overlooked.

JOHN AS WITNESS AND FRIEND

Mary Coloe

The Fourth Gospel is the most historical of all the Gospels. While it has been entitled "the spiritual Gospel," its depth of spiritual insight does not in any way detract from its focus on the actual life and death of Jesus of Nazareth.[1] In fact, this Gospel proclaims that history is now the locus of the divine presence. In the flesh of Jesus, we have the eternal Word of God. For this reason, history is now radiant with the glory of God: "The Word became flesh and dwelt among us, and we have seen his glory, glory as of the only begotten" (1:14). The event of the incarnation undergirds the principle that will govern the telling of this Gospel's story.[2] Words and deeds, places and times will be both mundane, in that they refer to things of this world, and symbolic, in that they, at the same time, look to the transcendent to find their fuller meaning. There is a reality in the Gospel narrative that is both fully historical and, at the same time, transcends the historical. If this Gospel dispenses with history, it loses its christological credibility, for then the Word remains ephemeral, inchoate. Thus my reading of the Fourth Gospel begins with a presumption of its being deeply grounded in the remembered words and deeds of Jesus of Nazareth.[3]

Where this Gospel stands apart from the Synoptic Gospels is in its way of recounting the tradition that it has received. Whereas the Synoptics invite the reader into a symbolic world in the many parables of Jesus recounted as part of the narrative, the Fourth Gospel uses the narrative itself to invite the reader into its symbolizing dynamic. The story of Jesus is from the beginning, the history of the Word-made-flesh. In this essay I shall demonstrate this juxtaposing

---

1. The designation "the spiritual Gospel" was first given by Clement of Alexandria (ca. 200 C.E.); Eusebius, *Hist. eccl.* 6.14.7.

2. This principle for the uniquely Johannine way of recounting the tradition of Jesus was termed the "Sacramental Principle" by Sandra Schneiders (1977, 221–35), in an essay that remains one of the clearest expositions of the symbolic character of the Fourth Gospel.

3. On the trustworthiness of the Fourth Gospel regarding historical, social, and geographic details, see Brown 1966–70, 1:xlii–xliii; 2003, 90–111.

of history and symbol using the figure of John the Baptist, to illustrate the way the Fourth Evangelist uses the narrative, drawing on traditional material, to tell the story of the Word, in the story of Jesus.[4] The narrated word will reveal the incarnate Word.

JOHN IN THE TRADITION

In the Christian liturgical year, Advent focuses on John the Baptist. This placement of John before Christmas reflects the traditional interpretation of John presented in the Synoptics, that John is the herald, the precursor. He is the one who comes before "to prepare the way of the Lord." So strong is this tradition of John's role as the forerunner that it is regularly taken to reflect the historical and sequential reality: first John baptized Jesus, then John was arrested, then Jesus began his ministry of preaching in Galilee. This is the sequence we find in the Synoptics. The single dissenting voice is that of the Fourth Gospel, which in the past has been too readily dismissed as "unhistorical" and "spiritual" because of its symbolic language; however, as I noted above, history and symbol are not mutually exclusive.

THE PROLOGUE

John is described as "a man sent from God" (1:6), and his role is "for testimony, to bear witness to the light, that all might believe through him" (1:7). This verse clearly names who John is, not John the Baptizer but simply John, the witness. Still within the Prologue, John witnesses directly and says, "this was he of whom I said, 'he who comes after me ranks before me, for he was before me'" (1:15). This brief verse raises a number of critical issues: (1) To whom is John referring by this expression? (2) What is meant by the expression "comes after me"? Does it mean discipleship? In the context of the Christian proclamation of Jesus and of the Fourth Gospel's theology of the preexistent Word, the verse as it now stands is a reference to the divine Word, who ranks higher than John and whose existence has already been situated "in the beginning."[5] But the statement is more complex

---

4. I shall not attempt a reconstruction of the historical Baptist. For those wanting historical assessment of what evidence we have, I recommend Meier 1994, chs. 12 and 13, esp. 101–5. More recently, Catherine Murphy's work (2003) provides a helpful introduction to redaction criticism in its evaluation of Baptist material. There is also a short study of the Baptist material from a historical perspective in Moloney 2000, 42–58. My interest is to take up two images from the early tradition and to see how the Fourth Evangelist has used this traditional material for his christological purposes.

5. Brown (1966–70, 1:56, 63–65) discusses the understanding of this expression in a temporal sense, referring to the preexistent *logos*.

than this. This verse is one of very few in the Fourth Gospel that has a close parallel in the Synoptics, as the following table shows.

John 1:15, 27	Mark 1:7	Matthew 3:11	Luke 3:16
15 (John testified to him and cried out, "This was he of whom I said, 'He who comes after me ranks ahead of me because he was before me.'")	He proclaimed, "The one who is more powerful than I is coming after me; I am not worthy to stoop down and untie the thong of his sandals."	"I baptize you with water for repentance, but he who is coming after me is mightier than I, whose sandals I am not worthy to carry; he will baptize you with the Holy Spirit and with fire."	"I baptize you with water for repentance, but one who is more powerful than I is coming after me; I am not worthy to carry his sandals. He will baptize you with the Holy Spirit and fire."
27 "… the one who is coming after me; I am not worthy to untie the thong of his sandal."			

The Fourth Gospel shares with Mark and Matthew a statement put on the lips
of John about "one coming after me" (this sequence is implied in Luke); a statement of unworthiness to untie his sandals (in all Synoptics); and a comparison
made indicating that the coming one is more deserving of honor.[6] In assessing the
evidence, on the grounds of multiple attestation, John Meier concludes "we have
good reason to accept this as substantially the Baptist's own teaching" (1994, 33;
see also Murphy 2003, 57). But what would John have meant by this in its original
setting? Again, drawing on Meier's work, this statement probably indicates John's
expectation of the dawn of the eschatological age and John's awareness that there
was one coming that would have a greater role in bringing this about (1994, 35).
According to the prophet Malachi, Elijah was to return before the day of the Lord:
"Behold I will send you Elijah the prophet before the great and terrible day of the
LORD comes" (Mal 4:6). It is possible that John, during his ministry, considered
that such an Elijah figure was soon to come and that his own ministry was in
preparation for that day.[7] Read in this light, his statement in John 1:15 would

---

6. A similar statement is found also in Acts 13:25.

7. There has been considerable debate about whether the expectation of Elijah was part
of Second Temple Judaism or owes its origin to early Christian teaching. A brief summary of
this debate is in Taylor 1997, 281–88. Taylor draws the following conclusion based on evidence
from Qumran and other intertestamental writings: "The main point to be derived from this

have had a temporal sense: "The one who comes after me (Elijah *redivivus*) is more important than me, for he was before me."[8] On their own, the words "who comes after me," as spoken by John, do not suggest discipleship but rather a statement about the temporal order: John first, then the coming one. Meier uses other material, particularly Jesus' baptism by John, to propose that there was a time when Jesus followed John in the sense that he shared John's view that Israel's end-time was approaching (Meier 1994, 106–9).[9] The question of whether Jesus stayed within John's circle of disciples meets with varying responses. Only the Fourth Gospel depicts Jesus carrying out a ministry of baptizing (3:22), and while there is no corroborating evidence, the principle of embarrassment argues for the historicity of this information.[10] But this activity alone does not indicate that Jesus was one of John's disciples in a formal sense. He may well have begun a ministry of preaching and baptizing independently of John. Weighing the evidence, I think there is a strong possibility that Jesus was a disciple of John for some period, but I speak of this as a possibility rather than probability.

Day 1: John and the Jewish Delegation

When the Gospel narrative begins, John appears in dispute with the Jerusalemites regarding his own identity. John does not identify the "one coming after" him explicitly as Elijah or the Son of Man but leaves this identity vague. What is clear, however, is that John, along with other Jews, is still expecting another figure to come, so he is not seeing himself in the role of Elijah *redivivus*. In fact, in the Fourth Gospel he explicitly denies this title. When asked by the delegation from Jerusalem, "Are you Elijah?" John replies, "I am not" (1:21). Given such a clear and resounding οὐκ εἰμί, why has the Christian tradition so strongly identified John as the forerunner, the prophet Elijah?

The association of John with Elijah comes as part of the post-Easter proclamation of Jesus as the Christ. In looking back at these two figures and attempting to clarify their roles and relationships, if Jesus was the Christ, then John must

---

brief survey of texts is that Elijah was expected by some Jews to come before the end, but how one imagined the end depended on many factors. There was no one, fully supported scenario among Jews of this time" (285).

8. The same temporal sense would apply to any apocalyptic figure: Elijah, Moses, Son of Man. None of these figures would have been considered by John to be his disciple (Meier 1994, 118).

9. Moloney (2000, 48–49) goes further in suggesting that Jesus was a follower of John in a serious sense without John being aware of his identity as "the one coming after me"

10. Meier 1994, 122. That Jesus' baptizing activity was embarrassing can be seen in the later correction of this information: "Although Jesus himself did not baptize, but only his disciples" (John 4:2).

have been the Elijah promised by Malachi.[11] So we must distinguish between the historical John, as far as can be ascertained, and John as a character created in the Synoptic texts. From the above discussion of the phrase about "the mightier one" coming after John, which we have argued was part of John's own teaching, it is clear that the historical John did not consider himself to be the Elijah figure; in fact, in Mark's Gospel Jesus is the one who is first considered to be Elijah (Mark 6:15; 8:28).[12]

It is likely that an early form of Mark introduced John simply as "the voice of one crying in the wilderness: 'Prepare the way of the Lord, make straight his paths'" (Mark 1:2).[13] This is almost identical to the way John is introduced in the Fourth Gospel. At a later stage, the lines from Malachi were added: "Behold I send my messenger before thy face, who shall prepare thy way" (Mal 3:1). This verse, which does not directly follow its introduction, "As it is written in Isaiah the prophet," expresses the post-Easter association of John with the apocalyptic messenger of Malachi. The presentation of John simply as the voice in the wilderness preparing for another greater one still to come, which is found in the pre-Markan tradition and in the Fourth Gospel, is therefore more likely to be historical than the later, clearly Christian, association of John and Elijah. As Barrett (1978, 144) states, "John sharply contradicts the earlier, and apparently growing, tradition, returning perhaps to a pre-Synoptic stage of Christian belief, before apocalyptic necessity called for the discovery of Elijah in some forerunner of Christ."[14]

Once the tradition made the John/Elijah association, in order to affirm its identification of Jesus as the Christ, this colored its presentation of both John and Jesus and their respective ministries. John/Elijah is the forerunner who prepares the way and then withdraws, which is essentially the picture of John presented in the Synoptics. But this sequence (first John, then Jesus, with John as the precursor) must be seen as a Synoptic interpretation and not taken uncritically to represent historical events.

---

11. On the association of Elijah and John in the early Christian community, see Hahn 1969, 365–72.

12. There are passages in the Synoptics where Jesus identifies John and Elijah (Mark 9:11–13; Matt 11:9–10; Luke 7:24–27) but Meier (1994, 141–42) argues that these sayings are "probably a Christian reflection added to an authentic logion of Jesus concerning the Baptist (Matt 11:7–9 par.)." For more details on the Markan redaction, see Ernst 1989, 30–34.

13. The quotation from Malachi is an awkward insertion, suggesting a later revision. Because the form of the quotation is identical to what is found in Matt 11:10//Luke 7:27, Mark may have relied on a source such as Q. In their introduction of John the Baptist, Matthew and Luke omit the lines from Malachi, since they do not follow Mark's introductory phrase, and a later copyist corrected the introduction to read, "As it is written in the prophets" (MSS A, K, P, W); see Robinson 1957–58, 267 n. 1; Metzger 1994, 62. For a further discussion of these verses with the suggestion that the Malachi citation is editorial, see Ernst 1989, 11–12.

14. See also Brown 1965, 139: "JBap seems to have conceived of his role only in terms of the Isaiah voice in the desert (a text associated with him in all four Gospels)."

After denying the titles that the Jerusalemites presented to him (John 1:20–21), John describes himself with the quotation from Isaiah referred to above, but with a significant change.

Isaiah 40:3 (LXX)	Mark 1:2–3	Matthew 3:3// Luke 3:4	John 1:23
	As it is written in the prophet Isaiah, "See, I am sending my messenger ahead of you, who will prepare your way; the voice of one crying out in the wilderness: 'Prepare the way of the Lord, make his paths straight,'"	This is the one of whom the prophet Isaiah spoke when he said, "The voice of one crying out in the wilderness: 'Prepare the way of the Lord, make his paths straight.'"	He said, "I am the voice of one crying out in the wilderness, 'Make straight the way of the Lord,'" as the prophet Isaiah said.
φωνὴ βοῶντος ἐν τῇ ἐρήμῳ ἑτοιμάσατε τὴν ὁδὸν κυρίου, εὐθείας ποιεῖτε τὰς τρίβους τοῦ θεοῦ ἡμῶν,		… as it is written in the book of the words of the prophet Isaiah, "The voice of one crying out in the wilderness: 'Prepare the way of the Lord, make his paths straight …'"	ἔφη, ἐγὼ φωνὴ βοῶντος ἐν τῇ ἐρήμῳ·εὐθύνατε τὴν ὁδὸν κυρίου, καθὼς εἶπεν Ἡσαΐας ὁ προφήτης.

The Fourth Gospel follows the LXX reading, as indicated by the use of the verb βοᾶν here, while this Gospel usually uses κράζειν (1:15; 7:28, 37; 12:44) or κραυγάζειν (11:43; 12:13; 18:40; 19:6, 12, 15). It does not use the verb prepare (ἑτοιμάσατε) but instead conflates the two clauses found in Isaiah to read, "make straight [εὐθύνατε] the paths of the Lord." In discussing this change, Menken (1996, 26–28) notes that the verb "to prepare" is used to describe the task of someone preparing something for another who is absent, and only when it has been accomplished does the other arrive. With the task of preparation finished, the one doing the preparation can depart. While this describes the role of a forerunner, which is how the Synoptics present John, it is not an appropriate description of John's role as described in the Fourth Gospel. John is to bear witness, which means he must know the one about whom he testifies. So in the Fourth Gospel, John cannot depart the scene as soon as Jesus appears. Instead, there are a series of encounters between Jesus and John (1:29–34, 35–37; 3:23, 27–30), and it is implied that there was a previous encounter when Jesus was baptized (1:32–34). The ministry of John and the early ministry of Jesus are contemporaneous. Menken concludes, "John the Baptist is not so much Jesus' precursor as a witness who appears next to Jesus" (1996, 31).

The change in the wording of the Isaiah prophecy, along with John's explicit denial of the role of Elijah, indicates to the reader that the Fourth Gospel need not follow the temporal sequence of the Synoptics. In breaking the John/Elijah nexus, the Fourth Evangelist is free to bypass Synoptic theological interpretation of John's role as the forerunner and can draw upon more historical memories. Of course, the Evangelist may also shape and present these memories in a way to augment his particular Christology. Further evidence will be needed to decide on the historical reliability of John's characterization, but at least this evaluation can be freed from the assumption that the Synoptic sequence is necessarily historical, thus no longer making the Synoptics the measuring stick for historicity.

Days 2 and 3: John's Witness

On the following day, Jesus is introduced into the narrative for the first time. At this point John witnesses to an event that had previously taken place when Jesus' identity was revealed to him (1:32–34). The next day John is with his disciples; when he sees Jesus again, and following his identification of Jesus as "the Lamb of God," these two disciples follow Jesus (1:35–39).[15] We hear nothing further of John until he returns in John 3, in the narrative about Jesus' early ministry. What I wish to emphasize is that John does not disappear completely from the Gospel when Jesus appears and begins his own ministry. There is no mention that John has been imprisoned. Furthermore, at some indefinite time prior to the start of the narrative, John and Jesus have already met at Jesus' baptism. Jesus invites two of John's disciples to follow him; then Jesus begins his own ministry while John continues his. The Fourth Gospel therefore differs from the Synoptics in two significant ways: the ministries of Jesus and John overlap; some of Jesus' first disciples came from a group around John, a possibility that "does not strain the imagination," as Moloney suggests (2000, 50). It was Raymond Brown (1979, 29, 32) who first proposed that some of the early members of the Johannine community may have been disciples of John, including the anonymous Beloved

---

15. It is beyond the scope of this essay to discuss the possible meaning of the phrase "Lamb of God." At the 2005 Colloquium in Leuven, a consensus was forming that this must be understood as a messianic title, couched as it is between John's denial that he is the Messiah (1:20, 25) and Andrew's statement to Simon, "We have found the Messiah" (1:42). This suggestion fits in with one made by Brown (1965, 137) that the expression refers to an apocalyptic lamb who destroys the evil of the world such as found in T. Jos. 19:8; 1 En. 90:38; and Rev 5:9.

Disciple.[16] His hypothetical reconstruction of the Johannine community offers a way of understanding the high esteem given to John in this Gospel, but also the consistent affirmation of Jesus' superiority over John: John is a burning lamp (5:35), Jesus is the light (8:12); John is the witness (1:15), Jesus is the coming one (1:30); John is the bridegroom's friend (3:29), Jesus is the bridegroom (3:29); John must decrease, while Jesus must increase (3:30).

Once we realize that the "John-then-Jesus" sequence of the Synoptics may be theologically driven to explain the relationship between the two men in terms of Elijah the forerunner, followed by the Messiah-Christ, then it is possible to weigh the evidence of the Fourth Gospel on its own merits. The chronology of all the Gospels places John before Jesus. In Mark and Matthew, John baptizes Jesus (Mark 1:9–11; Matt 3:13–17), and the criterion of embarrassment suggests that this scene is recounted because it has a basis in history. It is unlikely that an early Christian community would invent this episode (Meier 1994, 100–105; see also Murphy 2003, 59). But the Fourth Gospel depicts Jesus in the ambit of John for at least three days, then carrying out an independent ministry of baptism. How can this be evaluated?

John Meier addresses these questions by looking at the polemical nature of the Fourth Gospel's rhetoric in the description of John. He concludes that this rhetoric is necessary because the Fourth Evangelist seems to have had some opposition from some Baptist followers still claiming the superiority of John over Jesus (Meier 1994, 119).[17] While John himself is presented very positively, the view that John could be greater is strongly corrected at every opportunity. It is in the Evangelist's interests, therefore, to minimize the significance of John, in contrast to Jesus. If such is his pastoral situation, it would thwart his own goals if he created a narrative suggesting that in any way Jesus was a follower of John. It would suit his christological purpose to follow the Synoptic lead and have John disappear from the scene before Jesus begins his ministry. That he does not do this, but allows the potentially embarrassing scenario of John and Jesus carrying out similar ministries at the same time, argues for the historical plausibility of the Fourth Gospel's account. The criterion of embarrassment again argues for the probable historicity of some of John's disciples becoming disciples of Jesus. "Granted the theological program of the Fourth Evangelist, it is difficult to imagine him making up the story that some of the most important disciples of Jesus had first chosen the Baptist as their master" (Meier 1994, 120).

---

16. For a recent review of Brown's hypothesis on the historical development of the Johannine community and a survey of other reconstructions, see Brown 2003, 69–78. See also Tatum 1994, 163; Moloney 2000, 50–51, 57–58.

17. See also Brown's comments (2003, 156): "The cautions uttered against exaggerating the role of JBap and placing him on the level of Jesus may have arisen in Johannine history out of conflict with the sectarians of JBap, but in the final Gospel they are not addressed to such sectarians. They have a christological function of deepening the faith of John's Christian readers."

I am not arguing here that every aspect of the Fourth Gospel's presentation of John is historical, but that its overall schema of John and Jesus engaging in similar and contemporary baptizing ministries is quite probable, as is its description of Jesus' first disciples coming from the ambit of John.[18] I think that the Fourth Gospel is correct in claiming that John did not see himself as an Elijah figure but thought there was another coming soon who would fit this role. John's task was to ready the people for this coming one by being the "voice in the wilderness," as prophesied by Isaiah. That the historical John clearly identified Jesus as this coming one is highly questionable. In Matthew and Luke, John sends disciples from his prison to ask this question; Meier argues for the historicity of this scene using the criteria of embarrassment and discontinuity with later Christian apologetic (1994, 130–37). Moloney considers that John most likely "went to his death not certain that his former follower, now exercising a ministry of his own, was ὁ ἰσχυρότερος" (2000, 48). It is also reasonable to suppose that if John had recognized in Jesus the one he was awaiting, then he himself would have become Jesus' disciple, rather than simply sending two of his followers.

THE BRIDEGROOM'S FRIEND[19]

When John's disciples follow Jesus, the narrative focus shifts away from John to the opening account of Jesus' ministry. John returns to the narrative following the Nicodemus episode when some of his disciples raise their concerns regarding Jesus' popularity. In this context John describes himself as the friend of the bridegroom who has been sent before the Christ.

All four Gospels have sayings applying the image of the bridegroom to Jesus within a context of a comparison being made between Jesus and John.

---

18. Taylor (1997, 288–99) argues otherwise and accepts the Synoptic chronology that John was imprisoned before Jesus began his baptizing ministry. While recognizing the christological agenda of the Fourth Gospel, I do not think she pays sufficient attention to the christological agenda of the Synoptics in casting John in the role of Elijah, the forerunner.

19. In discussing marriage customs at the time of Jesus, it must be recognized that there are few, if any, texts from this period providing conclusive evidence of the social customs. What follows draws on scholarship based on references to marriage found in the biblical literature over a range of centuries and also what was codified in the Mishnah in the postbiblical era. A law code from Sumerian times indicates that the role of the bridegroom's friend was a very ancient custom that extended beyond Israel and included other Middle Eastern nations. I am presuming here that some of the customs described were preserved during the Second Temple period. See van Selms 1950, 65–75. For the narrative significance of this image, see Coloe 2007, chs. 2 and 3.

Mark 2:18–20	Matthew 9:14–15	Luke 5:30–35	John 3:25–30
[18] Now John's disciples and the Pharisees were fasting; and people came and said to him, "Why do John's disciples and the disciples of the Pharisees fast, but your disciples do not fast?" [19] Jesus said to them, "The wedding guests cannot fast while the bridegroom is with them, can they? As long as they have the bridegroom with them, they cannot fast. [20] The days will come when the bridegroom is taken away from them, and then they will fast on that day."	[14] Then the disciples of John came to him, saying, "Why do we and the Pharisees fast often, but your disciples do not fast?" [15] And Jesus said to them, "The wedding guests cannot mourn as long as the bridegroom is with them, can they? The days will come when the bridegroom is taken away from them, and then they will fast."	[30] The Pharisees and their scribes were complaining to his disciples, saying, "Why do you eat and drink with tax collectors and sinners?" [33] Then they said to him, "John's disciples, like the disciples of the Pharisees, frequently fast and pray, but your disciples eat and drink." [34] Jesus said to them, "You cannot make wedding guests fast while the bridegroom is with them, can you? [35] The days will come when the bridegroom will be taken away from them, and then they will fast in those days."	[25] Now a discussion about purification arose between John's disciples and a Jew. [26] They came to John and said to him, "Rabbi, the one who was with you across the Jordan, to whom you testified, here he is baptizing, and all are going to him." [27] John answered, "No one can receive anything except what has been given from heaven. [28] You yourselves are my witnesses that I said, 'I am not the Messiah, but I have been sent ahead of him.' [29] He who has the bride is the bridegroom. The friend of the bridegroom, who stands and hears him, rejoices greatly at the bridegroom's voice. For this reason my joy

has been
fulfilled.[30] He
must increase,
but I must
decrease."

Meier argues for the authenticity of the bridegroom image within a saying of Jesus in response to questions about fasting: "The sharp antithetical metaphors of fasting and a wedding, compressed into a single rhetorical question, are typical of the forceful rhetoric and parabolic speech of Jesus" (1994, 448).[20] Without going into the possible meaning this image may have had for Jesus, I wish to focus on the way the image was developed in the post-Easter communities, particularly the community behind the Fourth Gospel. The image of the bridegroom has its background in the spousal imagery used in the Old Testament to describe the relationship between God and Israel (Hos 1–2; Jer 2:2; Isa 61:10). In the post-Easter preaching this image was one of many such biblical images transferred by the Christian communities to describe the relationship between Jesus and the *ekklēsia* (2 Cor 11:2; Eph 5:27). The Ephesian imagery draws on the marriage custom where the young woman prepares for her wedding by bathing before being led in procession and presented to her husband (Boismard 1961, 292).

> Husbands, love your wives, just as Christ loved the church and gave himself up for her, in order to make her holy by cleansing her with the washing of water by the word, so as to present the church to himself in splendor, without a spot or wrinkle or anything of the kind—yes, so that she may be holy and without blemish. (Eph 5:25–27)

The washing "of water with the word" is a reference to baptism, indicating that this community at Ephesus linked baptism with the bridal bath and drew on marital imagery to speak of Christ's love for his church. When turning to the bridegroom imagery in the Fourth Gospel, we find a similar baptismal context. There appears to be a genuine memory behind this episode. It recalls some rivalry between the disciples of these two men, who, at least for some period of time, were involved in similar baptizing ministries and yet had different practices. The Fourth Gospel takes up the image of the bridegroom, which the evidence suggests was originally a saying of Jesus, but places this on the lips of John. Now it is John who makes the contrast between himself and Jesus, with Jesus as the bridegroom, while he has the role of the bridegroom's friend.

---

20. Meier 1994, 448. While arguing for the authenticity of an original core saying, Meier also shows how later tradition has made use of this saying for apologetic reasons.

THE ROLE OF THE "FRIEND" IN BETROTHAL AND MARRIAGE CUSTOMS

Marriage in biblical times was a purely social institution with no religious ceremonies, since there is nothing in the Torah stipulating how marriages were to be celebrated.[21] It was an arrangement entered into by two families. While each village no doubt had its own local variations, the following description provides a general pattern for this arrangement.

Marriage involved first a formal betrothal, with the wedding following after a period of at least a year (Stapfer 1885, 160, 162). Arrangements for the betrothal were made with the heads of the families of the young man and the young woman (Gen 24:1–4; Judg 14:1–3); if the father was absent, the arrangements became the duty of the mother or the elder brother (Gen 21:14–21; see Trumbull 1894, 12). In these negotiations the two fathers did not deal directly with each other but through deputies (Trumbull 1894, 17), probably to avoid any loss of honor if the negotiations broke down.[22] This was one of the tasks of the bridegroom's friend (Wight 1953, 127). The deputy would be informed of the dowry and how much of that would be paid at the time of betrothal and how much at the actual wedding. The father of the groom and this friend/deputy formally went to the house of the intended bride to begin discussions about the appropriate dowry that the bridegroom would pay and that would revert to the wife in case of divorce (Collins 1997, 109). When the purpose of the visit was explained, the bride's father would send for a deputy to speak for him (Trumbull 1894, 18). When the two deputies were present, the negotiations began until there was consent about the marriage and the dowry, then the deputies and the fathers drank together as a sign of the covenant now agreed upon. At this point the couple was considered engaged until a more formal betrothal ceremony could take place. In earlier times the betrothal was a spoken pledge before witnesses (Ezek 16:8; Mal 2:14), but after the exile a written document was drawn up in the presence of the families of the bride and the groom and of other witnesses (Stapfer 1885, 161; Collins 1997, 109). According to Turnbull (1894, 20), it was the deputies who drew up the formal contract, which was signed by the two fathers and then "committed into the trusty hands of the best man" (Jeremias 1967, 1101 n. 20). During this ceremony, the young man would give the young woman a ring, some other wealthy article, or a written promise of marriage as an initial sign of commitment; part of the dowry could

---

21. See Trumbull 1894; Collins 1997, 107; Stapfer 1885, 159, 165. Trumbull describes customs among Arabs in the Middle East in the nineteenth century C.E., but his description seems to accord with customs found in the biblical literature.

22. "Few events held more potential for the transfer of honor than marriage. Conversely, for a father, especially of the bride, few events would have been as laden with anxiety as marriage.... [E]very juncture presented a possibility for shame and social disaster. In such an environment it is a miracle that anyone would want to enter the process of negotiating a marriage" (Satlow 2001, 104).

also be given at this stage with the promise of the rest at the time of the wedding.[23] At this time a pledge would be spoken.[24] A typical pledge was, "She is my wife and I am her husband" (Collins 1997, 108). The betrothal was a formal and binding agreement that could only be broken by divorce or death (Yamauchi 1978, 244–45; Stapfer 1885, 162; Trumbull 1894, 26).

It is clear from this description that the bridegroom's friend had a very significant role in the proceedings even prior to the wedding. As friend, he was the one who dealt directly with the family of the young woman. His negotiations played a crucial part in the father's granting consent. It is for this reason that there were ancient laws forbidding the father, if he refused the request of the intended bridegroom, to give his daughter to the bridegroom's friend. "If a son-in-law [intended] has entered the house of his [intended] father-in-law and has performed the betrothal gift, and afterwards they have made him go out and have given his wife to his companion—they shall present to him the betrothal gift which he has brought and that wife may not marry his companion" (van Selms 1950, 65–70). The term "companion" in this passage refers to the formal role called today in Western cultures the "best man" or in the Fourth Gospel the "friend of the bridegroom" (3:29). By virtue of the friend's role in the prebetrothal arrangements, he could never be the husband, even if the proposal was turned down. The bride could never be his.[25]

The wedding ceremony itself involved a joyous procession of the young woman from her father's house to the bridegroom's home, which was his ancestral home, since the young man usually stayed within the house of his parents, his father's house. She was conducted to her new home by her relatives with songs and dancing.[26] This procession traveled slowly, so that the entire village could see the finery and wealth of the young bride, and it would usually arrive at the bridegroom's home late in the day for the wedding ceremony, which "was always in the evening at sunset" (Stapfer 1885, 163; Trumbull 1894, 39–44). Sometimes the groom himself would come to lead the bride, and sometimes this role would

---

23. The account of the betrothal of Isaac and Rebecca is similar to this description. Abraham's servant acts as the go-between and gives Rebecca a golden ring and bracelets. When her father has agreed to the betrothal, the servant produces more jewels of silver and gold as gifts to Rebecca and her family (Gen 24).

24. Samples of written pledges from the fifth century B.C.E. have been found in Egypt (see Yamauchi 1978, 246). Collins (1997, 111–12) also describes contracts from the early second century C.E.

25. This is the situation described in Judg 14, when the woman Samson claims for his wife is given instead to the best man, so that Samson considers himself blameless for his actions against the Philistines (Judg 14–15). See also van Selms 1950, 71–74.

26. Wight 1953, 131–33. Trumbull (1894, 45–58) describes a wedding procession he observed in the Arabian Desert. While this took place in the nineteenth century, the description of events parallels many biblical passages.

again be given to the bridegroom's friend (Boismard 1961, 292).[27] While the procession was a public feature of the wedding, the most solemn moment came when the bride entered into the home of the bridegroom (Wight 1953, 133; Stapfer 1885, 163): "she was taken in procession to the home of the bridegroom, and it was from that moment that she was considered finally married" (Boismard 1961, 292, my trans.). Here she waited with her attendants while festivities continued outside. Throughout the procession her face was veiled, for now only her husband could see her face within his house (Stapfer 1885, 164). Often the bridegroom would travel in his own procession, arriving at the home some hours later in the evening. He was then led into the bridal chamber by the best man, and it seems that the best man awaited the call of the bridegroom to fetch the nuptial sheet to testify to the virginity of the bride (Jeremias 1967, 1101; Satlow 2001, 175–77).

JOHN: WITNESS AND FRIEND OF THE BRIDEGROOM

The details given above on the customs surrounding betrothal and marriage shed light on the Fourth Gospel's presentation of John. John identifies himself using two images, "the voice" (1:23) and "the friend of the bridegroom" (3:29), while the narrative calls him a "witness" (1:19, 32–34). Evidence about marriages in the Second Temple period is primarily legal in character, and within the legal formalities of the betrothal, witnesses are a necessary part of the contractual arrangements that stipulated the dowry and inheritance rights. During the wedding the bridegroom's friend witnesses that the marriage has been consummated. When looking at John's role through the lens of social customs surrounding marriage, his role as witness and friend of the bridegroom come together.

John is the first to arrive on the scene, and he has been sent by God (1:6). Jesus is first introduced into the narrative through John's voice (1:26–27, 29–30). John describes what he experienced at the baptism and reveals Jesus as the one who outranks him. He then reveals Jesus' identity as "the Son of God" (1:31–34). John acts in this narrative in the traditional manner of a deputy or friend of the bridegroom sent by the groom's father to initiate proceedings that will hopefully lead to betrothal and marriage. He then, as friend of the groom, directs disciples to Jesus (1:35–36), as the friend would direct or lead the young bride to the bridegroom's place. We are told that the disciples saw where Jesus was and stayed with him (1:39). The time detail is given: "about the tenth hour," that is, late afternoon, which would be the traditional time for a wedding celebration. The time detail, which seems to have no other narrative purpose, is one indicator to the reader that the Evangelist may be working with symbolism; that is to say, the meaning

---

27. Boismard refers also to a number of rabbinic texts where God is considered to have had the role of the friend of the bridegroom when, following the creation of Eve, God presented her to Adam.

of this detail is to be found beyond the actual narrative.[28] Once the disciples and Jesus have been brought together, John withdraws from the narrative, which now shifts its focus from John to Jesus.

Without going into details I draw the reader's attention to the overall movement of the narrative, beginning with John's witness and concluding with his self-identification as the bridegroom's friend. Through John disciples are introduced to Jesus; they then participate in a wedding where Jesus acts as the bridegroom in providing the wine for the festivities (2:1–11).[29] The Cana pericope concludes with an affirmation of faith: "his disciples believed in him" (2:11). The following narrative comment should not be overlooked: "After this he went down to Capernaum, with his mother and his brothers and his disciples; and there they stayed for a few days" (2:12). The disciples have now been drawn into the family of Jesus.

The narrative so far has followed the customs of a Middle Eastern marriage, from the initial witness of John, to disciples being directed and led to Jesus, a wedding celebration, and the inclusion of disciples in Jesus' household. These are the preparatory stages for the final solemn moment in a wedding, when the bride enters the home of the bridegroom, which is his father's house. Following the festivities, the groom also enters the bridal chamber, and that, in some cases, is the first time the groom actually sees his new wife. The moment when the bride's veil is lifted is a key moment for their relationship.[30] He will see her face for the first time, and she will read his response to her in his face. It is a revelatory moment for them both.

From Capernaum, Jesus and his disciples travel to Jerusalem and enter his "Father's house" (2:16), the temple of Jerusalem. Here, in his Father's house, Jesus reveals his identity explicitly for the first time. The temple that had been called "the Lord's house" can be called by Jesus "my Father's house," because he is Son (1:14, 18). As the Son in whom the Spirit dwells, Jesus is now the locus for God's presence in history, so that by the end of the pericope the meaning of the temple shifts from a building to his own person. The encounter within the Father's house

---

28. In an article on Johannine symbolism, Juan Leal (1960) offers four criteria that can indicate when the narrative has a symbolic as well as a literal meaning: (1) inconsequential details that seem to play no part in the narrative; (2) a discourse set within the narrative of an event such that they are mutually illuminating; (3) when the Evangelist accentuates the importance of a person who has no significant role in context; (4) when later liturgical and Christian expressions are used.

29. Jesus' role as the bridegroom is implied at Cana when the head steward goes to the bridegroom to congratulate him on producing good wine late in the festivities. This would indicate that the bridegroom has the task of providing wine, and in this case it is Jesus who has provided the good wine. See Moloney 1998b, 68–69, 72–73.

30. Trumbull (1894, 43, 58) notes that in many parts of the East the "specific celebration of the marriage rite is called today 'the lifting of the veil' or 'the uncovering of the face.'"

has been a decisive moment of revelation. The nuptial imagery does not dominate this scene as it did at Cana, but the naming of the temple as "my Father's house," the significant revelation of Jesus' identity as the temple within his Father's house, and the narrative sequence of this scene following the wedding festivities at Cana suggest to me that the narrative has not lost sight of this image, and it will in fact come to the forefront again in the next chapter.

Following these events within the temple, the marital imagery continues in Jesus' encounter with Nicodemus, where Jesus teaches the necessity of being "born anew" and Nicodemus ponders the impossibility of returning to the mother's womb (3:3–5). The language of birth dominates the first part of the discourse, where the setting is a conversation between two people (3:1–10),[31] while the second part, which can be called discourse (3:13–21), introduces the theme of eternal life (3:15, 16).[32] Birth and new life are the final testimony to a complex social process that began with an initial approach by the bridegroom's friend to the home of the intended bride. The birth of a child fulfills the marriage blessing that the bride would bear many children (Gen 24:60; Ruth 4:11).[33] The Gospel narrative has taken us through the stages in this process: a first meeting, initiated by John, with initial signs and the promise of greater things to come; a wedding, with entry into the Father's house; and finally birth. After the episode with Nicodemus, John returns to the narrative for the last time and concludes his testimony by identifying himself as the friend of the bridegroom, a friend whose role is now complete: "he must increase, but I must decrease" (3:30). The narrative has moved from John as witness to John as friend, and in between it has drawn upon nuptial imagery that can be shown schematically as follows:

1:19–34	John (witness)
1:35–51	disciples of John/Jesus
2:1–12	wedding
2:13–25	my Father's House
3:1–21	birth
3:22–24	disciples of John/Jesus
3:25–36	John (friend of the bridegroom)

---

31. The conversational tone comes to an end after 3:10, where there is a shift from singular to plural.

32. For further discussion of the birth imagery in this scene and its relationship to baptism, see Lee 2002, 68–71, 147.

33. Yamauchi 1978, 247. By rabbinic times the blessing, called "the groom's blessing," was a major feature of the wedding celebration and was recited several times over the days of the feasting; see Satlow 2001, 178.

Conclusion

The Fourth Gospel has drawn upon historical memories in its characterization of John. Rather than interpret John as Elijah, this Gospel has used what is
probably a pre-Synoptic designation of John as "the voice crying in the wilderness," which probably goes back to John's own testimony. In its interpretation
of the relationship between John and Jesus, the Fourth Gospel utilizes another
remembered saying from the Jesus tradition, this time a saying of Jesus using the
metaphor of the bridegroom. These sayings have provided the Fourth Evangelist
with two images from the tradition that he develops in an extended metaphor of
Jesus as the bridegroom and John as the witnessing "voice" of the bridegroom's
friend. Using this nuptial imagery, rather than that of the Synoptic forerunner,
the Fourth Evangelist is able to incorporate into his narrative further historical
reminiscences that the Synoptic Gospels must omit if they are to maintain the
Elijah/Christ model. The Fourth Gospel, therefore, is able to show that John and
Jesus were both involved in baptizing ministries at the same time, that this was a
cause of some tension between their disciples, and that some disciples of John left
him to become followers of Jesus.

Far from being "unhistorical," the Johannine narrative has drawn on historical reminiscences from the Jesus tradition, bringing together history and symbol
in a narrative that not only tells a story about what happened but also offers
insight into the meaning of what happened. Jesus, the divine Word incarnate,
enacts the prophetic words of the Old Testament describing God's betrothal to
and love of Israel. Within the sequence under consideration in this essay (John
1:1–3:36), the nuptial symbolism is explicit only in the wedding at Cana and in
John's concluding words, but its presence is felt from the moment John is introduced as the man sent by God as witness (1:6–7), and I suggest that a first-century
audience/reader, familiar with Jewish marital customs, would have picked up the
allusion. The marital imagery makes apparent the underlying narrative logic of
the events across these chapters beginning and ending with John. Ricoeur speaks
of the need to link together the action kernels that constitute a narrative's structural continuity;[34] symbols, in a particular way, hold the actions of a narrative
together by providing a deeper network of associations than simple chronology.
Reading a narrative, alert to its historical and symbolic potential, enriches the
reading experience by offering a second dimension. The artistry of this Fourth
Evangelist offers such a stereoscopic vision, well symbolized in his traditional
image: the eagle.

---

34. Ricoeur 1976, 85.

THE SYMBOLOGY OF THE SERPENT
IN THE GOSPEL OF JOHN

James H. Charlesworth

Over the past two decades, specialists on the Gospel of John have customarily focused on the translation, composition-history, and exegesis of this masterpiece. Less attention is addressed to the symbolic world of the Evangelist. That dimension of Johannine studies is now much clearer, thanks to archaeological research and the study of symbolism (see Charlesworth 2006 and 2008), otherwise known as symbology. The present work will illustrate this emerging clarity by exploring the deeper and fuller meaning of an incredibly rich and well-known section of the Fourth Gospel: John 3:13–17.

Such a study is warranted, since over the last decade some scholars, especially D. Moody Smith, Urban C. von Wahlde, and Paul N. Anderson,[1] have pointed the way for an improved understanding of the Gospel of John by recognizing that in many ways what is reported in the Fourth Gospel has as strong a case of representing reliable history as comparable sections of the Synoptic Gospels. More and more Johannine specialists rightly are perceiving that the Fourth Evangelist seems to know Jewish customs and the architecture of Jerusalem better, in some cases, than the authors of the Synoptics, intermittently describing features of this city missed by Josephus. Archaeological research and discoveries have also made a significant impact on Johannine studies.[2] The essays in this volume significantly advance this new dimension of a reappreciation of the historical elements in the Gospel of John.

The present study of Johannine symbology evolves out of the recognition that the Fourth Evangelist lived in a symbolic world appreciably different from

---

1. See esp. the chapters by von Wahlde and Anderson in *Jesus and Archaeology* (Charlesworth 2006, 523–86 and 587–618).

2. Many of those who contributed to *Jesus and Archaeology* stated and demonstrated, surprisingly, that the Fourth Evangelist knew Jerusalem intimately. His descriptions help us comprehend some pre-70 monumental elements of the Holy City that are being unearthed now and have come to light over the past decade.

ours, achieving an elevated perception of symbolic language and theology. There can be little doubt that John 3:14–15 was carefully couched by the Fourth Evangelist and reflects the symbolic culture of the first century c.e. My translation here indicates the key symbolic words in italics.[3]

> And as *Moses lifted up the serpent in the wilderness,*
> So *it is necessary* for *the Son of Man to be lifted up*
> In order that *all who are believing* in him may have *eternal life.*

Clearly, the Fourth Evangelist is developing a thought based on the well-known story in Num 21. According to this tradition, Moses made a metal serpent and placed it on a staff, so that all who had been bitten by burning-serpents would not die. At first glance, the Evangelist's analogy between this unusual object and Christ seems confused. If the snake symbolizes evil, as is often the case in biblical imagery, the possibility that the Fourth Evangelist is comparing "the serpent" and Jesus the "Son of Man" seems unthinkable. In the first century c.e., however, serpents seldom symbolized evil.

Serpent symbolism was multivalent at the time the Gospel of John was being written and shaped.[4] Yet too many Johannine experts have inadvertently assumed that the negative portrayal of the serpent in books like the Apocalypse of John is the proper perspective from which to understand John 3. In point of fact, as detailed below, serpent imagery in the first century c.e. almost always denoted something positive, such as health, wisdom, beauty, rejuvenation, and resurrection. What, then, is the meaning of John 3:14–15?

The consensus position on this important question has been conveniently summarized by D. Moody Smith, one of the most distinguished Johannine scholars today. Commenting on John 3:14, he notes:

> The biblical scene in view here [at John 3:14] is Num 21:8–9, where the Lord instructs Moses to make an image of a serpent and elevate it on a pole, so that the rebellious Israelites, against whom the Lord had actually sent serpents in the first place, might, if snake bitten, look on it and live. The analogy with the work of the crucified Jesus, the Son of Man who is lifted up, is very striking indeed. It is a classic typology. The element that is new in John, and characteristically Christian, is the emphasis on belief, which is absent from the story in Numbers. (*Of course, comparisons of Jesus with the serpent are misplaced; the analogy applies only to being lifted up*). (Smith 1999, 98, emphasis added)

---

3. I am influenced by the division of texts provided by Boismard and Lamouille 1986, 29.

4. Xavier Léon-Dufour (1990) has written an insightful study of symbolism in the Fourth Gospel but does not discuss the symbol of the serpent in John 3:14.

Smith's reading reflects the consensus view that John 3:14–16 does *not* actually compare Jesus to Moses' serpent. Particularly here, Smith specifically states that John is comparing Moses' act of raising the snake to the crucifixion of Jesus, with no intention to correlate Jesus himself with the bronze serpent; put another way, the analogy is limited entirely to the action, not to the object of the action. In Smith's view, such a comparison would be "misplaced." Yet this conclusion begs a number of important questions. Did John think of Moses' serpent as a *typos* of Jesus, and if so, what meaning did he see in the analogy? If John understood the connection between Christ and the snake primarily in terms of the fact that both were "lifted up," how should the term "lifted up" be understood? Does "lift up" refer to the lifting up on a cross—a meaning this verb (ὑψόω) never carries outside the Johannine corpus—or does it also denote Jesus' "lifting up" into heaven and returning to the Father? Is there any connection between "the serpent" (3:14) and "eternal life" (3:15)?

The remainder of this essay will attempt to answer these questions by reflecting on the wider meaning of serpent symbolism at the time the Fourth Gospel was written and on the actual grammatical and poetic structure of John 3:14–15.

JOHN AND ANCIENT SERPENT SYMBOLISM

The interpretation of John 3:14 entails not only seeking to indwell the complex symbolic language of the Evangelist's time but also searching for the meaning of a symbol: the serpent. Four components must be considered in this analysis: the symbol maker (the Fourth Evangelist), the structure of the symbol itself, the meaning of the symbol, and the interpreter of the symbol (in antiquity and today). In view of space limitations, primarily the third component will be emphasized here.[5] In what ways does the symbol of the serpent reveal or point toward meaning in John 3? To address this question, three fundamental points will be demonstrated here: (1) The serpent was frequently a powerful and positive symbol in the Fourth Evangelist's culture; (2) the verb "lifted up," which, as Smith notes, is a key component of the analogy between Jesus and Moses' serpent, has more than one meaning in the Fourth Gospel; (3) the poetry and grammar of the passage draw a clear parallel between the serpent and Jesus.

1. CULTURAL SYMBOLISM

Over the years, I have often asked research assistants and colleagues what comes to mind when they hear "Jesus, the serpent." They answer, immediately and with

---

5. The other themes are dealt with extensively in my new book, analyzing the serpent symbolism of John 3:13–17 in the light of good and evil associations in the ancient Greco-Roman world (Charlesworth 2008).

no apparent reflection, "Jesus, the Devil." If, however, we were able to ask members of the first-century Johannine community what they thought if they heard that a man was considered a serpent, they most likely would answer that he was divine. Three pieces of evidence from the first-century world may conveniently illustrate this point.

1.1. The first emperor of Rome, Augustus (63 B.C.E.–14 C.E.), was considered a god. The Roman historian Suetonius (ca. 69–140 C.E.), in his informative work, *The Twelve Caesars*, records the following startling account of the birth of Augustus Caesar:

> Then there is a story which I found in a book called *Theologumena*, by Asclepiades of Mendes. Augustus' mother, Atia, with certain married women friends, once attended a solemn midnight service at the Temple of Apollo, where she had her litter set down, and presently fell asleep as the others also did. Suddenly a *serpent* glided up, entered her, and then glided away again. On awakening, she purified herself, as if after intimacy with her husband. An irremovable colored mark in the shape of a *serpent*, which then appeared on her body, made her ashamed to visit the public baths any more; and the *birth of Augustus* nine months later suggested a *divine paternity*.[6]

The story of Augustus's birth from a serpent was well known and widely assumed to be accurate.[7] It shaped beliefs, myths, and reflections on other individuals deemed divine. Augustus was none other than the son of Apollo and grandson of Jupiter and Latona. In evaluating this story of Augustus's "divine paternity" by the great god, Apollo/Zeus, it is relevant to observe that Suetonius's account of the lives of the Caesars continues until the death of Domitian in 96 C.E.—in other words, up through the time when the Fourth Gospel, or its second edition, most likely reached completion. In the Evangelist's day, the divinity of Augustus was widely expressed in terms of serpent imagery.

1.2. Also about the time the Gospel of John achieved its present form (ca. 95 C.E.), Philo of Byblos was working on his compositions. Philo discussed the divine nature of serpents, suggesting that the serpent is immortal because it sheds its skin and appears once again youthful and without blemish.

In his monograph *Ethothion*, which is now lost but preserved in excerpts by Eusebius, Philo claims to "demonstrate" that the serpent is "immortal and that it dissolves into itself ... for this sort of animal does not die an ordinary death unless it is violently struck. The Phoenicians call it 'Good Demon.' Similarly the

---

6. Suetonius, *Aug.* 100; trans. Graves 1989, 104–5, emphasis added.

7. It is possible that Suetonius's statement, "Everyone believes this story," refers not only to the astrologer's claim about Augustus, which immediately precedes it, but also includes the story of the birth of Augustus from a snake.

Egyptians give it a name, *Kneph*, and they also give it the head of a hawk, because of the hawk's active character."

According to Eusebius, Philo called the serpent "exceedingly long-lived, and by nature not only does it slough off old age and become rejuvenated, but it also attains greater growth [lit. "becomes young again"]. When it fulfills its determined limit, it is consumed into itself, as Taautos himself similarly narrates in his sacred writings. Therefore, this animal is included in the rites and mysteries."[8]

These excerpts from Philo of Byblos are critical to the present study at several points. First, they offer valuable insights on the mythologies and symbolic theology of the contemporaries of the Fourth Evangelist. Second, there can be no doubt that this perspective on the serpent was thought to belong not only to the Greeks, Syrians, and Egyptians but also to the Phoenicians and others. Third, and most important, the serpent was lauded for its ability to symbolize new life, rejuvenation, and immortality.

1.3. As a third significant example, a review of the serpent imagery at Pompeii helps us grasp the wider Roman culture of the Fourth Evangelist. The serpent was extremely popular at Pompeii. Images of serpents loom large in murals painted on the exterior walls of houses and also appear within houses in small temples. Serpent iconography graces elegant gold rings, bracelets, and armlets.[9] At Pompeii there was a cult of the serpent. The serpent almost always symbolized life, eroticism, beauty, new life, and protection. Pompeii was destroyed in 79 C.E.; what remains helps us contemplate the world of serpent symbolism that shaped the Fourth Evangelist's symbolism.

If this brief survey were expanded into an exhaustive discussion of first-century C.E. iconography in Persian, Greek, Aramaic, Hebrew, and Latin texts, it would immediately become clear that the Fourth Evangelist and those in his circle, community, or school were reminded almost daily that the serpent symbolized immortality, reincarnation, and perhaps resurrection.

Since John 3:14–15 portrays Jesus as a type of the serpent raised up by Moses, it is imperative to explore the possibility of a remnant of ophidian Christology in the Fourth Gospel. Surely after one has immersed oneself in ancient serpent symbology and the intricate symbolic universe of the Fourth Evangelist, serpent symbology was most likely imagined by some members of the Johannine circle as they heard such words as "I am the way, the truth, and the life" (John 14:6) and "I am the *resurrection* and the *life*; he who believes in me, though he die, yet shall he live, and whoever lives and believes in me shall *never die*" (11:25). The Fourth Evangelist's favorite word for life is ζωή. While this noun

---

8. For the Greek and English text of these excerpts, see Attridge and Oden 1981, 64–65.

9. I am grateful to the officers of the Archaeological Museum in Naples for the opportunity to study minutely the gold jewelry from Pompeii and nearby villages that disappeared in 79 C.E.

appears four times in Mark's Gospel, seven times in Matthew, five times in Luke, and thirty-seven times in the entire Pauline/Deutero-Pauline corpus, John uses ζωή thirty-six times. In the Evangelist's time the serpent was the quintessential symbol for "life"; hence, one should not be blind to the possible christological ophidian symbolism in this noun.

Before proceeding to examine the theological symbolism of the key words in John 3:14–15, attention must be given to the meaning poured into the grammar and syntax of the verses.

2. "Lifted Up"

The Fourth Evangelist three times mentions that Jesus would be "lifted up" (John 3:14; 8:28; 12:32–34). Commentators often assume that this verb refers only to the crucifixion, largely on the basis of contextual evidence from the second and third references. In 8:28, Jesus tells "the Pharisees" that they "will lift up the Son of Man," a statement that can scarcely refer to God's exaltation of Jesus, as is the case with the similar language in Acts 2:33 and 5:31. Even more explicitly, when Jesus states at John 12:32–34 that "when I am lifted up from the earth, I will draw all to myself," the Evangelist adds, "He said this to show by what death he was about to die." At John 8:28 and 12:32–34, the verb "lifted up" clearly refers to Jesus' death. But should this nuance be read back narrowly into 3:14?

In my view, such a reading would violate the integrity of John 3 and miss the *double entendre*: Jesus was lifted up on the cross and thereby exalted on his way to heaven and back to his Father. As Theodor Zahn explained in 1921, "the lifting up is to be understood as the elevation into heaven, the return of Jesus from the earthly world to the otherworldly realm of God" (1983, 204). It must be stressed again, against the tide of recent research, that "to lift up" in the Fourth Gospel denotes not simply crucifixion but also a lifting up on the cross that symbolizes Jesus' exaltation and return to heaven. This point has been recognized and stressed by a number of scholars. Ernst Haenchen wisely pointed out that the Fourth Evangelist avoids mentioning the crucifixion, except in the passion narrative. He refers rather to "its [the verb "lifted up"] divine meaning, the exaltation" (1984, 1:204). Long ago, B. F. Westcott astutely perceived that the words of John 3:14 "imply an exaltation in appearance far different from that of the triumphant king, and yet in its true issue leading to a divine glory. This passage through the elevation on the cross to the elevation on the right hand of God was a necessity … arising out of the laws of the divine nature" (1919, 53). R. J. Burns insightfully states that the Evangelist uses "lifting up" to refer "not only to Jesus' death by crucifixion but to his resurrection as well."[10] George Beasley-Murray correctly

---

10. Burns 1990, 84; perhaps Burns sees this connection because she is primarily an Old Testament specialist.

claims, "To the lifting up of the snake on a pole that all may live corresponds the lifting up of the Son of Man on a cross that all may have eternal life" (1987, 50).

Yet while the eyes of the Hebrews who trust God's promise look up at the copper serpent, and while the Johannine Jews gaze up to the exalted Jesus—the Son of Man and Son of God—there is a difference. In the Septuagint version of Num 21:8, the stake on which the copper serpent is raised is called a "sign" (probably of God's healing power). The "signs" in the Fourth Gospel, Jesus' mighty works (John 5:31–47), play a revelational role in John distinct from the miracles of the Synoptics. These signs (σημεῖα) witness to Jesus, who is not a sign himself, but the One to whom the signs point, according to God's plan (2:11, 23; 3:2; etc.). In light of this insight, and recognizing the stress on Jesus' incarnational and physical nature, it seems difficult to comprehend how Johannine experts can miss the narrative force of John 3:13–16. The Fourth Evangelist does not wish simply to draw attention to the physical "lifting up," but he is also focusing the reader's mind on things above (3:12) and proclaiming that Jesus' crucifixion was not a failure, but his hour of triumph.

According to the Fourth Evangelist, the image of the serpent in Numbers is a foreshadowing of Christ. Specifically, in Num 21 and John 3, the serpent symbolizes God's salvation. As Saint Augustine (354–430 c.e.) stated in his homilies on the Gospel of John: "Just as those who looked on that serpent perished not by the serpent's bites, so they who *look in faith on Christ's death* are healed from the bites of sin."[11]

3. POETRY AND *PARALLELISMUS MEMBRORUM*

Often lost or unobserved by New Testament critics is the poetic structure of John 3:14–15. The content is structured harmoniously in parallel lines of thought so that each word is echoed in the word that follows (*parallelismus membrorum*).[12] As repetition (or echoing) of thought or sound is the heart of all poetry, so parallelism is the hallmark of poetry in biblical Hebrew. Two familiar excerpts from the Psalms may be cited to illustrate this literary structure.

Line 1: Your kingdom is a kingdom for all eternity,
Line 2: And your dominion is for all generations.
Line 3: The Lord upholds all who fall,
Line 4: And raises up all bowed down. (Ps 145:13–14, translation mine)

---

11. Augustine, "On the Gospel of John," 12.11; the quotation is from NPNF 7:85.
12. *Parallelismus membrorum*, or *isocolon*, is thought, written or oral, that is focused on coordinated lines of similar length within an isolated linguistic group of words; see Watson 2000, esp. 260–61.

The thought in line 1 reappears in line 2, and that of line 3 is repeated in line 4. The fourfold repetition of "all," often not represented in translations, also helps to clarify the parallel thought. That is, each line is a universal statement, applying to all places, times, and persons. A similar pattern may be observed in Ps 8:5(4).

Line 1: What is man ['nwsh]   that you are mindful of him,

Line 2: And the son of man [bn-'dm]   that you care for him?

The poetry presents a parallelism; the poetic form is synonymous parallelism. The first two beats in each line are synonymous: the "man" in the first line is synonymous with "the son of man" in the second line. The two beats at the end of each line are also synonymous: God is "mindful" of the human and does "care" for him.

As Martin Hengel (1989b) has demonstrated, the Fourth Evangelist knew the "Old Testament" and its literary forms well. It is no surprise, therefore, to find Hebrew poetic forms appearing in the Fourth Gospel, especially *in the words of Jesus*. The Fourth Evangelist chose synonymous *parallelismus membrorum* to emphasize the divine words directed by Jesus to Nicodemus. Note the poetic structure of John 3:14–15, following the Greek order (my translation).

And as Moses lifted up   the serpent in the wilderness,

thus it is necessary to be lifted up   the Son of Man

that all who are believing in him   may have life eternal.

The parallelism is so clear that it needs no discussion. It is also obviously synonymous. "And as Moses lifted up" is synonymously parallel to "thus it is necessary to be lifted up." Most importantly, "the serpent in the wilderness" is synonymously parallel to "the Son of Man." The poetic structure of the passage is carefully structured to clarify the virtual identity of "the serpent" and "the Son of Man." Moreover, grammar also points out this fact. Both "serpent" and "the Son of Man" are clearly in the objective case (accusative) and conclude the thought in their respective lines. Thus, grammar and poetic structure clarifies that the Fourth Evangelist has paralleled the serpent in thought and symbolism with the Son of Man.

SUMMARY

We began this study with questions that arose from focused reflections on John 3:14–15. Our central question may be rephrased: How, why, and in what ways, if at all, is Jesus compared to Moses' upraised serpent? The following summary points may be highlighted in answer to this question, with particular emphasis on the significance of this study for considerations of Johannine Christology—arising historically from a Jewish setting and delivered within a Hellenistic setting.

(1) The serpent was a symbol of immortality or resurrection in many segments of the culture in which the Fourth Gospel took shape. This dimension of serpent symbolism may be seen as undergirding the thought of the Fourth Evangelist. Indeed, the Gospel of John appears to be a blurred mirror in which we see reflected discussions on this topic in the Johannine community, school, or circle. There should be no doubt that some who read the Fourth Gospel in antiquity would have seen Jesus in light of serpent symbolism characteristic of its life-availing associations within the Hellenistic world.

(2) In John's view, the serpent raised up by Moses is a *typos* of the Son of Man, rooted in a deeply Jewish understanding of the Messiah/Christ. As God gave life to those who looked up to the serpent and believed God's promise (Num 21:8–9), so Jesus gives life to all who look up to him and believe in him. Further, by looking up to Jesus, lifted up on the cross, one is looking not only at an antitype but also looking up to heaven—the world above. It is from there that the Johannine Jesus has come and is returning. In the words of conservative Old Testament scholar R. K. Harrison (1992, 279): "In the same way that the ancient Israelite was required to look in faith at the bronze serpent to be saved from death, so the modern sinner must also look in faith at the crucified Christ to receive the healing of the new birth (John 3:14–16)."

(3) Trust, or believing, is required so that God through the serpent and Jesus can provide life to all who look up to the means of healing and new life, including eternal life. No other New Testament author employs the verb "to believe" as frequently and deeply as does the Fourth Evangelist. He chooses it, accentuates it pervasively, and indicates the dynamic quality of "believing" by avoiding the noun "faith."

Therefore, while many Johannine scholars today assert that John 3:14 refers only to the "lifting up" of Jesus physically, it seems clear that Johannine typology entails *both* Jesus' being lifted up *and* his portrayal as the serpent on the pole or cross. According to the Fourth Evangelist, Jesus was the One-Who-Was-to-Come, while the prophet Isaiah, one of John's favorite biblical authors, claimed that the One-Who-Was-to-Come would be a snake:

Rejoice not, all you of Philistia,
Because the rod that struck you is broken;
For out of the serpent's root shall come forth a pit viper,
And his offspring shall be a flying serpent. (Isa 14:29)

In his homily 37 on the Gospel of John, John Chrysostom attempts to explain why Jesus did not simply tell Nicodemus directly: "I am about to be crucified." Jesus wanted his hearers to think about the analogy with the Old Testament because "the old order was akin to the new." Parallels are evident not only between the "lifting up" of the serpent and the manner of Jesus' death but also between the serpent and Christ himself. "In the former," Chrysostom says, "the uplifted serpent healed the bites of serpents; in the latter, the crucified Jesus healed the wounds inflicted by the spiritual dragon. In the former, there was the uplifted brass fashioned in the likeness of a serpent; in the latter, the Lord's body formed by the Spirit" (trans. Goggin 1957–59, 1:262–63).

Is it possible that the Fourth Evangelist has adequately represented some teaching of Jesus that has been lost? Perhaps. Remember that Jesus did refer to the serpent, even as presented in the Synoptics. He considered the serpent to be a symbol of wisdom: "Be wise, therefore, as serpents" (Matt 10:16). Did the historical Jesus preach on the symbolic meaning of Num 21 and the elevation of the serpent? Perhaps. No one can claim that this is impossible and that the Fourth Evangelist had no Jesus tradition from which to craft his own creation. Most of Jesus' teachings were lost when those who heard him died; as the Fourth Evangelist, or most likely his editor, reminded his community (and us): "There are also many things which Jesus did [and said]; were every one of them to be written, I suppose that the cosmos would not be able to contain the books that would be written" (John 21:25).

The Woman at the Well:
John's Portrayal of the Samaritan Mission

Susan Miller

The account of the meeting of Jesus and the Samaritan woman (John 4:4–42) portrays the positive response of a Samaritan woman to Jesus' mission. The Samaritan woman recognizes Jesus as the Messiah, and she then tells others in her town about Jesus. As a result of her actions, Jesus stays two days in the Samaritan town, and more Samaritans come to faith in him. There is no account of a Samaritan mission, however, in the other Gospels. Mark does not make any reference to the Samaritans, while Matthew includes a prohibition to the disciples not to enter a city of the Samaritans (Matt 10:5). Luke contains positive accounts of Samaritans (Luke 10:29–37; 17:11–19), and Jesus travels in Samaria, but he is rejected by a Samaritan village because his face is set toward Jerusalem (9:51–56). Acts, moreover, describes the progression of the early church in Judea and Samaria after the death of Jesus (Acts 1:8; 8:1), and the mission of Philip there is supported by the later mission carried out by Peter and John (8:4–25).

These references suggest that Jesus did not initiate a mission to the Samaritans. The positive account of the meeting between Jesus and the Samaritan woman was developed to support a later mission carried out by the early church. Scholars such as Wayne Meeks (1967), Charles Scobie (1973), and Raymond Brown (1979) propose that Samaritans influenced the formation of the Johannine tradition prior to the writing of the Gospel. Several commentators, including Brown (1966–70), C. K. Barrett (1978), and Andrew Lincoln (2005), believe the meeting of Jesus and the Samaritan woman may be historical but that it also reflects the theological concerns of the Evangelist. This essay aims to identify the later theological developments within the narrative and to assess the features that may contribute to an understanding of the historical Jesus. John highlights current tensions over the mission to the Samaritans that are supported by an examination of the charge against Jesus that he is a Samaritan (8:48). John, however, demonstrates accurate knowledge of Samaritan beliefs concerning their descent from the tribes of Ephraim and Manasseh, accompanied by the correct reference to the site of their temple on Mount Gerizim. It is thus plausible that a conversation between Jesus and a Samaritan woman indeed took place and even referred to these issues. The final section proposes that Samaritans regarded themselves as descendants of Jacob and that they were attracted both to Jesus' eschatological focus on the restoration of Israel and also to his critique of the Jerusalem temple.

A Comparison of Mark's Account of the Syrophoenician Woman with John's Account of the Samaritan Woman

John's account of the Samaritan woman may be compared to the meeting of Jesus and a Gentile woman in Mark 7:24–30. In Mark, a Syrophoenician woman approaches Jesus and requests that he cast a demon from her daughter. At first Jesus is reluctant to heal the child, but he is convinced by the woman's clever replies. In response, Jesus moves into Gentile areas and proclaims the gospel. Mark and John both depict the meeting between Jesus and someone who differs from him in terms of gender as well as race. The two narratives, moreover, present conversations that focus on the sharing of water or food, and they raise the question of Jesus' attitude toward the purity laws. In Mark, Jesus declares all food clean (7:19), while in John he ignores any concerns about purity by seeking to drink from the Samaritan woman's water jar. In both Gospels an encounter between Jesus and a woman is used to support the expansion of Jesus' mission.

Mark's account of the Syrophoenician woman includes a sharp contrast between the woman and Jesus in terms of gender and race. Mark describes the woman as Ἑλληνίς, Συροφοινίκισσα τῷ γένει (7:26). In John's Gospel the woman lives in Sychar, a city of Samaria, and she is described as a Samaritan woman (ἡ Σαμαρῖτις, 4:9). The woman draws attention to the differences between Jesus and herself by asking him how it is that he, a Jew, asks for a drink from her, a Samaritan woman (4:9). What does the term "Samaritan" mean? Scholars distinguish between inhabitants of Samaria and those who are defined by their religious identity as Samaritans (Hjelm 2000; Meier 2000). The Samaritans accept only the Pentateuch as authoritative and believe that the temple should be located on Mount Gerizim. According to 2 Kgs 17, the Assyrians took people from Samaria into exile and settled people from other nations on the land. Conflict over the identity of the Samaritans is indicated in the writings of Josephus, who gives a negative interpretation of Samaritans. He argues that Samaritans only claim to be descendants of the tribes of Ephraim and Manasseh when Jews are prospering and that they deny shared descent when Jews are in difficulties (*Ant.* 9.291; 11.340–341). In John's Gospel, the Samaritan woman claims descent from Jacob (4:12), the father of the twelve tribes of Israel, but tensions over the relationship between Jews and Samaritans form the background to her conversation with Jesus.

Mark's account of the Syrophoenician woman focuses on tensions between Jews and Gentiles. The Syrophoenician woman asks Jesus to cast an unclean spirit from her daughter. Jesus, however, replies with a parable: "Let the children be fed first, for it is not right to take the children's bread and throw it to the dogs" (Mark

7:27). The term "children" refers to the children of Israel (Deut 14:1; Isa 1:2; Hos 11:1); "dogs" occurs in other biblical passages as a term of abuse for Gentiles (1 Sam 17:43; 2 Kgs 8:13), and it is associated with impurity, as in the teaching of Jesus: "Do not give what is holy to dogs" (Matt 7:6). The sharing of meals between Jews and Gentiles was a contentious issue in the early church (see Gal 2:1–14; Acts 10). The Syrophoenician woman responds to Jesus' parable by arguing that even the dogs under the table may eat the crumbs from the children's food. Jesus has argued that he gives priority to the Jews over the Gentiles (see Rom 1:16). The woman acknowledges the priority of the children but also shows that both Jews and Gentiles may be fed at the same time. Jesus implies that the dogs are scavenger dogs outside the house. The woman refers to household dogs under a table, and in this way she transforms the metaphor into a story in which both groups are located within the household.

John's Gospel similarly presents a conversation that focuses on the sharing of water. On this occasion Jesus is the one who initiates a meeting with the Samaritan woman. The conversation between Jesus and the Samaritan woman begins with his request for a drink of water (4:7). In response, the woman points out that Jews and Samaritans do not share drinking vessels (4:9). The verb συγχράομαι has been translated as "to have no dealings with," but David Daube (1950) rightly notes that the woman is referring particularly to the sharing of a drinking vessel, and the verb may be better translated as "to use together." This translation is supported by the woman's comments that Jesus has no bucket, and he must rely on her water jar in order to drink some water (4:11).[1]

Jesus offers the Samaritan woman life-giving water. Natural water is replaced by the water that may well up within a human being, bringing life. The discussion about water raises the question of the observance of purity regulations. Jews and Samaritans both accept the Pentateuch but follow different interpretations of the purity laws.[2] The term "living water" occurs in the purity regulations that require running water (Lev 14:5–6, 50–52; 15:13; Num 19:17). In John 7:38, "living water" (ὕδατος ζῶντος) is used of the Spirit that will be given to those who believe in Jesus. Jesus refers to one drink of water that is able to prevent anyone from feeling thirsty again (ὃς δ' ἂν πίῃ ἐκ τοῦ ὕδατος, 4:14). As Barnabas Lindars notes (1972, 183), the use of the aorist subjunctive πίῃ rather than a participial construction implies that one single drink is sufficient to overcome an individual's thirst. Jesus'

---

1. Bruce M. Metzger (1994, 177) notes that verse 9b is omitted by several witnesses. It is accepted in the UBS text because asides are a characteristic feature of John's Gospel, and it may have been omitted by some scribes because they did not believe that it is an accurate description of relations between Jews and Samaritans.

2. For an account of the observance of purity regulations by Samaritans in the first century, see the archaeological excavations of ritual baths used by Samaritans at Qedumim (Magen 1993b, 181–92).

saying has an eschatological focus pointing forward to his death. The water Jesus brings is able to purify, and there is no need for repeated washings.

Jesus asks the Samaritan woman to call her husband, and when he reveals his knowledge that she has been married five times, she recognizes him as a prophet (4:16–19). She then expresses her expectation that the Messiah is coming, which leads to Jesus' affirmation that he is the Messiah (4:25–26). The term "Messiah" is anachronistic because the Samaritans did not expect a Davidic Messiah. They looked forward to the advent of a prophet like Moses, as described in Deut 18:15–18. The Samaritans called this figure the Taheb, which means "the one who returns" or "the one who restores." The Samaritan Pentateuch includes a reference to this prophet in the tenth commandment, with a citation of Deut 18:15 following Exod 20:21. Evidence for the eschatological beliefs of the Samaritans may be seen in Josephus's account of the man who led crowds of Samaritans up Mount Gerizim with a prophecy that he would discover the temple vessels hidden there by Moses (*Ant.* 18.85–89). This expedition was violently crushed by Pilate, whose soldiers killed many Samaritans. Samaritan beliefs associate the prophet with the task of restoring worship. This feature is supported by Josephus's account and is also indicated by the Samaritan woman's introduction of the topic of worship.

In the course of the conversation, the woman refers to the different views of Jews and Samaritans about the correct location of the temple (4:20–24). The Jews worship in the temple in Jerusalem, whereas the Samaritans believe that the temple should be located on Mount Gerizim.[3] As in Mark's account of the Syrophoenician woman, Jesus in John affirms the priority of the Jews ("salvation is from the Jews," 4:22) but prophesies the replacement of the temple. Jesus proposes that a time will come, and is now here, when worshipers will not worship on Mount Gerizim or in the temple in Jerusalem (4:23). Each individual may worship in spirit and truth. The discussion about water enables Jesus to challenge the purity regulations that maintain boundaries between Jews and Samaritans. Earlier in John, Jesus had prophesied the destruction of the Jerusalem temple, stating that it would be replaced by his body (2:19–21).

Mark's account of the Syrophoenician woman focuses on the eschatological significance of the bread. The woman's insight suggests that both Jews and Gentiles may eat from the one loaf. The Syrophoenician woman convinces Jesus that the time has come to carry out the mission to the Gentiles. Jesus can carry out a mission to Jews and Gentiles at the same time. The discussion about bread foreshadows the Last Supper, when Jesus identifies the bread with his body (Mark 14:22). He prophesies that he will not drink wine again until he drinks it new in the kingdom of God (14:25). Jesus' mission will culminate in the new age when

---

3. For a description of archaeological excavations that have identified the site of the temple on Mount Gerizim, see Yitzhaq Magen 1993a, 134–48, and the work of Robert J. Bull 1975, 54–59; 1977, 460–62.

Jews and Gentiles will share the messianic feast together (Isa 25:6; 1 En. 62:14; 4 Ezra 6:51; 2 Bar. 29:5–6). There is a similar eschatological focus in John's Gospel. The life-giving water that Jesus brings represents eternal life and the abundance of the new age (John 7:37–39). In this way both Gospels link the change or overcoming of the difficulties in relations between the groups to Jesus' death. Through his death a new group of people is created who do not adhere to the old boundaries. They share the same relation to him in terms of their faith in his death and resurrection.

Our analysis indicates that Mark's account of the Syrophoenician woman and John's description of the Samaritan woman both emphasize differences between Jesus and the women in terms of race and beliefs. The narratives focus on the sharing of bread and water, respectively, and these concerns relate to the overcoming of boundaries between Jews and Gentiles, and Jews and Samaritans, within early Christian communities. A comparison of the two accounts suggests that John has shaped the meeting of Jesus and the Samaritan woman in order to address concerns over the Samaritan mission. The overcoming of these concerns is related to Jesus' death and resurrection, implying that John's narrative reflects later theological understandings of the significance of Jesus' death. In the next section we shall compare the structure of Mark with that of John. To what extent has John developed the account of the Samaritan woman by the literary structure of his Gospel?

JESUS' DEBATES WITH THE PHARISEES

Both Mark and John depict meetings between Jesus and a woman of a different race. These stories act as turning points in each Gospel, and they impact the direction of Jesus' mission. Mark's account is situated in the context of Jesus' debates with the Pharisees over purity issues. These debates function on the level of the Markan community to justify their own mission to the Gentiles (see 13:10). In Mark's Gospel, a debate between Jesus and the Pharisees refers to the issue of washing hands before eating (7:1–20). Jesus responds with a parable stating that nothing from the outside may cause impurity but that what comes from the inside causes impurity (7:15). This parable is concluded with the statement that Jesus declares all foods clean (7:19). In the next passage Jesus goes into the vicinity of Tyre but does not want anyone to know (7:24). Once the food is declared clean, a path is made for the healing of the girl with an unclean spirit (Marcus 2000, 465–66).

Is there any indication of conflict between John's community and the Pharisees? When Mark's account of the Syrophoenician woman is compared to John's story of the Samaritan woman, there are similarities on the level of each community. The account of the Samaritan woman is placed after the account of the Pharisee Nicodemus, who approached Jesus at night (John 3:1–21). Nicodemus accepts that Jesus has carried out signs, but he is unable to understand Jesus' teaching about the necessity of being born again. The Samaritan woman thus responds to Jesus with more faith and understanding than the leading Pharisee, Nicodemus.

In the following verses Jesus withdraws to Samaria after the Pharisees learn that he is making disciples and baptizing a greater number of people than John the Baptist (4:1). John 1 has a debate between representatives of the Pharisees and John the Baptist. Messengers from the Pharisees ask John why he is baptizing people if he is not the Messiah, Elijah, or the prophet (1:25). In John 4 the description ἔδει (it was necessary, he had to) implies a sense of threat indicating that Jesus has to leave Judea on account of opposition to his mission. Baptism, moreover, is a point of conflict between Jesus and the Pharisees because John's baptism occurs once and marks a person's entry into a new state of purity.[4] The conflict between Jesus and the Pharisees focuses on definitions of purity. On the other hand, the meeting of Jesus and the Samaritan woman enables him to overcome concerns about purity.

The conflict between Jesus and his opponents is further illustrated in a later debate (John 8:12–59) in which Jesus is accused of being a Samaritan (8:48). Why is this charge included in the debate? There is no indication in the Gospel that more than one Samaritan village has responded to Jesus. The accusation may therefore reflect a later period when a number of Samaritans were associated with Jesus. Jesus' opponents in this debate are described as "Pharisees" (8:13) and "the Jews" (8:22), who upon their convincement are described as "Jews who had believed in him" (8:31). These references may imply that the debates represent later conflicts at the time of the Johannine community. In John 8 the charge of being a Samaritan is particularly linked to the accusation of being demon-possessed, but why are these two charges connected?

In Mark's Gospel scribes from Jerusalem accuse Jesus of being possessed by Beelzebul and casting out demons by the prince of demons (3:22). This charge is linked to a charge of deceiving people and disobedience to the law (see Deut 18:19–20). In John's Gospel Jesus responds to his opponents by stating that whoever keeps his word will never die (8:51). At this point his accusers reaffirm the charge that he is possessed by a demon. They argue that Abraham and the prophets died and question Jesus, "Are you greater than our father Abraham who died?" (8:53) Abraham is regarded as the first Jew, and Jews claim descent from Abraham. The debate focuses on the fact that Abraham has died and concludes with Jesus' claim to preexistence and divinity: "Before Abraham was, I am" (8:58).

The debate between Jesus and his opponents in John 8, moreover, has several verbal similarities with the conversation of Jesus and the Samaritan woman in John 4. The Samaritan woman asks Jesus a similar question: "Are you greater than our father Jacob who gave us the well, and drank from it himself, and his sons, and his cattle?" (4:12; see also 8:53). The woman's description of Jacob as

---

4. Jonathan Klawans (2000, 139) describes John's baptism as a "ritual of moral purification."

"our" father indicates that she traces her descent to the twelve tribes of Israel. In both passages, the status of the patriarchs is redefined in relation to that of Jesus. Whereas his opponents reject Jesus on account of his claim, the Samaritan woman accepts him. In John 4 Jesus' conversation with the Samaritan woman leads to his revelation of his identity as the Messiah: "I am who is speaking to you" (4:26; see also 8:58). In John 8 his opponents reject Jesus' claim to Abrahamic authority, whereas the Samaritans believe that they share Abrahamic descent with Jesus. This debate raises the question of whether or not the historical Jesus regarded the Samaritans as descendants of Abraham, an issue that we will explore in the final section.

The Historical Jesus and the Samaritans

The Synoptic Gospels record only one visit to Jerusalem, whereas John's Gospel is more historical, mentioning several visits. It was customary for Galileans to travel through Samaria to reach Jerusalem in order to celebrate festivals, and it is likely that Jesus and his disciples would take this route (see Josephus, *Ant.* 20.118; *Life* 269). Whereas Mark and Matthew describe a mission of Jesus in Galilee and one journey to Jerusalem, Luke's Gospel refers to Jesus' visits to Samaritan villages (9:51–56). Although members of one village reject Jesus' disciples, he does not leave Samaria but responds by proceeding to another village. John P. Meier thus argues that Jesus traveled through Samaria and had a positive attitude toward Samaritans (2000, 202–32).

Why does Jesus have a positive attitude toward Samaritans? Meier notes that Jesus' choice of twelve disciples has multiple attestation in the New Testament (1997, 635–72). The Synoptic Gospels and Acts contain lists of the names of the Twelve, and John also refers to the Twelve (6:67; 20:24). The criterion of embarrassment is indicated by the account of the betrayal of Jesus by Judas, one of the Twelve, because it is unlikely that Jesus' followers would create this tradition. E. P. Sanders has argued that Jesus' choice of twelve disciples is intended to foreshadow the restoration of Israel (1985, 98–106). In Matthew and Luke, moreover, there are eschatological sayings referring to the twelve disciples judging the twelve tribes of Israel (Matt 19:28; Luke 22:30). The significance of the number twelve to the early church is evident in the decision to choose another person to replace Judas (Acts 1:15–26). Several Old Testament passages refer to the restoration of the twelve tribes in the end-time (Isa 27:12–13; Hos 11:11; 2 Macc 1:27). David Catchpole argues that Jesus may have included Samaritans in his mission strategy (2006, 188). Our analysis of John 4 indicates that the Samaritan woman identifies herself as a descendant of Jacob (see Josephus, *Ant.* 9.291; 11.341). She may thus represent the views of Samaritans who were attracted to the mission of Jesus in terms of the restoration of Israel.

In John's Gospel Jesus looks forward to a time when his followers will no longer worship in the Jerusalem temple (4:21–23). Scholars such as E. P. Sanders (1985, 61–76) have argued that Jesus' action of overturning tables in the temple and casting out the merchants (Mark 11:15–19; Matt 21:12–17; Luke 19:45–46; John 2:13–22) may be interpreted as a prophetic sign representing the destruction of the temple. Stephen's speech in Acts 7 is given in response to the accusation that he claimed Jesus would destroy the temple (6:14). Several scholars have identified Samaritan eschatological beliefs within this speech (Spiro 1967, 285–300; Purvis 1975, 161–98; Coggins 1982, 423–34). Stephen refers to the Samaritan Pentateuch by stating that Moses prophesies that another prophet will be raised up (Acts 7:37; see also Deut 18:15). Stephen's speech also places a strong focus upon the patriarchs, and he begins his historical account with the figure of Abraham (7:2–8), who is an ancestor of both Jews and Samaritans. He records the role of Joseph (7:9–16), who is the father of Ephraim and Manasseh, and his emphasis on the patriarchs expresses an understanding of identity based on descent. Stephen, moreover, distances himself from the temple. He states that the temple was built by Solomon but argues that God does not dwell in a house made with hands (7:47–48). At the same time, he stresses the promises of the land of Israel to the patriarchs. After the martyrdom of Stephen, the early Christians are persecuted, and this situation leads to the mission to Samaria (7:54–8:1). Our analysis of Stephen's speech thus supports the presentation of Samaritan beliefs in John 4 concerning descent and the temple. These concerns may point to the reasons why some Samaritans were attracted to Jesus' mission of restoration to Israel.

Conclusion

Our analysis supports the historical plausibility that Jesus met a Samaritan woman at Jacob's well. The account of the meeting of Jesus and the Samaritan woman contains accurate geographical information concerning the site of Jacob's well, and Jesus' visit to Samaria is supported by Luke's description of the presence of Jesus in Samaria (9:51–56) as well as by Josephus's references to the custom of Galileans to travel through Samaria to Jerusalem for the celebration of festivals (see *Ant.* 20.118; *Life* 269). John's account, moreover, includes accurate presentations of Samaritan beliefs such as their expectation of a prophet like Moses and their conviction that the correct location of the temple is on Mount Gerizim. John's portrayal of the meeting of Jesus and the Samaritan woman, however, also reflects later theological developments. A comparison of Mark's account of the Syrophoenician woman with John's account of the Samaritan woman suggests that narratives featuring women have been employed to support the validity of the mission to the Gentiles and Samaritans, respectively. Concerns over purity regulations are transcended by Jesus' eschatological gift of life-giving water. The boundaries between Jews and Samaritans are overcome through the death and resurrection of Jesus. The accusation that Jesus is a Samaritan (John 8:48), moreover, reflects the later association of Jesus with Samaritan followers.

What are the implications of our examination of John 4 for an understanding of the historical Jesus? The account of the meeting between Jesus and the Samaritan woman raises the question of the descent of the Samaritans from Jacob, and the historical Jesus is associated with the restoration of Israel. His choice of twelve disciples is intended to relate to the twelve tribes of Israel, and the Samaritans regarded themselves as descendants of Ephraim and Manasseh. In John 4 Jesus prophesies a time when his followers will no longer worship in the Jerusalem temple. Jesus' action in the temple in all four Gospels has been interpreted as a prophecy of the destruction of the temple. This feature of the mission of the historical Jesus may have paved the way for Samaritans who rejected the location of the temple in Jerusalem. In this way the account of the Samaritan woman does contain insights into the perspective of the historical Jesus, suggesting that he welcomed Samaritans in his mission to restore Israel.

The Royal Official and the Historical Jesus

Peter J. Judge

One would be hard-pressed nowadays to find many commentators with the opinion that John's story of the cure of the royal official's son (John 4:46b–54) is not the same event as the cure of the centurion's boy at Capernaum in the Synoptics (Matt 8:5–13; par. Luke 7:1–10). Unmistakable similarities abound: some kind of officer at Capernaum approaches Jesus to seek healing for a member of his household; the sick person is healed instantaneously without Jesus going to the house of the officer; and the issue of faith is a focal point in all three versions of the story. Yet, in spite of these similarities, significant differences in detail remain between the three versions: in Luke, the man is represented by delegations of Jewish elders and then by friends, so that he never encounters Jesus personally, as he does in Matthew and John; for Matthew//Luke the man is (apparently) a Gentile centurion, while in John he is a royal official whose ethnicity is not specified; in the Synoptics, Jesus is dissuaded from coming to the house with the suggestion that Jesus need only "say a word" (Matt 8:8; Luke 7:7) followed by an appreciation for the power of an authoritative word—an exclamation that causes Jesus to marvel at a faith the like of which he has not found in Israel—while in John the official persists with his request for Jesus to "come down" (John 4:47) in spite of an apparent initial rebuke by Jesus and comes to full faith upon being tested; Matthew includes an additional saying by Jesus about those who will "come from east and west and will eat with Abraham, Isaac, and Jacob in the kingdom of heaven" (Matt 8:11), a saying that Luke has in a different form in a completely different context (Luke 13:29) and that John does not include at all; and, finally, although each version reports the fact of the healing, the wording of each report is quite distinct, so that we have three very differently worded narrative conclusions. All of this raises questions about what we can know of the historical details of the event as we sift through the presentations of the three Evangelists. More specifically, how historical is John's account? Might the report of the episode in the Fourth Gospel bring us closer to the historical event in the life of Jesus than do the Synoptics?

My short answer is—probably not. In the first volume of these papers on John, Jesus, and history, John Painter contributed a fine essay in which he expresses his view that finding the "historical Jesus" in the Gospel of John involves one inextricably, perhaps hopelessly, in the difficulty of distinguishing historical accuracy from theological interpretation. Yet, much like the probability that Plato gives us a "more authentic understanding of Socrates" than the more conventional or perhaps even *historical* Socrates of Xenophon's *Recollections* and *Defense before the Jury*, the Fourth Evangelist may well give us a *real* Jesus even though he may not give us a factually *accurate or historical* Jesus (Painter 2007, 231). Thus, John's is not an "arbitrary presentation of the story of Jesus. Rather, the evidence suggests that John is a radical interpretation of the Jesus tradition in which the Evangelist is so certain of his understanding of Jesus that he freely transmits the tradition, providing insight in his own words" (Painter 2007, 235). At the end of his piece, Painter concludes:

> It seems to me that John goes to great lengths to make clear how certain events have transformed the memory of Jesus now embodied in this Gospel. John has written with the intent that this transformation should be carried through in a thoroughgoing fashion. We might say that, for John, this is the real Jesus revealed through resurrection, glorification, and departure and through the inspiring presence of the Spirit of Truth…. Based on the recognition of how the power of the resurrection and the experience of the Spirit have transformed the Johannine story, we may doubt that significant use will be made of it in historical Jesus research. (Painter 2007, 245)

John's late post-Easter interpretation of Jesus may be the most perceptive among the Gospels, even if not the most historical. This means that, when it comes to the Gospel of John especially, we ask the wrong question if we are simply interested in *what* happened. Nevertheless, as Painter stresses in several places, we are not dealing with memory gone wildly astray; the Evangelist perceptively and creatively shapes the *what*—the historical content of the tradition—to convey the far more important *why and wherefore*—the deeper understanding of how these events were then and remain now good news in the perspective of the Beloved Disciple.

This seems to me a very acceptable and useful hermeneutical approach to questions of John, Jesus, and history. How might it apply, then, to the Fourth Gospel's treatment of the royal official? Like Professor Painter, I think John has taken an episode from the tradition about Jesus and given it a fuller, we might say, more Johannine, interpretation. Painter indicated his sense that John made use of "Synoptic-like" traditions or "nuggets" and that the author knew one or more of the Synoptics by the time he finished his work, but that "John was independent of the Synoptics in the fundamental shaping of the Gospel" (Painter 2007, 234).[1]

---

1. Painter references the work of D. Moody Smith, who provides a very cogent and readable discussion of the issues and recent debate on the relationship of John and the Synoptics, with the conclusion: "It is not possible to prove that John did not know any of the Synoptics,

It may not be possible to show that John depended upon the Synoptics in every pericope, but I am more inclined to explore the possibility of seeing a real use of the Synoptic Gospels by John especially in those passages that evince the amount of similarity we see here.[2] If we proceed on a pericope-by-pericope basis, without forcing all pericopes therefore into the Procrustean bed of one overarching theory, I think the case can be made for a certain *rélecture* by John of portions of the Synoptic Gospels. The story of Jesus and the royal official may be a good case in point.

The method of working here is not a simple source- and redaction-critical analysis by which an author is shown to have redacted or edited a clearly distillable source text. I see it rather as a literary application of Painter's basic historical outlook that John provides us with "perhaps the most perceptive interpretation of Jesus," even though it may not be the most historically factual presentation. I wonder whether we can describe a certain trajectory from the life of Jesus to the Gospel of John that wends its way through Q and the Synoptic Gospels. Can we say in some way that in this episode the witness of the Fourth Gospel connects us with an encounter between Jesus and a Galilean official in such a way as to demonstrate awareness of previous iterations of the story but also to provide a deeper, more lasting appreciation of the *real* meaning of the story, at least from the Johannine perspective?

Somewhat ironically, one bit of historicity that John may well preserve for us is the identity of the person who comes to Jesus to seek a healing. The man in John 4:46 is described as a βασιλικός. His identity is indeed ambiguous. What is his role, and what is his ethnicity? While it seems to be of central importance in the Synoptics that the man is a Gentile, in John this content is not stated directly. Francis J. Moloney is representative of the position that in John, too, the official is a Gentile—"a final example [in John 4] of the reception of the word of Jesus from the non-Jewish world" (Moloney 1998b, 153).[3] John P. Meier, on the other hand,

---

and improbable that his Gospel was published without cognizance of them," but viewing John as an independent Gospel "is a better working hypothesis for exegesis than the assumption that the late-first-century author was writing with the Synoptic Gospels principally in view, whether to supplement, correct, or displace them. *John does, in fact, interpret them*, but whether that is by the intention of humankind or the providence of God is likely to remain a moot question" (D. M. Smith 2001, 241, emphasis added). My inclination would be that John's interpretation is more than coincidental.

2. It is interesting to read the claim by Obery M. Hendricks Jr., in his introduction to "The Gospel according to John" in the 3rd edition of the *New Oxford Annotated Bible*: "Although some scholars deny any dependence of the Fourth Gospel upon the Synoptic Gospels, *most* scholars accept the Fourth Gospel's dependence upon the Synoptics; at the least, they hold that its writer was aware of them" (Hendricks 2001, NT 147).

3. In an earlier work, Moloney explains with greater detail that, while "the *basilikos* may be either Jewish or Gentile," the implied reader of the Gospel knows that Jesus has left the world of Judaism behind and traveled through Samaria and now to Galilee, where "the reader accepts

is just as insistent that the official is Jewish: "no Gentile speaks directly to Jesus during the public ministry" until the arrival of some Greeks seeking Jesus in John 12:20–26 brings about the arrival of Jesus' "hour" (Meier 1994, 722). Nevertheless, as Meier points out, *historically* the officer's ethnicity is ambiguous at best, given the situation in Capernaum as a Galilean border town under the control of Herod Antipas.[4]

For John, the issue is not the man's ethnicity in the same way that it is for Matthew and Luke. At stake is the fact that he is a Galilean, and John, I suggest, leaves his religious and ethnic identity *intentionally* ambiguous. At the end of John 4, the βασιλικός steps out from among a new group who respond to Jesus— the Galileans—a group of mixed background, marginalized, mongrelized, and (like the Samaritans) theologically suspicious as far as Judeans were concerned. Parallel to the report that the Samaritans came to Jesus because they heard about him but then advanced to a fuller faith because they heard Jesus' word (4:39–42), in this story a Galilean approaches Jesus after hearing about him but advances to full faith on the same basis (4:43–54). The nature of this faith must be shown

---

this figure from Capernaum, a town where a military presence was called for, as a Gentile" (1993, 183).

    4. Meier further explains: "the ethnic origin of the centurion (or, alternatively, the royal official) remains ambiguous when we try to probe the earliest attainable tradition or a hypothetical historical event. However, no such ambiguity attends the stories as they now stand in Matthew and Luke, or even in John. Both Matthew and Luke, in various ways, make clear that the centurion is a Gentile.... Matters are not quite so clear in John, who does not specify the ethnic origin of the royal official. Yet the overall redactional theology of John makes it likely that the Fourth Evangelist understands the official to be a Jew (Meier 1994, 721–22). Udo Schnelle thinks the official in John is a Gentile because of the connection with the Synoptic story. Nevertheless, he emphasizes that John never really tells us anything about the man's ethnicity and that clearly "the father's origin no longer has the significance in John that it had in the Synoptic tradition" (Schnelle 1992, 83 n. 49).

    It is interesting to note the somewhat attractive evidence presented by David Catchpole for the argument that the officer was not a Gentile in the Q tradition: "it is worth noting that the term [ἑκατοντάρχης] in itself stands simply for 'an officer commanding 100 men' and is ethnically neutral," with the additional comment that this fact is implicitly recognized when commentators derive the fact that the soldier was a Gentile more from the formulation of Luke 7:9b (which Catchpole sees as Lukan) than from the term itself (Catchpole 1992, 527 [= 1993, 292] and n. 49). One of Catchpole's main points is that the centurion's expression of unworthiness "is oriented to christology and not to any sense of Gentile inferiority" (1992, 539 [= 1993, 307]) so that this story in Q is about the outstanding quality of his faith and not his faith as a Gentile. It is Matthew and Luke who have emphasized his "Gentile-ness." Moreover, "What is of concern is πίστις, as Q 7,7b–9 establishes. In that respect the later version of the same tradition in John 4,46–54 is a closer parallel. John 4,48 succeeds in making πίστις the central concern in a setting whose horizon is from start to finish so Jewish that the Jew/Gentile distinction simply does not arise" (1992, 526 [=1993, 291]). For his acknowledgement of John's literary dependence upon the Synoptic Gospels, see Catchpole 1992, 521 (= 1993, 285).

to be genuine in the Johannine perspective, and the ensuing sign story forms yet another parallel—this time with the opening sign at Cana, where, after a certain expression of hesitancy on the part of Jesus, those who "see" the sign come to full faith in him (2:1–11). These two Cana episodes bracket a series of episodes that illustrate what genuine faith in Jesus is and what it is not (Moloney 1993, 178–79; 1998b, 151).

Jesus testifies that "a prophet has no honor in the prophet's own country" (John 4:44), a difficult saying to be sure. Jesus is known throughout John's Gospel to be from Galilee/Nazareth (1:45–46; 6:42; 7:3, 41–42, 52; 18:5, 7; 19:19). So if the saying is used with the same meaning as in the Synoptic parallels (Matt 13:37; Mark 6:4; Luke 4:24), it produces something of a non sequitur, with Jesus going to the very place where he says he will find no honor (4:43) and the report in the following verse that "the Galileans welcomed him" (4:45). This leads to the frequent interpretation that, since we are told at the very beginning (1:11) that he came to his own who did not accept him, "his own" are the Judeans/the Jews (οἱ Ἰουδαῖοι) and the πατρίς of Jesus is Israel in general; moreover, since at this point in John's Gospel Jesus has already spent a good amount of time in Judea, he comes from there as far as the story is concerned (Moloney 1993, 181; 1998b, 152; Keener 2003, 629). On the other hand, if we can read the γάρ of 4:44 with an anticipatory sense, as Gilbert Van Belle, drawing on an impressive history of interpretation, has shown, it would carry the meaning "now," "yet," "admittedly," or even "although" (Van Belle 1998, esp. 36–39). There is then no contradiction between Jesus' saying and the reception the Galileans give him. The saying does not explain why Jesus leaves Judea for Galilee, nor does it set up a contrast between Judea and Galilee. Rather, it expresses something especially Johannine, giving a different twist to the Synoptic understanding of the saying. We are told in John that Jesus does not seek honor in the usual sense of that word (see 5:41). Therefore, the saying in 4:44 is not about Jesus' concern over having *no* honor but about the *kind* of honor the Galileans will accord him.

> Verse 44 can be understood as an important hint for the reader about the faith of the Galileans. It is on the occasion of Jesus' return to Galilee that the evangelist reminds us of His saying that a prophet is not honoured in his own country. The saying explains why the Galileans do not honour Jesus suitably; their faith is insufficient because it relies on signs. True faith consists in believing in His word. This word is then illustrated in the story of the βασιλικός (Van Belle 1998, 35).

The recollection of the feast in Jerusalem (4:45) recalls the suspicion of Jesus in 2:23–25, and so, as we see in the ensuing episode with the royal official, the faith of the Galileans must be tested and not accepted immediately prima facie. Just as Nicodemus represents those who saw Jesus' signs in Jerusalem and expresses a faith that needs correction (3:1–2, following on 2:23–25), so the official is representative of the Galileans whose acceptance of Jesus is insufficiently based on signs and must be tested. The Galilean official undergoes and passes the test and moves to a deeper level of faith based on Jesus' word, just as the Samaritans did in 4:41–42.[5]

The official's story began its literary history in the Q sayings document as an exchange between Jesus and a centurion that reveals the man's confidence in Jesus and presumably results in the healing of the man's "boy." Matthew and Luke each gave the dialogue from their source a narrative framework. It seems to me that there are elements in John's version that conform to redactional elements in Matthew and Luke, respectively. Moreover, in reshaping the episode as it comes to him through the Synoptics, John radically turned the story on its ear, so to speak, so that, "In the synoptic version the centurion's faith is never in question. Here the official's faith is the question," as D. Moody Smith puts it (1999, 126).

The Critical Edition of Q offers the following reconstruction of the story in the Synoptic sayings source:

> Q 7:1, 3, 6b–9, ?10?
> 1 [[And it came to pass when]] he … ended these sayings, he entered Capernaum. 3 There came to him a centurion exhorting him [[and saying: My]] boy [[<is> doing badly. And he said to him: Am I]], by coming, to heal him? 6b–c And in reply the centurion said: Master, I am not worthy for you to come under my roof; 7 but say a word, and [[let]] my boy [[be]] healed. 8 For I too am a person under authority, with soldiers under me, and I say to one: Go, and he goes, and to another: Come, and he comes, and to my slave: Do this, and he does «it». 9 But Jesus, on hearing, was amazed, and said to those who followed: I tell you: Not even in Israel have I found such faith. ?10? <..>. (Robinson, Hoffman, and Kloppenborg 2000, 102–17; Johnson 2002, 401; see also Judge 2004).

This brief dialogic exchange—resembling Matthew for the most part—puts all the emphasis on the centurion's faith, or at least a faith that is confident in Jesus' ability to heal, and, even more, that only a word is necessary; Jesus need not touch, nay even come near, the boy. As many observe, it is hardly a miracle story at all. The reconstruction of an original narrative conclusion is even left in doubt.

Two comments on the reconstruction are thus in order. First, Jesus' reply to the centurion in Matt 8:7 is included in the reconstructed Q passage and

---

5. Van Belle 1998, esp. 34–35. See also Neirynck 1979, 114–16. Raymond Brown explains, "in their estimation of enthusiasm based on miracle, iv 44–45 and ii 23–25 have much in common. These two passages also have a similar function in the outline of John. After the description in ii 23–25 of those in Jerusalem who believed in Jesus because of his signs, one of these 'believers,' Nicodemus, came to Jesus with his inadequate understanding of Jesus' powers. Jesus had to explain to Nicodemus that he was really one who had come from above to give eternal life. So also, after the description in iv 44–45 of the Galileans who welcomed Jesus because of his works, a royal official from Galilee comes to Jesus with an inadequate understanding of Jesus' power. Jesus will lead the man to a deeper understanding of his function as a giver of life" (Brown 1966–70, 1:188).

punctuated as a question, indicating hesitancy on the part of Jesus. It is true that even H. J. Held, who generally pointed to Matthew's redactional preference for dialogue over narrative in healing stories, hesitated to exclude such dialogue from tradition in situations (like the centurion story) when Matthew's tradition already placed conversation, and not the miracle, at center stage. Yet Held went on to say that it is Matthew who "brings out the conversational character of these stories most clearly" (Johnson 2002, 155). So, while most interpreters quite rightly view Luke's double delegation as redactional, that does not automatically make the entire conversation in Matthew's version traditional. Matthew may well have enhanced a direct speech request by the centurion in Q with the motif of Jesus' hesitancy in Matt 8:7, just as the Evangelist does later in Matt 15:22–24, *adding* dialogue that heightens the same motif of hesitancy about contact with a Gentile—in this case the Syrophoenician woman of Mark 7.[6]

Some also include the indignant rebuff of Matt 8:7 in Q because it "approximates the tradition behind John 4:48" (Johnson 2002, 159)[7] or because "the presence of this implied rejection here in Q is needed to explain the Lukan redactional interpolation of the emissary of the Jewish elders to dissuade Jesus from taking the position expected at this point in the story."[8]

On the one hand, it can be observed that even those who accept a Johannine signs source regard John 4:48 as redactional and not a traditional element in the story. For those who do not accept such a source, it is even more appealing to examine John's version of the story in the light of Matthean redaction. On the other hand, do we need Jesus' reluctant question (in Q) as background for an anticipated but unexpressed reluctance that motivates redactional delegation(s) in Luke? Luke certainly is concerned with the Jewish-Gentile continuum throughout his work, and he does present Jesus here and elsewhere as avoiding contact with Gentiles. Jesus' indignant reluctance in Q is thus not needed as motivation for this Lukan motif. Moreover, we could investigate other, more positive motives for Luke's redaction; his accent on the centurion's character and virtue and his heightening of the worthiness/unworthiness motif already present in the centurion's

---

6. Johnson 2002, 162: evaluator Hoffmann assigns a C rating to Q 7:3 in direct address, declaring that, while Luke's version is redactional, the decision on the traditional or redactional character of Matthew's direct address must remain open.

7. Johnson assigns a B probability, with reference to Jeremias 1956.

8. Robinson, in Johnson 2002, 219; see 161: "Matt 8:7 needs to be presupposed in Q to suggest the Lukan delegations." See also Robinson, Hoffman, and Kloppenborg 2000, xcii: "Matt 8:7 is to be understood as a question expressing reserve, in the light of Luke 7:3–5 (the appeal of the Jewish elders to persuade Jesus to overcome such reserve and help a Gentile) and John 4:48 (Jesus' rebuff to the Gentile official for demanding a sign, in the same healing narrative), and the analogous reserve of Jesus toward the Syrophoenician (Mark) or Canaanite (Matthew) woman (Mark 7:27; par. Matt 15:26), in a structurally parallel, but distinct healing of a Gentile from a distance." Nevertheless, Robinson's confidence in the verse's presence in Q is only C.

words come to mind, to name just two. Further, might we not expect Luke to have reproduced Jesus' verbal reply after Luke 7:5 if he knew it in Q, since he could have read it as a positive response? In fact, with Robert Gagnon, we can observe that "the pericope makes perfectly good sense without Matt 8:7–8a."[9] We do not need Matt 8:7 to explain Luke's redaction. Rather than being a traditional part of the story, Jesus' hesitation is due to Matthean redaction, and John 4:48, at least in part, would be inspired by Matt 8:7, if familiarity can be inferred.

My other comment has to do with the narrative conclusion. As indicated above, *The Critical Edition of Q* (followed by the reconstruction in Q *7:1–10* in the Documenta Q series) is firm in assigning no concluding statement to the pericope in Q. Yet many commentators and the evaluators of the data base in Q *7:1–10* (Johnson 2002) conjecture that for various reasons there must have been some narrative conclusion in the Q pericope. Nevertheless, the absence of verbal agreement between Matt 8:13 and Luke 7:10 is problematic.

Elsewhere I have tried to establish the notion that both verses can be taken without great strain as the redactional compositions of the respective Evangelists (Judge 1989, 487–89; quoted in Johnson 2002, 359–61). Without repeating the details here, my essential position was that Matthew added the conclusion in Matt 8:13 in a fashion similar to what he does with Markan miracle stories, particularly that on behalf of the Syrophoenician/Canaanite woman (Mark 7:29–30; diff. Matt 15:28). Admittedly, "Matthew has largely altered Mark 7:29–30" so that Mark is not immediately seen as a direct influence on Matt 8:13 (Johnson 2002, 370). My argument, however, would be not that Matthew was explicitly working backward from a later text in the Markan order (or his redaction of same) but that his awareness of the healing at a distance in Mark 7 already sparked ideas of how he might change it and that he anticipated such with his rendition of the centurion's story. We need not think of Matthew working along through Mark piece by piece, giving no thought to what came later until he arrived there. Put in another way, it was not a concluding text in Q 7:10 that influenced Matthew's reworking of Mark in Matt 15:28; rather, it was the Evangelist's own composition of Matt 8:13 (in a formulation that became typical for him) that provided his conclusion to the Q episode, where there was none originally.

Conversely, it might be argued that Luke "missed" a conclusion in Q, but Jesus' praise for the Gentile centurion's expression of faith likely reminded Luke of Jesus' similar approval of the Syrophoenician woman's saying in Mark 7:29. Though Luke does not have a parallel to Mark's Syrophoenician woman, Luke probably knew the story in Mark and was influenced to bring his own story of

---

9. Gagnon 1994, 137, also quoted in Johnson 2002, 158–59. Furthermore, Gagnon observes, the verbal agreements/synonyms that remain—ἐλθὼν, θεραπεύσω/διασώσῃ, and the repetition of ὁ ἑκατόνταρχος/ἑκατοντάρχης (Matt 8:8a//Luke 7:6) are not traditional but are simply coincidental, due to the Evangelists' respective redactional activity.

the centurion to a conclusion in a way analogous to Mark 7:30. It was not neces-sary for Jesus to go to the centurion's house, but Luke's narrative introduction to the dialogue now made it natural in his redactional conclusion for the envoys to return there and find the servant in good health. James Robinson notes the Lukan character of the language in Luke 7:10 and the Markan influence on Luke's syntax with the conclusion: "There is nothing in Luke 7:10 to be ascribed to Q" (Johnson 2002, 399). Note the similar comment a decade earlier: "Stating the fact that the boy was actually healed, if in Q at all, seems hardly more than an afterthought" (Robinson 1992, 365).

I think the case can be made that these and other redactional elements in Matt 8 and Luke 7 have had some influence on the writing of John 4:46–54. The royal official comes to Jesus because he "heard that Jesus had come from Judea to Galilee." Like the Samaritans who came to Jesus because they heard from the woman in the previous episode, the official also "hears" of Jesus. Verse 47a is closely linked in the narrative with verse 45: the official approaches Jesus because he heard from the Galileans of all that Jesus had done in Jerusalem. There is here also an echo of the redactional verses in Luke's account (7:2, 3), where the Evan-gelist tells us that the centurion has heard of Jesus and approaches him because his boy is near death—a note of urgency that John takes over as well (4:47, 49). Like the Samaritans, the official's faith is deepened because of his own hearing of Jesus' word (cf. 4:41–42 with 50, 53; see Moloney 1993, 187). This is an important theme in the Fourth Gospel, as Craig Koester (1989) has demonstrated: for exam-ple, the disciples in John 2:11, 22 come to a genuine faith because they believe the word Jesus spoke.

Unlike his interactions with the Samaritans, however, Jesus seems at first to respond negatively to the request. He rebukes the man and with him the sur-rounding Galileans—warning "you people" against "signs and wonders" (4:48), that is, warning that true faith cannot be based on witnessing signs (see also 3:3). "This rebuke enables the author to state clearly the major theme of the pas-sage: authentic belief" (Moloney 1998b, 153). Here we begin to perceive the truly Johannine character of the story, the structuring of which has been aptly described nearly thirty years ago by Charles Giblin (1979–80, esp. 204–6) and more recently reiterated by Francis Moloney (1993, 184–91; 1998b, 153–56) and John Painter (1996, 357–61). As with the first Cana sign, there is an initial request to Jesus, who replies with a testing objection, which is overcome in some way by the quester. Jesus then complies with the request, but in his own way that makes clear that we have moved with the Evangelist to a new level of significance. As Painter (2007) pointed out in the delivered version of his John, Jesus, and History paper, Jesus' objection in John 4:48 is no "clumsy redaction" of an earlier source's story. Rather, it is an integral part of John's "most perceptive interpretation" of (this event in the life of) Jesus.

Again, we have a very Johannine pattern and theme, but in telling this par-ticular tale the Evangelist could well have been influenced by Jesus' hesitant objection in the redactional Matt 8:7. The difference, however, is that in Matthew it is a question of a religious/ritual barrier between Jesus the Jew and the Gentile centurion, which the centurion breaks through by volunteering a solution that reveals his belief in Jesus the miracle worker, while in John the real issue is the quality of the man's faith in Jesus himself. In the Synoptics, the centurion expresses his confidence and faith in the healing power of the word of Jesus; John, typically, gives the initiative to Jesus, who tests the man's faith by setting up an obstacle for him to overcome. For John, it is Jesus who elicits a response from the man, rather than the other way around, and it is Jesus who commands that the man "go," rather than the centurion dissuading Jesus from coming to his house or persuading him that there is no need to come. Instead of the official instructing Jesus to "say the word," Jesus in John speaks a word that evokes the faith of the official and eventually all his household. I come back to Moody Smith's concise statement: "In the synoptic version the centurion's faith is never in question. Here the official's faith is the question" (1999, 126).

John's rendition of the resolution of the story carries traces of elements that I consider redactional in the Synoptics, particularly their narrative conclusions. These include the motif of the "hour" when Jesus spoke and the boy was healed, the return to the house to find the boy well, and the idea of someone coming from the house—not as in Luke to request Jesus' help or to ask him to "only speak the word"—but in John to confirm the healing of which Jesus spoke on his own initiative.[10]

There is no question that we have a very Johannine story through and through; the Evangelist rewrote the story to give it completely new emphasis. The royal official believes the word of Jesus just as the disciples do in John 2: they believe what Jesus told them in John 1, and the sign in 2:1–11 confirms their faith (Koester 1989). They also believe the "word of Jesus" in 2:22 (Moloney 2005b, 463–64) against the background of those who challenge Jesus (2:18–21) and those who saw the signs but of whom Jesus was skeptical. The official believes "the word that Jesus spoke," and his faith is confirmed by the sign, so that "he himself believed, along with his whole household" (4:53). His faithful response is featured against the background of the Galileans who welcomed Jesus because "they had seen all that he had done" (4:45), but who also needed to come to a deeper faith on the basis of his word.

I come back here to Painter's insightful and engaging approach: John was so certain of his understanding of Jesus that "he freely transmits the tradition, providing insight in his own words" (Painter 2007, 235). For me, at least part of John's tradition is not merely Synoptic-like but a profound reflection upon the Synoptic Gospels themselves. In this view, John does not put us in touch with a more factually accurate history of Jesus but with a deeper appreciation of the historic Jesus.

---

10. See esp. Neirynck 1984; 1979, 93–120.

Aspects of Historicity in John 1–4: A Response

Craig R. Koester

The manner in which modern scholars investigate questions of historicity is one that the Fourth Evangelist would find peculiar. In contemporary research, the historical Jesus is the pre-Easter Jesus, and questions of historicity focus on how much we can know about the ministry of Jesus prior to his death. The writer of the Fourth Gospel, however, assumes that truly understanding the pre-Easter Jesus involves a post-Easter perspective. At points this Gospel specifically draws later insights into the meaning of Jesus' words and actions and acknowledges that Jesus said and did things that were not understood prior to his resurrection (John 2:22; 12:16). In some passages, the line between the pre-Easter and post-Easter Jesus is blurred, so that during the course of his ministry Jesus speaks as if he has already returned to the Father (3:10–15; 17:11). Therefore, sifting through the details of John's narrative in order to identify the earliest forms of traditions about Jesus would seem to run counter to the Evangelist's own approach to understanding history.

What brings contemporary questions of historicity into closer alignment with the concerns of the Fourth Evangelist is the recognition that the Gospel tells the story of a particular person: Jesus of Nazareth. The Gospel includes more than Jesus' sayings or general religious instruction; it narrates a life. Following this same tradition, the Johannine Epistles emphatically reject the idea that the message of Jesus can be dissociated from his coming "in the flesh" (1 John 4:2–3; 2 John 7), and "flesh" presupposes the historicity of a life that took place at particular times and places. The Fourth Gospel interprets the story of Jesus, yet it also assumes that there is a story to interpret and that the Gospel's message is integrally connected to Jesus of Nazareth (John 1:45; 18:5, 7; 19:19). John's Gospel both preserves and interprets the tradition (Martyn 1968; Thompson 1996; Moloney 2005a, 45–65).

The seven essays considered here use various methods to identify early traditions about Jesus and his followers. To determine that something is an early tradition does not necessarily mean that it is historically accurate, and assessing the historical plausibility of the material is therefore another step. These authors rightly understand that when assessing historicity, one can at most claim greater or lesser degrees of probability for one's conclusions. Some of the essays deal with matters unique to John, while others attempt to sort out issues of agreement and disagreement with the Synoptic Gospels. We will consider each of the essays in turn, asking about the contributions made by each of them, as well as identifying some of the questions and issues that remain.

Craig Keener explores the interplay of history and theology in his study of the Gospel's Prologue. The statement "we beheld his glory" (John 1:14) suggests both an eyewitness claim and a theological interpretation of that claim. The use of the first-person plural in "we beheld" was common in various genres where an author wanted to show direct knowledge of the events being described. In fictitious narratives the "we" would presumably be fictitious, but Keener does not think this is the case with John. Although space does not allow him to develop the point, he maintains that the writer of the Fourth Gospel identifies himself with those who actually witnessed the ministry of Jesus. The claim to have seen "glory" in Jesus' ministry moves further into the realm of theology, since not everyone who witnessed the events could claim to have seen Jesus' glory revealed in them. The intense debates in the Gospel show that many people could agree *that* Jesus performed a given action, yet they could construe the meaning of the action in dramatically different ways (e.g., 5:16–18; 9:18–34; 11:45–48). Moreover, even those who believed eyewitnesses were able to comprehend many of the revelatory dimensions of Jesus' life and work only in retrospect. For Keener, John presents an independent tradition that is probably no less historical than those found in the Synoptic Gospels. But since the Prologue has no real counterpart in the Synoptic tradition, its implications for questions of historicity must be considered in other ways.

Much of Keener's essay is devoted to the theological lenses that shape the Fourth Evangelist's presentation of the tradition. Seeing the glory of Jesus is a key element in the Prologue, and seeing the divine was a weighty theme in Greek and Hellenistic Jewish spirituality. What makes John distinctive in this cultural milieu is that he locates the revelation of God in the person of Jesus. Philosophical sources may refer to the soul's contemplation of divine realities, and Jewish sources tell of Moses' vision of divine glory on Sinai, but for John the deepest vision of God comes from seeing the revelation of God's character in history—in the person of Jesus. This means that the vision of God is never unmediated; it occurs in and through Jesus. This conviction assumes its most radical form in the Gospel's insistence that those who see divine glory will see it in the crucifixion itself. The crucifixion is not separated from the life that precedes it or the exaltation that follows, but it means that people meet God in the suffering and disgrace of a Roman execution.

Reading the Prologue in light of Keener's essay raises the important question as to what is essential in the historical claims made about Jesus. In the Prologue we find that the statement about seeing Jesus' glory is preceded by the reference to his "flesh" (1:14). If Jesus is a person of flesh, then there is a particularity to what the Gospel says about him. Patterns of thought that are reflected in a range of Jewish and Greco-Roman texts may help to disclose who Jesus is, but Jesus himself is the given. So how much about the particular person named Jesus does this Gospel presuppose, and how much connection with the human Jesus is required for the Gospel's message to have integrity? In the Fourth Gospel, "flesh" includes Jesus' genuine humanity. This is borne out by the ensuing narrative, where friend and foe alike agree that Jesus is a human being. Their disagreements concern what more can be said about him.

"Flesh" also includes mortality, and the Gospel also presupposes the historicity of the specific means by which Jesus was put to death: his crucifixion. The presupposition that Jesus was crucified undergirds the Gospel's treatment of "glory." As Keener points out, Jesus' glory is not limited to crucifixion, but it does encompass crucifixion. Without the presupposition that Jesus truly was executed, the Gospel's claims about the nature of his glory would be decisively altered. The Prologue leaves us wondering what else might be considered an essential dimension of Jesus' "flesh." For example, those who are truly human have some sort of ethnic identity, and it seems essential to affirm that Jesus was Jewish. Are there other dimensions of his "flesh" or humanity that might be deemed essential? Responding to such questions would take one well beyond the opening verses of the Gospel, but the Prologue's incarnational theology makes asking such questions important (Thompson 1988, 33–52).

A related issue involves the role of eyewitness testimony in the community of faith. The use of the plural "we" or "us" in the Prologue is remarkably fluid. To say "we beheld his glory" (1:14) might suggest that eyewitnesses are speaking, but then to say "we all have received grace upon grace" (1:16) extends the plural beyond eyewitnesses, since the recipients of grace include all members of the believing community. Similarly, the Gospel's conclusion links the Gospel's tradition to the Beloved Disciple, who is said to have been beside Jesus at the Last Supper, thereby affirming a link between the Gospel's message and the human being named Jesus (21:24a). Yet the same passage also claims, "we know that his testimony is true," reflecting a wider circle of believers, at least some of whom were probably not eyewitnesses (21:24b). Just as the Gospel fuses the pre-Easter and post-Easter Jesus, it connects the pre-Easter and post-Easter faith community. The Gospel assumes that it is essential for the message it transmits to be linked to Jesus and his earliest disciples, but the Prologue leaves us wondering about how much of a link is needed for the Gospel's message to have integrity.

Mark Appold shifts our attention to the interplay between Gospel studies and recent work in archaeology. The Gospel of John has long been noted for its detailed knowledge of topography (Kundsin 1925; Koester 1995). Appold's focus is the town of Bethsaida, on the northeast side of the Sea of Galilee. Bethsaida is mentioned in all four Gospels and some extrabiblical sources, but John is unique in identifying Bethsaida as the home or workplace of Andrew, Peter, and Philip (1:44). The narrative in which these figures are brought into the circle of Jesus' followers is theologically shaped, yet Appold sees beneath it a tradition that has connections to the historical Jesus. There does not seem to be any apparent theological motivation for linking these disciples to Bethsaida, which enhances the likelihood that it reflects early tradition that might be historically accurate. Appold notes that the Synoptic Gospels link the early disciples more closely to Capernaum but does not attempt in his essay to work out the discrepancy. Taking up this issue at some point, however, would help to strengthen the case for a Bethsaida connection.

Recent archaeological work has helped to disclose aspects of cultural and economic life at Bethsaida. The town was inhabited until the early centuries C.E., but afterward no building took place on the site. In the first century, it was evidently a fishing village of perhaps two hundred people. Its residents were also involved in agriculture, but there is no evidence of a thriving economy. The town had a Jewish population, but it was open to the influences of the adjacent Gentile region. Appold points out that the names of the three Bethsaida disciples are Greek in character, which would suit the Hellenized social context of Bethsaida.

The reminiscence of a connection between some of Jesus' early disciples and the town of Bethsaida does seem historically plausible for the reasons Appold suggests. The more difficult questions arise when considering the rest of the call narrative in John 1:35–51. Appold rightly notes that the Fourth Gospel's portrayal of the early disciples is shaped by issues that were important at the time of writing. One of these concerned the rivalry between the followers of John (the Baptist) and the disciples of Jesus (see 3:22–26), and the Evangelist makes clear that John's role is to direct people to Jesus (1:6–8, 15; 3:28–30). According to the call narrative, Andrew of Bethsaida was once a follower of John (the Baptist), but at the beginning of the Gospel he follows Jesus and calls him "Messiah" (1:40–41). This scene is important for the Fourth Evangelist, since it shows someone leaving John and going to Jesus, which serves as an example for others. It is quite possible for something to be historically accurate while representing a larger theological claim (Koester 2003, 7–8, 33–39). The question here is whether Andrew's initial connection to the Baptist reflects historical tradition, especially since this is not evident in other early sources that mention Andrew. The question is complicated by Andrew's immediate use of a messianic title for Jesus, which seems to reflect later theological shaping.

Another question concerns the number of disciples who might have had connections to Bethsaida. The call narrative specifically mentions the three disciples, but it also notes that Andrew was accompanied by another disciple, whose name is not given (1:35–42). It is possible that this unnamed disciple is to be understood as the Beloved Disciple, who often appears with Peter in John's Gospel. What is more problematic is the suggestion that he be identified as John the son of Zebedee, which might mean that he and his brother James would also come from Bethsaida. Although a later reference to the sons of Zebedee, along with two unnamed disciples, makes this connection possible (21:2), studies of the Beloved

Disciple's identity make the connection with the son of Zebedee less than plausible (Brown 1979, 31–34; 2003, 189–99). When considering links to Bethsaida, it seems best to work with the three disciples whom the Fourth Gospel explicitly identifies with the place.

Bethsaida's role in the interplay between history and theology in John might also follow the insight that it was a community on the boundary between Jewish and non-Jewish areas. The Greek character of the names of Philip and Andrew is clear, and when the Greeks approach Philip at the end of Jesus' public ministry, the Evangelist reminds readers about the connection with Bethsaida (12:20–22). The Gospel's narrative about the coming of the Greeks is highly stylized, and it carries considerable theological freight. Nevertheless, it may help to show how an early tradition about the disciples' origins in a border town was developed in order to make a larger theological claim about the importance of Jesus for those outside the traditional Jewish community.

James McGrath provides a study of the temple cleansing and Jesus' statement about destroying and rebuilding the temple (2:13–22). His approach takes up one of the principal questions pertaining to the historical study of Jesus, namely, the relationship of traditions found in John to those in the Synoptic Gospels, Paul's writings, and the Gospel of Thomas. McGrath's work gives support to John's independence from the Synoptics, which has been affirmed by many (Smith 1992; Thatcher 2006, 3–11). He notes that in John's account of the temple cleansing there are unique details that do not seem to be derived from the Synoptics and yet do not appear to have been introduced for theological reasons. Such details include the whip of cords, the oxen, and the sheep. John may have derived these from an independent tradition. Moreover, John and the Synoptic writers weave different Old Testament passages into their accounts. Whereas Mark uses Isa 56 and Jer 7, John draws on Ps 69 and Zech 14; yet John's selection of texts does not seem to have a strong connection to his distinctive theology. McGrath makes a strong case that John has drawn on an independent interpretive tradition.

A distinctive feature in John's account is that Jesus speaks about his opponents destroying the temple and himself raising it up in three days. In contrast, the Synoptic form assumes that Jesus was falsely accused of saying that he would both destroy and rebuild the temple (Matt 26:59–61; Mark 14:55–59; see also Acts 6:14). In order to show that the Johannine form could be quite early, McGrath compares it to Pauline statements that speak of God destroying those who would destroy the temple (with the Christian community understood to be the "temple"; 1 Cor 3:17; see also 2 Cor 5:1–4). The parallel is intriguing, but the contexts of Paul's remarks do not make a clear connection to the Jerusalem temple or to Jesus traditions (Thiselton 2000, 316–18). More would need to be done to show that Paul is actually appealing to the Jesus tradition, rather than using temple imagery in a broader sense. Likewise, to bolster the case that John's version of the saying is quite early, more would also have to be done to account for the Synoptic form of the saying. Since the Synoptics state that the saying about the destruction of the temple was ascribed (falsely) to Jesus, it is arguably the more troubling form of the saying. From this perspective, the Johannine version actually eases some of the tension. To strengthen the case for the early character of John's version, a plausible case would have to be made as to the origins of the Synoptic version.

When dealing with the placement of the story, McGrath notes that Mark established the outline of Jesus' ministry that was adapted by Matthew and Luke, so that the basic New Testament chronologies are only those of Mark and John. He also notes that both John and the Synoptic authors were capable of arranging sequences for theological reasons. In Mark's account, Jesus' ministry takes place over a rather short period of time that includes only one visit to Jerusalem. Many scholars, however, find John's depiction of a longer ministry to be more plausible. John's mention of the temple being constructed for forty-six years would place the temple cleansing at around 27–28 C.E., which would fit well at the beginning of Jesus' ministry. John's early placement of the temple cleansing warrants historical consideration. McGrath rightly refrains from claiming too much about the amount of historical information that might be gleaned from John, but he also offers a salutary reminder that many involved in Jesus research might be too dismissive of John. Modest claims about the plausibility of early traditions in John might be the best way to encourage greater usage of the Fourth Gospel in Jesus research.

Mary Coloe turns our attention to traditions concerning John the Baptist, who plays a large role in the Fourth Gospel. Like McGrath, she develops a case that the material in the Fourth Gospel is largely independent of that in the Synoptics. She points out that all of the canonical Gospels attribute to the Baptist a saying in which he speaks of the superior figure coming after him (Matt 3:11; Mark 1:7; Luke 3:16; John 1:15, 27). This substantial agreement suggests that this saying reflects the Baptist's own teaching. The Gospels diverge, however, over the Baptist's relationship to Elijah. The Synoptic tradition identifies the Baptist with Elijah, who was to return prior to the end of the age, according to Mal 4:4–5. In the Fourth Gospel, however, the Baptist denies that he is Elijah (John 1:21). Those who think that John knew one or more of the Synoptics might argue that the Fourth Gospel's refusal to identify the Baptist with Elijah is a response to the Synoptic tradition. Coloe, however, proposes an alternative. She maintains that the identification of the Baptist with Elijah need not have been made by the Baptist himself and that it probably arose in the post-Easter tradition of the church. Therefore, in refusing to identify the Baptist with Elijah, the Fourth Gospel may stand in line with the earlier tradition, which is plausible. It also seems likely, however, that the Fourth Gospel makes such a direct rejection of the Elijah connection because the status of the Baptist was disputed at the time the Gospel was written. Accordingly, the Fourth Gospel may be asserting a substantially early tradition in which John the Baptist was not identified with Elijah, in light of later claims that he was Elijah.

Coloe observes that the Gospels have different ways of relating the ministries of John the Baptist and Jesus. The Synoptic accounts create a fairly neat sequence, in which John's ministry ends as Jesus' ministry begins. In the Fourth Gospel, however, there is a significant period of overlap, when both John and Jesus teach and baptize. This leads to confusion in their respective roles, which the Fourth Gospel attempts to clarify (3:22–30). Coloe points out that the sense of clear temporal succession in the Synoptics might have less to do with historical tradition and more to do with the Synoptic writers' desire to show how John the Baptist's ministry leads to that of Jesus. The Fourth Gospel, however, preserves a tradition that acknowledged that the two figures worked at the same time and in some similar ways. Since the tradition concerning these parallel ministries created problems that needed to be addressed, it might well have been historical.

Another example of a point where the four Gospels seem to develop an early tradition in different ways concerns the comparison of Jesus to a bridegroom. In the Synoptic sayings, Jesus identifies himself as the bridegroom, whereas the Fourth Gospel presents John the Baptist as the one who makes this connection (Matt 9:15; Mark 2:19; Luke 5:34–35; John 3:29). In this case, Coloe finds it most probable that the Synoptics preserve the earlier form of the tradition and that the Fourth Gospel has developed it independently in a different direction. This again seems plausible, and the result is that interpreters are encouraged to see the theological dynamics at work in the way that all four Evangelists develop the traditions about the Baptist. A question that goes beyond the scope of her essay is how these early traditions might relate to the overall picture of John the Baptist in a particular Gospel. Some of the most pointed questions about historicity revolve around portrayals of John the Baptist's preaching. In the Synoptics, the Baptist preaches a baptism of repentance, whereas the opening chapter of the Fourth Gospel has him identify Jesus as the redemptive Lamb of God. Calling Jesus "the Lamb" fits well with the post-Easter perspective of the church, but its relationship to the Baptist's own preaching is problematic (Brown 1966–70, 1:58). Here the Fourth Gospel shows evidence of some early traditions with considerable theological reshaping.

James Charlesworth takes a different approach to the question of history in his study of the symbolism of the serpent in John 3:14–15. The passage involves a typology in which Jesus is said to be "lifted up" as Moses once lifted up the serpent on the pole (Num 21:9). Instead of asking at the outset whether this might draw on an early Jesus tradition, Charlesworth assumes that the passage is the work of the Fourth Evangelist. His interest concerns the meaning of the imagery. He notes that many interpreters assume that the serpent is a symbol for evil and therefore think that John 3 only compares the actions of "lifting up" that took place in the story of Moses and the passion of Jesus. He points out, however, that serpent symbolism was multivalent and that there might be a more direct comparison between the serpent and Jesus himself. Citing passages from various ancient sources, he suggests that the serpent could connote divine paternity and immortality. While this point is broadly true, the imagery can better be explicated through a reading of Num 21 and the Jewish traditions that informed its later interpretation.

Next, Charlesworth considers the significance of Jesus' being "lifted up." Later references in the Gospel make clear connections with the crucifixion, when Jesus' opponents will lift him up to die (John 8:28; 12:32–34). The question is whether this is the point in 3:14–15, and Charlesworth seems to give a mixed answer. He argues that the expression "lift up" helps to show that "Jesus' crucifixion was not a failure but his hour of triumph" (69), which I think is correct; however, he also maintains that it "symbolizes Jesus' exaltation and return to heaven" (68). This does not seem likely, since the force of the passage comes through the comparison of the physical elevation of the serpent on the pole and the elevation of Jesus on the cross (Moloney 1996, 193). For the Evangelist, both of these are sources of life. Identifying the "lifting up" with the crucifixion rather than the ascension best fits Charlesworth's own emphasis on the parallelism in the passage, which shows that both the serpent on the pole and Jesus on the cross give life to those who turn to them in faith.

At the end of the essay, Charlesworth does make brief mention of the question of connections to the historical Jesus. The way he poses the question is by asking whether we can assume that it is impossible that the Fourth Evangelist might have presented a teaching of Jesus that was otherwise lost. In response, he observes that Matt 10:16 preserves a saying in which the followers of Jesus are told to be wise as serpents. He insists that it is within the realm of possibility that the Fourth Evangelist might have known a saying of Jesus concerning the serpent in Num 21, but the essay itself does not attempt to show how this possibility might be taken as a genuine probability. His work is primarily an exploration of how the serpent image would have functioned in the communication between the Evangelist and readers in the post-Easter church.

Susan Miller explores John's narration of Jesus' encounter with the Samaritan woman in John 4. At the level of sources, she observes that none of the other Gospels speak of a Samaritan mission, that Matthew includes a prohibition against entering a Samaritan city (Matt 10:5), and that Luke says that Jesus was rejected by a Samaritan village (Luke 9:51–56). Nevertheless, Luke does include positive references to Samaritans, and Acts says that the early church extended its mission work there (Luke 10:29–37; 17:11–19; Acts 1:8; 8:1). Accordingly, one question is whether John's account of Jesus in Samaria has more do with an early Jesus tradition or whether it is mainly a reflection of the post-Easter church's mission there. Many interpreters assume that the encounter primarily reflects post-Easter realities, especially since Jesus' comments to the disciples anticipate the later mission of the church (John 4:31–38; Brown 1979, 34–40). Miller and others, however, find it historically plausible that Jesus himself had an encounter with a Samaritan woman. Evidence for this includes the remarkable accuracy of the geographical references to Jacob's well, the Gospel's familiarity with Samaritan beliefs about the location of worship and the coming of an eschatological prophet, and the fact that some Galileans did travel through Samaria on their way to and from Jerusalem. What complicates the effort to ascribe the historicity of the scene to the historical

Jesus, however, is that the Evangelist's familiarity with Samaritan topography and thought could stem from the post-Easter mission of the church rather than early traditions about Jesus' own ministry in the region.

Miller also suggests another, less direct way of linking the scene to the historical Jesus. She finds that the outlook of Jesus in John 4 seems congruent with early traditions about him. She points to evidence that the historical Jesus took an interest in Samaria. The most significant argument is that Jesus chose twelve disciples, evidently foreshadowing his hopes for the restoration of all Israel; this would include the tribes that had once settled in Samaria. From this perspective, John 4 shows Jesus putting this hope into practice. Another point is that early traditions about Jesus indicate that he anticipated the end of temple worship in Jerusalem. According to some interpreters, his cleansing of the temple functions as a prophetic sign that portends the coming destruction of the temple and the cessation of worship there. Similarly, John 4:21 tells of the coming hour when worship will no longer take place in Jerusalem or on Mount Gerizim. What may be said, then, is that Jesus' encounter with the Samaritan woman seems to include some elements that are congruent with early traditions about Jesus, as known from other sources.

Much of Miller's essay considers the theological shaping of the narrative, which she agrees took place in response to later issues that were raised by the church's Samaritan mission. She notes that both Mark's account of the Syrophoenician woman (Mark 7:24–30) and John's account of the Samaritan woman deal with matters of gender and ethnicity. Each account deals with food or water, and each shows how Jesus (and his followers) must reach across traditional boundaries. The critical response of the Pharisees, who charge that Jesus is a Samaritan (John 8:48), suggests that in post-Easter conflicts Jesus and his followers were denigrated as Samaritans, who were not considered authentic children of Abraham. That John 4 gives Samaritans an important place within the Christian community seems clear, and the encounter is rich with themes from Johannine theology. Given the complexity of the material, however, identifying earlier traditions in this episode and distinguishing them from later theological reflection remains difficult.

Peter Judge focuses attention on Jesus' healing of the royal official's son (John 4:46–54). The official comes from Capernaum to Cana, where Jesus simply says the word and the boy is healed. Here again John's relationship to the Synoptic Gospels is a major question. The Synoptics include a similar episode in which Jesus heals a boy in the household of a centurion at Capernaum without actually going to the man's house (Matt 8:5–13; Luke 7:1–10). Each version of the story has distinctive elements, but most interpreters find it quite likely that John and the Synoptics draw from a common tradition. In contrast to some of the essays we have considered above, however, Judge's work finds that John often seems to be dependent on the Synoptic Gospels, though it is difficult to distinguish layers of tradition and interpretation. Judge's reading suggests that John does not dismiss the importance of the tradition but transmits and develops it in order to disclose its significance.

Judge initially observes that the royal official's ethnic identity is ambiguous in John's account. This is one point in the essay where he finds that John might take us back to a very early version of the story. In the Synoptic accounts the man is a Gentile, but in John this is not so clear. Judge notes that some interpreters assume that the official is Jewish, while others consider him a Gentile. This division of opinion underscores an ethnic ambiguity that John may have preserved and that the tradition tried to clarify. What is more important in the Fourth Gospel is that the official is a Galilean. The Johannine account is prefaced by the saying that "a prophet has no honor in his own country" (John 4:44), a traditional saying that is also attested in the Synoptics (Mark 6:4; Luke 4:24). If Jesus' own country is Galilee, then the royal official from Galilee presents a test case. The Galileans may appear to honor Jesus by welcoming him, but it appears that their faith depends on signs and therefore is insufficiently based. Accordingly, John develops the story so that it becomes an account of a person's faith being tested and moved to a deeper level, based on Jesus' word.

Tracing the development of the story in the various Gospel traditions, Judge turns to a recent reconstruction of the episode as it appears in Q, together with the redactional elements added by Matthew and Luke. The critical reconstruction of Q proposes that Jesus' initial response to the man shows hesitancy. Judge finds it more likely that the hesitancy comes from Matthew's redaction. If so, then Jesus' rebuff to the official in John 4:48 might have been influenced by the hesitancy reflected in Matthew. The difference between the accounts is that in Matthew the hesitancy arises because of the religious barriers separating the Jewish Jesus from the Gentile centurion, whereas in John the issue concerns the quality of the man's faith in Jesus. What is not entirely clear is whether we are to assume that John knew a form of the story that was independent of the Synoptics and left the official's ethnic identity unspecified or that John also knew the Synoptic version, which influenced him at points (Anderson 2006b). Given the differences, I find it most plausible to think that John worked with a tradition that came to him independently of the Synoptics and less likely that he worked with the Synoptics themselves. Nevertheless, this raises again the basic question about the interrelationships among the Gospels and the traditions upon which they drew. Oral and written forms of the Jesus stories may have circulated side by side, and this in turn makes tracing the various forms of influence extraordinarily complex.

The essays considered above all recognize the ways the Fourth Evangelist creatively shapes a portrayal of Jesus in John 1–4, and all find evidence that he did so by drawing on earlier traditions. For those engaged in the broader field of historical Jesus studies, this means that here are good reasons to continue considering where and how the Fourth Gospel might include early traditions concerning Jesus, his disciples, and John the Baptist. Given the difficulty in reaching consensus about what constitutes an early tradition, claims about the findings must remain modest, yet giving John a larger place in the discussion enriches the process. For those focusing primarily on Johannine studies, the search for early traditions and the assessment of their historical character are but aspects of a much larger interpretive enterprise. Conclusions are difficult to reach, and the most that can be said is that certain findings have a greater or lesser degree of plausibility. In the end, however, asking the question of historicity is important, since it reminds interpreters that John's account is tied to a Jesus who was truly flesh and was crucified under Pontius Pilate. In its creative retelling of the story from a post-Easter perspective, the Fourth Gospel assumes that its message is integrally connected to the person and work of the pre-Easter Jesus.

PART 2
ASPECTS OF HISTORICITY IN JOHN 5–12

INTRODUCTION TO PART 2:
ASPECTS OF HISTORICITY IN JOHN 5–12

Paul N. Anderson

John 5–12 covers the middle section of Jesus' ministry, including three trips to Jerusalem (John 5; 7; 12), intense debates between Jesus and the religious leaders in Jerusalem (John 5; 7–10), the feeding of the five thousand and related events (John 6—the sea crossing, debates as to the meaning of the feeding, and the confession of Peter), the healing of a lame man by the Pool of Bethesda (John 5), the healing of a blind man and his washing in the Pool of Siloam (John 9), the raising of Lazarus from the dead (John 11), the anointing of Jesus' feet by Mary of Bethany, Greeks coming from afar to meet Jesus, his triumphal entry into Jerusalem (John 12), and the emergence of plans to kill Jesus (John 5; 7; 8; 11; 12). In addition to these events, Jesus' teachings play an important role in this section of the Fourth Gospel. In debates with Jerusalem leaders, controversy over his being "one" with the Father who sent him take the center stage in John 5; 7–10; and 12. After the feeding of the five thousand, Jesus' bread-of-life discourse and related dialogues occupy over half of the seventy-one verses in John 6. In John 8:12, Jesus declares himself to be the light of the world, while the sin of the religious leaders in the next chapter is that they claim "We see" (John 9:41). In John 10:1–9, Jesus declares himself to be the gate of the sheepfold, while he soon thereafter declares himself to be the good shepherd who lays down his life for his sheep (10:10–18). Prior to the raising of Lazarus, Martha makes a pivotal christological confession, and Jesus declares, "I am the resurrection and the life" (11:25–26). Jesus' agony is expressed before his final entry into Jerusalem (12:23–33), and Jesus' closing words at the end of John 12 provide a summary of his mission, closing what has been called the Johannine "book of signs" (12:44–50). As such, several historical questions press their way into the foreground when considering the middle section of the Gospel of John.

First, the presentation of Jesus as traveling to and from Jerusalem poses a striking contrast between John and the Synoptics. Jesus' visit to Jerusalem in John 5 is presented as at least a second visit following the first visit in John 2, and due to the hostility to his mission among the Jerusalem religious leaders (the *Ioudaioi*), his further visits to the south are questioned severely by those around him (7:1–10; 11:1–16). Jesus' entry into Jerusalem on a colt in John 12 is the fourth recorded visit to Jerusalem in the Johannine narrative, lending credibility to his statement that he had taught openly in synagogues and in the temple (18:20). Here one must choose between the Synoptic and the Johannine renditions of Jesus' ministry itinerary; one cannot have it both ways. Either Jesus visited Jerusalem several times during his ministry, or he visited only once—when he was arrested, tried, and crucified. Because Matthew and Luke follow Mark's itinerary, the question comes down to analyzing John and Mark together. On this point, many scholars believe that John's presentation is closer to a realistic rendering of what an observant Jew would have done before the fall of Jerusalem in 70 c.e. Not only once a year at Passover, but visiting the temple several times a year—especially during religious festivals—seems a likely thing for an emerging religious leader to have done in Jesus' day. It is also interesting to note that in all four Gospels, after Jesus rode into Jerusalem on a donkey's colt with crowds chanting "Hosanna!" and paving the street with garments and foliage, the Romans did not arrest him as a threat. The answer to this question, as posed by Paula Fredriksen (1999; 2007), lies in the likelihood of the Johannine presentation: Jesus had probably been there before, and thus the threat he posed was felt to be minimal. Here the Johannine rendering seems historically preferable to the single-Jerusalem-visit itinerary of the Synoptic Jesus.

A second problem, though, follows the solution to the first. If Jesus indeed traveled to Jerusalem more than once, how did he arrive back abruptly in Galilee at the beginning of John 6? Further, the Jewish leaders in John 7 appear to be still debating Jesus' healing on the Sabbath—performed in John 5—while John 7:1–10 clearly presents a debate about Jesus *returning* to Jerusalem. As the living-water motif of John 4 fits well with the living-bread themes of John 6, some scholars have sought to explain these aporias (perplexities in the text) by inferring a changing of the Johannine order: perhaps the original order was John 4; 6; 5; 7, which was rearranged by a later editor. Then again, the manna and sea-crossing themes, as well as the crowd's desire to coronate Jesus as the Mosaic prophet in John 6:14, follow directly on Jesus' assertion that "Moses wrote of me" (5:46). That being the case, it seems that John 6 follows John 5 with intentionality, even referring to a plurality of healings (6:2, implying those performed in John 4 and 5), suggesting a simpler set of composition possibilities. What if an earlier edition of the Johannine narrative was supplemented by the additions of several sections of material, including John 6? This matter cannot be solved here, but it does illustrate the fact that questions of historicity and chronology emerge from features *within* the Johannine text, not simply as a factor of comparing John and the Synoptics.

A third problem relates to John's distinctive selections of material. Why are there no exorcisms, teachings on the kingdom of God, or presentation of the transfiguration in this section? If John's tradition indeed represents an alternative perspective on the ministry of Jesus, how could it possibly have omitted core elements of that ministry? Conversely, why are some of the prominent features of John 5–12 completely missing from the Synoptics? The two healings in Jerusalem, Jesus' claims about himself using distinctive "I am" references, and his raising of Lazarus from the dead would all feature prominently in any Jesus narrative connected with history—if indeed these things really happened in history and were known. Again, one way scholars have dealt with the diversity of selection between John and the Synoptics is to ascribe to the Fourth Evangelist's interests theological motives instead of historical ones. The assumption is that John crafts things in keeping with the narrator's theology, while the Synoptics proceed with historical interests, proper. The problem with this approach is that the Synoptics are equally as theological as John, and John has much more archaeological and topographical detail than all the Synoptics put together. Indeed, some theological crafting is likely in every Gospel, but other explanations include access to traditions with particular geographical provenances, access to different traditions and sources, and alternative presentations as an intentional factor of familiarity and complementarity. Indeed, the Johannine narrator acknowledges other renderings of Jesus' ministry (20:30–31), and the final editor declares intentional selectivity, perhaps as an answer to original questions about the narrative's distinctiveness (21:24–25). The Johannine-Synoptic selection differences, though, remain an interpretive and historical challenge.

A fourth problem relates to the similarities between John and the Synoptics. The feeding of the five thousand is included in all four canonical Gospels, and in Matthew, Mark, and John it is followed by a sea crossing. Does this imply Johannine familiarity with, or even dependence upon, Synoptic traditions? When comparing the feedings in Mark 6 and John 6, even some of the details are similar: the plentitude of grass (Mark 6:39; John 6:10) and the cost of feeding such a multitude (Mark 6:37; John 6:7). If these similarities imply traditional familiarity, might John's narrative be seen as a spiritualized incorporation of Mark? Yet despite several similarities between John 6 (the feeding of the five thousand, the sea crossing, a discussion of the feeding, and the confession of Peter), Mark 6 (the feeding of the five thousand and the sea crossing), and Mark 8 (the feeding of the four thousand, discussions of the feeding, and the confession of Peter), none of them is identical, making close derivation an unlikely inference. These seem to be three independent renderings of a similar set of events. Regarding possible traditional influence, however, why not assume that one or more Synoptic tradition made use of John's tradition, that influence went in more than one direction, or that intertraditional contact happened in several ways at several times? Reductionist theories may fail at precisely this point: they fail to account for the complexity of multiple possible inter-Gospel relationships. For now, however, the similarities as well as the differences between John and the Synoptics pose a historical problem.

A fifth problem involves the Johannine-Synoptic differences, especially at places where things are otherwise similar. Staying with John 6 for a moment,

John 6 includes the feeding of the five thousand, the sea crossing, a discussion of the feeding, and the confession of Peter; Mark 6 includes the feeding of the five thousand and the sea crossing; and Mark 8 includes the feeding of the four thousand, discussions of the feeding, and the confession of Peter. Did Jesus perform two feeding miracles, as listed in Mark and Matthew, or are these parallel traditions that Mark seeks to preserve? Clearly Matthew stays closer to Mark than Luke does, but why does Luke depart from Mark and include only one feeding (as in John), moving Peter's confession to follow the feeding of the five thousand (as it does in John)? Differences also extend to theological content and implications. In Mark 8:29 Peter confesses that Jesus is "the Christ"; in Matt 16:16 Jesus is "the Christ, the Son of the living God"; and in Luke 9:20 Jesus is "the Christ of God." In John 6:69, however, Jesus is "the Holy One of God," a title found elsewhere in Hebrew and Christian Scriptures only on the lips of the demoniac in Mark 1:24 and Luke 4:34. If the Johannine Evangelist was familiar with Mark, why is Peter rendered as speaking like the Markan demoniac instead of the Markan Peter? Differences *and* similarities between John and the Synoptics present problems for narrow dependence-oriented theories, but they may also point the way forward in other ways.

A sixth historical problem with the presentation of Jesus in John 5–12 is the plentitude of southern, Judean material. In fact, only a few scenes in John (1:43–51; 2:1–12; 4:1–54; 6:1–71; 7:1–10; 11:1–16; 21:1–25) are set in the north; the rest is in Transjordan, Judea, or Jerusalem. This fact has led some scholars to infer that the Fourth Evangelist must have been from the south, Judea, instead of from the north, Galilee. Whatever the case regarding the location of the narrator, the content of the tradition does indeed pose a striking contrast to the primarily northern ministry of the Synoptic Jesus. But this precisely is the historical question. Did Jesus' ministry include outreach to Judea as well as to Galilee and the Decapolis? If so, John's presentation appears to expand the reach of Jesus' ministry, if the Synoptics were known by the Evangelist or his audience. Even the north-south antipathy reflected in the Judeans' ambivalent response to the Galilean prophet (John 7) bears a good deal of religious and political realism when viewed from this perspective. In John, the northern prophet is portrayed as ministering in the south and raising consternation long before the foreboding events of the passion narrative.

A seventh historical problem with this section is an indirect result of the primary Johannine historical interest within the last four decades. The new light cast upon the Johannine situation as a function of J. Louis Martyn's treatment of John 9 involving two levels of reading, augmented by Raymond Brown's illumination of the Johannine situation on the basis of his reading of the Johannine Epistles and other texts, has led to the eclipsing of the originative level of history in favor of focusing on its finalized level of history. Indeed, some dialogical relationship with Jewish communities around the time of the narrative's finalization (say, in the 80s or 90s C.E.) can be inferred in a mirror-reading of the story. Not only is synagogue expulsion a threat to the Johannine audience if they confess Jesus openly as the Messiah (John 9:22; 12:42; 16:2), but those struggles, says the narrator, went back to the days of Jesus and his immediate followers. While scholars have contested the particulars of synagogue expulsion and Jewish-Christian dialogue, originative history questions still remain. *Was* there a blind man whose healing became a threat to religious authorities during the time of Jesus? If so, how might the threatening of the Jerusalem authorities in John 9 be related to their being threatened by the healing of the lame man on the Sabbath (John 5) and the raising of Lazarus from the dead (John 11)? Whatever the case, the relation between the originative and delivered levels of history must be considered, not only the second level of history, but also on the first. Historical situation research, even if successful, cannot replace originative inquiry.

This issue points to an eighth question, involving the relation between history and theology in the Johannine narrative. Put bluntly, given that the Fourth Evangelist clearly believes Jesus to be the Messiah, are the presentations of Jesus as making high theological claims for himself (note the "I am" statements of John 6:20 and 8:58, Jesus' claim to be "working" with the Father in 5:17 resulting in accusations that he claimed to be "equal to God" in 5:18, and his own claims to be one with the Father in 10:30) and the wondrous miracles of Jesus distinctive to John (healing a man by the pool of Bethesda in 5:1–9, giving sight to a blind man in 9:1–7, and raising Lazarus from the tomb in 11:1–44) reports of what happened in history, or do they reflect embellished renderings of Jesus' words and deeds? While the Markan Jesus emphasizes messianic secrecy, the Johannine Jesus majors in messianic disclosure. The Synoptic Jesus speaks in parables and aphorisms, while the Johannine Jesus develops "I am" metaphors. While the Markan Jesus resuscitates the daughter of Jairus having said she is "sleeping" (Mark 5:39), the Johannine Jesus raises the brother of Mary and Martha from the tomb having clarified that "Lazarus is dead" (John 11:14). Of course, all nine of the Johannine "I am" metaphors are also found in the Synoptics in some form, as are *egō eimi* statements of Jesus and references to Exod 3:14 (Mark 12:26), and the Synoptic Jesus certainly performs miraculous signs in what is unlikely to have been an exhaustive record. While most scholars argue for some sort of independent tradition underlying the Johannine Gospel, the relation of the Evangelist's theological interests to the construction of his narrative remains an abiding question requiring the attention of Johannine and Jesus scholars alike.

These and other questions are addressed by the essays in part 2 of the present collection, as they engage aspects of historicity in John 5–12. In the first paper, Brian D. Johnson elucidates the historical realism of the Jewish feasts presented in the middle part of Jesus' ministry. In particular, the Feasts of Tabernacles, Dedication, and Passover are analyzed from a socioreligious perspective and then connected with the narrative presentation of Jesus' multiple visits to Jerusalem and participation in these festivals as a means of furthering the narrator's purposes. Johnson also develops further his analysis of first-century Judaism

(Johnson 2006) by showing how a first-century Galilean leader might have been received in Jerusalem, including how Jewish images of value might have been appropriated by Jesus in articulating his mission. Whether or not Jesus' multiple trips to Jerusalem in John represent a strict chronology or a more general presentation of his fulfilling the theological themes of the particular feasts narrated, Johnson shows how they functioned in the narrator's presentation of likely historical events in compelling ways for later audiences.

Craig A. Evans addresses a handful of issues particular to John 6, contributing to a sense of coherence within the Johannine tradition. Having produced a number of studies on John and the Synoptics (1993; 1999; 2001) and extensive treatments of historical Jesus research (1995; 1996; 2008), Evans here focuses on the sacramental associations in John 6 (see Evans 2002). If more formalized presentations of a eucharistic meal setting are more likely to represent Christian theological developments, as rendered in the Synoptics, might the absence of an institution of the Last Supper as a meal of remembrance in John and the more informal feeding of the multitude argue for historical realism in John? Evans also unpacks the political and religious realism of the presentation of Jesus as fulfilling the typologies of Elijah and Moses in John 6. As the prophetic agent from God, Evans shows how the presentation of Jesus in John 6 fits entirely well within conventional prophet-associations, as described by Josephus, including Jesus' commissioning of the twelve as a sign of the restoration of dismembered Israel.

Given the strong likelihood that a devout Jewish leader from Galilee would have traveled to Jerusalem several times a year and that Jesus' ministry probably lasted more than one year, Sean Freyne takes the discussion further by showing how a Galilean leader would likely have been received in Jerusalem by the religious elite—both positively and negatively. Building on his earlier work (1988; 2001a), Freyne develops the contextual plausibility of a northern prophet's ironic rejection in Jerusalem. While finding his Davidic credentials lacking, the Judean leaders fail to note Jesus' fulfilling the biblical typology of the prophet like Moses (Deut 18:15–22) and accuse him of being insufficient in keeping the law of Moses. Having established his own picture of Jesus as a Galilean prophetic leader, however, Freyne (2001b; 2004) suggests several ways the Jesus presented in John indeed reflects the realism of first-century C.E. Palestine. Representing a Judea preceding the fall of Jerusalem in 70 C.E., John's presentation of the Jesus of Galilee poses a remarkable contrast to the Jesus (ben Sirach) of Jerusalem. Rather than being presented as a cultured religious authority, the Johannine Jesus comes across as one of the people of the land (ʿam haʾarets)—an unlikely image to have been concocted for rhetorical purposes. In that sense, Freyne elucidates the religio-geographical realism of the Johannine presentation of the northern prophet spurned by the southern religious leaders.

Reporting on the latest archaeological discoveries in Jerusalem, Urban C. von Wahlde sheds light on the historical realities associated with the Pool of

Siloam in Jerusalem. Where the explanatory statement, "which means 'sent'"
(John 9:7), has been patently dismissed as having no historical relevance because
of its clearly symbolic and theological character, the archaeological discoveries
since 2004 and von Wahlde's analysis of them pose a serious challenge to such
moves. While the northern Pool of Siloam has been known for more than a century, the identification of the larger southern pool as a *miqveh*—a pool used for
ritual purification—bears considerable implications for understanding the larger
set of events reported in John 9. Rather than seeing the primary level of meaning
as a reflection of the debates between later Johannine Christians and the local
synagogue in Asia Minor or some other Diaspora setting, the originative history of the events takes on new significance. Jesus' sending of the man to wash
in the Pool of Siloam and to show himself to the priests would have restored him
socially and religiously, and such a detail would not have made sense outside of
Palestine or after the fall of Jerusalem. In addition to von Wahlde's major contribution to Johannine archaeological and topographical studies (2006), this study
makes major inroads not only into Johannine historicity but also into socioreligious understandings of Jesus' historic ministry.

A second analysis of John 9 is contributed by Edward W. Klink III, but it
focuses on the second level of Johannine historicity—that of its intended audience. Following recent critics of the Martyn/Brown hypothesis, namely, that a
second level of reading John's text should be seen against a Jewish-Christian set
of tensions in the last decade or two of the first century c.e., Klink asks what
sort of tensions would have been experienced by Jesus and his followers "even
back then," decades before the finalization of the Johannine narrative. Indeed, if
Jesus were associated with high theological claims about himself, his movement
would likely have been regarded as unorthodox. The point is that in-house tensions between local synagogue leadership and the Jewish followers of Jesus would
have been experienced at earlier stages of the tradition's development, perhaps
even suggesting something of the original conflicts encountered by Jesus and
his followers a half century or more before the Johannine Gospel was finalized.
If Jesus was regarded by religious authorities as a *mesith*—someone who leads
people astray—tensions with his followers are certainly understandable, whether
or not there were ever widespread expulsions of followers of "the Nazarene" from
local synagogues in Asia Minor or elsewhere. If tensions between the Jesus movement and orthodox Judaism were earlier as well as later within the developing
Johannine tradition, might they have even rooted in the historic and provocative
ministry of Jesus himself?

Addressing one of the most difficult issues in the Fourth Gospel, Richard
Bauckham focuses on John 11 and 12, seeking to account for the Lazarus material in John, which is completely missing in the Synoptics. Picking up on the
presentations of Mary and Martha in John and Luke and the anointing of Jesus
presented in all four Gospels, albeit differently, Bauckham seeks to identify and
analyze connections between the Johannine narrative and the Bethany family.

Given the occurrence of these names in Palestine in the first century (Bauckham 1998b), Bauckham asserts the reliability of at least the names representing real people during this time, bolstering the scene's credibility. He also resorts to "protective anonymity" as a means of accounting for other characters named in John that are unnamed in Mark. Within Bauckham's larger approach (2006; 2007; 1998a), if John's narrative was crafted as an augmentation and corrective to Mark, and if it also served a historiographic function, might John's narrative have been intended to pose an alternative history, explaining its echoes of—and contrasts to—the Markan narrative?

Ben Witherington III continues the investigation of the Johannine Lazarus tradition by connecting it with the question of John's authorship. Given the problems with the traditional view of authorship, Witherington picks up on the mention that Jesus "loved" Lazarus (John 11:3, 5), connecting him with the Beloved Disciple (21:24). While other theories of John's authorship abound, Witherington thereby seeks to account for the distinctively Judean material in the Fourth Gospel, the origin of this distinctive tradition, and the transcendent character of John's theological presentation of Jesus. In doing so, Witherington builds upon his earlier monograph on the wisdom tradition in John (1995b), suggesting how such a transformative experience as being brought back to life from the depths of the tomb might account for John's distinctive presentation of Jesus and his ministry. He also builds upon his earlier monograph on women around the ministry of Jesus (1984) in his treatment of Mary and Martha. Jesus' connection with the family of Bethany accounts not only for the inclusion of the Lazarus material in John, but it also explains, in Witherington's view, John's distinctive presentation of Jesus and his ministry.

A third analysis of the Lazarus material is offered by Derek M. H. Tovey, who poses a means of distinguishing history from fiction by asking whether there is a "referential" feature of the narrative. According to Tovey, if a narrative appears to be alluding to something particular in the consciousness of the author and the audience, that makes it a different sort of narrative than an abstract story plucked out of the blue. While confirming that such a feature does not determine anything about the historicity of a story as such, it at least shows evidence of history-reference markers in the text, calling for a preliminary consideration of the narrative as such. In doing so, Tovey builds upon his earlier monographs on narrative artistry and the presentation of Jesus in the Fourth Gospel (1997; 2007) and concludes that John's narrative here is closer in its form to theologized history than historicized theology. Whether or not this proves anything about the historicity of the contents is another matter; Tovey simply seeks to advance the discussion by identifying the telling character of the narrative's genre.

The essays in part 2 are responded to by Paul N. Anderson, who identifies strengths and weaknesses in each of the papers. In addition to commenting upon historical and literary bases for John's theology, Anderson draws into play his own attempts at assessing aspects of historicity in the Fourth Gospel with implications for John's composition and Jesus research (2006a; 2006b; 2006c). In doing so, he picks up on some issues and extends the discussion to include degrees of plausibility in the arguments both engaged and advanced.

The Jewish Feasts and Questions
of Historicity in John 5–12

Brian D. Johnson

1. Overview of the Jewish Feasts in John 5–12

Jewish feasts are mentioned frequently throughout the Gospel of John. These references occur from the first Passover, mentioned as the setting of the temple incident in John 2, to the final Passover, which provides the setting of John 12–19. The following table includes every explicit mention of a Jewish feast in John's Gospel.

2:11, 23	Passover
4:45	reference back to Passover
5:1	unnamed feast
5:9, 10, 16, 18	Sabbath
6:4	Passover
7:2	Tabernacles
7:22, 23	Sabbath
7:37	last and greatest day of the feast
9:14, 16	Sabbath
10:22	Dedication
11:55; 12:1	before the Passover
13:1	Passover
18:28, 39; 19:14, 31	Passover and Sabbath

As Stephen Motyer (1997, 36) has observed, "the festivals are closely woven into the structure of the Gospel." John 5–12 particularly contain a concentration and progression of feasts. The final explicit mentions of the feast of Passover are in the context of the narration of Jesus' death, as is also the case in the Synoptic Gospels.

The frequency of the mention of the Jewish feasts in John 5–12, and the associations made between these feasts and the teaching and action portrayed in connection with them, show intentionality in their presentation throughout

John's Gospel. Various understandings of the function of the Jewish feasts in the narrative have been proposed. Some scholars have understood these as primarily temporal and spatial markers for the action and teaching of Jesus. When thought of in this way, the feasts provide a progression through the year of Jesus' actions. Others have suggested that the feasts sometimes simply provide occasions for Jesus to be in Jerusalem. Examining the use of the feasts in the narrative itself provides reasons why both of these understandings of the function of the feasts are not likely. First, the actions and teachings of Jesus have thematic connections to the feasts that are portrayed, and elements of the teachings and actions of Jesus bear a direct relationship to the feasts that they accompany in the text. The clearest example of this is the Feast of Tabernacles and the events and teachings of John 7–8, but even the brief mention of the Passover in John 2 seems to add to the development of this theme in relation to the identity of Jesus. Second, elements from the feasts themselves are used to further the Johannine presentation of Jesus' identity. More than serving as temporal or spatial settings, the feasts themselves provide content for the portrayal of Jesus in John's Gospel.

In considering this initial overview of the Jewish feasts in John's Gospel, one element of the question of historicity already emerges. In the Synoptic Gospels, only the Sabbath and Passover are explicitly mentioned. In contrast, the Gospel of John has numerous mentions of various feasts. Furthermore, these mentions are distributed throughout John's Gospel, rather than centering only on the passion account. This presents Jesus as having a fuller interaction with the temple and temple worship than is portrayed in the Synoptics. This description accords well with an understanding of Jesus' Jewishness, specifically a custom of participation in feasts, as mentioned also in the Synoptics.[1] These multiple trips to the temple accord well with the sense that Jesus customarily attended the Jewish feasts (Freyne 2004, 152–53), and it also explains the virulence of the conflict that is reported between Jesus and the Jewish authorities—even in the Synoptic Gospels.[2] The prevalence and distribution of the Jewish feasts thus suggests a significant aspect of historical reliability in the Gospel of John's presentation of this element of Jesus' life.

The rest of this essay will examine three particular ways in which the Johannine presentation of the Jewish feasts will impact the issue of historicity. First, the issue of Jewish feasts and the chronology of Jesus' ministry will be considered. Second, a focus on the Jewish feasts will be proposed as a way to assess the plausibility for the setting of the narrative accounts in a time roughly contemporary

---

1. E.g., Luke 2:42; see also John 7:1–13 and note that John's Gospel already portrays Jesus as not going to Judea because of conflict with the authorities there.

2. "As Scott Holland insisted, the Synoptic chronology is a mystery to itself, full of hints which are not self-explanatory. Above all the Synoptists are saying to us in all sorts of subtle ways of Jesus in Jerusalem, 'He has been here before'" (Robinson 1985, 135)

with Jesus' life. This is not a common way to ask the question of historicity, but it provides another approach to the subject. This approach is, at least in some ways, better suited to assess the reliability of John's Gospel than the models that have grown out of comparing and contrasting it over and against the Synoptic Gospels. Third, the presentation of the feasts in John's Gospel and the narrator's comments and interpretation will be considered in order to assess the historical likelihood of the setting of these feasts within the life of Jesus.

2. THE JEWISH FEASTS AND CHRONOLOGY IN THE GOSPEL OF JOHN

The Gospel of John has most evoked questions of historicity in the area of chronology. The three Passover accounts mentioned in John's Gospel have been used widely and for a long time to reconstruct the three-year chronology of Jesus' ministry. However, that the Jewish feasts are presented with thematic connections to the surrounding material should caution scholars against using these three mentions too confidently in making chronological reconstruction. Thematic use would not by itself eliminate the possibility that these feasts present some sort of timeline, but specific examples show that any such timeline might be difficult to surmise. Here are two brief examples.

2.1. THREE PASSOVER CONTEXTS

In the first context in which it occurs, Passover is mentioned twice (John 2:13–23) in a way that brackets the temple incident. Inclusios in John's Gospel help give the reader clues as to how to interpret a passage. This account is interpreted in light of Passover and is also an important element in this Gospel's temple theme. So John 2:12–22 is an important introduction to two central themes to the Gospel of John's presentation of the identity of Jesus: the theme of the feasts and the theme of the temple.[3] There are also proleptic elements in the presentation of the temple incident. Not least is the element of the disciples' "remembering" his statement about his three-day rebuilding of the temple after Jesus had been raised from the dead (see Johnson 2001). This indicates that the temple incident is linked to the final Passover. If this is the case, the Passover of John 2 is not a separate Passover at all but a thematic, rather than chronological, arrangement of material.[4] The irony of this is that the historical element most often derived from John's Gospel—the three-year ministry—may not have been intended to be understood in this way at all. It is possible that only two historical Passovers are intended and

---

3. For these themes and their connections, see Coloe 2001; Kerr 2002; and Johnson 2001.
4. John 20:30–31 indicates both selection and choice in the Evangelist's arrangement of material.

that the triple mention is a narrative feature used to highlight two themes regarding Jesus' identity.

2.2. THE UNNAMED FEAST OF JOHN 5:1

The unnamed feast cannot contribute as a chronological marker in the narrative, precisely because it is unnamed. Many attempts have been made to identify this feast, and nearly every conceivable possibility has been suggested.[5] Any attempt to identify this feast specifically is ultimately unsatisfying. Any proposal that adequately interprets the unnamed feast must deal with two items: (1) the feast occurs in a narrative where feasts have thematic value; and (2) it is not named. Martin Asiedu-Peprah, in his work on the Sabbath controversies, argues that "at a deeper level, the mention of a feast is intended to place the whole of chapter 5 within a specific religious-cultural setting." He argues that "a Jewish feast always depicts a certain understanding of the people in relation to their God and to his saving work past and present." In reference to this particular example, he further argues, "this unnamed feast provides an excellent setting for the Johannine Jesus to make his Christological claims, which seek to deepen the understanding of 'the Jews' in relation to the intimate relationship between the Father and himself in the work of salvation" (2001, 54). So what may be in mind here is a statement in relation to the whole concept of the Jewish festivals without reference to a specific feast.[6] This approach has value in that it takes seriously the mentioning of "the feast," as well as the failure to designate the specific feast. If it is impossible to identify this particular feast, it follows naturally that it is impossible to determine how it contributes to a chronology of Jesus' ministry. This again suggests that it is not reliable to put Jesus' ministry into any kind of chronological framework based upon the Jewish feasts.

3. HISTORICAL TRAJECTORY AND THE JEWISH FEASTS IN THE GOSPEL OF JOHN

The Jewish feasts are directly connected to the actions and sayings of Jesus for which they provide settings in the narrative. They are important for understanding the significance of what Jesus does and what he says. Therefore, some knowledge of the practices, themes, and didactic content of the Jewish feasts as they were practiced in a first-century context is necessary. The reconstruction of the practices connected with the Jewish feasts in the first century is a field of study that is not without its own inherent difficulties. The writings that are concerned with the proper practice of the Jewish festivals, and which are often

---

5. "The unidentified feast of 5:1 has been identified with Purim, Pentecost, Tabernacles, … Rosh Hashanah" (Keener 2003, 1:635).

6. This approach is also advocated by Kerr 2002, 207.

called upon to provide background information for these festivals in the Gospel of John, postdate the life of Jesus and even the destruction of Jerusalem. As Adele Reinhartz has written, "the mining of rabbinic sources, all of which postdate the New Testament, for the background to the earliest period of Christian history is a dangerous occupation, to be undertaken only when the rabbinic source is also paralleled in a first-century Jewish source such as the writings of Josephus or the Genesis Apocryphon" (Reinhartz 2005, 109). Therefore, when considering the potential historical accuracy of these accounts set within Jesus' life, the question also becomes what can be said about the practice of the Jewish feasts within the early first century. The rabbinic literature does appeal to traditions that are set as early as this period, but it is difficult or impossible to determine with accuracy the reliability of these traditions. Ironically, those who ask questions of the historical setting for these accounts in Jesus' life are left with a similar set of questions as those who would seek to understand the practice of Second Temple Judaism within the early first century (see Rubenstein 1995, 85). This may seem like an insurmountable difficulty, but it also suggests the potential for corroborative movement toward a solution.

Reinhartz makes a fascinating and helpful suggestion in response to Burton Visotsky's essay in the Raymond Brown memorial volume. She suggests that the Gospel of John could be "a potential source of knowledge of first-century Judaism" (Reinhartz 2005, 110). This is an intriguing and exciting suggestion, with potential for a completely new approach to the question of historicity in John's Gospel! This section of the essay will pursue Reinhartz's line of enquiry in connection with the Jewish feasts and will suggest one modest additional point. Simply put, this suggestion is to include the information available from the Hebrew Bible and the Second Temple literature in this discussion, with the purpose of charting a trajectory in the development of the practice, content, and significance of the Jewish feasts in John. This is a question of historicity in relation to the Gospel of John, but it is a different approach than the standard doubting of John first, accepting nearly all other sources as inscrutable. It seeks to adduce whether or not this Gospel's presentation of the Jewish feasts is consistent with the stage along the trajectory that would be expected in the early or mid-first century C.E. While not a specific question of historicity, it is more a general question of plausibility or implausibility of the historical setting of the accounts.[7] Furthermore, this would allow us to understand the Gospel of John's later formative influence as well. Perhaps most important, it would pose a means to open a fruitful and satisfying dialogue among students of the Hebrew Bible, Second Temple Judaism, early Christianity (particularly the Gospel of John and the Apocalypse of John, elucidating the feast imagery employed in both writings), and early and medieval rabbinic Judaism focused on the issue of reconstructing the development of the

---

7. This is similar also to the approach proposed by Theissen and Merz 1996, 117.

Jewish feasts. As a test case, the following is an attempt to apply this approach to the three Jewish feasts mentioned specifically in the Gospel of John: Tabernacles, Dedication, and Passover.

3.1. TABERNACLES

John 7 is set in the context of the Feast of Tabernacles. The high point of the narrative is John 7:37–39, where Jesus stands on the last day of the feast and shouts: " 'Let anyone who is thirsty come to me, and let the one who believes in me drink. As the scripture has said, "Out of the believer's heart shall flow rivers of living water." ' Now he said this about the Spirit, which believers in him were to receive; for as yet there was no Spirit, because Jesus was not yet glorified." Which Scripture is mentioned here is debated, but many understand an allusion to Zech 14:8 because of the reference to "living water(s)" flowing from Jerusalem. Zechariah 14 is closely connected to the Feast of Tabernacles, mentioning it three times (Zech 14:16, 18, 19).[8] These passages imagine a time when "all of the nations" will come to Jerusalem to keep Tabernacles and the punishment that will come upon the nations—especially Egypt—if they fail to keep the Feast of Tabernacles.

Jeffrey L. Rubenstein (1995) has written a study on Sukkot that is related to this suggestion. His book is a detailed attempt to analyze and trace the development of the practice of the Feast of Sukkot throughout the Second Temple and early rabbinic periods.[9] In his analysis of the Second Temple material, he references John 7 and connects it to Zech 14.[10] In his later tracing of the development of Tabernacles, Rubenstein discusses the water libation ceremony and the accompanying prayers for winter rains. These become a part of the festival practice at some point. While Rubenstein notes that "no non-rabbinic source explicitly mentions the libation," many commentators on the Gospel of John use the libation ceremony as a context for, and an explanation of, Jesus' statement. It is in a situation such as this that we can evaluate the trajectory of thought indicated in John's Gospel. For example, Rubenstein understands that "Zechariah 14 and John 7 indicate a connection between Sukkot and rain, but neither illuminates the specific rituals" (1995, 121). Jesus' statement in John 7 may thus illustrate a point between the development of thought in Zech 14 and the later rabbinic sources. This statement in John 7 points toward a developing practice of the libation ceremony. Archaeological evidence has also been adduced to suggest that the libation ceremony is a pre-70 C.E. practice. Anita Engle, for example, has

---

8. This is out of only nine uses of the word σκηνοπηγία in the LXX.

9. The more of these excellently detailed studies that become available, the more we will be able to say about the Jewish feasts in this period of time.

10. Rubenstein particularly thinks Zech 14 is the reference because of "living water flowing out" mentioned both in John and Zechariah.

written on the discovery of glass bottles (or amphorisks) with tabernacle symbols on them, which may have been sold as souvenirs to travelers who had come to Jerusalem for the Feast of Tabernacles.[11] This is another example of the possibilities for cross-fertilization of disciplines with relation to this question.

To give another brief example, many commentators connect Jesus' statement, "I am the light of the world" (John 8:12),[12] with the lighting of lamps at night during the Feast of Tabernacles, as this practice is mentioned in the Tannaim (m. Sukkah 5:2–4). It may also be a parallel to Zech 14:7, which speaks of a day when it will be light even in the evening (Brown 1966–70, 1:343). The Gospel of John's statement placed on the lips of Jesus shows again this kind of intermediary position and the suggestions of later development that is seen explicitly in the later Tannaitic literature.

Granted, this type of approach will be less than satisfying for those who are looking for absolutely solid historical grounding for the actions and statements of Jesus. This approach, for example, does not differentiate between an event of Jesus' life and an event narrated in relationship to Jesus by his early followers. Given a general sense of the trajectory of thought and practice in relation to the feasts, this approach provides a plausible historical setting for this account. Even if not satisfying, it does take seriously the limitations of the evidence available to us, and it is perhaps a step toward a more robust reconstruction of the development of the Feast of Tabernacles. Additionally, this approach sets the evidence within its proper historical order rather than trying to read potentially earlier texts in light of possible later "evidence."

3.2. DEDICATION

Turning to the Feast of Dedication mentioned in John 10:22, the connections between Jesus' teaching and this feast have not been nearly as clear. Little has been written on this, especially when compared to the amount that has been written on the Passover and Tabernacles contexts.[13] The connections between those feasts and the actions and teachings of Jesus cause one to wonder what potential points of contact there might be in this context of Dedication. James VanderKam (1990, 212) proposes a potential connection here. He argues that language parallels suggest that the Jewish accounts of Antiochus IV Epiphanes and Dan 7, 8, and 11 are to be brought to mind. He concludes, "It seems no accident that John dated Jesus' assertion of his divinity to the festival of Hanukkah

---

11. Engle 1977, 117–22; cited in Keener 2005.

12. John 8:12 should be read as following 7:52, as the Pericope Adulterae breaks the flow of the context.

13. For example, this is the sparest part of Yee 1988, which is otherwise a thorough treatment.

when the blasphemies of Antiochus IV, the self-proclaimed god manifest, were remembered" (1990, 213). So, according to VanderKam, Jesus is portrayed as legitimately claiming for himself what Antiochus IV had illegitimately claimed. VanderKam's argument is intriguing. He may be right in focusing attention upon the period of the Maccabean revolt, but the focus should rather be placed upon the Maccabean rulers themselves.

The good shepherd discourse of John 10:1–21 can thus be understood in connection with the Feast of Dedication.[14] If this discourse is connected with Dedication, then Jesus' claim to be a "good shepherd" (10:11) is in contrast to "all who came before" (10:8). This may be another example of Jesus' being presented as a ruler for the people, but a different kind of ruler than was commonly understood (18:33–37). The Maccabees, who are remembered by the people at Dedication, ruled because of the political power and military force they could muster, while Jesus becomes the true shepherd of the people by laying down his life. The image of those who came before as thieves and robbers may emphasize a rule brought about and characterized by violence, to be contrasted with the authentic leading of his people—like a shepherd caring for his flock. This is similar to VanderKam's suggestion, in that it has Jesus arguing for legitimacy over against illegitimacy; in this case, however, it would seem to pose a contrast to the group remembered positively at the Feast of Dedication.[15]

Dedication is somewhat different from the Feasts of Tabernacles and Passover because it owes its origins to the events recorded in 1 and 2 Maccabees, rather than more established feasts stipulated in the Hebrew Bible. As mentioned above, VanderKam notes verbal parallels to the Maccabean accounts. It is also interesting and suggestive that the Maccabean account connects Dedication closely with Tabernacles (2 Macc 1:18), which is paralleled in the Gospel of John with the close connection between the Tabernacles and Dedication contexts.[16] This suggests the possibility that the account in John 10 is drawing upon the language of the Second Temple literature, though it should be noticed that the word Dedication (ἐγκαίνια) can also be found in the context of Ezra's dedication of the temple (Ezra 6:16–17 LXX). Brown (1966–70, 1:402) suggests parallels to the tabernacle (Num 7:10–11) and temple (1 Kgs 8:63) dedications as well.

For two reasons, the Feast of Dedication had a much smaller role in post-70 C.E. Jewish practice. First, because Dedication is so centered on temple practice and in fact is centered on the existence of the temple itself, it played a much

---

14. I have argued for this elsewhere: Johnson 2006, 96–97.

15. See also Blomberg 2001, 162, who sees the connection with "the warrior-deliverers of the Maccabean family," although he connects the earlier passage with Tabernacles rather than Dedication (158).

16. So close is the connection here that commentators often have difficulty deciding which pericope goes with which account.

smaller role after the temple's destruction. Second, the connection with rebellion against the oppressive power became much less popular after 70 C.E. (Schauss 1975, 228–29). Even in Josephus's writings, the practice of this festival seems somewhat unclear (*Ant.* 21.323). The casual mention of Dedication and the thematic connections here suggest a setting before 70 C.E. and therefore potentially set within Jesus' own lifetime.

3.3. Passover[17]

The Passover accounts also show points on the trajectory between the Hebrew Bible's establishment of the Passover feast and the rabbinic halakah. There are some suggestive connections with the Gospel of John's presentation of Passover, but at least one significant question is also raised. The question concerns the use of palm branches in connection with Passover (John 12:13). The mention of palm branches in the triumphal entry is unique to John's Gospel. This and the cry "Hosanna" suggests to Rubenstein (1995, 86) that the account of the triumphal entry fits a Tabernacles context better than a Passover context. Blomberg suggests that the use of palm branches here "harks back to the custom, attested during the Hasmonean dynasty, of celebrating military victories and welcoming national rulers with similar festivity" (2001, 179). Perhaps, then, the palm branches are not being used in direct connection with the Passover feast at all here. This, of course, does not eliminate the question of how the palm branches came to be present in Jerusalem (see also Keener 2003, 2:869). On the other hand, this is the one feast setting that the Gospel of John has in common with the Synoptic accounts. So, by one criterion for determining the historicity of a passage in John's Gospel, namely, its connection with the Synoptic tradition, the account of John 12:12–19 fits well; however, by the criterion introduced and used in this essay, there is a difficulty. When focusing on this detail of the practice of the Jewish feast of Passover, there is at least a difficulty with the Johannine presentation of the event.

The Gospel of John does mention other details that seem to accord with the practice of Passover. For example, this Gospel specifically mentions that hyssop (ὕσσωπος) is used to lift the sponge to Jesus' lips (John 19:29). Also, it is John's Gospel that uniquely mentions the crurifragium ("breaking of the legs") and the connection with the "prophecy" of Exod 12:46 in connection with the Passover lamb (John 19:36). Of course, both of these details could be understood as later additions of details that have more to do with the Hebrew Bible's account than with practice contemporary to the life of Jesus.

When considering the Johannine presentation of Passover and contemporary practice of the Jewish feast, the most intriguing connection comes from Josephus, who describes practices connected with Passover (*Ant.* 3.248–249). He specifically

---

17. On the connection between Passover and Gospel of John, see Segal 1963, 36–37.

mentions the sacrifice of lambs by burning, which he describes as being "for sins" (ὑπὲρ ἀμαρτάδων). This accords well with the Johannine presentation of Jesus as the lamb who takes away "the sin of the world" (John 1:29).

4. HISTORICAL SETTING AND THE JEWISH FEASTS IN THE GOSPEL OF JOHN

The Jewish feasts in John's Gospel also provide a way to propose more likely settings of these accounts, suggesting their broad plausibility. This section will provide a narrowing of this breadth by suggesting that there are limited time frames of plausibility within which these accounts can be set. In making these assessments, each of these feasts mentioned in John's Gospel depends upon the temple complex and continuing temple practice for its setting and background. Thus, each of these feasts is set in a pre-70 C.E. context, when the temple still stood and temple worship continued to take place, as John's Gospel is increasingly thought to have been written by someone familiar with these practices and places at first hand (Bauckham 2006, 384). While some features of the Fourth Gospel make it clear that it was written after 70 C.E., the same details suggest that these accounts may have arisen closer to the aftermath of the destruction of the temple—perhaps even in response to this event—than has been recently assumed (see Motyer 1997, passim). At the level of the narrative, the accounts of these feasts are set within the ministry of Jesus. John's Gospel is interesting because issues of knowledge, testimony, memory, and belief are brought into the foreground, so that there is a certain transparency of witness, narrator, author, and reader within this Gospel. Time is seen to elapse between what has been witnessed, what was remembered, and what is written (see Thatcher 2005, passim). These temporal gaps provide some sense of the setting of these accounts, and the Jewish feasts in John's Gospel provide one locus for considering this issue.

4.1. TABERNACLES

As mentioned above, the narrative that includes Jesus' statement regarding living water is set on the temple grounds, during the Feast of Tabernacles, particularly "on the last day of this feast, the great day" (Ἐν δὲ τῇ ἐσχάτῃ ἡμέρᾳ τῇ μεγάλῃ τῆς ἑορτῆς). Jesus is said to have made a bold and emphatic statement regarding his identity in relation to the meaning and practice of Tabernacles—perhaps the libation ceremony or at least some incipient form of prayer for winter rains based upon the promises and content of Zech 14. Then, in John 7:39, the narrator breaks in to interpret this saying in relation to the giving of the Spirit after Jesus' glorification. In the thought-world of John's Gospel, the glorification of Jesus points to his death and resurrection and the events surrounding them. Thus, we are moved within the narrative time from an occasion where Jesus was alive in the temple to a later time at, or possibly after, Jesus' death when the Spirit has come. In the narrator's thought process, as it is presented here, this retrojection is based upon an earlier historical event from a later position after the giving of the Spirit, which in the context of the Johannine thought-world immediately follows Jesus' resurrection (John 20:21–23). This is interesting at a narrative level, because within the Gospel of John there is no other place for this account to make sense than within the lifetime of Jesus.[18]

What makes this even more intriguing is that, if we were to remove the narrator's statement in 7:39, there would be no indication that anything in this account was to be understood in relation to the giving of the Spirit or to anything having to do with the Spirit at all. The preceding context, Jesus' statement, and the subsequent discourse all revolve around the issue of Jesus' identity. While Jesus mentions his death and glorification in such a way that we could imagine the Spirit being mentioned, the focus instead is upon Jesus' identity and his relationship to the Father. So what does this suggest? Perhaps the narrator's statement is interjected based upon a later interpretive remembering from a period after Jesus' death. Notice what this presents: we have the time frame of the account's composition, which reflects upon an earlier time frame of a perception of the giving of the Spirit. This remembering in turn is separated from the time of Jesus' statement, which is presented as being before the Spirit had come and consequently is prior to Jesus' death.

Obviously, this by itself is only suggestive. It could simply be another instance of verisimilitude, intended to push the setting of this account into the lifetime of Jesus himself. It is interesting, however, that apart from the narrator's statement the account is not about the Spirit at all. There does not seem to be a massive reworking of this material to make it suit the Evangelist's purpose. If this account had been created by the author out of whole cloth, it is odd that this interpretation was not placed on the lips of Jesus or even as a subject of the later discussion. After all, there are places within the discourse where such a statement would have fit. Jesus' death and glorification become part of the discussion in the subsequent account. Even when Jesus appeals to the testimony of two witnesses (8:17–18), it is the testimony of himself and the Father that is called upon. Again, this is nothing more than suggestive, but there is certainly a sense in this statement of an earlier account and discourse of Jesus related to the issue of his identity and a subsequent "Spirited" remembering of this account interpreting Jesus' statement as referring to the giving of the Spirit; then we have a subsequent writing of these with a perception that the giving of the Spirit had happened at an earlier time. Remember, the statement is that the Spirit "was not yet [οὐδέπω] given."[19] Because of this, a strong inference can be made that this account is set within the life of Jesus, which is later interpreted by his followers in light of

---

18. For a similar approach to the concept of "the Twelve," see Gnilka 1997, 182–87.

19. It is interesting that of the four times οὐδέπω is used in the New Testament, three are in the Gospel of John (7:39; 19:41; 20:9). Equally interesting to notice is its fourth use in Acts 8:16!

their experience. The account of Jesus' presence at the feast, his symbolic action (standing and shouting on the greatest day of the feast), his saying connected with Zech 14, and the libation ceremony are all most plausibly understood in the context of Jesus' own life.

4.2. DEDICATION

As suggested above, Jesus' teaching in connection with Dedication is best understood as Jesus' contrasting himself with the Maccabean rulers and suggesting that he comes as a different kind of Messiah. This passage has no direct mention of memory. There is, however, clear illustration within the later narrative that the disciples who are portrayed as witnesses to these events continued to misunderstand Jesus' teaching with relation to this point. Consider Peter in the upper room: "I would lay down my life for you" (13:37). I understand this not so much as referring to a sacrificial death but as Peter being willing to die in revolutionary conflict. The Gospel of John also uniquely notes that it is Peter in the garden who strikes the blow that cuts off Malchus's ear. This is not presented as an act of self-defense or as the defense of Peter's rabbi; instead, it is better understood as the first strike in an abortive revolt. The idea that Jesus' messianic teaching was misunderstood is not only portrayed elsewhere in the Gospel of John (6:15; 18:33); it is also consistent with the Synoptic picture of the disciples' misunderstanding. Although there is no specific statement of memory here, a connection is still implied between the setting of Jesus' utterance and the subsequent understanding and experience of the disciples after Jesus' resurrection. Here again we see an apparent gap between Jesus' teaching and subsequent understanding. In John's Gospel it is in a postresurrection context that Peter is reinstated and, perhaps most provocatively, commissioned to follow Jesus as a shepherd of subsequent believers in a way commensurate with Jesus' being the good shepherd of his sheep.

5. CONCLUSION

The Jewish feasts in the Gospel of John provide provocative areas for considering the historicity of the accounts of Jesus' life. While further work could be done, four preliminary conclusions can be drawn. (1) The widespread and systematic use of the Jewish feasts in the Gospel of John's presentation accords well with the picture of Jesus as a first-century Galilean Jew who regularly participated in pilgrimages to Jerusalem for the feasts. This Gospel's presentation of Jesus' connection to the feasts is more robust than those found in the Synoptic accounts. (2) The thematic use of these feasts makes it difficult to argue for a temporal or spatial setting for Jesus' ministry. It is crucial to begin with the narrative purpose of the feasts as they are presented before attempting to understand any chronology they may present. The irony of this is that historical Jesus studies have frequently used this chronological aspect of the historicity of John's Gospel, even when rejecting the events and speeches narrated. (3) The Jewish feasts are used in connection with Jesus' actions and teachings in a way that is consistent with our understanding of first-century practice in relation to these feasts. This would lend credibility to the accounts as they are portrayed. More pointedly, I contend that it would be valid to use John's Gospel as a source for historical information regarding the practice of the Jewish feasts in the early first century C.E., especially when a trajectory of thought and practice can be established from a period earlier than the later rabbinic period. This goes against standard approaches used by most historical scholars, yet earlier Johannine evidence of a particular practice in regard to the Jewish feasts might suggest whether later accounts are plausible or credible as presented. In regard to the Jewish feasts, and as far as the practice of these feasts can be understood for the relevant period, John's Gospel shows a high degree of plausibility. (4) The Gospel of John's strategy of using the Jewish feasts suggests that they are recollections from before 70 C.E. and further remembrances from a time before the Spirit was understood to be given to Jesus' believers in a Johannine thought-world. That is, these narratives portray a time before his death and therefore within his lifetime. Again, while this analysis does not prove that these accounts definitively represent the ministry of the historical Jesus, it does suggest that scholars should at least allow the possibility that these accounts might indeed represent actual events from within Jesus' lifetime.

Feeding the Five Thousand and the Eucharist

Craig A. Evans

The purpose of the present study is to explore the possibility that the feeding story of John 6, which is made up of the multiplication of the loaves and fishes and the "eucharistic" discourse,[1] may constitute tradition that predates the Synoptic Gospels, where the feeding story is separate from the Eucharist.

It is natural to assume that the Fourth Evangelist has linked what is disparate in the Synoptics, but we might also wonder if in John 6 we have not a *late* combination of feeding miracle and eucharistic discourse but an *early* tradition that has been edited to reflect interest in Jesus as the giver of the new covenant. Thus, the bread of the "Eucharist"[2] has become the manna of the wilderness. Or, to put it the other way around: perhaps the manna of the wilderness—a typology that originated in Jesus himself—contributed to eucharistic ideas. It will be useful to explore this possibility in the context of restorative movements mentioned by Josephus.

We have approximately contemporary examples of individuals who appeal to exodus and conquest typologies. We immediately think of John the Baptist at the Jordan, Theudas at the Jordan, and the anonymous Jew from Egypt who spoke of the walls of Jerusalem falling down. Our sources mention other prophets who speak of salvation in the wilderness. These typologies need to be reviewed in more detail.

According to tradition shared by Matthew and Luke (what is usually identified as the Q source), the Baptist warns the Jewish people not to presume upon God's grace by saying, "We have Abraham as our ancestor." No Jew can say this, John the Baptist asserts, because "God is able from these stones to raise up children to Abraham" (Matt 3:9; see also Luke 3:8). Reference to "these stones" in the

---

1. For discussion of the possible eucharistic elements in John 6 (esp. with respect to 6:51–58), see Brown 1966–70, 1:274; Barrett 1978, 297; Schnackenburg 1980–82, 2:55–59. Many others, including Ignatius and Justin Martyr, have seen eucharistic elements in the bread discourse. However, several scholars have challenged features of this line of interpretation; among others, see Anderson 1996, 110–36.

2. If indeed "Eucharist" is the appropriate word.

context of the Jordan River may well have alluded to the story of Joshua building a monument of twelve stones when the twelve tribes of Israel crossed the Jordan to enter the promised land. On this occasion Joshua says to the people, "When your children ask their parents in time to come, 'What do *these stones* mean?' Then you shall let your children know, 'Israel crossed over the Jordan (River) here on dry ground'" (Josh 4:21–22, emphasis added; see also Deut 27:4; Josh 4:2–23). The symbolism of twelve stones also appears in the story of Elijah, who led the struggle in Israel against adoption of foreign gods (see 1 Kgs 18:31: "Elijah took twelve stones, according to the number of the tribes of the sons of Jacob"), who for a time lived near the Jordan River (see 1 Kgs 17:3–5) and even parted its waters (see 2 Kgs 2:8), and whose disciple Elisha also parted the water (see 2 Kgs 2:14) and later ordered the Syrian captain to be baptized in the Jordan River (see 2 Kgs 5:10–14). This is significant, for the clothing of John the Baptist resembles that of Elijah (Mark 1:6; see also 2 Kgs 1:8), and Jesus himself identifies John as the famous prophet of old (Mark 9:11–13).

It seems clear that John's preaching and activities were significantly informed by biblical symbolism, especially the symbolism of the Jordan River and, by inference, the tradition of the twelve stones (Trumbower 1994; Dunn 1994; Evans 2002). Jesus' appointment of twelve disciples (see Mark 3:14–19; 6:7) provides significant support for this line of interpretation. Most commentators rightly recognize that the number twelve was intended to symbolize the twelve tribes of Israel, implying that the goal of the ministry of Jesus was the restoration of the whole of the nation. Other prophetic figures mentioned in Josephus, invariably in highly negative, prejudicial language, had similar goals and in some instances utilized similar biblical symbolism. We may survey four of these figures in chronological sequence.

(1) During the administration of Cuspius Fadus (44–46 C.E.), Josephus tells us of a man named Theudas who urged the people to take up their possessions and meet him at the Jordan River, where at his command the waters would be parted (*Ant.* 20.97–98). The Roman governor dispatched the cavalry, which scattered Theudas's following. The would-be prophet was himself decapitated and his head put on display in Jerusalem. Acts 5:36 tells us that he had a following of about four hundred men. Although he regarded himself as a "prophet [προφήτης]," Josephus calls Theudas an "impostor [γόης]" who "deceived many." Theudas's claim to be able to part the Jordan River is an unmistakable allusion either to the crossing of the Red Sea (Exod 14:21–22) or, more likely, to the crossing of the Jordan River (Josh 3:14–17), part of the imagery associated with Israel's redemption (see Isa 11:15; 43:16; 51:10; 63:11). In either case, it is probable that Theudas was claiming to be the prophet "like Moses" (Deut 18:15–19; see also 1 Macc 4:45–46; 9:27; 14:41), who could perform signs like those of Moses' original successor, Joshua (see Graupner and Wolter 2007).

(2) During the administration of Antonius Felix (52–60 C.E.), a Jewish man from Egypt made an appearance in Jerusalem. He stationed himself on the Mount

of Olives, which overlooks the Temple Mount, and summoned people to himself, claiming that at his command the walls of the city would fall down, permitting him and his following to enter the city and, presumably, to take control of it. Governor Felix promptly dispatched the cavalry, which routed and dispersed the following. However, the Egyptian Jew himself escaped. In the parallel account in *Jewish War* Josephus calls this man a "false prophet" and "impostor" who, with a following of thirty thousand, "proposed to force an entrance into Jerusalem and, after overpowering the Roman garrison, to set himself up as tyrant over the people" (*J.W.* 2.261–263). The hoped-for sign of the walls falling down was probably inspired by the story of Israel's conquest of Jericho, led by Joshua, the successor of Moses (Josh 6:20). This Egyptian is mentioned in other sources as well. According to Acts 21:38, a Roman tribune asked the apostle Paul: "Are you not the Egyptian, then, who recently stirred up a revolt and led the four thousand men of the assassins out into the wilderness?" (see Barrett 1994–98, 2:1025–26; Fitzmyer 1998, 700). It is interesting to note that, according to the accounts in Acts and *Jewish War*, the Egyptian summoned people "out into the wilderness." This wilderness summons, as well as the Joshua-like sign of the walls falling down, is very likely part of the prophet-like-Moses theme, or some variation of it, that evidently lay behind much of the messianic speculation of the first century C.E. Moreover, the fact that this Jewish man was known as the man from Egypt might also have had to do with some sort of association with Moses, who also came out of Egypt, to begin his preparation for the deliverance of Israel.

(3) Similar confrontations took place during the administration of Porcius Festus (60–62 C.E.). In a context in which he described the troubles brought on by the *sicarii*, Josephus reports that Festus sent armed forces against a throng of people deceived by an impostor who had promised salvation and "rest" if they followed him out into the wilderness (*Ant.* 20.188). It is likely that this "impostor" was another messianic prophet, probably in keeping with the prophet-like-Moses theme (as the wilderness summons would seem to indicate). The impostor's promise of rest, moreover, may have had something to do with Ps 95:7b–11, a passage warning Israelites not to put God to the test, as they did at Massah and Meribah "in the wilderness," and consequently fail to enter God's "rest" (see Exod 17:1–7; Num 20:1–13).[3]

(4) Finally, Josephus tells us of one Jonathan, who, following the Roman victory over Israel and the capture of Jerusalem (70 C.E.), fled to Cyrene, North Africa. According to Josephus, this man, by trade a weaver, was one of the *sicarii*. He persuaded many of the poorer Jews to follow him out into the desert, "promising to show signs and apparitions" (*J.W.* 7.437–438; *Life* 424–425). The Roman

---

3. Although the parallel is not precise, it is worth noting that this passage is cited and commented upon in Hebrews (3:7–4:13), a writing in which Jewish Christians are exhorted not to neglect their "salvation" (2:3) but to "strive to enter that rest" (4:11).

governor Catullus dispatched troops who routed Jonathan's following and eventually captured the leader himself (*J. W.* 7.439–442).[4] Although Josephus does not describe Jonathan as a prophet (false or otherwise), it is likely that this is how the man viewed himself, as the desert summons would imply.

The activities of the several men who have been considered above clarify and place in context the preaching and activities of John the Baptist (see Horsley 1984; 1985). The location of the Baptist's ministry at the Jordan River, the reference to "these stones," and the promise of one to come, who will be far mightier than the Baptist himself and who will immerse the people with spirit and fire—not water—strongly suggest that John was one of several men who anticipated the restoration of Israel and imagined it in terms of past acts of salvation. The Baptist was not only guided by Jordan typology (especially as seen in the stories of Joshua and Elijah) but was probably guided by the language and imagery of some of the classical prophets, such as Malachi, who inveighed against divorce and adultery (Mal 2:16; 3:5) and foretold the day of the Lord (Mal 3:1), the coming fiery judgment (Mal 3:2–3; 4:1–2; see also Heb 3:19–20), and the return of Elijah the prophet (Mal 4:5–6; see also Heb 3:23–24). The prophet Isaiah also contributed to John's language, as seen in the quotation of Isa 40:3 and in other allusions (see Isa 30:27–28, which speaks of fire, wrath, coming, spirit, and water; see Evans 2002, 53–61).

One must remember that the accounts of Josephus are hardly unbiased. Josephus has little sympathy for eschatology and messianism. Although his portrait of John is somewhat sympathetic, the eschatological element—including the biblical typology that undergirds it—is carefully expunged. As for the other would-be prophets of deliverance, Josephus is harsh in his criticism, regarding them and others like them as ultimately responsible for the rebellion against Rome and its catastrophic results.

At this point we may ask: Which elements of John the Baptist's typology, if any, were taken over by Jesus? I believe there are several that are attested in the Synoptic and Johannine Gospels. First of all, I think Jesus' appointment of *twelve* apostles symbolized the restoration of Israel and in all probability coheres with the *twelve* stones, which are explicit in Joshua and implicit in John the Baptist. Just as Joshua's twelve stones symbolized the twelve tribes of Israel, so Jesus' appointment of the Twelve symbolized the tribes.[5] Major scholarship today accepts the historicity of the Twelve, even if the actual membership of this select group of

---

4. For analysis of these figures and their place in Jewish life in late antiquity, see Horsley 1987; Horsley and Hanson 1985.

5. See esp. Horbury 1986; Allison 1998, 141–45. See also McKnight 2001, who argues that the appointment of the Twelve has less to do with the twelve tribes per se; rather, the focus is on covenant leadership, as seen in T. Judah 25:1–2; T. Benj. 10:7; and many passages in the Dead Sea Scrolls (e.g., 1QS 8:1; 1QM 2:1–3; 4Q159 frgs. 2–4, lines 3–4; 4Q164 4–6; 11Q19 57:11–14). True enough, but even Qumran's twelve-symbolism, as concerned with covenant renewal as it

disciples varied somewhat.[6] Jesus' "use of the conception 'twelve' points towards his understanding of his own mission. He was engaged in a task which would include the restoration of Israel" (Sanders 1985, 106).

The "twelve" symbolism is deeply entrenched in the Hebrew Scriptures and the intertestamental literature.[7] Early on we hear of the twelve spies sent to reconnoiter the land of Canaan, the "promised land": "These were the names of the men whom Moses sent [שָׁלַח/ἀπέστειλεν] to spy out the land. And Moses changed the name of Hoshea the son of Nun to Joshua. Moses sent them to spy out the land of Canaan, and said to them, 'Go up there into the Negeb, and go up into the hill country...'" (Num 13:16–17; see also Deut 1:23: "I selected twelve of you, one from each tribe"). Appointing a number of men, sending them out, and naming them are features echoed in Jesus' appointment of his twelve (see Mark 3:14–17; 6:7; esp. Matt 10:1–4).

It is probable that the designation "apostle," meaning "one who is sent," derives from the story of Moses sending the twelve spies (see also Isa 61:1–2: "He has sent me to preach"). Sending forth twelve apostles, representing the twelve tribes of Israel, across the Jordan River into the promised land constitutes the very typology that forms the backdrop to the ministries of John and Jesus, when viewed together.

The Old Testament's symbolism of the number twelve at many points augments this typology and in some places probably contributes to the twelve stones/twelve tribes/twelve apostles symbolism of John and Jesus. According to Exod 28:21, "There shall be *twelve* stones with names corresponding to the names of the sons of Israel; they shall be like signets, each engraved with its name, for the twelve tribes" (see also Exod 39:14). We are told that "Solomon had *twelve* officials over all Israel, who provided food for the king and his household" (1 Kgs 4:7). According to 1 Kgs 18:31, "Elijah took *twelve* stones, according to the number of the tribes of the sons of Jacob, to whom the word of the Lord came, saying, 'Israel shall be your name.'" With restoration in view, the prophet Ezekiel says: "Thus says the Lord God: 'These are the boundaries by which you shall

---

is, nevertheless harks back to the twelve tribes. All twelve tribes, guided by righteous and qualified leaders, will be restored and renewed.

6. See Jeremias 1971, 234–35; Meyer 1979, 153–54 ("beyond reasonable doubt"), 293 (ancient and widespread tradition; multiple attestation; not easily accounted for as creation of early church); Sanders 1985, 95–106 ("virtually certain"); Gnilka 1997, 182–87; Meier 1997; Reiser 1997, 258–62; Becker 1998, 27–28. Against Vielhauer 1965, 68–71, who thinks the tradition of the Twelve is a post-Easter construct, Gnilka incisively asks: "How is it to be explained that a body created after Easter was projected back into Jesus' life and that Judas, who handed Jesus over, is consistently called 'one of the twelve'?" (1997, 182). Objections to the historicity of the Twelve invariably stumble over the consistent inclusion of Judas.

7. The question of the Old Testament background of the idea of "twelve" apostles is simply not explored in Klein 1961; this is an astonishing omission.

divide the land for inheritance among the *twelve* tribes of Israel'" (Ezek 47:13). Centuries later, the author of the Psalms of Solomon anticipates the coming of the messianic son of David, who will redistribute the twelve tribes on their respective portions of the land (Pss. Sol. 17:26, 28; see Atkinson 1999; Werline 2000, 786–88).

Jesus anticipates the day when his twelve apostles will "sit on twelve thrones to judge the twelve tribes of Israel" (Matt 19:28//Luke 22:30). The restoration of Israel is clearly in view.[8] It is in this light that the parable of the Wicked Vineyard Tenants (Mark 12:1–12) should be interpreted. When Jesus threatens the ruling priests, "He will come and destroy the tenants and give the vineyard to others" (Mark 12:9), he is predicting the removal of the ruling priests and their replacement either with his own twelve apostles (as the Q tradition just mentioned suggests) or perhaps with a new and obedient order of priests. For obvious reasons, identity with the twelve tribes of Israel was not particularly meaningful for Gentile Christians, but the *theologoumenon* remained in vogue among Jewish Christians for some time (see Jas 1:1: "To the twelve tribes in the Dispersion"; 1 Pet 1:1: "To the exiles of the Dispersion").

The Fourth Evangelist also knows of the tradition of the Twelve (see John 6:13, 67, 70, 71; 20:24). It is interesting to note that most of these references occur in John 6, in which the Evangelist provides his version of the feeding of the five thousand. Not only do the first and most of the references to the Twelve occur in this chapter, but it is a chapter rich with exodus and wilderness typology.

When the people see the miracle of the multiplication of the loaves and fish, described as a "sign," they proclaim, "This is indeed the prophet who is to come into the world!" (John 6:14). It is probable that this confession alludes to the Mosaic promise in Deut 18:15: "The LORD your God will raise up for you a prophet like me from among your own people; you shall heed such a prophet" (see 18:18: "I will raise up for them a prophet like you from among their own people; I will put my words in the mouth of the prophet, who shall speak to them everything that I command").[9]

The description of this miracle, as well as several others, as a "sign" is itself an allusion to the signs in the wilderness that God performed through Moses (see LXX Deut 29:2–3: "You have seen all things that the Lord did in the land of Egypt before you to Pharaoh and his servants, and all his land; the great temptations which your eyes have seen, the signs, and those great wonders…").

---

8. "Judging the twelve tribes" should be understood in the sense of administering the tribes, as did the judges in the book of Judges. See 4Q159 frgs. 2–4, lines 3–4: "And […te]n men and two priests, and they shall be judged by these twelve." For further support for this line of interpretation, see Allison and Davies 1997, 55–56.

9. Rightly Anderson 1996, 174–75, and many others.

The day after the feeding of the five thousand, Jesus urges his followers not to labor for the food that perishes but to labor for the food that endures to eternal life (John 6:27). The crowd responds by asking what sign Jesus performs (surely ironic, given the sign Jesus performed the day before) and reminding him: "Our ancestors ate the manna in the wilderness; as it is written, 'He gave them bread from heaven to eat'" (John 6:31, quoting Ps 78:24). Jesus corrects the crowd by explaining that it was not Moses who provided the bread, but God who provides the true bread from heaven. When the crowd requests this bread, Jesus replies, "I am the bread of life. Whoever comes to me will never be hungry, and whoever believes in me will never be thirsty" (John 6:35). Thus Jesus is compared to the manna, as bread given from heaven, but he is superior to the manna, in that the manna is a type of bread that perishes, not the type of bread that endures to eternal life (Borgen 1965).

Exodus typology finds expression elsewhere in the Fourth Gospel. The most obvious example is in John 3, where Jesus says, "just as Moses lifted up the serpent in the wilderness, so must the Son of man be lifted up, that whoever believes in him may have eternal life" (3:14–15). The saying alludes to the bronze serpent made and set up by Moses "on a pole; and if a serpent bit anyone, he would look at the bronze serpent and live" (Num 21:9). Jesus too will be placed "on a pole," or cross, and those who look on him in faith will live—although eternally, and not merely in this life. The interpretative perspective of this Johannine material coincides with Aramaic tradition.[10]

In John 4 Jesus discusses living water with the Samaritan woman. In the immediate context, of course, Jacob's well provides the point of departure. Again we have significant coherence with Aramaic tradition. In John 7 Jesus again speaks of the provision of water that quenches thirst eternally: "Let anyone who is thirsty come to me, and let the one who believes in me drink. As the scripture has said, 'Out of the believer's heart shall flow rivers of living water'" (7:37b–38). The text may well allude to Isa 44:3 ("I will pour water on the thirsty land [or on him who is thirsty], and streams on the dry ground; I will pour my Spirit upon your descendants, and my blessing on your offspring"), but readers and hearers who only moments before heard Jesus promise that those who come to him will "never thirst" (6:35; see also 6:53–56) would have readily associated living water with the water Moses supplied the people in the wilderness (see Num 20:8–11).

---

10. The Johannine Jesus says "Moses lifted up." Numbers 21 in the Hebrew only says that Moses "set it on a pole." The Neofiti Targum, however, says Moses "put it on an elevated place," which coheres with the Johannine interpretive orientation. Targum Pseudo-Jonathan says that he who looks on the bronze serpent will live if "his heart was paying attention to the Name of the Memra of the Lord," which coheres at yet another point with the Johannine perspective, in that faith is required. The Fragment Targum speaks of looking on the serpent "in prayer."

We may wonder if the association of the feeding of the five thousand with Moses typology originated with Jesus himself, on analogy with the Moses/Joshua typology that probably underlay the public actions and teachings of men such as John the Baptist, Theudas, and the Jew from Egypt. Further, if Jesus himself interpreted the multiplied loaves in terms of the manna, he may well have suggested that the bread being provided in this eschatological time was of much greater significance, signifying eternal life. What was linked by Jesus is still linked in John 6, but in the Synoptic tradition (or, better, in Mark) it has become dislocated.

Over thirty-five years ago Paul Achtemeier (1970; 1972) suggested that underlying Mark 4–8 were two cycles of miracles, with five miracles in each cycle, and each cycle concluding with a feeding miracle (i.e., the feeding of the five thousand in Mark 6 and the feeding of the four thousand in Mark 8). Achtemeier plausibly speculated that the feeding miracles functioned as part of the celebration of the Eucharist, since, after all, a eucharistic-like discourse follows the feeding of the five thousand in John 6. Achtemeier's interesting suggestion may also explain—at least in part—the curious statement in Mark 6, where the Evangelist explains the fear and ignorance of the disciples as due to their not understanding "the loaves."[11] That is, because they did not understand the true significance of the loaves (signifying Jesus' sacrificial death), they were subject to fear and misunderstanding.

If Achtemeier is correct, and if the suggestion of the present essay has merit, then we may be in a position to take a fresh look at the eucharistic tradition as preserved in the Synoptic words of institution, possibly as related in some way and perhaps as having grown out of teaching that is preserved more or less intact, even if embellished, in the Fourth Gospel.

Historical Jesus research has tended to neglect the Fourth Gospel, often assuming that the differences between it and the Synoptic Gospels constitute evidence that the Fourth Gospel has little to offer. In the light of political realities in Palestinian Judaism and a comparatively primitive eucharistic association as reflected in John 6, perhaps this tendency reflects unwarranted assumption more than it does careful historical assessment.

---

11. "And he got into the boat with them and the wind ceased. And they were utterly astounded, for they did not understand about the loaves, but their hearts were hardened" (Mark 6:51–52). In the Markan and Johannine accounts the disciples are afraid on the occasion of crossing the Sea of Galilee (Mark 6:47–52//John 6:16–21). The feeding miracle in John 6 is said to have taken place near the time of the Passover (John 6:4). Accordingly, the discourse in John 6 is linked to Passover, just as the Synoptic words of institution are uttered on the occasion of the Passover.

Jesus and the Galilean 'Am Ha'arets: Fact, Johannine Irony, or Both?

Sean Freyne

In discussing the historical plausibility or otherwise of episodes or speeches in the Fourth Gospel, a number of important interpretative decisions have to be taken. These methodological issues cannot be discussed in detail in this essay. My own opinion, as stated in my study of Galilee and the Gospels, is as follows: "The fact that Galilee enters the ironic patterns that the author (John) seeks to develop, shows just how important the memories associated with the region were to Christian self-understanding, even when there is no concern to develop a realistic narrative of that setting" (Freyne 1988, 131–32). In other words, I am convinced that the enterprise of seeking genuine traces of the historical Jesus' Galilean sojourn in the Johannine Gospel is not a futile one, even when strategies different from those employed in dealing with the Synoptic Gospels need to be employed and different results are to be expected.

Two noticeable trends emerge in some recent discussions, each of which can provide us with a direction for the present enquiry, namely, the source/redaction critical and the contextual. I plan to adopt both strategies in my exploration of the significance of John 7 for a discussion of the historical Jesus. Both approaches seem necessary and complementary, since an attempt to separate tradition from redaction does not on its own take us very far, given the unique character of the Fourth Gospel. The contextual approach highlights the strong Palestinian coloring, even when the finished work is now usually attributed to a Diaspora setting. This raises the question as to whether this "coloring" might not go back to the earliest stages of the tradition, possibly emanating from the period of Jesus himself.

Source and Redaction Criticism

Since Bultmann's pioneering work, most of the focus has been on the so-called signs source. Even when reaction to his proposals for various sources of the Gospel has for the most part been negative, there seems to be a general acceptance of the idea of a signs source, even when its precise contours have remained somewhat elusive. Until recently, however, the main focus of historical enquiry has been on the history of the Johannine community rather than the historical Jesus. Both J. Louis Martyn (2003; first published in 1968) and Raymond E. Brown (1979) were early pioneers in that discussion, the former being mainly interested in the community's history in relation to the synagogue, while the latter sought to uncover the intracommunity disputes by engaging with the trajectory of both the Epistles and the Gospel.

In this exploration my focus is on John 7, where the question of Jesus' identity is under discussion, thus bringing us to the heart of the concerns of the John, Jesus, and History Group. In its present form the chapter has a complex and somewhat baffling structure, but John Ashton's analysis (1991, 330–36) serves as a useful starting point. He detects two independent blocks of material: one a controversy dealing with Jesus' identity as prophet and Messiah (7:14–31, minus 19b–24) and the other dealing with the Pharisees' and chief priests' concerns, leading to the attempt to have him arrested (7:32–52, minus 33–36). These two independent blocks of material (controversy and arrest) were prefaced by an account of Jesus going to the Feast of Tabernacles, thus preparing for the central proclamation of 7:37–39 in which Jesus claims to be the fulfillment of the religious aspirations of the festival.

This summary does scant justice to the details of Ashton's analysis, but it suggests that the question of Jesus' identity as both prophet and Messiah arose at a relatively early stage of the tradition and that this was linked to his coming to the notice of the religious leaders in Jerusalem because of an episode in the temple. The issue of his Galilean origins and background play a central role in both the controversy and arrest segments. As a Galilean he is presumed to be unlettered, a member of the so-called 'am ha'arets, and therefore a false prophet, deserving of death (7:15–16, 19–20). Neither could he be the Messiah, since the Scripture was clear that the Messiah must come from David's village (7:41–42). When Nicodemus, a member of the Council of the Jews, seeks to have him receive a hearing before the Council, he is also pilloried as being a Galilean, ignorant of the fact that no prophet could come from Galilee (7:52). The action takes place on two stages: Jesus and opponents—variously named as the Jews, the crowd, the people of Jerusalem—on the front stage, and his real opponents, the Pharisees and the chief priests, on the back stage plotting his arrest, with the temple guard acting as an ineffectual, though ironic, go-between (Dodd 1953, 347–48).

Before proceeding to ask the historical questions that this treatment raises with regard to Jesus, it is important to note briefly how the characterization of Galilee and Galileans in this chapter differs from that of the narrator/author in the rest of the work. As a geographical designation, it is the place of origin of Jesus' first disciples, who were from Bethsaida in Galilee, even though he encounters the first pair, Andrew and Peter, in Judea. However, on his first visit to Galilee he meets Nathanael, who was from Cana in Galilee (see 21:2), seated under a fig tree—a pose often adopted by students of Torah—and whom Jesus designates as "an Israelite in whom there is no guile." Nathanael responds with a confession of Jesus in standard Jewish messianic titles as "Son of God and King of Israel" (1:45–50). Others of his Galilean disciples share similar ideas. Andrew reports, "we have found the Messiah," and Philip declares, "the one whom Moses wrote about in the Law and the Prophets, we have found, Jesus, the son of Joseph from Nazareth" (1:41, 44–45).

Cana, Nathanael's hometown, is particularly favored over Capernaum or Nazareth. It is there that Jesus performs his first sign, thus revealing his glory, "so that his disciples believed in him" (2:11). He returns later, after a journey to Jerusalem and Samaria, to perform a second sign. This event is prefaced by the narratorial comment that "the Galileans received him" (4:45–46). This positive attitude is confirmed after the first feeding miracle, where the Galilean crowd, recognizing him as a prophet, wanted "to take him by force and make him king" (6:14–15). This survey suggests that for John, Galilee is "both a geographical region and a value term" (Ashton 1991, 300). By this Ashton means that "Galilean" stands for openness to Jesus and his messianic claims, unlike the Judeans, even when the acceptance of Jesus in these encounters was incomplete and in need of further deepening from the perspective of a full Johannine understanding. However, the outcome of the first Cana story suggests that this was indeed an attainable goal for them. The wine miracle at Cana in Galilee is described as "the first of Jesus' signs" by which "he revealed his glory and his disciples believed in him" (2:11), thus already achieving the purpose of the whole work as described at its first ending (20:30–31). It is surely indicative, therefore, that the second, later ending, in which Jesus confirms the disciples (including Nathanael; 21:1–25), is located by the Sea of Tiberias, even though most of the action of the work was in Jerusalem and Judea.

The links between the opening scene of discovery and recognition of Jesus by the Galilean disciples in 1:35–50 and the action of John 7 are clear. In both there is an air of anticipation regarding the coming one, either as prophet or Messiah. But whereas the Galileans excitedly declare their discovery and greet Jesus with standard messianic titles—Messiah, the Mosaic prophet, and son of God and king of Israel—the Judeans are divided: some prepared to accept him as prophet and Messiah and others rejecting the identification, either because of his lack of learning (knowledge of the Scriptures) or because he was a Galilean. The same titles—prophet and Messiah—occur in both scenes, but the outcome is quite different. Indeed, in a Judean context, acceptance of Jesus as Messiah leads to expulsion from the synagogue (9:22), whereas for the Galileans it signaled a further revelation to come of Jesus' true identity.

In an important article evaluating the various Judean reactions to Jesus, especially in John 7, Marinus de Jonge (1977, 77–116) has argued that the various depictions of the Messiah are insignificant in terms of developing an understanding of Jesus' true identity as far as the Johannine author is concerned. They are either ignored (7:41b–42; 12:34) or reinterpreted fundamentally (7:27), or they represent inadequate formulations of belief in Jesus, which are subsequently implicitly corrected (1:51; 7:31). Thus, in his view, Jewish formulations about the Messiah in the Fourth Gospel are made entirely subservient to the Johannine perspective of Jesus as being one with the Father. These inadequate formulations are introduced to address objections in debates with non-Christian Jews, functioning in a fashion similar to Justin's *Dialogue with Trypho*. They add "little or nothing to other expectations concerning the messiah known from other sources" (de Jonge 1977, 97).

While this judgment would seem to rule out any consideration of these opinions about the Messiah with regard to the historical Jesus, it ignores their significance in the context of the developing Johannine tradition. In opting for a gradual development of the distinctively Johannine point of view about Jesus, John Ashton (1991, 246–51) has astutely noted the a priori unlikelihood of any firm belief in Jesus' divinity being acceptable within a community dominated by the Jewish religious establishment. He suggests a number of instances where, within an early Jewish-Christian perspective, a recognition of Jesus as Messiah that falls far short of the full-blown Johannine Christology can be documented. If this indeed is the case, the fact that these earlier ideas about Jesus are not jettisoned, but rather are used to form the basis for the later development of the tradition, entitles us to ask whether the issue of Jesus as a Galilean prophetic Messiah might not have arisen at a very early stage indeed, perhaps already within his own lifetime, and that the Jerusalem elite sought to discredit utterly such suggestions (Freyne 2001b, 198–218).

The argument of those who did not want to accept Jesus as Messiah or prophet in John 7 is based on the fact that as a Galilean he did not fulfill the one essential condition for the Son of David: that he be from Judea—although it is nowhere stated that he should come from David's village (John 7:42, 52). That this objection is also being addressed in the Matthean infancy narrative suggests that it was current in those Christian circles that were engaged in debates with nonmessianic Jews. It should be noted, however, that royal Davidic messianism is only one version of the messianic myth that can be documented for this period, especially in the light of the messianic speculation at Qumran (Zimmermann 1998). Indeed *the nature* of Jesus' ministry would be as likely to disqualify him for the role of Davidic Messiah as would his *origins* as a Galilean. The expected Davidide was preponderantly seen as a warlike figure who would rid Israel of sinners, "smashing their arrogance like a potter's jar" and "destroying the unlawful nations with the word of his mouth" (Pss. Sol. 17:21–25). Yet the Johannine community knows of other alternatives, as the opening scenario of John the Baptist's and the Galilean disciples' encounters with Jesus makes clear. In particular, it is noteworthy that the prophet like Moses and the Messiah are often closely juxtaposed, if not interchangeable (John 1:20–22, 46, 49; 6:14–15; 7:40, 41, 52). It is only at the very end, in the highly dramatic scene with Pilate, that they are fused in the Johannine theological synthesis: Jesus has come into the world "to bear witness to the truth," and because his word is obeyed, he is a king, "but not of this world" (John 18:28–19:16).

The image of the warlike Messiah was based on the political circumstances of the day, as is clear from the allusions to Pompey's attack on Jerusalem and the imminent threat of Roman rule in Judea with the ending of the Hasmonean dynasty (Pss. Sol. 8:15–20; 17:2–9). Clearly, other images of the longed-for redeemer were based on different expectations, even if they were not the dominant ones. These included the establishment of justice for all, the restoration of the tribes and a return to the values of the covenantal community of the pre-monarchic period, and the reconciliation of the peoples within the greater Israel that stretched from the Great Sea to the Euphrates. Elijah, a northern figure, was associated with some of these hopes in various biblical allusions (Mal 4:5; Sir 48:4; m. Sotah 9:15). In all probability it is he who is hailed as Messiah in 4Q521, an apocalyptic fragment that bears a striking resemblance to the early Q description of Jesus' ministry within the setting of a messianic identity parade of sorts (see Matt 11:2–6; Luke 7:18–23), where Isa 61:1–2 provides the shared background for the Qumran and early Christian texts (Collins 1995, 117–22). Once the contours of Jesus' Galilean ministry as described in the Synoptics are judged in this light, there is every possibility that the question of his messianic status, in prophetic as distinct from royal terms, did arise in Galilee. Yet, as the country prophet who came to Jerusalem full of concern for its spiritual well-being (Matt 23:37; Luke 13:34), he was no more likely to receive a sympathetic hearing from the religious elite than did others of his ilk, such as Jeremiah from Anathoth, the prototype of such country prophets (Jer 26:11), or Jesus, son of Ananias, "a rude peasant," on the eve of the great revolt (Josephus, *J.W.* 6:300–311).[1]

CONTEXTUAL PLAUSIBILITY

It is time to turn to the other trend in Johannine studies mentioned at the outset and to ask what a consideration of the wider Galilean Jewish context, both literary and archaeological, might have to offer in terms of a plausible and intelligible reading of John 7.[2] Here I am interested in applying the criterion of contextual plausibility as formulated by Gerd Theissen and Annette Merz (1996, 117), which "requires only a demonstration of positive connections between the Jesus tradition and the Jewish context, i.e. between Jesus and the land, the groups, the

---

1. See Theissen 1976, 144–58; see also J. Z. Smith 1997, 233–47.

2. Hengel's 1993 study (see also 1989a) does not seem to have had the impact it deserves in terms of an alternative approach to the Fourth Gospel and its authorship. Hengel's suggestion regarding the identity of the Johannine author is, as he himself admits, highly speculative, but this does not detract from the important discussion of the Palestinian Jewish dimension of the work and its relevance for historical reconstruction of the Johannine school (1993, esp. 272–313; Hengel 1989a, 102–8). See also Hengel 1999.

traditions and the mentalities of Judaism at that time." In the context of this essay and the questions raised by John 7:15, 49, it is important to examine what was the actual situation of Jewish belief and practice in Galilee in the first century C.E. Too often, stereotypes of Galilee and Galileans, often stemming from the ancient sources, have been used uncritically by New Testament scholars in order to provide a suitable background for a particular portrayal of Jesus. One has only to compare the highly flattering picture of Galileans given by Josephus, a Jerusalemite priest acting on behalf of the provisional council as governor of the region in 66 C.E. (*J. W.* 3.41–43), with the negative views of the Jerusalem elite in John 7 to realize just how one-sided is the perspective that these sources often betray. This points to the need, therefore, for critical evaluation before one attempts to use John and Josephus for historical reconstruction. The same is equally true of the rabbinic sources, as we shall presently see.

The question of the *Ioudaioi* at 7:15 (πῶς οὗτος γράμματα οἶδεν μὴ μεμαθηκώς; "How does this man have such learning, when he has never been taught?") implies that Jesus has no authority to teach since he was not one of the *talmidê hakamîm.* The statement of the Pharisees later in the episode, that "this crowd who do not know the law are accursed" (7:49), confirms this understanding of the purport of the question. This reaction was based on the readiness of some of the "crowd" (ὄχλος—Galilean pilgrims, Jerusalemites, or both?) to agree that Jesus was the awaited prophet and Messiah. In terms of the current usage, this charge implies that Jesus and the crowd were deemed to belong to the *'am ha'arets letorah,* that is, people who were ignorant of the basics of Jewish identity, as distinct from the *'am ha'arets lemitswot,* people who did not strictly observe the commandments relating to tithing or purity laws. How likely is it that a charge in these specific terms relating to the *'am ha'arets* would have been levied against the historical Jesus in the 20s of the first century C.E.? Is not the tone and terminology more redolent of the 90s, reflecting the alleged conflictual atmosphere between the synagogue and the Johannine community?

The issue of Jesus' relationship with the *'am ha'arets* arose already in the late nineteenth century, when scholars—German Protestants, for the most part—argued that Jesus was a champion of the common people, in contrast to the legalistic impositions and hostile attitudes of the Pharisees toward them.[3] Such a presentation suited the anti-Jewish trends of scholarship of the period. Adolf Büchler, a leading Jewish historian, sought to refute these claims in his 1906 book, *Der galiläische 'Am ha-'Arets des zweiten Jahrhunderts,* arguing that all the references to the *'am ha'arets* on which Christian scholars had relied belonged to the Ushan period (i.e., after 135 C.E.). They were not addressed to the Galilean populace but to the descendants of the Jerusalem priesthood who had come to Galilee after the Bar Kokhba revolt and who did not observe the regulations con-

---

3. For example, Friedländer 1894, 37–58; Schürer 1907, 2:454–75; Bousset 1926, 187–89.

cerning the eating of the priestly *terumah* in ritual purity, unlike the members of the pharisaic *haburot*. While subsequent scholarship on the 'am ha'arets has been able to point out various flaws in Büchler's manipulations of the sources to suit his apologetic intention, his study did illustrate the need for more careful analysis, recognizing the possibility that the designation may have had different applications at different periods.[4] Christian scholars have often relied too heavily on Strack-Billerbeck, whose canvassing of rabbinic parallels to the Gospels treats the whole of the rabbinic corpus with little consideration of literary or historical variations.[5] In order to test the original historical plausibility of the charge against Jesus, one needs to examine the way in which the notion of the 'am ha'arets had evolved and was employed at different periods of Jewish history, including the pre-70 C.E. period.

The label 'am ha'arets took on a distinctively pejorative tone only in the immediate postexilic period, being applied by the returnees from Babylon to the non-Jewish residents of Judah and the neighboring peoples (Neh 10:29; Ezra 6:19–21; 9:1), whereas in the preexilic period it referred to an influential social stratum, probably a type of landed gentry within the Israelite kingdom ("the people of the land," 2 Kgs 11:14–20; 23:30). In between this early usage and its reappearance in the first century C.E., the term came to be used in inner-Judean circles, while retaining its pejorative overtones.[6] It was employed now to distinguish between strictly observant and less observant Jews, as these categories were classified by the Pharisees—the dominant religious group in the late Second Temple period, or alternatively, to those who were not just ignorant of Torah but willfully so—the 'am ha'arets lemitswot and letorah, respectively. It is this latter accusation that seems to lie behind John 7:15, 49, while the discussion of Jesus' lack of concern for purity regulations, as dealt with in the Synoptics (e.g., Mark 7), is more properly judged under the former category.

The argument has been made that it was in the Jamnia period that the category of 'am ha'arets letorah became particularly prominent. Prior to its destruction in 70 C.E., the temple with its system of sacrifices and festivals was the center of Judean life for all who would call themselves *Ioudaioi*, whether of Judean provenance or not. After the temple's destruction, the sage supplanted the priest, and the Torah scroll replaced the altar as the sacred center of Israel. Study rather than sacrifice was now the hallmark of fidelity and a sacred duty for all. The sages who established the center at Jamnia and their successors saw themselves as the leaders

4. Schürer (1906, 619–20) voiced this criticism in his review of Büchler's book; see also Meyer 1947, 169–99, esp. 181, n. 39; Oppenheimer 1977, 5–7, and passim.

5. See Strack and Billerbeck 1922–61, 2:494–519.

6. Hillel, a first-century sage, declared, "A coarse person will never fear sin, nor will an 'am ha'arets ever be pious" (Pirqe 'Abot 2:5). See also Oppenheimer 1977, 103. However, consistent with his idea that the notion of the 'am ha'arets letorah only emerged in the post-Jamnia period, he seeks to attribute the saying to a later third-century Rabbi Hillel (104–5).

of the nation, so that gradually they came to think of themselves as an elite class (Oppenheimer 1977, 172–87). After 135 C.E. they operated in Galilee of necessity, but their efforts to make the whole people a nation of Torah observers seems to have been less than fully successful, as the oft-cited saying attributed to Johannan ben Zakkai implies: "Galilee, Galilee, because you hate the torah your end shall be destruction" (y. Šabb. 16:8, 15d). While the historical Johannan belongs to the Jamnia period, the saying attributed to him and the anecdote relating to his unsuccessful sojourn in Galilee are more likely to reflect the situation in the second century C.E., when there are numerous expressions of the sages' total distrust, and even hatred, of the ʿam haʾarets letorah (Neusner 1985, 79–96).

In the light of this brief sketch of the development of the concept of ʿam haʾarets, it might appear that the charge against Jesus and other Galileans in John 7 fits neatly into this later context and is, therefore, a reflection of the struggles between synagogue and church at the end of the first and beginning of the second century, not a datum of the life of the historical Jesus. However, the claim of Oppenheimer and others that it was only in the Jamnia period that study of the Torah became significant within Judaism needs to be critically evaluated. For one thing, the rather rigid distinction between the two categories of ʿam haʾarets seems somewhat forced, in the light of descriptions such as b. Ber. 47b, t. ʿAbod. Zar. 3:10, and so on. As these texts indicate, the list of what constitutes an ʿam haʾarets includes *both* lack of knowledge and respect for the basics of the Torah (e.g., recitation of the Shema) *and* failure to observe the purity laws (e.g., eating food in ritual purity).

This is as we might have expected. Josephus repeatedly describes the Pharisees as "the most accurate interpreters of our laws" (*J.W.* 1.110; 2.162–166; *Ant.* 13.296; 18.12–19), implying an emphasis on study and learning, as well as their concern to extend the temple purity to the home and village.[7] Elsewhere Josephus boasts: "should anyone of our nation be questioned about the laws, he would repeat them all more readily than his own name" (*Ag. Ap.* 2.178). Of course, these statements cannot be taken uncritically either, in view of the fact that they are made by a self-confessed admirer of the Pharisees who is writing his apology in the 90s in Rome. However, it should be recalled that the second-century B.C.E. Jerusalemite Jesus Ben Sirach could extol the role of the sage and his pursuit of wisdom above every other profession (Sir 38:24–39:11). In doing so, he was clearly including himself in that class, as he offers an explicit invitation to others to come and "lodge in the house of instruction" (Sir 51:23). Thus, the linking of wisdom and Torah (Sir 24) generated an atmosphere of learning

---

7. For a fuller discussion of the Pharisees and their relation to the scribes, see Freyne 1988, 198–213. Saldarini 1999 is the most thorough discussion of the distinctions between Pharisees and scribes within Judean society, based on social-scientific models and a careful reading of the different sources.

in Palestinian Judaism, once it had come in contact with the Hellenistic *Zeitgeist* (Meyer 1947, 172–73; Hengel 1993, 143–52). Both wisdom and Torah-learning were necessary for the life of holiness. We do not have to wait until the second and third centuries c.e., therefore, to find the emergence of the scribal class as an elite social phenomenon in Judaism. In addition to Ben Sirach's school, the Theodotos inscription from Herodian Jerusalem refers to both the reading of the law and the teaching of the commandments as activities that were conducted in the building (*synagōgē*) that he had dedicated.[8] It was, therefore, a school as well as a place of meeting for religious purposes. The fact that the building complex also had guest rooms (*zenōna*) implies that visitors to Jerusalem lodged there, perhaps in order to study the Torah at the feet of an important teacher (such as the young Saul of Tarsus at the feet of Gamaliel; see Acts 22:3). In addition to this datable evidence, there are numerous references in rabbinic literature to houses of study (as distinct from synagogues) in Jerusalem during the period of the Second Temple. Clearly, the holy city was not just a temple city but also a place of learning and study at that time.

But what of Galilee? Is the attitude of the Pharisaic leaders and the chief priests toward "this crowd who do not know the law and are accursed"—which is linked to the jibe about Nicodemus being "a Galilean"—likely to be typical? What was the status of Torah-learning in the region in the first century? To begin with, it is important to note that the designation 'am ha'arets is never specifically applied to Galileans in the rabbinic sources. As a term of censure, if not opprobrium, its use was not restricted to any one region or class, and even the high priest could be an 'am ha'arets. As indicated above, circumstances dictated that many of the debates dealing with the issue took place in Galilee in the second century c.e., but that fact should not be projected back onto the first century to imply that all Galileans were deemed to be ignorant of Torah and unconcerned about purity matters. There is a growing consensus today that the ethos of first-century c.e. Galilee was Jewish, in the sense that the dominant strand of the population had Judean roots, with their ancestors settling there after the Hasmonean conquests (Freyne 2001a, 176–82; see also Reed 2000, esp. 23–61). Indeed, it is quite possible that the family of Jesus had been such internal migrants to Galilee. A reconsideration of Josephus's narrative of the Hasmonean expansion to the north, allied to the cumulative evidence of the intensive archaeological investigation of the region, has effectively sealed the fate of what has been described as *The Myth of a Gentile Galilee* (Chancey 2002 and 2005).

While E. P. Sanders's discussion of a common or normal Judaism, as distinct from the particular emphases of the various philosophies, is highly significant, it seems necessary to ask how this was seen differently at the center and

---

8. For a detailed discussion and interpretation of this important inscription, see Kloppenborg 2006, 236–82.

the periphery. Did all the stipulations apply equally in all the regions (Sanders 1992, 47–51)? The stipulation of attendance at the great feasts (e.g., the setting for the discussion John 7) must have been highly demanding, if not downright impossible, for many Galilean peasants, removed by as much as a seven-day journey from the holy city, if they lived in Upper Galilee. Attendance at all three feasts would have taken up to ten weeks for such people, at times when seasonal demands had to be met in terms of harvesting, tending of animals, and processing the grape crop. The discussion in John 7:1–11 about whether or not Jesus would go to Jerusalem for Sukkoth is highly charged with Johannine theological irony, yet issues of how to travel, to which festival, and how many from the village or household should make the journey must surely have been of real concern for those struggling to eke out subsistence from their traditional plots of land, not to mention the logistics of bringing agricultural tithes to Jerusalem.[9] That many did not, or could not, fulfill their obligations in this regard is clearly evidenced from Josephus's report that the servants of the high priests went down to the villages and forcibly confiscated the tithes (*Ant.* 20.181). In Galilee, paying the tithes to local priests does not seem to have been an option, but yet, if we are to believe Josephus, the Galileans were willing to discharge their obligation to him and his fellow priests who had come to the region in 66 C.E. (*Life* 63, 80).

For Jesus and the retinue who had left family, home, and lands to follow him, there were no such impediments. As mentioned previously, going to Jerusalem on the occasion of the great festivals was, for a country prophet, a highly significant opportunity to challenge the values that the aristocratic, priestly elite and their retainers enjoyed. The economics of pilgrimage cities, then as now, should not be overlooked when assessing the range of religious influence and control that such centers seek to generate over the populace at large!

Yet, equally, these practical difficulties for Galilean Jews—the attitudes they engendered and the perceptions they gave rise to—should not be overemphasized to the point of suggesting a climate of implacable opposition and hostility between Galilee and Jerusalem (Freyne 2001a, 289–311). The artifacts and other material remains in the archaeological record—stone jars, *miqva'ot* (or stepped bathing pools), coins, absence of pig bones in the deposits, and burial practices—all point to a Judean provenance. This evidence is scattered throughout the various subregions of Galilee, and while we are not yet in a position to offer a complete picture of the ethno-religious identities of all the ancient settlements that have been surveyed, there are unmistakable signs of a consistent pattern of Jewishness throughout the region. Places such as Gamla and Yotapata, both centers of strong

---

9. The mention in the Jerusalem Talmud of caravans of tithe-bearing carts traveling from various centers in Galilee (Migdal, Shiknin, and Cabul, *y. Ta'an* 4, 69a*) may represent a later, idealized picture, yet it does highlight the difficulty for Galilean peasants in transporting their agricultural offerings to Jerusalem.

resistance to Rome in 66 C.E.—the former producing a locally minted coin with an inscription in Paleo-Hebrew that reads "For the freedom of Zion, Jerusalem the holy"—shows that some centers in Galilee felt close, emotional ties with the symbolic world of the Jerusalem temple. The concern with purity maintenance that the *miqva'ot* and the remains of stone jars demonstrate—a point noted in the Fourth Gospel's mention of the six stone jars "according to the Jewish rites of purification" (John 2:6)—is indicative of the fact that the expansion of purity concerns associated with the Pharisaic movement had also occurred in first-century Galilee (Deines 1992; Kazen 2002, esp. 263–97).

This suggestion is further confirmed by the literary evidence. On two occasions Mark mentions scribes coming from Jerusalem to check on Jesus' activities in Galilee. The first reference is an attempt to discredit him as being in league with Beelzebul, the prince of demons (Mark 3:22), and on the second occasion they challenge his apparent lack of concern with purity issues (7:1–2). The former was clearly the more serious charge, akin to the Johannine reference to the *'am ha'arets letorah* being accursed (John 7:49), whereas the latter deals with the issues concerning the *'am ha'arets lemitswot*. Such "outreach" from the Jerusalem elite's retainers calls to mind the make-up of the Jerusalem delegation sent to remove Josephus from the governorship of Galilee in 66 C.E. Of the four members of the delegation, three were Pharisees (two described as *demotikoi*, i.e., plebeian, and one a priest), and the fourth member, Simon, was from the high priestly faction (*Life* 187–188). Once again we have an example of Jerusalem elites and retainers concerned with and being involved in Galilean affairs, and one must wonder whether or not the preponderance of Pharisees on the delegation might not tell us something about the extent of Pharisaic influences in Galilee.

Where did Jesus and his movement stand with regard to these concerns of the Jerusalem priestly and lay aristocracy? As regards the *mitswot* dealing with purity, opinions among scholars are still divided: Jesus was opposed to the Pharisaic purity halakot, replacing "the politics of purity with the politics of compassion" (Borg 1994, 112); Jesus was ambivalent, respecting certain aspects of the system (e.g., the rules dealing with the pronouncement of the priests regarding skin disease), but "he did not regard such (purity) concerns as central to his understanding of what constituted the Israel of God" (Dunn 2002, 467); "Jesus did not seriously challenge the law as it was practiced in his day even by the strict rules of observance of pietist groups—except on the issue of food" (Sanders 1990, 96). Since the issue of purity is not the subject of the charge against him in John 7, we can bypass this discussion for now, focusing instead on the more serious issue of both he and the Galileans being categorized as *'ammê ha'arets letorah*.

Unfortunately, we are ill-informed about schools and schooling in Judaism prior to the second century, when we hear of various rabbinic "houses of study" in Galilee, both communal ones and those belonging to individual rabbis. That there were centers of Torah-learning in Jerusalem during the days of the Second Temple has been mentioned already, but there is no comparable evidence for

Galilee during the same period. One inscription found at Daburra in the Golan proclaims, "This is the house of study of Rabbi Eliezer Ha-Kappar." This discovery has lead Dan Urman to hypothesize that perhaps there were others also in the region that have been wrongly identified as "prayer houses" rather than "community centers" or "study houses" (Urman 1993, 237–57). While there is indeed merit in this suggestion, it does not assist us in dealing with the situation in the first century. The one pre-70 c.e. building in the region, generally identified as a "synagogue," that of Gamla, could easily be a case in point, with its stepped benches around the walls facing an open space in the center. This suggests a more communal type of meeting place, which could also function as "a house of study," even though the excavators have designated a smaller adjoining room, also with benches, for that purpose (Gutman 1993, 2:459–63). At Tiberias, Josephus intimates, the meeting house could be described as a *proseuchē*, literally, a "house of prayer," yet it functions as a location for political business (*Life* 280). In terms of knowledge of the Torah in Galilee, it is interesting to note that on another occasion a certain Jesus, son of Sapphias, the leader of a revolutionary party in the city, could brandish a copy of the law of Moses as he harangued the populace (*Life* 134).

Apart from Luke's description of Jesus' visit to the synagogue at Nazareth, which also mentions a *book* of Isaiah (καὶ ἐπεδόθη αὐτῷ βιβλίον τοῦ προφήτου Ἡσαΐου καὶ ἀναπτύξας τὸ βιβλίον εὗρεν τὸν τόπον οὗ ἦν γεγραμμένον, Luke 4:17; see also 4:20), the Josephan reference is the only evidence we have for a copy of a sacred book in a Galilean context of the first century. We must, however, presume that Torah scrolls were more widely diffused than our evidence suggests, on the basis of various reports in Josephus (*J.W.* 2.229–230, burning of scroll by a Roman soldier in Caesarea Maritima; *J.W.* 7.150, display of a Torah scroll in victory parade after the Jewish War). In addition, Josephus assumes widespread knowledge of and respect for the twenty-two books that make up the Jewish Scriptures (*Ag. Ap.* 1.37–43). How and to what extent this ideal was achieved is a much more difficult question to answer. Catherine Hezser has challenged the widespread idea of Judaism as a religion of the book, which has been a standard view, based on the cultic reform of Josiah through the "discovery" of the book of Deuteronomy and Ezra's reading of the Torah in front of the congregation from morning until evening. Her argument, arising from comparable evidence of the period, is that Jewish society was no more literate than other parts of the Greco-Roman world. This means that only a small percentage—as little as 1 percent in some towns, increasing to a maximum of 5 percent in urban settings—were literate. While the numbers may have increased with the intensive urbanization of Palestine in the second and third centuries, one must also reckon with what has been described as the "secondary orality" of the rabbis in the same period (Hezser 2001, 34–36).

If these statistics are at all accurate, we would have to reckon with an oral rather than a literate culture in Galilee of the early first century, even if the situation had improved somewhat later, the main focus of Hezser's pioneering study. Furthermore, the ability to read (and write) would belong to the elite and retainer classes: royal officials, village scribes, priests, leading Pharisees, and the like. Such competency only helped to widen the gap between the urban and rural populations. However, this need not imply "ignorance of torah," given what we know about oral cultures and their capacity for memory, storytelling, and respect for tradition.[10] Harry Gamble draws attention to the fact that the early Christians were "bookish" (see, e.g., the appeal "according to the Scriptures" [κατὰ τὰς γραφὰς] as early as 1 Cor 15:3b–4), yet there is the "unquestionable fact that few Christians could read"—thereby replicating the situation in Judaism as a whole. Gamble goes on to remind us, however, that in using terms such as "literacy" and "illiteracy" we are in danger of overlooking an important aspect of the situation in the ancient world: the overlap between the oral and literary modes. There was a complex synergy between the two modes, both in terms of production and reception, since most writing was based on dictation aloud, just as texts were not read in silence but read aloud (Gamble 2004, 27–39, esp. 28–31). This aspect of ancient writing and reading points to the communal "outdoors" aspects of ancient societies, and the implications of this phenomenon extend to the dissemination of knowledge of, and familiarity with, communal stories. The role of the father of the household in terms of the Passover ritual is one concrete example of how faithful transmission of the tradition took place (Exod 13:8–10). In addition, the emergence of the Targums as Aramaic paraphrases of the synagogue readings, although difficult to date on the basis of our present textual evidence, was widespread and early. It demonstrates the insistence upon knowledge not just of the Torah but of the Prophets and other writings as well, something that the emergence of the Greek translations also underlines, well before the first century C.E.[11]

Jesus is repeatedly described as a "teacher" or engaged in teaching activity in the Synoptic Gospels, even when, as in Mark, we are not given much of the content of that teaching. The Fourth Gospel also acknowledges this aspect of Jesus' ministry, and John 7 in particular emphasizes the point. The verb διδάσκειν ("to teach") occurs three times in this chapter (7:14, 28, 35), initially sparking off the debate about Jesus' identity and climaxing in the prophetic action of crying out and teaching in the temple (ἔκραξεν οὖν ἐν τῷ ἱερῷ διδάσκων ὁ Ἰησοῦς καὶ λέγων, 7:28, see also 7:37). This performance leads to the report—spoken with typical Johannine irony and hyperbole—of the high priest's servants sent to arrest him: "Never has anyone spoken as this man" (οὐδέποτε ἐλάλησεν οὕτως ἄνθρωπος, 7:46; see also 4:42; 6:68). This reaction is similar to that found in the Synoptics, where both Mark and Matthew stress the contrast between Jesus' teaching and

---

10. See Dunn 2003a, 139–75, esp. 147–56 on the characteristics of orality.

11. See, in general, the articles by Tov and Alexander on the Septuagint and the Jewish Aramaic translations in Mulder 1988, 161–87 and 217–54, respectively.

that of the scribes (Mark 1:22, 27; Matt 7:28; see Luke 4:32, 36, although the contrast with the scribes is softened, but see also Luke 4:22).

What can be said about this contrast, and how might it have given rise to the charge that Jesus was a member of the 'am ha'arets letorah? Here it is only possible to make some suggestions. To begin with, we can definitely say that, on the basis of the evidence, Jesus' approach to Scripture was not the same as that of either the scribes or groups such as the Essenes. Efforts to see his teaching within the framework of a school system (Gerhardsson 1961; Riesner 1981) are unconvincing, since they fail to take account of his wandering ministry and his emphasis on deeds rather than learning, as Martin Hengel (1981, 42–57) rightly points out. While Jesus does allude directly to the Scriptures on occasion, his style of teaching is not primarily scriptural.[12] His most characteristic form of speech is perhaps the parable (māšāl). Even then his appropriation of a traditional form displays his own original style and perspective, what Gerd Theissen has called "Risikofreudigkeit," that is, a joyful celebration of risk-taking on behalf of the kingdom of God (1989, 354–55). It was this central conviction that determined Jesus' hermeneutical stance with regard to his own inherited tradition and that caused him to be highly selective with regard to those elements of that tradition that were to shape his own ministry.[13]

Such an independent perspective on what was, together with the temple, one of the central symbols for all Jews would inevitably have made Jesus highly suspect to the Jerusalem scribal authorities, whose role the Johannine Pharisees seem to represent (Saldarini 1999, 187–98). Indeed, the initial reaction of the Jerusalem crowd about Jesus' lack of learning is quite similar to that of his own family and townspeople in Mark 6:2–3. The pejorative note with regard to being a Galilean and the implication of belonging to the 'am ha'arets is additional in John. However, this does not necessarily mean that it is a Johannine creation. The Synoptics are also aware of regional differences with regard to accent (Matt 26:73; see also Mark 14:70; Luke 22:59), with at least a certain implication of inferiority, something that much later was developed in a highly negative way in rabbinic circles (b. Erub. 53a, b; see also b. Meg. 24b).

If we are to take seriously Jesus Ben Sirach's description of the scribe's role, in contrast to all manual activities, as typical of how Jerusalem-based scribes thought of their own activity, then the point of view of the Johannine Pharisees is

---

12. E.g., his dealing with the issue of divorce (Mark 10:6), the Shema and love commandment (Mark 12:29–31), the Sabbath, the Jonah story (Q: Luke 11:30; Matt 12:40–41), biblical characters such as the patriarchs (Matt 8:11; Luke 13:28), Solomon (Matt 6:28–29) and the Queen of the South (Q: Luke 11:31; Matt 12:42), the figures of the Son of Man in Daniel, Elijah, the Passover meal, etc.

13. In Freyne 2004, I have attempted to develop this approach with regard to Jesus' concern for creation over election, and the influence of Isaiah and Daniel on his approach and strategy, in his proclamation of the kingdom of God in Roman Palestine.

not at all surprising, nor indeed implausible for the actual career of Jesus. Indeed, once it is recognized that the historical Jesus' championing of the poor and the marginalized should be seen as a subtle attack on elitist values—at one and the same time appropriating them for those who had been marginalized as a result of elitist attitudes, but thereby also transforming them—then there was all the more reason to discredit Jesus by whatever means possible. One of the most prized values was that of wisdom and the education by which it was acquired (Theissen 1989, 253–55). Jesus of Nazareth declared that wisdom belonged to the very type of people whom Jesus of Jerusalem (Ben Sirach) had excluded! He invited those who were "weary and heavily burdened" to come to him in order to partake of the wisdom he had to offer. The spiritualizing tendency that sees these terms as psychological, rather than materialist, ignores the concrete images of Jesus' style and expression. Indeed, he had used the idioms and images of these peasant people to describe the kingdom that he proclaimed and its workings, thereby also giving real value to their everyday lives—lives that in Herodian Galilee were often drab and care-worn. To declare that these people were the wise and the blessed was not good news for those, whether in Galilee or Jerusalem, who owed their privileged positions to the exploitation of such people. This man was indeed accursed, in league with Beelzebul, for not merely making such assertions but actually enacting them through his charismatic healing and exorcisms.

CONCLUSION

In this essay I have adopted two different strategies for evaluating the likely historical value of John 7 for a discussion of the historical Jesus. Both approaches lead to promising but inconclusive results. Judging the plausibility of one or both approaches will depend on what stance one takes with regard to the Johannine project as a whole. My own position, stated at the outset, is to postulate an intimate nexus between the full-blown theological vision of John and the history of Jesus. This irony is not based on any modern form of skepticism; rather, it is the irony that inevitably arises from speaking about God as present in the world. The initial misunderstanding of various historical events or situations dealing with Jesus' Jewish identity triggers the epistemological current, whereby the deeper meaning of those events and situations can be illuminated. Thus they become signs of the glory (δόξα) of God at work in Jesus for those who are open to such an extraordinary revelation.

   That this literary strategy is no mere historical nostalgia, but an essential component of Johannine theology, is evident from the outset, when the Baptist addresses those from Jerusalem (Pharisees!) who had been sent to make enquiries about his identity: "Among you there stands one whom you do not know, the one who is coming after me" (John 1:26). Had this pronouncement been taken seriously, the debates of John 7 in Jerusalem would have taken on a different tone. Yet the Jerusalem crowd "knows" where Jesus is from, and thereby they can disqualify any claim about his being the Messiah: "We know where this man is from, but when the Messiah comes no one will know where he is from" (7:27). The two points of view are subtly contrasted: "Do not judge by appearances, but judge with right judgment" (7:24), is Jesus' advice to the Jews who first raised the issue of his lack of knowledge because of not having studied with the scribes (7:15).

These statements sound more like an in-house argument, as John Ashton suggests (1992, 137–51), than a bitter dispute with the synagogue. As such, they could be placed at any point on the trajectory that runs from the recognition by the Galilean populace of the historical Jesus as a prophet, who goes to Jerusalem on the occasion of a festival to challenge the religious authorities, to the time when messianic Jews (in the process of transmuting into Johannine Christians) began to develop an independent identity. In its present form, John 7 would appear to be nearer this latter point, but that does not mean that the earlier moments in the process were unimportant or redundant as far as the Johannine Christians were concerned. The full-blown Johannine incarnational theology is rooted in the history of Jesus the Jew, as this is narrated in the Gospel (Söding 2002b, 21–41). Indeed, if we are to take seriously the notion of remembering, which seems to have played an important role in the coming to full understanding of the Johannine disciples (John 2:25; 12:16), then the history of Jesus was essential to the theological highpoint of the Prologue: "The Word became flesh and dwelt among us" (1:14). As the Gospel narrative unfolds, the association between prophet and Messiah as applied to Jesus is gradually clarified. The Galilean disciples variously describe him as the prophet, the Messiah, and the king of Israel (1:41, 47, 49); the Galilean crowd recognizes him as prophet and wants to make him king (6:14–15); the *Ioudaioi* and the Jerusalem crowd are divided on the issue of whether he is the prophet or the Messiah—titles that are virtually interchangeable as far as the participants are concerned (7:26, 31, 40–41, 52). In the final scene with Pilate, Jesus himself defines his kingship in terms of the prophetic role: "You say I am a king. For this was I born, and for this I came into the world, to bear witness to the truth. Everyone who is of the truth listens to my voice" (18:37–38). Thus, John 7 forms a midpoint between the "naïve" Galilean declarations and the Johannine synthesis of the roles of Messiah, king, and prophet in terms of the Revealer. One suspects that this is not just a literary creation but reflects the actual experience of the founding member(s) of the Johannine community—an experience that originated already in the career of the earthly Jesus.

The Pool of Siloam: The Importance of the New Discoveries for Our Understanding of Ritual Immersion in Late Second Temple Judaism and the Gospel of John

Urban C. von Wahlde

The Pool of Siloam is one of the biblical sites adjacent to the Old City of Jerusalem that has been pointed out to visitors and pilgrims for centuries. It lies south of the Old City at the tip of the Ophel Ridge, in what is now the Arab village of Silwan. The pool is known locally by its Arab name, the Birkat Silwan. Visitors to the pool are directed to a fenced-in area near a Muslim school. A small, rusty sign identifies the place as the Pool of Siloam. In order to get near the pool itself, one must enter through a gate. Sometimes locked and sometimes open, the gate leads down perhaps twenty steps to the level of the pool. The pool itself is a small rectangular area with grates at both ends. At the northern end, the pool meets Hezekiah's Tunnel, built in the eighth century B.C.E. to bring the water from the Gihon Spring inside the city, so that the water supply could be protected during times when Jerusalem was under siege. At the southern end, the water drains into a channel that disappears underground and emerges about sixty yards farther to the east, flowing into the Kidron Valley. Such is the Pool of Siloam. Rather, such *was* the Pool of Siloam until the summer of 2004.

The Excavations from 2004 to 2006

In the spring of 2004, the public works department of the city of Jerusalem determined to replace a faulty sewer line along the rock scarp just to the south of the Pool of Siloam. In keeping with their ordinary practice, the city department allowed the Israeli Antiquities Authority (IAA) to conduct a salvage dig to either side of the place where the repairs were to take place.[1] The general area along the

---

1. A preliminary version of this study was presented at the Annual Meeting of the Society of Biblical Literature in Philadelphia, in November 2005. The present version represents an expansion and updating of a treatment of the pools that appeared in my chapter, "The Gospel of

Figure 1. A view of the traditional "Pool of Siloam" (the
Birkat Silwan), looking north. The mouth of Hezekiah's
Tunnel is under the arch. Photo U. von Wahlde.

rock scarp had been briefly explored by a number of earlier archaeologists who
had identified the area as a reservoir. This reservoir was known in Arabic as the
Birkat al-Hamra. Presumably, the archaeologists, Ronny Reich of the University
of Haifa and Eli Shukron of the IAA, expected to uncover more detail about the

John and Archaeology," in Charlesworth 2006, 523–86. No information regarding the southern
pool is included here that has not been published by the archaeologists or without their permission. The most extensive treatment of the excavations to date is Reich and E. Shukron 2006; see
also Reich and Shukron 2004; Shanks 2005. I am grateful to G. Rivkin for his translation from
the Hebrew of the article by Reich and Shukron 2006 and also to Alec Lucas, my graduate assistant at Loyola University of Chicago, for his assistance with the present essay.

Figure 2. The traditional pool looking south. The conduit leading
toward the Kidron Valley is beyond the grating. In the first century,
the pool was at ground level. The steps to the upper right of the
photo lead to the current ground level. Photo U. von Wahlde.

reservoir. What they found, though, was hardly a reservoir. As the excavations
progressed, it became apparent that it was a pool that contained steps all along
the northeastern side.

This side extended eastward until it met the modern road that extends to the
northeast and up the Kidron Valley. Two British archaeologists, Frederick Bliss
and Archibald Dickie, had explored the area in the late 1800s and had found a
large dam extending from the rock scarp across the Tyropoean Valley.[2] Just before

2. See Bliss and Dickie 1898. It was this dam that led to the theory that the area had been

the steps meet this dam, they turn southwest. Just how far they lead along the southwest side cannot be determined. This is because the salvage dig allowed only a moderate amount of excavation in that direction and also because the remainder of the area was an abandoned orchard that belonged to the Greek Orthodox Church; thus, permission could not be obtained to dig in the area.

As the excavation followed the steps to the northeastern corner, it became clear that they continued across the northern side of the pool also. Again, excavation was not allowed to continue far along that edge. Nevertheless, given the configuration of the area to the southwest, the archaeologists proposed that the original pool had extended across the Tyropoean Valley as far as the modern road known as the Ma'Alot Ir David, which begins opposite the Dung Gate and continues to the southern end of the Tyropoean Valley. The corners of the pool are not perfectly square but indicate that the pool was trapezoidal, following the contours of the valley. Reich and Shukron (2006, 93) estimate that the pool was approximately 50 x 60 meters (165 x 197 feet).

The steps themselves were evidently hewn from stone. In a first phase of their history, the steps were covered with a gray plaster. In a later phase, they were covered with stone pavers. Archaeologists, using metal detectors, discovered five coins from the reign of Alexander Jannaeus (103–76 B.C.E.) embedded in the plaster of the earliest layer, indicating that the plastering of the pool dated from some time during (or after) the reign of Jannaeus.

But this was not all. As the archaeologists excavated to the southeast, uncovering more steps leading down into the pool, they discovered that the steps were interrupted regularly by narrow landings. It became immediately apparent that the pool was in fact a large public *miqveh*, a pool for ritual bathing.[3] In fact, this *miqveh* immediately attained the status of being the largest public *miqveh* in first-century Jerusalem!

But just as the discovery of this pool enabled a whole new perspective on this part of the Ophel Ridge in the first century, it also gave rise to a number of new questions. Perhaps the most significant question concerned the identity of the pool that was employed during the Feast of Tabernacles to draw water for the Temple Mount ceremony: Was it the northern or the southern pool? In addition,

---

a reservoir. At the present time, the road runs across the top of the dam, so no remains of the dam are visible.

3. *Miqva'ot* are the subject of a separate tractate in the sixth division of the Mishnah (see Danby 1933, 732–44). The most thorough modern discussion of *miqva'ot* is said to be that of Ronny Reich (1990, Ph.D. dissertation, in Hebrew). An excellent discussion of *miqva'ot* can also be found in Sanders 1990, 214–36. Sanders follows Reich closely but puts the variety of practice reflected in the archaeological evidence into a very helpful context. See also Wright 1997, who gives a detailed analysis and critique of the criteria used by Reich in his dissertation for identifying ritual baths (see esp. 193–205). Most recently, see Gibson 2005, esp. 275 n. 6 for additional bibliography.

there was the question about the relation of the southern pool to the northern pool, the pool immediately adjacent to the exit of Hezekiah's Tunnel. Finally, there was the question about how these discoveries would impact the understanding of the role of the "Pool of Siloam" mentioned in the Gospel of John.

The excavation season in Jerusalem concluded with the end of summer in 2004. Reich and Shukron knew that they had discovered something important, and the news of the discovery was released to the press in July. At the time, I was finishing an article on "The Gospel of John and Archaeology" for a collection entitled *Jesus and Archaeology*, edited by James Charlesworth (2006). When I heard of the excavation, I contacted Charlesworth at Princeton, who acknowledged that he had heard about the discovery and was interested in seeing it first-hand. As a result, I was able to visit the site in February 2005 along with Charlesworth and to be given a tour by both Reich and Shukron.

Figure 3. The excavations looking east in February 2005. The concrete sewer encasement has not been removed but the steps and the southeast corner of the pool are visible. Photo U. von Wahlde.

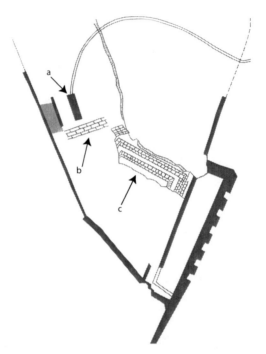

Figure 4. Diagram showing the relationship between
Hezekiah's Tunnel and (a) the "traditional" pool, (b) the
plaza, and (c) the newly discovered *miqveh*.

In the excavation seasons of 2005 and 2006, work continued at the site. The northeast corner was excavated, and a plaza along the northwest side of the pool—which had been discovered earlier—was fully excavated. This plaza was traced to the northwest, coming eventually into contact with a series of steps leading to a major staircase, which in turn led north to the Temple Mount. Drains were found in the floor of the plaza intended to keep the plaza dry.[4] In addition, Reich and Shukron found remains of columns along the plaza and corresponding sockets for the beams that ran along the top of the columns. By examining the marking on the columns and the way they were fashioned, Reich and Shukron (2006, 94) dated them to the late Second Temple period.[5] An additional small

---

4. The presence of these drains indicates that activity at the site resulted in significant amounts of water being drained onto the plaza, a feature that further suggests that the pool was used for ritual bathing.

5. Thus Reich and Shukron conclude that these columns are from the original structure, not from the later portico of the Byzantine church erected above the northern pool by Empress Eudokia.

Figure 5. The steps of the pool, looking northwest in the summer of 2008.
The entrance to the plaza between the two pools is visible in the upper
center of the photo. Photo U. von Wahlde.

pool, apparently for foot washing, was found at the very base of the scarp. Finally, the course of the exit drain from the "original" pool (at the mouth of Hezekiah's Tunnel) was uncovered and traced to its exit at the Kidron Valley.

Because the work uncovering the plaza between the northerly and southerly pool led to the discovery of the street leading to the Temple Mount (and eventually to the discovery of the sewer that lay underneath that street), and because it is not possible to excavate the pool further to the southwest until permission can be obtained to do so, it is likely that there will be no more discoveries in the area for the immediate future. So there is time to reflect on what we have learned and the questions that have arisen about these discoveries—and their significance for the Gospel of John.

THE SOURCE OF THE WATER FOR TABERNACLES

The Feast of Tabernacles was an annual event celebrated by the Jews and contained a "water rite" that involved the Pool of Siloam. Originally, Tabernacles was

Figure 6. The plaza between the two pools as it
appeared in the summer of 2008. Photo U. von Wahlde.

an agricultural feast intended to celebrate the harvest, and the booths (or "tabernacles") were intended to symbolize the huts in which the harvesters slept in the
fields during the harvest. Later it was given a historical symbolism, and the huts
were understood to symbolize the dwellings of the early Israelites as they wan-
dered in the desert.

The feast lasted eight days, and the final and greatest day of the celebration
was thought of as a distinct feast in itself. Each day during the week-long feast, a
golden pitcher was filled with water at Siloam (m. Sukkah 4:9–10). This was carried in procession to the temple. When the procession reached the water gate, the
shofar was sounded. When the procession then reached the altar, the priest took
the golden pitcher and poured the water into a silver laver that had been placed
on the altar, along with another laver for the reception of a wine offering. Both the
water and the wine were poured into the lavers, and from there they were poured
out onto the altar. On the seventh day of the festival, the procession involving the
water was more elaborate and circled the altar seven times (m. Sukkah 4:5).

In its agricultural aspect, this water ceremony was connected with the hope
for rain for the crops in the coming year. In its eschatological aspect (evident
in Zech 14), the water that was prayed for was "eschatological" water, water that

Figure 7. An artist's rendering of the pool in its original state. The rock scarp is visible to the upper left, as is the massive dam wall across the southern end of the valley. Photo U. von Wahlde.

would supersede the gift of the water of the Torah that Moses had given, and was to flow forth from Jerusalem to the western sea (i.e., the Mediterranean) and to the eastern sea (i.e., the Dead Sea).

The water for this ceremonial use during Tabernacles had to be of the highest quality, and it was drawn from the Pool of Siloam, because the pool was the only source of fresh water in Jerusalem. Because the water flowed regularly, it was recognized as "living water" and thus of the highest grade of ritual purity. There can be little doubt that this water was drawn from the more northerly pool, directly at the mouth of Hezekiah's Tunnel.

THE RELATION OF THE NORTHERN TO THE SOUTHERN POOLS

As mentioned above, the northerly pool is much smaller than the southern pool, and the water from the Gihon Spring that flows through Hezekiah's Tunnel enters into this northern pool and then exits into a channel that leads to the larger, southern pool (the *miqveh*). In two articles published on the discoveries and in personal conversation, Reich has expressed the opinion that the northern pool

Figure 8. Steps have been excavated immediately to the east of the
northern pool. These steps lead to the Temple Mount. Under them
is an extension of the first-century sewer system leading out of the
city. Josephus reports that Jews hid in the sewers during the Roman
attack in 70 c.e. The steps are broken open periodically, presumably
by the Roman soldiers looking for refugees. Photo U. von Wahlde.

had no precise function other than as a conduit to the *miqveh* (Reich and Shukron 2006, 96; see also Shanks 2005, 22). Reich argues that the waters from the
Gihon are by definition "living waters" and so cannot be defiled.[6] However, I
would propose that another explanation is more likely.

According to the Mishnah (m. Miqva'ot), "living water" is water that occurs

---

6. Our most detailed source for information regarding the validity of water for use in
attaining ritual purity comes from the Mishnah. The use of rabbinic materials to determine
usage in the first century can be dangerous, since the Mishnah was not formally collected until
about 200 c.e. At the same time, the physical configuration of almost all *miqva'ot* conforms in
detail to rules that are articulated in the Mishnah, suggesting that there was very little change.
As Sanders points out (1992, 226), the configuration of ritual pools is explained by the regulations of the Mishnah. While the regulations cannot be dated to pre-70 c.e., the pools and their
configuration can be.

naturally ("given by the hand of God") and not gathered by bucket ("drawn by the hand of man"). Living water cannot be contaminated and always remains valid for ritual purification. Thus, the waters of a river were considered "living" because of the current in the river. Such water could not be contaminated ritually. The same was true of the waters in the sea. They also could not be rendered ritually impure. A third category of living water was that given in rainfall. It was also considered "living" because it was given by the hand of God and was also "running." Finally, water from springs was also considered "living," again because it was given by God and not provided by human effort.

However, there were certain circumstances under which living water ceased to be considered "living" and so could be contaminated. According to m. Miqv. 1:4, "The water in ponds, the water in cisterns, the water in ditches, the water in caverns, rain-ponds after the rain-stream has stopped, and pools holding less than forty *seahs* are alike in this, that while the rain continues all are deemed clean" (trans. Danby 1993, 732). While rainwater continues to flow, nothing can invalidate it, but once the water has stopped, it ceases to be "living water." It may still be "clean," but it is susceptible to contamination. If the pool or cistern or ditch or cavern had an exit through which the water could continue to flow, then the water would continue to be considered "living" as long as it flowed. But if the stream of water was stopped up, then the water became a "pool." Like the rainwater, it might be "clean," but it was no longer "living."

A second qualification of "living waters" concerned springs that were intermittent. According to m. Parah 8:9, "intermittent waters"[7] were not valid. That is, they were not valid for cases where "living water" was needed (see Danby 1933, 707 n. 9). "They are deemed intermittent waters that fail [even] once in a week of years; but they that have failed only in times of war or in years of drought are valid" (trans. Danby 1933, 707).

Although the Gihon Spring was the only source of water in Jerusalem, and although it regularly delivered abundant water, the Gihon was an intermittent spring. The Hebrew name of the spring is derived from the verb meaning "to gush forth." Thus the name itself seems to reflect its intermittent character. The intermittent nature of the spring has been noted regularly throughout history. In 333 C.E., the Bordeaux Pilgrim commented: "This spring flows six days and nights, the seventh is, indeed, a Sabbath: throughout the entirety, both night and day, it does not flow."[8] It is likely that this is an exaggerated view of the rhythm

---

7. "Lit. 'disappointing waters' whose flow is not to be relied upon. The term is derived from Is. 58.11" (Danby 1933, 707 n. 15).

8. *Itinerarium Burdigalense* 592.2–3 (CCEL 175:16): "et deorsum in valle iuxta murum est piscina, quae dicitur Siloa; habet quadriporticum; et alia piscina grandis foras. Haec fons sex diebus atque noctibus currit, septima vero die est sabbatum: in totum nec nocte nec die currit." The translations from the Latin are my own.

of the spring; nevertheless, it points to the fact that the flow into the pool was observed to be intermittent.

In the mid-fifth century, Eucherius, bishop of Lyons, commented in his description of Jerusalem: "at the base of the hill the spring of Siloam pours forth, which comes forth irregularly and flows off to the south."[9] Around 570 c.e., the anonymous pilgrim of Piacenza describes the pool(s) of Siloam and states that "in those pools, at fixed times, the spring pours forth much water."[10]

The geological reason for this irregularity is that the Gihon Spring is a siphonic spring created by underground water collecting in a karst.[11] When the water level reaches the top of the karst, it is siphoned off through cracks in the rock.[12] Thus, water gushes out into Hezekiah's Tunnel until the karst is emptied. At that point, the water ceases to flow until the karst fills again and the process is repeated. The water from the spring would be considered living water when it gushes, but after the flow stops, the water remaining would be considered a "pool."[13] The water in the northern Pool of Siloam would be considered "living" while the spring gushed forth, and it would continue to be considered "pure" (but not "living") even after the flow stopped, provided it was protected from contact with impurities. However, if it became impure, it would be rendered pure again by the next flow of the spring. Thus, it would be possible for the water in both the northern and southern pools to be rendered impure, but at the same time, it could be purified by the next flow of living water from Hezekiah's Tunnel.

However, the Mishnah also provided a ruling by which, if the water in a *miqveh* was contaminated in any way, it could be rendered pure again. This was done by means of establishing contact between the water of the *miqveh* and pure, ritually clean water in an adjoining pool, known as an *otzer*.[14] This contact would be created by a pipe connecting the two pools. According to the Mishnah, opening the pipe and allowing the water from the *otzer* to come into brief contact with

---

9. *Eucherii de Situ Hierusolimae Epistula* 9 (CCEL 175:238): "ad radices collis fons Siloa prorumpit, qui alternante aquarum accessu in meridiem occurrit."

10. *Antonini Placentini Itinerarium* 24 (CCEL 175:142): "nam in illis soliis certis horis fons ipsa inrigat aquas multas."

11. A "karst" may be defined as an area in a rock formation that has been hollowed out by the erosive power of water.

12. See Gill 1994; 1996, 128. Dan Gill is a senior geologist with the Geological Survey of Israel in Jerusalem.

13. Wilkinson (1978, 121) notes that Josephus (*J. W.* 5.145) calls the (northern) Pool of Siloam a *pēgē* ("spring") rather than a pool. Wilkinson suggests that by the time of Josephus, people may have thought that the water of the northern pool emanated from a spring at that place. This would not alter the view that the water in the northern pool was intermittent.

14. This was particularly useful in small, private *miqva'ot*, where the water in the *miqveh* needed to be replenished. The *miqveh* could be filled with drawn (and therefore "not pure") water, but then, by opening the channel to the *otzer*, the drawn water was brought into contact with the water in the *otzer* and was then considered ritually pure.

the water in the *miqveh* purified the water in the *miqveh* itself. While clearing out the channel between the northern and southern pools, Reich and Shukron discovered that the channel forked, with one branch leading to the southern pool and the other continuing along the scarp and into the Kidron. The two branches were the same size, and each channel had vertical notches cut into the sides opposite one another so that each branch could be closed by the insertion of a board into the notches. While this device could have had the more mundane purpose of preventing the southern pool from overflowing when water from the spring was abundant, it would also permit the kind of closure and contact required for an *otzer*.

However, as was indicated above, water from an intermittent spring was "living" only while the water was running. When the flow stopped, it remained pure (unless defiled), but it was no longer considered living water. As a result, it is very likely that the northern pool was not understood simply as a conduit from Hezekiah's Tunnel to the *miqveh* but was conceived of rabbinically as an *otzer* for the *miqveh* to the south.

Of course, the function of the northern pool as an *otzer* in no way prevented that pool from being used as the source of water for the water ceremony at Tabernacles. Since the water was pure and might well be "living" (running) at the time of the gathering of the water, it would be the purest, highest grade of water in the city and the water most apt for the water ceremony.

THE DEPRESSIONS IN THE STEPS OF THE SOUTHERN POOL

In articles in *Biblical Archaeology Review* and in *Qadmoniot*, Reich and Shukron raise the question of how the issue of privacy could be addressed in such a *miqveh*, given the Jewish abhorrence of public nudity.[15] For Reich and Shukron, this abhorrence of nudity makes it difficult to conceptualize the process of public immersion in such a pool. As a possible solution, Reich and Shukron have pointed to indentations in the stone steps, which they have described as "sockets," and have suggested that these were used to create some sort of screen to allow such ritual bathing in private.[16]

However, I would argue that the presumption that ritual bathing always had to be done in the nude is a false one and needlessly complicates our understanding of the process of immersion. While those purifying themselves in smaller, private *miqva'ot* undoubtedly did so without clothing, there are several indications that there was no *requirement* that ritual purification be done unclothed in order for the purification to be valid.

It must be said, first, that the Bible itself says nothing about this issue. How-

---

15. This position is also taken by Sanders 1992, 225, and Gibson 2005, 279.
16. Photos of these indentations are given in Reich and Shukron 2006, 94.

ever, we do have indirect information from other sources. While discussing the celibate community of Essenes, Josephus states that, when the men purify themselves, they wear a loincloth (*J. W.* 2.8.5 §129) given to them when they entered the community (2.8.5 §138). When discussing those Essenes who married, he states that when men purify themselves they wear a loincloth and that when women purify themselves they wear a dress (*J. W.* 2.8.13 §161). It is generally recognized that the rules of the community at Qumran regarding ritual purity were stricter than those of other sectors of Judaism (see Harrington 2004, 12–23). If this is so, then the fact that the Essenes could wear a loincloth/dress during ritual bathing would indicate that this was almost certainly possible also for other Jews whose interpretation of the law was less strict than that of the Essenes.

Evidence from the Mishnah provides a second, independent indication that clothing was allowed. Although composed later than the first century, m. Miqva'ot is the most detailed discussion of ritual bathing we have, and it agrees with what we know from other sources regarding ritual immersion in the first century. This tractate addresses the issue of what interposes between an unclean object and the water of purification and in doing so implies that clothing was allowed.

The main concern regarding ritual immersion was that the water be able to contact all parts of the person or object. For example, pitch that was stuck to a vessel would "interpose," and therefore the vessel would not be considered clean even after immersion, since the pitch prevented the water from reaching one part of the surface of the vessel.[17]

The same principle was applied to objects that would interpose between the human body and water. M. Miqv. 9:1–4 speaks of those things that interpose "in the case of a human creature" (Danby 1933, 742). For example, if a person clamped any parts of the body together (e.g., one's fingers or lips) so that water could not reach between the parts, or if a person immersed while holding some of one's hair in one's closed mouth, the person would not be rendered clean. But the Mishnah also addressed the issue of clothing. It was the common opinion of the rabbis that strips of wool or linen "interposed" between the skin and the water, so the person remained unclean. These would be strips that were bound closely to the skin, rather than loose clothing. The only reason for such a ruling would be that it was common for people to wear some items of clothing while immersing. However, Rabbi Judah argued that even strips of wool did not interpose, since the water could penetrate them (m. Miqv. 9:1). If this was true of strips wrapped closely to the body, then all the more so would a loose-fitting garment be allowed.[18]

---

17. M. Miqv. 9:5; see also the second part of m. Miqv. 8:5 regarding holding a vessel loosely during immersion (to allow water to contact the entire surface of the vessel).

18. It could well have been that clothes that were considered impure would also be purified by the immersion process.

Third, it is significant that many of the *miqva'ot* discovered by archaeologists have a low partition down the center of the stairs. It is recognized that this partition was to separate those entering the pool from those exiting. If the pool was in use by a number of people at the same time, certainly the people would not have been totally unclothed. Thus, it seems that the very structure of the *miqva'ot* suggests that some sort of a loose garment was worn into the pool.

Finally, E. P. Sanders proposes that not all elements of the strictest interpretation of the rules for ritual purity were observed by all Jews. Beginning during the Maccabean period, attitudes toward purity began to change. What had been originally intended for the priests began to be legislated for others. The priests were bound to the strictest interpretation; next were the Pharisees; finally, there was the general populace.[19] While it is true that the rules were being extended to include new groups of people, Sanders is probably correct that the rules of purity would be less rigorously enforced for the general populace than they would be for the priests. This also argues for the allowance of some clothing rather than none at all. Again, if the Essenes represent the strictest interpretation of ritual bathing and they allowed clothing, then we can be reasonably certain that other more lenient sectors would do so also.

In first-century Palestine, clothing typically consisted of two garments: an undergarment (the *chitōn* or *hypendytēs*) and an outer garment (the *himation* or *ependytēs*). The *chitōn* was the basic garment, worn against the skin, and consisted of a flat panel of cloth in front and rear, sewn at the shoulder line with an opening for the head and wide enough to extend beyond the shoulder and cover the upper arm. Although for older persons it might extend to the ankles, on a younger male the tunic might reach only to mid-calf. It was held in place by a belt and was often gathered up so that it flowed over and hid the belt. The *himation* was a long, rectangular cloth that served as the outer garment and could be worn either across both shoulders or off one shoulder to expose the upper part of the tunic underneath. It could be pulled up over the head in inclement weather.

Both of these garments were loose-fitting and would allow proper circulation of water during immersion. Of course, only one garment would need to be worn. One can imagine that a male would wrap the *himation* around himself as a loincloth and immerse, replacing the *chitōn* after he emerged from the water.[20] Thus he would have dry clothing next to the skin and the *himation* could be allowed

---

19. The extension of this practice to the general populace is almost certainly what is referred to in Mark 7:3 as "keeping the tradition of the elders" (as opposed to commandments).

20. This would seem to be the arrangement envisioned in the Gospel of John (21:7), where Peter, who was in a boat fishing, having been informed that Jesus was on shore, "tightened his outer garment around himself (for he was wearing only that) and threw himself into the sea" (Σίμων οὖν Πέτρος … τὸν ἐπενδύτην διεζώσατο, ἦν γὰρ γυμνός, καὶ ἔβαλεν ἑαυτὸν εἰς τὴν θάλασσαν). Literally, the text says that Peter was naked (γυμνός). However, the text probably means that Peter was wearing the *ependytēs* as a loincloth as he worked (because the *hypendytēs*

to dry, perhaps while over the shoulders. Alternatively, the man could remove his belt and *himation* and then immerse while wearing only the *chitōn*. After emerging from the pool, he would take up his belt and *himation* and simply allow the *chitōn* to dry in the air. In either case, the immersion would be valid because of the loose-fitting clothing, and the problem of public nudity would be avoided.

There is also a third possibility that may be even more likely. It was thought that the clothing of ordinary people was almost always in a state of uncleanness. If a person immersed and then put on unclean clothing, one would again be rendered impure. However, if immersion was done while clothed, both the person and the clothing would be rendered pure.

As a result, it seems unlikely that a provision would have had to be made at a large, public *miqveh* for the privacy necessary for immersion while totally nude. It may be that the indentations in the stone were part of a kind of railing that would divide the steps so as to keep those entering the pool (and so unclean) separate from those exiting (and now clean). But this must remain speculative. Certainly such railings were not essential, and there are no remains of such railings evident either at the *miqveh* in the southern basin of Bethesda or in the *miqveh* near the Hulda Gates.

The History of the Water Installations in the Birkat al-Hamra

Although it has only recently been discovered that the Pool of Siloam was a *miqveh* from the second century B.C.E., this is hardly the whole of the pool's history. Rather, the area had a long history before the second century B.C.E.; this not only aids our understanding of the pool itself, but it is also a significant contribution to the understanding of water installations in the city of Jerusalem in general. Finally, this history further aids our understanding of the development of attitudes toward ritual purity within Judaism in the two centuries before Jesus.

First Period (ca. 1900 b.c.e.–ca. 721 b.c.e.)

As pointed out above, the Gihon Spring is the only continuing source of water in the Ophel Ridge and is almost certainly the reason that the earliest city was located there rather than on Mount Zion, the hill to the west, which is more easily defended than the Ophel. Because the Gihon Spring is the only source of water, it was determined to gather its waters more efficiently than could be done at the mouth of the spring itself, so a channel was cut through the rock along the eastern side of the Ophel Ridge. The channel is identified variously as "Channel II," "Solomon's Tunnel," "the Siloam Channel," and the "Tunnel of Achaz." For part of

---

would have been awkward). Then, before he entered the water to swim to shore, he tied the *ependytēs* tighter around him.

its run the channel is open on the top, while at other places it is a true tunnel.[21] It leads to the area of the Birkat al-Hamra and exits near the southeastern corner of the rock scarp. Reich and Shukron have dated this channel to approximately 1900 B.C.E. The exit point for this channel is still quite evident today, even from a distance. In their excavations in 1894–97, Bliss and Dickie uncovered a massive dam crossing the Tyropoean Valley just to the east of this outlet, confirming that in the earliest period the area had served as a reservoir (the Birkat al-Hamra).

SECOND PERIOD (CA. 721 B.C.E.–CA. 100 B.C.E.)

The second period of installations in the area is represented by the construction of Hezekiah's Tunnel. This took place about the year 700 B.C.E. The purpose of the tunnel was to provide water that was safeguarded the entire length of its movement from the Gihon Spring to the tip of the City of David. At that time, a pool was constructed there (the Birkat Silwan).

At roughly the same time, the Birkat al-Hamra was allowed to dry up and fall into disuse. Kathleen Kenyon excavated the western part of the Birkat al-Hamra in the 1960s and reported evidence that the area was dry during that period.

THIRD PERIOD (CA. 100 B.C.E.–70 C.E.)

In the third period of the area's history, the Birkat al-Hamra was rehabilitated and turned into a stepped pool. As mentioned above, the *terminus post quem* for the construction of this stepped pool is approximately 100 B.C.E., as determined by the Hasmonean coins found in the plaster of the lower part of the pool. Recall that during its existence, the steps in the pool were resurfaced with rock once after the original plastered construction. During this period, both the Birkat Silwan and the Birkat al-Hamra were in operation. What is most important for our purposes is that the second pool had been converted from a reservoir to a very large stepped pool.

This period ended with the destruction of the city by the Romans in 70 C.E. In fact, Josephus writes that the Romans "set all on fire as far as Siloam" (*J. W.* 6.7.2). That the pool went out of use at this time is attested by the presence of coins dating from the second, third, and fourth years of the first Jewish Revolt in debris in the pool. The one commonly shown is a *prutah*, from the second year

---

21. In those places where the channel was open to the sky, it was roofed over by immense boulders that were wedged into the top and then covered with soil and plants. Periodically, "windows" were cut into the side to allow water to irrigate the fields along the eastern slope of the Ophel. It was probably those windows that irrigated the King's Garden, which lay along the southern end of the Ophel.

of the revolt. Thus during this third period both pools were in use, but water was supplied only by Hezekiah's Tunnel.

FOURTH PERIOD (70 C.E.–430 C.E.)

We know nothing about the pools from the destruction of the city of Jerusalem until the early fourth century. With the conversion of Constantine to Christianity and the devotion to the holy sites shown by his mother, Helena, interest in the Holy Land was stimulated, and devout individuals began to visit Jerusalem and to write accounts of their visits. Even so, the only report from this period is the account of the Bordeaux Pilgrim, who visited Jerusalem in 330 and reported two pools at the site.

FIFTH PERIOD (430 C.E.–2004 C.E.)

After a passage of time about which we know very little, a fifth period begins with the account of the visit by Bishop Eucherius around 430. He also visited Siloam, but in his account he mentions only the northern pool and says the water from that pool drained off into the Kidron Valley. About seventeen years later, the empress Eudokia built a church extending partly over the northern pool. From that time on, the northern pool continues in existence and is mentioned repeatedly in commentaries and other studies as "the Pool of Siloam." There is no mention of a southern pool at this time or in the future—*until* the excavations of 2004.

Thus we can see that from pre-Israelite times, this area had been used to store the abundant but precious water from the Gihon Spring. But with the increased concern for ritual purity in the century before Jesus, what had previously been a reservoir was converted to an enormous public *miqveh*. Thus, the pool stands as a monument to, and as archaeological evidence for, the statement of m. Šabb. 13b that during this period "purity broke out in Israel."

THE POOL AND THE GOSPEL OF JOHN

Finally, we turn to the value of the discoveries at Siloam for the Gospel of John. The first benefit from the discovery is the simple confirmation that the reference to the Pool in the Gospel of John is not fictional. But in one sense, that was already known—or at least half of the story (the northern pool) was known.

The second benefit is that now we have much more precise knowledge about the nature of what actually existed at Siloam, so we are able to understand more fully what the first-century reader would have understood when he or she heard that the man blind from birth was sent to Siloam to wash. The Pool of Siloam was not simply some undeveloped pool where water emerged from the rock face of the hillside and where it was possible to gather water. In the time of Jesus, there was an entire complex surrounding the pools, a complex that was much more imposing than it is today. It was the terminal point of a monumental staircase leading up to the Temple Mount. In addition, the pool area itself consisted not just of one pool but of a fully developed *otzer* and *miqveh* complex, surrounded by a stone plaza and evidently having a portico on at least one side. The fine construction of the drains in the stone pavement, as well as the size of the *miqveh* itself, indicate that this was a major part of the religious life of first-century Jerusalem.

But why did Jesus send the man to the Pool of Siloam to wash? If the purpose of the washing were simply to remove the mud Jesus had placed on his eyes, any source of water would have been sufficient (see Reich and Shukron 2006, 96). However, because the man was blind, he would have been presumed to be in a perpetual state of uncleanness. The blind were considered constantly impure because they were not able to see the myriad sources of impurity that they would confront in their daily life. If they were to touch the impure, they would be rendered unclean; further, if they were to walk into a house where there was a corpse or unknowingly be touched by the shadow of a corpse, these acts would also render them unclean—without ever knowing it. Ritual washing before entering the temple area would be a special need for such people.[22]

To send the man to a *miqveh* would be understandable, since the man would be presumed in need of ritual cleansing. To send the man to the *Pool of Siloam* would be all the more appropriate, since it was the place par excellence for cleansing. Even though the Pool of Bethesda, north of the Temple Mount, was a *miqveh* and would have served for a mud-washing, the Pool of Siloam was fed by the waters of the Gihon; the water there had a special quality to it, since it would be rendered clean every time the spring gushed forth.

To be ritually purified would mean a temporary reprieve from the man's presumed impurity. However, when the man washes he finds more than ordinary purity; he finds that he has been cured of the very infirmity that had made him constantly impure ritually. He is now radically cleansed in a way that the *miqveh* of Siloam could never do.

Thus, our appreciation of the healing in John 9 is increased significantly by the discovery that this pool was more than simply a pool: it was a *miqveh*. And in such a context, the precise implication of the man's blindness also becomes all the more significant, since he would be presumed more than ordinarily in need of ritual purification.[23]

---

22. Reich and Shukron (2006, 96) understand the sending of the man to the pool as ordering the purification necessary after a healing. However, the man is not cured until after he washes the mud from his eyes.

23. As I hope to show in a future article, the Pool of Bethesda, now also recognized to be a *miqveh*, had a history similar to that of the Birkat al-Hamra, and the fact that the Gospel of John, alone among the Gospels, makes reference to Jesus' activity at these two *miqva'ot* is quite significant for not only confirming the topographical accuracy of the Gospel but also for revealing an interest in the relationship between Jesus' healing and the activity associated with such *miqva'ot*.

The Overrealized Expulsion in the Gospel of John

Edward W. Klink III

Introduction: J. Louis Martyn and the "Expulsion from the Synagogue"[1]

When reading John 9, Martyn finds as blatantly anachronistic a key term in 9:22, ἀποσυνάγωγος ("from the synagogue"; also in 12:42 and 16:2a). Although in the narrative this term describes an event during Jesus' earthly ministry, for Martyn (2003, 65) it is most certainly dealing with an event that could not have occurred until decades after Jesus' life. Martyn is convinced that the first-century readers of the Fourth Gospel would have seen the "expulsion from the synagogue" term as an anachronistic insertion into the narrative. In many ways, the "expulsion from the synagogue" in 9:22 is the key to his reading of the Fourth Gospel. Although Martyn's understanding of ἀποσυνάγωγος has been heavily criticized by historians of first-century Judaism and early Christianity, his reading is still the dominant reading of this Gospel. Because of the tendency for the second level of history to eclipse the first, such criticisms provide warrant for a fresh appraisal of the historical "glimpses" provided by the Fourth Gospel's narrative. This essay will argue that Martyn has guided us to an overrealized reading of the "expulsion from the synagogue" passages.

Consensual Criticism of a Consensus

Among his critics, there has been almost unanimous agreement that Martyn's treatment of the Birkat Haminim in John 9 is historically inaccurate.[2] Several major critiques of Martyn's use of the Birkat Haminim have challenged its his-

---

1. For a more extensive version of this essay, see Klink 2008.
2. Martyn was not the first to place these "expulsion" passages in the context of Jewish-Christian dialogue involving the Fourth Gospel. The earliest example can be found in Wrede 1933, who argued that Jews in John reflected a Johannine conflict with contemporary Judaism. But it was Carroll 1957 who aligned the "expulsion" passages with the Birkat Haminim. At nearly the same time Smith 1959 made a similar connection.

torical inferences,[3] and several other studies have challenged its analysis of early Jewish-Christian relations.[4] Although Johannine scholars were enthusiastic for a proposal that seemed to work, rabbinic experts and other historians have been less than persuaded. Several irresolvable problems were noted concerning Martyn's thesis: doubt concerning the kind of general authority to be given to the Jamnia Academy within the first century; the date of the Twelfth Benediction and the improbability of it being composed as early as the 80s of the first century; the lack of direct evidence that the Benediction was formulated for the purpose of removing Christians from the synagogue or that it was ever used that way; the inability to limit the meaning of *minim* to anything less than "heretic"; and the late date of the pertinent sources.

The developing response over the last few decades to Martyn's thesis and the Johannine link to the Jewish-Christian split can now be stated in two related points.[5] First, interpreters have consistently credited Christianity, their primary interest, with too great a role in Jewish developments after 70 C.E. As Stephen Wilson (1995, 180–81) argues, the Jamnia sages "were not obsessed with Christians and certainly not with them alone. Apart from promoting a number of complex and necessary adjustments to postwar conditions, they also had to deal with Gnostics, apocalypticists, hellenizers, and various other 'nonrabbinic,' but thoroughly Jewish, groups." A statement by Reuven Kimelman is more to the point: There is a "lack of evidence for any formative impact of Christianity on any major element of tannaitic Judaism.... This itself is sufficient to question the thesis that *birkat ha-minim* was primarily directed against Christianity. We must be careful of anachronistically overestimating the impact of Christianity on Judaism in the first two centuries" (Kimelman 1981, 233, emphasis added).

Second, the influence of the Jamnia sages between 70 and 135 C.E. and beyond should not be overestimated. Again, according to Wilson (1995, 181), "The rabbinic account of the *Birkat ha-minim* is ... a retrospective, punctiliar summary of what was in reality a lengthy process. The spread of their influence was gradual and almost certainly did not encompass all Jewish communities until well beyond the second century." Daniel Boyarin (2001) wants to make Wilson's conclusion even more explicit, claiming that the process was lengthy and that the earliest evidence is from the mid-third century, not before. The above discussion of problems might be described as a rethinking of how Judaism worked toward

---

3. For the critiques of Martyn's use of the Birkat Haminim and its general use in the first century, see Stemberger 1977; Schäfer 1978; Kimelman 1981; Horbury 1982; Katz 1984; Wilson 1995; Motyer 1997; and Boyarin 2001. Yet even amidst all these reservations, Martyn 2003 (60 n. 69, 61–62 n.75) only speaks with caution, and Meeks 1985 (93–115) merely prefers to think of a linear development in which the promulgation of the Birkat Haminim was a culmination rather than the beginning of a development.

4. Mayo 2006; also Aune 1991; van der Horst 1998.

5. The following is adapted from Wilson 1995, 180–81.

self-definition. The overrealized role of the Birkat Haminim as argued by Martyn is unable to accurately depict this Jewish-Christian controversy of identity.

"Expulsion" in the Johannine Narrative

A further critique of Martyn's thesis is the almost complete narrative impotence of the "expulsion" motif in the rest of the Fourth Gospel.[6] If the "expulsion from the synagogue" is a hermeneutical key to the Gospel, as argued by Martyn and assumed thereafter, then it should be evident in the whole narrative of John, not just in that one pericope. Even more, the "expulsion" motif should be a controlling force over the rest of the narrative; other passages should, by necessity, function in light of the reality posited behind John 9.

One of the only treatments of the disjunction between the reading by Martyn and the rest of the Johannine narrative has been done by Adele Reinhartz (1998; 2004), where she applies Martyn's two-level reading strategy to the whole of the Gospel of John. Reinhartz examines two passages in particular and subjects them to the two-level reading strategy proposed by Martyn. The first passage Reinhartz examines is John 11:1–44, the story of the raising of Lazarus. This passage tells of the sisters, Mary and Martha, who are in mourning for their recently deceased brother, Lazarus. Although apparently known to be related to Jesus, even called his beloved, these women have clearly not been excluded from the Jewish community, as evidenced by the fact that they are comforted in their grief by "many of the Jews" (11:19). As Reinhartz explains,

> If we apply the two-level reading method to this passage, we arrive at a scenario whereby the sisters represent the Johannine believers, of the Johannine community towards the end of the first century, and the Jews who comfort them represent the majority of the Jewish community that does not believe Jesus to be the messiah. If, as the consensus view asserts, Christ-confessors had already been excluded from the synagogue and hence from the Jewish community as a whole, how is it that these two women are surrounded by Jewish mourners? (2004, 9–10)

The second passage Reinhartz examines is John 12:11, which states that on account of Jesus "many of the Jews were going over to Jesus and putting their faith in him." They believed in Jesus because they witnessed Jesus raise Lazarus from the dead. As Reinhartz explains,

> In this case, the narrator, perhaps representing the views of the evangelist and/or the Johannine community, views belief in Jesus as the Christ as incompatible

---

6. For a more detailed analysis of the key texts that Martyn uses to establish the community's plot, see Klink 2007.

with membership in the Jewish community, yet it does not refer in any way to an official Jewish policy of expulsion. On the contrary, it refers to Christ-confessing Jews as deserters—presumably from the Jewish community. (2004, 10)

Neither of these two passages is able to function with Martyn's two-level reading. In fact, if we are consistent with Martyn's reading strategy, we get two different "glimpses" of the Johannine situation, and a third if we include Martyn's own examination of the specific "expulsion from the synagogue" passages. Thus, it appears that we have either a very complex set of relationships between the Jews and Johannine Christians portrayed in the narrative, or the historical reconstruction proposed by Martyn is impossible to harmonize with the narrative as a whole.

Even more might be deduced by examining the narrative progression in John. Martyn's analysis of the narrative parts creates a completely different narrative whole. It is interesting that several times Martyn claims (2003, 85) that he is not doing decoding work. Martyn's reconstruction would construct the narratives in the following chapter order: 9, 12, 16, 5, and 7. Although first in the narrative order, chapters 5 and 7 are actually later stages in the Johannine community's experience, according to Martyn. It is 16:2b that links the three "expulsion" passages (9:22; 12:42; 16:2a) with chapters 5 and 7. Thus, the progression necessarily moves against the flow of the first level of the narrative, but when the narrative shows a necessary progression in its development, Martyn's narrative "reordering" becomes problematic. For example, an examination of the character of Nicodemus reveals that it is developed as the narrative progresses: chapters 3, 7, and 19. The narrative assumes that the reader has followed its own progression. Helpful here is the discussion of the narrative's progression or plot development by Alan Culpepper (1983, 89–97), who argues that John has a narrative development that is vital to its individual parts. Martyn disrupts the narrative's plot development for his own plot—a plot not found in the narrative of the Fourth Gospel. The realization that the Martyn "expulsion" thesis has been so successfully criticized, at the level of both history and narrative, forces us to examine further the exact nature of this "expulsion from the synagogue."

"Expulsion" in Judaism and Earliest Christianity

What the consensual criticism and narrative analysis has demonstrated is that Martyn has been anachronistic in positing a broad Jewish-Christian conflict from as late as the fourth century onto a late-first-century Johannine text. This is no small miscalculation that merely requires an adjustment on the same line of linear development, as Barnabas Lindars (1981, esp. 50–51) and especially Wayne Meeks (1985, 102) have argued; it reflects a distortion of the type of Jewish-Christian tension reflected in the Gospel. We hardly need Martyn's thesis to tell us that the Fourth Gospel reflects tensions between Jews and Christians.

What is needed is a fresh examination of the possible concepts of "expulsion" in the first century and a reflection on the nature of a heretic, or *min.*

THE CONCEPT OF EXPULSION

The problem with the term ἀποσυνάγωγος is that we have no other literary evidence for its potential sense. Recent study has furthered our understanding of Jewish conflicts, even conflict between differing Jewish groups. The historical criticisms mentioned above tend to emphasize one important point: the Jewish-Christian conflicts in the first century reveal complex tensions that appear to have been intra-Jewish in nature. It was a familial conflict. As Kimelman (1981, 239) explains, "there is abundant evidence from patristic sources that Christians were frequenting the synagogues quite often. Indeed, there is far-flung evidence that it was the church leadership that strove to keep Christians away from the synagogue and not Jews who were excluding them." Although this evidence is from after the first century, it may show a more accurate linear progression—one of continuing conflict through interrelation and dialogue. Although a shift eventually occurred, it was not until long after the first century. In fact, Daniel Boyarin (2001, 438–39) argues convincingly that the evidence from Justin Martyr and other sources reflects not a Jamnia-type break between Jews and Christians but a gradual development of the idea of a "heretic." According to Boyarin, it was not until the third or fourth century that "heretic" meant anything different from "a party or sect marked by common ideas and aims." Thus, as Boyarin (2001, 439–40) explains, "It follows that in the later part of the first century the notion of heresy had not yet entered (pre)-rabbinic Judaism, and that the term *min*—only attested … in the late second-century sources—is in fact a later development in Jewish religious discourses."

The evidence[7] from the second to the fifth century "makes it apparent that Christians and Jews continued to have contact with each other well into the fifth century" (Wilken 1971, 36) and that both Christians and Jews devoted a good part of their exegetical, theological, and "ecclesial" endeavors to dealing with their continued shared existence. This is a difference in kind from Martyn's thesis, which posits two distinct and unrelated entities in conflict during the first century: Judaism and Christianity. The linear progression modification of Meeks is only different in degree, for he too is forced to assume a fairly monolithic understanding of each group, just at a more localized level. But the evidence does not seem to reflect such a reality, at least not for a full century or more after John. Rather, the evidence from history reveals a familial conflict that took centuries to define.

---

7. For specific examples, see Klink 2008.

"Heretic" as an Intra-Jewish Concept

It appears, then, that our examination of the Jewish-Christian conflict represented by John must take into account the intra-Jewish nature of such first-century tensions. What has been at the center of the discussion is the enigmatic term *minim*. Thus far we have confirmed that the term can only anachronistically be limited to "Christian" in the late first century. Rather, it seems to have been used with the more generic sense of "heretic." A recent article by David Instone-Brewer (2003) provides some helpful definition to the use of the term even *before* 70 c.e. Instone-Brewer examines the fragment of one version of the Eighteen Benedictions, which he calls "Schechter's Geniza fragment,"[8] that appears to preserve wording originating from the Second Temple period. When comparing the fragment with the earliest Babylonian version of the Benedictions, Instone-Brewer (2003, 34) notes that there is a change in language about the temple, specifically in benediction 14, where the Geniza fragment assumes that the temple is still standing, whereas the Babylonian version, with its phrase "return in compassion and build her soon in our days," assumes it is destroyed. This strongly suggests that the text of the Geniza fragment originated before 70 c.e. More important, and directly related to this essay, is what Instone-Brewer suggests concerning the use of the term *minim* in benediction 12, namely, that the term refers to the Sadducees when they had the high priesthood during the Second Temple period. Instone-Brewer (2003, 42) admits that the term *minim* was flexible, and "In later rabbinic writings the ... term ... *Minim* continued to be used, either as a general reference to 'heretics,' or as a reference to Christians." This shows at least two things. First, the term *minim* performed an important function in the midst of intra-Jewish conflict between various "groups" and was flexible enough to be able to refer to a diverse number of groups: Sadducees, Samaritans, and Christians all had the honor.[9] Second, the term both originated and functioned before 70 c.e., well before the time scholars assume the Gospel of John was written, in the earlier part of the Christian movement.

The above discussion has only confirmed that the Jewish-Christian conflict portrayed in the Gospel of John must reflect an intra-Jewish tension that was common in and around the time of the Gospel's origin. Not only does the historical evidence require the rejection of a singular expulsion verdict as argued by Martyn, but it also requires the rejection of the modified version proposed by

---

8. As Instone-Brewer admits, "The origins and original wording of the Eighteen are probably now impossible to reconstruct, though their form goes back before the first century.... However, it is also likely that the areas where variation was permitted were carefully limited, and local versions would become popular and semi-fixed" (2003, 26).

9. Instone-Brewer 2003, 39. For similar evidence from the Mishnah, see Boyarin 2001, 440–46.

Meeks and others, who see the verdict as a linear progression between two established groups. Rather, the Jewish-Christian tension in the first century was part of the larger intra-Jewish tension between related members with common familial roots. To describe the warring parties as unrelated groups is anachronistic.

A Most Common Anachronism: John, Jesus, and History

As we return to the enigmatic "expulsion from the synagogue" passages in the Fourth Gospel, we approach them with a refreshed paradigm for understanding the Jewish-Christian conflict in the first century as an intra-Jewish conflict in existence well before 70 c.e. An immediate result of the above discussion is that the term ἀποσυνάγωγος, which according to Martyn reflects a tension that could not have occurred before the late first century, can no longer qualify as an anachronism.[10] On the contrary, tension in and around "the synagogue" was a most common event between Jewish groups, including first-century Christians, a group defining itself both within and beyond what we now call Judaism. This explains why the rest of the Johannine narrative not only is unaffected by what should have been the controlling influence of the "expulsion" passages but also is seen to conflict with the second-level drama assumed by Martyn.

So what kind of tension is John portraying? One of the key issues for Martyn was the use of the adverb ἤδη ("already") in 9:22. For Martyn, ἤδη emphasizes that the "agreement" or "decision" made by the Jews had been reached at some time prior to John's writing, but if this "decision" was the Birkat Haminim, such a suggestion is blatantly anachronistic. However, if we cannot begin with the assumption that the "agreement" is as formal as the Birkat Haminim, then we need not read the expression as an anachronism. Martyn understands this agreement to be specifically for John and his readers, but the above examination of expulsion and heresy forces a rethinking of such a conclusion. It would appear that it is better to assume that the Jewish-Christian conflict portrayed in John was a general feature of intra-Jewish disputes in the first century. Even more, although these disputes certainly intensified as "Christianity" grew and became more unified, it is likely that the tension had existed from the very beginning of the Christian movement. As Philip Alexander explains:

> It is abundantly clear from the New Testament itself that Christianity before 70 not only attracted support but also encountered strong and widespread opposition within the Jewish community. That opposition ranged from central authorities in Jerusalem to the leaders of the local synagogues. It extended from Palestine to the Diaspora. *It began in the time of Jesus himself and continued unabated in the period after the crucifixion.* (1992, 19)

---

10. This corrects Martyn at the literary level as well; see also Hägerland 2003.

More specifically, D. Neale has argued convincingly that during Jesus' lifetime he was considered to be a *mesith*, one who led people astray, based upon an examination of the Gospel accounts with reference to Deut 13. According to Neale,

> The examination of some New Testament texts that reflect a negative response to Jesus in light of literary traditions about the *mesith* … shows a reasonable possibility that the hatred reserved for the biblical *mesith* could have been directed toward Jesus. Furthermore, some enigmatic aspects of the public response to Jesus' ministry are made comprehensible in the light of this interpretation. Deuteronomy 13 and the subsequent *mesith* tradition provide a valuable addition to our basis for understanding the familial turmoil, civic unrest and personal struggle with loyalty at which the gospels hint.[11] (1993, 101)

Such an understanding of Jesus requires only that he was viewed as a problem, a *mesith*, in his Jewish-familial context. Martyn (2003, 77–79) notices similar language in the Fourth Gospel and claims that the phrase that describes Jesus as the one who is "leading the people astray" in John 7 "reflects the contemporary drama" in John's own day. Yet Martyn is willing to admit that Paul himself had been called a deceiver (2 Cor 6:8; 1 Thess 2:3).[12]

Maybe even more important to our reading of John 9 is Neale's discussion of the treatment of those connected to the *mesith*. The rabbinic evidence explains that both the family of the apostate and the town that welcomes him is guilty by association. According to Neale (1993, 91), "The fierceness of the punishment for the *mesith* or those who tolerate his activity is remarkable. Judicially both the perpetrator and those who tolerate the crime are the subject of extreme punishment." This would explain much about the Pharisees' approaching the blind man's parents, their fearful reaction, and their attempt to defer to their grown son. Rather than being an anachronistic intrusion into the narrative, John 9 is looking more and more like familial turmoil common to the first century.

We do not need to look far for similar evidence of familial tensions involving Jesus, for such evidence is found also in the Synoptics: "Blessed are you when people hate you, and when they exclude you, revile you, and defame you on account of the Son of Man" (Luke 6:22; see Beasley-Murray 1999, 154). Even C. H. Dodd, when remarking on 9:22, states, "We must … conclude, it seems, that the prospect of such exclusion was before Christians of Jewish origin early enough, at least, to have entered into the *common tradition* behind both Luke and John" (Dodd 1963, 410, emphasis added). What makes such evidence compelling is that, when setting out his methodology in *History and Theology in the Fourth*

---

11. See also b. Sanh. 43a for evidence in Jewish tradition that Jesus was executed for "deceiving" Israel.

12. For a comparison of similar Jewish tensions between John and the early Pauline evidence, see Wenham 1997.

Gospel, Martyn (2003, 31) declares that "by comparing John with the Synoptic Gospels we can identify many pieces which are obviously *traditional*." Thus, using Martyn's own method, it would seem that 9:22 might actually meet his criterion of "traditional melodies."[13]

For the Johannine narrative, then, the use of "already" is important; rather than trying to explain the readers' current situation back to them, the narrative is purposefully attempting to show the necessary similarities between the experiences of Jesus and those who decide to follow him.[14] This understanding of the familial turmoil is exactly what Martyn is unable to explain. Although Martyn certainly paints a picture of conflict in John 9 that is possible, once one leaves that chapter the reader is unable to make sense of the rest of the narrative without splicing it into two distinct levels, into a narrative order that is out of sequence with the Johannine narrative's own plot development. Even more, because of the influence given to chapter 9, the rest of the chapters must in some way reflect the life of the second level, that of the Johannine community. But if our reading is correct, this move by Martyn misses the rhetoric of these passages precisely because of an overrealized understanding of "expulsion." In contrast, the present essay is arguing that these passages reflect familial turmoil as various "groups" of the Jewish family are confronted by Jesus, a *mesith* or *min* in their midst, allowing the reader to experience the point of tension through the narrative. Such tension is forced upon the reader, who is asked at the end of the Gospel to realize that the entire work was written that they might believe that Jesus is the Jewish Messiah, not a *mesith* or a *min*.

It seems necessary, therefore, to rethink the historical reconstruction normally applied to ἀποσυνάγωγος in the Johannine narrative or projected onto the circumstances surrounding the finalization of the Johannine Gospel. This rethinking in no way tries to remove Jewish-Christian tension and conflict from the realm of the Gospel; it seeks only to locate it on a trajectory that is "already" rooted in the Johannine Jesus, one of many who may have qualified as *minim* in first-century Judaism. It is also necessary, it seems, to give the narrative its voice back, for its explicit development of Jesus is intimately tied, not just loosely affiliated, to the current experiences of the readers. Although the Johannine Evangelist is certainly formed by his situation, he also seems to be arguing for a future formation linked to Jesus himself—even shared experiences between Jesus and the Johannine readers. Such a clear Jewish-Christian or intra-Jewish

---

13. Martyn 2003, 31. One need not assume that John's perspective or circumstances did not circumvent the "telling" of this tradition, but certainly it has to be regarded as tradition-like enough to be of a firm historical nature.

14. For a specific example of this reading in the traditional material in John 15:18–16:4, see Klink 2008.

tension over identity is as pertinent in the late first century as it was during Jesus' own ministry.

Conclusion: A Theological Interest in History

John Ashton provides an interesting reason for accepting Martyn's reading of the Fourth Gospel: "Martyn goes on to build an impressive case, which carries conviction because of ... the satisfactory ways it accounts for one of [John's] most puzzling features: Why is the Gospel at once so Jewish and yet so anti-Jewish?" (Ashton 1991, 109). But this is exactly what our reading has tried to correct. It is specifically the intra-Jewish, familial turmoil that allows John to portray itself as both Jewish and anti-Jewish simultaneously. Historically, the Fourth Gospel portrays familial turmoil rooted in a long history of intra-Jewish tension involving heresy and group identity. John's narrative reflects its own identity-forming portrayal of the conflict between what later became the early Christian movement as distinguished from its parent Judaism. As a Gospel, John attempts to link the turmoil experienced by the readers with the experiences of Jesus himself. This does not take away from the fact that real "expulsions" of whatever kind were taking place behind the Johannine narrative, as witnessed elsewhere in the early Christian movement, for this was part and parcel of what Jesus himself experienced—and what those who have threatened any established religion have faced for generations.

THE BETHANY FAMILY IN JOHN 11–12:
HISTORY OR FICTION?

Richard Bauckham

According to the Gospel of John, Jesus counted among his close friends three siblings, Lazarus and his sisters Martha and Mary, who lived in the village of Bethany near Jerusalem. This essay is primarily concerned with the historicity of this family, but this can scarcely be separated from the historicity of the events in which they are involved in John's narrative: the resuscitation of Lazarus by Jesus and the anointing of Jesus by Mary. It is true that the historicity of these events could be defended, while regarding the family as a Johannine invention. John, it might be argued, has a habit of identifying characters who were anonymous in the tradition with known disciples of Jesus: the generalized "disciples" of Mark 6:35–38 are identified as Philip and Andrew in John 6:5–8; the man who injured the high priest's servant in Gethsemane, anonymous in the Synoptics (Matt 26:52; Mark 14:47; Luke 22:50), is identified as Peter in John 18:10–11. Perhaps he has done the same in the story of the anointing of Jesus by a woman who is anonymous in Matt 26:7 and Mark 14:3.[1] Perhaps he knew a story in which Jesus raises an anonymous man from death and has identified this man as Lazarus. But in that case we should know nothing about the Bethany family (except perhaps Luke's story about Martha and Mary: Luke 10:38–42). It would be very hard to tell whether John knew of their existence apart from the stories he tells of them or whether he borrowed the sisters from Luke's narrative and invented their brother Lazarus. In this essay I shall consider the historicity of the Bethany family along with the events in which the Gospel of John portrays them as major participants.

1. THE PERSONAL NAMES

1.1. Many scholars have been much too impressed by the fact that the name Lazarus occurs not only in John 11–12 but also in Luke's parable of the rich man

---

1. In my view, Luke 7:36–50 narrates a different story (many think the four anointing stories in the four Gospels all derive from one event), but here too the woman is anonymous.

and Lazarus (Luke 16:19–31). But we now know that the name Lazarus (Eleazar)[2] was the third most popular male name among Palestinian Jews (Simon and Joseph were first and second): 6.32 percent of Jewish men bore the name (166 occurrences in a database of 2,625).[3] If anything, what is surprising is that only two persons in the Gospels bear this name,[4] not that as many as two do. The coincidence of name between John's character and the poor man in the Lukan parable, supposed by so many scholars to be significant (e.g., Lincoln 2005, 42), is therefore not in the least remarkable. Nor is the alleged thematic connection between the two convincing. The proposed return of Lazarus in the parable is not a return to earthly life after temporary death but a temporary visit by the dead Lazarus as a ghost or in a dream.[5] His visit is not regarded as a sign that the rich man's brothers need in order to believe. The point is rather that Lazarus will be able to tell them about the fate that is awaiting them in the afterlife unless they reform. None of this is at all like the resuscitation of Lazarus in John 11 (so also Beasley-Murray 1987, 200). It is true that Lazarus in the parable is the only occurrence of a personal name in any Gospel parable, but there are other explanations more plausible than that it has been borrowed from John 11 or from a story lying behind John 11.[6] So there is no reason either to suppose that John borrowed the name from the parable or that an early tradition about Jesus' resuscitation of a man called Lazarus lies behind the parable. Sometimes adequate information renders banal what might otherwise seem significant coincidences.

---

2. The form Λάζαρος is colloquial (also found in Greek in Josephus, *J. W.* 5.567; cf. Λαζαρ on an ostracon from Masada; whereas elsewhere Josephus has Ἐλεάζαρος). "The Palestinian Hebrew/Aramaic dialect tended to drop the א prefix" (Ilan 2002, 29). This is an example of the fact that the New Testament "often preserves less official orthography which coincides with the common pronunciation rather than the traditional or official spelling found in Josephus" (Ilan 2002, 18).

3. I am using the tables of names in order of popularity in Bauckham 2006, 85–92. These were compiled from the data in Ilan 2002, an invaluable reference work. My statistics are a little different from hers because I have differed from her in a few aspects of the criteria used for calculating statistics (see Bauckham 2006, 68–83). Consequently, whereas I put Eleazar third and Judah fourth in order of popularity, Ilan puts Judah third and Eleazar fourth. But both calculations put them very close together (Bauckham: Eleazar 166 occurrences, Judah 164; Ilan: Judah 179, Eleazar 177).

4. There are eight Simons and six Josephs in the Gospels and Acts.

5. The reading ἀπελθῇ should be preferred to ἀναστῇ in Luke 16:31; see Tanghe 1984.

6. There may be a purely narratological reason. The theme of reversal of fortune would make it misleading to call "the poor man" poor after his death. The story is easier to tell if the man has a name. However, it is also relevant to notice that in popular stories about the return of a dead person, the sort of stories of which this parable is an example, he or she is almost always named, since the stories either purport to be true anecdotes about known people or else are fictional imitations of such true anecdotes. Giving the poor man a name may therefore belong to the genre of this kind of story (see Bauckham 1998b, 115–16).

1.2. Mary was the most common female name among Palestinian Jews: 21.34 percent of Jewish women were called Mary (70 occurrences in a database of 328). Martha was the fourth most common: 6.10 percent of Jewish women were called Martha (20 out of 326).[7] These statistics have some relevance to the relationship of the Bethany family in John to the story of Martha and Mary in Luke (10:38–42). It would not be at all surprising if there were more than one pair of sisters called Mary and Martha in Jewish Palestine at this time. But it would be more surprising if two such pairs of sisters were both nonitinerant disciples of Jesus and, moreover, lived as adults in the same home. What makes the identity of the sisters in Luke with those in John undeniable is the correspondences in the characterization of them, to be discussed below.

1.3. Our evidence for naming practices among Palestinian Jews of this period enables us to rule out one suggestion for harmonizing John and Mark: that "Lazarus was a former leper also known as Simon (double names were not uncommon)" (Keener 2003, 1:861).[8] Double names were certainly common, but they fall into two categories. Many Palestinian Jews used a Greek or (less commonly) Latin name as well as their Semitic name. Second, since a small number of names were very common, a patronymic or a nickname of some kind was often used with or instead of a very common name. In some families, a family nickname became virtually a surname. But Simon was the most common Jewish male name and Lazarus the third most common, and there is no reliable evidence of the use of two common names for the same person (Bauckham 2006, 108–10). The practice would serve no purpose.

1.4. Throughout the four Gospels the recipients of Jesus' healings and exorcisms in stories of those events are not usually named. In the Synoptics, the only exceptions are Jairus (Mark 5:22; Luke 8:41)[9] and Bartimaeus (Mark 10:46).[10] John's Gospel fits the same pattern: he does not name the steward or the groom at the wedding, the royal official or his son, the lame man healed by Jesus, or the blind man healed by Jesus. Lazarus, Mary, and Martha are the only exceptions (the two sisters count as recipients of the miracle because they had their brother restored to them). It should be noted that these examples of naming and not naming certainly do not support a claim that adding names was a tendency of the Gospel traditions. (The evidence in general shows that sometimes names are added and sometimes omitted—there is no consistent tendency; see Bauckham

---

7. Salome (58 occurrences) and Shelamzion (24 occurrences) are second and third. Since the database for women's names is much smaller than that for men's, the proportions are somewhat less certainly indicative of those in the whole population.

8. In the medieval period this identification led to the common belief that Lazarus was a leper (Gardner-Smith 1938, 46).

9. I count Jairus as a recipient because his daughter was restored to him.

10. According to Luke 8:3, Jesus had cast demons out of Mary Magdalene, but the story is not told.

2006, 42–45.) Moreover, it is not plausible that John has given Lazarus, Mary, and Martha their names only because they are relatively individualized characters in a relatively long narrative. The same is true of the blind man in John 9.

1.5. I have argued elsewhere that the occurrence and nonoccurrence of names in stories in the Gospels may be partially explained by supposing that the named characters were members of the early Christian communities and themselves told the stories of the events in which they had been participants. So long as they were known figures, their names remained attached to their stories as indications of the eyewitness sources of these stories (Bauckham 2006, ch. 3). The same explanation easily fits the case of Lazarus, Martha, and Mary.

1.6. If we take broader account of the occurrence and nonoccurrence of personal names in John, we find that, apart from publicly known persons (John the Baptist, Caiaphas, Annas, Pilate, Barabbas), almost all the named characters are disciples of Jesus. The only exception is Malchus (18:10).[11] A closer look at the disciples (itinerant and nonitinerant) shows that only three of those who are prominent in John are also prominent in the Synoptics: Peter and Mary Magdalene, who seem to have been universally treated as the most prominent of Jesus' male and female disciples, respectively, and Judas Iscariot, for obvious reasons. Disciples who appear only in the lists of Twelve in the Synoptics acquire prominent roles in John: Philip (1:43–46; 6:7; 12:21–22; 14:8), Thomas (11:16; 14:5; 20:24–29; 21:2), the other Judas (14:22; cf. Luke 6:16), and Martha and Mary (11:1–12:8). Also prominent is Andrew (1:40; 6:7; 12:22), mostly detached from his brother Peter, with whom he is always found in the Synoptics. By contrast, the sons of Zebedee, so prominent in the Synoptics, appear only once, at the end of John (21:2). But then there are the disciples peculiar to John: Nathanael, Nicodemus, Mary of Clopas, and Lazarus. These differences from the Synoptics suggest that the sources of the Johannine traditions come from a circle or circles of disciples of Jesus different from the circles from which the Synoptic traditions derive (especially the inner three of the Twelve: Peter, James, and John).[12] These would be the circles in which the Beloved Disciple moved and acquired those traditions of which he was not himself a direct witness. Finally, we should note that four of the disciples peculiar to John were nonitinerant disciples resident in the Jerusalem area: Nicodemus, Lazarus, Martha, and Mary. If we accept the now quite widely held view that the Beloved Disciple himself was a Jerusalem resident, his personal knowledge of those four disciples makes very good sense. Perhaps we should add that, if he was the owner of the house where the Last Supper took place, he must have belonged to an at least moderately wealthy family, as must also have been

---

11. It is possible that Malchus became a member of the early Jerusalem church.

12. A parallel that may merit some attention is the way different early accounts of Francis of Assisi derive from different circles of his disciples.

true of Nicodemus, Lazarus, Martha, and Mary.[13] Thus the Bethany family fits very well into the pattern of John's use of personal names.

2. RELATIONSHIPS WITH LUKE AND MARK

A common view is that John borrowed Martha and Mary from Luke, invented Lazarus or at least gave him a name, used Mark alone as his source for the anointing, embellishing Mark's story by naming the anonymous woman Mary, and, finally, located the family in Bethany because Mark located the anointing there.[14] We must tackle these possibilities by examining the relationships of the two Johannine narratives—the raising of Lazarus and the anointing—to Luke's story of Martha and Mary and Mark's story of the anointing. The aim here is not to prove that John's narratives are reliable but to establish that their relationships with the Synoptic narratives are not obstacles to considering them basically reliable.

2.1. MARTHA AND MARY IN LUKE AND JOHN

Whereas John locates the home of the sisters and their brother in Bethany, Luke 10:38 refers only to "a certain village" in a context that gives no indication that it is near Jerusalem. This merely shows that the tradition Luke knew gave no specific location for the story. (The difference does establish that Luke's story is not dependent on John, for Luke is not likely to have ignored John's specific location of the family in Bethany.)

That Lazarus does not appear in Luke's story of the sisters (where Martha "received him as a guest": 10:38)[15] is not at all a plausible argument against his historicity.[16] In Gospel pericopes as brief and focused as Luke 10:38–42, extraneous details unnecessary to the story are not to be expected.

There are no convincing verbal contacts between Luke's story and John 11–12, though two have been suggested.[17] (1) In Luke 10:39 Mary "sat at the feet" of Jesus, while in John 11:32 Mary "fell at the feet" of Jesus. But these are dif-

---

13. For the Bethany family, note the extreme value of Mary's perfume (12:3). Other evidence for their relatively high social status is given by Witherington 1995b, 200, though his argument that their house could accommodate a banquet for at least fifteen people assumes, perhaps incorrectly (see below), that the dinner in John 12:2 is located in their house.

14. E.g., Lindars 1972, 384–86, who thinks that the name Lazarus may have been in the miracle story John used. For a different account of how John created the story of the raising of Lazarus out of Synoptic elements, see Brodie 1993, 86–88.

15. Many manuscripts add εἰς τὴν οἰκίαν, with or without αὐτῆς, or εἰς τὸν οἶκον αὐτῆς, but the shorter reading is preferable (Metzger 1975, 153; 1994, 129; though other scholars disagree) and does not necessarily suggest that the house was hers in any exclusive sense.

16. *Contra* Esler and Piper 2006, 76.

17. Brown 1966–70, 1:433; Lindars 1972, 385; Barrett 1978, 411.

ferent idioms with quite different meanings: to sit at someone's feet is to listen their teaching (so also Luke 8:35; Acts 22:3), while to fall at someone's feet is an expression of humility and devotion (so also Mark 5:22; 7:25; Luke 8:41; 17:16; Acts 5:10; 10:25). Both are common. (2) In Luke 10:40 Martha "was distracted with much serving" (διακονίαν), while in John 12:2 Martha "served" (διηκόνει). These words are so common in the general sense of domestic work or, more especially, preparing a meal that the *verbal* coincidence is unremarkable. (The substantive resemblance is more remarkable; see below.)

Most commentators have noticed the consistency of the characterization of the two sisters in the two Gospels but are sharply divided on its significance.[18] Whereas some scholars take it to be strong evidence of the historicity of John's portrayal of the sisters,[19] others think it shows that John borrowed them from Luke.[20] (The case is similar, on a smaller scale, to the strikingly consistent portrayal of Peter across all four Gospels.) In assessing this issue, we should take care to avoid allowing our reading of the characterization in one Gospel to affect our reading of the characterization in the other Gospel. A composite picture of the two sisters based on both Gospels can easily mislead.[21] In fact, the commonality between the two Gospels in this respect is striking but limited. It seems clear in both Gospels that Martha is the elder sister, since in Luke Martha appears first, and Mary is then introduced as her sister (Luke 10:38–39), while in John references to both sisters usually place Martha before Mary (John 11:5, 19).[22] She may well be considerably older. In both Gospels she takes responsibility for domestic work, especially preparing meals for guests (Luke 10:40; John 12:2). The fact that in John she goes out to meet Jesus, whereas Mary stays at home (11:20), may be due to her responsibility, as elder sister, for managing the household and its affairs (especially now that her brother has died), as may also her words in John 11:39.[23] In John, at least, there is no suggestion that she is less devoted to Jesus than her sister is, but in both Gospels Mary, unlike Martha, expresses her devotion to Jesus in overt ways other than domestic work (listening to him teaching,

---

18. The issue is similar to a more remarkable instance of consistent characterization across the Gospels: that of Peter. See now especially Wiarda 2000.

19. Stauffer 1974, 223–24, quoted in Witherington 1984, 115; Stibbe 1994, 101; and Twelftree 1999, 309–10.

20. E.g., Lincoln 2005, 333, 340.

21. Thus it would be easy to parallel Martha's outspoken complaint to Jesus in Luke 10:40 with her complaint to Jesus in John 11:21 (see also 11:39), but this would overlook the fact that, in John, Mary makes the identical complaint as her sister (11:32). This mistake is made, e.g., by C. J. Wright, quoted in Morris 1969, 170–71.

22. John 11:1–2 is an exception because the author evidently expects his readers to know of Mary already (even if not by name, if they knew her from Mark) but not of Martha.

23. Another feature of the characterization of Martha in John, her "discerning faith" (Culpepper 1983, 141–42), does not appear in Luke.

Luke 10:39; falling at his feet, John 11:32; anointing him with the expensive perfume, 12:3), and Jesus defends her unconventional expressions of devotion (Luke 10:42; John 12:7).[24]

It is important to note that, as usually in ancient narrative, the character of the sisters is portrayed by their actions and words, not by explicit character description. What is common to both Gospels in Martha's case really comes down to her responsibility for the household, while what is characteristic of Mary are her two rather unconventional acts of devotion (sitting like a disciple at the feet of her teacher, anointing him with costly perfume). These acts of Mary are central to the two narratives in which they occur, and so the consistent characterization of Mary would have been embodied in the tradition of the two stories quite independently of each other. That Martha was the older sister and the one with domestic responsibility is similarly integral to Luke's story, and it is important, if not wholly necessary, to John's narrative of the raising of Lazarus.[25] There is nothing very subtle about this characterization of Martha. It could easily correspond to historical reality, and it could easily have belonged to both stories quite independently of each other. We may conclude that what is common to the characterization of the two sisters in the two Gospels does not at all require that John borrowed this characterization from Luke.[26]

2.2. Timing and Location of the Anointing in John and Mark

There is enough verbal agreement between John 12:1–8 and Mark 14:3–9 to make it more probable that John knew Mark's account (see especially John 12:3a and Mark 14:3b) than that both depended on a common oral source.[27] This does not, however, preclude the possibility that John also had independent knowledge of the event. But in that case we must consider two respects in which John is supposed to contradict Mark. First, whereas Mark seems to date the event two days before

---

24. The commonly expressed view that in both Gospels Martha is the more active and Mary the more passive figure neglects the anointing, where Mary on her own initiative performs a bold and unconventional act.

25. A number of scholars have argued for an original (pre-Johannine) form of this story in which Martha did not appear (e.g., Fortna 1988, 94–108; Latourelle 1988, 233–34; Meier 1994, 819–22), though Mary did. I think attempts to reconstruct an original story are hopelessly speculative. See the survey and critique in Marchadour 1988, ch. 2.

26. I am open to the argument that Luke was influenced by John (Matson 2001; Anderson 2006b, 212–17), but I do not think it can apply in this instance. It seems quite implausible that Luke should have composed his story of Martha and Mary on the basis of John's portrayal of the sisters. Different stories about them must have been handed down as distinct traditions.

27. Gardner-Smith's case (1938, 42–50) is probably the least convincing part of his argument for John's complete independence of Mark. Both his argument and that of Dodd 1963, 162–73, are in reality strong arguments for the view that John's account is not solely dependent on Mark's, rather than the view that John had no knowledge of Mark whatever.

Passover (14:1), John dates it six days before Passover (12:1). Second, whereas Mark places the event in the house of Simon the leper (14:3), John appears to place it in the house of Lazarus and his sisters (12:1–2). Of course, it is quite possible that John corrected Mark's account on the basis of what he considered better information. But in fact the contradictions, when more closely examined, turn out not to be real contradictions at all.

In the first place, Mark makes the supper at Bethany the "filling" in a typical Markan "sandwich" (an ABA pattern, thus: 14:1–2 + 14:3–9 + 14:10–11). He frames the event with the two stages of the plot against Jesus: (1) the authorities determine to put Jesus to death but hesitate to provoke the people to riot (14:1–2); (2) Judas offers to betray Jesus, thus enabling the authorities to arrest him secretly, away from the crowds (14:10–11). Markan "sandwiches" are contrived for thematic rather than chronological reasons. Thus, for example, the sandwiching of Jesus' demonstration in the temple (11:15–19) between the two-stage narrative of the cursing of the fig tree (11:12–14, 20–21) makes the fig tree a symbol of the temple, which would not be at all evident otherwise. Similarly, the sandwich in 14:1–11 creates a thematic rather than chronological link between the anointing and the plot against Jesus (exactly what this link is will be discussed in the next section). Recognizing that Mark's apparent chronology here is artificial makes it entirely possible that John is historically correct in placing the anointing prior to the triumphal entry. It is an example of John's habitual precision in chronological and geographical matters, a precision that distinguishes John markedly from the Synoptics.

Second, John does not in fact locate the supper in the house of Lazarus and his sisters. He certainly places it in Bethany (John 12:1–2), as does Mark, but the house is unmentioned. That "Lazarus was one of those at the table with" Jesus (12:2) indicates, if anything, that Lazarus was not the host (Brown 1966–70, 1:448; Blomberg 2001, 176). The impression that the house is that of Lazarus and his sisters has probably been produced primarily by the statement that "Martha served" (12:2). But we must envisage a quite major social occasion, which the house of Lazarus and his sisters may not have been large enough to accommodate. We can easily imagine Martha helping to prepare, or even taking charge of preparing, the meal even though it was held in a neighbor's house.[28] Finally, and perhaps most tellingly, the subject of "made [ἐποίησαν] a meal for him" (12:2) cannot be Martha and Lazarus, since at this point only Lazarus has been mentioned (12:1). The plural verb has an indefinite subject, indicating that the dinner was arranged and Jesus invited by Bethany villagers, not exclusively Lazarus and

---

28. See Carson 1991, 428: "a village dinner honouring a celebrated guest might well draw in several families to do the work, and the presence of Lazarus at any Bethany dinner designed to honour Jesus would scarcely be surprising."

his sisters (Bernard 1928, 415). Thus, if John knew Mark's account, it is not necessary to suppose that he deliberately contradicted Mark in this respect.

3. The Silence of the Synoptics

The weightiest argument against the historicity of the raising of Lazarus (apart from naturalistic objections to the miraculous) has always been its absence from the Synoptics (e.g., Casey 1996, 55). There are a number of commonly deployed responses to this argument. It is rightly pointed out that the presence of a tradition in only one Gospel is no necessary argument against its historical value (e.g., Latourelle 1988, 230–31). More specifically, the Synoptic Gospels focus on the Galilean ministry,[29] whereas the raising of Lazarus belongs to the Fourth Gospel's greater attention to events in Jerusalem and Judea. Moreover, the Synoptic Gospels locate only one specific miracle in the vicinity of Jerusalem: the healing of the blind man or men near Jericho (called Bartimaeus only in Mark 10:46–52; anonymous in Luke 18:35–43; two men in Matt 20:29–34). It seems to have been Mark's compositional decision (followed by Matthew and Luke) to limit the narration of miracles to the earlier stages of Jesus' ministry (up to 9:29), breaking this rule only in the case of Bartimaeus for a specific reason: to introduce the theme of Jesus' Davidic kingship that features prominently in Mark's passion narrative. Since Matthew and Mark do have one resuscitation miracle (Jairus's daughter) and Luke two (Jairus's daughter and the son of the widow of Nain), they may not have wished to include another (e.g., Twelftree 1999, 309).

However, although these arguments carry some weight, they do not reckon fully with the fact that John portrays the raising of Lazarus as an especially impressive miracle and also gives it a key role in the sequence of events that led to Jesus' death. Many scholars think that John has exaggerated the miracle he found in the tradition and has given it a role in his overall narrative that it did not have in pre-Johannine tradition.[30] In that case, its nonappearance in the Synoptics could be adequately explained by the arguments adduced above. But if the miracle was as dramatic and crucial to the course of events as John represents it, the silence of the Synoptics is less intelligible. Ben Witherington puts the issue thus:

> If … this story was but one of a number of stories of Jesus' raising the dead that were told and retold in the early church as self-contained narratives, there is no compelling reason why the Synoptic writers would have had to include

---

29. E.g., Witherington 1984, 104; Stibbe 1994, 103; Blomberg 2001, 55.

30. Some argue that the story was added in a second edition of the Gospel to a narrative that originally followed the same sequence as Mark: the triumphal entry, cleaning of the temple, and the chief priests' plot. Only in the second edition did the raising of Lazarus acquire the key role in leading to the chief priests' plan to put Jesus to death (Brown 1966–70, 1:429–30; Lindars 1972, 379–82; Witherington 1984, 104–5).

the Lazarus story if they knew it. If, on the other hand, the Lazarus narrative was known to other evangelists and this episode was *the* event that triggered the events that led to Jesus' death and resurrection, it is very difficult to see how the Synoptic writers could possibly have afforded to omit the story. (Witherington 1995b, 196)

If, as I have suggested, John's knowledge of the events involving the Bethany family derives from the Beloved Disciple's own familiarity with the family, it is not so easy to leave aside the place that the raising of Lazarus has in the Gospel's account of the development of events. It will not do to put this down to John's alleged concern with theology rather than history. Caiaphas's words in 11:49–50 are instructive: at one level they make good sense as a statement of political expediency provoked by the fear that Jesus' popularity will lead to popular revolt, and it is only on a second, ironic level that they also express the divinely ordained reason why Jesus had to die. John is deeply concerned with the theological reasons for Jesus' death, but he evidently purports also to provide a straightforwardly historical explanation, in the sense of an account of how one thing led to another. His Gospel portrays the opposition of the Jewish authorities to Jesus, first aroused by his demonstration in the temple (2:18–20), mounting in a series of clashes during Jesus' periodic visits to Jerusalem. The report of the raising of Lazarus is, so to speak, the last straw because it is no longer simply a matter of the Jewish leaders' theological objections to Jesus' actions and claims, but now also of the specter of popular revolt aroused by the huge following in Jerusalem that the reports of the raising of Lazarus have created for him. Dealing with Jesus thus becomes a matter of urgency, the more so when Passover approaches and Jesus returns to the Jerusalem area. This account does not make everything hang on the raising of Lazarus. In 11:47 the assembled Jewish leaders refer to Jesus' "many signs," not only that of Lazarus.[31] But the raising of Lazarus was a focus of popular attention, especially as it was possible to see the recently dead man now alive and well (12:9).

While not all scholars find this a convincing historical account of how the Jewish authorities became determined to put Jesus to death (e.g., Lindars 1972, 380–82), there can be no doubt that it does offer a *historical* form of explanation, which is arguably more convincing than Mark's, in which it seems to be Jesus' demonstration in the temple alone that provokes the authorities to plot his death (Mark 11:18). John's account, by explaining the enthusiasm for Jesus that gripped not only pilgrims from Galilee but also the people of Jerusalem at the approach of Passover, plausibly shows how the authorities could have viewed Jesus as a danger and have expected to convince Pilate that he was. Moreover, since John's account

---

31. Where John has the crowd at the triumphal entry going to see Jesus because they had heard of the raising of Lazarus (John 12:18), Luke has them praising God "for all the deeds of power they had seen" (Luke 19:37).

of the raising of Lazarus and the subsequent decision of the authorities makes Jesus already a wanted man as soon as he arrives in the Jerusalem area, the atmosphere of danger and subterfuge that already attends Jesus' preparations for the triumphal entry in Mark 11:1–6 actually becomes more intelligible if we assume some historical substance to the narrative of John 11:1–54.[32] But in that case, why did Mark himself not tell that story?

4. Protective Strategies in Gospel Passion Narratives

In a significant essay on the Markan passion narrative, which he argues took shape in the Jerusalem church in the 40s C.E., Gerd Theissen makes use of the notion of "protective anonymity."[33] He applies this primarily to two anonymous characters in Mark's account of the arrest of Jesus in Gethsemane (Mark 14:43–52): "one of the bystanders" who cut off the ear of the high priest's servant (14:47) and "a certain young man" who escaped arrest by fleeing naked (14:51–52). Theissen points out how difficult it is to tell whether either or both of these are disciples of Jesus. He offers an explanation of both why they are anonymous and why their relationship to Jesus is left so unclear.

> It seems to me that the narrative motive for this anonymity is not hard to guess: both of them [had] run afoul of the "police." The one who draws his sword commits no minor offense when he cuts off someone's ear. Had the blow fallen only slightly awry, he could have wounded the man in the head or throat. This blow with a sword is violence with possibly mortal consequences. The anonymous young man has also offered resistance. In the struggle, his clothes are torn off, so that he has to run away naked. Both these people were in danger in the aftermath. As long as the high priest's slave was alive (and as long as the scar from the sword cut was visible) it would have been inopportune to mention names; it would not even have been wise to identify them as members of the early Christian community. Their anonymity is for their protection, and the obscurity of their positive relationship with Jesus is a strategy of caution. Both the teller and the hearers know more about these two people.[34]

This argument, among others, suggests to Theissen that the tradition has its origin in Jerusalem during the lifetime of these two persons: "Only in Jerusalem

---

32. See Robinson 1985, 222–23, which takes this argument further.

33. Theissen 1991, ch. 4: "A Major Narrative Unit (the Passion Story) and the Jerusalem Community in the Years 40–50 C.E."

34. Theissen 1991, 186–87. With regard to the man with the sword, Theissen is far from the first to make this argument. For example, Swete 1909, 352, already wrote: "During the early days of the Church of Jerusalem when the evangelical tradition was being formed, prudential reasons (cf. Jo. xviii.26) may have suggested reticence as to the name of the offender and even the fact of his connection with the Christian body."

was there reason to draw a cloak of anonymity over followers of Jesus who had endangered themselves by their actions" (1991, 188–89). Theissen adds to the case another, very different instance of anonymity in Mark's passion narrative (1991, 171–74). Although Mark refers by name to Pilate (15:1) and evidently expects his readers to know that Pilate was the Roman governor, in the case of the high priest Caiaphas he does not give his name but refers merely to "the high priest" (14:53).[35] The continued hostility of Caiaphas and other high priests from the family of Annas to the Christian community in Jerusalem, up to at least 62 C.E. (VanderKam 2004, 478), would have made it diplomatic for Christian traditions formed in Jerusalem in that period not to refer explicitly to the name of Caiaphas in an account of the death of Jesus.

Theissen himself does not take the notion of "protective anonymity" further, but there is at least one other anonymous person in Mark's passion narrative who could be regarded as complicit in the events that led to Jesus' arrest and could therefore have needed the protection of anonymity: the woman who anointed Jesus (Mark 14:3–9).[36] Like the two nameless men in Gethsemane, this woman is peculiarly unspecified. Not only is her name not given, but there is no indication at all who she is. Her introduction in verse 3 is remarkably abrupt and unexplanatory: "a woman came." Whether she belongs to the household or is a guest or has simply come in from the town is unexplained, as is her connection with Jesus. But what makes her anonymity quite extraordinary, and not at all comparable with the many unremarkable cases of anonymity in Mark's Gospel, is the words of Jesus that conclude the pericope: "Truly I tell you, wherever the good news is proclaimed in the whole world, what she has done will be told in remembrance of her" (14:9). This statement that her story will be told not merely to make known what she did, but "in remembrance of *her*," seems in straight contradiction to her anonymity in the story, and commentators have often noted the problem without offering any convincing solution. It is true that in ancient narrative women are more often anonymous than men, but this type of prejudice is unlikely to be present in this particular narrative, which ends by commending the woman so highly and in terms unique within this Gospel.[37]

A solution can be found in Theissen's notion of protective anonymity. At the time when this tradition took shape in this form in the Jerusalem church, this

---

35. The other Evangelists name him Caiaphas (Matt 26:57; Luke 3:2; John 18:13–14, 24), although Luke does not name him in the passion narrative itself (22:54), and readers of Luke might have difficulty knowing whether Annas or Caiaphas was in charge of the proceedings that condemned Jesus.

36. The argument that follows is presented in a little more detail in Bauckham 2006, ch. 8.

37. It is tempting to compare "in remembrance [μνημόσυνον] of her" with "Do this in remembrance [ἀνάμνησιν] of me" spoken by Jesus at the Last Supper, but among the Gospels only Luke, who does not have these words about the woman, has Jesus say, "Do this in remembrance of me" in his Last Supper narrative (22:19; the words are in the longer text).

woman would be in danger were she identified as having been complicit in Jesus' politically subversive claim to messianic kingship. Her act, in its context of the last days of Jesus in Jerusalem, would easily be seen as the anointing entailed by the term *Messiah*, comparable with the anointing of kings in the Hebrew Bible.[38] The woman was acknowledging or even designating Jesus as the Messiah ben David. She may have acted purely on her own initiative, or she may have planned it in association with others who wished to take Jesus by surprise and so encourage him to undertake the messianic role about which he seemed ambivalent. Admittedly, it would no doubt be very surprising for the Messiah to be anointed by a woman, but she could have been seen in the role of a prophet, like Samuel, inspired by God to recognize and designate his Anointed One (see 1 Sam 16:1–13).[39]

Not all scholars who think the woman's act had messianic significance in its original historical context think that Mark's narrative preserves that significance (e.g., Elliott 1973–74, 105–7; Schüssler Fiorenza 1994, 95), while not all scholars who think Mark sees messianic significance in the anointing think this was originally intended or perceived (e.g., Cranfield 1963, 415). There are several reasons for denying that the anointing, either historically or in Mark's story, carries messianic significance: (1) anointing the head in the context of a banquet was by no means confined to kings (Corley 2003, 66–67; France 2002, 552) but was a common custom at feasts; (2) the messianic significance is not explicit in Mark's text;[40] (3) Mark's narrative "goes on to interpret the festal gesture in terms of death and burial rather than of messianic commissioning" (France 2002, 552). The first point is correct and therefore means that the messianic significance is not self-evident but dependent on the context, including the wider context in Mark's passion narrative outside this story itself. The second point can be answered by referring to Mark's narrative of Jesus' riding the colt into Jerusalem. The messianic significance is left implicit, but it can hardly be doubted that it is implicit. The story of the anointing is similar. The third point poses a false alternative. What happens in the story is that Jesus recognizes the messianic significance of the anointing but interprets it according to his own understanding of his messianic vocation as entailing suffering and death. Just as readers of Mark know that Jesus' riding into Jerusalem on a colt does not signify messianic triumph of the generally expected kind, but constitutes a journey to his death, so the messianic

---

38. Most recently Evans 2001, 359, with references to others who argue for this view; see also Broadhead 1994, 37 n. 2. For the anointing of kings in the Old Testament, see 1 Sam 10:1; 16:1, 13; 1 Kgs 1:39; 19:15–16; 2 Kgs 9:3, 6; Ps 89:20.

39. So Schüssler Fiorenza 1985, xiii–xiv; Horsley 2001, 217–18. Schüssler Fiorenza's view is repeated, with updated references, in Schüssler Fiorenza 2003, 240–42.

40. Presumably this is why many commentators do not even mention the possibility; see also Neagoe 2002, 146–47.

anointing by the woman is redirected by Jesus toward his burial, coherently with the characteristically Markan connection between messiahship and the cross.

What has not been generally recognized is the significance of Mark's placing of this story between his account of the plot by the Jewish authorities to arrest and kill Jesus (14:1–2) and his account of Judas's visit to the chief priests in order to offer to hand Jesus over to them (14:10–11). I have already pointed out that this is a typically Markan "sandwich" composition, indicating a close connection of meaning between the story that forms the two outer parts of the story that is sandwiched between them. We should surely understand that Judas reported the incident of the anointing to the chief priests, for whom it must have constituted significant evidence that Jesus and his disciples were planning an imminent messianic uprising. Perhaps we should also suspect that it was this incident—with its unavoidable confirmation by Jesus that he would undertake the messianic role only on his own terms as a vocation to die—that led Judas to defect. Thus the anointing provides both added cause for the chief priests to take swift action against Jesus and also the means to do so in the shape of Judas's offer.

That the anointing is related in this way to the actions of the chief priests and Judas is not, of course, explicit in the story, but this is not a valid objection to it. There is similarly no explicit connection between the story of the withered fig tree and the demonstration in the temple, but most commentators believe that, by means of the Markan "sandwich" construction, the former functions as a comment on Jesus' attitude to and action in the temple. But we should also notice the surely studied reserve in Mark's passion narrative as to what led the Jewish authorities to suppose both that Jesus was so dangerous that action must be taken swiftly and that a charge of claiming messiahship could be made to stick and represented to Pilate as a political challenge to Roman rule. There are three events in Mark's narrative that explain this: Jesus' entry into Jerusalem; his demonstration in the temple; and his anointing by a woman. But in all three cases the messianic significance is notably subdued in Mark's telling. The author seems wary of making explicit the aspects of these events that made them construable as evidence for the charge on which Jesus was put to death: that he was claiming to be the messianic "king of the Jews" and planning an uprising.

The messianic significance of all three events would have been clear to Mark's first readers or hearers, but Mark's apparent strategy of leaving it for them to perceive, rather than himself highlighting it, coheres rather strikingly with the strategy of "protective anonymity" in relation to certain characters in this narrative. What put these persons in danger in Jerusalem in the period of the earliest Christian community would be their complicity in Jesus' allegedly seditious behavior in the days before his arrest. Furthermore, all members of the community were potentially at risk for their allegiance to a man who had been executed for such seditious behavior. We can readily understand that, just as the pre-Markan passion narrative protected certain individuals by leaving them anonymous, so it protected the community by not making too obvious the messianic meaning of the events that had constituted the chief priests' evidence for treating Jesus as a dangerously seditious figure. Just as the members of the Jerusalem church who first heard the narrative would know who the anonymous persons were, so they would understand the messianic significance of these events without needing it spelled out for them.

We are now in a position to understand why it is that several of the persons who are anonymous in Mark's passion narrative are named in John.

woman who anoints Jesus (Mark 14:3)	Mary, sister of Martha (John 12:3)
man who wields a sword (Mark 14:47)	Simon Peter (John 18:10)
servant of the high priest (Mark 14:47)	Malchus (John 18:10)

These should not be regarded as instances of some alleged tendency for names to get added in the tradition. There is little evidence of such a tendency before the fourth century (see Bauckham 2006, 43–45). Moreover, such an explanation neglects the specificities of these particular cases in the passion narrative. As we have seen, there may be very good reasons for the anonymity of these characters in Mark, while, conversely, such reasons would no longer apply at the date and in the place at which John's Gospel was written. Given, as we have argued, that John has independent access to such traditions, there is no difficulty in supposing that the names in John are historically accurate.

In the light of the messianic character of the anointing, John's dating of this event before the triumphal entry makes good historical sense. Jesus is anointed as the Messiah in Bethany the evening before riding into Jerusalem as the Messiah. But in spite of this plausible sequence of events, John has actually obscured the messianic significance of the anointing more than Mark has. Mary of Bethany does not anoint Jesus' head but his feet, wiping them with her hair. Whatever the explanation for the coincidence[41] with Luke's otherwise very different story of an anointing of Jesus by an anonymous woman (Luke 7:38),[42] the effect of this feature in John is to highlight Mary's extravagant devotion to Jesus rather than the messianic meaning of anointing.[43] She takes the role not of a prophet but of a servant. She performs the role of a servant washing a guest's feet—a role

---

41. But even so there is the contextually appropriate difference that Luke's woman sheds tears on Jesus' feet, whereas there is no suggestion in John that Mary weeps. Nor does Mary kiss Jesus' feet, as Luke's woman does (Luke 7:38).

42. There are a variety of views on the tradition history, depending on such judgments as whether or not there was only one anointing or two and whether or not John knew Luke's Gospel. Many think of some kind of "cross-fertilization of the two anointing stories" (Witherington 1984, 113) in the tradition.

43. Scholars who find messianic significance in the anointing in John 12 include Barrett 1978, 409; and Köstenberger 2004, 361. Those who think that John 12 certainly cannot suggest royal anointing include Dodd 1963, 173; and Lincoln 2005, 337.

distinctively that of a servant or slave[44]—but does so in an extraordinarily lavish way.[45] (But it is not clear that letting down her hair would be seen as scandalous, as most scholars suppose, if Mary was unmarried, as most likely she was: see Keener 2003, 1:863.) Various reasons why John's account focuses on the anointing of the feet are plausible. It is possible that Mary anointed more than Jesus' feet but that John focuses on the feet because he wishes to stress her humble devotion to Jesus and has in mind the significance of footwashing in his Last Supper narrative (e.g., Conway 1999, 152). The significance could be that she anointed *even* Jesus' feet. If, as we have suggested, the Beloved Disciple was close to the Bethany family, he may have wished to emphasize as much as possible Mary's remarkable love for Jesus. It is also possible that referring to the feet rather than the head of Jesus is actually another protective strategy that originally served to veil the seditious nature of the act. Mark's version protects Mary by not naming her; John's names her (and identifies her by reference to her brother and sister) but hides the messianic significance of her act. In that case John's version, like Mark's, was originally formulated in a context of danger to those who had aided and abetted Jesus.

Finally, there may be a more theological point. If the significance is not that Mary anointed only the feet but even the feet, then her action is more appropriate for anointing for burial than anointing the head would be. This reading would be consistent with the way that John's account ends, not with commendation of the woman, as in Mark, but with, first, Jesus' words about his burial,[46] then the assertion that Jesus will be leaving them (12:7–8). The whole story in John functions as another of the many passion predictions in this Gospel and serves to interpret Jesus' riding into Jerusalem the next day as the arrival of a king already anointed for his burial. It is in this sense that John's Mary is a prophet: she performs a prophetic sign of Jesus' destiny.

If we accept that in Mark's passion narrative Mary's anonymity is protective and that John correctly identified her, there is a further consequence that will complete our argument for the historical value of John's account of the Bethany family. Lazarus would have needed "protective anonymity" in a passion narrative originating in Jerusalem in the 40s even more than his sister Mary would. John's Gospel explicitly reports, already before the death of Jesus, that "the chief priests planned to put Lazarus to death as well" (12:10). Lazarus could not have been protected in the early period of the Jerusalem church's life by telling his story but not naming him. His story was too well known locally not to be easily identifiable as his, however it was told. For Lazarus, "protective anonymity" had to take

---

44. See Thomas 1991, ch. 3; Bauckham 1999, 412–14.

45. For (rare) parallels to the anointing of the feet in antiquity, see Coakley 1988, 247–48.

46. The seemingly intractable problem of the precise meaning of John 12:7 cannot be discussed here.

the form of his total absence from the story as it was publicly told.[47] By the time John's Gospel was written, after 70 C.E., there would of course be no longer any such need for protection. John was free to fill an awkward gap in Mark's (and Matthew's and Luke's) account of the events leading to Jesus' execution.

In conclusion, the difficulties usually perceived in accepting the historicity of the events in which the Bethany family take part in John's narrative, as well as the historicity of all three family members themselves, can be adequately met. They belong to a range of indications that the author of this Gospel was especially well informed about persons and events in Jerusalem and its vicinity.[48]

---

47. This has already been suggested by Harris 1986, 312; Keener 2003, 1:836.

48. A slightly different version of this essay was published as chapter 8 of Bauckham 2007.

What's in a Name? Rethinking the Historical Figure of the Beloved Disciple in the Fourth Gospel

Ben Witherington III

"This is the disciple who is testifying to these things and has written them,
and we know that his testimony is true." (John 21:24)

The environment in which the New Testament was written was both oral and rhetorical in character. Texts, especially religious texts, function differently in oral cultures that are 90 percent illiterate and in which even the texts that exist are oral texts, meant to be read aloud. These important insights, when coupled with the realization that orally delivered and rhetorically adept discourse and storytelling was at the heart of first-century culture, should long ago have led us to a new way of reading the Gospels themselves.

First, the telling of the story of Jesus was from the beginning crucial for the new Christian movement, well before the whole story was written down in any one fashion. Margaret Mitchell in a seminal essay has shown that in various places in the Pauline corpus, "Paul grounds his arguments solidly upon an underlying gospel narrative, which he accesses through various forms of rhetorical short-hand—brevity of speech, synecdoche, and metaphor. Though Paul is thoroughly consistent in his frame of reference—the gospel narrative—his references to it are fluid and flexible" (Mitchell 1994, 88). A good example of this sort of short, rhetorical citing of the gospel can be found in 1 Cor 15:3–8, where Paul mentions the climax of the gospel narrative: the death, burial, and resurrection of Jesus and its immediate sequels, the appearances of Jesus. The gospel story apparently first appeared in written form in these Pauline summaries as highly rhetorical discourses, framed as letters.

What this meant, of course, is that there was permission to tell the story in rhetorically effective and persuasive ways, even when, and perhaps especially when, the story involved the memoirs of someone who actually heard Jesus in person—an eyewitness and earwitness of some part of Jesus' life and teachings. I would submit that there is no more rhetorically effective (and affective) telling of the gospel story in long form, although edited down on the basis of rhetorical and other considerations (see John 20:30; 21:25), than the Gospel of John. What we have in this Gospel is not the boiling up of a story on the basis of shards of information but rather the boiling down of copious notes, memoranda, and eye-witness accounts from the Beloved Disciple and putting them into an rhetorically effective order and shape by some final editor (on which more will be said at the end of this essay). I also submit that when one looks at the Gospel of John as an oral document that was meant to be heard rather than read privately or individu-ally, and heard in the order in which it is now presented, certain things come to light, including fresh insights into the identity of the Beloved Disciple.[1]

The Problem with the Traditional Ascription to John Zebedee

Martin Hengel (1989a) and Graham Stanton (1997), among other scholars, have reminded us in recent discussions of the Fourth Gospel that the superscripts of all four of the canonical Gospels were in all likelihood added after the fact; indeed, they may originally have been added as document tags to papyrus rolls. Even more tellingly, they were likely added only after there were several familiar Gospels, for the phrase "according to…" is used to distinguish a particular Gospel from other, well-known ones.

This means, of course, that all four Gospels are formally anonymous, and the question then becomes how much weight one should place on internal evidence of authorship (the so-called inscribed author) and how much on external evi-dence. In my view, the internal evidence should certainly take precedence in the case of John's Gospel, not least because the external evidence is hardly unequivo-cal. This does not alleviate the necessity of explaining how the Gospel came to be ascribed to someone named John, but we will leave that question to the end of our discussion.

As far as the external evidence goes, it is true enough that various church fathers in the second century thought that John son of Zebedee was the author. There was an increasing urgency about this conclusion for the mainstream church after the middle of the second century c.e. because the Fourth Gospel seems to have been a favorite among the gnostics, and therefore, apostolic authorship was deemed important if this Gospel was to be rescued from the heterodox. The ten-dency to associate authenticity and accuracy with apostolicity and eyewitness

---

1. One of the clear clues that we are dealing with oral stories that were written down sepa-rately and then later combined in a full Gospel narrative meant to be delivered orally is, of course, the pericope about the woman caught in adultery. This unit appears not to have made the original cut of what would be included in this Gospel narrative, but it nonetheless was viewed as a beloved and valid part of the testimony of the Beloved Disciple. So it became a text looking for a home, which led to its inclusion in various places in John (often but not only at 7:53–8:11) and even in several Lukan manuscripts.

testimony is evident throughout this church crisis, but the emphasis on eyewitness testimony is already evidenced in Luke 1:1–4 and in various places in the Pauline corpus. It was not an urgency first forced on the church by the gnostic crisis.

Irenaeus, the great heresiarch, around 180 C.E. stressed that the Fourth Gospel was written in Ephesus by one of the Twelve: John. It is therefore telling that this seems not to have been the conclusion of perhaps our earliest witness, Papias of Hierapolis, who was surely in a location and in a position to know something about Christianity in the provenance of Asia Minor at the beginning of the second century C.E. Papias ascribes this Gospel to one elder John, whom he distinguishes presumably from another John, and it is only the former with whom he claims to have had personal contact. Eusebius, in referring to the preface to Papias's five-volume work, stresses that Papias only had contact with an elder John and one Aristion, not explicitly with John of Zebedee (*Hist. eccl.* 3.39.3–7), who is distinguished by Eusebius himself from the John in question. It is notable as well that Eusebius reminds us that Papias reflects the same chiliastic eschatology as is found in the book of Revelation, something at which Eusebius looks askance. According to Eusebius, it is clear that Papias only knew the "elders" who had had contact with the "holy apostles," not with the "holy apostles" themselves. Papias had heard personally what Aristion and the elder John were saying, but had only heard about what the earlier apostles had said.[2]

As most scholars have now concluded (e.g., Schoedel 1992), Papias was an adult during the reign of Trajan and perhaps also Hadrian, so that his work, cited centuries later by Eusebius, should probably be dated to about C.E. 100, which is to say only shortly after the Fourth Gospel is traditionally dated. All of this is interesting in several respects. In the first place, Papias does not attempt to claim too much, even though he has great interest in what all the apostles and the Twelve have said. His claim is a limited one: of having heard those who had been in contact with such eyewitnesses. In the second place, he is writing at a time and in a place where he ought to have known who it was that was responsible for putting together the Fourth Gospel; equally clearly, he reflects the influence of the millennial theology that within the New Testament we find only clearly in the book of Revelation, and not in the Fourth Gospel. This suggests that the John he knew and had talked with was John of Patmos, and that this was the same John who had something to do with the production of the Fourth Gospel. It is significant that Hengel (1989a), after a detailed discussion, concludes that this Gospel must be associated with John the Elder, who was not the same as John son of Zebedee. More on this will be said in due course. As I have stressed, while Papias's testimony is significant and early, we must also give due weight to the internal evidence in the Fourth Gospel itself, to which we will turn shortly. One more thing: Papias fragment 10:17 has now been subjected to detailed analysis by

---

2. On this entire matter and on the reliability of Papias, see now Bauckham 2006.

Michael Oberweis (1996), who draws the conclusion, rightly in my judgment, that Papias claimed that John son of Zebedee died early, as a martyr, like his brother (Acts 12:2). This counts against both the theory that John of Patmos was John of Zebedee and the theory that the latter wrote the Fourth Gospel.

The Growing Recognition of the Judean Provenance and Character of This Gospel

In his new commentary on the Gospel of John, Andrew Lincoln has concluded that the Beloved Disciple was a real person and "a minor follower of Jesus during his Jerusalem ministry" (2005, 22). While Lincoln sees the Beloved Disciple traditions as small snippets of historical tradition added to a larger core of the Gospel that did not come from this person, he draws this conclusion about the Beloved Disciple's provenance for a very good reason. This figure does not show up at all in this Gospel's telling of the Galilean ministry stories, while, on the other hand, he seems to be involved with and know personally about Jesus' ministry in and around Jerusalem.

One of the things that is probably fatal to the theory that John son of Zebedee is the Beloved Disciple and also the author of this entire document is that none, and I do mean none, of the special Zebedee stories from the Synoptics are included in the Fourth Gospel (e.g., the calling of the Zebedee brothers by Jesus, their presence with Jesus in the house where Jesus raised Jairus's daughter, the story of the transfiguration, the request for special seats in Jesus' kingdom when it comes, and so forth). In view of the fact that this Gospel places some stress on the role of eyewitness testimony (see especially John 19–21), it is strange that these stories would be omitted if this Gospel were indeed written by John of Zebedee, or even if he were its primary source. It is equally strange that the Zebedee brothers are so briefly mentioned in this Gospel (only in John 21:2) and that John is never explicitly equated with the Beloved Disciple, even in the appendix (see 21:2 and 7, although the Beloved Disciple could certainly be one of the two unnamed disciples mentioned in 21:2).

Also telling is the fact that this Gospel includes none, or almost none, of the special Galilean miracle stories found in the Synoptics, with the exception of the feeding of the five thousand/walking on water tandem. Rather, the author of this document includes stories such as Jesus' meeting with Nicodemus, his encounter with the Samaritan woman, the healing of the cripple by the pool of Bethesda, the healing of the man born blind, and the raising of Lazarus. What all these events have in common is that *none of them transpired in Galilee.*

When we couple these features with the fact that our author seems to have some detailed knowledge about the topography in and around Jerusalem and the historical particulars about the last week or so of Jesus' life (e.g., compare the story of the anointing of Jesus by Mary of Bethany in John 12 to the more generic account in Mark 14), it is not surprising that Lincoln and others reflect a growing trend in recognizing the Judean provenance of this Gospel. Recognition of this provenance clears up various difficulties, not least of which is the lack of Galilean stories in general in this Gospel and more particularly the lack of exorcism tales, none of which, according to the Synoptics, are said to have occurred in Jerusalem or Judea. Furthermore, this Gospel has absolutely no emphasis or real interest in the Twelve as such or in their being Galileans. If the author were a Judean follower of Jesus and not one of the Twelve, and if he in turn were sticking to the things he knows personally or has heard directly from eyewitnesses, this is understandable. This brings us to the question of who this Beloved Disciple might have been.

THE FIRST MENTION OF "ONE WHOM JESUS LOVED"—JOHN 11 OR JOHN 13?

It has been common in Johannine commentaries to suggest that the Beloved Disciple as a figure in the narrative does not show up under that title before John 13. While this case has been argued thoroughly, it overlooks something very important. This Gospel was written in an oral culture for use among non-Christians as a sort of teaching tool to lead them to faith. It was not intended to be handed out as a tract for the nonbeliever to read, but nevertheless its stories were meant to be used orally for evangelism.

In an oral and rhetorically careful document of this sort, the ordering of things is especially important.[3] Figures once introduced into the narrative by name and title, or by name and an identifying phrase, may thereafter be identified by only one or the other, since economy of words was at a premium when writing a document of this size on a piece of papyrus (John 20:30–31). This brings us to John 11:3 and the phrase ὃν φιλεῖς ("the one whom you love"). It is perfectly clear from verses 1 and 3 that the sick person in question, first called "Lazarus of Bethany" and then called "the one whom you love," is the same person; in the context, the mention of sickness in each verse makes this identification certain. This is the first time in the entire Gospel that any individual is said to have been loved by Jesus. Indeed, one could argue that this is the only named person in the whole Gospel about whom this is specifically and directly said. I would stress that in a rhetorically saturated environment, the audience would be well aware and attuned to the fact that the first mention of crucial ideas, persons, and events was critical to the understanding of what was being suggested and how it was meant to persuade the audience.

---

3. Think, for a moment, of the highly schematized nature and arrangement of the Gospel: we have seven sign miracles climaxing in the grandest one—the raising of Lazarus; seven "I Am" sayings; and seven discourses linked to the "I Am" sayings in one way or another. Clearly, schematization and internal signals by a key word or phrase are major rhetorical traits of this Gospel.

This brings us to John 13:23, where we have the by-now-familiar reference to a disciple whom Jesus loved (ὃν ἠγάπα this time), who is reclining on the bosom of Jesus, by which is meant that he is reclining on the same couch as Jesus. The disciple is not named here, and notice that nowhere in John 13 is it said that this meal transpired in Jerusalem. It could just as well have transpired in the nearby town of Bethany, and it need not even be an account of a Passover meal. John 13:1, in fact, says that it was a meal that transpired *before* the Passover meal. This brings us to a crucial juncture in this discussion. John 11 refers to a beloved disciple named Lazarus; John 12 mentions a meal at the house of Lazarus. If someone heard these tales in this order without access to the Synoptic Gospels, it would be natural to conclude that the person reclining with Jesus in John 13 was Lazarus. There is another good reason to do so as well. It was the custom in this sort of dining that the host would recline with or next to the chief guest. Then the story told in John 13 likely implies that the Beloved Disciple is the host. But this in turn means that he must have a house in the vicinity of Jerusalem, which probably eliminates *all* the Galilean disciples.

This identification of the Beloved Disciple as Lazarus not only clears up some conundrums about this story, but it also neatly clears up a series of other conundrums in the Johannine passion narrative. Some examples: (1) It was always problematic that the Beloved Disciple had ready access to the high priest's house (John 18:15–16). Who could he have been to have such access? Surely not a Galilean fisherman! John 11:36–47 suggests that some of the Jewish officials who reported to the high priest had known Lazarus and had attended his mourning period in Bethany. This in turn means that Lazarus likely had some relationship with them. He could have had access to Caiaphas's house, being a person of high status known to Caiaphas's entourage.[4] (2) If Lazarus of Bethany is the Beloved Disciple, it also explains the omission from this Gospel of the Garden of Gethsemane prayer story. Peter, James, and John were present on that occasion, but the Beloved Disciple was not. (3) It also explains John 19:27. If the Beloved Disciple took Jesus' mother "unto his own" home (it is implied), this surely suggests some locale much nearer than Galilee, for the Beloved Disciple shows up in Jerusalem

---

4. I was asked, when I presented this paper, "Would Lazarus not have known about the threat against his life by these very people, and would that not have prevented him from going to the high priest's house?" This is a reasonable question, but one must realize that Lazarus in the story has just been raised from the dead. What had he to fear from further death threats? He was instead concerned about the danger his beloved friend Jesus faced. Another question asked is, "If Lazarus had been ill, and then dead, would he not have been unclean, and thus not allowed into the high priest's house?" The text of John 18:15 actually only mentions his coming into the courtyard, but more importantly, Lazarus would have likely gone through the *mikveh* rituals prescribed by the priests after his being raised in order no longer to be considered ritually unclean, and the priests would likely have known of this fact. See, for example, what Jesus says in Mark 1:44: "Go, show yourself to the priest, and offer for your cleansing what Moses commanded."

in John 20 immediately thereafter, and of course Mary is still there, according to Acts 1:14, well after the crucifixion and resurrection of her son. (4) How is it that the Beloved Disciple gets to the tomb of Jesus in John 20 *before* Peter? Perhaps it is because he knows the locale. He indeed knows Joseph of Arimathea and Nicodemus, being one who lived near and spent much time in Jerusalem and with various elders in Jerusalem. One more thing about John 20:2, about which Tom Thatcher kindly reminded me: here the designation of our man is double—he is called both "the other disciple" and "the one whom Jesus loved" (τὸν ἄλλον μαθητὴν ὃν ἐφίλει ὁ Ἰησοῦς, only this time the verb is φιλέω). Why has our author varied the title at this juncture, if in fact it was a preexisting title for someone outside the narrative? We would expect it to be in a fixed form if it were some kind of preexisting title. Notice now the chain of events: Lazarus is identified in John 11 as the one whom Jesus loves, and here "the other disciple" (see John 20:1–2) is identified as the one whom Jesus loves, which then allows him to be called "the other disciple" in the rest of this segment of the story, but at 21:2 we return once more to his main designation: the one whom Jesus loved is Lazarus. All of this makes good sense if all of John 11–21 is read or heard in the sequence in which we now find it. (5) The old problem of the fact that the Synoptics say that all of the Twelve deserted Jesus once he was taken away for execution, even Peter, and record only women being at the cross, is not contradicted by the account in John 19 if in fact the Beloved Disciple, while clearly a man (called Mary's "son" in John 19:26, so not Mary Magdalene!), is Lazarus rather than one of the Twelve. (6) Finally, if indeed the Beloved Disciple took Mary into his own home, then we know where the Beloved Disciple got the story of the wedding feast at Cana—he got it from Mary herself. I could continue mounting up small textual details that are best explained by the theory that Lazarus is the Beloved Disciple, but one more conjecture must suffice for now (before we deal with some larger issues in regard to this Gospel that are explained by this theory, in particular the appendix in John 21).

Scholars, of course, have often noted how the account of the anointing of Jesus in Bethany as recorded in Mark 14:3–11 differs from the account in John 12:1–11, while likely still being the same story or tradition. Perhaps the most salient difference is that Mark tells us that the event happens in the home of Simon the Leper in Bethany, while John 12 implies that it happens in the house of Mary, Martha, and Lazarus in Bethany. Suppose for a moment, however, that Simon the Leper was in fact the father of these three siblings. Suppose that Lazarus himself, like his father, had also contracted the dread disease and succumbed to it (and from recent archaeological and medical work on ancient corpses from the region, we now know with certainty that the deadly form of Hanson's disease did exist in the first century C.E.). This might also explain why none of these three siblings seems to be married. Few have remarked about the oddness of this trio of adults not having families of their own, but rather still living together; however, it is not at all odd if the family was plagued by a dread disease that made them unclean on a continual or regular basis. It also explains why these siblings never travel with Jesus' other disciples and why other people never get near this family until the fateful day recorded in John 11, when Jesus raised and healed Lazarus. Jesus, of course, was not put off by the disease and so had visited the home previously alone (Luke 10:38–42). But other early Jews would certainly not have engaged in betrothal contracts with this family if it was known to be a carrier of leprosy.

How Seeing That Eyewitness as Lazarus Himself Explains Both the Ending of the Gospel and Its Character

Most scholars agree that John 21 makes it clear that, while the Beloved Disciple is said to have written down some Gospel traditions, he is no longer alive when at least the end of this chapter was written. The claim "we know his testimony is true" is a dead giveaway that someone or ones *other* than the Beloved Disciple put this Gospel into its final form and added this appendix, or at a minimum the story about the demise of the Beloved Disciple and the conclusion of the appendix. This line of reasoning I find compelling. It also explains something else. We may envision that whoever put the memoirs of the Beloved Disciple together is probably the one who insisted on calling him by that term.

In other words, the Beloved Disciple is called such by his community, perhaps, and by his final editor certainly. It is not a self-designation. Indeed, it is unlikely to have been a self-designation in a religious subculture where humility and following the self-sacrificial, self-effacing example of Jesus was being inculcated. This then explains one of the salient differences between 2 John and 3 John and the Gospel of John. The author of those little letters calls himself either the "elder" or "the old man," depending on how one wants to render πρεσβύτερος. He nowhere calls himself the Beloved Disciple, not even in the sermon we call 1 John, where he claims to have personally seen and touched the Word of Life—in my view, a claim that he saw and touched Jesus. We must deal, then, with at least two persons responsible for the final form of the Fourth Gospel, while only one is necessary to explain the epiphenomena of the Johannine Epistles. This brings us to a particular question about the story itself in John 21:20–24.

Why does the final editor of this material take such pains to deny that Jesus predicted that the Beloved Disciple would live until Jesus returned? Is it because there had been a tradition in the Beloved Disciple's church that he would live until then, and if so, what generated such a tradition? Not, apparently, the Beloved Disciple himself. If he had by now passed away, this would have caused anxiety among the faithful about what Jesus had actually said about his future in 30 c.e., especially with implications for the Beloved Disciple. I would suggest that no solution better explains all the interesting factors in play here than the proposal that the Beloved Disciple was someone whom Jesus had raised from the dead, and so quite naturally there arose a belief that surely he would not die again before Jesus returned. Such a line of thought makes perfectly good sense if the Beloved Disciple had already died once and the second coming was still something eagerly anticipated when he died a second time. Thus, I submit that the proposal that Lazarus was the Beloved Disciple and the author of most of the traditions in this Gospel is the theory that best clears up the conundrum of the end of the appendix, written after his death.

On this matter, there is one more thing to say. It is of course true that the Fourth Gospel takes its own approach to presenting Jesus and the gospel tradition. I am still unconvinced by the attempts of Lincoln (2005) and other scholars to suggest that the author of the Fourth Gospel drew on earlier Gospels, particularly Mark. I think he may well have known of such Gospels, may even have read Mark, but he is certainly not dependent upon the Synoptic material for his own Gospel. Rather, he takes his own line of approach and has an abundance of information that he is unable to include in his Gospel, including much non-Synoptic material (see John 20:30; 21:25), because of the constraints of writing all this down on one papyrus. He did not need to boil up his Gospel based on fragments and snippets from the Synoptics. On the contrary, he had to be constantly condensing his material, as is so often the case with an eyewitness account that is rich in detail and substance. But it is not enough to say that the author was an eyewitness to explain the Fourth Gospel's independence and differences from the earlier Synoptics. There are other factors as well.

As I pointed out over a decade ago, the Fourth Gospel is written in a way that attempts to present the Jesus tradition in the light of the Jewish sapiential material (Witherington 1995b). Jesus is presented in this Gospel as God's Wisdom come in the flesh, serving up discourses like those of personified Wisdom in earlier Jewish wisdom literature, rather than offering aphorisms and parables as in the Synoptics. I have suggested that this reflects Jesus' in-house *modus operandi* for his private teaching of his own inner circle of disciples. We need not choose between the public form of wisdom discourse found in the Synoptics (i.e., parables and aphorisms) and the private form of wisdom discourse in John (e.g., John 14–17) when trying to decide which went back to the historical Jesus: both did, but they had different *Sitzen im Leben* and different functions. I have concluded that even this line of thinking is insufficient to explain the differences from the Synoptics we find in the Fourth Gospel. A final factor comes into play here.

If our author, the Beloved Disciple, had been raised by Jesus not merely from death's door but from being well and truly dead, this was bound to change his worldview! It became quite impossible for our author to draw up a veiled-Messiah portrait of Jesus, as we find in Mark. No, our author wanted and needed to shout from the mountain tops that Jesus was "the resurrection," not merely that he performed resuscitations. In the experience of this witness, he was indeed what Ernst Käsemann once said (1968, 9) about the presentation of Jesus in the Fourth Gospel: he was a God bestriding the stage of history. Just so, in Johannine perspective, and our author pulls no punches in making that clear in various ways in his Gospel, especially by demonstrating that the mind and plan of God known as God's Wisdom is now said to come from Jesus. He is the incarnation of the great I Am.

The Beloved Disciple would not have been pleased with modern minimalist portraits of the historical Jesus. He had had a personal and profound encounter of the first order with both the historical Jesus and the risen Jesus, and he knew that they were one and the same. This was bound to change his worldview. It is no accident that the Book of Signs in the Fourth Gospel climaxes in John 11 with the story of Lazarus's own transformation, just as the Book of Glory climaxes in John 20 with the transformation of Jesus himself. Lazarus had become what he admired, and he had been made, to a lesser degree, to be like Jesus. That is why he would have nothing to do with mincing words about his risen Savior and Lord. Rather, he would walk through the door of bold proclamation, perhaps even to the point of adding the Logos hymn at the beginning of his Gospel. This was the Jesus he had known and touched and supped with before and after Easter, and he could proclaim no lesser Jesus.

This then leads us to the last bit of the puzzle that can now be solved. How did this Gospel come to be named according to John? My answer is a simple one: because John of Patmos was the final editor of this Gospel after the death of Lazarus. Once Domitian died, John left Patmos, returned to Ephesus, and there lived out his days. One of the things he did was edit and promulgate the Fourth Gospel on behalf of the Beloved Disciple. Somewhere very near the end of John's own life, Papias had contact with this elderly John. It is not surprising, since this contact seems to be brief, that Papias learned correctly that this John was not the Zebedee-descended John and that this elderly John had something to do with the production of the Fourth Gospel. This, I think, neatly explains all of the various factors involved in our conundrum. It may even have been Papias who was responsible for the wider circulation of this Gospel with a tag "according to John." It is not surprising that Irenaeus, swatting buzzing gnostics like flies, would later conclude that the Fourth Gospel must be by an apostle or one of the Twelve.

If I am right about all this, it means that the historical figure of Lazarus is more important than we have previously imagined, both due to his role in founding churches in and around Ephesus and, of course, his role in the life of Jesus and of Jesus' mother. Jesus must have trusted him implicitly to hand over his mother to him when he died. This likelihood, then, accounts for much of the historical origin of John's distinctive tradition, staking out its own claims to historicity as an independent memory. It also accounts for the theological and Judean character of John's material in a highly plausible way. Lazarus was far more than just one more recipient of a miraculous healing by Jesus. He was "the one whom Jesus loved," as the very first reference to him in John 11:3 says. We have yet to take the measure of the man. Hopefully now, we can begin to do so.[5]

---

5. See now my archaeological thriller, *The Lazarus Effect* (Eugene: Pickwick, 2008), for a fuller development of the implications of this thesis

On Not Unbinding the Lazarus Story:
The Nexus of History and
Theology in John 11:1–44[1]

Derek M. H. Tovey

As I prepared this paper, a joke often came to mind of a traveler on his way to a city, finding himself lost in the countryside (perhaps I should say "boondocks"— we might imagine a traveler to Washington, D.C., somewhere in the Appalachian Mountains). He stops to ask directions of a local he finds leaning on a fencepost. "Tell me," he asks, "how do I get to Washington, D.C.?" "Well," comes the reply, "if I was going there, I wouldn't start from here."

The story of the raising of Lazarus must be one of the most problematic in the Fourth Gospel when addressing the issue of the relationship of the material to an event in the life of the historical Jesus. If one wishes to argue positively, as I will here, for the historicity of the Lazarus story as an event in the life of the historical Jesus, one faces many obstacles (one might say "roadblocks") on the way to one's destination. Moreover, as I shall argue below, when it comes to reading the story under the conventions of post-Enlightenment, "scientific" historiography, there is a sense in which one cannot "start from here." I shall raise the question whether we need to find a form of history that encompasses the possibility of events such as the return to life of a deceased man and, equally, if not more importantly, allows for the depiction of the historical figure of Jesus to include actions, and categories of description, not normally accepted within "scientific" historiography.

---

1. The word "nexus" in the title and this essay may be taken to refer both to the bond or link between history and theology (and, one might add, history and narrative artistry, though there is not space to explore this aspect here) and to the fact that history, theology, and narrative artistry are interconnected. Under the aspect of "history" it would be possible to discuss the history of the literary tradition (essentially what Meier 1994 does in treating this pericope) or the historical situation within the Johannine community to which the Evangelist might have directed his story of the raising of Lazarus. I am concerned here, however, with the material's connection with an event in the life of the historical Jesus.

The problems associated with any endeavor to establish the historicity of this pericope revolve around two fundamental issues. First, does the Evangelist (or "implied author")[2] intend a referential function in this story, or has the story been crafted out of theological motivations, so that any referential function the story may be presumed to have has been subsumed under other purposes? I shall elaborate on this below.

Second, if the Evangelist does intend a referential function, how might we recover such historical data as the story may contain? This issue is generally addressed by exploring the "sources" or traditions behind the story to recover a core of historical tradition that points to an event in the life of the historical Jesus. On the way to such an outcome, one must grapple with a number of difficult questions that can only be noted here. First is the question of the thoroughly Johannine cast of the material, noted long ago by C. H. Dodd (1963, 30, 32, 228; see also Meier 1994, 800–801). Next, the vexed question of the Fourth Gospel's relation to the Synoptic Gospels must be considered, for if we could determine whether and how the author of the Fourth Gospel was drawing upon the Synoptics, would we then be able to describe the influences and intertextual motivations by which the author constructed his account (on the relation of John 11:1–44 to Luke 10:38–42, see, e.g., Brown 1966–70; Dunkerley 1959)?

Once a careful recovery of the historical data has been completed, one remains confronted by the epistemological questions deriving from the philosophy of history that has operated since the Enlightenment. How do we judge evidence that runs beyond the bounds of the categories of what constitutes "history" as we conceive of it (that is, events that do not arise out of human or "natural" causes and effects and that are not open to investigation and explanation under the rubrics of analogy, contingency, and all of that)? This problem is illustrated most clearly in the work of John Meier.[3] In about thirty-four pages of careful argument, he is able to claim that the nature of the tradition makes him inclined "to think that the Lazarus story ultimately reflects some incident in the life of the historical Jesus" (Meier 1994, 831). But in the next sentence he writes that "the question of what actually happened cannot be resolved by us today." The most that can be said is that "this event was *believed* by Jesus' disciples even during his lifetime to be a miracle of raising the dead" (emphasis added). Indeed,

---

2. I shall use the terms "Evangelist" and "implied author" more or less interchangeably here. I prefer the term "implied author," which is the intratextual "profile" of the extratextual "author" (conventionally called "the Evangelist"). For more on the implied author, see Tovey 1997, 45–46; 2007, 12, 41.

3. But see also Barnabas Lindars's assessment of the fact that the way in which the Evangelist has developed the Lazarus story has "deprived us of any hope of recovering the truth of what actually happened. All we know is that people in NT times felt that return to life was not impossible in certain circumstances, and that Jesus was credited with having raised the dead on one or two occasions" (1972, 386).

the most that can be established, Meier is careful to say at the outset of his discussion of all the stories of raisings from death in the Gospels (and, I submit, this applies *mutatis mutandis* to exorcisms and other healing miracles as well, indeed, to all miracles), is "that some of these stories may go back to events in the life of Jesus, events that he and/or his disciples *interpreted* as the raising of the dead to life" (Meier 1994, 775; emphasis added). The most that we can do, then, is establish a belief, an interpretation, or an explanation against which other beliefs, interpretations, or explanations may be offered. I shall return to this issue toward the conclusion of this paper.

TEXTUAL INDICATIONS OF HISTORICAL REFERENCE

As regards the issue of whether or not the Evangelist intends a referential function in this story, it seems to me that the tendency of much current scholarship is to focus on the symbolic and theological value of this story, while leaving aside the question of its historical value. This arises not simply because of perceived difficulties in making the Fourth Gospel cohere with a construction of Jesus based on the Synoptic accounts but because it would seem that the Evangelist's own treatment of the story, especially as it is set within the wider Gospel narrative, lends itself to interpretation under symbolic and theological categories.

So, for example, James P. Martin (1964) sees the story of Lazarus as addressing the problem of the delay of the Parousia in the early church. Sandra Schneiders (1987) sees the Lazarus story as one directed at spirituality: the personal appropriation of faith in Jesus as the resurrection and the life. Philip F. Esler and Ronald Piper (2006) apply social-science analysis to examine how the narrative's use of Lazarus, Mary, and Martha as "prototypes" speaks to the intended readers' situation and their questions about their social identity and postmortem destiny.[4] Wendy Sproston North (2001, esp. 54–57) sees the story, in part, as an invitation for the disciples to tread the way of martyrdom, in faithfulness to and imitation of Jesus and for the sake of witness.

Such readings can be exegetically fruitful, and they can make sense of a number of the pericope's *aporiae*. It is tempting to abandon attempts to anchor the story as an event in the life of Jesus and explore these further. Nevertheless, I argue, the Evangelist's (or, the implied author's) speech-acts drive the interpreter to ask the question about the referential character of this story.

To begin with, the implied author puts statements in the mouths of Jesus, the narrator, and Martha (at 11:39) that press the point that Lazarus's death is to be understood as an actual and unmistakable physical death, which Jesus reverses by

---

4. The authors say that they are not attempting to "say something about the historical Jesus" (Esler and Piper 2006, 46). The question as to whether these characters were also real people is left somewhat open (see, e.g., 76).

an act of revivification.[5] This is despite the fact that the implied author also develops the story, including some of the dialogue, in a way that appears to prepare for a symbolic and theological interpretation of Jesus' death. I refer to how the narrator says that, while the disciples take Jesus' words as a reference to natural sleep, Jesus means that Lazarus has died (11:13). This is followed by the statement that Jesus clarifies the misunderstanding by saying plainly (παρρησία): Lazarus is dead (11:14).

However, Jesus has already set up the disciples for this misunderstanding by saying earlier (11:4) that Lazarus's illness would not result in death (οὐκ ἔστιν πρὸς θάνατον). Thus, his plain-speaking at 11:14 forces the reader to consider alternative meanings to Jesus' earlier words. Readers infer either that the death of Lazarus is to be reversed or that the "death" spoken of is some other type of death (hence the symbolic and theological readings).

The fact of death is also stressed in the dialogue between Jesus and Martha at Lazarus's tomb. When Jesus commands that the stone be removed from the tomb's entrance, Martha immediately remonstrates: "Lord, already there is a stench because he has been dead four days" (11:39). In fact, as the mourners make their way to the tomb, the death of Lazarus has already been confirmed when some say, "Could not he who opened the eyes of the blind man have kept this man from dying?" (11:37).

The implied author's narrative strategy to this point in the Gospel suggests that if he had wished to downplay the concreteness of the revivification of Lazarus in favor of some of the more symbolic, theologically motivated purposes proposed by interpreters, he could have done so. For example, the first exchange between Jesus and Martha (11:20–27), which many commentators rightly see as the climax of the pericope, would have afforded an excellent opportunity to develop an extended discourse (as, for example, in John 5 or 6). Lazarus's return to life could have been alluded to without dwelling on it in the concrete terms this story provides, hence freeing the implied author to draw out the symbolic aspects.

The implied author tells a story of the raising of a dead man in concrete terms for two reasons. First, he wants this story to be a theological and narrative counterpoint to the resurrection of Jesus. I shall draw out the significance of this later. Second, he desires to show that, among the signs that Jesus performs, signs that act as proofs, if you will, for the reader to accept his assertions that Jesus is the Christ (and come to believing faith, 20:31), is the raising of a dead man.

That the implied author works with traditional material in providing this sign has been well established by scholarship. We may quickly rehearse the arguments.

---

5. Here I follow Esler and Piper, who reserve the term "resurrection" for the state of "being raised on the last day" (2006, 1 n. 1). Lazarus is raised to a mortal life and will eventually die again. Furthermore, the term "resurrection" is best reserved for the resurrection of Jesus (which is resurrection to a new form of life beyond death).

To begin with, a tradition of stories in which Jesus raises the dead is attested to by Mark 5:21–43 (par. Matt 9:18–26; Luke 8:40–56) and by Luke 7:11–17. Luke 7:22 and Matt 11:5 provide a report of Jesus' ministry where, among other things, Jesus is said to raise the dead (Lincoln 2005, 332; Schnackenburg 1990, 2:341).

Furthermore, scholars are able to agree that we can recover a primitive story (a "source," if you will) once the Johannine features of the pericope have been "stripped away" (Beasley-Murray 1987, 185). Moreover, despite a range of opinions as to which parts constitute the source material, scholars are able to reconstruct a reasonably consistent outline, or basic structure, to this primitive story (Beasley-Murray 1987, 185; Meier 1994, 892 n. 118; Haenchen 1984, 2:68).

The presence in the story of Mary and Martha, sharing the same general characteristics as found in the portrayal of them in Luke 10:38–42, suggests a common tradition here, which is based upon the memory of an historical pair (Byrne 1991, 74–75). That all three names (Mary, Martha, Lazarus) have been found in ossuary inscriptions near Bethany indicate that historical persons bearing those names existed, though we cannot assume that the inscriptions are those for the characters found in the Gospel (Blomberg 2001, 165). Meier points out that Lazarus (Eleazar or Lazar) was in any case a common name "for Jewish men in Palestine around the turn of the era" (1994, 825). The proleptic mention of Mary at 11:2 as the one who anointed Jesus with perfume might indicate a tradition known to the intended readers.[6]

An analysis of the names along the lines that Richard Bauckham has suggested (2003; 2006) may provide a further set of criteria by which we might determine traditional material that is rooted in some sort of "extratextual" data and that points to what Samuel Byrskog has described as the "extrafictional reality or history" behind the narrativized oral history.[7] Bauckham's argument is that named characters may appear in the Gospel narratives because they were eyewitnesses "who not only originated the traditions to which their names are attached but also continued to tell these stories as authoritative guarantors of the traditions" (2003, 44; see also 2006, 39). He seeks to establish that, contrary to earlier assumptions that names were added as traditions developed, they were as likely to be eliminated in later tradition. In fact, names tended to drop out of the canonical Gospel material (at least as far as the Synoptics are concerned) as the status of named characters as remembered informants and eyewitnesses diminished or was "obscured" (2003, 49–50). If anything, the tendency to invent names

---

6. It might also be a narrative device (prolepsis), or evidence of the editing (misediting?) of sources; discussion is divided, for which see the commentaries.

7. For the terms "extrafictional reality" and "extrafictional history," see Byrskog 2000, 41, 47, along with comments on the relationship between the "narrativized and intratextual use of autopsy" with "its extratextual and extrafictional significance" (2000, 303).

for characters unnamed in the canonical Gospels seems to have been a practice that became popular from the fourth century C.E. onward (2003, 48–49).

Bauckham's argument that the feature of naming needs explanation, given that it is usual that recipients of healings and exorcisms remain unnamed, has weight. The explanation he advances, that an individual is named because of his or her role as a witness involved as a central participant in the event, is plausible (2003, 57; 2006, 52–54) and every bit as strong as earlier suggestions that such detail adds "novelistic interest" or is a tendency in the development of tradition (2003, 46; 2006, 40–41).

Unfortunately, while Bauckham identifies recipients of Jesus' healing, including revivification (and here he names Lazarus), as examples of named characters whose inclusion in the Gospels may stem from their role as eyewitnesses, he does not develop the argument with regard to Lazarus in any detail. His explanation, that the absence of the Lazarus story in Mark (puzzling, given the importance attached by the Fourth Evangelist to this event as a key event leading to Jesus' death) arises from the need to protect Lazarus (2006, 196), is speculative at best.

Furthermore, several comments Bauckham makes give me pause when considering the application of his hypothesis to the Lazarus story. First, in a footnote to the observation that the practice of giving invented names to unnamed Gospel characters is a late phenomenon, Bauckham states that this practice "must be distinguished from the invention of new characters with names" (2003, 49 n. 81). Thus, we must first establish that the character of Lazarus is not an instance of the invention of a new named character. Second, Bauckham maintains that in Jewish practice, the giving of names to characters not named in Scripture was common. So, he goes on, "it would not be surprising to find Christians doing the same in the case of Gospel narratives from an early date" (2003, 49 n. 81). While Bauckham states that the evidence suggests that this did not happen, it might be the case that the author of the Fourth Gospel is influenced by this common Jewish practice. Thus, further research is required on this point. One might also ask whether the Fourth Gospel contains early instances of the habit Bauckham identifies as late, namely, the giving of invented names to unnamed characters.[8]

---

8. As tendencies may be observed to move in either direction, it is important at this point to test the strength of Bauckham's arguments that in the early period the tendency is for named characters to become unnamed as their significance as witnesses weakens or is forgotten (2006, 42, 46) and, conversely, that the invention of names for unnamed characters is a much later phenomenon (2006, 43–44). What is further required is a set of criteria by which it can be determined, if possible, where names are used in a way that shows that they function referentially to historical figures and when they are used for "fictive" purposes. Establishing such criteria would require analysis of literature across a range of genres and a span of two or three centuries on either side of the first century. One working hypothesis to begin with might be to explore the referential status of named characters that are associated with particular localities. Analogies with modern historical novels might also be helpful if it can be established that there

The argument of this essay to this point may be summarized as follows. Strong arguments have been mounted by scholars that the Lazarus story derives from primitive tradition.[9] If Bauckham's hypothesis is correct, the primitive nature of this tradition, and its connections with an historical event, is strengthened by the presence of named characters whose status is to be understood as guarantors of the tradition. While aspects of what I have described as "the implied author's speech-acts" might be motivated by considerations of narrative artistry, the structure of the story suggests that the implied author intends to assert that the event concerned an actual death followed by an actual act of revivification. However, even if we establish that the nature of the textual evidence indicates that the pericope is neither a pure invention of the implied author nor based on an invented tradition of an earlier generation, but is referential upon an event in the ministry of Jesus when he raised a dead man, that is about as far as we can go. We cannot easily go beyond this to speak of "what actually happened" in that event.

This is the case not simply because of the difficulties we have determining the nature of texts. It is inherent in the nature of history itself. Sometimes biblical scholars express the idea that the stories we have in the Gospels are not like the kind of evidence we would have if a video camera had been on hand to capture the event, as if video footage would help solve the problem of obtaining good history. While at one level it is true that having video footage might help with obtaining a sense of the outward features of the event (the data or "the facts"), what the sentiment as expressed generally obscures is the fact that we would still need to "make meaning" of the event. We would still need to *interpret* what was captured on camera (and surely we would require not one but hundreds of video cameras to adequately provide a comprehensive idea of what happened). If, for the sake of the argument, it were possible to show images of Lazarus emerging from the tomb in all his wrappings, it would not for a moment do away with the debate about what actually happened and what it meant.[10]

---

are certain habits of mind that are trans-historical and trans-cultural and that determine the way in which historical characters function in fictional contexts as against invented nonhistorical characters. That is, are there controls upon the liberties that an author feels can be taken when using a historical character in an invented setting?

9. I have largely taken the substance of these arguments for granted, as they are so widely discussed in the scholarly literature. More points than space allows might have been brought in. Meier 1994 provides a comprehensive overview.

10. Commentaries, monographs, and articles provide something of the character of the debate that might ensue. Once scholars decide that there may be some historical basis to an account of a revivification, some hazard guesses as to what might "actually have happened": the possibilities include "suspended animation," recovery from deep coma, or that a report of a seriously ill man healed by Jesus became a story about a revivified man (Dunkerley 1959, 325; Meier 1994, 775). In the case of the revivification of Lazarus, the length of time he is "supposed" to have been dead provides a difficulty, though one might posit that a mistake had been made, that it was conceivable that he had been put in the tomb too hastily, and that he had actually

THE LAZARUS STORY AS "THEOLOGIZED HISTORY"

It is to the interpretive and explanatory aspects of historical discourse that I want to turn in conclusion. For, whatever judgments we might make about elements of the story as historical datum, however we may judge the implied author to have configured the sequence of those elements in the interests of his theological and rhetorical aims, it remains the case that the implied author selects this "sign" (this account) as part of his overall illocutionary act of convincing the reader of the particular construction he wishes to put upon the historical event of the life and death of Jesus. Indeed, he writes this account from a perspective that is after what he would call "the glorification" of Jesus (that is, postresurrection).

In fact, as many commentators have noted, the implied author tells this story and crafts it in such a way as much for what he wants to say about the meaning and significance of his main character, Jesus, in the light of his death and subsequent resurrection. The "event" of the death and subsequent resurrection of Jesus is as much the focus of this story as is the revivification of Lazarus. In a very real sense, in terms of the assertions made by the implied author in 11:1–44, the historicity of Lazarus's revivification depends upon the historicity of his later account of the resurrection of Jesus.[11]

That the text's focus is upon the death and resurrection of Jesus is supported by such elements as the fact that Jesus declares Lazarus's death to be for the "glorification" of "the Son of God" (11:4), the discussion about the danger in which a return to Judea will place Jesus (11:7–10), the ringing declaration by Jesus in 11:25, saying "I am the resurrection and the life," and the subtle comparisons between the description of the raised Lazarus emerging in his wrappings and the later description of the wrappings in Jesus' own empty tomb (11:44; see also 20:6–7). We might also possibly add, depending on how we read it, the description of Jesus' own perturbation of spirit both prior to and on arrival at Lazarus's tomb (11:33, 38).[12]

All this amounts to a construction put upon the life and being of a historical person. To that extent, it is an exercise in historical interpretation and explanation. It is this author's attempt to convey what he understands to be the historic

---

been in a coma. One would, however, need to explain plausibly how members of the family and others had concluded that Lazarus had died.

11. Of course, this statement contains several problems, not least what one means by "the resurrection of Jesus" and how one understands it as a historical event. However we might wish to understand the problematic phrase "the resurrection of Jesus" as an item of tradition, we would be hard pressed to find one more multiply attested in the New Testament.

12. Analysis of 11:1–54 (arguably the textual parameters required by the narrator's discourse) would include among the evidence for this focus the plot to kill Jesus subsequent to his revivification of Lazarus, Caiaphas's "prophecy" (11:49–50), and the narrator's comment (11:51–52).

meaning and significance of Jesus, whom the Evangelist wishes us to know is to be understood under the descriptors of Christ, Lord, and Son of God and for whom the metaphor that he is "the resurrection and the life" is appropriate. It is, if you will, a theologically motivated (and committed) form of historical interpretation and explanation. It is what I would call "theologized history." It is here, too, that Bauckham's thesis in *Jesus and the Eyewitnesses* is important, for it establishes the whole Gospel as a work deriving from eyewitness testimony, amounting to a "disclosure" of the Jesus of testimony.[13]

The problem is that as "theologized history" it is a form of history that does not easily fit within the bounds of our notions of historical discourse. Consequently, we find our options limited to two broad strategies. The first is either to dismiss its claims as historically untrue and inaccurate[14] or, and I think this is the more usual approach among current scholars, largely to ignore or sideline the question of history in favor of exploring the narrative's theological or ideological interests. The other strategy is to attempt to distill out the historical data from the theological material in the hopes of reconstructing "history" of a scientific sort. One then has two types of material: one type can be labeled "history" and the other "theology." Material of the "history" type can then be used to construct another, different historical explanation of Jesus. But that will be what it is: a different historical explanation, not *the* historical explanation to be set alongside the Fourth Gospel's theological explanation. It, like all historical reconstructions, including a theologized historical reconstruction, will stand or fall not only on its handling of the evidence (insofar as that has been adequately recovered) but also on how plausibly it stacks up against a reader's apprehension of reality.

There is a further consideration: for some types of historical evidence and for some types of historical event, we may only proceed to a final judgment on the basis of testimony by a witness or witnesses. As Richard Bauckham says, "As a form of historiography testimony offers a unique access to historical reality that cannot be had without an element of trust in the credibility of the witness and what he or she has to report" (2006, 505). This trust is not to be uncritical, nor need the testimony remain untested; however, in some instances, trust in the testimony of the witness may be the only way forward. The subtleties of this situation are many, not the least that the subjectivity and worldview of the one receiving the testimony always remain in play. One may find a witness credible but the content and character of the testimony incredible.

---

13. Bauckham 2006, esp. 505–8 (I take the word "disclosure" from him). Bauckham's thesis is a cumulative one and is comprehensively argued on the basis not only of all four Gospels but on a survey of evidence in noncanonical writings and the early Christian witnesses and church fathers. I consider that the overarching thesis he presents helps strengthen the case for the overall historicity of particular stories within the Gospel (such as the Lazarus story), even though attention to the detail may require some nuances.

14. This is the approach of Casey 1996.

Where does this bring us in our attempt to find an event in the life of the historical Jesus in the Fourth Evangelist's story of the raising of Lazarus? I argue that the concrete manner in which the implied author speaks of the death of Lazarus, and the fact that the story contains material that by wide consensus goes back to a story of a raising in the tradition, means that the implied author includes this story among his "signs" because he understands it to refer to an actual event when a dead man was raised by Jesus. In terms of what may be the yield of historical data from this story, I argue that we have good reason (on the various grounds laid out above) for accepting that the event recounted here involved a family at Bethany bearing the names Mary, Martha, and Lazarus.

Determining whether or not, or how far, the event unfolded in the manner recounted by the Evangelist would require further discussion of the relationship between the narrative dynamics of the story (set within the wider framework of the Gospel's narrative) and its referential function. This cannot be attempted here. We may not be able finally to determine how far the details supplied by our Fourth Evangelist are true to the event, but that some such event happened is made almost certain by evidence of tradition, multiply attested.

The implied author intends by this story to say something about the significance of Jesus' death, for which Lazarus's revivification is the precipitating cause. More particularly, he wishes to bring into focus the new understanding of Jesus' true identity that the resurrection of Jesus brings and to which the raising of Lazarus acts as a counterpoint.[15] My argument here is that the claims made for Jesus by the story are made about a historical figure that must either move the story of Jesus' life into the realm of legend and fantasy or remain claims of a historical nature that do not fit within the accepted categories of post-Enlightenment historical discourse.

This being the case, the challenge for us is to find a way of thinking about history that will enable us to deal with a form of historical discourse that brings theological explanations to bear upon the account of the life of a historical person. Under the "canons" of history that we have become accustomed to work with, there is no way, other than agnostically, that we can answer the question: Did Jesus raise Lazarus from the dead? Here scientific historiography reaches its Rubicon, the kind of impasse at which Meier finds himself.[16] The nexus between

---

15. It is the implied author's narrative artistry in wanting to bring the raising of Lazarus into contiguity with his passion narrative (as well as making this "sign" the climax of all the signs in the Book of Signs) that gives rise to this particular configuration of the Gospel's plot. Actual chronology may be reconfigured to achieve this end: in fact, the whole narrative may be configured around the events of one particular Passover. For further elaboration of this, see Tovey 1997, 229–41.

16. Meier 1994 is not alone here; see also Lindars 1972, 386; Byrne 1991, 82–83. A recent article by Gregory W. Dawes has some bearing on the issues with which I am concerned here. He argues that if the Evangelists intended their narratives to refer to history (even if we must

history and theology in our material is too tight, and it is a nexus that goes all the way back into the earliest tradition.

I suggest that what is required is a fresh way forward, one that asks what forms of interpretation and explanatory work might be allowed under a more capacious description of "history." If "scientific history" cannot bridge the Rubicon, perhaps a form of history that admits theological interpretation and explanation might. Or, following Bauckham, a form of history that listens to the testimony to Jesus handed down by (or from) eyewitnesses.

---

judge that in fact the narratives do not actually do so), "[t]he interpreter who wishes to respect the evangelists' intentions may not simply set aside, as theologically irrelevant, the question of the historicity of these stories" (2006, 174). However, he goes on to state that, even though we may not conclude that they had no concern for history, we may yet judge that "they had very different standards by which they made their judgments of historical plausibility" (2006, 175). Thus, in a sense, we arrive at the same position effectively as that of Meier, Lindars, and others. We do not share the same criteria for historical plausibility as the Evangelists, so we may (or must?) set aside their narratives as history. While I would agree with some of Dawes's arguments, I believe that a different position may be taken on how we are to judge what is "solid, sober history" if we approach the question of "historical plausibility" under an understanding of how "history" may be done under criteria other than those traditionally supplied by scientific historiography. See Dawes 2006, 163–64, for his comments about "solid, sober history."

ASPECTS OF HISTORICITY IN JOHN 5–12: A RESPONSE

Paul N. Anderson

In responding to the eight essays in part 2 of this volume, I am impressed at the variety of approaches to aspects of historicity in the Gospel of John. Employing religious-anthropological, archaeological, contextual, and historical-critical studies, these essays cover the middle section of the Fourth Gospel, which includes three of Jesus' four trips to Jerusalem and rising opposition from the Judean religious leaders. The one miracle narrated in all four canonical Gospels—the feeding of the five thousand—and its attending features makes John 6 the premier locus of Gospel-comparison analysis, yet the Lazarus story of John 11 has captured the attention of three of our eight essays in this section. In addressing aspects of historicity in John 5–12, a number of advances are made with a variety of methodological approaches in play.

In the first essay, Brian Johnson highlights the diversity of Jewish feasts presented in John. In contrast to the Synoptics, which mention only the Sabbath and the Passover, John also mentions the Feasts of Tabernacles and Dedication and an unnamed feast. In arguing for the essential plausibility of Jesus' multiple visits to Jerusalem and public ministry during the various feasts, Johnson asserts that their primary value is theological and content-oriented rather than spatial or temporal.

Johnson's first conclusion—that John's presentation of Jesus as a Galilean Jew who "regularly participated in pilgrimage to Jerusalem for the feasts"—is robust in its plausibility. Even though the Synoptic presentation of a single Passover coming at the culmination of Jesus' ministry appeals to many scholars, it is highly unlikely that an observant Jew from northern Palestine would *not* have participated in more than one Passover feast in Jerusalem; further, if Jesus participated in Passover celebrations, he probably attended other festivals as well. While the Johannine feasts indeed play theological roles in the narrative, however, chronological markers are not absent. Thus, the Johannine multiple-visit presentation sketches a textured backdrop, heightening political and religious understandings of the religious leaders' decisive opposition to the northern prophet.

Johnson's second conclusion—that the presentation of the Johannine feasts "makes it difficult to argue for a temporal or spatial setting for Jesus' ministry"—is mixed, however, in its strengths. While the narrator's theological and dramatic interests affected his use of feasts as vehicles to move the narrative forward, this does not eclipse the chronological markers within the text. A chronologically fitting progression between the Feasts of Tabernacles (John 7), Dedication (John 10), and Passover (John 13) is certainly apparent, and the Feast of Dedication is even situated *correctly* in winter (10:22). The main chronological question is what to do with the first two Passover references in John 2 and 6. Here Johnson fails to develop the implications of the Passover reference in John 6, and then he overextends his argument in claiming that an inclusio between John 2 and the passion narrative suggests that "the Passover of John 2 is not a separate Passover at all." Two points here deserve to be made.

First, while John 6 appears to have been inserted between John 5 and 7 (so, whether it serves an explicitly chronological purpose within the narrative is questionable), the Passover reference in 6:4 still appears to be chronologically sound, at least seasonally. The plentiful grass (John 6:10; Mark 6:39) suggests a springtime setting, and the number of only men being counted (a reference to potential soldiers?), who are then set in "groups" (companies?) of fifty and one hundred (Mark 6:40), has led some scholars to associate this event with Galilean hopes of a Passover political deliverance. The crowd's wanting to rush Jesus off for a political coronation (John 6:14–15) contributes to the political realism of the Johannine presentation of these events, which is also palpable in John 2 and 11–12.

Second, Johnson's assertion that an inclusio as a narrative feature eclipses or discredits the historicity of a presentation is somewhat fallacious. This may be the case, but it is never necessarily so. Whether or not John's three Passovers represent two or three Passovers in history, the claim that the Johannine *narrator* conceives of the events in 2:13–23 as happening at the *same* Passover as in John 11–19 is highly problematic for several reasons. (1) The reference to many having believed because of the signs Jesus was doing in Jerusalem at the Passover in John 2:23 is followed by the claim that Jesus did not entrust himself to the people (2:24–25), implying the continuity of his ministry after the original Jerusalem incident. (2) John 4:2–3 declares that Jesus left Judea and departed for Galilee through Samaria (also claimed in 4:47, 54); the only trip to Judea mentioned since the Cana wedding is his trip to Jerusalem in John 2—a direct spatial and temporal claim. (3) John 4:45 states that the Galileans had witnessed the sign Jesus *had performed in Jerusalem at the festival*, which clearly implies that the temple incident was earlier, not later. (4) The Jewish leaders in Jerusalem begin plotting to kill Jesus already in John 5:18, an unlikely response to an otherwise benign healing, despite the seriousness of Sabbath-law infractions. It implies an earlier offense—hence, an earlier temple incident rather than a later one. While Johnson correctly notes connections between the first and last Passovers in John, it is problematic to say that the Fourth Evangelist saw them, or portrayed them, as the same festival.

Johnson's third conclusion—that the Fourth Gospel's presentation of the feasts is consistent with first-century Jewish practice—is sound, and his inference that it might even illumine first-century Judaism is suggestive. Especially fruitful could be social-science analyses of religion, politics, and power within first-century Palestine. However, this might also suggest that heroic welcomes may have involved the waving of palm branches, even at Passover, despite their traditional associations with Tabernacles, calling into question Johnson's own questioning of John 12:13.

Johnson's fourth conclusion—that the Johannine presentation of the feasts reflects a pre-70 Jewish situation and even a set of precrucifixion perspectives—is also on target. The Evangelist's many earlier-versus-later interpretive comments acknowledge theological understandings, but they also distinguish them from first impressions, which arguably suggest traditional primitivity. In presenting the religious realism of the Jewish feasts in John's Gospel, Johnson elucidates their place in the Johannine narrative, while also suggesting ways they might provide valuable historical knowledge about first-century Judaism and the historical ministry of Jesus.

Craig Evans's impressive essay on John 6 raises several implications for aspects of historicity in John and the Synoptics. Rather than taking the so-called "eucharistic" features of the narrative as later additions to the text, Evans asks whether the manna theme might have been a primitive association, perhaps even made by Jesus himself. Evans's drawing in of contemporary messianic figures presented by Josephus strengthens his case. Indeed, the prophetic heroes of the Hebrew Scriptures provided the backdrop for nationalistic, religious, and political messianic movements within the Judaism of Jesus' day, and this certainly functioned in ways similar for John the Baptist and Jesus alike. Evans correctly notes that these Moses- and Elijah-associations are rife within John 6, while more muted in the Synoptic renderings, arguing for John's more primitive and coherent presentation of these events. Several implications follow.

First, the overall Johannine rendering of the feeding, sea crossing, discussions of the loaves, and Peter's confession are *more unified and fully presented* in John 6 than in the Synoptics. Indeed, what is truncated and disjointed in the Synoptics among the five feeding accounts (Matt 14:15–21; 15:29–38; Mark 6:33–44; 8:1–9; Luke 9:12–17), five sea-crossing accounts (Matt 8:23–27; 14:22–33; Mark 4:35–41; 6:45–52; Luke 8:22–25), two discussions of signs and loaves (Matt 16:1–12; Mark 8:11–21), and three confessions of Peter (Matt 16:16; Mark 8:29; Luke 9:20) is integrated and meaningfully narrated in John as a coherent whole. This suggests Johannine traditional integrity rather than a disjointed set of disparate sources and forms of material. Luke apparently departs from Mark and sides with John, describing one feeding and sea crossing instead of two and moving Peter's confession to follow the feeding of the five thousand (instead of the four thousand), as it is in John 6 (Anderson 1996, 167–220; 2006b, 101–26).

Second, Evans correctly judges the associating of Jesus with the Mosaic prophet of Deut 18:15–22 to be a prevalent and contemporary Palestinian messianic understanding, rather than a later christological addition to the text. This motif is entirely missing from the New Testament's christological hymns (Phil 2:5–11; Col 1:15–21; Heb 1:1–4), but it *is* a messianic motif argued by Peter and Stephen in Acts (3:22; 7:37). This suggests its primitivity, perhaps even going back to the self-understanding of Jesus and ways he conceived of his own ministry (Anderson 1999). This also would account for how the feeding incident was misinterpreted nationalistically, as the crowd wanted to rush him off as a prophet-king like Moses in John 6:14, causing Jesus to flee their designs on his future (6:15). This self-effacing action by Jesus is entirely parallel to the secrecy motif in the Synoptics, cast in an alternative-yet-realistic way.

Third, Evans's correct connecting of the "eucharistic" motif with the feeding of the multitude makes several historical advances, although they could be put a bit differently. (1) I might soften the cultic emphasis of the "eucharistic" feeding, seeing it as tied more closely to table fellowship associated with the Jewish understanding of eating bread together in the presence of God (Gen 18:5; Ps 23:5; Job 42:11). The meal here seems closer to other alimentary meals than to a cultic or symbolic one (Luke 5:29; Acts 2:42–47; note 1 Cor 11:17–22, *before* Paul advises believers to eat at home in 1 Cor 11:23–34, instituting a symbolic meal). (2) The appeal to ingest the flesh and blood of Jesus in John 6 is more directly a reference to the willingness of believers to undergo suffering and martyrdom if required by the truth rather than a cultic requisite. This is precisely the meaning of participating with Jesus in his baptism and in drinking his cup as declared to the Zebedee brothers in Mark 10:38–39, as the "bread" Jesus offers is his flesh given for the life of the world on the cross (John 6:51; see Anderson 1996, 110–36, 194–220). (3) This being the case, the absence of the words of institution in John 13 may reflect a more primitive memory from a cultic perspective than the more formalistic Synoptic presentations, which have clearly co-opted the Jewish Passover meal into a Christian meal of remembrance. John's cultic informality thus appears more primitive and undeveloped than in parallel traditions.

Here Evans's focus on the eschatological emphasis of Jesus' ministry comes into clearer focus. Rather than seeing Jesus as conducting a political maneuver over the Romans or winning a midrashic triumph over Jewish leaders, his emphasis on not what Moses gave but on what the Father *now is giving* (John 6:32) throws the scandal of the Revealer into sharp relief. As the eschatological agent from the Father, Jesus declares the eschatological availability of divine instruction (John 6:45; see Isa 54:13), which must have scandalized original Jewish audiences as it did later Christian ones. Challenges related to the Torah's authority and even wonder-cravings are debated by means of standard manna rhetoric (Anderson 1997, 11–17), and some of these presentations may even reflect originative, as well as developing, Jewish argumentation. By showing the overall coherence, Jewish political realism, and eschatological challenges of Jesus in John 6, Evans contributes profound and important insights into the historical ministry of Jesus.

Sean Freyne's essay on the ironic Judean rejection of the Galilean prophet brings to bear a lifetime of critical scholarship on our subject. As the leading authority on first-century Galilean religion and society, Freyne argues that the narration of Jesus' inflammatory reception in Jerusalem in John 7 bears a striking resemblance to how the historical ministry of Jesus as a northern prophet would have been experienced, and responded to, by Judean leaders originally. In doing so, he approaches his task by means of two critical strategies: source/redactional analysis and contextual plausibility.

From a source/redactional perspective, Freyne suitably adopts a more synchronic approach rather than a diachronic one[1] and correctly focuses on the material most likely to be considered traditional. Indeed, the Johannine presentation of Jesus as both "prophet and Messiah" coheres more closely with the mission of the historical Jesus than later Davidic associations. While Freyne shows how Jewish messianic expectations in the first century c.e. were diverse religiously and geographically, he also shows how particular typologies evolved and developed from one epoch to another.

This raises several questions for further consideration. (1) Parallel to Qumran-Jerusalem religious debates, might there have been a similar set of Galilean-Jerusalem messianic debates, which make several features of John 5–12 understandable? If so, this would also explain the Galilean prophet's critique of religious leadership in Jerusalem and why Jesus was experienced as a threat. (2) Could it be that the Johannine presentation of Jesus as fulfilling the typology of the Mosaic prophet rooted in Deut 18:15–22 also represents a closer portrayal of Jesus' self-understanding of his mission than alternative messiologies, such as the Davidic king? This seems likely, despite the fact that the authority of Moses played an accentuated role during the Jamnia period. (3) As such, might challenges to the northern prophet on the basis of a Davidic typology[2] have been employed by Judean leaders in staving off the messianic claims of Jesus and his followers? As a response, critiques such as those of the Jerusalem leaders in John 7:42, the Matthean tripling of the six Markan references to David, and the Lukan doubling of references to David were marshaled accordingly in the later Gospel traditions. The Johannine response, other than marshalling Davidic associations from Zechariah and a few other references, simply argues for Jesus' messianic authenticity on the basis of the Mosaic agency typology, which is why the oneness of the Son and the Father is argued within the developing Johannine tradition (Anderson 1999).

---

1. With Ashton (2007, 11–53, 233–40), I find Bultmann's inference of multiple sources underlying the Johannine narrative to be lacking in terms of critical evidence (Anderson 1996, 70–167); thus, the Johannine tradition is rightly considered autonomous.

2. Contrary to Freyne's claim, the Mic 5:2 prediction of a ruler coming from Bethlehem, David's hometown, does seem to have posed a messianic warrant; the question is whether it was regarded with the same weight beyond Judean Judaism.

In his development of the *contextual plausibility* of Jesus as the northern prophet, Freyne astutely appropriates the criterion for determining historicity put forward by Theissen and Merz. Here Freyne approaches the issue by asking how likely it is that the historical Jesus might have been marginalized by a pejorative label such as *'am ha'arets* in the third decade of the first century c.e. This seems likely, especially if he was garnering a following in Jerusalem, thus posing a threat to the religious establishment and their biblical warrants for their stances and status. Such was argued against Peter and John in Acts 4:13–16, and it is not unlikely that such a challenge may have been levied against Jesus as one who taught with authority without having achieved formal educational endorsements.[3] Jesus may have also been accused of cultic deficiency (*'am ha'arets lemitswot*), as reflected in the Johannine memory.[4]

While stories of tensions between Jewish leaders and Jesus played vividly when confronting Jewish authorities in Asia Minor, they did not begin there. In his compelling essay, Freyne shows many ways such tensions would also have been intrinsic to the historic ministry of Jesus, reflecting understandable conflicts between the established Jewish leaders of Jerusalem and the rustic prophet from the hinterlands. Indeed, the irony would have been thick in earlier *and* later stages of the Johannine tradition, as Diaspora "experts" on Scripture failed to connect Jesus with the prophet about whom Moses wrote (John 1:45; 5:46). Geographic irony, however, slices evenly the other way as well. In declaring their knowledge of Jesus' origin topographically (7:27), the Judean leaders expose their ignorance of his missional origin as being sent from the Father in keeping with the Mosaic prophet typology. While laced with theological meaning, the Johannine Jesus' ambivalent reception in Jerusalem also betrays aspects of historicity, in both originative and developing terms.

The essay by Urban von Wahlde on the second pool recently discovered below the traditionally identified Pool of Siloam breaks new ground in terms of

---

3. Parallels with Acts 4:1–31 corroborate Freyne's analysis, as Peter and John are imprisoned by the religious leaders *in Jerusalem* for teaching about the messianic identity and mission of Jesus Christ of Nazareth (the Galilean prophet) and are dismissively regarded as being *ignorant and unlettered* (ἀγράμματοί ... καὶ ἰδιῶται; Acts 4:13). Like Jesus in John 7, Peter and John are also regarded as *'am ha'arets letorah*, as Galilean itinerants before the Jerusalem authorities.

4. The case could also be made for the Johannine Jesus challenging Jewish cultic norms, as his first sign made merriment out of *purification* jars (John 2:6), he cleansed the *temple* as an inaugural prophetic sign (2:13–23), his spoken ministry took place in the *temple* (2:19; 5:14; 7:14, 28; 8:20; 10:23; 18:20) and around Jerusalem *feasts* (2:23; 5:1; 7:2, 14), the debate between John the Baptist's disciples and a Jewish leader from Jerusalem was over *purification* (3:25), Jesus' healings on the *Sabbath* were regarded as breaking cultic norms (5:5–18; 9:14–16), *washings* accompany Jesus' miracles (9:7, 11), and Jesus poses an alternative form of *cleansing* (13:10–11; 15:3). Indeed, even the Jewish leaders' opposition to Jesus in John 7:21–24 appears to be a direct result of his having broken the Sabbath by healing the invalid on the *Sabbath* in John 5.

archaeology and Johannine studies alike. While the northern pool was excavated over a century ago, the discovery of the southern pool in 2004 is highly significant for a variety of reasons. Because it is much larger than the upper pool and more clearly functioned as a *miqveh* used for ceremonial bathing, with running (living) water flowing through it, the command of Jesus to the blind man to wash in the Pool of Siloam makes better historical sense as a result of von Wahlde's work. As a means of attaining purification, the transformation of the man's religious status—not simply his restored sight—must be viewed as a matter of pointed discussion between the religious leaders and Jesus in John 9. Whereas modern interpreters have characteristically doubted the historicity of the narrative because of the narrator's explicit comment on the meaning of the name Siloam, "sent" (9:7), von Wahlde's essay obliterates the basis for such moves. The name of the pool is indeed theological, but there also was a real pool by that name. Its newly discovered features call for a radical reevaluation of the originative historical backdrop of John 9.[5]

The evidentiary work of von Wahlde requires little comment, as it stands well on its own merits. It will also be interesting to follow any future archaeological developments in Jerusalem to see what further insights and discoveries emerge. Especially relevant, however, is his treatment of what constitutes "living water" in terms of Jewish purification rites. If a stagnant pool of water could be purified by an *otzer*, or a small adjoining pool replenishing the *miqveh*, the added knowledge about the Pool of Siloam as a pool of purification adds several levels of meaning to the Johannine narrative.

First, the archaeological implications of this new discovery are astounding! The vast system of pools as means of purification give a much fuller picture of activities associated with pilgrimages to Jerusalem and the importance of the larger temple complex. Because the materials (coins, debris, etc.) found in the larger pool demonstrate that its use was discontinued following the destruction of Jerusalem by the Romans in 70 c.e., this confirms its use in Jerusalem *before* 70 c.e. The Siloam references would thus have made no sense to audiences in Asia Minor or elsewhere in the 80s and 90s of the first century, unless the narra-

---

5. Similar fallacious reasoning has at times been exercised by scholars who have taken the five porticoes around the Pool of Beth-zatha in John 5:2 to be a theologizing reference rather than a historical one. The thinking has simplistically assumed that, because pentagonal structures were uncommon in Palestine and the Greco-Roman world (a fact), the five porticoes "obviously" must have referred to legalistic paralysis in bondage to the fivefold Law of Moses, causing the man to languish for thirty-eight years, as did Israel in the wilderness. Jesus therefore delivered the man by grace, and he overcame both legalism and its paralyzing effects in becoming a follower of Jesus. As meaningful as such interpretations might be to dehistoricizing scholars, the discovery of two pools side by side, with three rows of columns running lengthwise and two other rows at right angles (thus supporting *five* porticoes), has made such theological speculation come across as naïve and wrongheaded.

tor and audiences alike had been familiar with pre-70 Jerusalem. With Albright's important essay half a century ago, von Wahlde's essay argues for the primitivity of John's tradition.[6]

Second, connections between the curative and transformative power of the "troubled waters" of the Pool of Bethesda in John 5 and Jesus' commanding the blind man to wash in the Pool of Siloam in John 9 illumine the salutary character of purification issues alluded to in both stories. In addition, Jesus' declaring in the temple that from one's innermost being shall flow "rivers of living water" (7:38) takes on new meaning in the light of von Wahlde's work. Jesus offers spiritually from within what the restorative and empowering work of "living water" avails from without. Archaeological history here clarifies an important Johannine theological point.

A third contribution of von Wahlde's work clarifies the religious and societal implications of the pool cleansing in John 9, explaining why the blind man appeared before the priests and why he was interrogated so severely. Not only was his sight restored, but his deliverance from his physical ailment also brought restoration religiously and socially. As the Jerusalem leaders had been threatened by the healing of the paralytic in John 5, were they again scandalized in John 9 by Jesus' demonstration of curative power, which threatened their religious prescriptions for healing, cleansing, and restoration? Add the detail that *both* healings were performed on the Sabbath, in Jerusalem, and the very structures of religious authority and promise are threatened, being outperformed by the nonauthorized Galilean prophet. Jesus' work brought about the wholeness claimed to be dispensed by religious and cultic prescriptions alone, and it did so in unauthorized ways—even in transgressing Sabbath laws.

While strict advocates of naturalistic measures of historicity will demur at the healings of Jesus in all four canonical Gospels, the archaeological backdrop of Jesus' Jerusalem ministry in John presents a Jesus every bit as historically engaged as the Synoptic Jesus. On contributing fresh insights into the threatening of religious structures and authorities by the charismatic leader and his ministry, von Wahlde's essay may only be the tip of the iceberg.[7]

Edward W. Klink III's essay picks up where the previous one leaves off. Given that the primary historical treatment of John 9 over the last four decades has engaged the work of J. Louis Martyn (1968) distinguishing two levels of his-

---

6. Von Wahlde's raising our awareness of the work done on the Pool of Siloam and its implications for Johannine studies promises to do for John 9 what the work of Albright (1956) did for John 5.

7. One wonders, for instance, what sort of insights would emerge if von Wahlde would perform this sort of analysis upon all twenty of the Johannine topographical and archaeological sites he treats in his important contribution to Charlesworth's *Jesus and Archaeology* (von Wahlde 2006). In the Scripture index of that collection there are half again as many references to the Gospel of John as there are to the other three Gospels *combined*!

tory—the originative history and the history of the contemporary audience at the time of the narrative's delivery—Klink's focus is a worthy one, historically. While Martyn did not claim to diminish the historicity of the originative events, the robust impact of developing the second level of history has tended to function in that way among many interpreters. Klink sets out to rectify that tendency by showing that a central aspect of Martyn's thesis—the mass expulsion of Jesus adherents from local synagogues—is an overreading of the evidence. Put otherwise, contravening evidence of Christian-Jewish cooperation during the late first century calls for a revised approach to the history of the Johannine situation and the contextual backdrop of John 9.

Helpful within Klink's approach are several things. First, he reminds us that Martyn was not the first to argue such a theory, and he points us to other treatments for further consideration. Second, he represents clearly several of the major critiques of Martyn's thesis, especially those by Kimelman, Wilson, Reinhartz, and Boyarin, showing a convergence of disenchantment with Martyn's hypothesis. Third, he shows how the larger narrative is disrupted if John 9 is either removed from its place or taken to be the hermeneutical key for interpreting the rest of the Johannine *Ioudaioi*-engagement scenarios. The many positive presentations of "the Jews" in the Fourth Gospel call into question a pervasive adversarial stance against Jewish members of the Johannine audience. Fourth, Klink helps us think about what excommunication and being declared a "heretic" might have meant as intra-Jewish realities in contemporary settings, qualifying our understandings of the issues. Finally, and most significantly, Klink argues that intra-Jewish tensions were likely earlier than the 80s and 90s of the first century, reflecting a long history of religious tensions, rather than an abrupt one. For the purposes of the John, Jesus, and History Project, this likelihood bolsters the connections between the first and second levels of Johannine history.

While the overall thrust of Klink's work is compelling, questions regarding his treatment of the subject nonetheless emerge. The first problem involves an "overreading" of Martyn—if not by Klink, certainly by Martyn's critics, whose views Klink incorporates somewhat uncritically. To be fair, Martyn never claimed that expulsions from the synagogue in the Jamnia period were pandemic or universal; nor did Martyn's supporters assert that they were thoroughly effected in particular contexts. Therefore, citing examples of close Jewish-Christian relations as evidence against *any* expulsion of Jesus-adherents from Jewish synagogues fails to convince in the opposite direction. It may even qualify and support Martyn's essential thesis, in that *territoriality exists only among members of like species*. Therefore, familial closeness with Jewish communities would have exacerbated the tensions over Johannine Jewish believers' claiming Jesus to be the Messiah. Put otherwise, how many devout first-century Jewish synagogues would have tolerated the reading of the Johannine Prologue by its members *within* the Jewish meeting for worship? Arguments against *any* disciplining of Christian ditheism within first-century Judaism come across as overstated and unrealistic. While Klink does not commit this error, some of the most ardent critics of Martyn appear to, thus making some of their critiques less than compelling.

A second overreading of Martyn fails to account for the presence of believing *Ioudaioi* on the second level of discourse. Just as Raymond Brown's treatment (1979) of Nicodemus as a representative of "crypto-Christians" (who in later decades feared to confess Jesus openly for fear of suffering alienation from their leading religious peers) posed a more textured inference of Jewish-Johannine relations, so do the presentations of believing and friendly *Ioudaioi*. Even some of the Jews in Jerusalem believed in Jesus as the Messiah (John 7:31; 8:30–31; 10:42; 11:45), although it is emphasized that, while many of the leaders believed, the Pharisees did not believe (7:48; 12:42). The point is that if the Johannine-Jewish dialogues were highly dialectical, some excommunication from some synagogues may have been happening,[8] some Jewish authorities and commoners may have been warm to the Jesus movement, some may have offered assistance and support to individuated Johannine believers, and some may even have believed in Jesus privately while being reluctant to profess their loyalty openly. Rather than overturning Martyn's work, the recent critiques do more to qualify it as a dialectical set of engagements thoroughly represented by the diverse presentations of Judean responses to Jesus in John.[9]

Again, the most important contribution of Klink's work qualifies the Jewish-Johannine relationships as being much broader and more complex than an acute set of excommunication debates in the Jamnia period alone. These tensions were much earlier and later, and they were multileveled and multifaceted. With the work of Instone-Brewer, Alexander, and Neale, the marginalization of the *minim* within Judaism would have extended to Jesus-adherents shortly after his ministry—perhaps even reflecting critiques of the northern prophet of Galilee himself,

---

8. At this point, Kimelman's comment (1981) about Christian leaders' pressuring their members not to affiliate with the Jewish synagogue is plausible, especially if it involved abandoning the emerging Christian community. This is precisely what I believe was happening in the situation of 1 John 2:18–25 (Anderson 1997; 1999). Having departed from the Jewish community, either volitionally or forcibly, some Johannine members apparently abandoned their fledgling community and returned to the synagogue, seemingly allowed to do so if they would diminish their belief in Jesus as the Christ. As the Jewish challenge to perceived ditheism was levied in support of Jewish monotheism and singular allegiance to "the Father," the Elder levies the monotheistic claims of the proselytizers directly back in the opposite direction (1 John 2:23): "No one who denies the Son has the Father; everyone who confesses the Son has the Father also." To deny the Son, who represents the Father authentically (Deut. 18:15–22), is to forfeit the focus of one's goal of pleasing the Father; conversely, to embrace the Son is to be embraced by the Father as his children (John 1:12–13).

9. This, I believe, is also a better way to read Wayne Meeks's position. It is significant that Moody Smith (1996) continues to assert the historical plausibility of the basic Martyn hypothesis, despite its recent challenges; Klink thus overstates the case that criticisms of Martyn's claims have been universal.

as developed above by Freyne. That being the case, these tensions were early as well as late, thus elucidating what may also have been the first level of Johannine history as well as later ones. On this matter, Klink's essay serves the John, Jesus, and History Project well, in that it illuminates the originative features of Johannine historicity, as well as its later ones. The fallacy, of course, is to assume that the illumination of one level of history eclipses all others.

Richard Bauckham's essay on the Bethany family in John 11–12 puts the question directly: Are the differences between John and the Synoptics around these events and the varying presentations of characters best explained as John's account being a factor of fiction rather than history? Bauckham's conclusion is negative, and this judgment is well-founded. For one thing, the raising of Lazarus seems a more plausible explanation for the Jewish leaders' conspiring to put Jesus to death—or at least one less likely to have been "concocted" (using Bretschneider's term)—than the Markan temple incident. A threat to the religious leaders' spiritual authority would have been far more of a challenge than a mere temple disturbance. Noting also the structuring of the Markan narrative, we see in this case an example of Mark's crafting *his* chronology around thematic interests as a central focus. Moreover, Mark's saving all the Jerusalem events—and nearly all of the judgment sayings of Jesus—for the culmination of Jesus' ministry during a "single" visit to Jerusalem reflects not a factor of strict chronology but of narrative denouement. Thus, with reference to the number of days before the Passover, as well as the events leading up to the arrest of Jesus, the Markan presentation, followed by Matthew and Luke, betrays features of conjectural arrangement and narrative climax more so than the Johannine rendering.

A second contribution of Bauckham's approach involves his attempts to reconcile the Johannine and Synoptic accounts on the basis of intertraditional contact. Strongest is his inference that the Johannine Evangelist was familiar with the Markan narrative, though not dependent on it. This raises questions, of course, as to *why* John's presentation is so different from Mark's account. If the Fourth Evangelist was familiar with Mark, was his distinctive narrative augmentive or even corrective? Certainly John 11 should be seen as an addition of narratives not included in Mark, similar to the other four signs in the first edition of John.[10] One might even see the exclamation of the steward in John 2:10, prefiguring Jesus' saving the best for last, as an indirect reference to the climactic Lazarus miracle, although it could also be a reference to the death and resurrection of Jesus. By

---

10. If indeed John 6 and 21 (along with the Prologue and John 15–17) were added to the first edition of John after the death of the Beloved Disciple, the first edition of John was likely the second Gospel narrative to be gathered, and all five of its signs are nonrepetitive of the Markan miracles. The first two signs (John 2; 4) fill out *the early ministry of Jesus* before the narrated events in Mark 1; the other three signs (John 5; 9; 11) fill out *the southern ministry of Jesus* in contrast to a largely northern ministry in Mark.

implication, the Johannine rendering poses an alternative narration to the Markan rendering of Jesus' ministry, with its own claims to traditional knowledge.

Bauckham is less certain about the Johannine-Lukan connection. While he rightly notes the Lukan additions to Mark's narrative, the most conspicuous feature of Luke's departure from Mark receives little attention. Given that Mark's presentation of the event as a head-anointing clearly inaugurates Jesus as a royal Messiah figure (followed by Matthew), why would Luke change the event (I think it *was* the same event) to a more servile anointing of Jesus' feet? Luke probably had a traditional reason for doing so rather than a rhetorical one. Given John's rendering, the fact that Luke departs from Mark and sides with John in an unlikely-to-be-concocted move suggests Luke's access to, and dependence upon, the Johannine tradition.[11] That being the case, Luke's additions of Mary and Martha as sisters playing similar roles, a parabolic story about a dead man named Lazarus, and even an attributed motive for the woman's anointing of Jesus suggest Luke's familiarity with the oral rendering of the Johannine tradition. While the case cannot fully be argued here, the anointing of Jesus' feet by a woman such as Mary (now *which* Mary was that?) suggests Luke's familiarity with, and indebtedness to, the Johannine rendering in presenting his "orderly" report, in which he includes that which has been seen and heard by eyewitnesses and servants of the λόγος (Luke 1:2).

Less convincing is Bauckham's inference of protective anonymity as a basis for omitting names of characters in the story, although he correctly resists inferring the adding of names by a narrator. When Matthew and Luke incorporate Mark, they more commonly omit names, places, times, and illustrative details rather than add them. This being the case, the predominance of graphic details in the Markan and Johannine accounts suggests primitive oral tradition rather than later additions (Anderson 1996, 94–104). Some of these details are even shared between Mark and John, though never presented identically, suggesting contact during the oral stages of the pre-Markan and early Johannine stages of their respective traditions. Given the more common Markan tendency to include details omitted by Matthew and Luke, the more plausible inference is that Mark's failure to include the name of the anointing woman was a feature of ignorance rather than protection. The strongest feature of Bauckham's account is the likelihood of particular, grounded Johannine familiarity with the Lazarus family of Bethany. Based on his analysis, the Johannine presentations of detail and relationships bear the trademarks of independent, traditional knowledge.[12]

---

11. The thesis that Luke allegorizes and moralizes around Johannine narrations bears greater plausibility than the inference that John fabricates moralizingly innocent historical narrative out of Lukan paraenetic scenarios. For a fuller development of Luke's dependence on the Johannine oral tradition, see Anderson 2006b, 101–26.

12. Kundsin's (1925) argument for geographically localized traditions may also account for Johannine distinctive material not found in the Synoptics.

One final point deserves to be made here about the historicity of the foot anointing in John and Luke rather than the more royal head anointing in Mark and Matthew. As Freyne has argued above, the Jerusalem leaders' claim that Jesus could not be the Messiah on the basis of his being a northern Galilean rather than coming from David's city in the south is answered by Mark and, more fully, by Luke and Matthew. While all four Gospels present Jesus' entry into Jerusalem as an enactment of Davidic typologies from Zechariah, Mark's and Matthew's pre-senting Jesus as receiving a royal anointing appears to be rooted more clearly in apologetic interests than historical ones. Rather than following royal rhetorical developments, Luke here follows the more modest and servant-oriented Johan-nine rendering of a foot anointing, even moving Jesus' admonition to his disciples to serve one another to the Last Supper context—as it is in John.

These and other features, as argued by Bauckham, should give us pause before consigning the distinctive-yet-similar material in John 11–12 to the canons of fiction rather than history. Again, they may be fictive, but such is less than demonstrable on the basis of Johannine-Synoptic contrasts alone. Especially with reference to the Johannine familiarity with the family of Bethany, something rooted in personal knowledge and history is here apparent.

Following Bauckham's lead on Johannine links with the Lazarus family, Ben Witherington III drives the connections further. If the unnamed Beloved Disciple can be identified as the source of the Johannine tradition, and also connected directly with Lazarus (whom the text singles out as one whom Jesus loved: John 11:5, 36), not only might the historicity of the Johannine tradition be explained, but also the origin of John's southern (Judean) material and anti-Petrine bias. This approach is not new, but Witherington argues it here vigorously with a particular interest in establishing a basis for aspects of historicity in John. As such, it has several appeals.

First, if the Fourth Gospel was written by an eyewitness from the south, this would explain the presence of the rife archaeological detail in the narrative; the focus on Jesus' visits to Jerusalem; the emphases on the feasts, Jesus' ministry, and related events in Bethany; the Beloved Disciple's access to the high priest; Jesus' entrusting his mother to someone living nearby; the Jerusalem authorities' animosity against Jesus and his followers; and other Judean features of the Johan-nine text.

A second appeal to this approach is its attempt to solve the "problem" that every scene in which the sons of Zebedee are mentioned in the Synoptics is miss-ing from the Gospel bearing the name "John." How could this writer, if he is the same person referred to in the Synoptics, *not* tell any of the stories related to scenarios in which he is directly involved in the Synoptics? Further, how could a member of the Twelve challenge the role of Peter and apostolic authority? With-erington's answer: the author was an eyewitness but not one of the Twelve.

A third appeal of the Lazarus hypothesis is that it might account for the distinctive theological slant of the Johannine narrative. After all, how might one who has undergone a life-after-death experience have thought about Jesus' words and works? To use Robert Browning's famous imagery in *A Death in the Desert* (1864), what were once "guessed as points" were later known as stars. Might the transcendental perspective of someone like Lazarus be responsible for the highly theologized Johannine narrative, despite its accompanying mundane features? Worse inferences have been made. With Witherington, the Johannine Elder does appear to be the final editor of the Johannine Gospel and the three Epistles.

Despite these attractive features, however, the case for Lazarus being the Fourth Evangelist is less than compelling. This is not Witherington's fault; he argues his thesis with creativity and verve. Rather, it is a factor of the reality that all of the strengths attributable to the Lazarus hypothesis could just as easily be argued for another individual. Does the mention of Jesus' loving Lazarus (as well as Martha and Mary in John 11:5) really prove that the Beloved Disciple was Lazarus? Why not Mary or Martha? Does the presence of Judean detail in John *prove* the narrator had to have been someone living in the south instead of one visiting Jerusalem and its environs, as most devout Galilean Jews would have done? Was it only Jesus but none of the Twelve who knew the Bethany family and situation, or might other members of the Galilean band also have known Bethany and Jerusalem's environs? Because Judas Iscariot was the *one* member of the Twelve who came from Judea, does this prove that he is the most likely Fourth Evangelist among them on that basis? Further, why does Jesus commission Peter and John (Luke 22:8) to find a place for the Last Supper? Unless the man they spoke with was an agent of the Lazarus family, it would seem that Peter and John were the hosts of the meal, not Lazarus or Simon the Leper. Finally, in Acts 1:14 Mary is with the disciples and Jesus' brothers in Jerusalem; it says nothing of she or they having established residence there. The criteria used by Witherington to pinpoint Lazarus need not point to Lazarus alone; it could also point to others, and often more fittingly so.

A second drawback of the Lazarus hypothesis is that it creates a new set of problems that Witherington leaves unaddressed. If Lazarus as the Beloved Disciple really was a close companion of Peter, as referenced explicitly in John (13:23–38; 20:1–10; 21:1–24), why is he nowhere mentioned in the Synoptics as a follower of Jesus? Conversely, the sons of Zebedee are mentioned many times as being in the company of Peter as the "inner ring" among the Twelve (Mark 1:29; 5:37; 9:2; 13:3; 14:33), and Acts mentions Peter and John together eleven times (Acts 1:13; 3:1, 3, 4, 11; 4:1, 13, 19; 8:14, 17, 25), so the Lazarus hypothesis on the basis of presentational textual evidence fares less well than the traditional view. Indeed, it could be that someone who was *not* one of the Twelve played a role as the exemplar of discipleship—leaning against the breast of Jesus at the Last Supper, present at the cross, entrusted with custody of Jesus' mother, visiting the tomb after the crucifixion, and fishing with the disciples after the resurrection (in *Galilee*)—but the Lazarus hypothesis creates new problems not addressed by Witherington.

Third, Witherington's treatment here fails to consider alternative views adequately. He does not, for instance, challenge the view of James Charlesworth (1995) that the Beloved Disciple was Thomas, nor does he consider the one disciple present at the beginning and end of Jesus' ministry who is not one of the Synoptic Twelve, namely, Nathanael. How about John Mark and his mission to the Gentiles? Further, Witherington's dismissal of John the son of Zebedee as a possibility for the narrative source of the Johannine tradition—mirroring Pierson Parker's touting (1962) of the "one assured result" of modern biblical critical scholarship—borders on the cliché.[13] Of Parker's twenty-one reasons why John the son of Zebedee could not have been the Johannine Evangelist, none of them is compelling.[14] It could even be that John's juxtaposition of Peter and the Beloved Disciple reflects a dialogue within the apostolic band rather than assuming a pristine unanimity about power, authority, and governance among the Twelve.[15] Likewise, the death of the Beloved Disciple would have been a problem for early Christians if he were standing there in the situation mentioned in Mark 9:1—the last hope for the Parousia prior to the death of the last of the Twelve—which is clarified as an alternative meaning in John 21:18–23. It need not imply Lazarus; it seems to have implied one of the Twelve, echoing and correcting Mark.

---

13. Rudolf Schnackenburg considers Parker's essay (1962) "possibly the most complete collection of the reasons which seem to exclude the authorship of the son of Zebedee" (Schnackenburg 1980, 1:92), while also judging the essay to be fraught with weaknesses and finally unconvincing. Of course, Parker's larger interest was to show that the Johannine Evangelist was John Mark, accounting for its Hellenistic character, which required a deconstruction in order to clear space for an alternative view of authorship.

14. Worse, some of Parker's assertions reflect less than adequate critical thought. (1) A fisherman must have been an ignoramus; a bit classist—never mind that Zebedee was an employer of several workers (including Peter) and would likely have had material resources as a business owner enough to provide for educating his children. (2) The omission of Markan material implies that John could not have been the author; an argument from silence—never mind the fact that the one disciple mentioned in the Synoptics as being uncomfortable with other exorcists (and their exorcizing work, proper?) is John the son of Zebedee (Mark 9:38; Luke 9:49), posing a plausible accounting for the absence of exorcisms in John. (3) The argument that John the son of Zebedee died at the same time as James (around 44 C.E.) is taken at face value; flawed historiography—never mind the fact that its inference is based primarily on a ninth-century borrowing of a fifth-century misreading of a second-century comment by Papias upon an indirect reference to the martyrological fates of the sons of Zebedee as a fallacious reading of Mark 10:39, when the second-century views of John's death locate it during the reign of Trajan around 100 C.E. (e.g., Irenaeus, *Haer.* 2.22.5).

15. *Contra* Raymond E. Brown (1979), the juxtaposition of Peter and the Beloved Disciple in John does not represent a critique of Petrine hierarchy from outside the apostolic band; more compellingly, it reflects a dialectical critique from within the apostolic band, seeking to correct problematic features of rising institutionalism in the late first-century church (Anderson 1997, 24–57).

Especially if the first edition of the Johannine Gospel was designed as a complement to Mark, most of Witherington's objections to the Fourth Evangelist having been a member of the Twelve on the basis of Synoptic silences fall by the wayside.[16] In addition to the prevalent second-century opinion connecting John's authorship with John the apostle, an unwitting first-century clue to Johannine authorship has been overlooked by all sides of the debate.[17] The only time John speaks in Luke's second volume is at Acts 4:19–20, where Peter and John utter characteristically Petrine and Johannine sayings. The first saying, arguing in Platonic terms the priority of obeying God rather than humans (4:19), is replicated as a Petrine statement also in Acts 5:29 and 11:17. The other statement, however, "we cannot help from speaking *about what we have seen and heard*" (4:20), is replicated as a Johannine saying twice in 1 John 1:1–3. As a first-person plural past reference, this same phrase is not uttered identically elsewhere in Luke-Acts (despite some 150 hearing verbs and 250 seeing verbs, although see the second-person instances in Luke 7:22 and Acts 22:15); rather, its closest parallels are when Jesus declares what he has "seen and heard" from the Father (John 3:32) and when the Johannine Epistle writer says, "we declare to you *what we have seen and heard* so that you may also have fellowship with us" (1 John 1:3). Problematic as it may be, this first-century presentation of John the apostle uttering an unmistakably Johannine saying—a full century before Irenaeus—approximates a fact.

The point here is that John's *non*authorship might not be as much of an open-and-shut case as critical scholars have thought, thus challenging the certainty with which alternative theories are advanced. Nonetheless, Witherington's overall approach is worthy. Like Charlesworth, he is on the right track arguing for a personal source and perspective accounting for the bulk of the Johannine tradition as an alternative to the Markan (or Petrine) account. In that sense, the arguing of Lazarus or Thomas or Nathanael—or even the son of Zebedee himself—deserves critical consideration as at least one factor in the distinctive presentation of Jesus in the Johannine Gospel. While I might argue that the critical case is much stronger for the son of Zebedee than recent scholarship has assumed, Witherington nonetheless is on the right track in asserting an independent memory of Jesus and its alternative perspective as the basis for the Johannine tradition.

Derek Tovey's essay directly takes on the issue of the historicity of John's Lazarus tradition, and he does so appropriately by considering the narrative's epistemological character. While this is the most historically problematic of the Johannine scenarios from a naturalistic standpoint, it is precisely the sort of treatment needed for assessing aspects of John's historicity. In doing so, Tovey

---

16. With Bauckham (1998a), if the first edition of John was produced for hearers and readers of Mark, its noncongruity with Mark is intentional as an alternative presentation, rather than a scandal.

17. This thesis is first argued in appendix VIII of Anderson 1996, 274–77.

addresses the problems engaged negatively in the post-Enlightenment programs of Strauss, Baur, and others, while bringing to bear recent interdisciplinary treatments of Johannine historiography by Meier, Sproston North, Esler and Piper, Byrskog, and Bauckham. Tovey thereby concludes that the Johannine Lazarus scenario fits better into the category of theologized history than historicized theology, and he does so compellingly.

While Tovey indeed acknowledges the typological function of the characters in the Lazarus story, he asks whether the subjects of the story betray a referential character. In other words, do they reflect real persons, places, and events supposedly known or knowable by early audiences, as opposed to fictive features never intended to be encountered by later audiences? This is an important matter, as the "theological purpose of the Evangelist" is all too easily employed uncritically by biblical scholars as a feature of theologizing speculation gone awry.[18] In doing so, Tovey acknowledges the author's reasons for telling his story in "concrete terms" while also assessing the traditional character of the material.

Tovey also notes the frequent presence of the names of Mary, Martha, and Lazarus on ossuaries of the day and sides with Bauckham on their being presented as guarantors of the Johannine tradition. In addition, the presence of details characteristic of pre-70 C.E. Judea suggests the primitivity of the Johannine narrative, although Tovey also rightly acknowledges the fact that little more can be ascertained as to "what actually happened." In that sense, Tovey's analysis presses the issue of what is meant by "history," and he calls for a more adequate means of approaching Gospel historiography, including interpretive and experiential features in the mix rather than limiting subjective memory and reflection to objectivistic and naturalistic measures alone. While Tovey does not claim to make much advance upon the question of whether the reported events took place in history, he advances the inquiry by assessing the epistemological character of the Lazarus material.

Indeed, the question of why the Lazarus story is missing from the Synoptics is an enduring one, and Tovey could have done more with the question of whether its inclusion in John is designed to augment, or even supplant, the ministry of Jesus in Mark. If the rising of Jairus's daughter in Mark 5:22–43 might have evoked the impression that Jesus performed a resuscitation of the "sleeping" girl, the Johannine story of Lazarus leaves no doubt. Lazarus had been dead four days, heightening the striking character of the purported event. Nonetheless, his pointing out the reference in the Q tradition (Matt 11:5; Luke 7:22) that the dead being raised provides external attestation to precisely the sort of thing that is reported

---

18. Four gradations of symbolization can be identified in the Johannine text: explicitly symbolic, implicitly symbolic, possibly symbolic, and nonsymbolic (Anderson 2006c). However, just as symbolic presentation does not demonstrate a detail's ahistoricity, neither does a detail's symbolic innocence determine its historicity.

in John 11. With Tovey, not only did the Johannine account of Lazarus prefigure the resurrection of Jesus, but it also testified to the signs-producing authority of Jesus in presenting him as the Messiah. Like fiction, there is no such thing as nonrhetorical history. In that sense Tovey's work suggests that we have in John not only a "narrative mode and theological claim" but a "narrative mode and historical claim."[19]

In conclusion, the eight essays in part 2 of this collection all advance our knowledge of aspects of historicity in John. As an independent perspective and presentation of the ministry of Jesus, the middle section of the Fourth Gospel heightens the reader's sense of its political and religious realism. By using a variety of approaches, the scholars in this section shed valuable light upon the northern prophet's ministry and conflicts in Galilee and Judea alike. Implicit are aspects of the Johannine tradition's dialogical engagement with other traditions, but those do not appear to reflect dependence. In all, the Fourth Gospel retains its own voice and points with dramatic flair to the Christ of faith *and* the Jesus of history.

---

19. Here, of course, the important work by Gail O'Day (1986) is expanded to include history as well as theology as a claim of the Johannine narrator. While theology is indeed pervasive as a central interest of the Johannine narrative, so are its claims to historicity—wrongly or rightly.

PART 3

ASPECTS OF HISTORICITY IN JOHN 13–21

INTRODUCTION TO PART 3:
ASPECTS OF HISTORICITY IN JOHN 13–21

Paul N. Anderson

John 13–21 covers the last week of Jesus' ministry, following his entry into Jerusalem (12:12–19), to include his last discourses with his followers (John 13–17), his arrest and trials (John 18–19), his crucifixion and burial (John 19), and his resurrection and appearances to his followers (John 20–21). Within John's treatment of the Last Supper in John 13, Jesus does not institute the Eucharist as a meal of remembrance but washes the feet of his disciples. In John 14–16, Jesus foretells the sending of the Holy Spirit and prepares his followers for the challenges they will face after his departure, leading to his prayer for their unity in John 17. There is no anguish at Gethsemane or on the Mount of Olives in John, although the arrest of Jesus is made in an unnamed garden in John 18. As the trials develop in John 18–19, Jesus is interviewed first by Annas, the father-in-law of Caiaphas, who then sends him to Caiaphas, and the trial before Pilate exposes Pilate's incomprehension of the truth—equally advocating Jesus' "kingdom" being one of truth. In John alone is Pilate's dictum regarding Jesus' being "the king of the Jews" rendered in Hebrew, Latin, and Greek (19:19), do soldiers gamble for the seamless robe of Jesus, is his mother entrusted to a disciple, are the legs of the other crucified victims broken, and is Jesus' side pierced, out of which flow blood and water (19:23–37). While Peter and the Beloved Disciple arrive at the empty tomb, it is Mary Magdalene to whom Jesus appears first, and she becomes an apostle to the apostles (20:1–18). In John the postresurrection Jesus commissions his followers with apostolic agency in Jerusalem (20:19–29) and appears a third time to them in Galilee, whereupon they experience a wondrous catch of fish numbering 153 (21:1–14). In what seems a second ending to the Gospel, the final chapter of John comments upon the selective inclusion of events and seems to acknowledge the death of the Beloved Disciple, who is also credited as the authorial source of the tradition (21:18–25). From these presentations in John 13–21, several historical problems arise.

First, John's presentation of the Last Supper (John 13) is strikingly at odds with the Synoptic presentations in several ways. Whereas all three Synoptics and Paul present the institution of a meal of remembrance wherein the bread and the cup take on special significance for the remembering of Jesus' sacrifice for believers, John's narrative is innocent of cultic associations in ways that pose historical problems for interpreters. Did the Jesus of history institute a meal of remembrance or not? If not, why is it included in the Synoptics? If so, why is it missing from John? Here John's presentation is remarkably *un*theological from a cultic perspective. If John's tradition originated in the memory of the Beloved Disciple who leaned against the breast of Jesus at the Last Supper (13:23; 21:20, 24), how could he have missed the institution of the Eucharist if it really happened? Was he dozing? Conversely, if Jesus really anointed the feet of Peter and his disciples (13:3–17), how did such an event not get picked up in the Synoptics? While the feet of Jesus are anointed by a woman in John and Luke (Mark and Matthew present it as the anointing of Jesus' *head*), it is only in John that Jesus washes the feet of his disciples. So, is this presentation rooted in history or in the theological interests of the Fourth Evangelist? On more than one account, what really happened at the Last Supper becomes a question of historical interest when comparing John and the Synoptics.

A second historical question involves the dating of the Last Supper. Was it a Passover meal, as presented in the Synoptics, or did it take place the evening before the Passover, as presented in John? The dating of the event could also affect the presentation of the meal as a more symbolic religious meal of remembrance, complete with the breaking of unleavened bread and the drinking of several cups of wine as Jewish participants in the Passover meal would have recalled the delivering works of God in Egypt, to which Jesus is presented as adding the significance of his own sacrificial death. In John, however, the Last Supper is presented as happening before the Passover (13:1), and John clearly presents the crucifixion on the day of Preparation (19:14, 31, 42). John even portrays with a sense of realism the reluctance of Jewish leaders to enter the household of Pilate lest they be defiled and hindered from eating the Passover that year (18:28), and John presents realistic religious concerns for getting Jesus off the cross before the Sabbath, suggesting that it coincided with a high festival that year (John 19:31; see Num 9:6). Some argue that John's account has moved the event to the day of Preparation for theological reasons, presenting Jesus as the Paschal Lamb, as that was the day on which the Passover lambs were sacrificed. That detail, however, is not found in John, but in Mark 14:12, followed by Luke 22:7. A second attempt to reconcile the dates argues for the use of two different calendars, arguing for Nisan 14 and 15 as alternative dates for the Passover, accounting for the Johannine-Synoptic difference. A third approach sees the Synoptics as presenting the Last Supper as a Passover meal as a means of establishing Christian eucharistic practices for religious reasons, rather than historical ones. Then again, Mark refers to the day of the crucifixion as the Day of Preparation (before the Sabbath; Mark 15:42), and Matthew also locates the death of Jesus on the Day of Preparation, following which the chief priests and Pharisees appeal to Pilate to make the tomb secure, which he does (Matt 27:62–66). It thus appears that there is some ambivalence within the Synoptics on the date of the crucifixion, not just between them and John. So, which Last Supper and crucifixion chronology is more plausible: the Synoptics' or John's?

A third problem follows from the first two. The implication of washing the feet of his disciples is Jesus' instruction for them to love one another as his primary ethical command (John 13:15–35; 15:9–12). Note the striking contrast between loving those within one's community and the command of the Synoptic Jesus to love one's enemies and to pray for and do good to one's adversaries (Matt 5:44; Luke 6:27, 35). From the perspective of moral-development theory, John's Jesus seems to exhibit a more insular and self-oriented ethic rather than a more mature and self-effacing one. The Johannine Jesus and the Synoptic Jesus both emphasize the need to love sacrificially, but two different ethical teachers seem to be represented here. Of course, loving one's own does not preclude loving the world for whom Jesus died (John 1:10–12; 3:15–17; 10:10–18; 15:13). Yet John's Jesus portrays "the world" not only as the realm of hostility to the Revealer and his followers but also as the object of his loving mission (15:19; 16:33; 17:6–26). So, not only does the Johannine Jesus fail to speak in parables about the kingdom of God, but he also emphasizes love of the community over love of the world. One can understand the concerns of Johannine Christianity fostering such an ethos, but how close is it to the teachings and mission of the Jesus of history?

A fourth historical question involves the fact that John's presentation of Jesus' last words to his disciples is so clearly Johannine that it seems to originate more directly from the ministry of the Fourth Evangelist than from the Jesus of history. By the time of the writing of the Johannine Epistles, the "new commandment" to love one another (John 13:34–35; 15:12, 17) has become the old commandment: "the message you have heard from the beginning" (1 John 3:11; 2 John 1:5) that community members should love one another (1 John 3:11–16, 23; 4:7–12; 2 John 1:5). The "I Am" sayings ("I am the way, and the truth, and the life," 14:6; "I am the true vine, and my Father is the vinegrower," 15:1) seem distinctively Johannine over and against the teachings of the Synoptic Jesus. Also, while the Synoptic Jesus likewise is presented as making long discourses about matters ultimate during his final visit to Jerusalem (Mark 13; Matt 23–25; Luke 20–21), the discourses of Jesus in John 14–16 are very different from the aphoristic and parabolic teacher we find in the Synoptics. The Father-Son relationship is especially accentuated in John 14–17, especially with reference to the agency of the Son as the central feature of his mission coming from and returning to the Father. The exhortation to ask, that it might be given (Matt 7:7; 21:22; Mark 11:24; Luke 11:9), is taken further by the Johannine Jesus (John 14:13–14; 15:7, 16; 16:23–24), who describes the sending of the Holy Spirit as the object of the believer's petition (Luke 11:13; John 14:16). From there the Johannine treatment of the Holy Spirit as the advocate/comforter/helper (ὁ παράκλητος) is developed as an encouragement to believers in the Johannine audience (John 14:16–26; 15:26–27; 16:7–15), although the speech-empowering work of the Holy Spirit is predicted by Jesus in all four Gospels (Mark 13:11; Matt 10:19–20; Luke 12:11–12; John 16:13). The question, of course, is the degree to which these teachings in the final Johannine discourses represent the Jesus of history or the Jesus of the Johannine Evangelist.

A fifth historical question relates to the editorial composition of John 13–21. Several aporias (perplexities) in the text have raised questions for scholars over the last two centuries and more, evoking diachronic approaches to John's composition as solutions. In John 14:31 Jesus says, "Rise, let us be on our way," but they do not reach the garden until 18:1. Do chapters 15–17 represent "the sermon in the alley," or do they reflect the last words of a leader before his death—crafted with pauses and elaborations for dramatic effect? Another possibility is that John 15–17 was added to the text as part of a later edition, along with chapter 21 and other material. Another question is why Jesus declares, "But now I am going to him who sent me; yet none of you asks me, 'Where are you going?'" (16:5), despite the fact that Simon Peter has just recently asked, "Lord, where are you going?" (13:36). Was the text disordered and reordered wrongly, was Jesus not paying attention, or does this perplexity reflect a diachronic relationship between the material in John 13 and 16, alleviated by seeing one passage or the other as part of another source or edition? A third literary problem is that there seem to be two endings to the Johannine Gospel. At the end of John 20 the Evangelist concludes: "Now Jesus did many other signs in the presence of his disciples, which are not written in this book. But these are written so that you may come to believe that Jesus is the Messiah, the Son of God, and that through believing you may have life in his name" (20:30–31). That being the case, John 21 appears to represent an addition, the end of which imitates the first ending: "But there are also many other things that Jesus did; if every one of them were written down, I suppose that the world itself could not contain the books that would be written" (21:25). If the Gospel of John, however, went through more than one edition or had a more extensive diachronic history of composition, this raises questions about the historicity of its material. Does it reflect the interpretive memory of firsthand encounters of the Jesus of history, or does it represent more than one editorial hand or sources with a multiplicity of perspectives? Here literary questions converge with historical ones.

A sixth set of issues relates to the historical character of the arrest, trials, and death of Jesus in John. In contrast to the Synoptics, John has no sleepy disciples in the garden, nor does Jesus suffer anguish over his fate. A strikingly large cohort of soldiers bringing lanterns and torches is sent to arrest Jesus (18:3), yet in response to their quest for Jesus of Nazareth, where he responds "ἐγώ εἰμι" (18:5, 6, 8), they fall to the ground as experiencing an epiphany—and then arrest Jesus. These features seem elevated in John. On the other hand, multiple cases of archaeologically correct references and the featuring of graphic, mundane details provide the Johannine passion narrative its own claims to firsthand historical knowledge. The names of both parties in the ear-severing incident are mentioned as "Peter" and "Malchus" (18:10), Annas is described as the father-in-law of the high priest Caiaphas (18:13), the cold temperature explains why Peter and others were gathered around a charcoal fire (18:18), the judge's bench used by Pilate is described as situated upon the stone pavement (λιθόστρωτος) and also by its Hebrew name *Gabbatha* (meaning "ridge of the house," 19:13), the Hebrew name of the place where Jesus is crucified (*Golgotha*) is translated for Hellenistic audiences as "the place of the skull" (19:17), the fuller explanation of why the soldiers cast lots for Jesus' clothes is supplied—the seamless robe (John 19:24; cf. Mark 15:24), Pilate's inscription posted on the cross is said to be rendered in Hebrew, Latin, and Greek (John 19:20), the religious reasons for breaking the legs of the other two victims and getting the body of Jesus buried that very day are given (19:31–34), water and blood are described as pouring forth from the pierced side of Jesus (19:34), the weight of the embalming spices is described as being around a hundred pounds (19:39) along with the linen-wrapping burial customs of the Jews (19:40), the linen wrappings are seen by Peter and the other disciple in the empty tomb (20:5–7), Jesus shows the disciples and Thomas the nail wounds in his hands and the piercing wound in his side (20:20–27), the number of the great catch of fish is given as 153 (21:11), and the postresurrection Jesus is described as eating fish and bread with his disciples (21:13). These details could have been added as a factor of the historicizing of a drama, but does their apparent realism argue more plausibly for a dramatization of history? As well as the most theological of the canonical passion narratives, John's is also the most mundane.

A seventh set of historical issues relates to the authorship of the Fourth Gospel and explicit references to eyewitness and firsthand testimony. Firsthand reporting is explicitly asserted in John 19:35, as a witness to blood and water flowing from the side of Jesus. Several assertions are made by the final narrator: (1) "he who saw this has testified so that you also may believe"; (2) "his testimony is true"; and (3) "he knows that he tells the truth." This eyewitness is unnamed, although the fact that the Beloved Disciple has just been entrusted the custody of Mary has led to their being associated together (19:26–27). In addition, an explicit attribution of authorship is made at the end of the Gospel (21:24), making three assertions as well: (1) "this is the disciple who is testifying to these things"; (2) "and [he] has written them"; and (3) "we know that his testimony is true." The connection is also made earlier between this figure and the Beloved Disciple who leaned against the breast of Jesus at the Last Supper (21:20; 13:23, 25), although he remains unnamed. It is also the fact, however, that 21:20–23 describes a discussion between Jesus and Peter regarding the fate of the Beloved Disciple, and the narrator clarifies that Jesus never promised that he would not die; does this imply that he *had* died by the finalizing of John 21? Whoever wrote and finalized the Fourth Gospel, we have a third-person attestation to firsthand witness and the authorial hand of an intimate associate of Jesus—unlike each of the Synoptic Gospels—which is why the distinctive Johannine presentation of Jesus remains a source of historical puzzlement and interest.

While some of these issues remain unaddressed in the present collection, many of them are addressed in creative and incisive ways. Jaime Clark-Soles opens up this section with an assessment of the degrees of plausibility regarding the historicity of the Johannine footwashing narrative. Acknowledging the fact that because this narrative is distinctive to John's Gospel it is omitted from most recent treatments of the historical Jesus, she questions whether this is a worthy judgment critically. While its narration clearly served didactic functions in its later Hellenistic Johannine situation, Clark-Soles examines its contextual realism to assess whether such an event is likely to have happened in Palestine. Noting that Synoptic criteria for determining Johannine historicity are often lacking in their serviceability, she poses some of her own ways forward for consideration. Separating features of the narrative into different gradations of plausibility (most likely, somewhat likely, less likely) and explaining the bases for her judgments, Clark-Soles offers an exemplary way forward in assessing critically aspects of John's historicity. From thence she expands helpfully upon the meaning of the narrative for later interpreters.

Moving further into the Johannine Last Supper discourses, Bas van Os considers the great discourses of Jesus in the light of postresurrection appearance themes and Synoptic comparisons/contrasts. Working with a two-edition theory of John's composition, van Os is able to trace developmental features in the later material accounting for the Johannine "relecturing" of earlier themes, which actually show a remarkable resemblance to the final teachings of Jesus in the Synoptics. In addition, a genre analysis of the function of resurrection dialogues in extracanonical sources casts light on the sort of development likely to have occurred within the evolving situation of Johannine Christianity itself. That being the case, van Os shows how the Johannine paraphrasing of earlier Jesus tradition was recrafted to fit later needs within its emerging situation, accounting for aspects of both history and theology in the formation of the Johannine Last Supper discourses.

With a special focus on the love commandment of Jesus in his final discourses, Richard A. Burridge shines the light hard on the similarities and differences between the exhortation of the Johannine Jesus to love one another and the Synoptic Jesus' commandments to love one's neighbors and enemies. Is this really the same Jesus talking? Building upon his earlier treatment of the Gospels as fitting into the genre of Greco-Roman historical biography (2004) and his focus on the ethical instruction of Jesus in the Gospels (2007), Burridge shows how reading the Fourth Gospel as biographical history, not an abstract ethical treatise, addresses this impasse. Rather than seeing the love of one another as being antithetical to the love of others in the world, Burridge shows the congruity between both emphases. By means of sacrificially loving those closest at hand, the love of God for the world is expressed incarnationally, which also results in the love of others. Despite the absence of parabolic forms and aphoristic presentations of Jesus' teachings in John, its ethical content is not antithetical to the teachings of Jesus in the Synoptics, but a complement.

Moving to the question of chronology, Mark A. Matson addresses the issue of the dating of the Last Supper in John as juxtaposed against presentations in the Synoptics. Having argued elsewhere for the plausibility of the Johannine early temple incident over and against the chronology of the Synoptics (2001b), here he turns to the other enduring chronological question when comparing John and the Synoptics together. Having concluded that the date of the Last Supper really is a problem between John and the Synoptics, resisting harmonization, Matson draws on other sources to help make the judgment. Matson also challenges views that "paschal theology" played any significant role in the presentation of the Johannine narrative, arguing for internal consistency with the rest of the Fourth Gospel's presentation of the passion and death of Jesus. In addition to finding the Johannine passion narrative to have been a likely source for Luke (2001a), Matson here also favors Johannine priority and considers the Johannine dating of the Last Supper more plausible than that of the Synoptics.

Addressing the Jewish trials of Jesus in John, Helen K. Bond assesses degrees of plausibility and aspects of historicity in the Johannine passion narrative as compared to the Synoptics. Building upon her works on Pilate, Caiaphas, and the crucifixion of Jesus in John (1998; 2004; 2007), Bond concludes that John's rendering is more reliable historically, despite its clearly theological thrust. While the Synoptic account bears a number of historical oddities, the Johannine account is straightforward. The lack of need for a Jewish trial in John, given the earlier sentencing of Jesus to death in John 11, makes the Johannine rendering seem rooted in traditional reference rather than theological concern. Bond thus notes the religious and political realism of the Johannine rendering, including the Annas-Caiaphas relationship and the informal nighttime trial of Jesus. The charge of being a false prophet and seducing the people—featured distinctively in John—lends insight not only into aspects of John's historicity but also to an understanding of the ministry of Jesus and its perceived effects in history.

Jeffrey Paul Garcia approaches aspects of historicity in John 19–20 by applying midrashic analysis to the presentation of the nail and piercing wounds of Jesus as an alternative explanation to their having happened in fact. Given that the nails and piercing details are missing from the Synoptic accounts, that "crucify" in Greek need not imply the use of nails but could simply refer to hanging, and that rope was often used to attach victims to crosses over more costly nails, Garcia argues against the historicity of the Johannine presentation. Further, as only one crucifixion victim in Jerusalem is known to have a spike pierced through his heel (Yehochanan, three decades or so after the death of Jesus) despite many bones found in ossuaries, Garcia reads this archaeological silence as an indication of the rarity of the practice. Finding, however, ample reason to infer the Johannine Evangelist's use of Jewish Scripture to make his points, Garcia sees in the citation of Zech 12:10 in John 19:37 a Johannine midrashic operation that added the nails/piercing details as the basis for their origin in the Johannine narrative. The fact that the flesh wounds of Jesus posed proof of Jesus' resurrection to his disciples in John 20 demonstrates the rhetorical interests of the narrator in including these details. Thus, according to Garcia, the nails and piercing motifs in John 19–20 originated not in history but in the midrashic embellishment of the Evangelist.

Addressing the restoration of Peter in John 21, Michael Labahn employs Jean Zumstein's *relecture* analysis (Zumstein 2004a) as a means of clarifying earlier meanings and later developments in the Johannine tradition. Here, in an innovative interdisciplinary way, Labahn explores the dialogical relationship between "facts" from the ministry of Jesus and their later meaning, interpretation, and use in the evolving Johannine tradition. In the present essay he develops further his earlier treatment of Walter Ong's theory of "secondary orality" and applies it to the Johannine and Lukan great-catch-of-fish narrative, but more centrally he shows how John 21 builds a new story upon the memory of an older one. In that sense, John 21 may be seen as an interpretive recasting of John 1–20 by another author, who has performed a redrawing of the Johannine story for a later situation. In laying out his case, Labahn shows how *relecture*, historic memory, and repetition and variation create an "orientation for the present" wherein the transformation of Peter from a sinner into a leader becomes a model for future community members as the past is fulfilled in the present.

R. Alan Culpepper concludes this section by focusing on John 21:24–25 as the closing "seal" (*sphragis*) whereby the final editor testifies to the truthfulness of the Johannine story of Jesus on behalf of the Johannine community. By drawing in literary parallels of closure statements, especially in Luke, Paul, and noncanonical literature, Culpepper shows how authenticating final statements in ancient literature functioned to provide a literary seal of veracity as a means of bolstering the testimony at hand. Disagreeing with Bauckham and others who see the third-person attestation as an author's way of speaking indirectly about himself or herself, Culpepper argues that the final editor is here testifying to the veracity of the Beloved Disciple's witness on behalf of the Johannine community. Exposing a multiplicity of relationships, the editor and his community provide the plurality of witnesses needed to validate the testimony of the Beloved Disciple, but the editor also serves as a bridge between that figure and the later Johannine audiences. Culpepper also advances our understanding of what Johannine historicity is and what it is not. Rather than a historical chronicling of data, the witness of the Beloved Disciple articulates the meaning of events and sayings, validating the historical significance of the subjective. As such, Johannine historicity cannot be confirmed with certainty; one can only attest to the authenticity of its witness—precisely what the final Johannine narrator has performed in declaring, "His testimony is true."

The essays in this section are responded to ably by Gail R. O'Day, who discusses the above essays within two larger analytical categories into which she groups them. Grouping Clark-Soles, Garcia, Matson, and Bond within approaches seeking to determine the *historical plausibility of Johannine depictions of the historical Jesus* in relation to various texts and subjects, O'Day assesses the degree to which each of these authors is successful in his or her analysis. Grouping van

Os, Culpepper, Burridge, and Labahn under the rubric of *the genre of the Gospels and aspects of historicity*, O'Day bridges the disciplinary divides of literary and historical studies effectively. In doing so, she also provides a set of rubrics for assessing the effectiveness of other treatments of aspects of historicity in the rest the Fourth Gospel as well.

John 13: Of Footwashing and History

Jaime Clark-Soles

Prodigious are the questions generated by this passage (John 13:1–20), and only slightly less prodigious are the publications devoted to it. Textual, anthropological, theological, literary, and exegetical analyses abound; only the historical remains largely untouched. When the historical is mentioned, however, treatments most often refer to the history of the Johannine situation, *not* to the historical Jesus or the historicity of the underlying Johannine tradition. Of all the questions one could ask, we shall attend most closely in this essay to these two. (1) Is it historically plausible that Jesus washed the feet of his disciples? Why or why not? (2) If he did, what might he have signified by this act?

In approaching this historical investigation, it must be acknowledged that many recent treatments are devoid of nuance. They simply make a judgment for or against John's presentation without saying much about degrees of certainty and strengths and weaknesses of one's arguments. In my approach, I hope to rectify those practices by arguing critically a nuanced approach in which gradations of plausibility are stated and explained. My argument runs thusly: (1) it is reasonable to assume that the historical Jesus performed a footwashing; (2) in doing so, Jesus may have signified one or more themes that would have been available to a Galilean Jew of the first century, namely, friendship, sacrificial love, and purification; and (3) the later Johannine community then expanded upon those themes and others that I shall mention later. In short, I argue that Jesus performed the deed, and it proved patient of polysemy for the author or authors of the Fourth Gospel.

1. The Structure of the Pericope

At the outset, some attention must be paid to the structure of the pericope, even if briefly. The footwashing story may be broken down as follows:

A. Introduction (John 13:1–3)

Generally considered a "second prologue" introducing the Book of Glory, verses 1–3 indicate Jesus' knowledge of his fate, his love for the disciples, and the devil's designs on Judas.

B. Narrative of Jesus' Deed (13:4–5)

Jesus pours water into a basin and washes his disciples' feet.

C. Dialogue with Peter (13:6–10a)

Calling Jesus "Lord," Peter questions whether Jesus is going to wash his feet, apparently seeing himself as set apart. Peter resists (the footwashing); Jesus insists (on doing it). Peter insists (add hands and head); Jesus resists (no need to do anything but the feet). Jesus distinguishes between the footwashing (νίπτω) and a full bath (λούω).

D. From Peter to Judas (13:10b-11)

Jesus declares all the disciples clean, except Judas.

E. Transition (13:12a)

Verse 12a provides a brief transition from the *act* of footwashing to its *interpretation* (13:12b–20), in Jesus' words.

2. The Historical Jesus in Galilee

Before offering my own constructive argument, it is important to note three points with respect to various recent Jesus-questers. First and famously, Jesus-questers tend to discount the Gospel of John as source material for reconstructing the historical Jesus. The John, Jesus, and History Project has been addressing this lacuna for years through meetings and publications. While the "third-questers" have been a bit more generous in their treatments of John than the first two quests for Jesus, they still have not done much with the footwashing. They take seriously the Jewishness of Jesus, but in evaluating the Johannine tradition in the light of Greco-Roman Mediterranean culture, they miss many of the Jewish features of the narrative—hence, overlooking the footwashing within their Jesus research.

Second, instead of sidestepping the issue, as many third-questers have done, the Jesus Seminar has ruled decisively *against* the Johannine footwashing as a historical possibility: "The narrative setting is the product of the evangelist's imagination, and the content of Jesus' instruction reflects the evangelist's theology, not the vision of Jesus. The Fellows designated the entire passage black" (Funk et al. 1998, 418). It is worth noting, however, that their argument actually focuses on Jesus' *instruction* in the footwashing (he emphasized loving one another instead of loving enemies, etc.), not the footwashing act itself. This is odd, as their second volume is devoted explicitly to the *acts* of Jesus.

Third, what might happen if accepted criteria for determining historicity were used on the passage? Jeremy Press argues that using John P. Meier's "primary criteria" of historicity,[1] including multiple attestation, embarrassment,

---

1. See Meier (1991, 168–77; 2001, 11–12) and the more extensive application of Meier's criteria to the Johannine footwashing in the riveting unpublished paper by Jeremy Press (2007). Press follows Anderson's critique of recent Jesus research (Anderson 2006b) and

discontinuity, and coherence, does not lead to particularly impressive results for the footwashing one way or the other. He concludes that because the criteria have been determined largely by study of the Synoptics, Q, and the noncanonical Gospels, John does not fare well in terms of contributing to the picture of the historical Jesus. For this to change, Johannine scholars should fully develop a historical Jesus that starts with John; they should develop criteria for determining *Johannine* historicity. In addition, historical Jesus scholars should be involved in the re-Johannification of Jesus project and the details of historically reliable material from John (with Press 2007). If one cannot get very far with the canons and procedures of typical Jesus research when studying John, then one must take a different approach involving at least the following four features.

2.1. GALILEE AS MORE JEWISH AND LESS HELLENIZED THAN PREVIOUSLY THOUGHT

Any argument about the historical Jesus depends first upon the cultural milieu in which the scholar finds him. This may be the single most important decision the historical Jesus scholar makes, as it will largely determine the Jesus who emerges. Clearly, Jesus was a Jew from Galilee. But we must ask archaeologists and Roman historians many questions: What was first-century Galilee like? Was it mostly Jewish, mostly pagan, or about evenly mixed? To what extent was the Galilee of Jesus' day Hellenized? Was Jesus of Nazareth likely to have spoken Greek? Would he have come into contact with those espousing the ideals of Hellenistic philosophy?

It has been quite commonplace to assume a heavily Hellenized Galilee, but Mark Chancey's recent work militates against such a view.[2] In *The Myth of the Gentile Galilee* (2002), Chancey not only employs the usual literary data, but he also supplies scholars with the most recent archaeological data regarding Galilee.[3] Using what he calls a "thoroughly historical" approach, which is distinct from sociological, anthropological, and cultural-theory approaches, Chancey inquires after the nature of the Galilean population. He finds "ample

---

seeks to rectify the dehistoricization of John and the de-Johannification of Jesus with a more "nuanced" approach—one that would take John seriously within the mix. He even suggests Anderson produce a historical treatment of Jesus that *starts* with John, leading to what Anderson calls a *fourth* quest for Jesus (Anderson 2007a, 288).

2. Consider Chancey's pointed comment: "The belief that pagans made up a large part, perhaps even the majority, of Galilee's population in the first century C.E.—a view that has influenced generations of New Testament scholars—exists despite the evidence, not because of it" (2002, 167).

3. Chancey's second book, *Greco-Roman Culture and the Galilee of Jesus* (2005), argues that the influence and absorption of Greco-Roman culture in Galilee occurred in the second and third centuries C.E., but not the first.

evidence in Galilee for Judaism and minimal evidence of paganism"; as a result, he insists that "discussions of the region in New Testament scholarship should always reflect the Jewish identities of the overwhelming majority of its inhabitants" (2002, 6). In his most recent book, *Greco-Roman Culture and the Jesus of Galilee* (2005), Chancey investigates the degree to which Galilee was affected by Greco-Roman culture. He helps us to "differentiate between Hellenistic and Greco-Roman culture, on the one hand, and pagan practice, on the other" (2005, 7). He notes that while Martin Hengel's statement is true, that "All Judaism was Hellenistic Judaism" (Hengel 1974a, 104), nevertheless "not all Judaism was affected by Hellenism in the same ways or to the same extent" (Chancey 2005, 225). He complains that "we scholars have been quicker to recognize the diversity in the *Judaism* of Hellenistic Judaism than in the *Hellenism* of Hellenistic Judaism" (2005, 229). Contrary to the notion that Jesus would have attended classical plays and regularly heard popular philosophers preaching on the corners of Sepphoris, Chancey contends that Jesus' Galilee was not Hellenized or Romanized at the deep level often assumed by scholars, the level that one would begin to see in the wake of the 120 C.E. stationing of a Roman legion in the area and that would characterize the later Roman era.

The relation of Galilee's population to Greco-Roman influence is an important topic here because it deeply impacts the plausibility of various parts of the footwashing story. The notion that Galilee was populated primarily by Gentiles, or even that there was a highly visible and large Gentile minority, is no longer tenable after Chancey's study. Furthermore, if Greco-Roman notions, ideals, and cultures were not readily adopted by the majority of that Jewish population, then any depiction of the historical Jesus that relies heavily on a primary backdrop of Hellenistic moral philosophers is less plausible than depictions that situate him squarely within what Sanders has called "common Judaism."

2.2. Chronological Development of Johannine Tradition

While the nature of first-century Galilee is an important initial consideration, the Hellenistic development of the Johannine tradition also deserves attention. This accounts for the fact that Jewish and Palestinian elements in the Johannine narrative appear to be translated for later, Hellenistic audiences. Anderson (2006b, 193–95) has convincingly argued that the first written version of John (roughly 80–85 C.E.) emerged from a Palestinian context. The Johannine community, or at least part of it, later operated in Ephesus, where another set of issues arose for the community (e.g., dealing with the synagogue in a non-Palestinian context, the Roman government under Domitian, and docetizing Gentile Christians). During this time the Johannine Epistles were composed. At the end of the century, the final version of the Fourth Gospel was compiled. So, the first layer of the Gospel would have been formed in a Palestinian context, where footwashing was apparently practiced.

2.3. Jesus the Jew Washes the Feet of His Disciples

There are several factors of historical realism in this narrative. To begin, note the *cultic realism* of the action. John Christopher Thomas (1991) has demonstrated that footwashing occurs in the Hebrew Bible and early Judaism for various reasons. It appears in cultic settings, such as when priests were expected to wash their hands and feet before entering holy places (Exod 30:17–21; 40:30–32 [MT, but not LXX]; 1 Kgs 7:38; 2 Chr 4:6; Josephus, *Ant.* 8.87). Footwashing and purity are connected here. Philo connects these purity concerns with leading a moral life (*Vit. Mos.* 2.128). Issues related to purity and cleansing are rife within the four Gospels' presentations of Jesus. So Jesus' cleansing his disciples' feet is not at all out of character with a Jew of Palestine.

In addition, the narrator's featuring factors of personal hygiene and comfort contribute to the *mundane realism* of the presentation. Anyone who has walked a mile or two in Palestine knows of the need to clean up, even after a short walk, before sitting down to a meal. What would be unlikely is that guests at a meal would not wash suitably before sharing table fellowship together. Thomas (1991, 31–35) lists numerous examples of footwashing in the context of personal hygiene and comfort. The highly untheological and mundane character of this activity makes the imputing of a theological motive for its fabrication an implausible'inference.

Further, the *domestic realism* of this event lends to the plausibility of the occurrence of the footwashing, according to Thomas (1991, 31–40). Footwashing appears most frequently within a domestic setting in the Hebrew Bible. Most often, servants perform the service, such as servants washing the feet of Abram's guests (Gen 18:4). At other times, however, a text is ambiguous regarding who does the washing—servants of the host or the guests themselves—such as when Lot invites the strangers to wash their feet (Gen 19:2) and when Laban offers Eleazar the chance at clean feet (Gen 24:32). Joseph's brothers are offered the same (Gen 43:24), and Abigail offers to wash the feet of David's servants (Judg 19:21; 1 Sam 25). The Testament of Abraham, roughly contemporaneous with the final form of the Fourth Gospel (ca. 100 C.E.), finds Abraham washing the feet of the angel Michael. Joseph and Aseneth (between first century B.C.E. and second century C.E.) depicts footwashing in the light of service rendered as an act of hospitality. In contrast to these renderings, the Johannine footwashing embellishes the theme of love, which probably belongs to a later interpretive layer—the same layer informing us that Jesus loved his disciples to the end (John 13:1). Whether or not the historical Jesus picked up on that theme, the later author certainly does.

2.4. Broader Contextual Realism

As noted above, while I have been convinced by Chancey's rendering of Galilee, such that I am reluctant to make too much of pagan literature in treating the historical Jesus, it is significant that footwashing also appears in Greco-Roman sources: "Footwashing was a widespread practice in the Greco-Roman world. It appears in a variety of contexts, from ritual purification to personal comfort" (Thomas 1991, 55). If one subscribes to an extremely Hellenized Galilee, one could use the Greco-Roman material to argue that a Hellenized Jesus drew upon such notions.

In the Greco-Roman material, footwashing occurs in various contexts, including cultic ones: "During Strabo's time [64 B.C.E.–24 C.E.] it can be deduced that among the Greeks most individuals washed their feet before entering a holy place" (Thomas 1991, 43). Most frequently, however, footwashing appears in the context of a meal. Moreover, it is done by slaves or servants (1991, 50). In fact, Thomas shows how footwashing can be eponymous with slavery in Plutarch (46–120 C.E.), Catullus (84–54 B.C.E.), and Herodotus (484–425 B.C.E.). Thomas also adduces artistic depictions to make this point. On the other hand, occasionally an individual not obligated to do this act would do it as a sign of love (1991, 55). Regardless of one's stance on Jesus' level of Hellenization, both the Jewish and Greco-Roman literature manifest that footwashing was a common practice. This makes it likely the historical Jesus did it—neither the historical Jesus nor the Fourth Evangelist had to invent the idea.

This larger contextual realism is corroborated by other New Testament evidence that may contribute to our discussion of footwashing. In Luke 7:36–50, a sinful woman wets Jesus' feet with her tears and wipes them with her hair, working from a servile position as a female and a declared sinner. In contrast, Jesus complains that Simon did not give him any water for his feet (7:44). Note also Mary's anointing of Jesus in John 12. This is typical of what we see in Jewish and Greco-Roman literature, in that it occurs in the context of a meal. Hence, although we do *not* have multiple attestations of Jesus' washing the disciples' feet, we do for the commonplace nature of washing another person's feet as a sign of devotion or hospitality. Additionally, widows are said to perform it (1 Tim 5:10), which may add to the likelihood that John's rendering is historical, because there too it is an act of service. On the other hand, one could infer that since the Pastoral Epistles have a Diaspora setting, it would argue for a later church practice. But as Anderson routinely reminds us (2006b, 37, 84, 86, 187), just because the church later practices an act does not mean that Jesus did not do it, unless one wants to argue for a church that never adopted *anything* Jesus said or did.

In conclusion, given the cultural context, it is highly plausible that a Jewish person in first-century Galilee would perform a footwashing. Therefore, it is plausible that Jesus performed a footwashing as he gathered for a final meal with his disciples in Jerusalem. On the bases of Jewish and Hellenistic literature, religious and societal customs, other presentations of footwashing in the New Testament literature, and various aspects of historical realism, this scenario in John demands renewed consideration as a historical event in the ministry of Jesus despite its unique presentation in the Fourth Gospel.

3. The Meaning of the Footwashing for Jesus

If the historical Jesus indeed performed a footwashing, what might he have meant by it, given his cultural context? Here it is best to categorize potential significations on a continuum from most likely, to somewhat likely, to unlikely.

3.1. Most Likely Features

1. *Purity*. Given that footwashing appears to have been a regular practice in Judaism, that it is connected with purity concerns, that Galilee was a region firmly situated in Judaism, and that there is much evidence that ritual baths were available, I see no reason to doubt that the historical Jesus performed a footwashing with some notion of purification in mind. Purification in a cultic setting is tied to preparation of a spiritual sort.

All of the Gospels depict Jesus as interacting with notions of purity that come from his own Jewish tradition. It is reasonable, then, to hypothesize that the Jesus of history did perform the footwashing and that he spoke of the act as having to do with a cleansing of some sort. Notice, of course, that two different washing words are used in John 13: λούω and νίπτω. Scholars posit distinct meanings for each, tying λούω (bathing; 13:10) to a one-time event, namely, baptism, while connecting νίπτω (washing; 13:5–14, *passim*) to a repeated event in the life of the Johannine community, namely, footwashing. Such discussions are beyond our scope here. It is enough to say that Jesus, as a Jew, could easily have attached notions of purity to the act of footwashing.

2. *Honor*. Jerome Neyrey (1995) has shown us that actions such as footwashing mark relationships. By performing a footwashing on his disciples, the historical Jesus may have marked them as related to him in a special way; the action marks them as his followers and thus serves as a particular status marker, giving the disciples a "share" (μέρος; 13:8) in Jesus, giving them honor.[4]

---

4. Neyrey distinguishes between a ritual and a ceremony: a *ritual* is a singular event that changes the role or status of an individual, while a *ceremony* is an action repeated regularly that confirms the role and status of a person. Neyrey argues that Peter undergoes a transformation ritual in 13:6–11, whereas the disciples are instructed to practice a ceremony in 13:12–20. Given the prominence of Peter in the Synoptics, in at least some places in the Fourth Gospel, and in the noncanonical Gospels, one might make a case that the historical Jesus did, in fact, have a special encounter with the historical Peter that involved footwashing. If so, given the plausibility of Jesus' performing an act related to purification, I would not vigorously protest at a historical level the notion that Jesus could have had a special encounter with Peter, the aim of which was purification. The particular incident with Peter, however, is a bit harder to maintain on historical grounds than the notion of a leader performing a ritual act that marks the identity of a group *qua* group.

As soon as the conversation moves more fully into footwashing as a ceremony or sacrament of the Johannine community, the historical plausibility becomes more remote; not impossible, but more remote.[5] Neyrey speaks of λούω as baptism and νίπτω as the footwashing ceremony. At that level of discussion, it is more plausible to envision the habits and concerns of the Johannine community rather than the historical Jesus.

3. *Friendship.* If the historical Jesus aimed to denote a special relationship with his disciples through the footwashing, he may have been operating out of biblical notions of friendship. Most scholars turn immediately to the Hellenistic philosophers or Philo when they treat the theme of friendship. However, if Galilee was less Hellenized than previously thought, as Chancey maintains, then we are probably safer in ascribing Hellenistic philosophical categories to the later Johannine community in the Diaspora rather than the historical Jesus of Galilee.

While φιλέω language does not appear in John 13, it is a prominent theme elsewhere in the Fourth Gospel. The whole footwashing scene, not to mention the Farewell Discourse, is framed in terms of love. That being the case, φιλέω and ἀγαπάω language are related, if not synonymous (see esp. 21:15–17). Notice that the Johannine Jesus' focus on love also coheres with the Synoptic image of Jesus. Could this be because the historical Jesus himself emphasized friendship and love as fundamental aspects of his work and vision? If so, what would friendship look like for him?

There is no reason to doubt that the historical Jesus was shaped by the Hebrew Scriptures, which include major figures of faith depicted as friends of God (e.g., Abraham, Moses, and Job); the *topos* of friendship in wisdom literature (e.g., Sirach); and narratives that depict deep love, care, and loyalty among friends (Joseph and Aseneth; 1 Samuel). It is likely, then, that if the historical Jesus performed a footwashing, his action was informed by notions of friendship drawn from his Scriptures.[6] Moreover, particular footwashing stories appear in the Old Testament. Even if no one in first-century Palestinian Judaism was still practicing footwashing, what would have precluded Jesus of Nazareth from intentionally imitating a ritual drawn from his Scriptures? Why is it plausible to find a later author (the Fourth Evangelist) drawing upon the Hebrew Scriptures in his presentation but not plausible to find a Jew around 30 C.E. (Jesus) doing so?[7] As a factor of friendship and love, further meanings of Jesus' action may also be inferred.

---

5. On the footwashing as a sacrament for the Johannine community, see numerous authors, including Mary Coloe 2004, Sandra Schneiders 1981, and Francis Moloney 1991.

6. See also Gail O'Day's essay on "Jesus as Friend in the Gospel of John" (2004).

7. Perhaps what Sharon Ringe says about the Johannine community can be pushed back to the level of the historical Jesus: "Because at least the core of the community to which the Fourth Gospel was directed was Jewish, we can be reasonably certain that the author of the Gospel and

First, friendship functioned as a means of *status elevation*. The Jesus of history certainly had access to the traditions about humans achieving friendship with God, as such language is used of Abraham, Moses, and Job.[8] Friendship in that case involved a certain status elevation for the human being vis-à-vis God, while still retaining some features of hierarchy. Neither Abraham, nor Moses, nor Job became equal with God, but they shared a special intimate relationship— one superior to that of others. In John 13, Jesus does not appear to eradicate all hierarchy, as if there were no master or students, but he designates this group as having a special relationship with him. Washing someone's feet is a way of ascribing honor and, therefore, status to that person. The historical Jesus may have depicted himself as a friend of God in the biblical sense; the later community adapted and pushed this idea further, to the point of depicting Jesus as self-presenting as God rather than merely a friend of God. Jesus gains higher status, but the later tradition also elevates the disciples to complete unity with Jesus and God (John 17:20–26). Some third-questers depict Jesus as a radical egalitarian with thoroughly democratic tendencies; the Jesus who considers his followers to be "friends" (John 15:13–17) may lend weight to such portraits.

A second consideration relates to the connections between *friendship and wisdom*. Numerous third-questers find in the historical Jesus a figure heavily influenced by wisdom traditions; they would argue, in fact, that the historical Jesus consciously presented himself that way. With relation to the Gospel of John, Sharon Ringe tidily outlines the important connections between wisdom traditions and friendship in her appropriately titled book, *Wisdom's Friends* (1999). The *topos* of friendship occurs in various texts of the Hebrew Bible and is especially prominent in Sirach and Proverbs. In his article on "friendship" in Philo, Greg Sterling notes that φιλέω language occurs 159 times in the Septuagint. He writes, "The most extensive discussions of friendship in the LXX are Sir 6:5–17; 22:19–26; 37:1–6" (1997, 204 n. 5). Many of the passages demand further attention for a study of the historical Jesus in John (e.g., Sir 14:13: "Do good to a friend before you die, and reach out and give to him as much as you can"). What Sterling finds surprising is Philo's redefinition of friendship and kinship. "Philo speaks of friendship and kinship on the basis of commitment to God and elevates these bonds over the ties of blood and marriage" (1997, 218). This applies easily to Jesus, who in all of the Gospels does the same (Luke 14:26 and par.; Matt 8:22 and par.; Mark 10:29–30; Mark 3:33–35), as does Paul after him (see Paul's usage of familial language for Christians, the language of fictive kin; Paul is a father, a nurse, a brother; see also his household language in referring to Christians). It

---

the members of his community would have been familiar with the biblical materials related to friendship" (1999, 69).

8. Greg Sterling notes that "the reference to friendship with God was fairly widespread in antiquity" (1997, 217–18).

makes sense to infer that all of those witnesses do so because the historical Jesus did so.

4. *Sacrificial love.* A fourth possibility regarding the meaning of footwashing for the historical Jesus has to do with sacrificial love. This is closely tied to friendship, of course, but deserves separate mention. To claim this is to situate him squarely within early Judaism, since there are no occurrences in the Greco-Roman literature of a superior washing the feet of an inferior (Thomas 1991, 59).

Both 1 Samuel and Joseph and Aseneth depict women who, from a standpoint of love, adopt a servant's role. So, when David sends his servants to collect Abigail to be his wife, she says, "Your servant is a slave to wash the feet of the servants of my lord" (1 Sam 25:41). Aseneth says, "And you, Lord, commit me to him for a maidservant and slave. And I will make his bed, and wash his feet, and wait for him, and be a slave for him and serve him forever" (Jos. Asen. 13:15). It is important here, however, to maintain a distinction between autonomous love and simple servile degradation (e.g., a slave who was expected to wash the feet of her or his master's guests). Neither the Greco-Roman evidence nor the Mishnaic literature, both of which find washing another's feet degrading, approximates the dignity of servant love as portrayed in the LXX.[9]

If footwashing was not seen as disdainful in the LXX as it appears to be in the Greco-Roman and Mishnaic literature, then one must be careful about too boldly depicting a historical Jesus who simply takes the form of a slave, offering servile hospitality that degrades him in some way. Instead, it seems to be an act of sacrificial love. Once the story encounters a Greco-Roman setting, it becomes available for starker musings on the reversal of status or a critique of hierarchy and embracing of radical egalitarianism.

3.2. Somewhat Likely Features

The following three elements of the narrative are less plausible but still possible with respect to the historical Jesus:

1. *Humble service.* As stated above, this notion fits better in a later Greco-Roman setting than an earlier Galilean one. Since I have been convinced by Chancey that a Galilee of the Gentiles in Jesus' own time is mythical, any material more at home in a Greco-Roman setting is less plausible for the historical Jesus. It makes sense that a ceremony of footwashing as delineated by Neyrey postdates the historical Jesus and predates a so-called "sacrament of footwashing" that seems likely to have been practiced by at least the latest community associated

---

9. Beasley-Murray (1999, 233) fails to maintain such a distinction; see also Barrett 1978, 440.

with the Gospel.[10] This action also fits well as an enacted embodiment of Jesus' teachings elsewhere on greatness as a factor of becoming a servant to others.[11]

2. *Peter's being singled out.* It may be that the historical Jesus singled Peter out during the footwashing in some way that was remembered later by the participants. Peter looms large in each of the Synoptics, as well as noncanonical texts. Even if Jesus did in some way mark Peter especially in the event of a footwashing, one would be hard pressed to argue that it took the form as narrated by the Fourth Evangelist. The rhetorical style and technique is typically Johannine, which makes it more difficult to argue for its origination at the level of the historical Jesus. Elevating the status of Peter, especially vis-à-vis the Beloved Disciple, is a particular concern in a later stage of the Fourth Gospel. In this regard, John 13 relates well to John 21; both are later attempts to elevate Peter and accord him special honor and status.

3. *A meal context.* It may be that the footwashing occurred in the context of a meal, although determining the particular meal in which it took place requires a further level of investigation. Both the Jewish and Greco-Roman sources provide some evidence that would make a meal context likely, but given John's differences with the Synoptics, corroboration remains elusive. As John's presentation of a footwashing at the Last Supper, as well as the date on which it fell, bears heavy theological overtones, it is likely that this context belongs to later layers of interpretation rather than earlier ones. Again, this does not deny the possibility of the Johannine rendering as it is; it simply diminishes the plausibility of the footwashing within a particular meal context.

In addition to plausible and possible gradations of historical likelihood, the least likely measure of Johannine historicity involves those features that focus more on its meaning within the later Johannine tradition rather than the meaning of the event for the Jesus of history and his contemporary associates. As most commentators never consider aspects of the historical Jesus, they argue at the

---

10. In relation to the Jewish sources, however, while we may not have found the exact opposite attitude, certainly we have nothing to indicate that footwashing was always and everywhere considered a servile task, which only the lowest members of society could be forced to perform. The sources for footwashing's being considered such an odious task in Jewish circles come from Mishnaic and talmudic literature, which can only be dated later than John with any real confidence. Whether or not these attitudes can be retrojected into first-century Palestine should be questioned. What we do find is that in material earlier than John (the Hebrew Scriptures and some of the apocryphal literature), there is no indication that footwashing always had to be performed by a servant (indeed, sometimes even guests could wash their own feet, a situation that would be unthinkable for status equals in the Roman context, at the time of the writing of John; Press 2007, 15).

11. Here scholars draw upon the Synoptic conversations about greatness and service (e.g., Luke 22:24–30). Thomas (1991, 87) argues that Jesus dressed himself as a slave in the manner of a servant as depicted in Roman art. This argues for a later layer when Johannine Christians had access to works of Roman art.

level of the Johannine situation at various stages, or more often, the Gospel in its final literary form. As a result, the bulk of scholarship on John takes up issues that I would argue belong not to the historical Jesus but to later instantiations of the Johannine community/ies. I mention them below.

3.3. Less Likely Features

1. *The developed love theme.* It is not unreasonable to propose that when the historical Jesus washed the feet of his disciples, he set it into the context of love (φιλέω; ἀγαπάω). However, the thoroughgoing focus on this theme through the Fourth Gospel implies that the author had a particular interest in the issue and thereby diminishes the likelihood that the historical Jesus can be credited with a systematic concern for voicing concerns of love.

2. *The great reversal.* In addition, the "great reversal," in which the master takes the form of a slave and performs a degrading, servile act in order to level the playing field and herald radical egalitarianism and democratic ideals, is clearly an interest of the Johannine Evangelist. While some of this could have originated with the Jesus of history, it certainly would have played dramatically within a Hellenistic context beyond Palestine. As I have already argued, such notions make more sense in a Greco-Roman environment.

3. *Meal meanings, including open commensality.* The meal context also raises issues of open commensality. From a historical standpoint, however, it is not at all clear that the footwashing originally occurred in the context of a meal or whether the author has combined traditions into a narrative construct. If one were to make a convincing argument that the footwashing and meal went hand in hand, then John Dominic Crossan's vision of Jesus the egalitarian would enjoy further evidence—even as portrayed in John (Crossan 1991, 261–64), although John 13 seems to reference an intimate meal setting instead of an open one.

4. *Footwashing as prefiguring Jesus' burial.* This type of interpretation ties John 13 very closely with the previous chapter (12:1–8), in which Mary's νίπτω act foreshadows Jesus' νίπτω act, which foreshadows the passion. The elegant literary virtuosity involved in the threading of the theme actually argues against the historicity of this theological and dramatic association.

5. *Friendship as evinced by Hellenistic philosophy.* The historical Jesus is to be located in Galilee. The original stage of Johannine Christianity should be located in Palestine as well. Eventually, however, it seems that the community moved to a Diaspora setting.[12] At this point it is certainly reasonable to assume that notions of friendship common in Hellenistic philosophy influenced the ideas of friend-

---

12. I find Paul Anderson's recent chronology of the Johannine situation convincing (2006b, 196–99).

ship as presented in the Fourth Gospel. At this level, then, one would want to engage the materials that deal with friendship in the Greco-Roman sources.

6. *Baptismal imagery.* If sacramental associations are inferred with relation to the Johannine footwashing, these most likely also reflect later developments rather than earlier traditions. If indeed baptismal overtones were associated with the λούω verb (itself somewhat questionable), these most likely would have reflected later Christian developments of sacramental themes rather than interests of the historical Jesus himself, who according to John 4:2 did not baptize—only his disciples did.

7. *Featuring Judas, the traitor.* Within the context of the cleansing of Peter (13:10–11), references are made to the uncleanness of Judas. The footwashing scene may function in part to provide an explanation for the embarrassing fact that the historical Jesus was betrayed by one close to him: Judas Iscariot. Hence, Jesus' indications that, unlike Peter, Judas was not clean would have had special theological meaning within the developing Johannine tradition. By the time the Johannine Gospel was finalized, Judas is almost a caricature of betrayal (6:71; 13:2; 18:2), representing later perspectives rather than primitive ones.

8. *Footwashing as a ceremony* or *sacrament.* If baptism served as a transformation ceremony for Johannine Christians, then the institution of "the ceremony of footwashing," as described by Neyrey, belongs to a later layer of the community and does not go back to the historical Jesus. Of course, some will question whether such a meaning is implied at all in the Johannine text; but if it is, its development was later rather than earlier.

In considering gradations of plausibility regarding aspects of historicity related to the Johannine footwashing scenario, a variety of features fall on a continuum between meanings associated with the Jesus of history and meanings associated with the latest stages of the Johannine tradition. While Johannine theological meanings should not be imposed upon the historical Jesus, it is also problematic to exclude from the realm of possibility all features of this passage simply because it is included in John's Gospel. By means of locating the various features within the categories of plausible, possible, and less plausible, a more nuanced analysis of this pericope is critically performed.

CONCLUSIONS

On the basis of evidence from John 13, it is entirely plausible to suggest that Jesus washed the feet of his disciples at some point and time. In doing this, he may have been acting on the basis of concerns for purification and spiritual preparation, marking a special relationship between himself and those whom he washed, exhibiting and stressing ideas of friendship as they appeared in Hebrew Scripture, and, finally, exhibiting sacrificial love. The later community, then, did two things: it built upon Jesus' significations, and it created some of its own.

From this analysis, several preliminary suggestions follow regarding the Gospel of John and the quest for the historical Jesus. While it may be too soon to infer what kind of historical Jesus one finds on the basis of John 13 alone, if one were to one analyze each episode in the Fourth Gospel—to determine the level of historical plausibility for each—such a set of analyses would make a considerable contribution to historical Jesus studies. Only when all of that work is done could one begin to reconstruct a historical Jesus that takes seriously the Johannine evidence. In a word, this sifting is the very project that the John, Jesus, and History Group has been encouraging. Nonetheless, some preliminary comments are in order here.

1. We could comment on the value of conventional criteria for determining the historicity of Gospel materials: multiple attestation, discontinuity, embarrassment, and coherence. It is worth noting that both the new quest and the third quest are marked by variety both in terms of personalities and methods. When the approaches of these quests converged in the work of the Jesus Seminar, the criteria were largely set by that group and were almost reified; the criteria were established without consideration of possible Johannine historicity. As the Jesus Seminar moved on to other projects beyond the canonical Gospels, however, most current questers seem to acknowledge that the categories are not much more than suggestive, heuristic, and flexible and certainly not "scientific." Can new criteria for determining historicity be developed to serve more adequately a critical quest for the historical Jesus without being hampered by an anti-Johannine bias? If so, Jesus *and* Johannine studies would both be helped.

2. If Anderson is right about a bi-optic tradition, why not start with John and see what kind of historical Jesus emerges? This might even pose a new, first-century window into the Synoptic Jesus in ways not yet considered.

3. This Johannine Jesus would corroborate some third-quest portraits of Jesus, but some others less well. In John one finds a Jesus who aligns himself with Wisdom traditions, makes some egalitarian moves, and is not apocalyptic. This is largely the Jesus that many third-questers derive from the Synoptics, retaining the elements that make him a nonapocalyptic sage, while discarding the rest. The Johannine Jesus is much more amenable to such a portrait than is currently acknowledged. Ironically, many Jesus-questers who rule John out of the playing field strip the Synoptics, only to get a Johannine Jesus minus the long-windedness.

4. Scholars who allow for a Palestinian Jew not particularly fluent in Hellenistic moral philosophy, such as E. P. Sanders (1985, 123–56; sayings material is all focused on "kingdom" and Jewish apocalyptic; no section on wisdom in Sanders) or John P. Meier (2001, 1–4; Meier focuses entirely on Jesus' Jewishness and does not consider Hellenistic philosophy at all), might do well to incorporate the Fourth Gospel more directly into their syntheses. For instance, the Johannine Jesus, who is a Jewish Jesus, far from abolishing purity acts that draw social boundaries, might be seen to enact and transform them.

5. Those who posit a historical Jesus who was a radical egalitarian, promulgating democratic ideals at every turn, would find the Fourth Gospel conducive in some ways but not in others. Positively, for instance, if the historical Jesus *did* perform a footwashing in order to elevate the status of his disciples and confer upon them a part of his honor, this would speak to a notion of democratizing leadership. Negatively speaking, however, the move to democratizing leadership does not necessarily imply equality with Jesus; he continues to play the role of the master in John as he does in the Synoptics.

6. Because the Jesus of John 13 does not particularly cohere with a Jesus marked by the sophisticated thinking of Hellenistic philosophy, this is all the more reason for inferring a Palestinian origin of the Johannine scenario. While Hellenistic associations of friendship and reversal abound, the Fourth Evangelist's Jesus most likely belongs to the layer of the Johannine community after it has left Palestine. The mistake is to displace the earlier levels of traditional history on the basis of later ones.

7. This Jesus might well serve those who cast him in Wisdom's image. Truth be told, the Fourth Evangelist was the first obsessive quester. He employs ζητέω language ("to seek") far more than any other biblical writer. "'Whom do you seek?' Jesus asked. They answered: 'Jesus the Nazarene'" (18:4–5). Like us, they sought the historical Jesus of Nazareth. He responded, "ἐγώ εἰμι" (18:5, 6, 8), whereupon they drew back and fell upon the ground. An enigmatic one, this Jesus is, then as now.

It may be that even now he comes to us as one unknown; but let it never be said that he comes as one unstudied.

John's Last Supper and the Resurrection Dialogues

Bas van Os

1. Introduction[1]

In an appendix to *The Fourth Gospel and the Quest for Jesus*, Paul Anderson (2006b, 193–95) proposes a phased development of the Johannine corpus:

(1) First, the Johannine tradition is formed around the Beloved Disciple. This tradition interacts with other developing Gospel traditions, such as those that would be used in the Synoptic Gospels, especially Mark's.

(2) In response to the Gospel of Mark, and before Matthew and Luke were written, a first edition of the Gospel of John is written by the Johannine Evangelist; Q and Luke show dependence on the Johannine oral tradition.

(3) and (4) In the last decades of the first century, the Johannine elder writes the Johannine Epistles, while the Beloved Disciple continues to teach. There may have been some interaction with Matthean Christianity in this period.

(5) After the death of the Beloved Disciple, the Johannine Elder compiles and finalizes the Johannine Gospel, which includes later traditions shaped by the Beloved Disciple. It is in this edition, Anderson believes, that the Gospel prologue (1:1–18) and chapters 6, 15–17, and 21 are added to the original work.

(6) In the second century, Johannine traditions influence not only mainstream Christianity but also Docetist, gnostic, and Montanist Christians.

---

1. Part of this essay is based on "The Gospel of John and the Sophia of Jesus Christ: Evidence for Post-resurrection Discourses behind John 13–17?" a paper I presented at the 2005 SBL International Meeting in Singapore. I would like to thank those who have commented on it.

In this essay I shall first discuss the components of the Farewell Speech. Second, I shall argue that these components influenced the development of the genre of the "resurrection dialogues." Third, I shall outline the similarities between the Synoptics' account of the Last Supper and the Johannine framework in which the dialogues have been used. Finally, I shall assess what this may mean for Anderson's theory of Johannine composition and the quest for the historical Jesus.

2. The Discourses in the Farewell Speech in John 13–17

John starts his account of the Last Supper with the story that Jesus washed the feet of his disciples (13:1–20), after which Jesus foretells his betrayal (13:21–30). The discourse material that I shall review is found in the remainder of chapters 13–17, ending with the words, "After Jesus had spoken these words…" (18:1). The so-called Farewell Speech consists of four smaller discourses. First, there is a dialogue after Judas had left to betray Christ (13:31–14:31) in which Jesus tells his disciples that he will now go to his Father and that the Holy Spirit will teach them from now on. This dialogue ends, "I will no longer talk much with you…. Rise, let us be on our way" (14:30–31). We would now expect Jesus to go out as he does in 18:1, but to our surprise there is a long monologue (15:1–16:15), which again ends with the promise of the Spirit, because, "I still have many things to say to you, but you cannot bear them now" (16:12). After this monologue, there is again a dialogue (16:16–33), repeating much of what we saw in the first dialogue. The Farewell Speech then concludes with a lengthy prayer (17:1–25).

Apart from the surprising resumptions in the discourse material, there are other indications that the material is a compilation of various versions of older sources. Many sayings occur in two or more of the four discourses. Sometimes this creates a problem, as with Jesus' saying, "Little children, I am with you only a little longer. You will look for me; and as I said to the Jews so now I say to you, 'Where I am going, you cannot come'" (13:33). Even though Jesus then explains his saying in his first dialogue, he apparently needs to explain it again, when he repeats his saying in chapter 16.[2]

A similar problem arises with the question at the end of 16:5: "But now I am going to him who sent me; yet none of you asks me, 'Where are you going?'" The question is rather odd in light of the first dialogue, where it was already asked by both Peter (13:36) and Thomas (14:5).

---

2. John 16:16–18: "'A little while, and you will no longer see me, and again a little while, and you will see me.' Then some of his disciples said to one another, 'What does he mean by saying to us, "A little while, and you will no longer see me, and again a little while, and you will see me"; and "Because I am going to the Father"?' They said, 'What does he mean by this "a little while"? We do not know what he is talking about.'"

Scholars have come up with various solutions to this issue. Andreas Dettwiler (1995, 266–92), for instance, sees the second dialogue as *"relecture"* of the first dialogue.[3] He sees here the later work of a Johannine school. His views are discussed by Klaus Scholtissek, who suggests an additional possibility, called *"réécriture.* Here, one basic principle is taken up, varied, and expressed differently by one and the same author" (2004, 459).

Of course, these tensions did not stand in the way of the inclusion of these discourses in the final composition of John. Francis Moloney rightly takes the resulting composition as an "artistic and strategic whole" (1998, 4, quoting Segovia 1991), in which he even finds a chiastic structure (Moloney 2005, 260–83). Scott Kellum (2004) argues for the Farewell Discourse as a literary unity from the start. His stylistic analyses point to a single author behind the entire discourse. He also notes that the text makes sense as a coherent whole and that "Rise, let us be on our way" (14:31) has its proper function.

I agree that the account of the Last Supper and the Farewell Speech are a unified composition, but why, in that case, did the composer of the Farewell Speech not smooth over the differences noted above? It seems that the tensions within John 13–17 are well explained by Anderson's theory of Johannine composition. If the Johannine Elder worked with multiple traditions of the Beloved Disciple, he needed to rearrange the discourses, but he may not have felt free to change the words of these dialogues significantly. After all, he saw the Beloved Disciple as an authority and eyewitness (21:24; see also 1 John 1:1–3).

If at least some of the discourses have been inserted secondarily into John's passion narrative, as Anderson believes, the question must be asked what their original setting had been. Rudolph Bultmann (1962) proposed that the backbone of the Farewell Discourse came from an early gnostic non-Christian revelatory source. J. Hammer (1959) and W. J. P. Boyd (1967) both proposed a postresurrection setting for John 13–17, for instance in the apparition of Jesus to the five hundred brethren mentioned by Paul (1 Cor 15:6), but their arguments did not convince (Brown 1966–70, 2:582–86). Most scholars today opt for Johannine creation as an alternative to the Synoptic tradition and modeled to the existing genre of the farewell speech.[4]

3. The Gospel of John and the Genre of the Resurrection Dialogues

Since Brown's commentary on John, our knowledge of gnostic revelatory discourses and resurrection dialogues has increased significantly as a result of the

---

3. Dettwiler discusses the close literary and functional relationship with the gnostic Christian redeemer dialogues (1995, 21–27) but does not use these observations for his source theory.

4. George Parsenios (2005) even claims that the discourse is a conscious act of genre bending, combining not just Jewish testament but also tragedy, ancient consolation literature, and the literary symposium.

publication of the gnostic Christian writings in the Berlin Codex, the Nag Hammadi writings (see Layton 1987; Robinson 1988), and the Codex Tchacos. Wilhelm Schneemelcher (1990, 189–91) discusses the genre of the *Dialoge des Erlösers* (dialogues of the redeemer). Scholars see this genre as a gnostic *Weiterentwicklung* (development) of Greco-Roman genres like the dialogue. Pheme Perkins (1980) devotes a monograph to the genre and provides an overview of the ancient works concerned. Some of them were short writings with specific discourses of Jesus set in a single episode of the then-familiar Gospel narratives.[5] The recently discovered Gospel of Judas, for instance, is set in the last days before Jesus' passion. The Gospel of Mary is set just after appearances of the risen Jesus to her and to his disciples. Indeed, most revelatory discourses are placed between Jesus' crucifixion and his final ascension. In some instances this is linked to the remark about the risen Christ in Acts 1:3: "After his suffering he presented himself alive to them by many convincing proofs, appearing to them during forty days and speaking about the kingdom of God."

In her doctoral dissertation, Judith Hartenstein studies the earliest works of this specific subgenre, which she refers to as *Erscheinungen des Auferstandenen* (appearances of the resurrected one). The earliest preserved resurrection dialogues are *Epistula Apostolorum*, the Sophia of Jesus Christ, the Dialogue of the Savior, and the Gospel of Mary. Within this group, Hartenstein (2000, 313–14) concludes that the Sophia of Jesus Christ (NHC III,4 and BG 8502,3) is probably the earliest extant representative of this genre.[6] She also believes that Sophia developed out of the Synoptic resurrection appearances as the model for the other dialogues. But there is a problem with this proposition. Sophia cannot have been the model for the other early resurrection dialogues, as the other early works are often shorter, less coherent, and less structured. Furthermore, these other resurrection dialogues contain variants that are not found in Sophia. The question that I shall discuss below is whether the material in John 13–17 and 20–21 provides a better model out of which the early resurrection dialogues may have developed.

3.1. The Making of Sophia

In Nag Hammadi Codex III, the Sophia of Jesus Christ follows Eugnostos the Blessed (NHC III,3); the compilers of this codex in the fourth century will have

---

5. Only John (Apocryphon of John) and Thomas (Book of Thomas the Contender) see Jesus in a context not described in the New Testament.

6. Hartenstein's argument focuses on a comparison between the early Apocryphon of John and Sophia. Although the content of the Apocryphon is earlier than the composition of Sophia, this is not so for the framework of the Apocryphon. The framework is clearly secondary and not mentioned in Irenaeus's description of the gnostic myth in the Apocryphon.

recognized the literary relationship between the two. Eugnostos is a short treatise proclaiming a gnostic view of God and the cosmos. Sophia largely and often
verbatim takes over the teaching of Eugnostos[7] but sets it in the framework of a
dialogue with the risen Savior. Sophia is the result of seven editorial interventions
or groups of interventions that together turn the existing treatise into a resurrection dialogue:

(1) First a setting is provided for the discourse (90.14–91.20). After the
resurrection, Jesus' disciples and "seven women" go to a mount in
Galilee.[8] This apparition resembles most clearly Matt 28:16 but is
also related to Mark 16:7 and John 21.

(2) Second, Jesus appears (91.20–24) and greets his disciples with the
words: "Peace be to you! My peace I give to you." The first part of
the greeting formula, "Peace be to you," is identical to that in the
resurrection experiences in John 20:19–20, 26, and Luke 24:36. The
second part can be found only in John 14:27.

(3) Next the subject of the dialogue (91.24–92.6) is taken from Eugnostos and briefly introduced by a question of the Savior, "What are you
searching for?" to which Philip answers, "For the underlying reality of the universe and the plan." Even though the subject matter is
not identical, John 13–17 is the largest substantial block of esoteric
teaching in the canonical Gospels; none of the Synoptic resurrection
discourses have anything like it. The two dialogues are introduced
by a statement of Jesus, to which the disciples respond with questions, like "Lord, where are you going?" and "What does he mean
with...?"

(4) Revelation authority. In various instances in Sophia, the risen Jesus
claims unique knowledge of the other side.[9] Jesus says, "I am the
great Savior"; he came from the Light and is the interpreter sent
by the Boundless One, "so that I might tell you all things." Of the
canonical Gospels, this comes closest to the Gospel of John, where
Jesus is the great "I am." In John 13–17 Jesus is sent by the Father,

---

7. Occasionally we see adaptations of the teaching material from Eugnostos: the nature
of Sophia/Immortal Man (III,76.24–77.9), and the elaborate use of numbers (III,78.16–{V,8.6},
III,82.7–84.11, 84.17–85.6). Some parts are rearranged, such as V,8.18–26 and III,81.2–10.

8. There are two names for the mountain, or two mountains, and one name is "Mount of
Olives"; this example shows that Sophia is not directly dependent on just one Gospel account.
At some point in time, removed from the historical and geographical setting, Jerusalem and
Galilee traditions must have been brought together.

9. NHC III: 93.8–12, 94.10–14, 96.19–97.16, 101.9–15, 105.13–19, 106.5–9, 107.11–108.15;
the esoteric element is stressed with the formula "he who has ears..." in 97.19–24, 98.21–22, and
BG 107.16–18.

who reveals himself and the Father in him to those who love him.
Jesus says: "I am the way, the truth, and the light; no one comes to
the Father except through me" (14:6).

(5) In Sophia, twelve dialogue questions divide the original treatise and
the additional teaching at the end.[10] The disciples asking questions in
Sophia are the same as those in John 13–16 and 20, but most of them
do not feature as individuals in the Synoptic resurrection stories.

(6) Additional teaching (114.14–119.8). To complement Eugnostos,
Sophia not only includes the teaching of Eugnostos but makes Jesus
speak a significant amount of additional teaching with regard to the
roles of Jesus and his disciples. Their roles are also discussed in John
13–17.

(7) Ascension and start of the mission (119.8–16). The ascension is
absent in Matthew and Mark; we find it only in Luke 24 and Acts 1.
Also, John 21 stops before the ascension and the start of the mission.
Nevertheless, the ascension and the mission seem to be present in
John 13–17. A central theme throughout these chapters is that Jesus
goes to his Father. This seems to be even more imminent than in
chapters 18 and beyond: when Jesus dies on the cross he does not
go to his Father; he meets the disciples again. Also, in his apparition to Mary Magdalene, he says that she should not hold him, as
he must ascend to his Father. Furthermore, in 17:4 Jesus says he
"has finished the work" on earth, which logically would follow the
crucifixion scene in which Jesus on the cross utters the words "it is
finished" (19:30). The commission of the disciples in Sophia also
has a parallel in John 17:18.[11]

In summary, the editorial interventions that turned Eugnostos the Blessed into
the Sophia of Jesus Christ connect Sophia more to John or Johannine traditions
than to the Synoptic Gospels. Furthermore, as expected, the direction of influence is from John to Sophia, not vice versa. In John the questions seem to be an
intrinsic part of the dialogue itself, while in Sophia they were clearly added afterwards. In John their distribution is rather uneven, whereas in Sophia they divide
up the entire dialogue into twelve subunits.

---

10. NHC III: 93.24–94.4, 95.19–21, 96.14–18, 98.9–13, 100.16–21, 103.22–104.5, 105.3–10, 106.9–15, 108,16–23, 107.13–108.1 (BG), 112.19–113.2, and 114.8–14.

11. Compare Sophia 108.5, "You were sent by the Son, who was sent so that you might receive light," with John 17:18, "As you have sent me into the world, so I have sent them into the world."

3.2. The Influence of John on the Other Early Resurrection Dialogues

The *Epistula Apostolorum* is an early antignostic resurrection dialogue. The framework story seems to be the result of a deliberate harmonization and expansion of the resurrection accounts in the Synoptic Gospels (esp. in Luke) and in John. The questions are of the same type that we saw in Sophia and John 13–16. Jesus replies with lengthy monologues, replete with paraphrases from all four Gospels, the Acts, Paul's epistles, and a little from the Apocrypha. It seems that the author wanted to stay close to the type of Christian teaching that would later become part of the New Testament. The idea of a resurrection dialogue written by a "conservative" author can be explained as a counterattack on the gnostic resurrection dialogue. But the idea that such an author would dare to do so is better understood if there was a precedent in the Johannine tradition.

If we take John 20–21 and most of the discourse material in John 13–17 as part of Johannine resurrection traditions, it is possible to explain features in the other early resurrection dialogues that cannot be found in Sophia. (1) The Dialogue of the Savior opens with a monologue in which Jesus says, "the time has come to abandon our work." The work he refers to ("when I came, I opened the path and I taught them about the passage which they will traverse … who have known the Father") resembles John 14:6. The document also contains a short prayer and further teaching. Then follow two lengthy dialogues, of which the second is preceded by a special revelatory vision to a number of disciples. The dialogue units resemble those of John's Gospel more closely than the secondarily arranged theological discourses in Sophia (Koester and Pagels 1988, 244). (2) The Gospel of Mary, of which the first part is missing, seems to include a dialogue with the disciples after Jesus' appearance to Mary Magdalene alone, as in John 20. The story might, in fact, be a deliberate correction of John: Mary does not see Jesus with her physical eyes, but with her mind, and Jesus tells her, "blessed are you, that you did not waver at the sight of me" (Gos. Mary 10.14–15). It is tempting to see here a correction to the words spoken to Thomas in John 20:28–29.[12] I conclude that Johannine traditions may well be the more primitive model behind the early resurrection dialogues. The various elements found in the Farewell Discourse and in the resurrection appearances in John 20 and 21 can account for the form of Sophia, as well as the variants found in the other early resurrection dialogues.

4. The Framework of the Last Supper in John

I shall now assess the framework of the account of Last Supper in John if we delete

---

12. John 20:28–29: "Thomas answered him, 'My Lord and my God!' Jesus said to him, 'Have you believed because you have seen me? Blessed are those who have not seen and yet have come to believe.'"

the discourse material that may originally have had a postresurrection setting. I shall also point to a number of parallels between the Johannine account and the material found in the Synoptic Gospels.

The narrative of the Last Supper begins at John 13:1. The first seventeen verses concern the Johannine story about the footwashing, which may be related to Luke 22:27.[13] In the next section, John 13:18–30, Jesus predicts that Judas will betray him. It is interesting to note that Mark merely says that one of the Twelve will betray Jesus. Only in Matthew and John is Judas identified as the traitor. The first dialogue begins at John 13:31b. Only two verses clearly belong to a precrucifixion setting: "Peter said to him, 'Lord, why can I not follow you now? I will lay down my life for you.' Jesus answered, 'Will you lay down your life for me? Very truly, I tell you, before the cock crows, you will have denied me three times'" (13:37–38). Again I note that John accords more with Luke than with Mark. In Mark, the order of conversation is reversed. In Mark, the cock crows twice, in John and Luke only once.[14]

The framework account continues at the end of the dialogue: "And now I have told you this before it occurs, so that when it does occur, you may believe" (14:29). In the present context it follows the prediction of the coming of the Holy Spirit, which is a bit odd, as the coming of the Holy Spirit itself is sufficient to bring someone to believe. It makes more sense if verse 29 refers to the night of Peter's denial. This is then also the theme of the next two verses: "I will no longer talk much with you, for the ruler of this world is coming. He has no power over me; but I do as the Father has commanded me, so that the world may know that I love the Father. Rise, let us be on our way" (14:30–31).

As in Mark, Jesus and his disciples now stand up to leave the house. In Mark 14:26–27, Jesus predicts that they will all desert him: "When they had sung the hymn, they went out to the Mount of Olives. And Jesus said to them, 'You will all become deserters; for it is written, I will strike the shepherd, and the sheep will be scattered.'" This warning is also found in John 16:32–33.[15] The account of the Last Supper ends with John 18:1, which resembles Luke somewhat more than

---

13. Luke 22:27: "For who is greater, the one who is at the table or the one who serves? Is it not the one at the table? But I am among you as one who serves." Compare John 13:14: "If I then, your Lord and Master, have washed your feet, you also ought to wash one another's feet."

14. Luke 22:33–34: "And he said to him, 'Lord, I am ready to go with you to prison and to death!' Jesus said, 'I tell you, Peter, the cock will not crow this day, until you have denied three times that you know me.'" Matthew also features the single crowing of the cock (Matt 26:34).

15. John 16:32–33: "The hour is coming, indeed it has come, when you will be scattered, each one to his home, and you will leave me alone. Yet I am not alone because the Father is with me. I have said this to you, so that in me you may have peace. In the world you face persecution. But take courage; I have conquered the world!"

Mark.[16] None of the remaining passages in John 13–17 require a precrucifixion setting.[17]

5. The Composition of John and the
Implications for Historical Reconstruction

We have seen that the discourse material in John 13–17 does not always fit with the occasion of the Last Supper and that there seems to be some overlap between the various parts of the Farewell Discourse. In light of their influence on later resurrection dialogues, it is not improbable that a significant part of the discourse material in John 13–17 originally belonged to a postresurrection setting.

On the basis of this proposition, we can now assess Anderson's theory of Johannine composition for these chapters. First of all, the analysis presented here confirms the last steps of that theory. It seems that there were alternative versions of Jesus' resurrection dialogues. Although these traditions were formed with a large degree of freedom, their later use within the framework of the Last Supper was far more conservative. This is understandable if these traditions were ascribed to an authoritative source such as the Beloved Disciple. We also see how the Johannine traditions continued to influence second-century Christian writing, including the early resurrection dialogues.

It seems that all discourses were added in one or two stages to the narrative outline of the Last Supper. The question, therefore, is why these resurrection dialogues were taken out of their original setting and put into the narrative of the Last Supper. One explanation is that other groups, like the second-century gnostics, may have used the same format to introduce new teachings. As Tom Thatcher concluded, the very reason for writing John might have been the wish to protect the Johannine spiritual traditions against groups with a different theology who were "expanding and reconfiguring the memory of Jesus" (2005, 157). Another explanation is that the composer wished to contextualize Jesus' witness for those who were persecuted in his days. The Farewell Discourse seems to prepare them for this (Lincoln 2000, 245–52). By bringing forward the resurrection dialogues to a point in time before the crucifixion, a powerful example is given by Jesus to such "witnesses" and a consolation to those left behind: they will meet

---

16. Luke 22:39: "He came out and went, as was his custom, to the Mount of Olives; and the disciples followed him." Compare John 18:1: "After Jesus had spoken these words, he went out with his disciples across the Kidron Valley to a place where there was a garden, which he and his disciples entered."

17. It is of course possible that more passages belonged to the setting of the Last Supper, such as John 15:1–5, where Jesus declares himself the true vine. The metaphor itself is rather neutral in terms of setting and could originally have fit anywhere, including in the earlier ministry of Jesus. Perhaps the composer chose to use this passage as a Johannine alternative for the institution of the Eucharist in the Synoptic Gospels.

again in their Father's house and will love each other on earth.[18] Although the data is insufficient to discard the first option, I note that the second explanation finds some support in two passages in the monologue itself that predict persecution in the world and in the Jewish community (John 15:18, 20; 16:1–4). If so, these references may point to a rather late date of composition of the Johannine Last Supper narrative.[19]

The analysis presented here has some relevance for the ways that historians can use the Gospel of John in reconstructing Jesus' life. Anderson believes that John "has been exiled from the canons of historicity by critical scholars. They have indeed identified real problems to which they pose the solution of the dehistoricization of John" (2006b, 191). One of these problems has always been the stark contrast between John's victorious Farewell Speech and the Synoptic account of the Last Supper and the prayer in Gethsemane. But if we take the resurrection dialogues out of the narrative of the Last Supper, this contrast disappears. We also saw that the composer of the Farewell Discourse seems to have regarded his sources as authoritative, as befits the witness of one regarded as a Beloved Disciple of Jesus. It is therefore possible that the Gospel of John has preserved historical information about Jesus. On the other hand, the analysis also shows that the Johannine account was already "dehistoricized" to a significant extent by both the Beloved Disciple as well as the final composer. The Beloved Disciple felt free to produce various versions of Jesus' words that suited the later context of his community. The composer felt free to rearrange these sources and fit them into another framework, again with a view to the needs of his day. It remains difficult, therefore, to decide what in the Gospel of John is "historical" and what is not; however, a better understanding of the roles of the Beloved Disciple and the composer does give us some guidance in the process of reconstruction.

---

18. The elements of consolation and care for those left behind may also be present in the passage about the Beloved Disciple and Jesus' mother Mary at the cross (19:26–27).

19. One could argue that the references resemble the persecutions described in the letters to the churches in Asia Minor in the book of Revelation. For example, see Rev 2:9–10, 13; 3:9 (large-scale persecution, however, is not yet happening in Revelation; it is only expected, as in 3:10).

Imitating Jesus: An Inclusive Approach to the Ethics of the Historical Jesus and John's Gospel

Richard A. Burridge

From earliest days, John has been viewed as the "spiritual gospel" (πνευματικὸν εὐαγγέλιον), while the "external facts" (actually, "the bodily things" (τὰ σωματικὰ) were preserved in the Synoptics (a saying originally attributed to Clement of Alexandria by Eusebius, *Hist. eccl.* 6.14.7). Thus John has been seen as relatively late and Hellenistic, and primarily theological, while the Synoptics were seen as earlier and more Jewish, and therefore, according to this argument, more historical. Not surprisingly, then, John has been neglected in the various quests for the historical Jesus.

Nowhere is this contrast more obvious than with regard to the ethical teaching of Jesus. After all, at first sight John appears very different from the Synoptic Gospels with its omissions of the kingdom of God, exorcisms, parables, and pithy sayings, all of which are associated with the teachings of the historical Jesus. Chapters 13–21 in particular breathe a different atmosphere, where the Farewell Discourses contrast greatly with the Synoptics' blocks of ethical teaching in the manner of the Sermon on the Mount. Instead, John's high Christology and realized eschatology seem to result in an introverted, exclusive sectarian group that is opposed both to Judaism and the world and that has no general ethical instruction; instead, Jesus' double command to love God and neighbor, preserved in the Synoptics, is narrowed down into merely loving other members of the same community. This all seems a world away from the ethic of the historical Jesus. Therefore, it is little wonder that many people seem to think that John has no moral teachings and little relevance for anyone who wants to follow Jesus' ethics today.

Furthermore, the major specialists in New Testament ethics argue that a search for John's ethics is difficult or impossible. Thus Wayne Meeks states, "it offers no explicit moral instruction" (1996, 318), and Brian Blount's opening words are even more direct: "John does not do ethics. Or so it seems" (2001, 93). Wolfgang Schrage asks himself "whether a chapter on the Johannine writings even belongs in a book on the ethics of the New Testament" (1988, 297), while Frank Matera starts his study thus: "For anyone interested in the study of New

Testament ethics, the Gospel according to John is a major challenge.... In a word, there appears to be remarkably little ethical content in the Gospel according to John, and its most explicit ethical teaching raises a host of questions" (1997, 92). The "host of questions" to which Matera refers includes the negative attitude both to those who are termed "the Jews" and to the world, portrayed adversarially by this introverted group, who are commanded only to love each other within a narrow sectarian community. This all suggests a large gulf between the ethics of the historical Jesus and those of the Fourth Gospel.

However, I want to argue that such conclusions are a result of two genre mistakes made by many biblical interpreters. First, contrary to such approaches, the Gospels are not written in the literary genre of ethical treatises; second, Jesus is not simply, or even mainly, a moral teacher. While it may be true that the Fourth Gospel does not contain individual, pithy, ethical sayings of the historical Jesus of the sort contained in the Synoptic Gospels, these generic considerations require us to step back and look at the larger picture of what the Gospels are, if they are not ethical treatises, and to demonstrate why John's Jesus is not to be seen as primarily a moral teacher. In the light of these two considerations, we can then explore how the Fourth Gospel relates both to the ethics of the historical Jesus and to the other three Gospels. Obviously, such a large-scale approach properly requires a major treatment, which cannot be provided in a brief paper such as this. However, I hope here to outline my larger argument, which is described more fully in *Imitating Jesus: An Inclusive Approach to New Testament Ethics* (Burridge 2007).

1. The Gospels Are Ancient Biographical Narratives Rather Than Ethical Treatises

All of my academic work on the interpretation of literature, both in the field of New Testament and previously in my work as a classicist, has stressed the importance of literary genre in the interpretation of texts. Texts must be interpreted according to the conventions of the literary genre in which they were written. In my doctoral study, *What Are the Gospels?* (Burridge 1992), I argued that classical literary theory and a comparison with Greco-Roman biography leads to the conclusion that the Gospels are written in the same genre as other lives of famous men in the ancient world. Therefore, we must interpret the Gospels according to this genre, in the same way as other ancient lives were read. Greco-Roman biography is very different from modern examples, with the post-Freudian concern for personality and contemporary interest in "celebrity." The ancient biographers wanted to depict their subject's character with a portrait of them through combinations of their deeds and words—through anecdotes and stories, as much as their sayings or speeches. Furthermore, both the deeds and the words lead up to the person's death, dealt with in some extended detail in ancient lives, as in the Gospels; often the death will also reveal something further about the person's life or bring the author's major themes to a climax (see Burridge 2004, esp. 233–51).

So to find the heart of Jesus' ethic, we need to consider *both* his ethical teaching *and* his actual practice. As Luke puts it, "In the first book, I wrote about all that Jesus began to do and to teach" (Acts 1:1, RSV). Therefore, we have to look not only at Jesus' sayings and sermons but also at his actions—in healing, miracles, and the events narrated—in order to grasp the Evangelists' portraits, if we are properly to understand how Jesus' ethics fit into this. Often those who study New Testament ethics appeal to his words, like the Sermon on the Mount, which are indeed very demanding and rigorous. But to do that alone is to ignore the biographical genre of the Gospels and to treat them instead as mere collections of ethical teachings.

2. Jesus of Nazareth: Great Moral Teacher or Friend of Sinners?

2.1. Jesus' Teaching

If you asked most people about Jesus of Nazareth, you would find what Dale Goldsmith terms the "common assumption that Jesus was primarily, or most importantly, a teacher of morality" (1988, 177; see also Carter and Thompson 1990, 128). Yet, amazingly, the Gospels do not portray Jesus as just a teacher of morality. Furthermore, to read them as ethical treatises or for moral guidance is to make a genre mistake, for that is not what they are. They are biographical portraits of Jesus, which do include some examples of his teaching. However, Jesus' ethical teaching is not a separate and discrete set of moral maxims but part of his main proclamation of the kingdom of God as God's reign and sovereignty are recognized in the here and now since the end of everything is at hand. This is one of the key basic facts about Jesus agreed upon by all who engage in historical Jesus research. His preaching of the kingdom is primarily intended to elicit a whole-hearted response from his hearers to give up everything and follow him. This means that they have to live as disciples within the community of others who also respond and follow, rather than simply obeying a set of moral instructions. When he touched upon the major human moral experiences, such as money, sex, power, violence, and so forth, Jesus intensified the demands of the law with his rigorous ethic of renunciation and self-denial. At the same time, however, his central stress on love and forgiveness opened the community to the very people who had moral difficulties in these areas. Therefore, as befits a biographical narrative, we must now turn from Jesus' teaching to confront this paradox in his activity and behavior.

2.2. Jesus' Example

Jesus' demanding ethical teachings on things like money, sex, and power should require very high standards from those around him, with the result that ordinary fallible human beings would find him uncomfortable. However, when we turn from his words to the biographical narrative of his activity, the converse is true. It is religious leaders and guardians of morality who find him uncomfortable, while he keeps company with all sorts of sinners—precisely the people who are not keeping his demanding ethic. He is criticized as "a glutton and a drunkard, a friend of tax collectors and sinners" (Matt 11:19 // Luke 7:34). This is the second key fact agreed upon by most historical Jesus scholars, that Jesus brought together a group of followers among the poor and marginalized, the sort of people despised and disdained by the rest of society.

In his ministry, Jesus accepts people just as they are and proclaims that they are forgiven without the need to go to the temple or to offer sacrifice. His healing ministry is directed toward such people and the eucharistic words at the Last Supper suggest that he saw his forthcoming death as being "for" them. A biographical approach means that it is not enough simply to look at Jesus' words and moral teachings; to be properly biblical involves facing the paradox that he delivers his ethical teaching in the company of sinners whom he accepts, loves, and heals. Furthermore, a major purpose of ancient biography was *mimesis*, the practice of imitation, of following the subject's virtues. This is reinforced by the Jewish habit of *ma'aseh*, precedence, where the disciple is expected to observe and imitate his master as a way of imitating Torah and ultimately becoming holy as God is holy (see Lev 11:44–45). Therefore, to imitate Jesus, it is not enough simply to extract his ethical teaching from the Sermon on the Mount; we must also imitate his loving acceptance of others, especially the marginalized, within an open and inclusive community.

3. JOHN: BRINGING THE TRUTH IN DIVINE LOVE

3.1. CHRISTOLOGY

If the kingdom of God is central for the teaching of the historical Jesus, it is because of his stress on the in-breaking rule, or sovereignty, of God. For both Paul and the Synoptic Gospels, God's in-coming rule is best demonstrated in what has been achieved in the life, death, and resurrection of Jesus Christ—hence the importance of Christology for them all. What is interesting for the Fourth Gospel is how John, despite all his differences and particular concerns, including the apparent absence of teaching about the kingdom of God, nonetheless takes the same basic story of Jesus' deeds and words, his life and ministry, death and resurrection, and retells it for his purposes and his audience as being at the heart of what God is doing. In this respect, we have direct continuity between John and the other three Gospels, and Paul, with the historical Jesus. The language and the concepts may be different, but the essential theological purpose is the same.

However, not everyone agrees with this. Thus, Maurice Casey argues that "this Gospel's presentation of Jesus is seriously false" (1996, 62). Given John's frequent use of and focus upon "truth," this is a serious charge. Andrew Lincoln's answer is to go back to the Gospel's biographical genre and to argue that Casey has confused truth and falsehood with "the modern era's standards of historical accuracy" (2000, 356–77). John's portrait of Jesus is certainly more divine than the Synoptics' accounts, but this does not necessarily mean that it is not true, either theologically or historically, providing the latter is properly understood as the ancients understood "enquiry" (ἱστορία) within both history and biography. As both John A. T. Robinson (1985, 343–97) and E. Earle Ellis (2000, 88) argue separately, the Fourth Gospel makes "explicit" what is "implicit" in the other three.

We can characterize the main theme of John's Christology as being that *Jesus is divine love bringing us truth*. The Fourth Gospel is a biographical narrative of Jesus' life and teaching, his words and deeds. Marianne Meye Thompson is right to point to the divine source of both: "the actions attributed to God in the Gospel are made known to the reader by the words of Jesus and are embodied in the deeds of Jesus" (2001, 237). As the divine *Logos*, Jesus comes to show us God's love by his very incarnation among us, which is "full of grace and truth" (1:14, 17). Throughout his ministry, he showed God's love through his "signs" (deeds) and taught his truth in the dialogues and discourses (words). At the Last Supper, he loved "his own" even "to the end" (13:1), while lovingly explaining the truth in the Farewell Discourses. Finally, he demonstrated God's love by his death on the cross (3:16), a love that cannot be defeated by death, as the truth of all that he said and did was vindicated in his resurrection. Therefore, while John may not include the parables and teachings of the kingdom as in the Synoptics, this does not mean that his biographical account "offers no explicit moral instruction," to use Meeks's words (1996, 318). The whole portrait of the divine love bringing us truth is full of ethical implications in both words and deeds, if we want to know that truth and live in that love. John's ethical challenge is for us to imitate Jesus' self-sacrificial example of the divine love.

3.2. JOHN AND JUDAISM

Given all of the Jewish background, framework, and atmosphere found in the Fourth Gospel, we might reasonably expect a very positive attitude toward Judaism and the law—yet in fact this area poses one of the greatest ethical challenges about the Fourth Gospel, provoking enormous scholarly debate. The twenty-five collected papers of the Leuven Colloquium in 2000 on *Anti-Judaism and the Fourth Gospel* run to some 550 published pages, while their "select bibliography" contains around 400 items (Bieringer et al. 2001, 549–70)! As with the other Gospels, there is the usual debate about whether this is best described as "anti-Semitism," "anti-Jewishness," or "anti-Judaism" (see Lieu 2001, 128–31; Dunn 1992a, 177–211). Furthermore, there is the question of whether the author himself can be "anti-Jewish" at the same time as being so Jewish, or whether "the text itself can generate anti-Jewish prejudice, even if this prejudice was not present in the mind of the author" (Bieringer et al. 2001, 8; see 5–17). In addition, there is the entire *Wirkungsgeschichte*, the history of the influence of this text, down to and including the use of it made by the Nazis, and how we might interpret it today. Since this enormous debate affects Johannine scholarship in general, it is not surprising that it is also one of the most difficult areas to handle in any treatment of John's ethics.[1]

Most attempts to handle this issue revolve around possible historical reconstructions of the debate between the Johannine community and the synagogue. The various approaches to "reading at two levels," that of the story of Jesus and also of the history of the community, which have developed following the theories of J. Louis Martyn and Raymond E. Brown, are well-known.[2] Such community theories were popular through several decades of scholarship but then waned, so that more recently Robert Kysar (2005a, 237–45) could speak of the "rise and decline" of this hypothesis as an object lesson in scholarly fashions and trends.[3] However, while scholars now doubt whether there was a universal expulsion from the synagogue connected with the Birkat Haminim, the concept of a split has been retained in most approaches, even if on a more local scale. As Frank Moloney concludes, "one cannot explain the Johannine story without accepting that it was written against a background (however recent or remote) of a painful breakdown between two groups in the larger Jewish community" (2005c, 41; see also Tomson 2001, 290–332). At the center of these disagreements was John's biography of Jesus, as he developed his christological portrait of the divine love breaking into our world to bring us his truth.

Therefore, we are back to our basic argument about genre. If one reads the Fourth Gospel as a tract about Jewish-Christian relations (as some Nazis wanted to do), it is hard not to see it as principally anti-Jewish—and therefore not a document that could be usefully employed in Christian ethics. However, in fact, it must be read as a biography about the love of God breaking into our world in the person of Jesus the Jew, who was accepted by some Jews and rejected by others, a biography that was written by and for others who had also shared that experience of rejection. Therefore, most scholars are surely correct to conclude that we cannot exonerate either the author or the text of its anti-Jewish elements, which arise out of its central story of Jesus; however, this does not mean that the author,

---

1. See the treatment given it by Verhey 1984, 142–43; Hays 1996, 146–47; Blount 2001, 112–17; significantly, it is only given a brief mention in Schrage 1988, 317–18; and Matera 1996, 103.

2. Martyn's original version (1968) is updated in his third edition (2003); for how Brown refines his version over the years, see Brown 1966–70, 1:xxiv–xl; 1979, *passim*; 1997, 368–78; 2003, 58–86 and 189–219.

3. This was originally given as "Expulsion from the Synagogue: The Tale of a Theory," in the SBL Johannine Literature Section, Society of Biblical Literature Annual Meeting, Toronto, Ontario, Canada, 25 November 2002, when fascinating responses were given by J. Louis Martyn and D. Moody Smith; see further, Kysar 2005b, 65–81.

editors, and the text itself can be held responsible for all the later uses to which it has been put. In interpreting John in general, and especially in applying this Gospel to Christian ethics, we must be very aware of this dimension and allow for it, but that is no reason for giving up on, or ignoring, this Gospel. Furthermore, its basic message about the coming of divine life itself demands this. As the Leuven editors themselves conclude, "even if we cannot help but admit that the entire Gospel is affected by an anti-Jewish attitude, the text projects an alternative world of all-inclusive love and life which transcends its anti-Judaism. It is the world of the text, and not the world of the author that is a witness to divine revelation" (Bieringer et al. 2001, 44).

3.3. JOHN'S ATTITUDE TO THE WORLD

We look in vain for any treatment in John of the different ethical issues that feature in the other Gospels, such as wealth and poverty, marriage and the family, power and violence. Again, this leads to the accusation that John is concerned only for his introverted community in a world-denying ethic. While the Fourth Evangelist uses the word "world" (κόσμος) nearly eighty times (four times as often as in all the Synoptics together!), closer analysis reveals that it is by no means as negative a term, as is sometimes assumed. In fact, the Fourth Gospel contains three attitudes to the "world"—positive, negative, and neutral—in almost exactly equal proportions. It begins as either merely a neutral location or positively as the object of God's love and the mission upon which he sends Jesus. It is only as the conflict grows, and when the world rejects Jesus, that the term becomes negative and stands for the source of opposition, especially in these later chapters (13–21) and in the Farewell Discourses (13–17). This is foreshadowed, as the Prologue actually uses all three senses programmatically in one verse: "He was in the world [neutral, for Jesus' presence on earth], and the world came into being through him [positive, a loving assessment of creation]; yet the world did not know him [negative, for the refusal to recognize Jesus]" (1:10).

Nonetheless, while such opposition may lead "the world" to hate the new community, which has been formed by the divine love, there is nothing in John to suggest that Christians should reciprocate the antagonism (in the way that was true, say, of the sectarian attitude of the Qumran community, as seen in the Dead Sea Scrolls). The command to "love one another" may have its immediate location in the internal relationships within the community—but that love is also the only answer to the world's negativity and hatred. It is significant that, writing from his African American experience of oppression as his interpretative "lens," Brian Blount observes, "perhaps John already understood that the 'love for one another' that enabled his believing community to sustain itself and simultaneously resist the hostile world around it would also, by energizing an alternative reality and a competing force for change, transform that world" (2001, 108).

3.4. Imitating Jesus, Friend of Sinners, in an Inclusive Community

We have argued that this general impression of John writing for an introverted sectarian community in the midst of bitter wrangling against "the Jews," with no specific ethical instruction other than for an internal love for other members of his group, is somewhat of a caricature; closer analysis demonstrates that the Fourth Gospel is much more complex, and infinitely richer, than this stereotype might indicate. The overriding theme is about the love of God, coming to dwell among human beings in the person of Jesus of Nazareth and to teach his divine truth as the Evangelist's community was defining itself over against its fellow Jews. Out of this conflict come harsh words about "the Jews" and "the world" alike, yet John can also be very positive about both of them as the objects of God's love, as Jesus is sent to save *all* the world. This love is the dominating theme of John's ethics, as much as his wider theology.

Even if the Synoptics' phrase "friend of sinners" is absent, John's careful portrait of how Jesus treats individuals and encourages them to respond in faith coheres with it. The Fourth Gospel is full of this pastoral approach to individuals who have become some of the most-loved biblical characters, such as Nathanael (1:45–51), Nicodemus (3:1–10), the Samaritan woman (4:7–26), the paralyzed man at the pool (5:2–14), the woman caught in adultery (8:3–11), the man born blind (9:1–38), Martha, Mary, and Lazarus (11:1–44), and Peter (13:6–10; 21:15–22). In each case Jesus accepts the person as and where he or she is and gently teases the person into making a response of faith to what God is doing in and through him.

Furthermore, the community addressed is comprised of a disparate group who respond and follow. John is the only Gospel to use the actual word "example" (ὑπόδειγμα), which occurs in the famous story about Jesus washing his disciples' feet: "So if I, your Lord and Teacher, have washed your feet, you also ought to wash one another's feet. For I have set you *an example*, that you also should do as I have done to you" (13:14–15). Like most interpreters, Xavier Léon-Dufour (2005, 127) connects this to the "new commandment" to "love one another as I have loved you," which follows shortly (13:34; 15:12). While this may be the only time John mentions "example" explicitly, it gives a clue to the interpretation of his biographical portrait of Jesus throughout the Gospel. Thus Wolfgang Schrage (1988, 307) notes that "other soteriological and christological passages in John also introduce a call to *mimesis* (e.g., see 12:25–26, following 12:24)." The explication of the example as self-sacrificial reappears in the second version of the love command, which again gives the definition of such love as "to lay down one's life for one's friends" (John 15:12–13). Thus, following Jesus' example in the footwashing and obeying his "new commandment" means that the community of those who "love one another" must always be inclusive and open to the rest of the world. For John, Jesus is the Revealer who not only teaches us the truth of God but also shows us what the divine love is like, so that we can imitate him and so participate in the divine life.

Conclusion

At first sight, John's account appears very different from the Synoptic Gospels, given the absence of the kingdom of God, Jesus' parables and exorcisms, and no great blocks of ethical teaching in the manner of the Sermon on the Mount. Because these elements are central in most reconstructions of the historical Jesus, this absence of ethical concerns often forms a major plank in larger arguments about the relationships between John, Jesus, and history.

Instead of such teachings about the ethics of the kingdom, we find John's high Christology and a realized eschatology, which at first seem to advocate an introverted exclusive sectarian group, which is opposed both to Judaism and the world and which has no ethical instruction beyond a narrow love for other members of the community. Therefore, it is little wonder that many people seem to think that John has no moral teachings and little relevance for Christian ethics today—and they contrast this with the various interpretations of the historical Jesus as an ethical teacher.

However, studying John in more depth shows quite the opposite to be the case. While the Fourth Gospel may appear very different at first, at the literary level we have discovered just another reinterpretation of the same basic story. Like the other three canonical Gospels, John is a biographical narrative where Christology is absolutely central. In the Fourth Gospel, Jesus is depicted as the love of God coming to dwell among human beings to bring them his divine truth. He teaches the crowds and seeks out individuals, especially among the marginalized, who respond to him in faith. This basic picture not only coheres with the other three Gospels but also reflects the mission of the historical Jesus, according to many current interpretations of it.

Unfortunately, this mission also provokes hostile reactions that lead to his death on the cross. Most historical reconstructions of the circumstances of the Gospel's production and first circulation consider that this was also true for the Evangelist's community, who suffered persecution, particularly as they were undergoing the painful separation from the synagogue after the Jewish war and the destruction of Jerusalem. Such circumstances help to explain both the Gospel's stress on realized eschatology and its attitude toward Judaism and the world. Nonetheless, this can be overemphasized, as the Gospel still has both a future dimension and a positive attitude toward all people and the world as the object of God's saving love in Jesus. Although this Gospel is highly Jewish in its background, such is the impact of the new life brought by Jesus that it fulfills and replaces all the former ways, painful as that might be for some. Everything is now subordinated under the "new commandment" to love one another as he has loved us, which is why the Gospel does not need specific ethical instruction. Far from narrowing down the love command of the historical Jesus, the "new command-ment" is to be worked out through the believing community and in the world, which "God so loved" (3:16).

Finally, John's careful portrait of how Jesus treated individuals and the mixed, inclusive nature of his community form the perfect backdrop for his ultimately mimetic purpose in writing this biographical narrative. In their own distinctive ways, the three Synoptic writers, Paul, and the Fourth Evangelist are all concerned that we should follow Jesus' example of self-sacrificial love within a mixed, inclu-sive community of others who are also responding to his call and reaching out to his world. In this respect, there is clear coherence between the ethical concerns of John's Gospel and the activity of the historical Jesus.

THE HISTORICAL PLAUSIBILITY OF
JOHN'S PASSION DATING

Mark A. Matson

1. INTRODUCTION

The question of the historical value of material in the Fourth Gospel rests on two concerns that always lurk behind the discussions in the SBL group focusing on John, Jesus, and history. The first is the foundational question of how we evaluate the Gospels, or really any ancient writing, for "historical" material. That is, we must deal with the always-contentious issue of the criteria we use to determine Gospel materials' historical value.[1] The second question is how we account for the stark differences between John and the Synoptics.[2] One cannot venture far into any consideration of John's historical value without confronting the differences between John and the Synoptics (or indeed even noncanonical Gospels), while also considering the similarities in content and overall structure that John shares *with* the other Gospels.

With respect to John's relationship to the Synoptics, one could reasonably argue that the historical value of John is best evaluated precisely where it shows the greatest tension, or difference, with the Synoptics. John's material that stands in stark contrast to the Synoptics thus has a special place in the quest for Gospel historicity. It exposes John to the charge either that the material has been created or altered deliberately by the author, perhaps for theological reasons, or that the Fourth Gospel presents a significantly different tradition bearing an alternative

---

1. It is not possible to give a complete bibliography here, but the main criteria used by most historical Jesus scholars are addressed in brief fashion by John Meier 1991, 167–95; see also Theissen and Merz 1998, 90–124; Theissen and Winter 2002. A topical bibliography on the matter is indeed extensive, but these serve as adequate pointers to the essential issues.

2. This is also an impossibly large block of material. The best overall summary of the discussion in all its variations is by D. Moody Smith 2001. This issue is such an essential starting point in any historically critical study of John that all major commentaries address it and reach at least a starting hypothesis. See Brown 1966–70, 1:xxiv–xlvii; 2003, 90–114; and Schnackenburg 1968, 26–43.

perspective, against which to compare Synoptic and noncanonical depictions. The subset, however, of distinctive material in John that *is* similar to the Synoptics in some respects—and yet very different in others—is most intriguing. Here it is very difficult to avoid the either/or question, forcing a choice between John and the Synoptics, and the historical issues are thus intensified.

One of the most glaring factual differences between John and the Synoptics, within material that is generally considered comparable, involves the question of the dating of the passion, especially the timing of the final supper and Jesus' death, relative to the Passover celebration. To summarize the issue at stake, it is nearly impossible to reconcile the dating of the Last Supper and the crucifixion—and thus the entire passion dating—between John and the Synoptics. For the Synoptic Gospels, Jesus' final supper is on a Thursday evening, which, importantly, happens to be the first evening of Passover, Nisan 14.[3] Mark's Gospel makes explicit reference to the Passover dating early in the passion narrative, and in Mark 14:1 early hints of a looming arrest are expressed as occurring "two days before the Passover and the festival of Unleavened Bread." Mark's narrative of the Last Supper itself begins with the second and more explicit reference to the Passover date: the disciples ask about preparations because it is "the first day of Unleavened Bread, *when the Passover lamb is sacrificed*" (14:12). What follows then is a narrative description of the preparation for a Passover meal: the disciples being sent to locate the upper room, a projected dialogue with the owner of the upper room about Jesus' desire to "eat the Passover" (τὸ πάσχα μετὰ τῶν μαθητῶν μου φάγω; 14:14), and preparations for a "Passover" are all alluded to. The final meal that is eaten by Jesus and the disciples is also patterned somewhat after the Passover (absent any reference to a lamb), and thus the eucharistic language is based to a great extent upon the structure of such a meal.

In contrast, John's Gospel presents a final meal that has only vague references to what could be discerned as a Passover feast, and there is no institution of the Eucharist or comparable language (instead we find a footwashing scene and subsequent instructions). Therefore, the meal generally does not resemble the Synoptics' account except in the barest of points, which would have been shared with almost any meal. More importantly, the Fourth Evangelist then explicitly marks out the chronological progression of the final days so that there is little question that the final meal was not Passover but was celebrated *the day before Passover*, that is, on Nisan 13. John's account begins in 13:1 by introducing the meal as taking place "before the Passover" (πρὸ δὲ τῆς ἑορτῆς τοῦ πάσχα). More explicitly, at the trial before Pilate, the high priests are unwilling to enter the Praetorium to prosecute Jesus' trial because it might make them unclean, for

---

3. For the biblical dating, see Lev 23:4–8: the Passover lamb is offered on the 14th, and the Feast of Unleavened Bread begins on the 15th (see also Num 28:16–17).

they *had not yet celebrated the Passover* (John 18:28). Moreover, Jesus is finally condemned to crucifixion at noon (sixth hour) of the "Preparation day of the Passover" (19:14). Thus, in John's chronology, Jesus is crucified on Nisan 14, at approximately the same time that the Passover lambs were being sacrificed in the temple (that is, at just before evening of the 14th).

In the events leading up to and including Jesus' death, then, we are confronted with a stark choice between alternate chronologies that, from a historical perspective, one must address directly: which, if either, of the depictions has a better claim to a historical basis? The thesis of this paper is that John's chronology has at least as good a claim to being historically accurate, and when taken as a whole, a better case can be made for the historical plausibility of John's chronology than for the Synoptics' chronology. This conclusion does not arise from any single new issue, but rather from the accumulation of all the data that relates to the dating of the Last Supper and crucifixion.

2. Is There an Irreconcilable Conflict?

While the differences between the Johannine and synoptic chronologies surrounding the Last Supper and crucifixion are considerable, some conservative scholars have sought to harmonize them. Some assert that John's account of the final meal can easily be understood as a Passover meal, since it bears many of the marks of the Synoptic meal.[4] Attempts to reconcile John and the Synoptics are not new, but I find these efforts at harmonization unconvincing. Especially in John, (1) the absence of any specific eucharistic language, or any figurative value attached to the meal elements, makes it hard to reconcile with the Synoptic meal; (2) the reference that the meal took place "before" the Passover (13:1) makes it other than a standard Passover meal. Moreover, the explicit reference to Jesus' trial before Pilate in John 18:28 says it took place before the Passover.

Nonetheless, harmonization is still attempted. Craig Blomberg, for instance, argues that the reference in 18:28 to "eating the Passover" in the future is referring to the entire feast of Unleavened Bread, not to Passover itself (Blomberg 2001, 237–38).[5] But this does not adequately explain why the priests would go to great

---

4. An example would be the treatment by Craig Blomberg (2001, 187–88), who interprets the final supper announced in John 13:1 as the Passover and suggests that references in 18:28 really are referring to the Feast of Unleavened Bread. A similar line of reasoning is found in Kostenberger 2004, 401–2, 524. But this is not new. Charles Torrey (1931, 227–41) had effectively argued that thesis, and much of his argumentation begins with the assumption that John and his audience "knew" (and accepted) the previous Synoptic accounts, so that knowledge is presupposed as a beginning point.

5. For Torrey (1931) also, the words φάγωσιν τὸ πάσχα in John 18:28, and παρασκευὴ τοῦ πάσχα in 19:14, refer not to the Passover meal itself, but to the Feast of Unleavened Bread. A similar perspective is presented a half-century later by Cullen I. K. Story (1989, 316–24).

lengths to avoid ritual defilement for the feast of Unleavened Bread. Surely this is best explained by their need to be present in the temple to sacrifice the Passover lambs, not some generalized concern for purity over the entire feast of Unleavened Bread. While individual items listed above might be explained away, when taken together they add up to a compelling argument that John and the Synoptics simply do not agree on the date of the final meal or the crucifixion of Jesus.

The Johannine and the Synoptic accounts thus resist harmonizing reconciliation; they do not agree on the date of the Last Supper and consequently portray very different supper emphases. The Synoptic Gospels center around a Passover feast in which some of the elements of the feast (bread and wine) are interpreted proleptically as memorials of Jesus' death, while in John's Gospel the Last Supper is the day before the Passover meal, Nisan 13. The meal is not eucharistic, since it is portrayed as a normal group meal, and the focus instead is on the footwashing as an example of service. The dating also cannot be reconciled, and this difficulty underscores the importance of this question for historical concerns. Put simply, which account offers the most likely representation of what actually happened at the time of Jesus' death? On which day was Jesus most likely killed? Is it more or less likely that Jesus' final meal was a Passover meal?

My examination of the historical value of John's presentation of the passion chronology will proceed along the following course: First, I shall look at any external evidence of the various chronological arguments. Here I shall consider the issue of the calendar itself, as well as references in other early documents, a comparison of very early eucharistic liturgies, and the evidence that might be adduced from the quartodeciman controversy. Then, I shall turn to more internal evidence, specifically the internal consistency of John's account and the Synoptics' accounts of the dating. Finally, I shall return to all of this in a more universal consideration of the overall plausibility of John's dating.

3. EXTERNAL EVIDENCE FOR JOHN'S CHRONOLOGY.

3.1. CALENDRICAL ARGUMENTS

The rather stark contrast between John and the Synoptics in the reckoning of the Last Supper (i.e., Nisan 13 versus 14) suggests at the outset an issue peculiar to the Jewish calendar. After all, the two accounts do agree on the same day of the week: the Last Supper in both is a Thursday evening, the crucifixion is on Friday, and the empty tomb is discovered on Sunday morning after the Sabbath has passed. Thus a solution has been sought by reference to features or peculiarities of the Jewish calendar. Perhaps the most noted of such proposals is the argument mounted by Annie Jaubert (1972, 62–75) shortly after the discovery of the Qumran scrolls.[6]

---

6. See also Jaubert 1965 and compare Ruckstuhl 1965.

Her argument is that the disjuncture of dates between John and the Synoptics was due to two different calendar systems: one followed by the Jewish leadership in Jerusalem, and one followed by Jesus. Specifically, Jaubert's argument held that Jesus followed an Essene 364-day solar calendar (according to her, an older reckoning of the Passover), such that Passover was celebrated on a different day than the calendar reckoned by the new moons of the lunar calendar that the Jewish hierarchy used (according to her, the newer reckoning of Passover).

This certainly has some attractive qualities, in that it has two very different ways of explaining the date of Passover. But scholars have generally not been persuaded by this proposal, for important reasons. First, it is based on speculation that Jesus would have followed an Essene calendar without much, if any, evidence for such an assertion. While we do have reason to think that the Essenes at Qumran had a conflict with the temple authorities, in part over calendrical disputes,[7] no such traces of Jesus' direct connection with the Essenes, or more importantly of any calendrical disputes, can be found in any sources dealing with Jesus.

Second, Jaubert's argument is extended in its complexity; it is based in part on John's interest in a subsequent meeting with the disciples eight days after the first resurrection appearances (20:26, καὶ μεθ' ἡμέρας ὀκτὼ), and this eight-day reckoning links up with the Essenes' counting for the celebration of Weeks following Passover. Thus, this eighth-day reference is a hint at another calendrical system that counts feast days differently than the major Jewish dating system in the Gospel (Jaubert 1972, 63–64). By her calculation, Jesus' Last Supper celebration followed an older Essene calendar, according to which Passover was actually on Tuesday night. The remark in John that on Friday the Passover had not yet been sacrificed is also correct, since the chief priests in this account held the Passover according to a Pharisaic calendar, but not the Zadokite (Essene) one. So, Jaubert posits:

> Jesus celebrates the Pasch on *Tuesday evening, the eve of the Pasch,* according to the *old* priestly calendar. He is arrested in the night between Tuesday and Wednesday. He dies on *Friday,* 14 *Nisan, the eve of the Pasch,* according to the *official* calendar. The old Pasch and official Pasch would accordingly, have been celebrated that year at a distance of three days from one another.... According to this explanation, then, *the Synoptic Gospels* preserved a primitive tradition corresponding to a Palestinian catechesis. In such a context, the Pasch celebrated by

---

7. The Qumran documents give substantial evidence of a conflict between the Teacher of Righteousness and the Wicked Priest concerning festal dates. Pesher Habakkuk in particular refers to such a conflict with the Day of Atonement. Other texts at Qumran make comments about Israel's "error" with respect to sacred times. So there was a substantial conflict. How widespread the conflict was, and whether the solar calendar had once been a major Jewish calendar system, are very hypothetical. See, e.g., the summary comments in VanderKam 1998, 115–16.

Jesus could be that of the old calendar. Explanations were, therefore superfluous. (Jaubert 1965, 97)

Third, further problems with Jaubert's thesis involve Jesus' practice as reported in the Synoptics—it is said to be following an old Essene calendar, without argumentation, but the Synoptic representation is still different. To make this work, Jaubert must create a space of three days between the Last Supper and the crucifixion. She must then amend the Synoptic Gospels' presentation. Moreover, while she bases much of this on hints in the Gospel of John (e.g., 20:26), she also recognizes that John is constructed around festivals in Jerusalem and that these betray little awareness of a calendrical conflict. Her view requires that all four of the Gospels have been edited to conform to the dominant Jewish calendar, although John and the Synoptics each do this in different ways, whereupon in this process any reference to a calendrical dispute is removed. Moreover, when we add the lack of clear evidence in the Gospels to any such dispute, her proposal seems to fail the simple test of reasonableness. For these and other reasons, Jaubert's approach has been less than compelling.

Another calendrical approach to resolving the chronological conflict is attempted by showing (by means of a retrojection of the Jewish calendar) which date, Johannine or Synoptic, is the most probable to have occurred within the window of time we think Jesus must have died. This approach has been broached most favorably in John A. T. Robinson, *The Priority of John* (1985, 153–56), and with more caution in Josef Blinzler, *The Trial of Jesus* (1959, 72–80).

The impetus for this approach lies in the fact that we now have the fairly sophisticated ability to predict the congruence of the lunar calendar against a projection of our current solar calendar for any period in the past, including the first century c.e. It is now relatively simple to know which dates, according to our current calendar system, were new moons and full moons, and thus to determine the beginnings of lunar months in antiquity. If we then project the current Jewish lunar calendar backwards to the period of 28 to 32 c.e., we theoretically should know which years Nisan 14 occurred on Thursdays and which on Fridays.

This is precisely what Robinson does (1985, 153), following astronomical calculations that were done by Parker and Dubberstein.[8] According to these calculations, on only three days in the period of 27–33 c.e. did Nisan 14 fall on either a Thursday or a Friday: it fell on a Thursday in 27 c.e., and it fell on a Friday in 30 and 33 c.e. A similar calculation is noted by Blinzler (1959, 77). Even Jeremias (1966, 41), who strongly argues for a Passover feast underlying the Last Supper, concedes that for the most part the data supports the Johannine date, though he suggests that the data on the timing of first sightings of the moon

---

8. Robinson here cites Parker and Dubberstein 1956; similar results are in Schoch 1928, 48–56, and Fotheringam 1934, 146–62.

might be incomplete.[9] For those who cite astronomical calculations, then, the conclusion is usually in favor of the Johannine chronology, since 27 C.E. is often regarded as being too early for Jesus' death. Blinzler thus concludes: "Hence, we find that the trial and crucifixion of Jesus very probably took place in the year 30, and presumably on the fourteenth of Nisan" (Blinzler 1959, 77).

All of the discussions that use astronomy to attempt to calculate the date of the crucifixion in terms of a lunar Jewish calendar have cautionary notes appended, usually dealing with the possible variation of the new moon's first sighting. Nonetheless, there is a certain confidence in the ability to calculate dates in the first century according to astronomical tables. Roger T. Beckwith (1989, 183–205), however, appropriately adds an even greater caution to this whole effort—one that clouds the whole endeavor (cf. Beckwith 1996). Simply put, the actual practice of the addition of leap months in antiquity creates so much variability in the calendar that a strictly astronomical approach is meaningless. If leap months were inserted in a formulaic way, the calculation of dates in antiquity would be relatively straightforward. But substantial evidence shows that, despite having a theoretical knowledge of when new moons appear, Jewish practice in the first century valorized actual sightings by priests, and even these sightings were mediated by subjective decisions about whether the new moon was sighted too early, relative to the seasons. That is, the purpose of the intercalation was to adjust the lunar calendar to the solar, but the determination of "spring" in the solar calendar was based on such issues as the maturity of the grain harvest and the fatness of lambs—these being held equally important as the actual dating of the spring equinox (see t. Sanh. 2.2; b. Sanh. 11b). Such subjective variables about when intercalated months were added, the potential of two back-to-back intercalated months, and even some controversy over the length of the intercalated months (a full lunar month, based on sightings, or alternatively a month fixed at 29 days or 30 days according to various sources), all mean that it is impossible to calculate with certainty when Nisan 14 fell in the period of Jesus' death.[10]

The use of chronology, then, provides almost no definitive help in resolving the conflict between John and the Synoptics, relative to the chronology of the passion week. Any resolution must come from other considerations.

3.2. EVIDENCE FROM SOURCES OTHER THAN THE FOUR GOSPELS

The issue of John's passion chronology affects the relationship between the Jewish Passover feast and the major twin events of the final supper and the crucifixion. If John is correct, the Last Supper was not a Passover meal, since Jesus was crucified

---

9. But see also the extended discussion on calendrical issues in Jeremias 1966, 36–41, and the discussion of Jeremias in Blinzler 1959, 78.

10. See especially the historical data on these in Beckwith 1989, 194–95.

in the afternoon of the Passover eve. Alternately, if the Synoptic chronology is correct, the final supper was indeed a Passover meal, and thus the crucifixion must have happened *on the day of Passover*.

Is there any external attestation to either of these dating systems outside of the canonical Gospels? As has been well documented over a number of years, we do have evidence to support various chronological schemes in other early sources that might provide some external evidence on the question.

1. *1 Corinthians.* Since our issue involves Jesus' Last Supper and the possible origination of the eucharistic memorial, a key "external" source to examine is Paul's first letter to the Corinthians, in which Paul passes on his tradition that Jesus "on the night he was betrayed" instituted a memorial feast (1 Cor 11:23–26). The language for the memorial is relatively close to that found in the Synoptic Gospels for the Last Supper, especially in Luke 22:17–20. A close analysis of the language of the various passages, although demonstrating some variants in the textual traditions, generally shows strong affinities with both Mark's version and Luke's longer version.[11] It is notable for our discussion of passion chronology that Paul does not refer to the Passover in his introduction to the eucharistic pattern but rather dates the event somewhat elliptically: "on the night he was betrayed." Does Paul not know this was a Passover feast? Does the feast indeed reflect the Passover itself?[12] While it is highly possible that Paul understood this initiating "remembrance meal" as a Passover meal and that it had some patterns based on this meal, this cannot be asserted with certainty, and the lack of direct language to a Passover in the "words of institution" may well reflect a different tradition from which he is drawing. Indeed, in light of 1 Cor 5 (see below), any overly firm conclusion about Paul's identification of the Last Supper with the Passover could be questioned.

In the same letter, another reference to the Passover may reflect a tradition closer to John than that found in the Synoptics. In 1 Cor 5:7–8, Paul uses extensive Passover terminology: "Clean out the old yeast so that you may be a new batch, as you really are unleavened. For our paschal lamb, Christ, has been sacrificed. Therefore, let us celebrate the festival, not with the old yeast, the yeast of malice and evil, but with the unleavened bread of sincerity and truth."

Granted, this passage does not specifically address the chronology of the crucifixion, nor does it explicitly refer to the Last Supper. But in its sometimes-related reference to Jesus as the paschal lamb, cast within a discussion that draws

---

11. One view of the relationship between Paul and the Gospels on the Eucharist can be found in Lietzmann 1979, 172–87 and 204–15. For another discussion on the relationship between 1 Cor 11 and Luke 22, see Matson 2001a, 180–84.

12. Of course Jeremias (1966) argues strongly that it is patterned after the Passover meal, but see alternatively Eduard Schweizer 1967, 29–32, for serious questions about this. Especially note that the bread and wine were standard parts of any meal and thus need not be specific to a Passover meal.

on unleavened-bread typology, we find a common tradition that sees Jesus linked to the lamb sacrificed on Nisan 14. The whole passage is tied to the central symbolism of the Passover feast (here with the paschal lamb and unleavened bread bound together in one image), and the readers are assumed or urged to celebrate a Passover feast, which presumes a knowledge and appreciation for this Jewish feast. Within the context of a Passover celebration, then, it is interesting that Jesus is typified as the "paschal lamb."[13] This may, of course, simply be an attempt at interpretation by analogy. But it is also very likely that underlying this reference is a tradition that Jesus died as a symbolic Passover lamb, an idea that would be more difficult to develop if his death had occurred the day *after* the slaughter of the Passover lambs.

2. *Talmud.* One of the few passages concerning Jesus in the baraitot of the Talmud addresses the chronological issue of Jesus' crucifixion:

> On the eve of the Passover, Yeshu (the Nazarean)[14] was hanged. For forty days before the execution took place a herald went forth and cried, "He is going forth to be stoned because he has practiced sorcery and enticed Israel to apostasy. Anyone who can say anything in his favor, let him come forward and plead on his behalf." But since nothing was brought forward in his favor, he was hanged on the eve of the Passover. (b. Sanh. 43a)

While caution must certainly be applied to evaluating material from the Talmud, especially because of its temporal remoteness and its often tendentious nature, this particular baraita seems to have originated independently and thus points to an early tradition about Jesus' crucifixion.[15] If it preserves an independent early tradition, it might inform our inquiry into the independence and historical value of the Johannine dating. In support of the baraita referenced above, we might note that the representation of Jesus as "practicing sorcery" and "enticing Israel to apostasy" both fit within the Gospels' representation of the reasons for the Jewish opposition to Jesus, at least to the degree that Jewish opponents of Jesus might have phrased their accusations against him. It is interesting also that while the rather self-serving mention of the forty-day notice and request for exculpatory evidence indicates that stoning would be the result of the charge (although see

---

13. The text says only that Jesus is "our pascha," but since the verb used is θύω, it is appropriate to translate pascha as "passover lamb."

14. Only one manuscript, the Munich manuscript, inserts the words "the Nazarean," which is probably a later addition, but it suggests that interpreters clearly saw this baraita as referring to Jesus of Nazareth.

15. In particular, Joseph Klausner, who is generally skeptical of most references that might be to Jesus in the rabbinic sources, nonetheless finds this one to have some relative historical value. Thus he makes a major distinction between the baraita on Jesus' execution and one that follows that supposedly deals with his disciples (Klausner 1926, 27–28). Less sanguine on the historical value is Meier 1991, 96–97; see also Theissen and Merz 1998, 74–76.

John 8:59; 10:31—the time delay would not, incidentally, cause problems to John's chronology, since only in the Fourth Gospel does the Jewish "trial" take place earlier than passion week; see John 11:47–53), the baraita nonetheless concludes that *hanging* was the mode of execution. It is possible, of course, that what is envisaged is death by stoning to be followed by a public humiliation by hanging. But whether there is a discrepancy in the method of execution in this passage or the public hanging is a humiliation after death, the passages seems to retain information about Jesus' crucifixion that would not have served later Jewish interests. If this baraita has any claim to deriving from an early period in the Jewish memory of Jesus—and I think its claim is strong—it clearly suggests that Jesus was crucified (or hung) on the day *before* the Passover, or Nisan 14, in agreement with John's Gospel.

3. *Gospel of Peter.* The extant fragment of the Gospel of Peter has generally been judged to be independent of the canonical Gospels. The historical value of the material has received varied assessments,[16] but it is generally accepted as relatively early and independent of the canonical Gospels.

In the early part of the extant fragment, at the conclusion of the trial scenes (which, interestingly, have Herod actually sending Jesus to his death), Pilate and Herod consent to give Joseph the body of Jesus for burial. As Herod consents, saying that he would have buried him anyway in order to avoid violating Deut 21:22–23, the narrator makes a generalizing comment: "And he turned him over to the people on the day before the Unleavened Bread, their feast [προ μιας των αζυμων της εορτης αυτων]." Here the first day of Unleavened Bread must certainly be the Passover celebration, and thus the Gospel of Peter knows of a chronology similar to John. If we follow Koester and allow that this may be an early independent tradition, then we have a second clear attestation for a chronology in which Jesus at least does not celebrate the Last Supper on the evening of Passover but rather is put to death on the day before Passover, Nisan 14.

3.3. Indirect Evidence: Early Church Practices

While the references in 1 Corinthians, the Talmud, and the Gospel of Peter provide external evidence of varying quality, there is some further evidence in the development of the eucharistic and Easter practices that might also suggest the independent and early use of John's passion dating tradition. Of course this could

---

16. On the positive side on the Gospel of Peter's originality, see Crossan 1988, xiii. Koester (1990, 216–50), however, thinks Crossan's claim that the canonical Gospels used Gospel of Peter as a source is too speculative, although he affirms that Gospel of Peter is independent and most original in its passion scenes. On the other hand, Theissen and Merz (1998, 50) generally dismiss its historical value, and Meier (1991, 116–17) dismisses it as dependent on the canonical Gospels.

mean simply that segments of the church knew the Gospel of John and were influenced at an early stage to follow its practice or theology. But it could also suggest that segments of the early church and John both relied on an early tradition, which would add another datum in favor of the historical value of such a tradition. What follows, then, is a consideration of a variety of evidence that the early church followed a tradition similar to John.

1. *The Didache on the Eucharist.* As noted before, it is striking in John's presentation that Jesus' final supper is not a Passover and that the last meal does not contain any language later identified with the Eucharist. In all of the other Gospels, Jesus' final meal is represented as a Passover meal, and his words over the bread and cup establish the basis for a later memorial meal. While it is not absolutely necessary that the "words of institution" of the Lord's Supper be linked with the Passover, the sacrificial metaphor of the body given (most clearly in Luke) and blood poured out "for others" fits very well within a Passover setting (Jeremias 1966, 41–48). Certainly in the Synoptic Gospels this metaphor is used proleptically for the upcoming passion of Jesus, so that the bread and cup come, on reflection, to symbolize Jesus' body "given up" in death on the cross. The Johannine version of eucharistic language in John 6, by contrast, uses the giving of manna in the wilderness as the entry point for identifying Jesus' flesh and blood as "true food." While associated with Jesus' death indirectly (6:51), and while John 6 is situated calendrically as taking place near the Passover (6:4), it is the exodus motif and the manna reference that are linked to the eating and drinking actions prescribed. Therefore, the closest eucharistic language in John is tied more directly to the exodus-deliverance and provision motifs of the Passover than its sacrifice-atonement associations. The "eucharistic" setting of John 6 is thus a common meal rather than a cultic one.

The Didache has an important witness to the early traditions of the Eucharist. Many see Did. 9 as presenting a substantially independent tradition within the early church, with a quite independent approach to theological grounding of the Eucharist. Niederwimmer (1998, 142–430) suggests that Did. 9 is not eucharistic but simply records prayers offered before an agape meal, and the Eucharist proper is alluded to in Did. 10. On the other hand, both Vööbus (1968) and Milavec (2003, 379–80) have argued persuasively, and I think correctly, that Did. 9–10 presents a Eucharist that predates a formal separation between the sacramental rite and the agape meal[17] Given that the Didache probably dates to the first century and seems to derive foundationally from independent Jewish traditions, it is probably a truly independent witness to an early church practice and perspective (Niederwimmer 1998, 52–54; Milavec 2003, 695–739).

---

17. See also on this issue John Riggs 1995, 256–83, though I do not entirely agree with his trajectory.

The eucharistic liturgy presented in this early document does not utilize the passion of Jesus as its metaphorical reference point. Instead, the wine (τὸ ποτήριον) is connected to the "holy vine of your son David, which you made known to us through your son Jesus" (Did. 9:2), and the "broken" bread (τὸ κλάσμα, not ἄρτος) does not symbolize the body of Jesus imagined through the eyes of the passion story but rather represents the unity of the church: "As this broken bread was scattered upon the mountains, and being gathered together became one, so may your church be gathered together from the ends of the earth into your kingdom" (Did. 9:4). Thus the celebration of the Eucharist is seemingly not grounded in the passion of Jesus, and may not even have a direct connection to the Passover, but rather is based on a tradition that connects Jesus' body to the church.[18]

What makes this interesting for our consideration of John's passion dating is the fact that it represents an early tradition in which the Eucharist is not linked to the Last Supper or to the passion, which is what we have in the Gospel of John, where eucharistic-type language is found associated with the feeding of the five thousand early in the ministry of Jesus and not connected to the passion narrative. Let me be clear, though. I am not suggesting here that the Didache is in any way dependent on the Fourth Gospel, although there are some broad symbolic points of similarity. While this has been suggested previously, I think this direct connection cannot be sustained (Vööbus 1969); however, that does not take away from the Didache's value as a witness to the relative plausibility of John's account, or at least a narrative account in which the passion and Eucharist precursor language are disconnected. For here in an independent and early witness to church tradition we find a Eucharist that is not grounded for its meaning in the passion. This testifies to a variety of traditions in the early church, some of which did not fundamentally link the passion and the Eucharist.[19]

2. *The Quartodeciman Practices*. An early controversy in the church dealt with the worship and liturgy on the occasion of the remembrance of Jesus' death and resurrection. This "quartodeciman controversy" is recorded in Eusebius, *Hist. eccl.* 5.23–25, and it involved the Roman bishop Victor's mandate to the churches in Asia to stop celebrating the Jewish Passover because it was a "heterodox" practice. The introduction to the controversy states that the churches in Asia focused on Nisan 14 as a central part of their celebration of Jesus' death and resurrection:

---

18. Of course here we find parallels in 1 Cor 10:17, although Paul still links it to the death of Jesus even while he uses "one body" language also. Of course, John also links the bread to the church by means of the mystical identification with Jesus: "those who eat my flesh and drink my blood abide in me, and I in them" (6:56), where "abiding" is John's later language for the bond that keeps Jesus' spirit connected to the church.

19. See Robert Richardson's added notes in Lietzmann 1979, 377–406.

At that time no small controversy arose because all the dioceses of Asia thought it right, as though by more ancient tradition, to observe for the feast of the Savior's passover the fourteenth day of the moon, on which the Jews had been commanded to kill the lamb. Thus it was necessary to finish the fast on that day, whatever day of the week it might be. (*Hist. eccl.* 5.23.1, Lake 1965, 503)

As Eusebius's discussion proceeds, it is apparent that this practice of the Asian churches is being contrasted with the alternative practice of ending the paschal *fast* on Easter, which was always a Sunday ("Lord's Day"). It is not obvious from Eusebius's description what specific kind of remembrance took place among the Asian churches. Was it a substitute for Easter on the Passover? Or was it a continued celebration of the Jewish Passover as opposed to (or in preference to) a Christian recognition of the resurrection? Or was it simply a conflict over the passion dating with reference to the Jewish calendar? The Asian practice, whatever it precisely was, was vigorously defended by Polycrates, according to Eusebius (*Hist. eccl.* 5.24.1–8), who also records that Irenaeus came to the defense of the Asian churches, not so much agreeing with their practice as asserting their right to practice it within a less monolithic concept of the developing catholic church (5.24.11–18). Ultimately, the dominant church did adopt the Roman tradition in the celebration of Easter.

The account in Eusebius is intriguing for several reasons. First, it appears that a substantial number of churches in Asia did keep the quartodeciman practice: "The dioceses in Asia" (τῆς Ἀσίας ἀπάσης αἱ παροικίαι) is a broad geographical identifier. Moreover, the reference to a plurality of bishops in Asia for whom Polycrates, bishop of Ephesus, spoke implies that the practice was fairly extensive within the region. Eusebius also notes in his introductory reference that he considered the practice to be ancient (ἀρχαιοτέρας), and in the bishops' response to the pressure to change they also are described as defending an old tradition that had been handed down over time. Polycrates' response, quoted in Eusebius, cites the long chain of tradition by which this form of commemoration of Jesus death was passed down:

Therefore we keep the day undeviatingly, neither adding nor taking away, for in Asia great luminaries sleep.... Such were Philip of the twelve apostles, and two of his daughters who grew old as virgins, who sleep in Hierapolis, and another daughter of his, who lived in the Holy Spirit, rests at Ephesus. Moreover, there is also John, who lay on the Lord's breast, who was a priest wearing the breastplate, and a martyr, and teacher. He sleeps at Ephesus. And there is also Polycarp at Smyrna, both bishop and martyr, and Thraseas, both bishop and martyr, from Eumenaea, who sleeps in Smyrna. And why should I speak of Sagaris, bishop and martyr, who sleeps at Laodicaea, and Papirius, too, the blessed, and Melito the eunuch, who lived entirely in the Holy Spirit, and who lies in Sardis waiting for the visitation from heaven when he will rise from dead? All these kept the fourteenth day of the Passover according to the gospel, never swerving, but following according to the rule of the faith. (*Hist. eccl.* 5.24.2–6)

What is clear from Polycrates' defense of the Asian churches' practice is that it is linked to a tradition that is traced all the way back to the disciples, including Phillip, one of the Twelve (called an apostle here), and John (not called an apostle but said to have been part of Jesus' group). The above reference to John, in terms that link it by direct allusions to the author of the Fourth Gospel (see John 13:23; 21:20),[20] is itself indicative of a deeper connection between the quartodeciman practice and the Fourth Gospel and its passion chronology. In Eusebius's discussion, it is also worth briefly examining Irenaeus's defense of the Asian churches. While Irenaeus agrees with the Western practice of Easter, he does recognize that the Asian churches have had their pattern for a long time. In particular, he notes that Polycarp (d. 156 C.E.) was adamant about the celebration on Nisan 14, "inasmuch as he had always done so in company with John the disciple of our Lord and the other apostles with whom he had associated" (*Hist. eccl.* 5.24.16). Irenaeus seems to admit that an ancient but distinctive tradition was a valid reason to allow for variety in liturgical practice.

The scholarly discussion about what exactly the quartodeciman practices were, and how they might be related to the issue of Gospel chronology, was active in the latter half of the nineteenth and first half of the twentieth centuries.[21] As noted above, a central question has been in defining precisely what significance the Asian churches attached to Nisan 14: Was it a commemoration of Jesus' death (in which case it relates directly to Johannine chronology), or was it a commemoration of the Last Supper (in which case it affirms the Synoptic chronology), or was it instead a Jewish-Christian celebration of the Passover with only a few typological connections to the passion (in which case the issue may have involved the strength of Jewish elements within Christianity)? A major effort in this early discussion was the formulation by Carl Schmidt, based on scanty references in ancient literature to what the quartodeciman practice was: (1) the quartodeciman observance of Nisan 14 celebrated the passion; (2) this was in harmony with Johannine chronology; (3) only one day, the 14th, was kept. The Asiatics fasted until the hour of the death of Jesus and later assembled for vigil, which terminated at the cockcrow. This moment signified the end of the Passion festival,

---

20. See Richard Bauckham's lengthy article (1993) dealing with Polycrates' letter embedded in Eusebius and how it might influence the debate on the authorship of the Gospel of John. He uses the evidence from Eusebius, together with traditions about Papias, to support Hengel's argument (1989a) for authorship of the Fourth Gospel by the Elder John, a disciple of Jesus but not one of the Twelve.

21. See, e.g., Drummond 1897; Richardson 1940; Strand, 1965. For a summary of much of this scholarship, see Lohse 1953.

which then concluded with a Eucharist and Agape (Richardson 1940, 178).[22] In contrast, however, Richardson suggested that the quartodecimans actually celebrated the Last Supper as Jesus' last Passover on Nisan 14, and thus they were following a Synoptic chronology rather than a Johannine one.

The discussion about the quartodeciman controversy has been raised anew, however, aided by significant new material. In particular the Passover liturgy of Melito of Sardis, *Peri Pascha*, has been reconstructed through a series of manuscript discoveries (Hall 1979). The publication of the reconstructed texts has been followed by an extensive examination of the *Peri Pascha* and the quartodeciman practices, notably a recent monograph by Alistair Steward-Sykes (1998, 206), who has confirmed Schmidt's conclusions cited above. That is, the quartodeciman practice did indeed focus on Nisan 14 as the celebration of Christ's death, interpreting him as the paschal lamb. This celebration also encompassed the resurrection as a unified celebration of the larger passion mystery (including the death, resurrection, and anticipation of return, all as elements of the passion). But the centrality of Nisan 14 for the quartodecimans, understood as an "Easter-type" celebration, raised the issue of the dating of the passion and thus led to the conflict with the Western tradition of celebrating Easter. It is clear that this quartodeciman practice was Johannine in its basic approach to the passion of Jesus, especially the chronology of the death of Jesus as it relates to the Jewish calendar and celebration of Passover.

Moreover, evidence of the extent to which the quartodeciman practice influenced the early church is also suggestive of the widespread nature of this tradition. As already indicated, Schmidt found the same emphasis in his examination of the *Epistula Apostolorum*. The Easter sermon by Pseudo-Hippolytus, εἰς τὸ ἅγιον πάσχα, is likely also to be quartodeciman in its outlook (Nautin 1950). Other studies present strong evidence that the Syriac churches retained quartodeciman liturgies until the time of Nicaea (Rouwhorst 1997, 82). Specifically, the writings of Ephrem the Syrian and Aphrahat show a similarity to Melito's *Peri Pascha*. It appears that the quartodeciman passion liturgy was fairly extensive in its reach and that this liturgy reflects a core narrative dating and approach that is found in John but not the Synoptic Gospels.

It is possible, of course, that all of these practices are simply the result of these churches choosing the Fourth Gospel over the Synoptics during the formative period when this liturgy developed. But since at least Melito's *Peri Pascha* betrays little direct quotation of the Fourth Gospel and yet shows strong similarity to its underlying mode of argumentation and chronology, I would argue that we may be seeing the pervasive influence of the Johannine tradition, not necessarily of the Fourth Gospel itself, on the liturgies in Asia and Syria. Certainly that is what Polycrates suggests in his response to Victor, and such a view

---

22. Cited from Richardson 1940, 178; originally in Schmidt 1919.

is also implied in Irenaeus's response to Victor's demand. That liturgies might contain very old and stable traditions is suggested in Rouwhorst's study of the Syriac liturgical traditions:

> A second reason (for the special interest in early liturgies) is that the liturgy is of particular importance because of its communal character. Liturgical rituals are performed, not by individuals but communities, by groups of believers, even when one must allow for the fact that not all of them participate in a ritual with the same degree of involvement. Moreover, rituals are characterized by a certain stability; usually they are not invented all of a sudden and at least their basic structures are not so easily changed. (Rouwhorst 1997, 73)

What the quartodeciman practice and the Didache liturgy both show is that there was an active liturgical tradition, especially in Asia Minor and Syria, that maintained a very different perspective on the Last Supper and the date of Jesus' death from the dominant "Western" liturgical traditions. These alternate traditions could generally be called "Johannine."

4. Internal Evidence for John's Chronology.

John's chronology, in which the Last Supper was eaten on Nisan 13 and Jesus' crucifixion took place on Nisan 14, has often been criticized as a theological construction by the Fourth Evangelist, even a deliberate refashioning of the Synoptic accounts. As C. K. Barrett has argued generally about John, but emphasized especially with regard to the final meal and the passion:

> It has already been shown that some of the historical differences between John and the Synoptic Gospels are not unrelated to John's theological interests. Indeed, if John knew the other Gospels (or at least Mark) every serious divergence between them must mean either that John had fresh historical information, or, as is often more probable, wrote from a different point of view with a different intention.... Again, the Johannine date of the Last Supper and crucifixion seems to be due to John's determination to make clear that Jesus was the true Paschal Lamb of God. (Barrett 1978, 51)

The question Barrett raises is whether there is evidence that John has shaped his chronology around the theological concern to portray Jesus as the paschal lamb.

4.1. Is John's Gospel Really Constructed around Jesus as Paschal Lamb?

A standard explanation for John's locating of Jesus' death on the day before the Passover is the assumption that the Evangelist is constructing his central narrative thrust around the idea of Jesus as the Passover lamb. Certainly John focuses more attention on the Passover as a Jewish festival than the Synoptics do, both in the passion narrative and in earlier material. It is noteworthy, of course, that John mentions the Passover several times in Jesus' ministry: the temple "cleansing" is set at the time of Passover (2:13, 23), and the feeding of the five thousand and the related discourse on Jesus' flesh and blood as true food and drink is set at a Passover time (6:4). We might also note that the passion narrative is anticipated by means of a number of references linked to the Passover: the order to arrest Jesus is given with the upcoming pilgrimage to Jerusalem at Passover in mind (11:55); the anointing at Bethany is specifically dated to "six days before Passover" (12:1); and the triumphal entry is linked to the "festival," which can only mean the Passover (12:12, 20). Moreover, the final meal in John is synchronized specifically as "before the feast of Passover," which would appear to be an explicit attempt to place the meal chronologically before the beginning of the feast, and the trial before Pilate is explicitly linked to the Passover, since the priests stayed outside Pilate's compound because they had not yet eaten the Passover (18:28). Finally, the crucifixion sentence is given on the "day of Preparation for Passover" (19:14). All of this points to John's deep awareness of and attention to Passover.

However, if Barrett's contention is correct, that the passion narrative is chronologically constructed to depict Jesus as the paschal lamb of God, one might have expected that John would focus more attention on that central connection. Instead, no explicit comment is made during the passion narrative that makes that logical connection, and this absence makes the conclusion that "Jesus as Passover lamb" is a major theme in John all the more tenuous.

Jesus' final meal focuses almost exclusively on the betrayal (the morsel given to Judas) and the footwashing, which serves as a moral example for the disciples. The issues that take place at the final meal are each presented with their own internal and self-consistent focus. There is no hint of any attempt to avoid Passover imagery or references, so if there was a theological effort to "refocus" attention from a Passover meal to something different, some trace of such a replacement or redirection should be evident in John's dinner account. The absence of such leads Haenchen, who is quite willing to find traces of editorial manipulation in the Gospel otherwise, to conclude, "An old source lies behind this account, which is already related to the footwashing rather than the Passover meal.... The alternative interpretation, that the story viewed him as the Passover lamb, is not hinted at in the Fourth Gospel" (Haenchen 1984, 2:105).

To be sure, several references in John might support Jesus as the paschal lamb. The first is the announcement by John the Baptist before Jesus' baptism: "Here is the Lamb of God who takes away the sin of the world" (John 1:29). This is problematic, in that the Passover lamb was not considered expiation for sin: it was not a sin or guilt sacrifice but rather a festival sacrifice that had a uniquely celebratory role in Jewish collective thought. Perhaps a more important theological or scriptural source for the reference to the "lamb of God" would be the suffering servant imagery, seen most clearly in Isa 53:4–7 (Schnackenburg 1968, 297–300).

Similarly, the reference at Jesus' death that the guards did not need to break his legs, so that the scripture might be fulfilled, "None of his bones shall be broken" (John 19:36), is often interpreted as referring to the Passover.[23] But this is not obvious either. The so-called "scripture" is not a known quotation; Exod 12:10, 46 and Num 9:12 are passages often referred to as the source of such Passover imagery, but none of them is exactly the same as the text in John (Schnackenburg 1990, 3:291). An equally plausible scriptural background, however, is the suffering-servant typology as found in Ps 34:20. In support of the latter, one should note that this suffering-servant understanding of Jesus' passion had already been cited in closely preceding passages: John 19:24 (citing Ps 22:18) and John 19:28 (citing Ps 69:21). This perspective would also fit closely with the subject of the other scriptural reference in this passage, Zech 12:10, which seems to refer to a similar "righteous sufferer." Certainly, if John 1:29 also referred to the suffering servant of Isa 53, it would explain the consistent focus on this figure in John's passion account, and it would be a focus on the suffering of the faithful servant, not a reference to Jesus as a Passover lamb.

The interpretation of the various scriptural references and allusions in John's passion narrative is not crystal clear. As Schnackenburg points out, "The preference for one passage as against another [that is, Exod 12:10 or 12:46 versus Ps 34:20] is, for most scholars, dependent on what conception they see behind the passage: Passover lamb typology, or, protection for the suffering righteous" (Schnackenburg 1990, 3:292). While one might see John as tendentiously creating the passion structure around the concept of Jesus dying as the Passover lamb, it is equally possible—perhaps even more probable—to see John's primary theological interpretation of the crucifixion as focusing on Jesus as the suffering servant, a theme that would recommend substantial revision of our view of John's sources and tradition.

It seems likely that if John were focusing on Jesus as a paschal sacrifice, he would underline or highlight the similarities with the Passover, especially since John is at such variance with the Synoptic tradition. John does have some explicit time markers in the Pilate trial and the crucifixion, yet at best these only hint at a temporal connection between the death of Jesus and the slaying of the Passover lambs. In John 18:28 Jesus is brought before Pilate early in the morning (πρωΐ); then in 19:14 Jesus is handed over for crucifixion at around noon, the sixth hour (ὥρα ἕκτη). This latter time is notably in conflict with Mark's time notations, which have Jesus crucified at nine in the morning (ἦν δὲ ὥρα τρίτη; 15:25) and a deep darkness covering the earth while Jesus is on the cross at the sixth hour (or noon) until the ninth hour (or three in the afternoon; 15:33). Perhaps John has moved his time period back in order for Jesus' death to take place at about the time of the slaying of the lambs, which was probably from 3:00 to 6:00 p.m. But what is remarkable is that John has only these two time markers early in the nar-

---

23. So, e.g., the *New Oxford Annotated Bible* at 19:36 notes simply: "Jesus fulfills the Passover (Ex 12:46; 1 Cor 5:7)."

rative, and then makes no specific reference to the time of Jesus' death. Again, the internal structure of John's account shows little apologetic interest in linking the Passover to Jesus' death; or, if such an apologetic interest is there, John is astonishingly subtle in his presentation.

4.2. IS JOHN'S ACCOUNT CONSISTENT WITH JEWISH TRIAL PRACTICE?

We might briefly also note an external historical feature that seems to affirm at least John's consistency, and perhaps causes problems for the Synoptic chronology. Here I speak of the probability of Jesus' trial taking place during a Passover time. This issue has two facets. The first is the question of legitimate jurisprudence: Would Jewish law have allowed for a trial of Jesus on the eve of Passover or on Passover itself? Based on later mishnaic regulations, it would seem that any such Jewish trial would be difficult.[24] But of course John presents the reader with no Jewish trial, and certainly not in the week before Passover. The closest thing to a Jewish trial mentioned in the Fourth Gospel is found in John 11:45–53. Here the council is called together with the high priest Caiaphas present, although Jesus is not present. The result of this "formal" tribunal is that they plan to put Jesus to death, but of course this all happens some time before Jesus' entry into Jerusalem in the week preceding the Passover. On the face of it, the regulations about Jewish trials on feast days present an argument in favor of John's consistency, if not the underlying historical plausibility of the competing accounts.

Jeremias argues effectively that having executions on feast days is not a problem, but the example he gives is of a person convicted of a major Jewish crime (e.g., idolater or false prophet) who is held until the Passover for public execution (Jeremias 1966, 78–79; Blinzler 1959, 76). But of course that is not the case here, since according to the Synoptics Jesus was arrested and tried after the Passover meal had already started. Indeed, even here John comes closer to the example given, if indeed the decision to have Jesus executed was made by a tribunal some days or weeks before Passover began (as John 11:45–53 suggests). Jeremias also argues that the prohibition against holding a trial during a major feast would have cut equally against John and the Synoptics, but that is not true either, since John has no Jewish trial in the Passover week.

While an execution during Passover may be theoretically possible, it is difficult to imagine that this would have been politically likely. The possible reaction against a Roman execution on a day that was treated as a Sabbath would have been politically difficult. Indeed, Mark's introduction to the arrest and trial contains the cautionary concern: "not during the festival, or there may be a riot among the people" (14:2). Of course, Mark's Gospel goes on to have Jesus executed after the

---

24. See, e.g., the discussion in Lindars 1972, 445, citing m. Sanh 6:1; however, the Mishnah does not address this issue directly. See also Blinzler 1959, 76.

Passover had begun! Yet John's Gospel does not present this problem, since Jesus dies before the beginning of Passover, the evening of Nisan 14.

A similar issue of chronological likelihood is to be found in the release of Barabbas, a feature found in all four Gospels. The idea of a customary release of a prisoner at Passover (see Mark 15:6) only makes sense if the prisoner is released *before* the beginning of the Passover feast, in order that he might join the celebration of the Passover with family (Blinzler 1959, 76–77). Again, this natural setting for a release fits poorly with the Synoptic presentation, since in each of them Barabbas would have been freed after the Passover feast, while in John this chronological relationship of freeing a prisoner before the Passover feast itself is maintained.

In summary, we have relative to the issue of internal consistency two issues, both of which support the plausibility of John's chronology.

1. While Jesus dies at approximately the same time as the Passover lamb in John, the Fourth Evangelist does not emphasize that feature at all. Indeed, there are real problems in connecting the motif of Jesus as "the lamb of God who takes away the sin of the world" with the Passover symbolism. The very lack of emphasis on the connection between the death of Jesus and the simultaneous Passover sacrifices gives John's account more internal historical credibility, since it argues against the motif of his death at Passover being theologically constructed.

2. At the same time, it would appear that the Synoptic representation *does* present problems with the chronology of the trial and the release of Barabbas, while the Johannine chronology does not. A Jewish trial on the eve of Passover after the meal appears to violate Jewish law, an execution on Passover would seem ill-advised politically, and the release of Barabbas makes little sense after the Passover meal is eaten. In each case, however, the Johannine chronology makes more sense: Jesus was not tried by the Jewish tribunal on Passover eve (such a trial had been held several days earlier), the execution takes place before Passover, and the release of Barabbas also takes place before the Passover meal. As a result, it seems that our investigation of a *theologically constructed account* should be directed at *Mark* rather than John. Does it not seem that Mark has apparently revised his traditions on the passion, and certainly his chronology, and given special importance to the Last Supper as a Passover? In this case, some of the internal inconsistencies may be due to Mark's forcing the passion to fit a Passover-meal design.

5. CONCLUSIONS

The issue of passion chronology involves a myriad of details related to the dating of Jesus' final supper and death. This fertile ground has been frequently plowed before, producing fruit on various sides of the argument. While one cannot "prove" the accuracy of John's passion dating, the largest number of corroborative details seems to point to John's dating as, at the very least, "plausible." Plausibility is a statement of probability, not fact. So let me highlight some of the conclusions that we have reached along the way in terms of probability.

1. It is nearly certain that John and the Synoptics relate two very different chronologies of Jesus' Last Supper and death relative to the Jewish calendar. To put this another way, it is highly improbable that John and the Synoptics can be harmonized on the date of Jesus' death.

2. While it is tempting to turn to astronomical calculations to certify the accurate chronology of Jesus' passion, that avenue is finally a dead end. On the face of it, it might appear that John's dating has a better chance of being accurate: most astronomical constructions of the period around 30 c.e. identify few if any possible days when Passover eve was on a Thursday and produce more "possible" days when Passover eve was on a Friday. Still, given the way calculations of new months and new years were actually performed in Jewish antiquity, the use of calendar retrojection is too uncertain to base any solid conclusion upon it. Thus, it is highly improbable that we can resolve the date of Jesus' death by a retrojection of our modern calendars.

3. Jaubert's attempt to find two calendars as a way of reconciling the problem is highly improbable. Not only is there no evidence, externally or internally, that competing calendars were involved in the Jesus movement, but her construction does not easily work without extensive editorial modification of all the Gospel accounts.

4. Evidence from texts other than the canonical Gospels provides some support for the Johannine chronology. While the eucharistic language in 1 Cor 11 apparently points to a Passover connection to the final meal, Paul also thinks of Jesus himself as the Passover sacrifice. We have, then, competing traditions in a single letter of Paul about the dating of Jesus' death relative to the Passover. Might this have influenced the Synoptic dating and presentation? At the same time, the Gospel of Peter and the one explicit baraita in the Talmud both support the Johannine dating, showing it was not alone.

5. Early church tradition paints a varied picture in its liturgical practice, and some of these liturgies support John's passion dating. While the traditional Christian Eucharist is linked to the Last Supper, there appear to be independent traditions (in the Didache and in John) that construct the eucharistic symbolism *without* the cultic Passover in mind. While the Didache's underlying symbolism is not necessarily Johannine, it can be seen as harmonious with John's view. To put this more strongly, it is highly probable that the earliest eucharistic celebration finds its genesis not in a final Passover celebration of Jesus and his disciples but rather was formed around the common daily meal of bread and wine, offered perhaps many times, but with an increasing sense of finality toward the end of his ministry.

Similarly, the extensive tradition of the quartodecimans is almost certainly related to John's dating of the Passover. The extensive and firmly held quartodeciman liturgy in the Asian churches into the late second century reflects a tradition that is also found in John, and it is highly probable that both John's dating and the quartodecimans' practice stem from early traditions that predate the Gospels.

6. While John is often dismissed as theologically constructed and thus unhistorical, John's passion narrative is more probably based on independent tradition than a thoroughgoing theological design. Not only does the linkage of Jesus as a Passover sacrifice who atones for the sin of the world seem theologically strained, but, more importantly, the Fourth Evangelist makes no effort to underline the point (while ἱλασμός is found in 1 John 2:2, it is found nowhere in the Gospel of John). It is highly unlikely that John constructed his chronology to fit a theological perspective only to forget to mention it at the climax, the *telos*, of the story.

7. At the same time, the Synoptic chronology has significant difficulties that make its internal consistency problematic. It is, then, moderately improbable that the Jewish leadership held a trial on the eve of Passover, improbable that they requested a public crucifixion on Passover, and improbable that Pilate waited until the Passover feast was over to make a public and symbolic release of a prisoner (Barabbas). In other words, the Synoptic chronology itself has serious difficulties, and it is highly probable that its dating is theologically constructed around Jesus eating a final Passover meal with his disciples.

Seven signs and seven conclusions—a Johannine symbol to be sure! Is John accurate in his depiction of the last week of Jesus' life? That is impossible to say for sure. Certainly his account is colored by his desire to bring readers to active belief and to instill an understanding of Jesus as the glory of God. Thus his account is, no doubt, constructed to achieve its end, but John's unique chronology resists compliance with the Synoptics or Paul—itself a factor of traditional considerations. In the light of critical analysis, John's dating of the crucifixion on Nisan 14 is not only plausible, it is even probable.

At the Court of the High Priest:
History and Theology in John 18:13–24*

Helen K. Bond

Despite a general preference for the Synoptic Gospels, several features of John's narrative have often commanded a certain historical respect: the lengthier ministry and its wider geographical location, the more complex relationship between Jesus and John the Baptist, the date of the crucifixion, and the passage that concerns us now—John's Jewish interrogation of Jesus (Smith 1993, 252–67). C. H. Dodd argued in 1963 that John's "account of the interrogation is drawn from some source, almost certainly oral, which was well informed about the situation at the time, and had contact with the Jewish tradition about the trial and condemnation of Jesus."[1]

Scholars today are less inclined to attempt to identify sources; they detect a Johannine coloring to the scene and are much more sophisticated in their treatment of "historicity" and verisimilitude. Yet, as Paula Fredriksen notes, "when the question turns to assessments of the Jewish trial in the Passion narratives ... most modern scholars ... unite in their opinion that, in this instance and on this issue—historical suitability—*John* is to be preferred."[2]

John's Account versus the Synoptics

Six reasons are often advanced for regarding John's interrogation as historical. After reviewing each in turn, I shall suggest that the scene is much more theologi-

* I would like to thank the British Academy for their generous Overseas Conference Travel Grant, which enabled me to attend the SBL meeting in San Diego, where this paper was presented.

1. Dodd 1963, 95–96. Dodd's assessment was followed by string of prominent scholars, e.g., Brandon 1968, 125–28; Barrett 1978, 523–24; Catchpole, 1970, 47–65; Millar 1990, 355–81.

2. Fredriksen 1999, 221, emphasis original. See also Brown 1994, 1:363, 404, 408; Senior 1991, 59; Keener 2003, 2:1086; Smith 1993, 264.

cal than is often supposed, but that John's theology does not necessarily drain the scene of all historical value.

1. The first reason why John's account is often preferred is *the problematic nature of the Synoptic account at this point*. Mark (followed closely by Matthew) presents a Jewish trial that breaks every legal ruling imaginable: it is held at night on the eve of a festival; members of the council are intent on a conviction, even arranging for false witnesses to be called; the high priest acts as a prosecuting attorney rather than a judge; and, in the end, after condemning Jesus on his own testimony, it is members of the council who set about beating and abusing him (Mark 14:53, 55–64). Earlier generations of scholars attempted to uphold the historicity of the scene, debating the validity of mishnaic law in the first century and asking whether the council followed Saducean rules. Recent literary studies, however, have shown that with "brilliant simplicity" (Brown 1994, 1:53) Mark constructs a final courtroom drama in which Jesus is set against Jewish authorities, who will stop at nothing in their desire to sentence him to death. It is a kangaroo court in which the Jewish leaders, true to character, behave despicably, and Jesus is convicted, anachronistically, for his Christian belief (Juel 1977; Bond 2004, 102–8).

Luke's account is different but no less problematic historically. He presents a small-scale interrogation by the Jewish leaders the morning after Jesus' arrest (Luke 22:66–71) as part of a four-scene trial narrative, which includes the historically questionable trial in front of Antipas and culminates in Pilate's decision that the demand of the Jewish crowd should be granted (23:25). The Lukan chief priests concentrate their questions on Jesus' identity, while several details from the Markan trial (such as the presence of the high priest and false witnesses, the accusation that Jesus spoke against the temple, and the charge of blasphemy) are reserved until the trial of Stephen in Acts 6:8–7:60. Luke clearly had a different agenda than Mark: he wanted to stress Jesus' innocence, an innocence that could only be maintained if Jesus had some semblance of a trial. So the Lukan Jesus is tried on three specific charges (Luke 23:2), all demonstrably false, and found innocent by two high-status male witnesses: Antipas and Pilate. Of course, Jesus will eventually be sent to the cross, but this is engineered in Luke's narrative through a combination of Jewish antagonism and Pilate's weakness (Neagoe 2002, 62–90; Bond 1998, 152–59; 2004, 112–16).

2. In contrast to the Synoptics, *John's account of Jesus before the high priest is simple and straightforward*, which is the second reason for preferring John at this point. There is no dramatic courtroom setting, no christological questions, no desperate attempt to convict Jesus through false witnesses, no accusations of blasphemy, and no abuse of the prisoner. Instead, Jesus stands alone in front of the high priest and a few attendants. What we have here is not a trial at all but a brief fact-finding investigation once Jesus has been taken into police custody. The high priest asks Jesus only about his disciples and his teaching, a necessary preliminary, one might think, before handing him over to Pilate the following morning.

3. The third reason for preferring John's account is *the lack of necessity for any kind of Jewish trial at this point in the Gospel.* It is commonly noted that the whole of Jesus' public ministry in John *is* a trial: Jesus' Jewish opponents continually bring accusations against him, and by chapter 11 the high priest has convened a Sanhedrin and sentenced Jesus to death in his absence (Harvey 1976; Lincoln 2000). Material connected with the Jewish trial in the Synoptics can be found scattered throughout the Gospel (Brown 1961). All the Fourth Evangelist needed to do was to refer the reader back to the trial in chapter 11, something he does quite clearly in 18:3; there was no need for Jesus to have any further hearing before the Jewish authorities. The presence of Roman soldiers in Jesus' arrest (whether historical or not) would naturally lead the reader to assume that Jesus would be taken into *Roman* custody, and it is the lengthy Roman trial that will dominate John's passion narrative. The most reasonable explanation for including the apparently lack-luster Jewish interrogation is that John is simply drawing on a tradition too well known to omit (rather like the episode with Barabbas in 18:39–40; so Bruce 1980, 11).

4. Fourth, it is often argued that *John's account has an air of authenticity about it* and that his narrative contains a number of details that cohere well with what we know of the religious and political situation of first-century Judea.

4.1. John accords a prominent place to the high priest (unlike Mark, who omitted his name, and Luke, who omitted him altogether). John knows that it was the high priest and his entourage (chief priests, advisers, and other aristocrats) who made the decisions and worked alongside the Roman governor for the good of Judea, a state of affairs outlined many times by Josephus (McLaren 1991).

At first glance, though, John's references to the high priesthood are rather strange. He seems to call Annas "high priest," for example, even though he has made it perfectly clear that Caiaphas was high priest that year (11:51; 18:13). Did the Evangelist think that two men could act as high priest simultaneously? Moreover, the expression "high priest that year" is odd: Did John hold the erroneous belief that the high priesthood, in common with a number of Roman priesthoods in Asia, was an annual appointment? For Dodd, these apparent "confusions" only added to the authenticity of the tradition, in that "an author composing freely would not be so likely to allow himself to fall into this kind of confusion as one who was incorporating material which, at a distance of place and time, he did not fully understand" (Dodd 1963, 94). Nowadays, however, scholars tend to have a more positive assessment of John's accuracy. It is true that Num 35:25 allowed for only one high priest at a time, but since the reign of Herod I high priests had been appointed and deposed at will, leading to an unprecedented situation in which a number of former high priests were still living. There is ample evidence from Josephus (*J.W.* 2.441, *Ant.* 20.205, *Life* 193), rabbinic tradition (m. Hor. 3:4), and perhaps Luke (Luke 3:2; Acts 4:6) that these former incumbents retained their former title and prestige, perhaps reflecting a view that a high priest, once appointed, could not be deposed by any foreign power (Mason 2003, 188). So the expression "high priest that year" is now generally interpreted as meaning that Caiaphas was high priest "that fateful year" (Brown 1994, 1:405). John's account of the high priesthood, then, seems to cohere well with historical fact.

4.2. John is the only ancient author to suggest a specific connection between Caiaphas and Annas (or Ananus I, as he is known in Jewish sources). Ananus was the first high priest appointed by Rome when Judea became a province in 6 C.E. Although he was deposed after nine years (for unknown reasons), he was extremely distinguished and had a prominent tomb, which Josephus referred to years later, to the south of the city (*J. W.* 5.506). Luke refers to him in his dating of John the Baptist's ministry (Luke 3:2) and in his account of the early church (Acts 4:6), and Josephus stresses his importance and ongoing influence through his five sons, each of whom succeeded to the high priesthood (*Ant.* 20.198). Although uncorroborated, John's suggestion of a connection between the two men would make good sense. Caiaphas's own family background is obscure,[3] but his rise to the high priesthood would be only natural if he were connected by marriage to the most important high-priestly dynasty of first-century Palestine (Bond 2004, 37). Even the Jesus Seminar saw no reason to doubt John's record at this point, awarding the detail one of the few red colorings in the whole Gospel (Funk et al. 1998, 429). And if Ananus and Caiaphas were related, Ananus's involvement in Jesus' trial (though mentioned by no other Evangelist) would be quite explicable. Caiaphas, as officiating high priest, had other duties to attend to on the night before Passover, and he might well have left this important yet sensitive matter in the capable hands of his father-in-law (Brown 1994, 1:363, 404, 408).

4.3. Furthermore, John's lack of a formal council at this point fits with a number of modern studies that question the existence of a fixed body known as "the Sanhedrin" (Goodman 1987, 113–18; Sanders 1992, 472–90; Goodblatt 1994). Instead, members of the aristocracy acted through ad hoc coalitions and alliances; the precise people involved depended on the nature of the issue. True to the spirit of the age, disputes were settled through diplomacy, negotiation, and compromise.[4] Historically, then, the high priest may have simply summoned a small body of councilors to help him determine the charge before passing Jesus over to Rome, which is precisely the outline of events described by John.

4.4. Finally, the Fourth Evangelist credits Caiaphas with the gift of prophecy in 11:51 and reminds the reader of his words again here. A number of contemporary Jewish texts similarly associate the high priest with prophetic powers (Hayward 1996, 70; Dodd 1962; Gray 1993, 7–34), suggesting that John's Gospel

---

3. A handful of rabbinic references may refer to him: t. Yebam. 1:10; y. Yebam. 1.6, 3.1; and m. Par. 3:5. For further discussion (and bibliography), see Bond 2004, 23–24, 164–65.

4. The reference to "*a* sanhedrin" in chapter 11 may well indicate a looser gathering, or a *consilium*, rather than a formal body known as "*the* Sanhedrin."

came from a community that knew these traditions and that had, at least at some point in the past, a certain respect for the priestly office.

The author of the Fourth Gospel, then, presents a much simpler picture of the Jewish trial, one that fits in well with what we know of first-century practices. But can we say more about this author and his sources?

5. John is the only Evangelist to explain how Peter got into the high priest's courtyard: he was admitted by a mysterious "other disciple" (ἄλλος μαθητής) with connections to the high priest (18:15). This disciple is commonly linked to the Beloved Disciple, the enigmatic figure who assumes a central role in the second half of the Gospel, and perhaps even to the Evangelist himself (see discussions in Charlesworth 1995; Blomberg 2001, 233–34; Keener 2003, 2:1089). Even if, following Dodd (1963, 87–88), we understand the "other disciple" to be an otherwise unknown Judean disciple, the implication is that at this point the Evangelist may have had access to good, historical, eye-witness information (either that of his own, or a trusted source). The vivid details of the scene—the charcoal fire (18:18) and the early hour (18:28)—appear to reinforce this view (Dodd 1963, 86; Burge 2001, 40).

6. The sixth and final reason why this scene is often regarded as more historical than its Synoptic counterpart is its apparent lack of theology. C. H. Dodd puts the matter clearly: "Where the Marcan scene has profound theological significance, John, the most theological of the evangelists, has given a version which has no theological content, but moves altogether on a matter-of-fact level" (1963, 92; see also 93). Raymond E. Brown likewise writes, "we find no clear Johannine theological motive that would explain the invention of the Annas narrative" (1966–70, 2:835). Finally, D. Moody Smith sums up the views of many when he writes, "John's account of Jesus' appearance before the high priest is almost completely different [from Mark's trial narrative] and, as commentators have noted, less theologically freighted than Mark's" (2001, 116). In a Gospel full of theological insight, the apparent lack of theology here is taken to imply that John was more dependent on tradition at this point, a tradition that may well go back to good historical memory.

Varying combinations of these six points have convinced many scholars that John's account of Jesus before the high priest has at least a claim to historical accuracy. Some, of course, have wished to harmonize John's account with the Markan/Matthean tradition, so that when Annas sends Jesus to Caiaphas in John 18:24 we are to read the Sanhedrin trial narrative into the story.[5] Such harmonizations have an ancient pedigree (traceable as far back as Tatian in the second century) but rather problematically produce a composite sequence of events unlike anything in any of the Gospels (see Brown 1994, 1:23–24, 417). Even more

---

5. So, for example, Bruce 1980, 11; Blomberg 2001, 232–35; Köstenberger 2004, 513; Carson 1991, 581; Benoit 1969, 79–85; Bauckham 1998a, 158.

difficult here is the fact that John already presented a full council meeting (albeit without Jesus) in 11:47–53. Whether the Fourth Evangelist is following a different tradition from the Synoptics or has deliberately relocated Mark's final courtroom scene,[6] there is absolutely no indication that he expected his readers to understand a Markan-style trial after 18:24. Logically, then, we have a fourfold choice: we can choose to follow John's account, Mark's (and Matthew's) account, Luke's account, or none of them (so Crossan 1994, 152; 1996, 147). Most commentators, for the reasons outlined above, favor John's.

But do these arguments really carry any weight? The first four arguments are strong, in my opinion; I would not argue with reading the Synoptics as dramatic courtroom fictions, nor with the apparent simplicity of, and lack of necessity for, John's account. Nor would I wish to dispute that John's account possesses an air of authenticity—though creating an air of verisimilitude, I must stress, is only that. All these details *prove* is that John was familiar with Judean ways and religious customs, not that he actually had any hard historical facts at his disposal. Quite possibly, as E. P. Sanders notes, "John was just more astute with regard to *Realpolitik* than were the other evangelists, and so wrote a story with greater verisimilitude" (1993, 72). I wish to remain agnostic over the "other disciple" (reason 5). At best, he is a witness to events outside rather than in the courtroom itself,[7] and even if he were in a position to furnish the Evangelist with reliable eyewitness testimony to the interrogation, I see no reason why the author would not have worked with it just as creatively as he does elsewhere. The weakest argument, in my opinion, is the sixth one listed above: that the scene lacks theology and so, on that basis, has a good claim to historicity. In the remaining sections of this essay, I wish to argue that the interrogation narrative is *highly theological* and to ask what implications this may have on the historicity of the scene. I shall start with a close reading of the text itself.

The Theology of the Trial in front of "the High Priest"

The problems regarding the identity of "the high priest" in John 18:19–24 are well known. As far as the flow of the narrative goes, the high priest must be Annas, and, as we have seen, there is plenty of evidence that former high priests retained their title even after they had been deposed. Yet Caiaphas was technically the high priest, and he is the only one specifically named as such by John (11:49;

---

6. For a survey of scholarship on the literary relationship between the Johannine and Synoptic passion narratives, see Smith 2001, 111–37; for a more complex relationship of "interfluence," see Anderson 2006b.

7. A point conceded by Richard Bauckham, though he goes on to argue that this disciple's relationship to the high priest "may well be intended to indicate access to information" (2006, 397–98).

18:13, 24). Scholars have detected some confusion here in John or his sources, and attempts have been made since the second century to rearrange the order of the verses so that Jesus appears in front of Caiaphas rather than Annas, though with little success.[8]

But perhaps the confusion is deliberate. In a Gospel that delights in word-plays and double meanings, John has introduced two high priests, who are connected by marriage and clearly share the same outlook and purpose: one is the most famous high priest of the first century; the other is "high priest that year." The note that Jesus was taken to Annas in 18:13 is immediately followed by a reference back to Caiaphas's prophecy (18:14; see also 11:50–51), meaning that when Jesus stands before "the high priest" in 18:19, the names of both men are in the reader's mind. What this ambiguity does, I suggest, is to deflect atten-tion away from the precise incumbent and onto the *office of high priest* (so also Escaffre 2000, 58–61). The short scene brings Jesus face to face with the supreme representative of "the Jews" for one final confrontation.

A face-to-face meeting is, of course, thoroughly Johannine. This Evange-list has a penchant for reducing scenes to one main protagonist (e.g., the visit of Nicodemus, who speaks in the plural, suggesting that the tradition recounted the visit of a number of visitors, 3:1–15; the presence of Mary Magdalene alone at the tomb, where the other Gospels have several women, 20:1, 11–18). Such a meeting allows an individual the space to encounter Jesus and to come to a deci-sion about him (3:17–21; Brown 1994, 1:413). Even if John's tradition included a larger courtroom scene at this point, the Evangelist may well have deliberately singled out the one person whose presence really mattered—the high priest—and brought him up against Jesus in a tense and dramatic moment. Perhaps, too, this is why the scene is not a trial as such; the Evangelist is not interested in the high priest as a "judge" (this is the role of Pilate, who will be found wanting in the next scene), but in the high priesthood itself.

Commentators often highlight the contrast between Jesus inside the high priest's palace and Peter outside in the courtyard. "Jesus stands up to his question-ers and denies nothing," writes Brown, "while Peter cowers before his questioners and denies everything" (1966–70, 2:842). Read in this way, the scene becomes a reflection of the trials of Johannine Christians at the hands of hostile authorities. Jesus is clearly the example to be emulated, while Peter shows that even one of Jesus' closest disciples could lose his courage under pressure. There is some valid-ity to this observation, but the contrast between the two men works much better in Mark, where Peter's denials are interwoven with a formal court hearing and his refutations contrast starkly with Jesus' powerful "I am" statement (Mark 14:62). In John's Gospel, Peter's strong and simple denials (οὐκ εἰμί; 18:17, 25; see also 18:27) are a much better parallel to Jesus' threefold ἐγώ εἰμι at the *arrest* (18:5, 6,

---

8. For discussions of this problem, see Schneider 1957, 116; Mahoney 1965, 137–44.

8), and the link back to the garden scene in 18:26 seems to confirm this connection. Jesus' confession in the garden defends his disciples (18:8), his "I am" saves their lives, even at the expense of his own, while Peter's "I am not" saves his own life but betrays his discipleship.

Why, then, does John interweave the denial scene with the interrogation? Why not simply group Peter's three denials together after the arrest, allowing his audience to make the connection clearly? The answer, it seems to me, lies with the high priest's opening question regarding Jesus' teaching and his disciples (18:19). Superficially this sounds rather banal until we realize, along with Wayne Meeks (1967, 60–61), that the high priest is drawing on the categories of the false prophet as condemned in Deut 13:1–5; 18:20: one who leads others astray (disciples) and falsely presumes to speak in God's name (teaching). Anyone familiar with Deuteronomy would understand the implication of the high priest's question, and the answer is not so much in Jesus' verbal response as in the interwoven story of Peter. At the precise moment that the high priest asks Jesus if he is a false prophet, we see his prophecy to Peter in 13:36–38 coming true. Jesus is clearly no false prophet, though his full identity will be made clear in the remainder of the scene.

It is often observed that, although bound throughout this exchange, Jesus' behavior is far from that of a common criminal: he is self-assured and speaks boldly and majestically to his high-priestly inquisitor. Like Wisdom in the Jewish Scriptures, Jesus has spoken openly in public places, inviting all to hear the message (Prov 8:2–3, 9:3; Wis 6:14, 16; Bar 3:37[38]). In a further christological link with the Prologue (John 1:1–18), Jesus' words echo those of God himself in Deutero-Isaiah,[9] reinforcing once again the unity between the Father and the Son. The high priest's attendant takes offense at Jesus, slaps him in the face, and asks if that is any manner in which to speak to the high priest (18:22).[10] The exchange invites readers to compare the two men and to see that the true ruler is not the high priest but the majestic figure of Jesus, who will not be intimidated but courageously speaks up for himself. Jesus has the last word in this encounter (18:20–21) and leaves as "the moral victor" (Haenchen 1970, 205). The high priest and his attendant, in contrast, are silenced.

On one level, this is a clear rejection of the truth and shows that the high priest falls under the condemnation of Jesus' words. All he can do is to send Jesus to Caiaphas, "high priest that year"—a designation that, though doubtless referring to that fateful year, may also be designed to underline the transitory nature of the office. Like the temple, the high priesthood has had its day, and its place in salvation has now been superseded by Jesus. John's silence regarding what hap-

---

9. LXX of Isa 45:18–19, also 48:16; noted by Brown 1994, 1:415 .

10. There is an allusion here to Exod 22:28 (which forbade cursing a ruler of the people) and perhaps also to Lam 3:30 and Isa 50:6.

pened in front of Caiaphas is surely not because he expects his audience to supply a Synoptic-style Sanhedrin trial or simply because of tradition. Rather, the reference to Caiaphas underlines the impotence of the high priest: whatever happened before him has no importance; the narrative gaze does not rest upon him. Faced with Jesus, the high priest loses his power and plays no further role in the story. Just as Jesus will later emerge as the true judge before Pilate, so he is the true high priest before Annas/Caiaphas.

All this, once again, fits perfectly with the rest of John's Gospel. The Evangelist continually juxtaposes Jesus alongside Jewish feasts and institutions, which are now fulfilled or transcended by his presence. So Jesus is the one who embodies the true meaning of the Sabbath (John 5), the Passover (John 6), Tabernacles (John 7–10), and Dedication (John 10–12). He transforms the water of Jewish purification into good wine (2:1–11), declares his body rather than the temple to be the site of true worship (2:19–22; 4:21–26), contrasts the bread of his body (presumably the Eucharist) with the manna given by Moses in the wilderness (6:25–65), claims priority and superiority over Abraham (8:56, 58), and dies as the new paschal lamb (1:29, 36; 19:14). What John is doing in this short interrogation scene, then, is bringing Jesus against yet another crucial Jewish institution—the high priest—and underlining, once more, Jesus' utter superiority. Everything Jewish Christians once looked to the high priest to achieve—intercession, sacrifice, reconciliation, cleansing, and forgiveness of sins—will now be accomplished through Christ.[11]

HISTORICAL REFLECTIONS

What does this say, then, about the historicity of the interrogation in front of the high priest? Just because something is theological, of course, does not in any way mean that it cannot also be historical (so Carson 1981, 104–7; Anderson 2007b, 2). John may have drawn theological meaning from actual historical events, or his theological agenda may have led him to present something that (perhaps unintentionally) turns out to be rather close to what happened. Yet as historians we need to be particularly wary of scenes (particularly uncorroborated ones) that exhibit a high degree of theology. Three elements in particular in the present scene are worth reflecting on.

The first is the setting: the quiet, ordered scene in which Jesus faces the supreme representative of "the Jews." We have noticed already that John likes to reduce scenes to a confrontation between Jesus and one other person. Is the setting, then, a historical reminiscence of a small preliminary interview or a Johannine creation in which Jesus faces the supreme representative of

---

11. For further connections between Jesus and the Jewish high priest in John, see Bond 2007.

"the Jews"? Similarly, the exchange takes place at night. Darkness and light are important dualistic motifs for this Evangelist, extending even to the settings of scenes. Nicodemus, a ruler of the Jews, and Judas operate at night; conversely, the Samaritan woman meets Jesus at noon (4:6; the appropriate hour in Greek thought for a theophany), and Jesus reveals his glory on the cross at the same time (19:14). When else, we might ask, would Jesus meet with the head of "the Jews" but at night? Even if John's tradition had Jesus interrogated the morning after his arrest (as in Luke), might not John have altered it to fit with his sense that the leader of "the Jews" could only function in the darkness?

Second is the presence of Annas. If what John wanted to do was to contrast Jesus with the Jewish high priest, why not introduce the most influential high priest of the first phase of Roman occupation—the founder of arguably the most significant priestly dynasty of the first century—the man we might call "the high priest par excellence"? Moreover, Annas may well have been infamous in Christian circles as the father of the high priest responsible for the swift removal of James, the leader of the Jerusalem church (a man also called Ananus; Josephus, *Ant.* 20.199–203); the very name, then, might well epitomize high-priestly animosity. Is it not curious that, although Annas was clearly well known to Luke (Luke 3:2; Acts 4:6), the Third Evangelist—despite a lengthy trial narrative—says nothing about Annas's involvement in Jesus' death?

Third, in a Gospel that delights in marriage imagery (Schneiders 1995, 356–57), why not explicitly connect Annas to Caiaphas ("high priest that year") through marriage? Surely it is strange that Josephus, who lauded Annas for his own high priesthood and that of his five sons (*Ant.* 20.198: "something that never happened before to any other of our high priests") forgot—or did not know—the connection between him and Caiaphas, the man who was probably in office at the time of Josephus's birth? Is it really credible that Josephus knew that Annas was the father of men who served for only a year or so (Eleazar, Jonathan, Matthias) but had no knowledge of the connection between him and the longest-serving high priest of the first century, a man who served for eighteen or nineteen years?

Of these three points, the second and third are the most problematic, though perhaps not insuperably so. Neither Mark nor Luke had any great interest in the identities of Jesus' Jewish opponents: Mark does not name "the high priest," and Luke omits him altogether (though Mark's nameless high priest will make an appearance as a literary device in Luke's trial of Stephen in Acts). Matthew did name the high priest, although it is uncertain whether this was a historical memory of Caiaphas's involvement or simply because, as a Jewish-Christian, Matthew knew that Caiaphas had been high priest at the time. There was, however, no role for Annas in the Markan presentation adopted by Matthew, so it is hardly surprising that he does not feature in the *dramatis personae*. The lack of corroboration of Annas's role at this point, then, is perhaps not as compelling as it may at first appear. On the matter of the relationship between Annas and

Caiaphas, it is worth noting that Josephus seems to have made use of lists of high priests, which he slotted into his narrative at appropriate points (Schwartz 1992, 212–13).[12] We cannot know how full these lists were; they may have mentioned important father-brother connections but not necessarily marital ties. Given that Josephus tells us very little about Caiaphas (or any other high priest, for that matter), his silence regarding Caiaphas's possible connection to Annas is not necessarily deafening.

Least problematic is our first consideration. The night-time setting clearly adds to John's theological presentation, but it is also corroborated by Mark's general outline (Luke probably relocated the Jewish hearing to the following morning so that it would form the first of a four-part trial before Jewish and Roman authorities). In 1 Cor 11:23, too, Paul recounts the tradition that Jesus was handed over at night. For a small ad hoc group of Jewish leaders (with or without Annas) to convene shortly after his arrest would not only make perfect sense, but it would also fit Josephus's contention that the "leading men" were instrumental in handing Jesus over to Pilate (*Ant.* 18.64).[13] It also, as we have seen, conforms to what we know of Jewish practice at the time. Despite the theology of the scene, then, the broad sequence of events may conform to what actually happened after Jesus' arrest.

The *content* of the scene is more difficult, but even here there may be elements of history that have not commonly been recognized. One such may be the matter of the charge—more specifically, the accusation—that Jesus was a "false prophet." Earlier in the Gospel the rather anachronistic sounding charges brought by "the Jews" are that Jesus claims to be the Christ and that he is a blasphemer (10:22–39, charges that appear again in a slightly different guise in the Roman trial, 18:33–38; 19:7–11). But if the reconstruction of the scene offered above has any merit, it is clear that the charge of being a false prophet was one that John wanted to counter, and it may well have been the actual charge against Jesus. B. Sanhedrin 43a, 107b has Jesus executed as a magician and a seducer of the people, that is, a false prophet, and a range of scholars (e.g., Wright 1996, 439–42) have, on quite different grounds, concluded that this—rather than the charge of blasphemy in Mark and Matthew—may have been the real accusation.

In conclusion, the *precise* course of events after Jesus' arrest is probably now irrecoverable. Our primary texts are such that it would be impossible to *prove* one narrative over another. What we can do, however, is to evaluate degrees of probability, and on this count, when it comes to Jesus before the high priest,

---

12. Josephus's summary of high priests in *Ant.* 20.224–251 may be drawn from such a list.

13. The authenticity of Josephus' *Testimonium Flavianum* (*Ant.* 18.63–64) is of course highly debated. A number of modern studies, however, have argued that, while the passage clearly shows signs of later Christian editorial work, the sentence regarding the involvement of the Jewish leaders may well be original; see Meier 1990; Carleton Paget 2001.

John's account performs relatively well. Despite the theology of his scene, the Fourth Evangelist's presentation of events does seem to possess a greater claim to historical accuracy than those of the Synoptic writers—though whether John had better traditions, a better sense of what commonly took place in such cases, or was (perhaps unconsciously) guided by his theological interests to present a scene that happened to cohere well with historical events is impossible to say.

SEE MY HANDS AND MY FEET:
FRESH LIGHT ON A JOHANNINE MIDRASH*

Jeffrey Paul Garcia

The unique quality of the Doubting Thomas pericope in the Gospel according to John is further distinguished by its preserving the only explicit reference to Jesus' nail wounds.

> But Thomas, who was called the Twin, one of the twelve, was not with them when Jesus came. So the other disciples told him, "We have seen the Lord." But he said to them, "Unless I see the mark of the *nails* in his hands, and put my finger in the mark of the *nails* and my hand in his side, I will not believe." A week later his disciples were again in the house, and Thomas was with them. Although the doors were shut, Jesus came and stood among them and said, "Peace be with you." Then he said to Thomas, "Put your finger here and see my hands. Reach out your hand and put it in my side. Do not doubt but believe." Thomas answered him, "My Lord and my God!" Jesus said to him, "Have you believed because you have seen me? Blessed are those who have not seen, and yet have come to believe. (John 20:24-29, emphasis added)

The Synoptic Gospels are silent regarding the use of nails or the wounds inflicted by them. Due to the common misreading of Jesus' postresurrection statement in Luke 24:39, "See my hands and my feet," John's creativity with the earlier accounts and his midrashic reworking have remained unnoticed. A critical assessment of the evidence for crucifixion in Judea during the Roman period will elucidate what was their method before and after the First Jewish Revolt (66–73 C.E.), as well as shed light on the Evangelist's re-presentation of Jesus' death according to a specific passage in the Hebrew Bible.

---

* For Santos Arroyo, אבי. I want to thank my professor and friend, Dr. R. Steven Notley, without whose encouragement, comments, and suggestions this study would not have come to fruition.

CRUCIFIXION IN THE BIBLE AND THE DEAD SEA SCROLLS

New Testament scholars have often read Jesus' statement in Luke 24:39, "See, my hands and my feet," as an implicit reference to the *stigmata* (see Hendriksen 2002, 1074; O'Collins 1999, 1:1209; Bock 1994, 2:1933; Fitzmyer 1985, 2:1576; Marshall 1978, 902; Plummer 1910, 559). Yet this interpretation conflicts with the context of the Lukan saying. Joel Green is correct to note that Jesus is offering "two proofs of his own materiality as evidence of his resurrected existence" (1997, 854; see also Nolland 1993, 1213). Jesus seeks *only* to dispel the disciples' fear that he might be a ghost (Luke 24:37).[1] "Touch me and see, *for a spirit does not have flesh and bones as you see that I have*" (ὅτι πνεῦμα σάρκα καὶ ὀστέα οὐκ ἔχει καθὼς ἐμὲ θεωρεῖτε ἔχοντα, 24:39). He further alleviates their incredulity by eating (ἔφαγεν "he ate") a piece of broiled fish in front of them (24:43). Thus, the presentation of his hands and feet is intended not as evidence of a particular method of crucifixion (i.e., with nails) but as a striking confirmation of his *bodily* resurrection.

The exact method of crucifixion is in fact not specified in the Gospel accounts. Although Martin Hengel (1977, 25) was right that the passion narratives are "the most detailed" of antiquity, the language employed by all the Evangelists is imprecise. The Greek verb σταυρόω ("to crucify"; Liddell, Scott, Jones 1996) does not specify the use of nails in crucifixion. The verbal derivative of σταυρός ("stake" or "cross") simply indicates that someone is somehow affixed to an upright stake. It should not be taken for granted, then, that the Greek term σταυρόω presupposes the use of nails. Clarifying the precise method of execution would be a matter of adding the qualifying verb προσηλόω ("to nail") or the prepositional phrase μετὰ ἥλους ("with nails"). The only time προσηλόω is found in the New Testament is on the lips of Paul, who speaks not of Jesus being nailed to the cross but rather of a *record of debt* (χειρόγραφον τοῖς δόγμασιν) that was charged against the church in Colossae (Col 2:14; *contra* Fitzmyer 1978, 508). Furthermore, neither in the Gospels nor in the rest of the New Testament—except for the Doubting Thomas account (John 20:25)—is the term ἧλος ("nail") used either in a generic sense or with specific reference to the crucifixion.

A closer look at the usage of σταυρόω in the Septuagint (LXX) is warranted here. The LXX translation of the book of Esther, the only composition to employ the term, sheds light on how the Greek verb was understood in the third century B.C.E. In the exilic narrative, Haman, enemy to the Jews and descendant of Agag the Amalekite (3:1), plots to have the Jews killed. After he fails, he is condemned by King Ahasuerus to be hung on the gallows (7:9, 10). For the translators of the Hebrew Bible, the king's command, "Hang him upon it [the gallows]" (σταυρωθήτω ἐπ' αὐτοῦ), seems to justify the use of σταυρόω. Yet it is κρεμάννυμι

---

1. Apparently, this was the understanding of a later scribe who inserted φάντασμα ("ghost," MS D) in 24:37, where other, more important manuscripts read πνεῦμα ("spirit").

("to hang up"; Bauer and Danker 1999, 941), not σταυρόω, that is utilized more often to describe execution by hanging (2:23; 5:14; 6:4; 7:10; 8:7; 9:13, 25). The verb finds a wide range of usage in the LXX, from the Deuteronomic decree to remove a "hung" corpse from a tree (Deut 21:22–23) to the Psalter's poetic imaginings (Ps 137:2). The synonymous use of both verbs indicates that σταυρόω was understood as execution by hanging, not nailing. Of course, σταυρόω, unlike κρεμάννυμι, denotes that the victim was hung on either a stake or a cross. Excluding the Greek additions to Esther (where σταυρόω is used again, but for which we have no Hebrew parallel), these Greek terms are always used to translate the Hebrew verb תלה ("to hang"; Koehler and Baumgartner 2000, 4:1738).

Evidence of the use of this Hebrew verb for crucifixion during the Hasmonean and Roman periods is attested in the Dead Sea Scrolls. Pesher Nahum, the Qumranic commentary on the biblical prophet (Nah 1:3–6; 2:12–3:14), preserves in a fragmented text a reference to the "Lion of Wrath" (כפיר החרון), who it is said "will hang men alive" (יתלה אנשים חיים; 4QpNah f3–4 i, 7–8). The pesher interprets Nah 2:12b, "he fills his cave with prey and his dwelling with torn flesh," as the "Lion of Wrath" who exacts vengeance "against the seekers of smooth things" (בדורשי החלקות) by hanging them alive. The qualifier "alive" or "living" is usually regarded as descriptive of an execution by hanging, perhaps crucifixion (see Berrin 2004, 165–92). While תלה should not be read unequivocally as referring to crucifixion, the prepositional phrase על העץ ("on the tree") in line 8 clarifies that the pesher text is speaking of crucifixion (see Zias and Charlesworth 1992, 277–78; Doudna 2001, 389–98). Scholars have read the "Lion of Wrath" as an allusion to the crucifixion of Pharisees under the orders of the Hasmonean monarch Alexander Yannai (Berrin 2004, 105; *contra* Doudna 2001, 627–37), a grizzly tale recounted by Josephus (*Ant.* 13.379–80).

The Temple Scroll (11QT), which possesses the Qumran congregation's halakah, provides the legal basis for having someone "hung on a tree" (i.e., crucified):

> If a man is a traitor against his people and gives them up to a foreign nation, so doing evil to his people, *you are to hang him on a tree until dead* [ותליתמה אותו על העץ וימת]. On the testimony of two or three witnesses he will be put to death, and they themselves shall hang him on the tree. If a man is convicted of a capital crime and flees to the nations, cursing his people and the children of Israel, *you are to hang him, also, upon a tree until dead* [ותליתמה גם אותו על העץ וימות]. (11QT lxiv 7–11)

While display of a body *after death* seemed to be common practice according to Deuteronomic and later rabbinic law (Deut 21:22; Berrin 2004, 170–71; see also Josh 8:27–29; Josephus, *Ant.* 4.202; m. Sanh. 6:4, b. Sanh. 46b), hanging someone "until dead" (וימת, line 11) was not. Execution by hanging (i.e., death occurs while the person is hanging, not prior) is a marked departure from both contemporary practice and later practice as stipulated by Israel's sages: "Four types of death penalty were handed over to the court: *stoning, burning, decapitation, strangulation*" (סְקִילָה שְׂרִיפָה הֶרֶג וְחֶנֶק; m. Sanh. 7:1). Baumgarten (1972) has questioned whether תלה in the scrolls is in fact a reference to crucifixion, and its use elsewhere should not be read as such; the verb must be defined by its context. Moreover, if the method of crucifixion involved the nailing of victims to a cross, one would expect to find the verb דקר ("to pierce"; see Zech 12:10) rather than תלה.[2]

The assumption that nailing was the primary method of crucifixion has unduly influenced the translation of several passages. Peter's speech after Pentecost references Jesus' crucifixion: "This man [Jesus], delivered over by the predetermined plan and foreknowledge of God, you *fastened* [προσπήξαντες] to a cross" (Acts 2:23, emphasis added). This is the only time the verb προσπήγνυμι ("to fasten" or "affix"; BDAG, 725) is used in the New Testament, and it is an unusual change from Luke's usual terminology.[3] It should be translated "to affix" or "to fasten to" (Fitzmyer 1998, 255), but *without* the implication of nails. Yet several English translations still render this verb "to nail" (see TNIV, NIV, NASB, NET, NCV).

Psalm 22 is either directly used or alluded to in the Gospels' depiction of the crucifixion (Matt 27:35, 46; Mark 15:24; Luke 23:34; John 19:24). The term כָּאֲרִי in Ps 22:16b (MT 17; 21:17 LXX), "a company of evildoers encircles me (כָּאֲרִי/ ὀρύσσω); my hands and feet have shriveled," has drawn the attention of scholars due to the different readings of the MT and LXX (see Swenson 2004; Strawn 2000; Kaltner 1998; Vall 1997). Early Christian interpreters read the Septuagintal rendering ὀρύσσω ("to dig" or "excavate") as piercing. An allusion to Ps 22:16b is found in the Epistle of Barnabas: "*Pierce my flesh with nails*, because a band of evildoers have risen against me" (5:13, emphasis added; see also Ignatius, *Smyr.* 1:1–2). To avoid the Christian apologetic use of this verse, the Hebrew text was pointed to read as a preposition and a noun: אֲרִי + כְּ ("like a lion"). While speculation continues, what is clear and commonly agreed upon is that neither the Hebrew nor the Greek text refers to piercing.

A scroll fragment that garnered much attention upon its discovery was the so-called "pierced messiah" text, which shares certain affinities with the War Rule (1QSM).

[... just as it is written in the book of] Isaiah the prophet, "And [the thickets of the forest] shall be cut down [with an ax, and Lebanon with its majestic trees

---

2. See Brad Young's (2006, esp. 194 n. 9) brief discussion on crucifixion in the Targumim.

3. The alternation between κρεμάννυμι and σταυρόω, which is witnessed in Esther, is also seen in Luke's Gospel. One of the criminals executed alongside Jesus is described as "hanging" on the cross, with the aorist of κρεμάννυμι (23:39), rather than the more common σταυρόω (23:33). The use of both Greek verbs suggests that Luke or his source(s) understood crucifixion as the act of hanging rather than nailing.

wil]l fall. A shoot shall come out from the stump of Jesse [and a branch shall grow out of his roots." This is the] Branch of David. Then [all forces of Belial] shall be judged, [and the king of the Kittim shall stand for judgment] and the Prince of the Congregation—the Bra[nch of David]—*will have him put to death* (והמיתו; DJD XXXVI, 239). [Then all Israel shall come out with timbrel]s and dancers.... (4Q285 f7, 1–6)

Eisenman and Wise initially interpreted the text as speaking about the death of a messianic prince, or as line 4 reads, the "Prince of the Congregation" (Vermes 1992, 81). The crux of the issue lies in how one reads the term והמיתו (*hemitu/hemito*) in line 4. "If read *hemitu*, the word could indicate the execution of the messianic figure. But if the reading is *hemito*, the verb would state that the messianic figure kills another male person" (Vermes 1992, 80). Eisenman and Wise's reading lead them to reconstruct line 5 to read "with wounds and stripes/piercings" (Vermes 1992, 81), and Eisenman (1993, 66) cited the suffering servant of Isa 53 as evidence that the slaying of a messianic figure was evoked elsewhere. Martin Abegg (1994, 87) convincingly argues, however, that according to the context of the tiny fragment, the messianic prince in line 4 should be understood as the one who is killing rather than being killed. The context of the Isaiah passage quoted in lines 1–3 "reveals that the Stem of Jesse 'will slay the wicked (ימית רשע) with the breath of his lips'" (Abegg 1994, 88). The "strokes and wounds" mentioned in line 5 of Eisenman and Wise's initial reconstruction can instead be restored to read "with timbrels and dancers" (בתופים ובמחוללות), in anticipation of the celebration of victory as preserved in the War Rule (Abegg 1994, 90; Schiffman 1995, 346). The linguistic evidence overwhelmingly indicates that the language for crucifixion in the scrolls, as well as the Hebrew Bible and the New Testament, is alluding to someone being hung from, rather than nailed to, a cross.

ARCHAEOLOGY AND HISTORY: THE CRUCIFIED MAN AND JOSEPHUS

Evidence for crucifixion as a form of execution outside of the New Testament is abundant, but our purposes here are narrowed to the practice within the confines of Judea before and during the First Jewish Revolt. If the Romans, from the time of their entry into Judea (63 B.C.E.), regularly employed nails during crucifixion, it finds no mention in the historical sources.[4] Both Paul Winter (1974, 95) and Joachim Jeremias (1966, 223) surmised that the crucifixion of Jesus was a bloodless act carried out with ropes. Yet it would seem that the discovery of a pierced heel bone from a burial cave in Giv'at ha-Mivtar contradicts Winter's and Jeremias's

---

4. However, there is evidence for nailing victims in a Pompeii inscription: *CIL* 4:2082, as quoted in Hengel 1977.

speculations. Of the ossuaries discovered there by archaeologist Vassilios Tzaferis, five contained the bones of individuals that bore "presumptive evidence of violent death" (Haas 1970, 43). One inscribed יהוחנן (Yehochanan) contained the remains of a small child and a man, presumably Yehochanan, whose heel(s) had been pierced by an iron nail (Hass 1970, 18; Tzaferis 1985, 44–53). Evidence for crucifixion was based solely on the nail that remained embedded in the heel bone (Tzaferis 1970, 31). It is unlikely that Tzaferis would have reached this conclusion if the nail had not been found. The only other marks of violence were "the comminuted tibiae and left fibula" (i.e., both the lower leg bones were severely splintered; Haas 1970, 51), which without the nail could be interpreted in any number of ways, since violence was no stranger to the land of Judea during the Roman period.

The two crucified men about whom we know the most, Jesus and Yehochanan, were both placed in burial caves. According to the Gospels, Joseph of Arimathea took Jesus' body and placed it in a new tomb (Matt 27:60; Luke 23:53). Yehochanan was secondarily interred in an ossuary, about a year after his death, and placed in a burial cave in a northern suburb of Jerusalem. It would then be reasonable to assume that petitions were made to the Romans in order to bury Jewish victims (see Josephus, *J. W.* 4.317), and in some cases the Romans obliged. But of all the excavated tombs from this period, only one has yielded evidence of crucifixion. This singular occurrence, which stands in contrast to the numerous ancient literary witnesses to crucifixion in Judea, indicates that nails were not used as widely as previously presumed. The contentions that nails were believed in antiquity to be powerful healing amulets (which they were; see m. Šabb. 6:10) or that they were used repeatedly due to the expense of their production are insufficient explanations. The remains of an individual who was nailed to a cross and then received a proper burial would still reflect the skeletal damage that corresponds to being pierced with nails. Apart from the bones of Yehochanan, which were found with a nail still attached, such evidence has yet to be presented.

Even with the discovery of the crucified man from Giv'at ha-Mivtar, the archaeological evidence for crucifixion is inadequate to determine its development. Josephus provides the literary-historical evidence for Roman crucifixion in Judea prior to and during the First Jewish Revolt. On almost every occasion when he speaks of crucifixion, he utilizes either σταυρόω (see *Ant.* 17.295) or ἀνασταυρόω ("to affix to the cross"; see *J. W.* 5.289). Hengel (1977, 24) notes that after the fifth century B.C.E., the verbs became synonymous with one another. On two occasions, however, Josephus substitutes his usual terminology with the more descriptive verb προσηλόω ("to nail").

In the tumultuous period leading to the revolt, Gessius Florus (64–66 C.E.) permitted his soldiers to sack Jerusalem's "Upper Market" and to kill anyone they encountered (Josephus, *J. W.* 2.305). The soldiers overran the Upper City, slaughtering its inhabitants. After scourging and crucifying many of the "peaceable citizens," Florus crucified men of the equestrian order:

The calamity was aggravated by the unprecedented character of the Romans' cruelty. For Florus ventured that day to do what none had ever done before, namely, to scourge before his tribunal and *nail* [προσηλόω] to the cross men of equestrian order, men who, if Jews by birth, were at least invested with the Roman dignity. (*J. W.* 2.308)

Josephus's unmistakable language shift from "crucifying" to "nailing" reflects part of Rome's "unprecedented character." Not only did Florus kill Jews who were Roman knights (Hengel 1977, 40); he compounded the tragedy by having them *nailed* to the cross. Prior to this occasion Josephus never deviates from σταυρόω and ἀνασταυρόω, yet here finds it necessary to describe crucifixion as being nailed: "The soldiers out of rage and hatred amused themselves by *nailing* [προσήλουν] their prisoners in different postures; and so great was their number, that space could not be found for the crosses nor crosses for the bodies" (*J. W.* 5.451). Josephus again opts to use προσηλόω. His linguistic switch is not one of synonymous words but reflects a new development in the method of crucifixion. It is not happenstance that the details of the revolt, and the period leading up to it, required a change in terminology that demonstrates the increased severity of crucifixion by the Roman soldiers. The use of προσηλόω signals a savage intensification of normal Roman practice within Judea. Otherwise, Josephus would have no need to distinguish his language.

To summarize, neither the Greek nor Hebrew verbs regularly used for crucifixion in the Second Temple period specify the use of nails. While the dating of the archaeological data is not precise, it belongs to the tumultuous period just before the revolt (Tzaferis 1970, 31). For Josephus, it would seem that σταυρόω and ἀνασταυρόω are insufficient means of expressing the use of nails during crucifixion. For this reason, he opts to use προσηλόω in order to describe Rome's cruel methods during the First Revolt, thus providing a historical attestation to a change in their method of execution nearly forty years after Jesus' death. Moreover, the use of σταυρόω, and the lack of any reference to nails in the Synoptic Gospels, suggest that Jesus was fastened to the cross with ropes.

THE JOHANNINE MIDRASH

What, then, are we to make of the Doubting Thomas account? Why does John introduce Jesus with nail wounds? Unraveling John's text involves understanding the Evangelist's creative exegesis of the Hebrew Bible. The Fourth Gospel records that soldiers came and broke the legs of those who hung alongside Jesus (19:32). Seeing that Jesus was already dead, the soldiers pierced his side (19:34). For John, these events are prophetic: "These things occurred so that the scripture might be fulfilled, 'None of his bones shall be broken.' And again another passage of scripture says, 'They will look on the one whom they have pierced'" (19:36–37). The citation of Zech 12:10 at the end of verse 37 and the piercing of Jesus' side are peculiar to John's Gospel. These unique elements of the crucifixion narrative consequently reveal the Evangelist's messianic understanding of the pierced figure in Zechariah and its fulfillment with Jesus' crucifixion.

The Doubting Thomas pericope is crafted to develop the unique Johannine messianic interpretation of Jesus as the pierced one of Zechariah. John's purpose with Thomas is not to specify the Roman method of crucifixion but creatively to rework the earlier Synoptic account, namely, Luke 24:36–43. The Fourth Evangelist's messianic understanding of the prophet and Luke's postresurrection appearance story are the driving forces behind John's portrayal of the doubting disciple.

Certain linguistic elements in the Thomas account signal which Synoptic narrative John is theologically reworking. In Luke's narrative, εἰρήνη ὑμῖν ("peace to you") is Jesus' greeting prior to presenting his hands and feet as evidence of the corporeality of his resurrection. Apart from this occasion, the Greek phrase is not found elsewhere in the Synoptics—at least not in Mark and Matthew; it is found in Luke 24:36. That John picks it up is evidenced in the three times Jesus employs it after his resurrection (20:19, 21, 26). Furthermore, along with his side wound, Jesus also reveals the wounds on his hands—a detail that is missing from his crucifixion account yet bears a striking similarity to Luke. The Johannine Jesus, with Luke, commands Thomas to see his hands. These linguistic components are unmistakable allusions:

- ▶ Luke 24:36, 39: εἰρήνη ὑμῖν ("Peace to you") / ἴδετε τὰς χεῖράς μου ("see [pl.] my hands")
- ▶ John 20:27: εἰρήνη ὑμῖν ("Peace to you") / ἴδε τὰς χεῖράς μου ("see [sg.] my hands")

Writing near the end of the first century, John also would have been aware of how the Jewish populace of Jerusalem was treated during the revolt, being nailed to crosses in different postures. These and other stories would undoubtedly have contributed to the Evangelist's description of crucifixion. Therefore, the unique elements of John's midrash are: (1) the utilization of Zech 12:10 as a messianic prooftext; (2) Luke's postresurrection narrative; and (3) the stories of Jewish crucifixion victims during the First Jewish Revolt.

John's theological rewriting of the earlier Gospel traditions is witnessed elsewhere in his Gospel. Scholars have wrestled with the differing chronologies for Jesus' final Passover celebration (Matson 2008, his essay in this volume; Sacchi 1992, 128–29; Miller 1983; Zeitlin 1932; Torrey 1931). Matthew, Mark, and Luke agree that Jesus celebrated a traditional Jewish Passover (Matt 26:17; Mark 14:12; Luke 22:15), while John places Jesus' last meal on the day prior ("Now before the feast of the Passover," John 13:1). Therefore, according to Johannine chronology, Jesus would have been crucified on Nisan 14, the day prescribed for the lamb to be sacrificed (Exod 12:6; m. Pes. 5:3, 5). The Fourth Evangelist's chronological modification likely reflects the early church tradition we find in Paul's writings: "For our paschal lamb, Christ, has been sacrificed" (1 Cor 5:7).

Should it be considered a coincidence that the evidence reviewed here for *nailing* victims to crosses in Judea all comes from decades *after* Jesus' crucifixion and just prior to the outbreak of the revolt? Furthermore, is it simply chance that John, who writes several years *after* the revolt, is the *only* Evangelist to portray Jesus with nail wounds? Surely not. His is the only Gospel to depict Jesus pierced on two separate occasions. The linguistic content of the Thomas account reveals which Synoptic narrative the Fourth Evangelist reworked (Luke's), while Josephus's linguistic variation indicates that nailing as a method of attachment to the cross was a development of a later period in Judea, that is, during the days of the First Jewish Revolt. Therefore, the Johannine midrash is a combination of unique elements that re-present Jesus' crucifixion according to the messianic interpretation of Zech 12:10. The atrocity perpetrated on the Jews for the first time during the revolt is where the Evangelist appropriates his departure from the Synoptic tradition. What is witnessed in the Fourth Gospel is a sophisticated interplay between exegesis and history. The layers of John's literary style are uncovered when one realizes that the details that comprise Jesus' encounter with Thomas are all intentional. They are meant to draw the reader's attention to Jesus' fulfillment of a messianic text, while also evoking the tragedy associated with witnessing a pierced victim of crucifixion.

The historicity of the Doubting Thomas account is a layered question. While it is clear that John is reworking an earlier Gospel narrative, thus not precisely recording a historical encounter with Thomas, his midrashic work is reflecting the interpretative history of the period in which he writes. A parallel interpretation of Zechariah is reflected in the Talmud (b. Sukkah 52b). Here the rabbis interpret the prophetic utterance as a reference to the Messiah ben Yoseph, who is to be slain in battle, thus ushering in the period of Messiah ben David. The death of the messianic figure seems to have developed early in the second century c.e. (Berger 1985, 143–48), not long after the Fourth Gospel was completed. John's midrash of Zechariah in the Doubting Thomas narrative is evidence that John utilized the creative interpretations of the Hebrew Bible that were developing to address the needs of the believing communities. The parallel interpretations likewise attest to the close contact that existed between the Jewish and Christian communities well after the destruction of the Temple (70 c.e.). The Thomas account's importance to the rest of the Fourth Gospel must not go understated. Uncovering the Evangelist's exegetical creativity raises important questions concerning his intentions when employing texts from the Hebrew Bible. Hopefully, this is the direction in which we are heading.

Peter's Rehabilitation (John 21:15–19) and the Adoption of Sinners: Remembering Jesus and Relecturing John*

Michael Labahn

John 21 may seem to be a surprising point of departure for a discussion about John and the historical Jesus.[1] Historical-critical scholarship, though challenged by conservative exegesis and/or by scholars using linguistic and narrative methods (e.g., Thyen 2005), still interprets John 21 as a later addition to the Gospel (e.g., Schnelle 2007a, 523–24). The judgment that John 21 has a secondary character is evident even in the more text-centered approaches of Francis Moloney (1998b, 545–47, 562–65) and Manfred Lang (1999, 294–95 n. 918).[2] So why take that chapter as a point of departure for raising the historical question with regard to the Gospel of John? I shall do so here because John 21 illustrates a number of key points concerning the narration of memories of the historical Jesus. As John 21 renarrates the older Johannine Jesus story, this chapter recalls "facts" about the historical Jesus in order to build new meaning and a new story through the repetition and variation of established themes.[3]

---

*My thanks are extended to Tom Thatcher for checking the English in this essay, to Felix Just for translating the German texts into English, and to the Katholische Universität Leuven for a travel grant that enabled my participation at the 2007 SBL Annual Meeting in San Diego.

1. On the use of the Gospel of John as a source for Jesus, see Smith 1993; Moloney 2000; Dunn 2003b, 165–67; and Anderson 2006b, who pleads for a more faithful approach in using the Gospel of John as a historical source in the search for the historical Jesus. While I do not deny that the Gospel of John may occasionally include significant information about the historical Jesus, I am focusing here on the information that is provided by the active memory of the Jesus communities. Note here Dunn's reference to "tradition [that] has been heavily worked upon *and* that is well rooted within earlier Jesus tradition" (2003b, 167). I would use the term "memory" here instead of "tradition."

2. "The addition of the appearance stories of 21:1–25 contradicts the storyteller's original narrative design" (Moloney 1998b, 564).

3. I borrow the terms "repetition and variation" here from Gilbert Van Belle's ongoing Leuven research project, "Repetitions and Variations in the Gospel of John" (see Van Belle, Labahn, and Maritz 2009)

MEMORIES OF JESUS: FACTS AND FICTIONS

In the popular rock ballad "Photograph" by the Canadian band Nickelback, Chad Kroeger sings about the experience of looking at pictures that evoke memories of a lost time.

> I miss that town
> I miss their faces
> You can't erase
> You can't replace it
> I miss it now
> I can't believe it
> So hard to stay
> Too hard to leave it
> If I could relive those days
> I know the one thing that would never change[4]

A song is a poem, and therefore a fictive text; sometimes, as here, it is a literary piece about things that have passed by. The song "Photograph" reflects on cherished events that human memory builds up from images of the past. The past is reviewed by the present, so that a new past is constructed by reorganizing memories and building a narrative from them that opens meaning in the present time. The songwriter even wonders at how he now misses the past things ("town" and "faces"). In the same way, it is important for any historical and exegetical approach to a text such as the Gospel of John to recall that narratives make sense out of memory by selecting and interpreting past facts (Goertz 2001, 24; Schröter 2007, 108).[5] Memory builds up the past and constructs meanings that evoke emotion, insight, and orientation in the present.

Jesus' public activity, with the meaning he communicated through his message that the kingdom of God was beginning in his words and deeds, made a lasting impression on those whom he addressed. Just as the imprint must always be distinguished from the original (Schröter 2007, 108–10), so the reception of an event is transformed in memory and renarration. This is true with regard both to Jesus himself and to those who keep his memory alive and communicate it to others. Each such communication is an attempt to create a new meaning, a meaning that takes over traditional material because its qualities are acknowl-

---

4. From the album *All the Right Reasons*, Roadrunner Records, 2005.

5. See Lorenz's observation, "Tatsachenaussagen sind immer bestimmte Interpretationen von Sachverhalten, in denen bestimmte Aspekte beleuchtet oder selektiert werden" (1997, 29: "Statements of fact are always particular interpretations of circumstances in which particular aspects are highlighted or selected").

edged—specifically, because it is acknowledged that traditions about the past can provide structure and orientation in the present.[6]

The search for the historical Jesus is mostly practiced as a search for so-called "facts." What happened first and last? What was said, what was done? Scholars search for events and for traditions that can be attributed directly to the figure that has been called, for a long time now, the "historical Jesus." However, this "historical" Jesus is none other than the one remembered by his earlier and later followers and opponents. The traditions about Jesus in early and late sources are nothing more nor less than pictures that keep the memories of Jesus meaningful in the present. There are very different pictures of Jesus even in the canonical Gospels, and even more in other early Christian texts where Jesus is remembered, including the Pauline texts and noncanonical documents. Such texts are "fictions" in the sense that each creates a narrative world of its own (see Assmann 1980, 14). This means that every draft of an interpretation of the Jesus event—whether literary or oral—is an interpretation with a significant distance from the historical event itself. Because this is the case, alternatives such as historical/nonhistorical and fact/fiction cannot assist us in the task of adequately describing the relationship between the remembered object and the actual past event (Schröter 2001, 6–36).

When the story of Jesus is told, the Jesus of history is present through narration. The facts are embedded in the traditions, memories, and interpretations. The latter are not without facts, but it is misleading to think that these facts could be safely and objectively distilled from their later interpretation by any historical method. In saying this, I do not advocate the application of a radical constructivism to Jesus research that might lead to a scientific agnosticism. For the sake of the present discussion, I assume that the available sources provide a good base to construct a plausible and broadly reliable picture of the Jesus of history. Nevertheless, such a picture remains a (re)construction that is open for scientific discussion on the basis of particular methods of analysis.[7] Therefore, even modern historians and exegetes establish different portraits of the Jesus of history due to their different methodological, historical, philosophical, and political presuppositions and their various starting points (see Witherington 1995a). The acknowledgment of these different presuppositions on interpretation has been viewed as the common sense of hermeneutics since Hans Georg Gadamer (1990, 270–311).

---

6. "Wäre da nicht das *Ereignis*, wir hätten nichts zu erzählen" (Moxter 2002, 67: "If the *event* did not happen, we would have no story to tell"). On the concept of the "construction of meaning" (*Sinnbildung*) from the perspective of New Testament exegesis, see Schnelle 2003, 11–18.

7. See here also John Meier's use of the term *reconstruction*, which for him establishes greater confidence in the character of the (re)construction of the Jesus of history (1991, 31).

With regard to the use of sources for the quest for the Jesus of history, even in later texts' motifs, aspects of his teaching, and stories of his work and deeds are remembered and retold. Even if the apparent plausibility of the Synoptic Gospels' records of the life of Jesus is supported by the fact that "they present the earliest narrative elaborations of the activity and destiny of Jesus, and at the same time possess a history-preserving character,"[8] it is also obvious that we must also listen to John, the narrator of the Johannine story of Jesus, and to his follower(s) who added John 21.

John 21 as a "Relecture" of John 1–20: Designing a New Story from Old Stories

Working from the perspective on memory outlined above, I shall now argue that John 21 is based on John 1–20 and retells aspects of the earlier narrated Johannine Jesus story.[9] In doing so, I first seek to demonstrate that John 21 is to be read primarily in relation to a previous story, not to "history," although of course this may not be a clear-cut alternative.

John 21 includes four distinct movements that fall into two major sections. The first section tells the story of the miraculous appearance of Jesus on the shore of the Lake of Tiberias (John 21:1–14). The second section (21:15–25), which builds on the narrative setting of the first, is about Peter, the Beloved Disciple, their relationship to Jesus, and the relationship of the Beloved Disciple to the Fourth Gospel. Each movement fills gaps that were left in the story of John 1–20. As such, the chapter should *not* be viewed, as older historical-critical exegesis has claimed, as foreign material written by a redactor who wanted to make the Gospel and its strange content usable and readable to the church. That kind of interpretation understands John 21 as late and secondary, added to the first and longest part of the narrative in order to deliberately correct or censure the older story. Here I shall offer a very different explanation of the relationship between this chapter and the remainder of the Gospel.

---

8. The Synoptic Gospels are documents that "die frühsten narrativen Verarbeitungen des Wirkens und Geschicks Jesu darstellen und zugleich einen historisch bewahrenden Charakter besitzen" (Schröter 2007, 106 n. 4).

9. "Die Endredaktion reiht sich in die ihr vorausgehende Traditionsfolge ein, indem sie die Interpretation weiterführt. Ihr Ziel ist es nicht, den ihr vorliegenden Text zu zerstören…, sondern ihn in Bezug auf die in der Schule betriebene theologische Arbeit und die auf der kirchlichen Ebene aufgetauchten Fragen zu rekontextualisieren" (Zumstein 2004d, 298: "The final redaction falls in line with the preceding development of tradition, in that it continues the process of interpretation. Its goal is not to destroy the previous text…, but rather to recontextualize it in view of the theological work of the Johannine School and the questions that arose in ecclesial contexts").

The Swiss scholar Jean Zumstein has offered a new approach to those parts of the Gospel of John that Rudolf Bultmann ascribed to a secondary *Kirchliche Redaktion* ("ecclesial redaction"), namely, the "second farewell discourse" (John 15–17) and the so-called "epilogue" (John 21).[10] Zumstein (2004b, 15–30) takes up a methodological approach that was previously used in Old Testament research called *"relecture."* Following this model, a new text rereads an older text and "writes it forth" (*Fortschreibung*). The material in the new text is not foreign to the older text; rather, it reads and transforms the older text, filling its gaps by giving new answers or by actualizing the previous text while correcting or adding new insights. *Relecture* is therefore not a source-critical method that seeks to ascribe texts to different hands, although in the case of John 21 it appears that the original author did not create the new text. *Relecture,* rather, describes the way that texts develop their thoughts by adding one text to another—the later text taking up the preceding one and accepting its basic setting and assumptions. The new text is intentionally based upon the older one and confirms its significance. This could well be the situation of John 21. John 20:30–31 forms the end of the earlier story, but a later reader, the author of John 21, filled narrative gaps, rescheduled subjects from the plot of John 1–20, and provided answers to questions that had arisen from the older story. This author is not a stranger to the Johannine narrative, but he *rereads* and *rewrites* the story.

The third appearance of Jesus to his disciples after his resurrection, as narrated in John 21, may well be read as a missionary commission, as symbolized in the miraculous catch of fish in 21:1–14 (see Söding 2002a, 209–10).[11] That is the hermeneutical frame into which the story of the rehabilitation of Peter (21:15–19) is integrated. In the earlier Gospel narrative, Peter failed by denying Jesus three times (18:17, 25–27), and he is not mentioned among those who stand beneath the cross (19:25). Yet, as if the Johannine narrative does not care about his denial any longer, John 20 portrays Peter as one of the first witnesses to the empty tomb, arriving there just after the Beloved Disciple (20:1–6). In view of this gap, any reader of John 20 may ask for more information about Peter's sin (see Lincoln 2005, 516; Claussen 2006, 66). Therefore, already John 21:7 (ἦν γὰρ γυμνός, καὶ ἔβαλεν ἑαυτὸν εἰς τὴν θάλασσαν—"for he was naked, and jumped into the sea") may refer to the shame of Peter's sin, which has been left unresolved in the preceding Johannine story (see Labahn 2006, 137; 2007b, 130; Zumstein 2004d, 310). It is up to a *relecture* of the Johannine story to clarify the relationships between

---

10. I have elsewhere taken this same approach to another passage widely ascribed to the "ecclesial redaction," John 6:51c–58, which I read as a sacramental *relecture* of the bread of life discourse earlier in the chapter (Labahn 2000, 76–78).

11. For a somewhat different reading see Culpepper 2006, who points to an "ecclesiological imagery" in John 21 that may include "the preaching mission."

Peter and Jesus, and also between Peter and the Beloved Disciple, who is presented as a privileged mediator in the earlier story (13:21–26; 18:15–16; 20:3–8).

Finally, the implied author of the book, who was not previously identified, is now revealed: the Beloved Disciple (21:24). As the many articles and books written on that figure attest, he remains a riddle, yet he was clearly an important character for the Johannine church, its tradition, and its Easter faith. John 21:20–24 thus clarifies several important points about that character's fate that were left unresolved in the earlier narrative.

If we accept that John 21 builds heavily on the gaps, open problems, and unanswered questions of John 1–20, we can see that it also directly borrows language, motifs, and stories from that pre-text. From a Leuven/Louvain perspective, it may be said that much of the John 21 material reflects "repetitions and variations."[12] In this case, the repetitions and variations are not limited to minor stylistic and linguistic features. The meal with the disciples in 21:12–15 is a repetition of the feeding of the multitude in John 6, as indicated by clear linguistic parallels.[13] The threefold question of Jesus addressed to Peter ("Do you love me?"), twice formulated ἀγαπᾷς με in 21:15–16, is changed to φιλεῖς με in 21:17. This is not only an adoption of the Fourth Gospel's technique of variation and repetition, but it also hints at and varies the threefold denial of Peter in the high priest's court (18:17, 25–27; see Neyrey 2007, 339). The reference to a "charcoal fire" (ἀνθρακιά) in 21:9 repeats a word from 18:18 that appears in the New Testament only in these two verses, preparing the reader for the encounter between Jesus and Peter in 21:15–19. The last verse of chapter 21 repeats the earlier ending at 20:30 by emphasizing the bulk of material about Jesus not included in this book. This repetition with variation also reminds the reader of the aim of the whole book without verbally repeating the words: the Gospel is written ἵνα πιστεύ[σ]ητε ὅτι Ἰησοῦς ἐστιν ὁ χριστὸς ὁ υἱὸς τοῦ θεοῦ, καὶ ἵνα πιστεύοντες ζωὴν ἔχητε ἐν τῷ ὀνόματι αὐτοῦ (20:31: "so that you may come to believe that Jesus is the Messiah, the Son of God, and that through believing you may have life in his name").

As shown above, much of the story of John 21 is closely related to John 1–20; indeed, many of the final chapter's ideas, words, and motifs are taken from John 1–20, perhaps with the exception of the story of the miraculous catch of

---

12. On repetition and variation as an element of Johannine style, see Van Belle 2005, 291–316; Van Belle and Maritz 2006, 337–38; Popp 2001.

13. John 21:13 (the bold is added to show the intertextual echoes and parallels): ἔρχεται Ἰησοῦς καὶ **λαμβάνει τὸν ἄρτον** καὶ **δίδωσιν** αὐτοῖς.

John 6:11: **ἔλαβεν** οὖν **τοὺς ἄρτους** ὁ Ἰησοῦς καὶ εὐχαριστήσας **διέδωκεν** τοῖς ἀνακειμένοις.

There are close links between John 21:1–14 and the entire context of John 1–20, and especially to John 6. See here Hasitschka 1999, 85–102; Malina and Rohrbaugh 1998, 288; Neirynck 1991, 604–5.

fish (21:1–14). Yet even that story is best explained as emerging from other pre-texts. Among other scholars, Frans Neirynck has argued that the author of John 21 has renarrated Luke 5:1–11 (1991, 605–9; see also, with different arguments, e.g., Blaskovic 1999, 83–87; Thyen 2005, 779). Although certain tensions in the text of the miraculous catch of fish point to the use of tradition, its source is not a primitive independent story about Jesus but a case of "secondary orality" (see Ong 1982) or "re-oralization" (Byrskog 2000, 138–44). As an interpretive model, secondary orality tries to understand the parallels and differences in words, plot, and structure between a written pre-text and later stories that are based on rec-ollections of that pre-text.[14] An approach to John 21 from the perspective of secondary orality suggests that the author of 21:1–14 has taken up a Johannine oral retelling of Luke 5:1–11 and renarrated this miracle story to support and strengthen the community's missionary activities (Labahn 2007b, 115–40).

My emphasis here on rereading, repeating and varying, and reusing tradition may suggest to some that one and the same author is responsible for John 21 and John 1–20. While this issue falls outside the aims of this paper, I judge it more likely that two separate authors were involved. The *hapax legomena*, words used only in John 21 but not in John 1–20, point in this direction (see the list in Brown 1966–70, 2:1079–80), as well as changes in the point of view of the narrator. Also, the fact that the book logically seems to end at 20:30–31 should not be quickly overlooked. In conclusion, I think it safe to say that the narrator of John 21 is part of the Johannine world of thought but is not the same as the author of John 1–20. His *relecture* is meant as a rewriting of the Johannine story.

A New Story Built on the Memory of an Old One:
The Adoption of Sinners into the Kingdom of God

Normally, a search for the Jesus of history entails a search for the so-called older/oldest traditions, which, it is supposed, may be separated from the literary sources and may refer to the most original form of memory. John 21 is concerned with the Johannine Jesus story and not so much with the historical Jesus. This fact must be kept in mind in asking what contribution John 21 can make to under-standing aspects of history in John and its portrait of the historical Jesus.

John 21:15–22: Re-adopting Peter

In the middle of John 21 we find an encounter between Jesus and Peter (21:15–

---

14. As, for example, in relating the Gospel of John to the Synoptic Gospels or understand-ing the evolution of the final text of the Gospel of John. For further discussion of secondary orality and the Gospels, see Labahn 1999, 195–96; 2000, 272–75; D. M. Smith 2001, 195–98; Williams 2007, 84–85.

19) that is based upon the narrative setting of the catch of fish scene (21:1–14). As mentioned earlier, this dialogue repeats, varies, and adds new implications to the denial of Jesus by Peter in the high priest's courtyard in John 18. Within the narrative flow of John 21, the recollection of John 18 is anticipated by the references to Peter's shame in 21:7 (being naked on the boat) and to the "charcoal fire" in 21:9. The short dialogue may suggest that Peter is becoming the shepherd of Jesus' flock (Schnelle 2004, 343; Talbert 1992, 260) and therefore stepping in some way into Jesus' role as the good shepherd (10:1–18). The interplay of the characters within the dialogue, however, suggests that John 21:15–19 is aiming first at another issue, the problem of Peter's denial, and then also at the evangelistic issue. Overall, then, "Peter will not be remembered as the one who betrayed Jesus but rather as the one to whom the risen Lord entrusted his followers" (Claussen 2006, 66). The dialogue answers still-open questions about Peter's failure and how to understand it by taking up and renarrating an aspect of the church's memory of Jesus: Jesus' adoption of sinners.

The narrator builds up an intimate scene, separating Jesus and Peter from the other disciples. Verse 15 explicitly mentions the end of the meal as a marker for the start of a new scene. Jesus then addresses Peter by his full name, "Simon son of John," so that the following question receives special weight: "Do you love me more than those others?" Peter replies, "You know, Lord, I love you." This confession is answered by the charge to shepherd Jesus' lambs. Up to this point, nothing in the discussion has referred to Peter's denial. It seems to be a dialogue about Peter's special future role or symbolic function as shepherd for the early Christian community in relation to other disciples, as indicated by πλέον τούτων ("more than these").

On the surface, 21:16–17 seems to add no new motifs—*if* one looks only at the immediate context but ignores its intratextual relationship. However, when viewed as a *relecture* of John 1–20, John 21 needs to be read against the background of the earlier Johannine Jesus story, which is also a story about his disciples. The remarks to follow will reflect this approach. Verse 16 repeats, as explicitly marked by the narrator's use of πάλιν δεύτερον ("again the second time"), Jesus' cheerful question. Now it comes to the surface of the story that the dialogue is not primarily about the charge to Peter to shepherd lambs, although this charge is repeated at the end of the verse. A somewhat different formulation of Jesus' question to Peter underscores that a problem is at hand, which may be found somewhere else in the Johannine narrative world. Jesus now simply asks, without reference to the other disciples, "Do you love me?"

When the question is raised for the third time (21:17), the reader has already been alerted that something special must be behind the discussion. Again, the narrator marks the question with τὸ τρίτον ("the third time"), which explicitly refers back to another threefold action: Peter's denials (see Lincoln 2005, 518; D. M. Smith 1999, 395). This time the question uses the other Johannine verb for "love" (φιλεῖς με; "Do you love me?"), but otherwise it simply repeats the content of 21:16. The change of verb does not imply a new meaning but rather is a stylistic variation (see Talbert 1992, 261; Lincoln 2005, 517), as there is also a change from τὰ ἀρνία μου ("my lambs," 21:15) to τὰ πρόβατά μου ("my sheep," 21:16, 17). In typically Johannine style, something already very evident is made explicit. Raising the question of one's love repeatedly offends any loving partner and leads to sorrow. This is exactly what the narrator now states: Peter felt sad because Jesus asked him for the third time, "Do you love me?" The exchange ends like the two verses before, but with Peter heightening the emphasis on Jesus' knowledge and showing that he has again come from denial into deep love, as is well known to Jesus and now also to the readers, who accept Peter as a shepherd. Peter's rehabilitation is thus complete.

In verses 18-19 the dialogue comes to an end with a reference to Peter's death, which seems only loosely connected to the preceding context because there is no verbal repetition and the logical progression is not obvious from the start. However, these two verses add a significant point to the themes developed in the dialogue in 21:15-17. Again, motifs and material from John 1-20 are taken up. In 12:32-33 Jesus refers to his own death on the cross, and there are sufficient verbal agreements between 12:32-34 and 21:18-19 to suggest a varied repetition of the announcement of the death of Peter, who, according to early Christian tradition also died on a cross (Acts of Peter 36-41; Tertullian, *Scorp.* 15.3; Eusebius, *Hist. eccl.* 2.25.8; 3.1.2).[15] Further, at John 13:38 Jesus challenges Peter's readiness to die for his master by the announcement of his threefold denial: "Will you lay down your life for me? Very truly, I tell you, before the cock crows, you will have denied me three times." In 21:18-19, then, the theme of Peter's death reappears.[16]

The inner logic of John 21:18-19, following 21:15-17, is that Peter will not only follow Jesus in his role as shepherd during his lifetime but will also become a good shepherd by imitating Jesus' death: "The good shepherd lays down his life for the sheep" (ὁ ποιμὴν ὁ καλὸς τὴν ψυχὴν αὐτοῦ τίθησιν ὑπὲρ τῶν προβάτων, 10:11). Peter's earlier willingness to die for his master ("I will lay down my life for you"; τὴν ψυχήν μου ὑπὲρ σοῦ θήσω, 13:37) will thus finally be fulfilled (see also Talbert 1992, 262), perhaps even implying a soteriological undertone regarding his community (see Zumstein 2004d, 308). John 21:18-19 interprets the phrase βόσκε τὰ ἀρνία μου ("Feed my lambs," 21:15) but also hints at the problem behind 21:15-17. Peter's new status is not, as Neyrey proposes (2007, 339), an indication

---

15. John 12:32-33: κἀγὼ ἐὰν ὑψωθῶ ἐκ τῆς γῆς, πάντας ἑλκύσω πρὸς ἐμαυτόν. τοῦτο δὲ ἔλεγεν σημαίνων ποίῳ θανάτῳ ἤμελλεν ἀποθνήσκειν.

John 21:19: τοῦτο δὲ εἶπεν σημαίνων ποίῳ θανάτῳ δοξάσει τὸν θεόν. καὶ τοῦτο εἰπὼν λέγει αὐτῷ· ἀκολούθει μοι.

16. On the interrelation of John 13:31-38 and 21:15-19, see van der Watt 2006, 42, who surprisingly does not discuss the relationship of John 21:15-19 to 18:15-17, 25-27.

of a new ability to "know the heart." Jesus' address to Peter is a rehabilitation of Peter after his denial, which could be called a forgiveness of the sin of denial and which is also shown in Peter's own death for his flock because of his faith in Jesus. He becomes a reliable follower and shepherd who is ready to die for his master. The result of rehabilitating Peter is that a former betrayer becomes a symbol of the later church leaders' responsibility for their community.

The Johannine technique of repetition and variation enables the narrator of John 21 to use his memories of the historical Jesus' adoption of sinners (see below) in solving a narrative problem in John 1–20. At the same time, the narrator establishes a new theme: the responsibility of church leaders for their community. Returning to the dialogue of 21:15–17, one recalls the threefold action of Peter in 18:17, 26–27, denying the Lord three times. In each instance, Peter is asked about his relationship to Jesus,[17] and each time he denies Jesus directly, or the narrator states the denial.[18] The second and third denials are not explicitly numbered in John 18, but they are marked as repeated actions, and the number is explicitly mentioned in the announcement of Peter's denial in 13:38 (ἀμὴν ἀμὴν λέγω σοι, οὐ μὴ ἀλέκτωρ φωνήσῃ ἕως οὗ ἀρνήσῃ με τρίς—"Very truly I tell you, before the cock crows, you will have denied me three times"). Jesus' three questions addressed to Peter in 21:15–17 follow the same pattern as those of the high priest's servants in chapter 18, and Peter's answers to Jesus represent his reply to his former denials. Peter loves Jesus and benefits from his new status as shepherd of Jesus' flock, yet only after being explicitly and dramatically reminded that he is the one who has denied Jesus.[19] Within the narrative flow, the dialogue moves between a failed Peter who knows his sin (cf. 21:7) and who returns to Jesus in love, and a betrayed Jesus who rehabilitates his disciple. Thus, Peter is marked as an outsider who was placed in the leading position, and the problem of Peter's failure in the denial sequence is answered by his threefold witness of love and Jesus' threefold commission.

In short, John 21:15–17 narrates how Jesus adopts the "sinner" Peter and gives him a new duty (see also 21:18–19). This development has not been anticipated earlier in John's Gospel—even the characters in John 5 and John 9 who are described with the terms "sin" (9:34, 41), "to sin" (5:14; 9:2, 3), and "sinner" (9:16, 24, 25, 31) provide no real parallel to Peter. Peter becomes a symbol that reminds community leaders that their position is based on love for Jesus and that it is

---

17. John 18:17: **μὴ καὶ σὺ ἐκ τῶν μαθητῶν εἶ** *τοῦ ἀνθρώπου τούτου;*

John 18:25: **μὴ καὶ σὺ ἐκ τῶν μαθητῶν** *αὐτοῦ* **εἶ;**

John 18:26: οὐκ ἐγώ σε εἶδον ἐν τῷ κήπῳ μετ᾽ αὐτοῦ;

18. John 18:17: **οὐκ εἰμί** / 18:25: **οὐκ εἰμί** / 18:27: πάλιν οὖν ἠρνήσατο Πέτρος.

19. "Ausgerechnet den, der in der Liebe zu seinem Herrn am meisten versagt hat, beruft der Auferstandene in seinen eigenen Hirtendienst" (Wilckens 1998, 327: "Of all people, the one who failed the worst in loving his Master is the one called by the Risen Lord to share in his own pastoral service").

received not by one's own honor but rather by the call of Jesus to faithful service. Such a duty is a responsibility that might even lead to death on behalf of the community and its Lord.

THE MEMORY OF JESUS ADOPTING SINNERS

Scholars have often been puzzled by the fact that the proclamation of God's kingdom, clearly a central activity for the historical Jesus, as evident from the Synoptic Gospels, is almost completely absent from the Gospel of John (see discussion in Kvalbein 2003, 215–32; Caragounis 2001, 125–34). The term βασιλεία τοῦ θεοῦ ("reign of God") is mentioned twice in John's Gospel (3:3–5), but in a slightly different sense from the portrait of Jesus' message in the Synoptics. Even in John, however, Jesus addresses people who lived on the margins of ancient Jewish society—the Samaritan woman (John 4), the paralyzed man (John 5), the man born blind (John 9)—and provides them with new hope and new life. In John 21:15–17, then, a basic aspect of Jesus' proclamation of God's kingdom is taken up and renarrated in a completely new and Johannine manner: the unconditional adoption of sinners into the kingdom of God.

While the issue cannot be explored in detail in an essay of this length, a number of scholars have suggested that Jesus in essence adopted sinners when he addressed the kingdom of God to marginalized people, poor people, and religious outsiders (see Dunn 2003b, 526–32; Holmén 2001, 200–220; Schnelle 2007b, 85–91; Zumstein 2004c, 91–94; Broer 1992). Jesus' behavior toward sinners is reflected in many Synoptic texts in different literary forms, including narratives and various types of sayings.[20]

Of basic importance here is Jesus' programmatic description of his mission in Mark 2:17b: "I have come to call not the righteous but sinners" (οὐκ ἦλθον καλέσαι δικαίους ἀλλὰ ἁμαρτωλούς; see Schnelle 2007b, 85). But what does this obligation entail? The famous and much-debated parable about a father and his two sons (Luke 15:11–32), which in my view could go back to the proclamation of the historical Jesus, illustrates the concept of adopting sinners into the kingdom of God. Within the narrative setting of this parable, a young man leaves his home, a step that is not inconsistent with the law and that reflects the economic situation of ancient Palestine (Pöhlmann 1979). However, the story later describes the young man losing the ground under his feet: "he squandered his property in dissolute living" (διεσκόρπισεν τὴν οὐσίαν αὐτοῦ ζῶν ἀσώτως, 15:13). In an economic crisis, the prodigal son remembers his father's house and returns to

---

20. See the sayings tradition (Matt 6:12 par.), including parables (Matt 18:23–30; Luke 15:4–7, 8–10, 11–32; 18:9–19), the miracle tradition (see Mark 2:1–12, esp. 2:5), the call to discipleship (Mark 2:14 par.), and the narrative tradition about Jesus' public meals with sinners (e.g., Mark 2:15–17 par.; see also Luke 7:36–50; 19:1–10).

it. Although neither the verb μετανοέω nor the noun μετάνοια appears, 15:18 describes some kind of repentance and an awareness of having sinned (ἥμαρτον εἰς τὸν οὐρανὸν καὶ ἐνώπιόν σου—"I have sinned against heaven and before you"), and in 15:19 the young man tells his father, "I am no longer worthy to be called your son" (οὐκέτι εἰμὶ ἄξιος κληθῆναι υἱός σου). The father opens his arms without condition (15:20) and sets the young man back into all his former rights as a son (15:22). Verses 18–19 are part of the young man's inner estimate of himself, while the direct confession of sin in 15:21 follows the father's acceptance. Jesus' special relationship to sinners seems to have been a problem in Christian proclamation, because opponents apparently grouped Jesus' community with "sinners"—he is, in fact, called "a friend of sinners" in Q (Matt 11:19 // Luke 7:34).

Of course, it is not possible to claim historical reliability for all or even most of the texts that reflect this theme. However, these texts reflect Jesus' adoption of sinners and thereby retell or renarrate elements of the memory of Jesus' activity. In sum, the broad range of these texts underscores Jesus' invitation to sinners and his offer to give them a new religious status if they follow his call into the kingdom of God and repent (Mark 1:15). By proclaiming the kingdom of God to outsiders, Jesus offered the possibility of a new beginning for those who otherwise would not have been able to establish a relationship with God. His blessings of the outsiders (see Matt 5:3–11; Luke 6:20–22) constituted a new relationship and provided a new status for the addressees.

According to the above reading of John 21:15–19, the memory that Jesus addressed his proclamation of the kingdom of God especially to the outsiders of society ("sinners") was still present in the community or communities behind the Fourth Gospel. The text of John 21, in rereading John 1–20, acknowledges the problem of Peter's failure and demonstrates awareness of his unresolved sin in his denial of Jesus (since failure to confess Jesus is a sin in the Johannine Gospel's message; see esp. 12:42–43). By recalling and reworking chapter 18, John 21:15–19 portrays Peter as a sinner or outsider who is addressed by Jesus. Thus, *John 21:15–19 clearly highlights an important aspect of the historical Jesus' proclamation of the kingdom in his words and deeds.*

CONCLUSION AND OUTLOOK

Building on the above observations, two conclusions may be drawn with regard to John 21 and the historical quest. First, the Johannine reception and renarration is a further witness for Jesus' behavior with regard to sinners and to their religious character as people who failed God's commandment. John 21:15–22 underscores the adoption of sinners by Jesus as that motif was available to be used in a new and different manner. The historical fact of Jesus' acceptance of religious and social outsiders is supported by John's Gospel and is mirrored in a fictional narrative (John 21) that builds up meaning for a new time and a new community.

Second, the reception further shows that the memory of Jesus was still open to creative renarration and was therefore still important, even for a community that reflected more on the *person* of Jesus than on his *proclamation* of the kingdom of God. A Johannine use of Jesus tradition would necessarily reflect Johannine language and thought. Therefore, Moody Smith's suggestion that the criterion of difference with Johannine Christology can be used for purposes of historical reconstruction appears to be very difficult to apply, in view of the permeation of the remembered material in the Fourth Gospel with Johannine themes (see D. M. Smith 1993, 256).

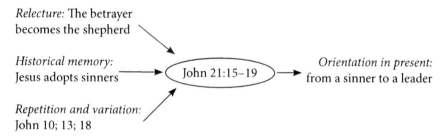

Relecture: The betrayer becomes the shepherd

Historical memory: Jesus adopts sinners → John 21:15–19 → *Orientation in present:* from a sinner to a leader

Repetition and variation: John 10; 13; 18

In sum, Zumstein's judgment that "the Johannine School did not have any direct access to the words and works of the historical Jesus" needs some reconsideration.[21] The Gospel of John is "a prime example for this process of re-narration and interpretation," as Zumstein notes,[22] of the public memory of Jesus that, going beyond Zumstein, is an effect of Jesus' activity and preaching and therefore represents historical memories.

Searching in early Christian texts for an understanding of Jesus' preaching and deeds is an expedition into renarrated memories and retold sayings. Embedded in memories, facts may have survived, and we can find these "facts" in new stories that no critical scholar may find historically reliable. However, scholarship dealing with the historical quest for Jesus must be open to different portraits and different kinds of renarration of Jesus, who was memorialized by a Johannine community for whom Christ was the center of belief and who dealt with their current situation by recalling relevant tradition.

Such an openness may not only read John 21:15–19 as evidence that the adoption of sinners was an important part of Jesus' preaching of the kingdom of God—a historical theme that remained alive in public Christian memory and ready to be renarrated—but it may also open the scholar's mind to other reflections about Jesus' proclamation and deeds in John's Gospel. One might refer, for

---

21. "[Z]war besass die johanneische Schule keinen direkten Zugang zu Verkündigung und Werk des historischen Jesus" (Zumstein 2004c, 100).

22. "[E]in Paradebeispiel für diese Wiederaufnahme und Interpretationsarbeit" (ibid.)

example, to Jesus' relationship to women, as reflected and renarrated in John 4:4–42 (see Ritt 1989, 287–306), and to the love commandment (John 5:42; 8:41–42; 14:15), which not only refers to Deut 6:4–6 (Labahn 2007a, 95–96) but also retells the story of God's love proclaimed by Jesus in his message of the kingdom of God (see Matt 5:44; Mark 12:28–34; see Labahn 2007a, 95–96; Schnelle 2006, 316–22). Especially the new commandment of Jesus in John 13:34–35 and the footwashing episode in John 13:1–15 may be read as a retelling or renarration of Jesus' ethical teaching. Overall, the search for a historical Jesus in the Fourth Gospel may not only open, in a limited manner, a door for new insights or corrections of constructions of Jesus based on the Synoptic Gospels; it may also, from time to time, give support to the Synoptic picture, while showing how the memory of Jesus remained alive and was renarrated in later communities who built up meaning for their present life based on their reliable experience with the memory of Jesus.

JOHN 21:24–25: THE JOHANNINE *SPHRAGIS*

R. Alan Culpepper

In *The Johannine School* (Culpepper 1975), I examined John 21:24–25 for clues to the composition history and setting of the Fourth Gospel. In *John the Son of Zebedee* (Culpepper 1994), I studied it in the context of the growth of the tradition and legends about John. In this essay, I propose to look at its function in providing closure for the Gospel. The focus of this paper was prompted in particular by Howard M. Jackson and Richard Bauckham, who have recently offered readings of the last two verses of John that call for a reappraisal of their testimony to the Gospel's authorship and its relation to historical tradition.

1. Recent Reappraisals of John 21:24–25

In an article entitled, "Ancient Self-Referential Conventions and Their Implications for the Authorship and Integrity of the Gospel of John," Howard M. Jackson (1999) asks: What ancient literary forms have appendices as a normative feature? He points to subliterary archival documents, papyrus texts including various sorts of formally registered public documents (contracts, deeds, wills, affidavits, etc.) that have a "subscription" (ὑπογραφή) adjoined to them. "Because such documents were drawn up by a public notary, they required the immediate suffixion of a supplemental section, consisting regularly of a brief summary and a signature, to tie declaratory parties personally and directly to the content of the body of the document" (Jackson 1999, 3–4). This literary convention spread from strictly documentary and purely juridical documents to the personal letter in the form of a postscript from the sender. Jackson concludes that "John 21 shares a sufficient number of characteristics in common both with the documentary subscription and the epistolary postscript to encourage the view that it was modeled after them and was intended to serve a similar purpose" (1999, 5). John 21:24 is therefore "a documentary ὑπογραφή ... a deposition of eyewitness testimony."[1]

---

[1]. Jackson (1999, 509 n. 8) affirms the work of Schenk 1992 but says Schenk confused the ὑπογραφή with a συγραφή.

Jackson continues: "John 21:24a also represents the signature and the statement of autography demanded of principals in the documentary subscription and common in epistolary postscripts (e.g., Gal. 6:11; Col. 4:18; 2 Thess. 3:17; Philem. 19)" (1999, 6). However, in John autography is claimed for the whole document, not just for the subscription.

Armed with these observations regarding the use of documentary subscriptions, Jackson offers the following interpretation of the "we" and "I" in John 21:24–25:

> The shift from the third person subject of γράφειν in verse 24 to the first person implied for γράφειν in verse 25 does not necessarily imply a change of subject, still less a redactional addition, as many have claimed.... The shift to the first person singular in verse 25 is explicable on the grounds of a shift from the one subgenre to the other, from the solemn, formal posture demanded of the documentary subscription being followed as a model in verse 24a to the more informal, familiar tone, characteristic of the epistolary postscript, evident in verse 25. (Jackson 1999, 8)

Jackson rejects the view that John 21 must be a later addition to the Gospel and that 21:23 presupposes the death of the Beloved Disciple (1999, 9, 21). The first-person plural in 21:24 "is best taken as an associative collective, where the 'you' is subsumed under the 'we' as the author's loyal Christian audience addressed directly in 19:35 and 20:31, the same audience as that addressed for the same reason by the same writer in 1 John" (1999, 23–24).

Moreover, Jackson rejects Kümmel's judgment that it is utterly inconceivable that the third-person singular in 21:24b is a self-reference, claiming that "authors of John's own time and culture regularly employed the third person singular self-referentially" (Jackson 1999, 24). Citing passages from Herodotus, Thucydides, and Xenophon, Jackson observes,

> If authors wished to have their readers accept as reliable and accurate any narrative of real events to which they had been eyewitnesses or in which they had themselves participated—i.e., historiographical narratives—it behooved them, then, to avoid the first person. It was for this reason that ... it became correspondingly *de rigueur* for writers of formal histories, or of personal reports or memoirs meant to be used by historians..., to adopt the detached persona of a third (i.e., different) person in referring to themselves in autobiographical contexts. (1999, 25)

One further move completes Jackson's argument. He claims that is "extremely unlikely that this 'title' [Beloved Disciple] ... is anything *other* than a self-designation," which the Evangelist chose to further his anti-Docetic agenda, because it emphasizes "his emotional and physical closeness to the earthly, fleshly Jesus" (1999, 31). The net gain of Jackson's work is that "all obstacles in the way of taking John 21:24 at its word and holding the Beloved Disciple to be the author of the

Gospel of John are removed" (1999, 33), and therefore the ancient narrative has a "high probability of historical accuracy" (1999, 34).

Richard Bauckham builds on Jackson's work in his *Jesus and the Eyewitnesses: The Gospels as Eyewitness Testimony* (2006). He agrees with Jackson that "these things" in 21:24 refers to the contents of the Gospel and that 21:24 claims that it was written by the Beloved Disciple himself. John 20:30–31 and 21:24–25 frame 21:1–23 and indicate "its status as an epilogue" (Bauckham 2006, 364). This "carefully designed two-stage disclosure of the Beloved Disciple's role in the production of the Gospel" moves from "are written" in 20:30–31 to "wrote" (2006, 366). Rejecting the alternative interpretations of the first-person plural, Bauckham contends that the "we" is not a genuine plural but stands for "I," calling it an example of "the 'we' of authoritative testimony" (2006, 370)—a substitute for "I" to give added force to the self-reference (2006, 371–72).[2]

Having concluded that the "we" and the "I" are synonymous, Bauckham argues that the "we" and the third-person reference to "the disciple who is testifying to these things and has written them" (the Beloved Disciple) are also synonymous. He offers the following justification for the change from the third-person reference to the Beloved Disciple to the first-person plural:

> The same person, the writer, speaks of himself first as "the disciple who is testifying to these things." This third person reference is necessary to make the transition from the narrative (up to 21:23) in which he had appeared as a character in the third person. Then, now revealed as the author and directly addressing his readers, he switches to the first person. He uses the first person plural ("we know") because this is Johannine idiom when solemnly claiming the authority of testimony. Finally, he uses the first person singular ("I suppose") as the natural way to address his readers when it is no longer a matter of solemn testimony. Awkward as these shifts seem to us, they are readily intelligible once we recognize the idiomatic "we" of authoritative testimony. (Bauckham 2006, 380)

In effect, Bauckham interprets John 21:24–25 as saying "I am the Beloved Disciple in the narrative, and I have written these things, and I know that my testimony is true." We must ask, therefore, how credible the readings offered by Jackson and Bauckham are.

2. Closure in the Other Gospels

John alone among the Gospels ends with a paratextual statement about the composition of the Gospel and its credibility. The writers of Matthew and Mark make no statement at the beginning or end of their respective Gospels claiming to give

---

2. Bauckham cites James Moulton, who claimed "examples from late Greek literature and from papyrus letters, which prove beyond all possible doubt that *I* and *we* chased each other throughout these documents without rhyme or reason" (Moulton 1908, 86, citing Dick 1900).

their own eyewitness account or that of another (Guelich 1989, xxix). Luke and John differ from the other two Gospels in that they contain self-referential statements, Luke in a prologue, John at the end. The prologue to Luke has often been identified as a statement that follows the conventions of historical writing, conditioning the reader to accept the narrative that follows as the work of a competent and reliable historian. Luke knows the tradition reaching back to "eyewitnesses and servants of the word," he has spent time "investigating everything carefully," he proposes to write an "orderly account," and he composes the account for the "most excellent Theophilus" so that he "may know the truth" about Jesus and the rise of the early church. Similarities as well as differences between Luke 1:1–4 and John 21:24–25 are obvious and instructive: (1) Luke refers to other accounts, which presumably served as sources; John does not; (2) both appeal to eyewitness tradition; (3) John identifies the eyewitness; Luke does not; (4) Luke has investigated carefully; the writer of the closing verses in John claims a personal knowledge of the tradition, if not of the eyewitness; (5) Luke speaks of the Gospel as an "orderly account"; John refers only to "these things" and speaks of "this book" and "the books" that could be written; (6) both assure the truth of what is written therein; (7) Luke names his patron or intended reader; John does not; and (8) John claims knowledge of other elements of the tradition that are not written in the Gospel; Luke does not.

Two other comparisons can be made, depending on whether one follows the conventional reading of John's last verses or that proposed by Jackson and Bauckham: (1) Luke speaks of the book(s) he was about to write; the scribe in John speaks of the book another person has written and books that might be written; (2) John appeals to the validation of others through the first-person plural, "we"; Luke does not.

The Gospel of John alone among the New Testament Gospels, therefore, appends a brief statement following the closing scene of the Gospel. John is also unique among the four Gospels in claiming to be the testimony of a particular eyewitness and in identifying that witness. As a literary addition to the Gospel genre, John 21:24–25 raises a variety of questions, including how these verses relate to the other closural devices in John and how they would have been understood in the first century. We turn therefore to the devices of closure in ancient literature.

3. The Mechanics of Closure

Writing on the "patterns of closure in ancient narrative," Massimo Fusillo found that the endings of ancient novels can be analyzed in terms of four elements: (1) *succession*, "a proleptic reference to the future of the story beyond the limits of the novel"; (2) *duration* of the closing scene or summary; (3) *perspective*, "i.e., whether or not we conclude with a character's point of view"; and (4) *voice*, "whether a narrator or character is speaking" (Fusillo 1997, 211). Of particular concern for the analysis of John 21:24–25 is the use and varieties of paratextual endings in ancient writings. Fusillo summarized Gérard Genette's definition of *paratext* as "the borderland of titles, subtitles, intertitles, epigraphs, prefaces, dedications, commentaries, and interviews" (Fusillo 1997, 211, citing Genette 1987; see also Estes 2008, 122). Unfortunately, Genette did not offer an analysis of paratexts as closural devices.

The paratext was typically incorporated into the text as part of the narration (Fusillo 1997, 211), and ancient novels often used paratextual devices to give a sense of historiographic authenticity to the fiction (212). Various types of closural statements and paratexts are relevant for understanding the ending of John, but it is also true that the following categories overlap because some paratexts serve multiple functions.

3.1. EXPLICIT

An *explicit* states that the narrative has ended:

- ▸ "So I will here end my story.… And here will be the end." (2 Macc 15:37, 39)
- ▸ "There you have, Philocrates, as I promised, my narrative." (Letter of Aristeas 322; *OTP* 2:34)
- ▸ "Here ends (the book) of Isaiah the prophet with his ascension." (Martyrdom and Ascension of Isaiah 11:43; *OTP* 2:176)
- ▸ "That is my story about Callirhoe." (Chariton, *Chaereas and Callirhoe* 8.8; Reardon 1989, 124)
- ▸ "Here ends the story of Apollonius." (The Story of Apollonius King of Tyre 51)

"An Ethiopian Story" by Heliodorus has an *explicit* that reveals the narrator-author's birthplace, his family, and, with the very last word, his name: "So concludes the *aithiopika*, the story of Theagenes and Charikleia, the work of a Phoenician from the city of Emesa, one of the clan of Descendants of the Sun, Theodosios's son, Heliodoros" (10.41; Reardon 1989, 588).

3.2. INCIPIT

An *incipit* affirms the narrator as a witness in historiographic and novelistic writings (Estes 2008, 122 n. 146):

- ▸ "I was his daughter-in-law and I was of his blood. The first things happened to him and all the latter things have been revealed, so let all these things from my mouth be accounted true." (Sibylline Oracles 3:827–829; *OTP* 1:380)
- ▸ "These are the revelations which Adam made known to Seth his son,

and his son taught his seed about them." (Apocalypse of Adam 7:17; *OTP* 1:719)

► "And I Nereus, his brother, with the seven male children accompanied by the poor and the orphans and all the helpless, we were weeping and saying...." (Testament of Job 53:1; *OTP* 1:868)

► "For this reason I have written out this, my testament, in order that those who hear might pray about, and pay attention to, the last things and not to the first things, in order that they might finally find grace forever. Amen." (Testament of Solomon 26:8; *OTP* 1:987)

► "I also saw there something like an invisible cloud.... And I have recounted in the books all their blessings.... Here ends the Revelation of the Secrets of Enoch." (1 En. 108:4, 10, 15; *OTP* 1:88–89)

► In addition, the Book of Thomas the Contender begins, "The secret words that the savior spoke to Judas Thomas which I, even I Mathaias, wrote down, while I was walking, listening to them speak with one another." (138.1–4; Robinson 1988, 201)

The first part of John 21:24—"This is the disciple who is testifying to these things and has written about them"—is an *incipit*, similar to the statements listed above, but what of the rest of the verse, which certifies the truthfulness of the Beloved Disciple's testimony?

3.3. Integrity Formula

An *integrity formula* assured the accuracy and truthfulness of the preceding account and at times warned the reader that its text was inviolable. David Aune found that integrity formulas were widely used in ancient writings:

► "in the OT wisdom settings, where it functions to protect the integrity of the divine instructions that have been transmitted by tradition" (Aune 1998, 1209): "Every word of God proves true.... Do not add to his words, or else he will rebuke you, and you will be found a liar." (Prov 30:5–6; see also Sir 18:6; 42:21)

► "at the conclusion of ancient treaties, where it has a juridical function: 'To this tablet I did not add a word nor did I take one out' is a statement found in a Hittite treaty" (Aune 1998, 1209).

► "in the writings of a number of Greco-Roman historians who use it to affirm accuracy in the use of sources and facts (...), though this did not really mean slavish accuracy" (Aune 1998, 1212): Dionysius of Halicarnassus describes the objective of the ancient historians as follows: "They all had the same aim: to make generally known the traditions of the past as they found them preserved in local monuments and religious and secular records in the various tribal and urban centres, without adding to or subtracting from them." (*On Thucydides* 5, cf. 16; LCL 1:473)

Following this review, Aune drew seven conclusions that are sufficiently relevant to warrant quoting in full:

> A consideration of all the pagan, Jewish, and Christian uses of the integrity formula discussed above leads to the following conclusions: (1) The integrity formula was so widely diffused throughout the ancient world that it would have been immediately comprehensible to people of diverse languages and cultures. (2) It was used either to guarantee that a text had not been tampered with or (when coupled with a curse) to prevent a text from being altered in any way. (3) In most instances, the integrity formula was used in conjunction with a sacred tradition, sacred text, or divine revelation, though it occasionally had other applications such as protecting the integrity of treaties. (4) The integrity formula implies that the text or tradition in connection with which it is used is *complete, definitive, and incapable of improvement*. (5) The integrity formula occurs with some frequency in the writings of Hellenistic historians to guarantee the accuracy of their use of sources. (6) Structurally, the integrity formula is generally placed at the beginning or conclusion of a text since such formulas usually have a metatextual character; that is, they describe the text to which they are attached. (7) In the case of John's [the Seer] use of the integrity formula, the author is not claiming canonical status for his book, i.e., equal status with the literature of the OT (against Windisch…), though he does appear to be giving it the status of a divine revelation that must be safeguarded from any alteration. (Aune 1998, 1212–13)

An interesting variation of the integrity formula occurs in the Letter of Aristeas, when after the Greek translation of the Hebrew scriptures was read the priests declared,

> Since this version has been made rightly and reverently, and in every respect accurately, it is good that this should remain exactly so, and that there should be no revision. There was general approval of what they said, and they commanded that a curse should be laid, as was their custom, on anyone who should alter the version by any addition or change to any part of the written text, or any deletion either. (Letter of Aristeas 310–311; *OTP* 2:33)

3.4. POSTSCRIPT

Ancient letters often closed with a *postscript* certification of authenticity (Jackson 1999, 6):

- ▶ "See what large letters I make when I am writing in my own hand." (Gal 6:11)
- ▶ "I, Paul, write this greeting with my own hand." (Col 4:18)

- ▶ "I, Paul, write this greeting with my own hand. This is the mark in every letter of mine; it is the way I write." (2 Thess 3:17)
- ▶ "I, Paul, am writing this with my own hand." (Phlm 19)

3.5. LIST OF WITNESSES

Legal documents typically listed witnesses at the end of the document, and in some instances a nonlegal document adopted this device.

- ▶ "When a man becomes surety, let him give the security in a distinct form, acknowledging the whole transaction in a written document, and in the presence of not less than three witnesses if the sum be under a thousand drachmae, and of not less than five witnesses if the sum be above a thousand drachmae." (Plato, *Laws* 12.953; Jowett 1937, 2:688)
- ▶ "Plato made a famous remark (*he* must be produced in the role of witness now that I am about to close) that it is trifles men buy with their lives. [The passage of Plato is otherwise unknown.] Yes, my friend Lucilius, if you judge rightly the madness of these people—that is, ours, for we wallow in the same herd—you will laugh all the more when you consider that things are acquired for living which are the very things for which life is destroyed." (Seneca, *Natural Questions* 5.18.16; LCL)
- ▶ "To-day a man was talking to me about a priesthood of Augustus. I say to him, 'Man, drop the matter; you will be spending a great deal to no purpose.' 'But,' says he, 'those who draw up deeds of sale will inscribe my name.'" (Epictetus 1.19.26; LCL 1:135; see also 1:136–37 n. 1)

Often, the first witness to sign was named the *syngraphophylax* (συγγραφωφύλαξ), which meant that he was the keeper of the contract (Grenfell 1902, 1:462; see also P. Petrie [Flinders Petrie Papyri] II.21 (d) 7–9, cited by Grenfell 1902, 1:450). Examples may be found in the Tebtunis papyri 104.34–35 and 105.53–54 (Grenfell 1902, 1:451, 458; Keener 2003, 1241, cites other examples). The editor describes the document: "The contract is endorsed on the *verso*, and below are the names of the contracting parties and of the six witnesses, arranged in four groups. Between the first and the last pair of groups was a clay seal, and beneath the seals passed the threads with which the roll was fastened up" (Grenfell 1902, 1:449–50).

3.6. COLOPHON

A *colophon* is a scribal addition at the end of a manuscript that typically attests to its origin or authenticity. In documents that were composed in stages, the distinction between a colophon and other paratexts depends on whether the scribe was also an editor or redactor. Esther is the only book in the Jewish canon whose Greek translation has a colophon. Addition F to the Greek version of Esther provides the date of the translation (ca. 114 B.C.E.) and the name and place of the translator (Moore 1977, 251–52; see also Bickerman 1944, 339–44).

> In the fourth year of the reign of Ptolemy and Cleopatra, Dositheus, who said that he was a priest and a Levite, and his son Ptolemy brought to Egypt the preceding Letter about Purim, which they said was authentic and had been translated by Lysimachus son of Ptolemy, one of the residents of Jerusalem. (Esther [Greek], Addition F, 11:1, NRSV)

E. J. Bickerman observed that "the concern with the pedigree of a manuscript appears whenever the authorship of a book or of a reading was challenged" (1944, 342). For example, "when Aulus Gellius quotes a variant reading in the Georgics (II, 246), he points out that his authority is a manuscript 'from the home and the family of Virgil'" (Bickerman 1944, 342, citing Gellius, *Noctes Atticae* 1.21.2; LCL 1:95). Similarly, when Origen quotes Symmachus, he states that he received the book from one Juliana, who inherited it from the author himself (Eusebius, *Hist. eccl.* 6.17; LCL 2:55). An extended colophon at the conclusion of the Martyrdom of Polycarp traces the early history of the document:

> Gaius transcribed these things from the papers of Irenaeus, a disciple of Polycarp; he also lived in the same city as Irenaeus. And I, Socrates, have written these things in Corinth from the copies made by Gaius. May grace be with everyone. And I, Pionius, then sought out these things and produced a copy from the one mentioned above, in accordance with a revelation of the blessed Polycarp, who showed it to me, as I will explain in what follows. And I gathered these papers together when they were nearly worn out by age, so that the Lord Jesus Christ may gather me together with his chosen ones into his heavenly kingdom. (Martyrdom of Polycarp 22; Ehrman 2003, 1:397–99)

3.7. SPHRAGIS

Signet rings were used to seal ancient documents and identify the author or sender through the imprint of his ring in the wax seal (Rev 5:1). Dionysius of Halicarnassus, for example, reports the following: "and when he [Brutus] found those [letters] written by his sons, each of which he recognized by the seals [σφραγίσιν], and, after he had broken the seals, by the handwriting, he first ordered both letters to be read by the secretary in the hearing of all who were present" (*Roman Antiquities* 5.8; LCL 3:23–25). The seal then became a metaphor for a validating paratext. Ancient poets and modern literary critics use the term *sphragis* (σφραγίς) or seal to refer to poetry at the end of a song that asserts the excellence of the song by "highlighting the skill of the poet, the tradition behind him, or the prestigious origin of the genre" (Rutherford 1997, 46). P. H. Schrijvers (1973, 149) observed that a *sphragis* in a strict sense ought to contain the name of the author,[3] but the term has come to be used more generally for validating paratexts. A *sphragis*, therefore, typically identifies the author and certifies the authenticity of the document or its contents (Carlson 2005, 54–56). The *sphragis* in Theognis of Megara, *Elegiae* 1.19–20, often serves as the classic example of this device: κύρνε, σοφιζομένωι μὲν ἐμοὶ σφρηγὶς ἐπικείσθω τοῖς δ' ἔπεσιν ("Cyrnus, let a seal I devise be laid upon these words"; Young 1971). The validating function of the closural *sphragis* in Pindar's odes is usually only implied. The *sphragis* in *Nemean* 8.48–53 is a notable exception, in that it speaks of the song and its origin:

> I am glad to cast a fitting vaunt upon your accomplishment, and many a man has with healing songs made even hard toil painless. Yes, truly the hymn of victory existed long ago, even before that strife arose between Adrastos and the Kadmeians. (Pindar, LCL 93)

Sphragides are not confined to the end of songs, however. Book 3 of the Sibylline Oracles contains the following *sphragis*:

> I who am a prophetess of the great God.
> For he did not reveal to me what he had revealed before to my parents
> but what happened first, these things my father told me,
> and God put all of the future in my mind
> so that I prophesy both future and former things
> and tell them to mortals.... so let all these things from my mouth be accounted true. (3:818–29; *OTP* 1:380)

The Book of Thomas the Contender 138.1–3 provides another example:

> The obscure sayings that the savior uttered to Jude Thomas, and which I, Mathaias, also wrote down. I used to travel and listen to them as they were talking to one another. (Layton 1987, 403)

Dionysius of Halicarnassus assures his reader:

> I could have written an essay on Thucydides which would have given you more pleasure than this one does, my good Quintus Aelius Tubero, but not one which was more in accordance with the facts. (*On Thucydides* 55; LCL 1:633)

It is worth noting that the verb σφραγίζω occurs twice in the Gospel of John,

---

3. Schrijvers cites E. Frankel 1957, 362–63: "On connait dans littérature ancienne l'usage assez répandu de 'sceller' le poème (et également le recueil) par voie de renseignements autobiographiques que le poète fournit sur lui-même a la fin d'un poème ou d'un recueil. La propriété littéraire est, pour ainsi dire, établie á l'intérieur de l'ouvrage littéraire en question.... la *sphragis* au sens strict du mot doit contenir le nom de l'auteur."

once in 3:32–33, "He testifies to what he has seen and heard, yet no one accepts his testimony. Whoever has accepted his testimony has certified [ἐσφραγίζειν] this, that God is true"; and once in 6:27, "For it is on him that God the Father has set his seal [ἐσφραγίζειν]."[4]

This review of closural statements allows us to analyze the form and function of John 21:24–25 in the context of paratexts at the end of other ancient writings. These verses do not state that the end of the Gospel has been reached, as do the *explicits* cited above. Like the *incipits*, however, John 21:24a affirms the role of the narrator/Beloved Disciple as a witness to the events recorded. In contrast to the *integrity formulas*, John 21:24–25 affirms the truthfulness and credibility of the Gospel account, not the authority or inviolability of its textual form. The question follows: Why was it necessary to affirm the truthfulness of the Beloved Disciple's witness so forcefully? *Postscripts* offer a variation on John's paratextual affirmation of authenticity, as do *lists of witnesses*, but the Gospel is neither a letter nor a legal document. The closing verses appeal to those who can certify its veracity, but they are not identified by name. Similarly, although the last two verses of the Gospel may be written by another hand, they are more like an *incipit* or *sphragis* than a *colophon* added by a copyist. Of the various closural statements, therefore, the *sphragis* offers the most appropriate parallels. John 21:24–25 does not contain the name of the author, but it does contain a reference to him through the epithet, "the disciple whom Jesus loved" (see 21:20). More significantly, John's closing verses fulfill the validating function of a *sphragis* by connecting the Gospel to an authorizing tradition and an authoritative eyewitness who was, they affirm, the author of the Gospel. We are ready, then, to examine the function of John's closing verses as a literary seal.

4. JOHN 21:24–25 AS A LITERARY SEAL

The Gospel of John develops a strong closure. In John 20 the risen Lord appears to Mary Magdalene and the disciples and fulfills promises he had made in the Farewell Discourse by sending them out just as the Father had sent him, conferring the Holy Spirit on them, and granting them authority in the forgiveness of sins (20:21–23). A week later the risen Lord appears again to the disciples (including Thomas), addresses the skepticism of Thomas, and pronounces a beatitude on all who would come later and believe without seeing (20:26–29). The statement of purpose at the end of this chapter recognizes that Jesus "did many other signs," makes reference to what is "written in this book," and states the purpose for writing the Gospel, making reference to the reader: "so that you may believe" (20:30–31). John 21 continues the crafting of closure by symbolically depicting the evangelistic mission of the church through the narrative of the

---

4. In the book of Revelation the verb occurs in 7:3–8; 10:4; 20:3; 22:10 and the noun in 5:1–9 *passim*; 6:1–12 *passim*; 7:2; 8:1; 9:4.

great catch of fish (21:1–14), resolving Peter's role through his threefold commissioning as a shepherd and an allusion to his death as a martyr (21:15–19), and resolving the misunderstanding surrounding the death of the Beloved Disciple (21:20–23). Jesus calls Peter to discipleship ("follow me," 21:19), evoking Jesus' calling of the disciples at the beginning of the Gospel ("follow me," 1:43, said to Philip). John therefore uses resolution of conflicts, completion of narrative gaps, prolepsis of events in the narrative future, reports of the deaths of the principal characters, and literary inclusios to develop a strong sense of closure.

The *sphragis* (21:24–25) completes the construction of closure by identifying the Beloved Disciple as the author, labeling the narrative as testimony, and reporting that the author's fellow believers certify that his testimony is true. The last verse returns to the earlier acknowledgement that there are other things that might have been reported that are not written (see 20:30) and closes with the first-person reference and the hyperbole, "I suppose that the world itself could not contain the books that would be written" (21:25).

What is obvious often goes unstated but is nevertheless significant. In contrast to the integrity formula in Rev 22:18–19, the concern here is not with the possibility that others may add to or take away from the Gospel narrative but that its report of Jesus' ministry, while selective, is true. The reasons for this concern are not stated and hence may only be inferred from the narrative itself, but both the labeling of the narrative as testimony (*martyria*) and the certification "we know that his testimony is true" (21:24) address the authenticity or truthfulness of the Gospel's account of Jesus.

We may now return to Bauckham's argument that in John 21:24–25 the author is identifying himself as the Beloved Disciple and speaking more formally in the first-person plural in verse 24 before reverting to the first-person singular in the more informal statement in verse 25. I believe the conventional reading of these verses is preferable for five reasons.

1. It is unlikely that readers would understand that "this disciple," "we," and "I" in the scope of these two verses all refer to the author. The history of interpretation itself shows how few readers have understood that there are not three persons or groups here but only one. Andrew T. Lincoln rightly contends that "the verse is more naturally read as making a distinction between the Beloved Disciple and his witness and the narratorial 'we' who are confirming that witness as true" (Lincoln 2002, 11).

2. Jackson and Bauckham are forced to interpret "the disciple whom Jesus loved" as an epithet chosen by the author so that he can write about his own role in the narrative in the third person rather than a title or honorary reference.[5]

---

5. Bauckham 2006, 400–401, claims that the argument that the author would not have been so presumptuous as to call himself "the disciple Jesus loved" "presupposes too modern a concept of appropriate modesty." "Howard Jackson is surely correct in concluding that it was

3. Contrary to Bauckham's interpretation (2006, 381), the "we" in John 1:14 can hardly be a "'we' of authoritative testimony" because the rest of the verse refers to the incarnate Word's dwelling "among us." The first-person plural references in the Gospel (3:11) are more naturally taken at face value as references to the author and those with whom he is associated—in context the Johannine community. Similarly, the author of 1 John speaks on behalf of the community (1:1–4, 5–10; 5:18–20), even in saying "we are writing these things so that our joy may be complete" (1:4), but he typically uses the first-person singular when referring to writing the epistle (1 John 2:1, 7, 8, 21, 26; 5:13, 16). Nevertheless, the first-person plural reference in John 21:24 has a meaning in context distinctive from its meaning elsewhere in the Gospel. The first-person plural in John 1:14, coming as it does in the opening verses of the Gospel, is open to various understandings. It may mean that "we" human beings have beheld God's glory. If one asks, which human beings, the context suggests "those who believed in his name," to whom Jesus "gave authority to become children of God" (1:12). It does not specifically mean the Johannine community at the time the Gospel was written. In contrast, the "we" in John 21:24 has precisely that meaning; it cannot mean all believers.

4. The law of two witnesses dictates that a Gospel cannot conclude with the author's testimony to himself. John's Gospel repeatedly appeals to the principle that one's testimony must be confirmed by the testimony of another (8:17). One witness testifies to the truth of another, and his testimony fulfills the requirement that a testimony be affirmed by two witnesses. John 21:24 is the final expression of the trial motif in the Fourth Gospel.[6] Jesus declares, "If I testify to myself, my testimony is not true" (5:31), and the Pharisees later respond, "You are testifying on your own behalf; your testimony is not valid" (8:13). The pattern in the Johannine writings is that multiple witnesses certify that Jesus' testimony is true. Verse 12 of 3 John offers an instructive parallel to the Johannine Gospel's *sphragis*. In 3 John the elder writes mostly in the first-person singular (vv. 1, 2, 3, 4, 9, 10, 13, 14) but uses the first-person plural when certifying Demetrius's truthfulness. Verse 12 makes four statements: (1) "*everyone* has testified favorably about Demetrius, and (2) so has the truth itself. (3) We also testify for him, and (4) you know that our testimony is true." The elder uses the first-person plural in references to testimony, presumably because it is important that the testimony be certified by more than one witness. Raymond Brown rejects the suggestion that "we" means "I" in 3 John 12, saying, "More likely the 'we' has the same sense as the 'us' in vv. 9–10,

---

not a title used by others but precisely a self-designation adopted by the author of the Gospel specifically for the purpose of referring to himself in his own narrative" (401–402, citing Jackson 1999, 31).

6. While Andrew Lincoln correctly asserts the function of 21:24–25 in relation to the trial motif in John, it does not necessarily follow that the paratext does not also function "as ordinary eyewitnessing that indicates the historical accuracy of the narrative's discourse." See Lincoln 2002, 10.

namely, the Presbyter speaking as a member of the Johannine School," so "III John 12d shows that the School of disciples related to the Beloved Disciple applied to themselves the claim of truth originally made for him" (Brown 1982, 724). Stephen Smalley agrees: "The first person plural in this part of the sentence … signifies the community of Johannine Christians.… The entire circle around the elder can vouch for Demetrius" (Smalley 1984, 362). Bauckham (2006, 372) responds that it is difficult to take the "us" in verses 9 and 10 as different from "the brothers" in verse 10, the traveling missionaries associated with the elder, and the "we" of verse 12 must be different from the "all" earlier in that verse. The syntax of the Johannine Epistles is notoriously problematic, and these verses are difficult on any reading. Nevertheless, it is clear that the elder is being emphatic about Demetrius's truthfulness, and his emphatic tone leads him to make repetitious assertions and adduce not only his own authority, which he is reticent to assert given the community's ecclesiology, but the authority of the entire community. Hence, he appeals to "our" authority (the authority of the community that he represents) in verse 9 and the offense of not receiving the brothers in verse 10. Verse 12 then affirms that Demetrius has the testimony of "all," the truth itself, and "we also testify for him." The verse follows an ABA pattern so that the latter part restates the first part. The elder makes his point emphatically (see a similar pattern in John 1:20, "he confessed, he did not deny, but confessed"). The witness of the community is true.

5. The relationship between John 21:24 and 19:35 shows that the "we" of the community voice supplies the needed second witness. In 19:35, the narrator speaks in an explicit comment or narrative aside: "(He who saw this has testified so that you also may believe. His testimony is true, and *that one* [ἐκεῖνος] knows that his testimony is true)." Is "that one" Jesus, God, or the eyewitness himself? Brown (1966–70, 2:936–37) and Schnackenburg (1982, 3:290) convincingly argue that the most natural reading is to take ἐκεῖνος as the eyewitness, presumably the Beloved Disciple. Bauckham agrees, adding that the verse "illustrates that, at least for some of the most important elements in the Beloved Disciple's testimony, there is no one other than himself who can vouch for the true of his witness. In both 19:35 and 21:24 all he can do is to solemnly aver that his testimony is true. Other people cannot corroborate this; they can only believe it" (2006, 380). In that case the Gospel would rest on only a single witness and hence would be open to challenge. Jackson recognizes the problem and therefore adopts the unlikely view that the ἐκεῖνος in 19:35 refers to Jesus because "the author's testimony by itself is not valid to establish his veracity" (1999, 32–33). I agree with his rationale but not his forced reading of ἐκεῖνος. The challenge the final editor of the Fourth Gospel faced is that the Gospel before him was vulnerable to the charge that it rested solely on the testimony of a single eyewitness: the Beloved Disciple, the eyewitness of 19:35. Regardless of how credible his testimony might be, without further corroboration his account would be suspect. The final editor solved this dilemma by adding the paratext in which he not only appeals to the Beloved Disciple's testimony but asserts that the community of believers who know that

disciple knows that his testimony is true. The Gospel rests not on one witness but on the testimony of a whole community. As Lincoln observes: "the last word about the epistemic status of the Gospel's testimony underscores not the Beloved Disciple's knowledge but that of the present community: 'we know that his testimony is true' " (2002, 24; see also 2000, 157, 172).

The Johannine *sphragis* implies a set of relationships. The writer is a member of a group ("we") who were sufficiently closely related to the Beloved Disciple to certify the truth of his Gospel. The intended readers, however, do not share in that relationship. On the other hand, the intended readers know who the "we" are and presumably will accept their certification. If this is a fair description of the implied relationships, it may help us to understand the setting more clearly. The challenge, then, is to discern the intended readers who would have needed the validation the *sphragis* provides and yet would have known those (the "we") who speak for the testimony of the Beloved Disciple. It is possible that the Gospel originally circulated within a community that knew the Beloved Disciple and then was edited (at which time some of the narrative asides, explanations, translations, and interpretations may have been added) and circulated to readers outside the community or set of Johannine communities. This new audience would not have known the Beloved Disciple and may have needed the kind of certification provided by the *sphragis*. On the other hand, would readers outside the Johannine community (or communities) have known the "we" so that the editor would not have needed to identify the group for which he speaks? Another possibility is that the editor who added the *sphragis* was writing as a member of the Johannine school and that he was addressing the rest of the Johannine community. Accordingly, after the death of the Beloved Disciple, the final editor prepared the Gospel for a new generation of members of the Johannine community (or communities), who would have known those who had been associated with the Beloved Disciple (the "we" of 21:24b) and would have respected their authority, even though by this time other Gospels, offering other interpretations of Jesus, may have made their way to the Johannine community.[7]

My argument, therefore, is that John 21:24 serves as a *sphragis*, a literary seal or certification of authenticity, in which the editor, speaking on behalf of the Johannine school affirms the truthfulness of the community's Gospel. The editor of the Gospel affirms that the conventions of good historiography have been followed, that the Gospel is based on the testimony of a reliable eyewitness, and that its account of Jesus' life is therefore credible. Such a certification may have been needed in part because the Beloved Disciple had died and other accounts or traditions that diverged from the Gospel were becoming known to the community.

---

7. I am grateful to John Painter, with whom I have had many conversations about John across the years, for helping me to define the views expressed in this paragraph.

Lucian of Samosata famously observed: "Facts are not to be collected at haphazard, but with careful, laborious, repeated investigation; when possible, a man should have been present and seen for himself; failing that, he should prefer the disinterested account, selecting the informants least likely to diminish or magnify from partiality" (*The Way to Write History* 47). Of such a historian it could be said, "he was truth all through" (61; Fowler and Fowler 1905, 2:131). Luke is not the only historian among the Evangelists. The final editor of the Fourth Gospel also knows how to establish the credibility of his narrative. Whereas Luke talked with "eyewitnesses and ministers of the word" and wrote an orderly account, the Gospel of John was written by an eyewitness himself, and its veracity was attested by the community around him (Thatcher 2006, 43–49). John's "history" is distinctively different from Luke's, however, in that instead of merely insisting on the accuracy of his report, John regards history as enlightened understanding of the events that transpired. John bears witness to a tradition that interpreted the historical events as they were remembered after the resurrection, in light of the scriptures, and through the guidance of the Spirit (see 2:22; 12:16; 20:9). For John history does not consist of a chronicle of historical data but the understanding of the events that exposed their true significance as the Beloved Disciple had come to understand it. In validating the significance of the subjective, John's Gospel is far ahead of its time. For our immediate purposes, however, John's recognition that the history that is being recorded is an interpreted history makes it all the more important that the credibility of the interpreter be certified by the community for whom and from whom he speaks.[8] Such history cannot be confirmed or documented by objective means; one can only testify to it. The Beloved Disciple, therefore, bore witness, and the Johannine school affirmed that his witness was true.

5. Epilogue

As an epilogue to this paper about an epilogue, I share the delightful experience of hearing Robert McDuffie, Distinguished University Professor of Violin at Mercer University, perform at the Kennedy Center in Washington, D.C., in fall 2007. The program concluded with "The Time Gallery" by Paul Moravec, a gifted contemporary composer. The program notes for the concert indicated that the piece concludes with an epilogue, "a commentary on the rest of the composition," in which all of the principal themes of the composition return, including the B-A-C-H [B-flat, A, C, B-natural] motif, which the composer included as a tribute to J. S. Bach, who has been described as "the spectator of all musical time and existence, to whom it is not of the smallest importance whether a thing be old or new, so long as it is true" (Rodda 2007, citing Clark 1969, 226).

---

8. See my comments on the construction of credibility in Culpepper 1983, 48–49.

ASPECTS OF HISTORICITY IN JOHN 13–21: A RESPONSE

Gail R. O'Day

The eight essays in part 3 focus on John 13–21. Two essays are on John 13 (Clark-Soles, van Os), two on John 18 and 19 (Bond, Matson), one on John 20 (Garcia), two on John 21 (Labahn, Culpepper), and one is an overview essay (Burridge).

These essays can also be grouped according to the basic orientation with which the authors approach the question of historicity. Four of the essays approach the topic of historicity from the perspective of the historical plausibility of events narrated in Fourth Gospel (Clark-Soles, Garcia, Bond, Matson). The other four essays take as their starting point questions of genre—the Gospel genre in general as well as subgenres in the Fourth Gospel (van Os, Culpepper, Labahn, Burridge). The essays in this second group are concerned with historical questions, but the decisive factors for determining (and defining) historical plausibility are at the level of the Fourth Gospel text and its history, not events in the life of Jesus. These two approaches to the question of John, Jesus, and history are not completely distinct—the essays in the first group attend to questions of genre, and the essays in the second group attend to questions of historical plausibility—but there is a significant and noticeable difference in methodological emphasis and governing presuppositions between the two groups of essays.

I begin with an overview of the four essays in group one, then turn to the essays in group two. I provide a brief summary of the key points and issues in each essay, but my main focus is to identify methodological issues and questions that move beyond each individual essay to the topic of John and the historical Jesus more generally.

GROUP ONE: THE HISTORICAL PLAUSIBILITY OF JOHANNINE DEPICTIONS OF THE HISTORICAL JESUS

Jaime Clark-Soles's "John 13: Of Foot Washing and History" takes the quest for the historical Jesus as its point of departure for investigating aspects of historicity in John. This can be seen in the essay's guiding question: Is it historically plausible that Jesus washed the feet of the disciples? Clark-Soles answers this question affirmatively, then examines what the act might have meant to the historical Jesus when he performed the footwashing.

Clark-Soles frames the conversation by addressing the ways in which traditional scholarly "quests for the historical Jesus," especially third-questers and the Jesus Seminar, are prejudiced against the Gospel of John in all dimensions of their work—from the utilization of criteria of historical plausibility to the very generation of these criteria. Because these criteria and their application are predetermined against finding historical plausibility in distinctly Johannine data, one must take another approach. Building from the work of Mark Chancey and Paul Anderson, Clark-Soles reads Jesus' life from the perspective of what would be historically plausible to posit of a first-century Galilean Jew (Chancey) as recorded in a tradition that has a Palestinian origin (Anderson). Read in this light, the footwashing can be taken as a historically plausible act by a first-century Palestinian Jew. To further support her thesis, Clark-Soles identifies a range of meanings that a first-century Jew might have attached to footwashing (purity, honor, friendship, sacrificial love). This set of possible meanings can be explained by Judaism without recourse to Hellenistic influence, a further indication that footwashing is a plausible first-century Jewish practice.

A signal contribution of this essay is its presentation of the footwashing as a plausible act in the ministry of Jesus. By cutting through presuppositions that almost by definition remove this act from consideration as an act practiced by Jesus during his ministry, Clark-Soles creates a new space for a conversation about the historical Jesus. By locating the historical Jesus in first-century Galilean Judaism and by showing that the footwashing had precedent in Jewish scriptural tradition and practice, Clark-Soles positions the footwashing within the range of things that the historical Jesus could have done. The historical Jesus is freed from constraints that remove this particular act from consideration as part of his ministry, so that a new dimension of the historical Jesus can be considered.

To make the case in the way she does, however, Clark-Soles has to separate the deed per se, the footwashing, from the interpretations given to it in the narrative of the Fourth Gospel. For Clark-Soles, the Evangelist and multiple successive communities reinterpreted the act, associating additional meanings with the act of footwashing (for Clark-Soles, these meanings are characterized by their "Hellenizing" tendencies). Clark-Soles assesses and evaluates a range of possible meanings for the footwashing, from historically likely or plausible to less likely, but the criteria by which she makes these assessments are not as clearly framed as those by which she establishes that the footwashing is a plausible act for a first-century Jew. For example, at the conclusion of the essay, she talks about the coherence between the Jesus who performs the footwashing and Jesus as a wisdom figure. This observation highlights an important dimension of Jesus in the Fourth Gospel and points to another way in which the Fourth Gospel can enrich historical Jesus conversations. Yet the very category of wisdom works against the Jewish/Hellenistic divide to which Clark-Soles seems drawn.

There is a gain to looking at the act of footwashing separate from its interpretation; the footwashing can be studied alongside, for example, other acts of table fellowship that are recorded in Jesus' ministry or other occasions when Jesus follows customs known in first-century Judaism. When the footwashing is fitted into a pattern of first-century Jewish life, the contours of the ministry of the historical Jesus expand. There is a cost to this approach as well, however, because Clark-Soles separates out the various interpretations and meanings that have accrued around the footwashing in ways that the Gospel narrative does not support. The various plausible meanings that Clark-Soles identifies (a fellowship meal, love, friendship, servanthood, and role reversal) are not as distinct or discrete in the storytelling of the Gospel as Clark-Soles seems to suggest. The determination of historical plausibility on the basis of the act of footwashing in isolation minimizes the significance of the placement of this act in the Gospel genre and of the storytelling of the Fourth Evangelist.

Jeffrey Paul Garcia's "See My Hands and My Feet: Fresh Light on a Johannine Midrash" takes a quite different approach to the question of historical plausibility. This essay takes one detail—the reference to nails in John 20:25—to assess John's historical reliability. The reference to "midrash" in the essay's title suggests that Garcia is primarily concerned with John's interpretive method, but the basic question that drives the essay is whether the reference to nails in John 20:25 constitutes reliable evidence that Jesus was nailed to the cross during the crucifixion. For Garcia, in the end, John's interpretive method ("midrash") is in conflict with any claims that can be made about the historical plausibility of John.

To make his case, Garcia reviews the first-century documentary evidence for the method of crucifixion. The method of crucifixion—whether a person was affixed to the cross by nails or was tied—is not specified in the other Gospel accounts, and Garcia's documentary survey finds no evidence in the period of Jesus to support nails as a method of crucifixion, in contrast to much documentary evidence to support hanging. Of critical importance for Garcia's thesis that the reference to nails in John 20 is historically unreliable is data from Josephus, who refers to the use of nails in the period after the death of Jesus to indicate the increased severity of crucifixion in the Roman Empire. Garcia posits that the reference to nails in 20:25 is a Johannine midrash on Zech 12:10 (part of the prophetic reference to "piercing") and postresurrection traditions in the Gospel of Luke, utilizing descriptions of crucifixion from John's own time, like those described by Josephus.

In this essay, what others have called "historical plausibility" is defined in terms of what I might call "facticity," and in this regard Garcia finds John wanting. The posited assumption behind this paper is that John is inherently nonhistorically reliable and that the Synoptic Gospels are the historical norm. For example, Garcia's working assumption is that John has modified the chronology of the passion for theological reasons and so is not historically reliable (contrast this approach with the Matson and Bond essays). Garcia continues the historical-critical trend, critiqued in the opening pages of Clark-Soles, of assessing historical plausibility on the basis of putative Synoptic historical neutrality: "Furthermore, is it simply chance that John, who writes several years *after* the revolt, is the *only* Evangelist to portray Jesus with nail wounds?" Matthew and Luke also write several years "after the revolt," yet John stands alone. For Garcia, the Fourth Evangelist is a sophisticated creator of midrash, utilizing creative interpretations of the Hebrew Bible to tell the story of Jesus, and this creativity outweighs any possibility that the Fourth Gospel could be a reliable source for historical traditions about Jesus.

The thesis of Mark A. Matson's essay, "The Historical Plausibility of John's Passion Dating," is that John's chronology of the passion, in particular the dating of the final supper and Jesus' death, has at least as good a claim to being historically accurate as the Synoptic chronology. For Matson, the places where John and the Synoptics starkly differ have a special role in the evaluation of John's historical value. In a comparative historical-critical method, the interpreter can explain the differences by saying that the Johannine material has been deliberately created or altered or by saying that the Fourth Gospel presents a different tradition that casts an independent perspective. The historical evaluative question becomes even more acute with material, such as the passion, that is similar in some respects yet also very different. Because the two chronologies conflict and cannot be reconciled, their respective historical value must be assessed.

Matson assesses external evidence (the Jewish calendar, comparison of very early eucharistic liturgies, evidence from the quartodeciman controversy), as well as internal evidence, specifically the internal consistency of the Gospel accounts. Among Matson's observations, for example, he notes: other early Christian (1 Corinthians, Gospel of Peter) and Jewish (Talmud) texts support the Johannine timing of Jesus' death; early Christian liturgical traditions in which the Eucharist is not linked to the Last Supper or to the passion; and the quartodeciman controversy that shows the existence of an active liturgical tradition that maintained a perspective on the Last Supper and the date of Jesus' death very different from the dominant "Western" liturgical traditions. Matson's assessment of the internal Johannine evidence is also carefully articulated. The timing of Jesus' death in John is commonly explained as an intentional theological revision, to position the death of Jesus at the same time as the slaughter of the paschal lambs. Matson shows that depicting Jesus as the paschal lamb is not a dominant Gospel theme and that details in John (e.g., Jesus' appearance before the high priest and the release of Barabbas, both of which occur before, not during, Passover) adhere with Jewish practices of the period. The cumulative data leads Matson to conclude that not only is the Johannine passion chronology historically accurate but that "when taken as a whole, a better case can be made for the historical plausibility of John's chronology than for the Synoptics' chronology."

This article offers a lucid and balanced assessment of the case for the historical plausibility of John's passion chronology. The details of Matson's analysis are nuanced and carefully articulated. The article's strengths are many. First, Matson frames his argument with the acknowledgment that his concern is historical plausibility. He is not confirming "facts," since that is rarely, if ever, possible with ancient texts; instead, he focuses on what is possible, given a judicious sifting of the available evidence. Second, Matson does not let the Synoptic model dominate as a historical and chronological norm but puts both chronologies under the same critical scrutiny. This evenhandedness is rare in studies on John and historical plausibility, since John's difference from the Synoptics is usually posited as a counter indication of any historical plausibility in John. Third, by taking the Johannine traditions as seriously as the Synoptic traditions, Matson creates new interpretive possibilities not only for John but also for the Synoptics. For example, the theological coloring of the Synoptic chronology comes into view in a way that is often ignored. This perspective allows for a fresh viewing of the multiplicity of early Christian traditions (even around something so seemingly "objective" as the passion chronology) and so enriches the data available for historical inquiry.

Yet even given these considerable strengths, Matson nonetheless ends his essay with sentences about how John is "colored by his desire to bring readers to active belief," written "to instill an understanding of Jesus as the glory of God," and "constructed to achieve its end." But which Gospel—canonical or noncanonical—is *not* constructed to achieve its end? Matson leaves somewhat unresolved the question with which his essay begins, "the foundational question of how we evaluate any of the Gospels, or really any ancient writing, for 'historical' material." The resolution of this central question is the struggle of all the essays in this volume.

The last essay in this group, Helen K. Bond's "At the Court of the High Priest: History and Theology in John 18:13–24," studies an episode in John's passion narrative, the Jewish trial before the high priest(s), that has generally been regarded by scholars as more historically plausible than the versions of the Jewish trial in the Synoptics. Bond examines this question afresh by providing a thorough and judicious review of the reasons conventionally offered in support of John's version of the Jewish trial (the problematic nature of the Synoptic accounts; John's simple and straight-forward account of Jesus before the high priest; the lack of necessity for any kind of Jewish trial at this point in John; an air of authenticity in John's account; John's explanation for Peter's entrance into the courtyard; and the apparent lack of theology in the Johannine account). Bond's careful historical analysis leads her to conclude that the first four arguments are strong ones, that she is agnostic over the role of the "other disciple" in gaining Peter access, and that the weakest argument is the last: that the account contains no theology. For Bond, the scene is more theological than is often supposed, but in a critical methodological turn she claims that John's theology does not necessarily drain the scene of its historical value. Like Matson, Bond is concerned to evaluate degrees of historical plausibility, and she argues that the presence of theology in a text does not automatically negate historical plausibility.

Bond then investigates what implications the theological intent of the interrogation scene has on the historicity of the scene. She provides a close and careful reading of John 18:13–24 that is persuasive. Her reading highlights the theological function of the Johannine ambiguity about the roles of Annas and Caiaphas. In Bond's reading, John's ambiguity about who is high priest "that year" deflects attention away from the actual incumbent and onto the office of the high priest. Just as in the trial before Pilate, John tells the story in such a way that Jesus emerges as the true judge and the true high priest. Other details of the story, aside from the ambiguity about the high priest, confirm this emphasis. Conventional scholarly wisdom holds that John interweaves Jesus' interrogation before Annas and Peter's denials to contrast Jesus' boldness and Peter's cowardice, but Bond argues convincingly that such a reading misses the true theological import of the scene. Instead, the scenes are interwoven to show that Jesus, not Annas, exercises the high priest's prophetic role. At the exact moment that the high priest asks him if he is a false prophet, his prophecy about Peter is shown to be true.

Bond provides a cogent and theologically compelling interpretation of this scene in John. Even in the face of a clear theological intent in the presentation of the Jewish trial, Bond maintains that theology and history do not negate one another. One can still assess for historical probability, since what can be seen as theologically motivated can be shown to have historical plausibility as well. All the reasons that are posited as evidence for the historical plausibility of the Johannine Jewish trial are not negated by its theology.

This careful essay models how to do historical reconstruction that is not afraid of theological interests and theological detail. Theological interests are not the only reason that the precise contours of a past event are not recoverable, and one of the signal contributions of this essay is the clarity with which Bond makes this case. Bond's integrated approach to questions of theological interest and historical plausibility widens the scope of historical Jesus conversations. The history and theology divide (recall the way Garcia frames his conclusions) is shown to be a false division when it comes to asking questions of historical plausibility. Bond's clear statement that even a theologically shaped text can still be assessed for historical plausibility creates a space for John to be considered a full partner in conversations about historicity.

And yet, as integrated as Bond's approach to historical plausibility and theological intentionality is, one is still left wondering about how Bond understands the larger questions of the relationship between history and theology that is at the heart of the Gospel genre. In the end, theology does not negate historical plausibility, although it cannot be determined which leads in the creation of individual Gospel stories: theological interests or historical traditions. According to Bond, John's trial scene is more historically plausible "despite the theology of the scene." Does Bond's "despite" mean that the basic theological functions of the Gospel genre must be overlooked to create a balance between historical plausibility and theological intent? This genre question is paramount in the essays that I have placed in group two.

GROUP TWO: THE GENRE OF THE GOSPEL AND ASPECTS OF HISTORICITY

Bas van Os ("John's Last Supper and the Resurrection Dialogues") is concerned with one particular Gospel subgenre: the resurrection dialogue that he sees as the basis of John 13–17. His argument about the historicity of the discourse material in John 13–17 depends on two methodological building blocks. The first is his assumption about the history of John's composition. Working from Paul Anderson's theory of the stages of the Fourth Gospel's composition, van Os posits that much of the discourse material in John 13–17 was inserted secondarily into the passion narrative by the Johannine elder, who worked with multiple traditions inherited from the Beloved Disciple. The second building block is his assumption about the form and original locus of the Johannine dialogue traditions. On the basis of his comparative exegetical analysis of the resurrection dialogues in the Sophia of Jesus Christ and the words of Jesus in John 13–17 and 20–21, van Os concludes that the Johannine traditions may well be the more primitive model behind the early gnostic resurrection dialogues and that the traditions in John 13–17 originally had a postresurrection setting.

With this background in place, van Os returns to John 13. By properly identifying most of the discourse material as resurrection dialogues, a historically plausible sequence of events at the Last Supper emerges that can be used by historians in reconstructing Jesus' life. He removes the postresurrection sayings from the narrative to arrive at a framework for the Last Supper that is remarkably similar to that found in the Synoptic Gospels. Proper identification of the genre and provenance of the discourse material also contributes to the history of the development of early Christian writings, because one sees in John a much more conservative use of resurrection dialogues than occurred in the second century. On a trajectory of theological appropriation, John's handling of received traditions appears more cautious than the freedom with which gnostics employed Jesus traditions.

On the one hand, van Os affirms the historical reliability of the Gospel of John: in addition to cohering with the outline of events at the Last Supper known from the Synoptic traditions, the composer of the Fourth Gospel appears to have regarded many of the traditions that he received (possibly from the Beloved Disciple) as authoritative, so he used them much more cautiously than later Christians would. Jesus traditions found in John can be trusted. On the other hand, van Os also asserts that the Johannine account of Jesus displays elements of "dehistoriciz-ing" at all stages of its composition. Both the Beloved Disciple and the composer are seen as free to put words in Jesus' mouth and to rearrange the sources in order to address the contextual needs of their audiences. In the end, van Os, like Garcia, decides that the unique interpretive work of the Fourth Gospel renders it untrustworthy for the work of historical reconstruction about Jesus. The Fourth Gospel is valued as a historical tool in reconstructing the history of interpretation of Jesus traditions, but falls below the Synoptic test of seeming "objectivity" for constructing the life of Jesus. The role of the Gospel genre—the intentional act of interpreting Jesus traditions—is identified by van Os, then seemingly rejected as a deterrent to historical reconstruction.

Like van Os, R. Alan Culpepper's essay, "John 21:24-25—The Johannine *Sphragis*," focuses on a subgenre within the larger Gospel genre as the starting point for his discussion of the historical reliability of John. Culpepper engages the recent work of two scholars (Howard M. Jackson and Richard Bauckham) who argue that John 21:24 is an autobiographical note indicating that the author of the Gospel is the Beloved Disciple. In this view, the Gospel of John is based on the eyewitness testimony of a follower of Jesus and makes that claim explicitly in the narrative. Culpepper challenges this perspective by examining afresh the genre of the Gospel's two concluding verses. He engages in a comparative study of the mechanics of closure in ancient novels and determines that the *sphragis* (which typically identifies the author and certifies ["seals"] the authenticity of the document or its contents) offers the best parallels to John 21:24–25.

John 21:24 fulfills the validating function of the *sphragis* by connecting the Gospel to an authorizing tradition and an authorizing eyewitness. For Culpepper, recognition of the end of the Gospel as a *sphragis* highlights the work of the community in the creation and reception of John. The writer is a member of a group of believers who were close enough to the Beloved Disciple to certify the truth of his Gospel, so that the Gospel's final editor, speaking on behalf of the Johannine school, affirms the truthfulness of the community's Gospel.

This comparative literary analysis leads Culpepper to critical methodological conclusions about how to evaluate aspects of historicity in John. The final editor's intentionality in employing the *sphragis* to establish the credibility of his narrative shows that "Luke is not the only historian among the Evangelists." In Culpepper's view, though, John operates with a very different understanding of history than Luke's, not history defined as the accuracy of the report but "as enlightened understanding of the events that transpired." For Culpepper, this makes John's understanding of history far ahead of his time, in that he is "validating the significance of the subjective." "Such history cannot be confirmed or documented by objective means; one can only testify to it."

Culpepper focuses on 21:24–25 to raise a basic question: Is an eyewitness required in order to have reliable testimony? Culpepper's point is that the validation of the community supersedes the question of whether or not the author is an eyewitness: the community trusts the testimony; the testimony is trustworthy. There is a certain circularity of logic in this perspective, but one that is in keeping with the intent not just of John but of all the Gospels. The communal embrace of the witness is essential to Gospel writing. Yet is John really alone among the Gospels in validating the subjective? It underinterprets Luke to say that he was "merely insisting" on the accuracy of his report; Luke's claim to accuracy is not an objective and historically neutral statement but is Luke's form of interpretation. If anything, Luke's claim in 1:1–4 shows his awareness of the competing subjectivities involved in history writing and is not a naïve valuation of the objective. The interpretive work in the Emmaus narrative in Luke 24 is no different from what John does in the Farewell Discourse and in chapter 21: the Evangelist positions Jesus to affirm the validity of the community's witness. Culpepper is correct that John was far ahead of the other Evangelists in making explicit that they were writing interpreted history and that the interpretation is an essential piece of the meaning, but he is wrong is distinguishing John's intentions so starkly from that of the other Evangelists.

What do Culpepper's rich and provocative findings mean for aspects of historicity in John? On the one hand, Culpepper offers a very radical answer: the historicity of John can be determined only in a community context, and the communal context serves as the seal of authenticity. On the other hand, by joining those who see John as unique on the question of interpretation and history, Culpepper leaves unresolved whether there is an unavoidable tension between the intents of the Gospel genre and the intents of historical record. Does the Gospel genre by definition preclude the possibility of historical reconstruction? And is this tension unique to John?

Richard Burridge's "Imitating Jesus: An Inclusive Approach to the Ethics of the Historical Jesus and John's Gospel" takes an overview approach rather than focusing on a discrete textual unit. Burridge's starting point is the Gospel genre, and he points to misperceptions about the nature of this genre as the reason why scholars discount John as a source of information about the historical Jesus and his ethics. The correct perspective is to recognize that the Gospels are ancient biographical narratives, not ethical treatises, and so they focus on words and deeds. As a result, Jesus' ethical teachings cannot be gleaned simply as a separate and discrete set of moral maxims but must be seen as a part of his integrated proclamation of the kingdom of God in action and in speech. That Jesus brought together a group of followers from among the poor and the marginalized is as much a source for constructing his ethics as his words are.

At the heart of Burridge's approach to questions of historical retrieval of Jesus' ethics is the centrality of Christology for the Synoptic Gospels, Paul, and John. For all of these New Testament writers, God's in-coming rule is best demonstrated in what God has achieved in the life, death, and resurrection of Jesus Christ. Each of these biblical writers may use different language and concepts, but their essential theological purpose is the same: to show how "Jesus is divine love bringing us truth." John's presentation of Jesus as divine love may differ in form from the other Gospels (e.g., no parables and teachings of the kingdom), but this does not mean there are no ethics. The Gospel of John is full of stories in which Jesus teaches the crowds and seeks out individuals from among the marginalized. John's goal, as is also the case with the Synoptics and Paul, is ultimately mimetic—that the community will follow the example of Jesus. Read through the lens of love and imitation, John's portrait of Jesus coheres with the activity of the historical Jesus.

This clear and lucid essay takes, as its title makes clear, an "inclusive approach" to questions of the historical Jesus. Instead of focusing on differences and emphasizing principles of dissimilarity, Burridge casts the net as widely as possible in constructing a picture of the historical Jesus and the New Testament's witness to Jesus. To speak of a historically reliable portrait means that despite differences in style and even content, all the New Testament writings share the same vision of Jesus. The question of historical reliability becomes a theological and ecclesiological question first, and the governing perspective is one of historical harmony and unity. For the Fourth Gospel, this approach provides a refreshing alternative and an important gain, because the Fourth Gospel is regularly treated as so different from the other canonical Gospels and Paul's letters as not to be a factor in conversations about New Testament ethics. Burridge argues persuasively that this is an ill-informed way to approach the Gospel of John.

Yet Burridge also manages essentially to skirt the question of the role of interpretation in shaping the historical record. By taking such an inclusive approach, one loses the sense that for John—and for the Synoptics and Paul—difference in literary articulation makes a difference for ethics. Why record these deeds in this way and not some other? Why provide this mimetic example and not that one? These questions make a difference in understanding the ways memories are remembered and renarrated in the early church. There is a commonality in the New Testament portrait of the ministry and ethics of Jesus, and the recognition of the inclusivity of that vision across textual differences is a significant contribution of this essay. It is significant for Johannine studies in particular, since John's share in the communal New Testament vision is so often disregarded due to methods that privilege dissimilarity, but it is also true that differences in historical memories matter.

It is precisely the question of historical memory that is at the center of Michael Labahn's "Peter's Rehabilitation (John 21:15-19) and the Adoption of Sinners." The underlying presupposition of Labahn's essay is that any past source is built on memory, on narrative, and on making sense out of it. Given this presupposition, Labahn challenges the basic operating principles of any quest for the historical Jesus—that one can find facts about Jesus. There are no unmediated facts about Jesus because "Jesus is none other than the one remembered by his earlier and later followers and opponents." Every interpretation of the Jesus event—whether literary or oral—is an interpretive model with a significant distance from the historical event itself. This means that approaches that pose historical/nonhistorical or fact/fiction as absolute alternatives are not helpful.

Labahn chooses John 21 as his heuristic lens on the question of historical memory because he sees John 21 as retelling aspects of the Johannine Jesus story narrated earlier. In particular, John 21:15–17 narrates how Jesus adopts the sinner Peter, accepting his offer of love, forgiving his denial, and setting him to new work. This narrative shows and tells more than something about Peter; it shows and tells something about Jesus. The idea that is renarrated in John 21 is that "Jesus in essence adopted sinners when he addressed the kingdom of God to marginalized people, poor people, and religious outsiders." Because John 21 is concerned with the Johannine Jesus story and not with history, a conventional "quest" approach to this story, in which one searches for older tradition that can be separated from its literary context, is not useful. Instead, one should note that Jesus' behavior toward sinners is reflected in many texts in different forms in all of the Gospels—in stories that celebrate Jesus' welcoming of sinners and in stories where Jesus' opponents use his communion with sinners to try to discredit him. All these texts—because of, not despite, their diversity and differences—reflect on Jesus' adoption of sinners and thereby retell or renarrate elements of the memory of Jesus' activity.

Labahn's conclusions are strikingly resonant with Burridge's inclusive approach. For example, like Burridge, Labahn notes that scholars are often puzzled that the proclamation of God's kingdom that is so central to the activity of the historical Jesus is nearly completely absent from John. Like Burridge, Labahn affirms that to define communality of tradition and emphasis so narrowly as to accept only certain categories of words and deeds is to miss the essentials. In John, as can be seen in 21:15–17, Jesus engages the outsider, the sinner and rejected one. Read from this perspective, in John 21:15–17 "a basic aspect of Jesus' proclamation of God's kingdom is taken up and renarrated in a completely new and Johannine manner." The retelling of John 21 shows the prominent place that Jesus' embrace of sinners had in the early Christian public memory of Jesus.

There is a significant methodological advance in this essay: instead of assuming that renarration automatically makes a story nonhistorically reliable, Labahn suggests that renarration may be the main way that historically reliable and enduring memories of Jesus and his ministry *can* be discovered. Instead of a literalistic approach to what constitutes historical narration, Labahn insists that all historical reconstruction, all history writing, is technically a fiction, because it is always a renarrated memory after the fact. Labahn shares with Burridge the methodological conviction that a reconstruction of the life and ministry of Jesus becomes a reconstruction of the ethical principles that guided Jesus' life and ministry, rather than a catalogue of individual deeds. For Labahn, more strongly than for Burridge, however, it is the diversity of the memories, not the underlying principles, that gives the portrait of the historical Jesus its vitality. Labahn's approach understands differences in stories to be an essential part of the act of remembering and essential to constructing a remembered portrait of the historical Jesus.

CONCLUDING REFLECTIONS

The essays in part 3 all highlight the need to include the Gospel of John as a serious conversation partner in any discussion of the historical Jesus. If all Gospels are assessed by similar standards and criteria of historical plausibility, then the conversation about what might have happened during the lifetime of Jesus shifts dramatically. When early Christian texts are not evaluated by whether or not they meet the Synoptic "norm" of what is historically plausible, but instead all texts are evaluated by the same criteria of careful review of external and internal evidence (best exemplified in the essays of Matson and Bond), then the balance of assumptions about what was historically plausible begins to shift. Including John as an equal player in the historical Jesus conversation means that assumptions and presuppositions about what is historically plausible begin to be revealed as exactly that: assumptions and presuppositions. All New Testament historians have to be more methodologically transparent when John is included in the conversation.

Yet the Gospel of John also makes another equally significant contribution to the question of how one evaluates any of the Gospels for historical reliability. The Gospel of John's hermeneutical sophistication, in repeatedly making explicit that it is engaged in interpretation of the Jesus traditions, places into evidence an important reality of all of the Gospel literature: there is no historical record without interpretation. While there may be a scale from less to more in the nature and quality of interpretation, there is no unmediated memory of Jesus anywhere in the New Testament. To single out John on this score is naively to overvalue the Synoptics and to distort the unavoidable and tensive interrelationship of history and theology throughout the New Testament. None of the Gospels is without interpretation; none of the Gospels is without a purpose other than historical reconstruction. To study John seriously from the perspective of historicity necessitates that the question of narrated historical memory is placed in the center of the conversation. That memory informs how history is recounted does not mean that historical plausibility cannot be assessed, but it equally means that questions of historical plausibility cannot be assessed apart from serious engagement with the diverse literary and theological forms through which these memories are communicated.

Michael Labahn writes, "I assume that the available sources provide a good base to construct a plausible and broadly reliable picture of the Jesus of history. Nevertheless, such a picture remains a (re)construction that is open for scientific discussion on the basis of particular methods of analysis." The contribution of this entire volume is that it provides constructions that are open for discussion *and* correction. The question of historicity in the Gospel portraits of Jesus will never be resolved absolutely, nor should it be. The essential task is to keep the discussion going with imagination and with an inclusive methodology that embraces both the diverse content and diverse interpretive strategies of the New Testament literature.

CONCLUSION

Aspects of Historicity in the Fourth Gospel: Consensus and Convergences

Paul N. Anderson

In reflecting upon the above treatments of aspects of historicity in the Fourth Gospel, a multiplicity of approaches and disciplines is here employed in getting at a common interest: the historical character of the Johannine tradition and ways in which it casts light upon the Jesus of history—his intentions, doings, teachings, travels, and receptions, as well as impressions, memories, interpretations, narrations, and writings about him in later settings. The division of the Gospel of John into three sections involving chapters 1–4, 5–12, and 13–21 works well as a means of dividing up the ministry of Jesus into early, middle, and late periods of his ministry as presented in John, although connections and echoes also reach from one section to another as a complete, larger narrative. By describing seven or eight historicity issues as introductions to each of the three parts, I have sought to alert the reader at least superficially to enduring issues related to historicity in John—raising issues both for and against it as a means of situating the essays within larger sets of discussions. Just as these nearly two dozen issues are not an exhaustive list of historical topics in John, it is not expected that they will all be addressed by the essays; nor is it inappropriate for any one of them to be addressed more than once or for essays to focus on more than one issue. Some subjects bear implications reaching in multiple directions, and taking note of that fact assists one's analysis. It is also hoped that some of the issues not touched on directly in the present collection will be addressed by further investigations and that future research will be stimulated in response to the present essays and their responses.

So, how do the essays stack up to their responders? By and large, the responders to the essays are quite affirming of the approaches the authors take and the conclusions to which they come. There are occasional places where our responders take issue with a point or two, but overall the responders contribute to the thrust of this collection, not only by commenting analytically on the essays in their sections but also by demonstrating how particular judgments seeking to ascertain aspects of historicity in the Fourth Gospel are made. In his response to the essays in part 1, Craig Koester begins with an insightful description of how the pre-Easter Jesus is presented as the post-Easter Jesus representing the over-all perspective of the Fourth Gospel. While recent quests for the Jesus of history have sought to divorce the former from the latter, the Fourth Evangelist does not do so overall, and even such an exercise does violence to the very data being assessed. This is a helpful reminder, as the Johannine narrator not only preserves history but also interprets it. In my response to the essays in part 2, I engage the strengths and weaknesses of each of the essays in that section. In doing so, I hope to affirm the arguments that seem plausible and even to suggest a few ways in which authors could have gone further. In challenging inferred weaknesses, I have sought to pose bases for consideration, especially as they relate to the com-position and authorship of the Fourth Gospel. In her response to the essays in part 3, Gail R. O'Day divides the essays in her section into two categories: those that assess degrees of plausibility with respect to particular features of historic-ity in the Johannine text, and those that approach the question of historicity by means of literary analysis, seeking to determine the form and function of particu-lar units. In doing so, she lays out a foundational pair of categories within which approaches to historicity in the Fourth Gospel may continue to advance.

From these analyses, general and particular impressions emerge. First, we find a general aspect of *consensus*; second, we find several *convergences* reflecting a variety of ways aspects of historicity in the Fourth Gospel might be addressed.

In reviewing the above essays and their responses, while this particular form of presentation does not lend itself to articulating a "consensus" on particular matters, one general consensus clearly emerges. With respect to the so-called "critical consensus" that the Fourth Gospel is "the spiritual Gospel" written by "the theologian" with no little or no interest in "history as such," the consensus of these papers, individually and collectively, poses the opposite view. The Fourth Gospel is clearly historical in its interest, as well as theological. Or, as Marianne Meye Thompson argued in volume 1 of *John, Jesus, and History* (Anderson, Just, and Thatcher 2007, 104–6), theological and interpretive narration *is* the way that the Fourth Evangelist writes history. Therefore, with reference to the schol-arly dehistoricization of John, the essays in this collection challenge that stance in a resounding way. By means of differing methodologies, perspectives, and approaches, all the essays in this volume argue that *Johannine historicity remains an important object of ongoing critical research*. If there is a single point of consen-sus within the present collection, this is it.

In addition, several convergences regarding aspects of Johannine historicity are here displayed in a collective though diverse set of ways. The first aspect of Johannine historicity involves an appreciation of John's *traditional historicity as an exercise in theological reflection*. As Craig Keener's opening essay reminds us, while the Johannine Prologue opens the Fourth Gospel as a confessional piece used in worship, it also bears witness to first-hand encounter with the object of its confession: the fleshly Jesus grounded in mundane history (Koester). As a deeply theological narration of a story rooted in history (Appold, Coloe, Bond), the narrator tells his story that members of the audience might believe (McGrath, Johnson, Matson, Garcia), and the repetition of earlier themes are developed in ways that make the past relevant for later audiences (Labahn, van Os). As events rooted in the past become exemplary patterns for later believers to emulate (Witherington, Clark-Soles, Burridge), the final editor testifies, along with the Johannine community, that the testimony of the Beloved Disciple is true (Culpepper). The truth at stake, however, is no mere objectivistic and impersonal set of data to be quantified, measured, and calculated. The truth attested is of value precisely because of its subjective character and personal implications—that is the sort of history the Fourth Gospel claims and shows itself to be. In that sense, the traditional memory of the Fourth Gospel moves from one level of experience to another: from encounter related to the ministry of Jesus or its attestations, to development within the evolving tradition, to delivery within its later contexts. Therein are Johannine history and theology interwoven together, from start to finish, and any effective analysis of Johannine history or theology must also take into account the other partner in this inextricable coupling of interests.

Second, John's *originative history* deserves consideration in addition to its delivered history. While the advances of the Martyn/Brown hypothesis have helped us think about the history of the Johannine situation, especially accounting for the crafting of some of its material around the time its final editions came together, the later stages of Johannine history cannot account for all the material in John—including religious tensions with Jewish leaders (Klink, Freyne) along the way. Clear references to earlier events confirm the "referential" character of much of John's material (Tovey, Labahn), suggesting the genre of the material, which is biographical history (Bauckham, Burridge). It is also a fact that when the developing character of the Johannine tradition is taken into consideration, conservatively involving at least two editions, development can be seen between the earlier and later material (Clark-Soles, van Os). This being the case, the inference of later material and perspective must not be allowed to eclipse earlier understandings and originative levels of history (von Wahlde, Bond). Johannine historicity must be considered comprehensively, including earlier and later material, as well as some that fits somewhere in between.

Third, a good quantity of the *distinctive material in John makes particular historical contributions* to our understanding of Jesus and his mission that other Gospels fail to make. The Bethsaida connections with several of Jesus' disciples (Appold) suggest a good deal about the socioreligious backgrounds of those who were closest to Jesus and who moved the Christian movement forward; Jesus' relation with John the Baptist (Coloe) is especially telling as it relates to a fuller understanding of Jesus' personal goals and mission; Jesus' use of the serpent symbolism of Num 21 reflects innovative typological uses of the Torah (Charlesworth); Jesus' trips to Jerusalem (Johnson, Freyne, Klink) say a good deal about the itinerary of Jesus and why he was both welcomed and resisted as a prophetic leader; the connections of Jesus with the Bethany family contributes an expanded understanding of his southern ministry (Bauckham, Witherington, Tovey), as do his Jerusalem healings (von Wahlde); the washing of his disciples' feet by Jesus offers valuable insight into the type of service Jesus advocated as central to authentic leadership (Clark-Soles); and the Johannine presentation of the Jewish trial and death of Jesus fills out the picture more fully and authentically than is rendered in the Synoptics (Bond, Matson). In each of these cases at least, material distinctive to the Fourth Gospel bears its own claims to historical knowledge and value, suggesting weighty implications for the historical study of Jesus.

Fourth, a closer look at the Johannine narrative exposes *a good deal of primitive, undeveloped material* over and against later and more developed features in the Synoptics and Paul's writings. In particular, the emphases upon Jesus' fulfilling Elijah typologies and the prophet-like-Moses agency schema (Coloe, Evans, Freyne), while prevalent in John, are left undeveloped in Christian confessional material. In contrast to pejorative references to serpent imagery in Revelation and elsewhere, the Johannine presentation of the uplifted serpent makes a redemptive association unaffected by later rhetorical concerns (Charlesworth). Likewise, John's sacramental and cultic innocence reflects primitivity instead of a highly developed presentation from a Christian religious standpoint (Evans, Anderson), and the Last Supper presentation of Jesus' washing the disciples' feet (Clark-Soles) is more likely to reflect Palestinian customs than later, Hellenistic ones. An informal set of Jewish trials suggests the religious realism of an awkward situation over and against the more formal and unlikely nocturnal Sanhedrin conference in the Synoptics (Bond), and the resuscitation of Peter as a redeemed sinner (Labahn) is an unlikely association to have been invented for rhetorical purposes alone. In these and other ways, much of John's distinctive material appears primitive and undeveloped—a likely place to look for information about the Jesus of history and the early movement in his name.

Fifth, Johannine *archaeological and topographical details* not only cast valuable light upon the historicity of the Fourth Gospel, but they also illumine features of the ministry of Jesus that would be otherwise unknown. Topographically, a Jesus who called disciples of John to be his followers in the Transjordan (Coloe) as men connected to a small fishing town named Bethsaida (Appold), who traveled through Samaria on the way to and from Jerusalem (Miller), and who visited Jerusalem several times during his ministry (Johnson, Freyne) shows a realistic Palestinian figure who commanded a following in the first third of the first century C.E. While other studies have developed other archaeological details, the discovery of the second Pool of Siloam in Jerusalem (von Wahlde) introduces new levels of understanding regarding the ministry of Jesus in Jerusalem. Not only did his healing ministries challenge Sabbath laws as in the Synoptics, but the revelation that the Pool of Siloam was a *miqveh*—a wading pool for purification and religious cleansing—features Jesus' goal of restoring the man societally and religiously, as well as physically. This discovery also elucidates some of the consternation felt by Jewish authorities in Jerusalem. While the man's recovering his

sight was experienced as a good thing, the fact that Jesus had performed the healing on the Sabbath as a nonauthorized, itinerant prophet challenged the effective
bases for their religious codes and structures. From ossuary and literary records,
plausible bases for the names Lazarus, Martha, and Mary can be found (Bauckham, Witherington), providing support for the Bethany narrative. Conversely,
the one archaeological discovery of a crucifixion victim in Jerusalem with a nail
through the heel, plus literary records suggesting the rarity of nailed crucifixions,
leads Garcia to doubt the Johannine reference to the nail wounds of Jesus. Jesus'
Jerusalem visits show features of first-hand knowledge before the destruction of
Jerusalem (McGrath, von Wahlde, Bond), and knowledge of these features must
be dated at the latest prior to 70 c.e. In these and other ways, archaeological and
topographical details internal and external to John promise to contribute greatly
to Johannine historicity studies and Jesus studies alike.

Sixth, Johannine *chronological plausibility* deserves a fresh look, especially
with regard to ways the Johannine itinerary of Jesus varies from that of the Synoptic Jesus. In contrast to recent approaches to the Fourth Gospel explaining these
differences as factors of the theological interests of the Evangelist, the scholars
in this volume largely take exception to those moves. Rather than reading paschal symbolism into the Baptist's testimony (Coloe), John's early temple incident
(McGrath) and the early dating of the Last Supper (Matson) argue for a good deal
of plausibility in the Johannine ordering of Jesus' ministry, attested in canonical
and extracanonical ways. While Johnson stops short of inferring a chronological
basis for the presentation of Jesus' visits to Jerusalem and the three references to
the Passover, it does seem plausible to infer multiple visits to Jerusalem (Freyne) as
reflected in at least the four visits described in John. Whether or not a three-year
ministry is confirmed by the Johannine rendering as opposed to the single-year
presentation of the Synoptics, a chronologically fuller ministry of Jesus does seem
to be indicated by his itinerant presentation in the Fourth Gospel. Further, the
sequence of the feasts (Tabernacles, Dedication, Passover) fits a basic chronological progression, although they need not reflect travels to Jerusalem all in the same
year. It is also a fact that the content of Jesus' teaching fits the particular feasts
that occasioned his visits (Johnson), so those connections convey a sense of religious realism within the narrative. Given that the Johannine presentation of the
crucifixion on Nisan 14 complies with ancient calendars and was appealed to in
the second century c.e., Matson finds ample reasons to side with the Johannine
dating of the Last Supper as not only plausible but even probable. In these and
other ways, Johannine chronology is seen less as a factor of theologizing speculation and more historically suggestive than recent studies have assumed.

Seventh, *Johannine-Synoptic similarities and differences* inform Johannine historicity in a variety of ways. On the one hand, parallels with Synoptic renderings
suggest a Johannine alternative presentation of an event similar to other ones: the
woman at the well is similar to the Syrophoenician woman in Mark and elsewhere
(Miller); the healing of the royal official's son from afar is similar to the healing

of the centurion's servant in Q (Judge); the feeding of the five thousand is parallel to all five Synoptic feeding narratives (Evans, Anderson); the healing of the blind man is similar to Synoptic healing narratives and concerns for ritual purity (von Wahlde, Klink); Jesus' being anointed (his head or his feet?) by a woman and some association with Mary and Martha in Luke (Bauckham, Witherington, Tovey) is interesting; the trials of Jesus are fraught with historical realism filling out Synoptic presentations (Bond); and the love commandments of Jesus in John reflect a community-appropriation of his teachings in ways that complement the Synoptic injunctions to love one's neighbors and enemies (Burridge). Some scholars take these similarities to imply Synoptic dependence (Judge), while most infer the independence of the Johannine tradition (e.g., Evans, von Wahlde, Bauckham, Witherington, Bond). At least one scholar (Garcia) found in John's distinctive presentation of the piercing wounds of Jesus a midrashic appropriation of a scriptural motif based on the silence of the Synoptics regarding the nail wounds and piercings of Jesus. Then again, are Synoptic parallels with John confirming of John's historicity or markers of its subservience to the Synoptics (van Os, O'Day)? In the light of these analyses, Johannine-Synoptic similarities and differences function to confirm John's historicity in some analyses and disconfirm it in others. Continuing to develop criteria for making solid judgments along these lines will be serviceable for all sides of the debate.

Eighth, Johannine *presentations of Jesus as a northern prophet engaged dialectically with Judean religious leaders* contribute greatly to an understanding of the historical ministry and reception of Jesus in ways rife with religious and social realism. In contrast to the Synoptic Jesus, who meets little serious resistance from religious leaders until the last week of his life, the Johannine presentation of a Jesus who launches a prophetic sign at the beginning of his ministry (McGrath) is striking. This provocative prophet who performs Elijah-type and Moses-type signs in the wilderness (Evans), attends feasts in Jerusalem (Johnson) in addition to the Passover (an unnamed feast, Tabernacles, and Dedication), is presented as the northern prophet who is disparaged by the Jerusalem leaders as one of the *'am ha'arets* (Freyne) or something of a heretic (Klink), and is tried and convicted by the Jewish leaders and turned over to the Romans (Bond) betrays a good deal of socioreligious realism. Even debates regarding Jesus' relation to the Father in John 5–10 should be understood not as advocating a metaphysically high Christology but as clarifying the Son's agency on behalf of the Father, which has become a religious and scriptural challenge to his contemporaries (Keener). The north-south tensions in John are far more pronounced than in the Synoptics, and this distinctive feature alone bears great potential for contributing to a fuller understanding of the intentions, deeds, teachings, and receptions of the provocative prophet from Galilee.

Ninth, approaches to *Johannine composition and authorship* impact one's understandings of John's historicity and the character of its presentation. While the text must be taken finally as it stands, appreciating the place of the Prologue and chapter 21 as likely additions to the text (Keener, van Os, Labahn, Culpepper), along with chapters 6 and 15–17 (Clark-Soles, van Os, Anderson), facilitates an appreciation for the development of the Johannine tradition and helps to account for its primary rough transitions. While scholars will disagree—even with some intensity—about the bases for inferring whom the Beloved Disciple might have been (Appold, Witherington, Anderson), acknowledging that the source of the Fourth Gospel's independent tradition is plausibly connected to an independent memory and reflection upon the ministry of Jesus may yet hold some promise in accounting for John's autonomy-yet-connectedness to the Synoptic renderings of Jesus' ministry (Bauckham). Even the third-person claim by the final editor that the author was originally a first-hand witness—apparently after that leader's death—reflects a community's attestation to the truthfulness of his testimony (Culpepper; see also Keener). Thus, the insistence upon personal encounter with the Jesus of history as the origin of the Johannine tradition becomes also the goal of the later narrative, engaging its later audiences with its flesh-becoming subject (Koester). Important here is understanding the relation between the literary form and its functions with relation to aspects of historicity (O'Day), and such a measure will be telling in its implications.

Tenth, *nuanced appraisals of John's historicity* are indeed possible, even profitable, when assessing aspects of history in John. In contrast to monological claims for or against Johannine historicity by traditionalist and critical scholars alike, a set of more measured approaches to the issue is evident in virtually all of the essays above. This marks a significant advance in the field because scholars can therefore say more directly why they agree or disagree with particular parts of an analysis instead of treating proposals in sweeping ways—either positively or negatively. While most of the essays discuss strengths and weaknesses of particular views and suggest degrees of plausibility regarding their own claims (O'Day), several essays engaging the Johannine Last Supper and passion narratives are exemplary in their attempts to produce such nuanced analyses with programmatic intentionality. Clark-Soles not only declares her intention to pose a nuanced analysis, but she also groups her own findings within three evaluative categories: most likely, somewhat likely, and less likely. Van Os applies what in his view is a plausible history of Johannine composition as a means of distinguishing earlier content from more developed content theologically, articulating thereby the bases for his judgments. Matson lays out an attempt to discern degrees of plausibility regarding the dating of the Last Supper in John, explaining also the evidence for and against particular inferences. Likewise nuanced is Bond's approach to the historicity of the Johannine Jewish trial narrative, where she assesses degrees of plausibility regarding her various conclusions. What is hopeful about these and other essays in this volume is that, while the claims made are clear and incisive, they are also measured and inviting of further analysis themselves. The benefit of such contributions is that future scholarship is enabled to move forward on the bases of the strongest inferences, while still being challenged by the questions and probings that remain. Both agreement and disagreement serve well when scholars articulate *why* they embrace the views they do, and understanding grows as new knowledge and disciplines cast light upon longstanding issues.

Indeed, not all the issues of Johannine historicity are either outlined or addressed in this volume; if they were, I suppose that all the libraries of the world would not be able to contain them (John 21:25)! Nonetheless, enough of them are addressed to show that the subject still has a good deal of life in it and to suggest that further inquiry ought yet to be conducted. While few of the essays above pose overstated claims regarding aspects of Johannine historicity demonstrated, they do suggest, collectively and individually, a variety of trajectories in which further investigations might serviceably proceed. In that sense, aspects of Johannine historicity are multiple, and a number of appropriate disciplinary tools deserve to be honed and employed in service to this critically neglected field of inquiry. This collection thus serves not as a last word on the subject but as a critical advance on an important dialogue.

Of course, the addition of the Fourth Gospel to the database of material contributing to the historical quest for Jesus will be a shock to the system of all three quests over the last two centuries or so, as much of the certainty of those quests has been forged on the anvil of John's historical disparagement. If the Johannine tradition, however, is seen as an independent Gospel tradition developing dialogically alongside the others, a good number of Jesus-assumptions will need to be rethought. Instead of beginning with the Synoptics and holding John hostage to a set of predisposed assumptions, what if we started with the Gospel of John in a fresh quest for the historical Jesus and proceeded from there to integrate inferences from the Synoptics in bi-optic perspective? It might require a *fourth quest* for Jesus—one with John *in* the mix—but this may be precisely what the inference of aspects of historicity in the Fourth Gospel requires.

EPILOGUE: WHENCE, WHERE, AND WHITHER FOR JOHN, JESUS, AND HISTORY?

Felix Just, S.J.

Where have we come from, where are we now, and where might we be headed with studies of the interrelationships between the Gospel of John and the historical Jesus? Readers of these first two volumes of collected essays, along with the many scholars who have attended sessions of the John, Jesus, and History Group over the past six years, are by now well versed in the discussions of the many complex questions surrounding the historicity of the Fourth Gospel. Yet it would be worthwhile for us briefly to reflect on the bigger picture and to consider the larger journey in which this collective work plays a role.

WHERE HAVE WE COME FROM?

Most biblical scholars are certainly aware of the recent past within New Testament studies: the Fourth Gospel was generally considered so "spiritual" or "theological" that its historical value was strongly questioned or even rejected. Indeed, a quick perusal of a large Johannine bibliography (e.g., on the Johannine Literature website: http://www.johannine.org) shows that very few historical investigations were published in the last century or more, up until recent years. We also know, as a corollary, how most historical Jesus studies in recent decades have routinely ignored the Fourth Gospel or even totally dismissed it from their list of possible sources for Jesus' life and ministry. Therefore, to have nearly five dozen essays and responses on subjects related to John, Jesus, and history within the past six years by an international group of first-rate Johannine and Jesus scholars is a significant start to something new, even if the work is by no means completed.

As evidenced by the many thought-provoking contributions in our first two volumes, more and more scholars are willing to reconsider the issues of historicity associated with the Fourth Gospel and are seriously attempting to tackle the difficult questions, without of course going to the extreme of uncritically accepting all aspects of the Johannine writings as completely historical. The papers presented at the John, Jesus, and History Group's sessions at the annual SBL meetings from

2002 to 2007 have encouraged and facilitated this dialogue, and the engagement at these sessions by large numbers of scholars also has led to innumerable subsequent conversations. The publication of most of these papers in the SBL Symposium Series, along with extensive introductions, invited responses, and reflective conclusions, has enabled the conversation on these issues to continue and to expand even further.

WHERE ARE WE NOW?

As Paul Anderson ably summarizes in his above conclusion, we now seem to have a consensus that exploring Johannine historicity in critical and disciplinary ways is a worthy venture, although we are still a good distance away from reaching a consensus on any of the disputed historical issues themselves. While he finds a good number of convergences among scholars regarding the need to engage particular issues, there continue to be considerable divergences about how to proceed in investigating John's historicity and its relevance for Jesus studies. Moreover, one might also ask if these investigations will make a significant difference for future biblical interpreters or if these discussions are simply adding more voices to the plethora of divergent opinions that increasingly fill the shelves of professors' offices and academic libraries. Let me phrase this concern somewhat differently: What concrete results have emerged so far from the John, Jesus, and History Project that most scholars would be able to agree upon? Not surprisingly, there is still no consensus on most historical issues surrounding the Fourth Gospel, either in the innumerable details or in the larger picture, which is of course also a reflection of the lack of consensus on Johannine literary and theological issues and approaches. Even among the many contributors to these volumes, one still finds a great divergence of views on such key literary-historical questions as the date and location of this Gospel's composition, whether it was composed all at once or in multiple stages, and the identity of the Beloved Disciple. Many concrete proposals have been put forth, both here and elsewhere, and greater clarity has been gained on certain issues, at least in how the questions should be framed. On the other hand, many tacit assumptions also continue to be made on some key historical questions, without the opportunity to discuss them thoroughly and systematically enough. To some readers, it may seem that we have raised many questions but provided few firm answers, and it remains to be seen if the answers that have been proposed will be widely accepted.

To take just one important example: Can we ever hope to find the answer, or at least to arrive at a working consensus, on the question about the identity of the Beloved Disciple? Some scholars would immediately say, "No!" while others believe that they already have the answer, whether it be John the son of Zebedee, Lazarus, Thomas, Paul, Mary Magdalene, or a host of other proposals that have been put forth over the centuries. As a case in point, the present volume not only contains a proposal by Ben Witherington that the Beloved Disciple was Lazarus of Bethany, but also a response by Paul Anderson, who compliments Witherington for some astute observations, yet ultimately rejects his arguments and contends that the Beloved Disciple was John the son of Zebedee. Would Witherington agree with Anderson's critiques and thus retract his own proposal? Or might he someday publish his own counterarguments, thereby strengthening his own position? Or would they just politely agree to disagree? Surely they cannot both be correct about the historical identity of "the disciple whom Jesus loved" (John 13:23; 21:7, 20–24), since no one has ever proposed that John, the son of Zebedee, is the same historical figure as Lazarus, the brother of Martha and Mary. More importantly, how might these two scholars be able to reach agreement with each other? In what venues could they discuss the relevant issues, and what would each one have to concede—or to accept as compelling evidence—for a working consensus to emerge? Would it help if we locked them into a room and not let them out until they agreed with each other, as done in papal elections? Would it speed things up if we deprived them of food and water until they reached a consensus, as the people of Rome purportedly sometimes did when the cardinal electors could not agree on their choice for a new pope? Or would more positive incentives be more effective these days, such as a book contract and speaking tour to allow our scholars to promote their newfound agreement?

Moreover, in our collective search for "the truth that will make us free" (see John 8:32), imagine what greater progress might be made in biblical studies if a larger group of scholars were willing to meet more regularly and to discuss thoroughly a focused question—such as the identity of the Beloved Disciple or other key historical questions—until they reached a consensus. For such a process to be fruitful, of course, all would need to come with open minds, truly wishing to find the solution, even if it ultimately differed from whatever theory they originally held. Yet is this not the promise and goal of the academic quest for truth? It would obviously be very time-consuming and difficult to do, given the currently dominant modus operandi of biblical scholarship—or most other humanities, for that matter. In contrast to the natural sciences and some social sciences, biblical conferences and publications are still predominantly based on the work and writings of individual scholars, with few opportunities for deeper discussions and more extended interactions. Conferences consist mainly of presentations of individual papers; although they sometimes include prepared responses or panel discussions, there is seldom time for in-depth analyses or resolutions of the differences between competing proposals. How might we move forward in finding modes of scholarship that are more truly cooperative and collaborative, and thus have greater prospects of reaching broader consensus, at least on the most important issues? Although their methods of voting and color-coding the results were not appreciated by many scholars, the dedication of the members of the Jesus Seminar in devoting much time and effort to their project over many years provides just one example of how scholars might work together more collaboratively.

The above musings are not a "call for papers" for some type of scholarly mega-conference on the identity of the Beloved Disciple; nor are they an invitation for scholars to join a new "Johannine-Jesus Seminar." Rather, they are intended to serve as a broader call for reflection on the questions posed at the beginning of this epilogue: Where have we come from, where are we now, and, most important, where and how might we go forward in order to make greater progress in biblical scholarship, especially as related to the Fourth Gospel and to the historical Jesus? These reflections are an invitation for all biblical scholars to consider how we might move beyond the currently dominant modus operandi of individual writers/presenters and individual reviewers/respondents toward more innovative ways in which the broader scholarly community can undertake the rigorous work of reaching agreements with broader consensus on the most central historical questions.

WHERE CAN WE GO NEXT?

What, then, are the next steps in the John, Jesus, and History Project? One has already been described by Tom Thatcher in his introduction to the present volume: the John, Jesus, and History Group's sessions from 2008 to 2010 will consider aspects of the life and ministry of the historical Jesus that may be understood more clearly through the Johannine lens. As the steering committee tried to envision these three years of inquiry, it seemed best to proceed by starting with the most solid historical base, namely, the passion narrative (2008), then moving to the works of Jesus (2009), and finally to the most speculative topic: the words of the Johannine Jesus (2010). The papers presented at these sessions are also scheduled to be published by the SBL, thus allowing even more scholars to continue to engage in these important discussions.

In addition to its own investigations, the John, Jesus, and History Group has actively sought to collaborate with other program units of the SBL in recent and future years. In 2007 we sponsored a major panel discussion of the Fourth Gospel and the Dead Sea Scrolls, which Mary Coloe and Tom Thatcher are editing for publication by Peeters, and we enjoyed holding joint sessions with the SBL's Johannine Literature Section. We also organized a major review session for the 2008 Annual Meeting of the SBL, featuring several key recent books on John, Jesus, and history topics, and we are sponsoring special sessions on Johannine archaeology and on methodological tools for determining Johannine historicity in 2009. We also hope to hold some joint sessions with the Historical Jesus Section in 2010, all in service to the quest for Jesus in Johannine perspective. Further questions and findings will certainly emerge from all these inquiries, but these are just a few of the venues presently underway or planned for the near future.

Another step beyond what is already planned might be the undertaking of a more thorough investigation of the Johannine Epistles, which have received only sporadic attention in the John, Jesus, and History Project so far, and possibly also the broader "Johannine" corpus (the book of Revelation, the Acts of John, and other more distantly related writings), to see if and how they might contribute, even in some small ways, to discussions of the historical issues involving the Fourth Gospel and its presentation of Jesus. A further major step, perhaps for the more distant future, would be for a team of scholars to attempt to "put it all together," taking all the results of these many papers and responses and compiling several book-length studies. One might involve a systematic investigation of all the historical aspects of the Fourth Gospel. Another might be a fresh portrait of the historical Jesus that, in addition to the Synoptics and other sources, takes seriously the evidence from John's Gospel.

There is one further step that I wish to propose, even though some scholars might consider this beyond the proper concerns of "the academy." One of the unfortunate features that have shaped most Jesus studies since the contributions of Reimarus is the posing of history and theology against each other, as if the two are so different that they cannot mix. Thus, theological disinterest has been privileged as the proper means of arriving at "objective" history, at the expense of any subjective or personal factors. This approach, however, fails to account for the inherently subjective character of history itself. Recalling the dual meaning of *Geschichte* in German, we need to remember that "history" always involves "stories" that are told by human beings in human language (i.e., unavoidably subjective and personal). Thus, in all of our academic interests, we regularly need to ask ourselves the question of relevance: So what? What difference does all of our high-level academic research and writing make for the average student in our classes and/or the average member of our congregations? What, if any, is the personal, existential, social, and/or pastoral import of our historical and theological studies? This is something that all of us, whether we consider ourselves to be primarily scholars or teachers, writers or pastors, need to keep in mind. Ironically, recent approaches to theology have been much more open and dynamic than the dominant approaches to history, which have still tended to be disjunctive—either/or instead of both/and. What we need is a more conjunctive approach to biblical historiography that includes the personal, the subjective, and the theological as central components of the historical investigation.

In my own teaching and preaching, I often emphasize that the proper Christian answer to any theological question is always both/and rather than either/or. The best Christian theology has always maintained that God is *both* transcendent *and* immanent, that Jesus is *both* divine *and* human, that the Eucharist is *both* a sacrifice *and* a meal, that the Bible is *both* the Word of God written under the inspiration of the Holy Spirit *and* written in human language by human authors, and so forth. In disputes over the many centuries of Christian history, one group often overemphasized one side of the coin and neglected the other side, while the opposing group did the reverse. With the more ecumenical spirit of recent decades, both parties in a theological dispute are now more often willing to admit that there is truth on both sides of the coin, which must always be held together, even if that may not always be easy. Applying these principles more directly to our current topic, it seems that in the past, many scholars overemphasized the historical nature of the Synoptic Gospels in supposed opposition to the theological nature of John's Gospel. In recent decades, however, we have not only rediscovered the theological purposes and influences behind the Synoptics, but more and more scholars are now also willing to reconsider the historical value of the Fourth Gospel.

It may seem obvious, but it still merits repetition and emphasis: *all* of the Gospels are *both* theological *and* historical. None is purely historical or solely theological. In addition to appreciating the great theological heights and depths of John's Gospel and its presentation of "the only begotten Son of God" (John 1:14, 18; 3:16, 18), we also need to deepen our understanding of John's portrayal of the historical "Jesus of Nazareth" (1:45–46; 18:5, 7). We invite you to participate in this endeavor, to continue searching with us and conversing with other scholars, as we together seek to recover the long-neglected historical dimensions of the Fourth Gospel.

Works Cited

Abegg, Martin G. , Jr. 1994. "Messianic Hope and 4Q285: A Reassessment." *JBL* 113:81–91.

Achtemeier, Paul J. 1970. "Toward the Isolation of Pre-Markan Miracle Catenae." *JBL* 89:265–91.

———. 1972. "The Origin and Function of the Pre-Markan Miracle Catenae." *JBL* 91:198–221.

Albright, William F. 1956. "Recent Discoveries in Palestine and the Gospel of St John." Pages 153–71 in *The Background of the New Testament and Its Eschatology: In Honour of Charles Harold Dodd*. Edited by W. D. Davies and D. Daube. Cambridge: Cambridge University Press.

Alexander, Philip S. 1992. "'The Parting of the Ways' from the Perspective of Rabbinic Judaism." Pages 1–25 in *Jews and Christians: The Parting of the Ways A.D. 70 to 135*. Edited by James D. G. Dunn. WUNT 66. Tübingen: Mohr Siebeck.

Alexander, Philip S., and Geza Vermes. 2000. "4Q285 Sefer ha-Milhamah." Pages 228–46 in idem, *Qumran Cave 4. XXVI: Cryptic Texts and Miscellanea, Part 1*. DJD XXXVI. Oxford: Clarendon.

Allison, Dale C., Jr. 1998. *Jesus of Nazareth: Millenarian Prophet*. Minneapolis: Fortress.

Allison, Dale C., Jr., and W. D. Davies. 1997. *A Critical and Exegetical Commentary on the Gospel according to Saint Matthew*. Volume 3: *Commentary on Matthew XIX–XXVIII*. ICC. Edinburgh: T&T Clark.

Anderson, Paul N. 1996. *The Christology of the Fourth Gospel: Its Unity and Disunity in the Light of John 6*. WUNT 2/78. Tübingen: Mohr Siebeck. Repr., Valley Forge, Pa.: Trinity Press International, 1997.

———. 1997. "The Sitz im Leben of the Johannine Bread of Life Discourse and its Evolving Context." Pages 1–59 in *Critical Readings of John 6*. Edited by R. Alan Culpepper. BIS 22. Leiden: Brill.

———. 1999. "The Having-Sent-Me Father—Aspects of Irony, Agency, and Encounter in the Johannine Father-Son Relationship." *Semeia* 85:33–57.

———. 2006a. "Aspects of Historicity in the Gospel of John: Implications for Investigations of Jesus and Archaeology." Pages 587–618 in *Jesus and Archaeology*. Edited by James H. Charlesworth. Grand Rapids: Eerdmans.

———. 2006b. *The Fourth Gospel and the Quest for Jesus: Modern Foundations Reconsidered*. LNTS 321. London: T&T Clark. Repr. in paperback, 2007.

———. 2006c. "Gradations of Symbolization in the Johannine Passion Narrative: Control Measures for Theologizing Speculation Gone Awry." Pages 157–94 in *Imagery in the Gospel of John: Terms, Forms, Themes, and Theology of Johannine Figurative Language*.

Edited by Jörg Frey, Jan G. van der Watt, and Ruben Zimmermann. WUNT 200. Tübingen: Mohr Siebeck.

———. 2007a. "Getting a 'Sense of the Meeting': Assessments and Convergences." Pages 285–89 in Anderson, Just, and Thatcher 2007

———. 2007b. "Prologue: Critical Views of John, Jesus, and History." Pages 1–6 in Anderson, Just, and Thatcher 2007.

Anderson, Paul N., Felix Just, S.J., and Tom Thatcher, eds. 2007. *John, Jesus, and History, Volume 1: Critical Appraisals of Critical Views.* SBLSymS 44. Atlanta: Society of Biblical Literature.

Appold, Mark L. 1976. *The Oneness Motif in the Fourth Gospel: Motif Analysis and Exegetical Probe into the Theology of John.* WUNT 2/1. Tübingen: Mohr Siebeck.

———. 2007. "Bethsaida and a Pre-Markan Tradition: Rethinking Mark 6:45–8:26." Paper presented at the Society of Biblical Literature International Meeting. Vienna, 26 July.

Arav, Rami, and Richard Freund. 1995–2009. *Bethsaida: A City by the North Shore of the Sea of Galilee.* 4 vols. Kirksville, Mo.: Truman University Press.

Ashton, John. 1991. *Understanding the Fourth Gospel.* Oxford: Clarendon; New York: Oxford University Press.

Asiedu-Peprah, Martin. 2001. *Johannine Sabbath Conflicts as Juridical Controversy.* WUNT 132. Tübingen: Mohr Siebeck.

Assmann, Aleida. 1980. *Die Legitimität der Fiktion: Ein Beitrag zur Geschichte der literarischen Kommunikation, Theorie und Geschichte der Literatur und der schönen Künste.* Texte und Abhandlungen 55. Munich: Fink.

Atkinson, Kenneth. 1999. "On the Herodian Origin of Militant Davidic Messianism at Qumran: New Light from *Psalm of Solomon* 17." *JBL* 118:435–60.

Attridge, Harold W., and Robert A. Oden, eds. 1981. *Philo of Byblos: The Phonician History.* CBQMS 9. Washington, D.C.: Catholic Biblical Association.

Aune, David E. 1991. "On the Origins of the 'Council of Javneh' Myth." *JBL* 110:491–93.

———. 1998. *Revelation 17–22.* WBC 52C. Nashville: Nelson.

Barrett, C. K. 1978. *The Gospel according to St. John: An Introduction with Commentary and Notes on the Greek Text.* 2nd ed. London: SPCK; Philadelphia: Westminster.

———. 1994–98. *A Critical and Exegetical Commentary on the Acts of the Apostles.* 2 vols. ICC. Edinburgh: T&T Clark.

Bauckham, Richard. 1988. "Jesus' Demonstration in the Temple." Pages 72–89 in *Law and Religion: Essays on the Place of the Law in Israel and Early Christianity.* Edited by Barnabas Lindars. Cambridge: James Clarke.

———. 1993. "Papias and Polycrates on the Origin of the Fourth Gospel." *JTS* 44:24–69.

———. 1998a. "John for Readers of Mark." Pages 147–71 in *The Gospels for All Christians: Rethinking the Gospel Audiences.* Edited by Richard Bauckham. Grand Rapids: Eerdmans.

———. 1998b. *The Fate of the Dead: Studies on the Jewish and Christian Apocalypses.* NovTSup 93. Leiden: Brill.

———. 1999. "Did Jesus Wash His Disciples' Feet?" Pages 411–29 in *Authenticating the Activities of Jesus.* Edited by Bruce Chilton and Craig A. Evans. NTTS 28.2. Leiden: Brill. Repr. as pages 191–206 in Bauckham 2007.

———. 2003. "The Eyewitnesses and the Gospel Traditions." *JSHJ* 1.1:28–60.

———. 2006. *Jesus and the Eyewitnesses: The Gospels as Eyewitness Testimony.* Grand Rapids: Eerdmans.

———. 2007. *The Testimony of the Beloved Disciple*. Grand Rapids: Baker.

Bauckham, Richard, and Carl Mosser, eds. 2008. *The Gospel of John and Christian Theology*. Grand Rapids: Eerdmans.

Bauer, Walter, and Frederick William Danker, eds. 1999. *A Greek-English Lexicon of the New Testament and Other Early Christian Literature*. 3rd ed. Chicago: University of Chicago Press.

Beasley-Murray, George R. 1987. *John*. WBC 36. Waco, Tex.: Word.

———. 1999. *John*. 2nd ed. WBC 36. Nashville: Thomas Nelson.

Becker, Jürgen. 1998. *Jesus of Nazareth*. Berlin: de Gruyter.

Beckwith, Roger. 1989. "Cautionary Notes on the Use of Calendars and Astronomy to Determine the Chronology of the Passion." Pages 183–205 in *Chronos, Kairos, Christos: Nativity and Chronological Studies Presented to Jack Finegan*. Edited by Jerry Vardaman and Edwin Yamauchi. Winona Lake, Ind.: Eisenbrauns.

———. 1996. *Calendar and Chronology, Jewish and Christian*. Leiden: Brill.

Benoit, Pierre. 1969. *The Passion and Resurrection of Jesus Christ*. Translated by Benet Weatherhead. London: Darton, Longman & Todd.

Berger, David. 1985. "Three Typological Themes in Early Jewish Messianism: Messiah Son of Joseph, Rabbinic Calculations, and the Figure of Armilus." *Association for Jewish Studies Review* 10.2:141–64.

Bernard, John Henry. 1928. *A Critical and Exegetical Commentary on the Gospel according to St. John*. Vol. 2. ICC. Edinburgh: T&T Clark.

Berrin, Shani L. 2004. *Pesher Nahum Scroll from Qumran: An Exegetical Study of 4Q169*. Leiden. Brill.

Bickerman, Elias J. 1944. "The Colophon of the Greek Book of Esther." *JBL* 63:339–62.

Bieringer, Reimund, Didier Pollefeyt, and Frederique Vandecasteele-Vanneuville, eds. 2001. *Anti-Judaism and the Fourth Gospel: Papers of the Leuven Colloquium, 2000*. Assen: Van Gorcum; Louisville: Westminster John Knox.

Blaskovic, Goran. 1999. *Johannes und Lukas: Eine Untersuchung zu den literarischen Beziehungen des Johannesevangelium zum Lukasevangelium*. Dissertationen 84. St. Ottilien: EOS Verlag.

Blinzler, Josef. 1959. *The Trial of Jesus*. Cork: Mercier; Westminster, Md.: Newman.

Bliss, Frederick Jones, and Archibald Campbell Dickie. 1898. *Excavations at Jerusalem, 1894–1897*. London: Committee of the Palestine Exploration Fund.

Blomberg, Craig L. 2001. *The Historical Reliability of John's Gospel: Issues and Commentary*. Downers Grove, Ill.: InterVarsity Press.

Blount, Brian K. 2001. *Then the Whisper Put on Flesh: New Testament Ethics in an African American Context*. Nashville: Abingdon.

Bock, Darrell L. 1994–96. *Luke*. 2 vols. BECNT 3. Grand Rapids: Baker.

Boismard, Marie-Émile. 1957. *St. John's Prologue*. London: Blackfriars.

———. 1961. "L'ami de l'Époux (Jo. iii 29)." Pages 289–95 in *A la rencontre de Dieu: Mémorial Albert Gelin*. Edited by André Barucq et al. Le Puy: Xavier Mappus.

Boismard, Marie-Émile, and Arnaud Lamouille. 1986. *Synopsis Graeca Quattuor Evangeliorum*. Leuven: Peeters.

Bond, Helen K. 1998. *Pontius Pilate in History and Interpretation*. Cambridge: Cambridge University Press.

———. 2004. *Caiaphas: Friend of Rome and Judge of Jesus?* Louisville: Westminster John Knox.

————. 2007. "Discarding the Seamless Robe: The High Priesthood of Jesus in John's Gospel." Pages 183–94 in *Israel's God and Rebecca's Children: Christology and Community in Early Judaism and Christianity*. Edited by David B. Capes, April D. DeConick, Helen K. Bond, and Troy A. Miller. Waco, Tex.: Baylor University Press.

Borg, Marcus. 1994. *Jesus in Contemporary Scholarship*. Valley Forge, Pa.: Trinity Press International.

Borgen, Peder. 1965. *Bread from Heaven: An Exegetical Study of the Concept of Manna in the Gospel of John and the Writings of Philo*. NovTSup 11. Leiden: Brill.

————. 1990. "John and the Synoptics." Pages 408–58 in *The Interrelations of the Gospels*. Edited by David L. Dungan. Macon, Ga.: Mercer University Press.

Bousset, Wilhelm. 1926. *Die Religion des Judentums*. Tübingen: Mohr Siebeck.

Bowie, Ewen. 1994. "The Readership of Greek Novels in the Ancient World." Pages 435–59 in *The Search for the Ancient Novel*. Edited by James Tatum. Baltimore: Johns Hopkins University Press.

Boyarin, Daniel. 2001. "Justin Martyr Invents Judaism." *Church History* 70:427–61.

Boyd, W. J. P. 1967. "The Ascension according to St. John: Chapters 14–17 Not Pre-passion but Post-resurrection." *Theology* 70:207–11.

Broadhead, Edwin K. 1994. *Prophet, Son, Messiah: Narrative Form and Function in Mark 14–16*. JSNTSup 97. Sheffield: Sheffield Academic Press.

Brodie, Thomas L. 1993. *The Quest for the Origin of John's Gospel: A Source-Oriented Approach*. Oxford: Oxford University Press.

Broer, Ingo. 1992. "Jesus und das Gesetz: Anmerkungen zur Geschichte des Problems und zur Frage der Sündenvergebung durch den historischen Jesus." Pages 61–104 in idem, *Jesus und das jüdische Gesetz*. Stuttgart: Kohlhammer.

Brown, Raymond E. 1961. "Incidents That Are Units in the Synoptic Gospels but Dispersed in St. John." *CBQ* 23:143–61.

————. 1965. *New Testament Essays*. Milwaukee: Bruce; New York: Paulist.

————. 1966–70. *The Gospel according to John*. 2 vols. AB 29–29A. Garden City, N.Y.: Doubleday.

————. 1979. *The Community of the Beloved Disciple*. New York: Paulist.

————. 1982. *The Epistles of John*. AB 30. Garden City, N.Y.: Doubleday.

————. 1994. *The Death of the Messiah: From Gethsemane to the Grave*. 2 vols. New York: Doubleday.

————. 1997. *An Introduction to the New Testament*. New York: Doubleday.

————. 2003. *An Introduction to the Gospel of John: Edited, updated, introduced, and concluded by Francis J. Moloney*. ABRL. New York: Doubleday.

Browning, Robert. 1864. *A Death in the Desert*. In *Dramatis Personae*. London: Chapman & Hall.

Bruce, F. F. 1976. "Myth and History." Pages 79–99 in *History, Criticism and Faith*. Edited by C. Brown. Downers Grove, Ill.: InterVarsity Press.

————. 1980. "The Trial of Jesus in the Fourth Gospel." Pages 7–20 in vol. 1 of *Gospel Perspectives: Studies of History and Tradition in the Four Gospels*. Edited by R. T. France and David Wenham. Sheffield: JSOT Press.

Büchler, Adolf. 1906. *Der galiläische 'Am-ha 'Arets des zweiten Jahrhunderts: Beiträge zur inneren Geschichte des palästinischen Judentums in den ersten zwei Jahrhunderten*. Repr., Hildesheim: Olms, 1968.

Bull, Robert J. 1975. "An Archaeological Context for Understanding John 4:20." *Biblical Archaeologist* 38:54–59.

———. 1977. "An Archaeological Footnote to 'Our Fathers Worshipped on this Mountain,' John 4:20." *NTS* 23:460–62.

Bultmann, Rudolf. 1958 [1934; 1926 in German]. *Jesus and the Word*. Translated by Louise Pettibone Smith and Erminie Huntress Lantero. New York: Charles Scriber's Sons.

———. 1962. *Das Evangelium des Johannes*. 17th ed. Göttingen: Vandenhoeck & Ruprecht.

Burge, Gary M. 2001. "Situating John's Gospel in History." Pages 35–46 in Fortna and Thatcher 2001.

Burns, Rita J. 1990. "Jesus and the Bronze Serpent." *The Bible Today* 28.2:84–89.

Burridge, Richard A. 2004. *What Are the Gospels? A Comparison with Graeco-Roman Biography*. 2nd ed. Grand Rapids: Eerdmans.

———. 2005. *Four Gospels, One Jesus: A Symbolic Reading*. 2nd ed. Grand Rapids: Eerdmans.

———. 2007. *Imitating Jesus: An Inclusive Approach to New Testament Ethics*. Grand Rapids: Eerdmans, 2007.

Byrne, Brendan. 1991. *Lazarus: A Contemporary Reading of John 11:1–46*. Zacchaeus Studies. Collegeville, Minn.: Liturgical Press.

Byrskog, Samuel. 2000. *Story as History–History as Story: The Gospel Traditions in the Context of Ancient Oral History*. WUNT 123. Tübingen: Mohr Siebeck.

Caragounis, Chrys C. 2001. "The Kingdom of God: Common and Distinct Elements between John and the Synoptics." Pages 125–34 in Fortna and Thatcher 2001.

Carleton Paget, James. 2001. "Some Observations on Josephus and Christianity." *JJS* 52:539–624.

Carlson, Stephen C. 2005. *The Gospel Hoax: Morton Smith's Invention of Secret Mark*. Waco, Tex.: Baylor University Press.

Carroll, Kenneth L. 1957. "The Fourth Gospel and the Exclusion of Christians from the Synagogues." *BJRL* 40:19–32.

Carson, D. A. 1991. *The Gospel according to John*. Leicester: Inter-Varsity Press; Grand Rapids: Eerdmans.

———. 2007. "The Challenge of the Balkanization of Johannine Studies." Pages 133–59 in Anderson, Just, and Thatcher 2007.

Carter, Charles W., and R. Duane Thompson. 1990. *The Biblical Ethic of Love*. American University Studies Series 7: Theology and Religion 79. New York: Lang.

Casey, Maurice. 1996. *Is John's Gospel True?* London: Routledge.

Catchpole, David R. 1970. "The Problem of the Historicity of the Sanhedrin Trial." Pages 47–65 in *The Trial of Jesus*. Edited by E. Bammel. London: SCM.

———. 1992. "The Centurion's Faith and Its Function in Q." Pages 517–40 in van Segbroeck 1992.

———. 1993. "Faith." Pages 280–308 in idem, *The Quest for Q*. Edinburgh: T&T Clark.

———. 2006. *Jesus People: The Historical Jesus and the Beginnings of Community*. London: Darton, Longman & Todd.

Chancey, Mark. 2002. *The Myth of a Gentile Galilee*. SNTSMS 118. Cambridge: Cambridge University Press.

———. 2005. *Greco-Roman Culture and the Galilee of Jesus*. SNTSMS 134. Cambridge: Cambridge University Press.

Charlesworth, James H., ed. 1983–85. *The Old Testament Pseudepigrapha*. 2 vols. Garden City, N.Y.: Doubleday.

———. 1988. *Jesus within Judaism: New Light from Exciting Archaeological Discoveries*. New York: Doubleday.

———, ed. 1990. *John and the Dead Sea Scrolls*. New York: Crossroad.

———, ed. 1992. *Jesus and the Dead Sea Scrolls*. New York: Doubleday.

———. 1995. *The Beloved Disciple: Whose Witness Validates the Gospel of John?* Valley Forge, Pa.: Trinity Press International.

———, ed. 2006. *Jesus and Archaeology*. Grand Rapids: Eerdmans.

———. 2008. *The Historical Jesus: An Essential Guide*. Nashville: Abingdon.

———. 2010 (forthcoming). *The Good and Evil Serpent: How a Universal Symbol Became Christianized*. ABRL. New Haven: Yale University Press.

Chernus, Ira. 1982. "Visions of God in Merkabah Mysticism." *Journal for the Study of Judaism* 13.1–2:123–46.

Clark, Kenneth. 1969. *Civilization*. New York: Harper & Row.

Clark-Soles, Jaime. 2003. *Scripture Cannot Be Broken: The Social Function of the Use of Scripture in the Fourth Gospel*. Leiden: Brill.

———. 2006. "'I Will Raise [Whom?] Up on the Last Day': Anthropology as a Feature of Johannine Eschatology." Pages 29–53 in *New Currents through John: A Global Perspective*. Edited by Francisco Lozada Jr. and Tom Thatcher. SBLRBS 54. Atlanta: Society of Biblical Literature.

Claussen, Carsten. 2006. "The Role of John 21: Discipleship in Retrospect and Redefinition." Pages 55–68 in *New Currents through John: A Global Perspective*. Edited by Francisco Lozada Jr. and Tom Thatcher. SBLRBS 54. Atlanta: Society of Biblical Literature.

———. 2007. "Johannine Exegesis in Transition: Johannes Beutler's Search for a New Synthesis." Pages 35–38 in *What We Have Heard from the Beginning: The Past, Present, and Future of Johannine Studies*. Edited by Tom Thatcher. Waco, Tex.: Baylor University Press.

Coakley, James F. 1988. "The Anointing at Bethany and the Priority of John." *JBL* 107:241–56.

Coggins, Richard J. 1982. "The Samaritans and Acts." *NTS* 28:423–34.

Collins, John J. 1995. *The Scepter and the Star: The Messiahs of the Dead Sea Scrolls and Other Ancient Literature*. ABRL. New York: Doubleday.

———. 1997. "Marriage, Divorce, and Family in Second Temple Judaism." Pages 104–62 in *Families in Ancient Israel*. Edited by Leo G. Perdue et al. Louisville: Westminster John Knox.

Coloe, Mary L. 2001. *God Dwells with Us: Temple Symbolism in the Fourth Gospel*. Collegeville, Minn.: Liturgical Press.

———. 2004. "Welcome into the Household of God: The Footwashing in John 13." *CBQ* 66: 400–415.

———. 2007. *Dwelling in the Household of God: Johannine Ecclesiology and Spirituality*. Collegeville, Minn.: Liturgical Press.

Conway, Colleen M. 1999. *Men and Women in the Fourth Gospel: Gender and Johannine Characterization*. SBLDS 167. Atlanta: Scholars Press.

Corley, Kathleen E. 2003. "The Anointing of Jesus in the Synoptic Tradition: An Argument for Authenticity." *JSHJ* 1:61–72.

Cranfield, Charles E. B. 1963. *The Gospel according to Saint Mark: An Introduction and Commentary*. 2nd ed. Cambridge Greek Testament Commentary. Cambridge: Cambridge University Press.

Crossan, John Dominic. 1988. *The Cross That Spoke*. San Francisco: Harper & Row.

———. 1991. *The Historical Jesus: The Life of a Mediterranean Jewish Peasant*. San Francisco: HarperCollins.

———. 1994. *Jesus: A Revolutionary Biography*. San Francisco: HarperSanFrancisco.

———. 1996. *Who Killed Jesus? Exposing the Roots of Anti-Semitism in the Gospel Story of the Death of Jesus*. San Francisco: HarperSanFrancisco.

Culpepper, R. Alan. 1975. *The Johannine School: An Evaluation of the Johannine-School Hypothesis Based on an Investigation of the Nature of Ancient Schools*. SBLDS 26. Missoula, Mont.: Scholars Press.

———. 1983. *Anatomy of the Fourth Gospel: A Study in Literary Design*. Philadelphia: Fortress.

———. 1994. *John, the Son of Zebedee: The Life of a Legend*. Columbia: University of South Carolina Press.

———. 2006. "Designs for the Church in the Imagery of John 21:1–14." Pages 369–402 in *Imagery in the Gospel of John: Terms, Forms, Themes, and Theology of Johannine Figurative Language*. Edited by Jörg Frey, Jan G. van der Watt, and Rueben Zimmermann. WUNT 200. Tübingen: Mohr Siebeck.

Danby, Herbert, trans. 1933. *The Mishnah*. Oxford: Clarendon.

Daube, David. 1950. "Jesus and the Samaritan Woman: The Meaning of συγχράομαι." *JBL* 69:137–47.

———. 1960. "Three Notes Having to Do with Johanan Ben Zaccai." *JTS* 11:53–62.

Dawes, Gregory W. 2006. "Why Historicity Still Matters: Raymond Brown and the Infancy Narratives." *Pacifica* 19.2:156–76.

Deines, Roland. 1992. *Jüdische Steingefässe und pharisäische Frömmigkeit. Ein archäologisch-historischer Beitrag zum Verständnis von Joh 2, 6 und der jüdischen Reinheitshalacha zur Zeit Jesu*. WUNT 52. Tübingen: Mohr Siebeck.

Dettwiler, Andreas. 1995. *Die Gegenwart des Erhöhten: Eine exegetische Studie zu den johanneischen Abschiedsreden (Joh 13,31–16,33) unter besonderer Berücksichtigung ihres Relecture-Charakters*. FRLANT 169. Göttingen: Vandenhoeck & Ruprecht.

Dick, Karl. 1900. *Der schriftstellerische Plural bei Paulus*. Halle: Niemeyer.

Dietzfelbinger, Christian. 1985. "Paraklet und theologischer Anspruch im Johannesevangelium." *Zeitschrift für Theologie und Kirche* 82.4:389–408.

Dillon, John. 1975. "The Transcendence of God in Philo: Some Possible Sources." Pages 1–8 in *Center for Hermeneutical Studies in Hellenistic and Modern Culture Colloquy* 16. Berkeley: Center for Hermeneutical Studies in Hellenistic and Modern Culture.

Dionysius of Halicarnassus. *The Critical Essays*. 1974. Translated by Stephen Usher. 2 vols. LCL. Cambridge: Harvard University Press.

———. *The Roman Antiquities*. 1937–50. Translated by Earnest Cary et al. 7 vols. LCL. Cambridge: Harvard University Press.

Dodd, C. H. 1953. *The Interpretation of the Fourth Gospel*. Cambridge: Cambridge University Press.

———. 1962. "The Prophecy of Caiaphas (John xi,47–53)." Pages 134–43 in *Neotestamentica et Patristica*. NovTSup 6. Leiden: Brill.

————. 1963. *Historical Tradition in the Fourth Gospel.* Cambridge: Cambridge University Press.

Doudna, Gregory L. 2001. *4Q Pesher Nahum: A Critical Edition.* Journal for the Study of the Pseudepigrapha Supplement Series 35. Copenhagen International Series 8. Sheffield: Sheffield Academic Press.

Drummond, James. 1897. "The Fourth Gospel and the Quartodecimans." *American Journal of Theology* 1:601–57.

Dunkerley, Roderic. 1959. "Lazarus." *NTS* 5:321–27.

Dunn, James D. G. 1991. "John and the Oral Gospel Tradition." Pages 351–79 in *Jesus and the Oral Gospel Tradition.* Edited by Henry Wansbrough. JSNTSup 64. Sheffield: JSOT Press.

————, ed. 1992a. *Jews and Christians: The Parting of the Ways A.D. 70 to 135.* WUNT 66. Tübingen: Mohr Siebeck.

————. 1992b. "Matthew's Awareness of Markan Redaction." Pages 1349–59 in vol. 2 of *van Segbroeck 1992.*

————. 1994. "John the Baptist's Use of Scripture." Pages 42–54 in *The Gospels and the Scriptures of Israel.* Edited by C. A. Evans and W. Richard Stegner. JSNTSup 104. SSEJC 3. Sheffield: Sheffield Academic Press.

————. 2002. "Jesus and Purity: An Ongoing Debate." *NTS* 48:449–67.

————. 2003a. "Altering the Default Setting: Re-envisaging the Early Transmission of the Jesus Tradition." *NTS* 49:139–75.

————. 2003b. *Jesus Remembered: Christianity in the Making.* Vol. 1. Grand Rapids: Eerdmans.

————. 2005. *A New Perspective on Jesus.* Grand Rapids: Baker.

Ehrman, Bart. 1999. *Jesus: Apocalyptic Prophet of the New Millennium.* Oxford: Oxford University Press.

————, ed. and trans. 2003. *Apostolic Fathers.* 2 vols. LCL. Cambridge: Harvard University Press.

Eisenman, Robert H. 1993. "Fragments: More on the Pierced Messiah Text from Eisenman and Vermes." *BAR* 19.1:66–67.

Eisenman, Robert H., and Michael Wise, eds. 1992. *The Dead Sea Scrolls Uncovered.* Dorset, U.K.: Element Books, Ltd.

Elliott, J. Keith. 1973–74. "The Anointing of Jesus." *ExpT* 85:105–7.

Ellis, E. Earle. 2000. "Background and Christology of John's Gospel: Selected Motifs." Pages 70–88 in idem, *Christ and the Future in New Testament History.* NovTSup 97. Leiden: Brill. Originally published in *Southwest Journal of Theology* 31.1 (1988): 24–31.

Engle, Anita. 1977. "*Amphorisk* of the Second Temple Period." *Palestine Exploration Quarterly* 109:117–22.

Epp, Eldon Jay. 1975. "Wisdom, Torah, Word: The Johannine Prologue and the Purpose of the Fourth Gospel." 128–46 in *Current Issues in Biblical and Patristic Interpretation: Studies in Honor of Merrill C. Tenney Presented by his Former Students.* Edited by G. F. Hawthorne. Grand Rapids: Eerdmans.

Ernst, Josef. 1989. *Johannes der Täufer: Interpretation-Geschichte-Wirkungsgeschichte.* BZNW 53. Berlin: de Gruyter.

Escaffre, Bernadette. 2000. "Pierre et Jésus dans la cour du grand prêtre (Jn 18,12–27)." *Revue théologique de Louvain* 31:43–67.

Esler, Philip F., and Ronald A. Piper. 2006. *Lazarus, Mary, and Martha: Social-Scientific Approaches to the Gospel of John.* Minneapolis: Fortress.

Estes, Douglas Charles. 2008. *The Temporal Mechanics of the Fourth Gospel: A Theory of Hermeneutical Relativity in the Gospel of John.* BIS 92. Leiden: Brill.

Evans, Craig A. 1993. *Word and Glory: On the Exegetical and Theological Background of John's Prologue.* JSNTSup 89. Sheffield: JSOT Press.

———. 1995. *Jesus and His Contemporaries: Comparative Studies.* AGJU 25. Leiden: Brill.

———. 1996. *Life of Jesus Research: An Annotated Bibliography.* 2nd ed. NTTS 24. Leiden: Brill.

———. 1999. "Jesus and Zechariah's Messianic Hope." Pages 373–88 in *Authenticating the Activities of Jesus.* Edited by Craig A. Evans and Bruce Chilton. NTTS 28.2. Leiden: Brill.

———. 2001. *Mark 8:27–16:20.* WBC 34B. Nashville: Nelson.

———. 2002. "The Baptism of John in a Typological Context." Pages 45–71 in *Dimensions of Baptism: Biblical and Theological Studies.* Edited by A. R. Cross and S. E. Porter. JSNTSup 234. Sheffield: Sheffield Academic Press.

———, ed. 2008. *Encyclopedia of the Historical Jesus.* New York: Routledge.

Fitzmyer, Joseph A. 1978. "Crucifixion in Ancient Palestine, Qumran Literature, and the New Testament." *CBQ* 40:493–513.

———. 1985. *The Gospel according to Luke (X–XXIV).* AB 28A. New York: Doubleday.

———. 1998. *The Acts of the Apostles.* AB 31. New York: Doubleday.

Flusser, David. 1988. *Judaism and the Origins of Christianity.* Jerusalem: Hebrew University, Magnes.

Fortna, Robert T. 1978. "Jesus and Peter at the High Priest's House: A Test Case for the Question of the Relation between Mark's and John's Gospels." *NTS* 24:371–83.

———. 1988. *The Fourth Gospel and Its Predecessor.* Edinburgh: T&T Clark; Minneapolis: Fortress.

Fortna, Robert T., and Tom Thatcher, eds. 2001. *Jesus in Johannine Tradition.* Louisville: Westminster John Knox.

Fotheringam. J. K. 1934. "The Evidence of Astronomy and Technical Chronology for the Date of the Crucifixion." *JTS* 35:146–62.

Fowler, Henry Watson, and Francis George Fowler, trans. 1905. *The Works of Lucian of Samosata.* Oxford: Clarendon.

France, Richard T. 2002. *The Gospel of Mark.* NIGTC. Grand Rapids: Eerdmans; Carlisle: Paternoster.

Frankel, Eduard. 1957. *Horace.* Oxford: Oxford University Press.

Fredriksen, Paula. 1999. *Jesus of Nazareth, King of the Jews: A Jewish Life and the Emergence of Christianity.* New York: Knopf.

———. 2007. "The Historical Jesus, the Scene in the Temple, and the Gospel of John." Pages 249–76 in Anderson, Just, and Thatcher 2007.

Freyne, Sean. 1988. *Galilee, Jesus and the Gospels: Literary Approaches and Historical Investigations.* Dublin: Gill & McMillan; Minneapolis: Fortress.

———. 2001a. "The Geography of Restoration: Galilee–Jerusalem Relations in Early Judaism and Early Christianity." *NTS* 47:289–31.

———. 2001b. "A Galilean Messiah?" *Studia Theologica* 55:198–218.

———. 2004. *Jesus, A Jewish Galilean: A New Reading of the Jesus Story.* London: T&T Clark.

Friedländer, Moriz. 1894. *Zur Entstehungsgeschichte des Christentums: Ein Excurs von der Septuaginta zum Evangelium*. Vienna: Hölder.

Fuglseth, Kåre Sigvald. 2005. *Johannine Sectarianism in Perspective: A Sociological, Historical, and Comparative Analysis of Temple and Social Relationships in the Gospel of John, Philo, and Qumran*. NovTSup 119. Leiden: Brill.

Funk, Robert W., and Roy W. Hoover. 1993. *The Five Gospels: The Search for the Authentic Words of Jesus*. New York: MacMillan.

Funk, Robert W., et al. 1998. *The Acts of Jesus: The Search for the Authentic Deeds of Jesus*. San Francisco: HarperSanFrancisco.

Fusillo, Massimo. 1997. "How Novels End: Some Patterns of Closure in Ancient Narrative." Pages 209–27 in *Classical Closure: Reading the End in Greek and Latin Literature*. Edited by Deborah H. Roberts, Francis M. Dunn, and Don Fowler. Princeton: Princeton University Press.

Gadamer, Hans Georg. 1990. *Wahrheit und Methode: Grundzüge einer philosophischen Hermeneutik 1*. Gesammelte Werke 1. Tübingen: Mohr Siebeck.

Gagnon, Robert A. J. 1994. "The Shape of Matthew's Q Text of the Centurion at Capernaum: Did It Mention Delegations?" *NTS* 40:133–42.

Gamble, Harry. 2004. "Literacy, Liturgy and the Shaping of the New Testament Canon." Pages 27–39 in *The Earliest Gospels*. Edited by Charles Horton. London: T&T Clark.

Gardner-Smith, Percival. 1938. *Saint John and the Synoptic Gospels*. Cambridge: Cambridge University Press.

Genette, Gérard. 1997. *Paratexts: Thresholds of Interpretation*. Translated by Jane E. Lewin. Cambridge: Cambridge University Press.

Gerhardsson, Birger. 1961. *Memory and Manuscript: Oral Tradition and Written Transmission in Rabbinic Judaism and Early Christianity*. Lund: Gleerup.

Giblin, Charles H. 1979–80. "Suggestion, Negative Response, and Positive Action in St. John's Portrayal of Jesus (John 2.1–11; 4.46–54; 7.2–14; 11.1–44)." *NTS* 26:197–211.

Gibson, Shimon. 2005. "The Pool of Bethesda in Jerusalem and Jewish Purification Practices of the Second Temple Period." *Proche Orient-Chrétien* 55:270–93.

Gill, Dan. 1994. "Jerusalem's Underground Water Systems: How They Met: Geology Solves Long-Standing Mystery of Hezekiah's Tunnelers." *BAR* 20.4:20–33, 64.

———. 1996. "The Geology of the City of David and Its Ancient Subterranean Waterworks." Pages 1–28 in *Excavations at the City of David 1978–1985, Directed by Yigal Shiloh. Volume 4: Various Reports*. Edited by Donald T. Ariel and Alon DeGroot. Qedem 35. Jerusalem: Institute of Archaeology, The Hebrew University of Jerusalem.

Glasson, T. Francis. 1969. "Colossians I 18, 15 and Sirach XXIV." *NovT* 11.1–2:154–56.

Gnilka, Joachim. 1997. *Jesus of Nazareth: Message and History*. Peabody, Mass.: Hendrickson.

Goertz, Hans Jürgen. 2001. *Unsichere Geschichte: Zur Theorie historischer Referentialität*. Reclams Universal-Bibliothek 17035. Stuttgart: Reclam.

Goggin, Sr. Thomas Aquinas, trans. 1957–59. *John Chrysostom: Commentary on St. John the Apostle and Evangelist*. 2 vols. New York: Fathers of the Church.

Goldsmith, Dale. 1988. *New Testament Ethics: An Introduction*. Elgin, Ill.: Brethren.

Goodblatt, David. 1994. *The Monarchic Principle: Studies in Jewish Self-Government in Antiquity*. Tübingen: Mohr Siebeck.

Goodman, Martin. 1987. *The Ruling Class of Judaea*. Cambridge: Cambridge University Press.

Graupner, Axel, and Michael Wolter, eds. 2007. *Moses in Biblical and Extra-Bible Traditions*. Berlin: de Gruyter.

Graves, Robert, trans. 1989. *Suetonius: The Twelve Caesars*. Revised with an introduction by Michael Grant. New York: Penguin.

Gray, Rebecca. 1993. *Prophetic Figures in Late Second Temple Jewish Palestine: The Evidence from Josephus*. Oxford: Oxford University Press.

Green, Joel B. 1997. *The Gospel of Luke*. New International Commentary on the New Testament. Grand Rapids: Eerdmans.

Grenfell, Bernard P., Arthur S. Hunt, and J. Gilbart Smyly, eds. 1902. *The Tebtunis Papyri*. London: Henry Frowde.

Guelich, Robert A. 1989. *Mark 1–8:26*. WBC 34A. Dallas: Word.

Gutman, S. 1993. "Gamala." Pages 459–63 in vol. 2 of Stern 1993.

Haas, Nicu. 1970. "Anthropological Observations on the Skeletal Remains from Giv'at Ha-Mivtar." *IEJ* 20:38–59.

Haenchen, Ernst. 1970. "History and Interpretation in the Johannine Passion Narrative." *Int* 24:198–219.

———. 1984. *John: A Commentary on the Gospel of John*. Edited by Robert W. Funk and Ulrich Busse. 2 vols. Hermeneia. Translated by Robert W. Funk. Philadelphia: Fortress.

Hägerland, Tobias. 2003. "John's Gospel: A Two-Level Drama?" *JSNT* 25:309–22.

Hagner, Donald A. 1971. "The Vision of God in Philo and John: A Comparative Study." *JETS* 14.2:81–93.

Hahn, Ferdinand. 1969. *The Titles of Jesus in Christology: Their History in Early Christianity*. Translated by Harold B. Knight and George Ogg. London: Lutterworth.

Hall, Stuart George. 1979. *Melito of Sardis: On Pascha and Fragments*. Oxford: Clarendon.

Hammer, J. 1959. "Eine klare Stellung zu Joh. 14.13b." *Bibel und Kirche* 14:33–40.

Hanson, Anthony. 1976. "John I.14–18 and Exodus XXXIV." *NTS* 23.1:90–101.

Harrington, Hannah K. 2004. *The Purity Texts*. Companion to the Qumran Scrolls 5. London: T&T Clark.

Harris, Murray J. 1986. " 'The Dead Are Restored to Life': Miracles of Revivification in the Gospels." Pages 295–326 in *The Miracles of Jesus*. Vol. 6 of *Gospel Perspectives*. Edited by David Wenham and Craig L. Blomberg. Sheffield: Sheffield Academic Press.

Harrison, R. K. 1992. *Numbers: An Exegetical Commentary*. Grand Rapids: Baker.

Hartenstein, Judith. 2000. *Die zweite Lehre: Erscheinungen des Auferstandenen als Rahmenerzählungen frühchristlicher Dialoge*. Texte und Untersuchungen zur Geschichte der altchristlichen Literatur 146. Berlin: Akademie.

Harvey, Anthony E. 1976. *Jesus on Trial: A Study in the Fourth Gospel*. London: SPCK.

Hasitschka, Martin. 1999. "Die beiden 'Zeichen' am See von Tiberias: Interpretation von Joh 6 in Verbindung mit Joh 21,1–14." *SNTSU* 24:85–102.

Hays, Richard B. 1996. *The Moral Vision of the New Testament: A Contemporary Introduction to New Testament Ethics*. San Francisco: HarperSanFrancisco; Edinburgh: T&T Clark.

Hayward, Robert (C.T.R.). 1996. *The Jewish Temple: A Non-Biblical Sourcebook*. London: Routledge.

Hendricks, Obery M., Jr. 2001. "Introduction to the Gospel according to John." Pages NT 146–47 in *The New Oxford Annotated Bible: New Revised Standard Version with the Apocrypha*. 3rd ed. Edited Michael D. Coogan, Marc Zvi Brettler, Carol A. Newsom, and Pheme Perkins. New York: Oxford University Press.

Hendriksen, William. 2002. *New Testament Commentary*. Vol. 3: *Luke*. Grand Rapids: Baker.

Hengel, Martin. 1974. *Judaism and Hellenism: Studies in Their Encounter in Palestine during the Early Hellenistic Period*. Vol. 1. Philadelphia: Fortress.

———. 1977. *Crucifixion*. Translated by John Bowden. Philadelphia: Fortress.

———. 1981. *The Charismatic Leader and His Followers*. London: T&T Clark.

———. 1989a. *The Johannine Question*. Philadelphia: Trinity Press International.

———. 1989b. "Die Schriftauslegung des 4. Evangeliums auf dem Hintergrund der urchristlichen Exegese." Pages 249–88 in *"Gesetz" als Thema Biblischer Theologie*. Vol. 4 of *Jahrbuch für Biblische Theologie*. Edited by M. A. Schökel et al. Neukirchen-Vluyn: Neukirchener.

———. 1993. *Die johanneische Frage: Ein Lösungsversuch*. WUNT 67. Tübingen: Mohr Siebeck.

———. 1999. "Das Johannesevangelium als Quelle des antiken Judentums." Pages 41–74 in *Jüdische Geschichte in hellenistisch-römischer Zeit: Wege der Forschung: Vom alten zum neuen Schürer*. Edited by Aharon Oppenheimer and Elisabeth Müller-Luckner. Schriften des Historischen Kollegs 44. Munich: Oldenbourg.

Hezser, Catherine. 2001. *Jewish Literacy in Roman Palestine*. TSAJ 81. Tübingen: Mohr Siebeck.

Himmelfarb, Martha. 1988. "Heavenly Ascent and the Relationship of the Apocalypse and the *Hekhalot* Literature." *Hebrew Union College Annual* 59:73–100.

Hjelm, Ingrid. 2000. *The Samaritans and Early Judaism: A Literary Analysis*. JSOTSup 303. Sheffield: Sheffield Academic Press.

Holmén, Tom. 2001. *Jesus and Jewish Covenant Thinking*. BIS 55. Leiden: Brill.

Horbury, William. 1982. "The Benediction of the *Minim* and Early Jewish-Christian Controversy." *JTS* 33:19–61.

———. 1986. "The Twelve and the Phylarchs." *NTS* 32:503–27.

Horsley, Richard A. 1984. "Popular Messianic Movements around the Time of Jesus." *CBQ* 46:471–95.

———. 1985. "'Like One of the Prophets of Old': Two Types of Popular Prophets at the Time of Jesus." *CBQ* 47:435–63.

———. 1987. *Jesus and the Spiral of Violence: Popular Jewish Resistance in Roman Palestine*. San Francisco: Harper & Row.

———. 2001. *Hearing the Whole Story: The Politics of Plot in Mark's Gospel*. Louisville: Westminster John Knox.

Horsley, Richard A., and John S. Hanson. 1985. *Bandits, Prophets, and Messiahs: Popular Movements at the Time of Jesus*. New Voices in Biblical Studies. Minneapolis: Winston. Repr., San Francisco: Harper & Row, 1988.

Horst, Pieter W. van der. 1998. "The *Birkat Ha-minim* in Recent Research." Pages 113–24 in *Hellenism–Judaism–Christianity: Essays on Their Interaction*. Edited by Pieter W. van der Horst. 2nd ed. Leuven: Peeters.

Horton, Charles, ed. 2004. *The Earliest Gospels: The Origins and Transmission of the Earliest Christian Gospels—The Contribution of the Chester Beatty Gospel Codex, P45*. JSNTSup 248. London: T&T Clark.

Ilan, Tal. 2002. *Lexicon of Jewish Names in Late Antiquity, Part 1: Palestine 330 BCE – 200 CE*. Texts and Studies in Ancient Judaism 91. Tübingen: Mohr Siebeck.

Instone-Brewer, David. 2003. "The Eighteen Benedictions and the *Minim* before 70 C.E."
	JTS 54:25–44.

Isaacs, Marie E. 1976. *The Concept of Spirit: A Study of Pneuma in Hellenistic Judaism and Its
	Bearing on the New Testament.* Heythrop Monographs 1. London: Heythrop College.

Jackson, Howard M. 1999. "Ancient Self-Referential Conventions and Their Implications
	for the Authorship and Integrity of the Gospel of John." *JTS* 50:1–34.

Jaubert, Annie. 1965. *The Date of the Last Supper.* Staten Island, N.Y.: Alba House.

———. 1972. "The Calendar of Qumran and the Passion Narrative in John." Pages 62–75
	in *John and Qumran.* Edited by James Charlesworth. London: Chapman.

Jeremias, Joachim. 1956. *Jesu Verheissung für die Völker.* Stuttgart: Kohlhammer. 2nd
	ed., 1959. English translation: *Jesus' Promise to the Nations.* SBT 24. Naperville, Ill.:
	Allenson, 1958.

———. 1966. *The Eucharistic Words of Jesus.* Translated by Norman Perrin. 3rd ed. New
	York: Charles Scribner's Sons.

———. 1967. "νύμφη, νυμφίος." *TDNT* 4:1099–1106.

———. 1971. *New Testament Theology: The Proclamation of Jesus.* New York: Charles Scrib-
	ner's Sons.

Johnson, Brian D. 2001. "The Temple in the Gospel of John." Pages 110–33 in *Christ's
	Victorious Church: Essays on Biblical Ecclesiology and Eschatology in Honor of Tom
	Friskney.* Edited by Jon A. Weatherly. Eugene, Ore.: Wipf & Stock.

———. 2006. "'Salvation Is from the Jews': Judaism in the Gospel of John." Pages 83–99 in
	New Currents through John: A Global Perspective. Edited by Francisco Lozada Jr. and
	Tom Thatcher. SBLRBS 54. Atlanta: Society of Biblical Literature.

Johnson, Steven R. 2002. *The Database of the International Q Project: Q 7:1–10: The
	Centurion's Faith in Jesus' Word.* Documenta Q: Reconstructions of Q through Two
	Centuries of Gospel Research Excerpted, Sorted, and Evaluated. Leuven: Peeters.

Jonge, Marinus de. 1977. "Jewish Expectation about the 'Messiah' according to the Fourth
	Gospel." Pages 77–116 in idem, *Jesus: Stranger from Heaven and Son of God.* SBL
	Sources for Biblical Study 11. Missoula, Mont.: Scholars Press.

Josephus, Flavius. *Jewish Antiquities.* 1986–98. Translated by Ralph Marcus et al. 9 vols.
	LCL. Cambridge: Harvard University Press.

———. *The Jewish War.* 1989–97. Edited and translated by Henry St. John Thackeray. 3
	vols. LCL. Cambridge: Harvard University Press.

Jowett, Benjamin, trans. 1937. *The Dialogues of Plato.* 2 vols. New York: Random House.

Judge, Peter J. 1989. "Luke 7,1–10: Sources and Redaction." Pages 473–90 in *L'Évangile de
	Luc/The Gospel of Luke.* Edited by Franz Neirynck. BETL 32. Leuven: Peeters.

———. 2004. Review of S. R. Johnson 2002. *ETL* 80:196–200.

Juel, Donald. 1977. *Messiah and Temple: The Trial of Jesus in the Gospel of Mark.* SBLDS 31.
	Missoula, Mont.: Scholars Press.

Kaltner, John. 1998. "Psalm 22:17b: Second Guessing 'The Old Guess.'" *JBL* 117:503–06.

Katz, Steven T. 1984. "Issues in the Separation of Judaism and Christianity after 70 C.E.: A
	Reconsideration." *JBL* 103:43–76.

Käsemann, Ernst. 1968. *The Testament of Jesus: A Study of the Gospel of John in the Light of
	Chapter 17.* Philadelphia: Fortress.

Kazen, Thomas. 2002. *Jesus and Purity Halakhah: Was Jesus Indifferent to Impurity?* Coni-
	ectanea Biblica 38. Stockholm: Almqvist & Wiksell.

Keener, Craig S. 1997. *The Spirit in the Gospels and Acts: Divine Purity and Power.* Peabody, Mass.: Hendrickson.

———. 2003. *The Gospel of John: A Commentary.* 2 vols. Peabody, Mass.: Hendrickson.

———. 2005. *1–2 Corinthians.* NCBC. Cambridge: Cambridge University Press.

———. 2007. "Genre, Sources, and History." Pages 321–23 in *What We Have Heard from the Beginning: The Past, Present, and Future of Johannine Studies.* Edited by Tom Thatcher. Waco, Tex.: Baylor University Press.

———. 2009. *The Historical Jesus of the Gospels.* Grand Rapids: Eerdmans.

Kellum, L. Scott. 2004. *The Unity of the Farewell Discourse: The Literary Integrity of John 31:31–16:33.* JSNTSup 256. New York: T&T Clark.

Kerr, Alan. 2002. *The Temple of Jesus' Body: The Temple Theme in the Gospel of John.* JSNTSup 220. London: Sheffield Academic Press.

Kimelman, Reuven. 1981. "*Birkat Ha-Minim* and the Lack of Evidence for an Anti-Christian Jewish Prayer in Late Antiquity." Pages 226–44 in vol. 2 of *Jewish and Christian Self-Definition.* Edited by E. P. Sanders et al. 3 vols. London: SCM.

Kirk, Kenneth E. 1934. *The Vision of God: The Christian Doctrine of the Summum Bonum.* Abridged ed. London: Longmans, Green & Company.

Klausner, Joseph. 1926. *Jesus of Nazareth.* New York: Macmillan.

Klawans, Jonathan. 2000. *Impurity and Sin in Ancient Judaism.* Oxford: Oxford University Press.

Klein, Günter. 1961. *Die zwölf Apostel: Ursprung und Gehalt einer Idee.* Göttingen: Vandenhoeck & Ruprecht.

Klink, Edward W., III. 2007. *The Sheep of the Fold: The Audience and Origin of the Gospel of John.* SNTSMS 141. Cambridge: Cambridge University Press.

———. 2008. "Expulsion from the Synagogue? Rethinking a Johannine Anachronism." *TynBul* 59.1:99–118.

Kloppenborg, John. 2006. "The Theodotos Synagogue Inscription." Pages 236–82 in *Jesus and Archaeology.* Edited by James Charlesworth. Grand Rapids: Eerdmans.

Koehler, Ludwig, and Walter Baumgartner, eds. 2000. *The Hebrew and Aramaic Lexicon of the Old Testament.* 5 vols. Leiden: Brill.

Koester, Craig R. 1989. "Hearing, Seeing, and Believing in the Gospel of John." *Bib* 70:327–48.

———. 1995. "Topography and Theology in the Gospel of John." Pages 436–48 in *Fortunate the Eyes That See: Essays in Honor of David Noel Freedman.* Edited by Andrew Bartelt et al. Grand Rapids: Eerdmans.

———. 2003. *Symbolism in the Fourth Gospel: Meaning, Mystery, Community.* 2nd ed. Minneapolis: Fortress.

Koester, Helmut. 1990. *Ancient Christian Gospels.* Philadelphia: Trinity Press International.

Koester, Helmut, and Elaine H. Pagels. 1988. "The Dialogue of the Savior (III,5): Introduction." Pages 244–46 in James Robinson 1988.

Köstenberger, Andreas J. 2004. *John.* BECNT. Grand Rapids: Baker.

Kuhn, Heinz-Wolfgang. 1995. "Bethsaida in the Gospels." Pages 243–53 in vol. 1 of Arav and Freund 1995–2004.

Kundsin, Karl. 1925. *Topologische Überlieferungsstoffe im Johannes-Evangelium: Eine Untersuchung.* FRLANT 22. Göttingen: Vandenhoeck & Ruprecht.

Kvalbein, Hans. 2003. "The Kingdom of God and the Kingship of Christ in the Fourth Gospel." Pages 215–232 in *Neotestamentica et Philonica: Studies in Honor of Peder*

Borgen. Edited by David E. Aune, Torrey Seland, and Jarl Henning Ulrichson. NovT-Sup 106. Leiden: Brill.

Kysar, Robert. 2005a. "Expulsion from the Synagogue: The Tale of a Theory." Chapter 15 in idem, *Voyages with John: Charting the Fourth Gospel*. Waco, Tex.: Baylor University Press.

———. 2005b. "The Whence and Whither of the Johannine Community." Pages 65–81 in *Life in Abundance: Studies of John's Gospel in Tribute to Raymond E. Brown*. Edited by John R. Donahue. Collegeville, Minn.: Liturgical Press.

Labahn, Michael. 1999. *Jesus als Lebensspender: Untersuchungen zu einer Geschichte der johanneischen Tradition anhand ihrer Wundergeschichten*. BZNW 98. Berlin: de Gruyter.

———. 2000. *Offenbarung in Zeichen und Wort: Untersuchungen zur Vorgeschichte von Joh 6,1–25a und seiner Rezeption in der Brotrede*. WUNT 2/117. Tübingen: Mohr Siebeck.

———. 2006. "Fishing for Meaning: The Miraculous Catch of Fish in John 21." Pages 125–45 in *Wonders Never Cease: The Purpose of Narrating Miracle Stories in the New Testament and Its Religious Environment*. Edited by Michael Labahn and Bert Jan Lietaert Peerbolte. LNTS 288. London: T&T Clark.

———. 2007a. "Deuteronomy in John." Pages 82–98, in *Deuteronomy in the New Testament*. Edited by Steve Moyise and Maarten J. J. Menken. LNTS 358. London: T&T Clark/Continuum.

———. 2007b. "Fischen nach Bedeutung—Sinnstiftung im Wechsel literarischer Kontexte: Der wunderbare Fischfang in Johannes 21 zwischen Inter- und Intratextualität." *SNTSU* 32:115–40.

Lake, Kirsopp, trans. 1965. *Eusebius of Caesarea: The Ecclesiastical History*. Cambridge: Harvard University Press.

Lang, Manfred. 1999. *Johannes und die Synoptiker: Eine redaktionsgeschichtliche Analyse von Joh 18–20 vor dem markinischen und lukanischen Hintergrund*. FRLANT 182. Göttingen: Vandenhoeck & Ruprecht.

Latourelle, René. 1988. *The Miracles of Jesus and the Theology of Miracles*. Translated by Matthew J. O'Connell. New York: Paulist.

Layton, Bentley. 1987. *The Gnostic Scriptures*. Garden City, N.Y.: Doubleday.

Leal, Juan. 1960. "El simbolismo histórico del IV Evangelio." *Estudios Bíblicos* 19:329–48.

Lee, Dorothy A. 2002. *Flesh and Glory: Symbolism, Gender and Theology in the Gospel of John*. New York: Crossroad.

Léon-Dufour, Xavier. 1990. "Spécificité symbolique du langage de Jean." Pages 121–34 in *La communauté johannique et son histoire: La trajectoire de l'évangile de Jean aux deux premiers siècles*. Edited by Jean-Daniel Kaestli, Jean-Michel Poffet, and Jean Zumstein. Geneva: Labor et Fides.

———. 2005. *To Act according to the Gospel*. Peabody, Mass.: Hendrickson.

Liddell, Henry George, Robert Scott, and Henry Stuart Jones. 1996. *A Greek-English Lexicon*. 9th ed. with revised supplement. Oxford: Clarendon.

Lietzmann, Hans. 1979. *Mass and Lord's Supper*. Leiden: Brill.

Lieu, Judith M. 2001. "Anti-Judaism in the Fourth Gospel: Explanation and Hermeneutics." Pages 126–43 in Bieringer et al. 2001.

———. 2005. "How John Writes." Pages 171–83 in *The Written Gospel*. Edited by Markus Bockmuehl and Donald A. Hagner. Cambridge: Cambridge University Press.

Lincoln, Andrew T. 2000. *Truth on Trial: The Lawsuit Motif in the Fourth Gospel*. Peabody, Mass.: Hendrickson.

———. 2002. "The Beloved Disciple as Eyewitness and the Fourth Gospel as Witness." *JSNT* 85:3–26.

———. 2005. *The Gospel according to St. John*. Black's New Testament Commentary 4. London: Continuum; Peabody, Mass.: Hendrickson.

Lindars, Barnabas. 1972. *The Gospel of John*. New Century Bible. London: Marshall, Morgan & Scott; Grand Rapids: Eerdmans.

———. 1981. "The Persecutions of Christians in John 15:18–16:4a." Pages 48–69 in *Suffering and Martyrdom in the New Testament*. Edited by William Horbury and Brian McNeil. Cambridge: Cambridge University Press.

Lohse, Bernhard. 1953. *Das Passafest der Quartadecimaner*. Gütersloh: Bertelsmann.

———. 1971. *Colossians and Philemon*. Philadelphia: Fortress.

Lord, Albert B. 1978. "The Gospels as Oral Traditional Literature." Pages 33–91 in *The Relationships among the Gospels: An Interdisciplinary Dialogue*. Edited by William O. Walker. San Antonio, Tex.: Trinity University Press.

Lorenz, Chris. 1997. *Konstruktion der Vergangenheit: Eine Einführung in die Geschichtstheorie*. Beiträge zur Geschichtskultur 13. Köln: Böhlau.

Lutz, Cora E., trans. 1947. "Musonius Rufus: The Roman Socrates." *Yale Classical Studies* 10:3–147.

Magen, Yitzhaq. 1993a. "Mount Gerizim and the Samaritans." Pages 91–148 in *Early Christianity in Context: Monuments and Documents*. Edited by Frédéric Manns et al. Jerusalem: Franciscan Printing Press.

———. 1993b. "The Ritual Baths (Miqva'ot) at Qedumim and the Observance of Ritual Purity among the Samaritans." Pages 181–92 in *Early Christianity in Context: Monuments and Documents*. Edited by Frédéric Manns et al. Jerusalem: Franciscan Printing Press.

Mahoney, Aidan. 1965. "A New Look at an Old Problem (John 18, 12–14, 19–24)." *CBQ* 27:137–44.

Malina, Bruce J., and Richard L. Rohrbaugh. 1998. *Social-Science Commentary on the Gospel of John*. Minneapolis: Fortress.

Marchadour, Alain. 1988. *Lazare: Histoire d'un récit, récits d'une histoire*. Lectio Divina 132. Paris: Cerf.

Marcus, Joel. 2000. *Mark 1–8: A New Translation with Introduction and Commentary*. AB 27. Garden City, N.Y.: Doubleday.

Marshall, I. Howard. 1978. *The Gospel of Luke: A Commentary on the Greek Text*. NIGTC 3. Grand Rapids: Eerdmans.

Martin, James P. 1964. "History and Eschatology in the Lazarus Narrative: John 11.1–44." *Scottish Journal of Theology* 17.3:332–43.

Martyn, J. Louis. 1968. "Attitudes Ancient and Modern toward Tradition about Jesus." *Union Seminary Quarterly Review* 23:129–45.

———. 1979. *The Gospel of John in Christian History: Essays for Interpreters*. New York: Paulist.

———. 2003. *History and Theology in the Fourth Gospel*. 3rd ed. New Testament Library. Louisville: Westminster John Knox.

Mason, Steve. 2003. *Josephus and the New Testament*. 2nd ed. Peabody, Mass.: Hendrickson.

Matera, Frank J. 1996. *New Testament Ethics: The Legacies of Jesus and Paul.* Louisville: Westminster John Knox.

Matson, Mark A. 2001a. *In Dialogue with Another Gospel.* SBLDS 178. Atlanta: Scholars Press.

———. 2001b. "The Temple Incident: An Integral Element in the Fourth Gospel's Narrative." Pages 145–53 in Fortna and Thatcher 2001.

Mayo, Philip L. 2006. "The Role of the *Birkath Haminim* in Early Jewish-Christian Relations: A Reexamination of the Evidence." *BBR* 16.2:325–44.

McGrath, James F. 2001. *John's Apologetic Christology: Legitimation and Development in Johannine Christology.* SNTSMS 111. Cambridge: Cambridge University Press.

McKnight, Scot. 2001. "Jesus and the Twelve." *BBR* 11:203–31.

McLaren, James S. 1991. *Power and Politics in Palestine: The Jews and the Governing of Their Land, 100 B.C.–A.D. 70.* JSNTSup 63. Sheffield: Sheffield Academic Press.

Meeks, Wayne A. 1967. *The Prophet-King: Moses Traditions and the Johannine Christology.* Leiden: Brill.

———. 1985. "Breaking Away: Three New Testament Pictures of Christianity's Separation from the Jewish Communities," Pages 93–115 in *"To See Ourselves as Others See Us": Christians, Jews, and "Others" in Late Antiquity.* Edited by Jacob Neusner and Ernest S. Frerichs. Chico, Calif.: Scholars Press.

———. 1996. "The Ethics of the Fourth Evangelist." Pages 317–26 in *Exploring the Gospel of John: In Honor of D. Moody Smith.* Edited by R. Alan Culpepper and C. Clifton Black. Louisville: Westminster John Knox.

Meeks, Wayne A., and J. Jervell, eds. 1997. *God's Christ and His People: Studies in Honour of Nils Alstrup Dahl.* Bergen: Universitetsvorlaget.

Meier, John P. 1990. "Jesus in Josephus: A Modest Proposal." *CBQ* 52:76–103.

———. 1991. *The Roots of the Problem and the Person.* Vol. 1 of *A Marginal Jew: Rethinking the Historical Jesus.* ABRL. New York: Doubleday.

———. 1994. *Mentor, Message, and Miracles.* Vol. 2 of *A Marginal Jew: Rethinking the Historical Jesus.* ABRL. New York: Doubleday.

———. 1997. "The Circle of the Twelve: Did It Exist during Jesus' Public Ministry?" *JBL* 116:635–72.

———. 2000. "The Historical Jesus and the Historical Samaritans: What Can Be Said?" *Bib* 81:202–32.

———. 2001. *Companions and Competitors.* Vol. 3 of *A Marginal Jew: Rethinking the Historical Jesus.* ABRL. New York: Doubleday.

Menken, Maarten. 1996. *Old Testament Quotations in the Fourth Gospel: Studies in Textual Form.* Contributions to Biblical Exegesis and Theology 15. Kampen: Kok Pharos.

Merkle, Stefan. 1994. "Telling the True Story of the Trojan War: The Eyewitness Account of Dictys of Crete." Pages 183–196 in *The Search for the Ancient Novel.* Edited by James Tatum. Baltimore: Johns Hopkins University Press.

Metzger, Bruce M. 1975. *A Textual Commentary on the Greek New Testament.* Stuttgart: Deutsche Bibelgesellschaft; London: United Bible Societies.

———. 1994. *A Textual Commentary on the Greek New Testament.* 2nd ed. Stuttgart: Deutsche Bibelgesellschaft; London: United Bible Societies.

Meyer, Ben F. 1979. *The Aims of Jesus.* London: SCM.

Meyer, Rudolf. 1947. "Der *Am ha-Arez:* Ein Beitrag zur Religionssoziologie Palästinas im ersten und zweiten nachchristlichen Jahrhundert." *Judaica* 3:169–99.

Milavec, Aaron. 2003. *The Didache*. New York: Newman.

Millar, Fergus. 1990. "Reflections on the Trial of Jesus." Pages 355–81 in *A Tribute to Geza Vermes: Essays on Jewish and Christian Literature and History*. Edited by P. R. Davies and R. T. White. Sheffield: Sheffield Academic Press.

Miller, Johnny V. 1983. "The Time of the Crucifixion." *JETS* 26.2:157–66.

Miller, Susan. 2004. *Women in Mark's Gospel*. JSNTSup 258. London: T&T Clark.

Mitchell, Margaret M. 1994. "Rhetorical Shorthand in Pauline Argumentation: The Function of the Gospel in the Corinthian Correspondence." Pages 63–88 in *Gospel in Paul: Studies on Corinthians, Galatians and Romans for Richard N. Longenecker*. Edited by L. Ann Jervis and Peter Richardson. JSNTSup 108. Sheffield: Sheffield University Press.

Moloney, Francis J. 1991. "A Sacramental Reading of John 13:1–38." *CBQ* 53: 237–56.

———. 1993. *Belief in the Word: Reading John 1–4*. Minneapolis: Fortress.

———. 1996. *Signs and Shadows: Reading John 5–12*. Minneapolis: Fortress.

———. 1998a. *Glory Not Dishonor: Reading John 13–21*. Minneapolis: Augsburg Fortress.

———. 1998b. *The Gospel of John*. Sacra pagina 4. Collegeville, Minn.: Liturgical Press.

———. 2000. "The Fourth Gospel and the Jesus of History." *NTS* 46:42–58.

———. 2005a. *The Gospel of John: Text and Context*. BIS 72. Leiden: Brill.

———. 2005b. "The Gospel of John as Scripture." *CBQ* 67:454–68.

———. 2005c. "'The Jews' in the Fourth Gospel: Another Perspective." Pages 20–44 in Moloney 2005a. Originally published in *Pacifica* 15 (2002): 16–36.

Moore, Carey A. 1977. *Daniel, Esther, and Jeremiah: The Additions*. AB 44. Garden City, N.Y.: Doubleday.

Morris, Leon. 1959. *Studies in the Fourth Gospel*. Exeter: Paternoster; Grand Rapids: Eerdmans.

Motyer, Stephen. 1997. *Your Father the Devil? A New Approach to John and "the Jews."* Paternoster Biblical and Theological Monographs. Carlisle: Paternoster.

Moulton, James H. 1908. *A Grammar of New Testament Greek*. 3rd ed. 3 vols. Edinburgh: T&T Clark.

Mowvley, Henry. 1984. "John 1.14–18 in the Light of Exodus 33.7–34.35." *ExpTim* 95.5:135–37.

Moxter, Michael. 2002. "Erzählung und Ereignis: Über den Spielraum historischer Repräsentation." Pages 67–88 in *Der historische Jesus: Tendenzen und Perspektiven der gegenwärtigen Forschung*. Edited by Jens Schröter and Ralph Brucker. BZNW 114. Berlin: de Gruyter.

Mulder, Martin Jan, and Harry Sysling, eds. 1988. *Mikra: Text, Translation, Reading and Interpretation of the Hebrew Bible in Ancient Judaism and Early Christianity*. Compendia Rerum Judaicarum ad Novum Testamentum 1. Assen: Van Gorcum; Philadelphia: Fortress.

Murphy, Catherine M. 2003. *John the Baptist: Prophet of Purity for a New Age*. Interfaces. Collegeville, Minn.: Liturgical Press.

Murphy-O'Connor, Jerome. 2000. "Jesus and the Money Changers (Mark 11:15–17; John 2:13–17)." *RB* 107:42–55.

Nautin, Pierre, ed., 1950. *Homélies Pascales*. Paris: Cerf.

Neagoe, Alexandru. 2002. *The Trial of the Gospel: An Apologetic Reading of Luke's Trial Narratives*. Cambridge: Cambridge University Press.

Neale, D. 1993. "Was Jesus a *Mesith*? Public Response to Jesus and his Ministry." *TynBul* 44:89–101.

Neirynck, Frans. 1979. *Jean et les Synoptiques: Examen critique de l'exégèse de M.-É. Boismard*. BETL 49. Leuven: Leuven University Press.

———. 1984. "John 4,46–54: Signs Source and/or Synoptic Gospels." *ETL* 60:367–75. Repr. as pages 679–88 in idem, *Evangelica II, 1982–1991: Collected Essays*. BETL 99. Leuven: Peeters, 1991.

———. 1991. "John 21." Pages 601–16 in idem, *Evangelica II, 1982–1991: Collected Essays*. BETL 99. Leuven: Peeters.

Neusner, Jacob. 1985. "The History of a Biography: Yohanan ben Zakkai in the Canonical Literature of Formative Judaism." Pages 79–96 in idem, *Formative Judaism: Religious, Historical and Literary Studies*. 5th series. Brown Judaic Studies 91. Chico, Calif.: Scholars Press.

Neyrey, Jerome H. 1995. "The Footwashing in John 13:6–11: Transformation Ritual or Ceremony?" Pages 198–213 in *The Social World of the First Christians: Essays in Honor of Wayne A. Meeks*. Edited by L. Michael White and O. Larry Yarbrough. Minneapolis: Fortress.

———. 2007. *The Gospel of John*. NCBC. Cambridge: Cambridge University Press.

Ng, Esther Yue L. 2002. *Reconstructing Christian Origins? The Feminist Theology of Elisabeth Schlüssler Fiorenza: An Evaluation*. Paternoster Biblical and Theological Monographs. Carlisle: Paternoster.

Niederwimmer, Kurt. 1998. *The Didache: A Commentary*. Hermeneia. Minneapolis: Fortress.

Nock, Arthur Darby. 1972. *Essays on Religion and the Ancient World*. 2 vols. Edited by Zeph Stewart. Cambridge: Harvard University Press.

Nolland, Thomas. 1993. *Luke*. WBC 35c. Nashville: Thomas Nelson.

North, Wendy E. Sproston. 2001. *The Lazarus Story within the Johannine Tradition*. JSNTSup 212. Sheffield: Sheffield Academic Press.

O'Collins, Gerald. 1999. "Crucifixion." *ABD* 1:1207–10.

O'Day, Gail R. 1986. *Revelation in the Fourth Gospel: Narrative Mode and Theological Claim*. Philadelphia: Fortress.

———. 1995. "The Gospel of John." Pages 491–865 in vol. 9 of *The New Interpreter's Bible*. Nashville: Abingdon.

———. 2004. "Jesus as Friend in the Gospel of John." *Int* 58:144–84.

Oberweis, Michael. 1996. "Das Papias-Zeugnis vom Tode des Johannes Zebedai." *NovT* 38:277–95.

Ong, Walter J. 1982. *Orality and Literacy: The Technologizing of the Word*. New Accents. London: Methuen.

Oppenheimer, Aharon. 1977. *The 'Am Ha-Aretz: A Study in the Social History of the Jewish People in the Hellenistic-Roman Period*. Leiden: Brill.

Os, Bas van. 2007. "Psychological Method and the Historical Jesus: The Contribution of Psychobiography." *HTS* 63:1.327–46.

Painter, John. 1996. "Inclined to God: The Quest for Eternal Life—Bultmannian Hermeneutics and the Theology of the Fourth Gospel." Pages 346–68 in *Exploring the Gospel of John: Essays in Honor of D. Moody Smith*. Edited by R. A. Culpepper and C. C. Black. Louisville: Westminster John Knox.

———. 2007. "Memory Holds the Key: The Transformation of Memory in the Interface of History and Theology in John." Pages 229–45 in Anderson, Just, and Thatcher 2007.

Parker, Richard Anthony, and Waldo Herman Dubberstein. 1956. *Babylonian Chronology 626 BC–AD 75.* Providence, R.I.: Brown University Press.

Parsenios, George L. 2005. *Departure and Consolation: The Johannine Farewell Discourses in Light of Graeco-Roman Literature.* NovTSup 117. Leiden: Brill.

Perkins, Pheme. 1980. *The Gnostic Dialogue: The Early Church and the Crisis of Gnosticism.* Theological Inquiries. New York: Paulist.

Pindar. *Nemean Odes, Isthmian Odes, Fragments.* 1997. Edited and translated by William H. Race. LCL. Cambridge: Harvard University Press.

Pliny the Elder. *Natural History.* 1938–83. Translated by H. Rackham et al. 10 vols. LCL. Cambridge: Harvard University Press.

Plummer, Alfred. 1910. *A Critical and Exegetical Commentary on the Gospel according to St. Luke.* ICC. Edinburgh: T&T Clark.

Pöhlmann, Wolfgang. 1979. "Die Abschichtung des Verlorenen Sohnes (Lk 15,12f.) und die erzählte Welt der Parabel." *ZNW* 70:194–213.

Popp, Thomas. 2001. *Grammatik des Geistes: Literarische Kunst und theologische Konzeption in Johannes 3 und 6.* Arbeiten zur Bibel und ihrer Geschichte 3. Leipzig: Evangelische Verlagsanstalt.

Press, Jeremy. 2007. "The Historicity of the Footwashing in John 13." Unpublished essay.

Purvis, James D. 1975. "The Fourth Gospel and the Samaritans." *NovT* 17:161–98.

Reardon, Brian P., ed. 1989. *Collected Ancient Greek Novels.* Berkeley and Los Angeles: University of California Press.

Reed, Jonathan L. 2000. *Archaeology and the Galilean Jesus: A Re-examination of the Evidence.* Harrisburg, Pa.: Trinity Press International.

Reich, Ronny. 1990. "*Miqva'ot* (Jewish Immersion Baths) in Eretz-Israel in the Second Temple Period and the Mishnah and Talmud Periods" [Hebrew]. Ph.D. diss. Hebrew University.

Reich, Ronny, and Eli Shukron. 2004. "The Siloam Pool in the Wake of Recent Discoveries." *New Studies on Jerusalem* 10:137–39.

———. 2006. "The Siloam Pool in the Second Temple Period in Jerusalem" [Hebrew]. *Qadmoniot* 38:91–96.

Reinhartz, Adele. 1998. "The Johannine Community and Its Jewish Neighbors: A Reappraisal." Pages 111–38 in *Literary and Social Readings of the Fourth Gospel.* Vol. 2 of *What Is John?* Edited by Fernando F. Segovia. SBLSymS 7. Atlanta: Scholars Press.

———. 2004. "Exclusion, Expulsion, Desertion: The Rhetoric of Separation in the Gospel of John." Paper presented to the John, Jesus, and History Group at the Annual Meeting of the Society of Biblical Literature. San Antonio, Texas. 21 November.

———. 2005. "John and Judaism: A Response to Burton Visotsky." Pages 108–16 in *Life in Abundance: Studies of John's Gospel in Tribute to Raymond E. Brown, S.S.* Edited by John R. Donahue. Collegeville, Minn.: Liturgical Press.

Reiser, Marius. 1997. *Jesus and Judgment: The Eschatological Proclamation in Its Jewish Context.* Minneapolis: Fortress.

Richardson, Cyril C. 1940. "The Quartodecimans and the Synoptic Chronology." *HTR* 33:177–90.

Ricoeur, Paul. 1976. *Interpretation Theory: Discourse and the Surplus of Meaning.* Fort Worth: Texas Christian University Press.

Riesner, Rainer. 1981. *Jesus als Lehrer: Eine Untersuchung zum Ursprung der Evangelien-Überlieferung.* WUNT 7. Tübingen: Mohr Siebeck.

Riggs, John. 1995. "The Sacred Food of Didache 9–10 and Second Century Ecclesiologies." Pages 256–83 in *The Didache in Context.* Edited by Clayton N. Jefford. Leiden: Brill.

Ringe, Sharon H. 1999. *Wisdom's Friends: Community and Christology in the Fourth Gospel.* Louisville: Westminster John Knox.

Ritt, Hubert. 1989. "Die Frau als Glaubensbotin. Zum Verständnis der Samaritanerin von Joh 4,1–42." Pages 287–306 in *Vom Urchristentum zu Jesus: Für Joachim Gnilka.* Edited by Hubert Frankemölle and Karl Kertelge. Freiburg: Herder.

Robinson, James M., ed. 1988. *The Nag Hammadi Library in English.* Revised ed. Leiden: Brill; San Francisco: Harper & Row.

———. 1992. "The Sayings Gospel Q." Pages 361–88 in van Segbroeck 1992.

Robinson, James M., Paul Hoffman, and John S. Kloppenborg. 2000. *The Critical Edition of Q: Synopsis Including the Gospels of Matthew and Luke, Mark and Thomas with English, German, and French Translations of Q and Thomas.* Hermeneia. Minneapolis: Fortress; Leuven: Peeters.

Robinson, John A. T. 1957–58. "Elijah, John and Jesus: An Essay in Detection." *NTS* 4:263–81.

———. 1985. *The Priority of John.* Edited by J. F. Coakley. London: SCM.

Rodda, Richard E. 2007. "Notes on the Program." *The Kennedy Center Playbill.* October 2007.

Rousseau, John, and Rami Arav. 1995. *Jesus and His World.* Minneapolis: Fortress.

Rouwhorst, Gerard. 1997. "Jewish Liturgical Traditions in Early Syriac Christianity." *VC* 51:82.

Rubenstein, Jeffrey L. 1995. *The History of Sukkot in the Second Temple and Rabbinic Periods.* Atlanta: Scholars Press.

Ruckstuhl, Eugen. 1965. *Chronology of the Last Days of Jesus.* New York: Desclee.

Rutherford, Ian. 1997. "Odes and Ends: Closure in Greek Lyric." Pages 43–61 in *Classical Closure: Reading the End in Greek and Latin Literature.* Edited by Deborah H. Roberts, Francis M. Dunn, and Don Fowler. Princeton: Princeton University Press.

Sacchi, Paolo. 1992. "Recovering Jesus' Formative Background." Pages 123–39 in Charlesworth 1992.

Saldarini, Anthony J. 1998. *Pharisees, Scribes and Sadducees.* Wilmington, Del.: Glazier.

Sanders, E. P. 1985. *Jesus and Judaism.* London: SCM; Philadelphia: Trinity Press International.

———. 1990. *Jewish Law from Jesus to the Mishnah.* London: SCM; Philadelphia: Trinity Press International.

———. 1992. *Judaism: Practice and Belief 63 BCE–66 CE.* London: SCM; Philadelphia: Trinity Press International.

———. 1993. *The Historical Figure of Jesus.* New York: Penguin.

Satlow, Frank P. 2001. *Jewish Marriage in Antiquity.* Princeton: Princeton University Press.

Schäfer, Peter. 1978. "Die sogannante Synode von Jabne: Zur Trennung von Juden und Christen im ersten/zweiten Jahrhundert nach Christus." Pages 45–64 in *Studien zur Geschichte und Theologie des Rabbinischen Judentums.* Arbeiten zur Geschichte des antiken Judentums und des Urchristentums 15. Leiden: Brill.

Schauss, Hayyim. 1975. *The Jewish Festivals: History and Observance.* Translated by Samuel Jaffe. New York: Schocken. Orig. 1938.

Schenk, Wolfgang. 1992. "Interne Strukturierungen im Schluss-Segment Johannes 21: Συγγραφή + Σατυρικόν/'Επίλογος." *NTS* 38:507–30.

Schiffman, Lawrence H. 1995. *Reclaiming the Dead Sea Scrolls: The History of Judaism, the Background of Christianity, the Lost Library of Qumran.* ABRL. New York: Doubleday.

Schleiermacher, Friedrich. 1864. *Das Leben Jesu: Aus Schleiermacher's handschriftlichem Nachlasse und Nachschriften seiner Zuhörer.* Berlin: Reimer. English translation: *The Life of Jesus.* Mifflintown, Pa.: Sigler, 1997.

Schmidt, Carl. 1919. *Gespräche Jesu mit seinen Jüngern nach der Auferstehung.* Leipzig: Hinrichs.

Schnackenburg, Rudolf. 1968. *The Gospel according to St. John.* Vol. 1. New York: Herder & Herder.

———. 1980–82. *The Gospel according to St. John.* 3 vols. New York: Crossroad. Repr. 1987, 1990.

Schneemelcher, Wilhelm 1999. *Neutestamentliche Apokryphen I: Evangelien.* 6th ed. Tübingen: Mohr Siebeck.

Schneider, Johannes. 1957. "Zur Komposition von Joh. 18,12–27." *ZNW* 48:111–19.

Schneiders, Sandra M. 1977. "Symbolism and the Sacramental Principle in the Fourth Gospel." Pages 221–35 in *Segni e Sacramenti nel Vangelo di Giovanni.* Edited by Pius-Ramon Tragan. Rome: Editrice Anselmiana.

———. 1981. "The Foot Washing (John 13:1–20): An Experiment in Hermeneutics." *CBQ* 43:76–92.

———. 1987. "Death in the Community of Eternal Life: History, Theology, and Spirituality in John 11." *Int* 41.1:44–56.

———. 1995. "Feminist Hermeneutics." Pages 349–69 in *Hearing the New Testament: Strategies for Interpretation.* Edited by Joel B. Green. Grand Rapids: Eerdmans.

Schnelle, Udo. 1992. *Antidocetic Christology in the Gospel of John: An Investigation of the Place of the Fourth Gospel in the Johannine School.* Translated by Linda M. Maloney. Minneapolis: Fortress.

———. 2003. *Paulus: Leben und Denken.* Berlin: de Gruyter.

———. 2004. *Das Evangelium nach Johannes.* Theologischer Handkommentar zum Neuen Testament 4. 3rd ed. Leipzig: Evangelische Verlagsanstalt.

———. 2006. "Johanneische Ethik." Pages 309–27 in *Eschatologie und Ethik im frühen Christentum: Festschrift für Günter Haufe zum 75. Geburtstag.* Edited by Christfried Böttrich. Greifswalder theologische Forschungen 11. Frankfurt: Lang.

———. 2007a. *Einleitung in das Neue Testament.* 6th ed. UTB 1830. Göttingen: Vandenhoeck & Ruprecht.

———. 2007b. *Theologie des Neuen Testaments.* UTB 2917. Göttingen: Vandenhoeck & Ruprecht.

Schoch, Karl. 1928. "Christi Kreuzigung am 14. Nisan." *Bib* 9:48–56.

Schoedel, William R. 1992. "Papias." *ABD* 5.140–42.

Scholtissek, Klaus. 2004. "The Johannine Gospel in Recent Research." Pages 444–72 in *The Face of New Testament Studies: A Survey of Recent Research.* Edited by Scot McKnight and Grant R. Osborne. Grand Rapids: Baker.

Schrage, Wolfgang. 1988. *The Ethics of the New Testament.* Translated by David E. Green. Philadelphia: Fortress. German original, 1982.

Schrijvers, P. H. 1973. "Comment terminer une ode?" *Mnemosyne* 26:140–59.

Schröter, Jens. 2001. "Die Frage nach dem historischen Jesus and der Charakter historischer Erkenntnis." Pages 6–36 in idem, *Jesus und die Anfänge der Christologie: Methodologische und exegetische Studien zu den Ursprüngen des christlichen Glaubens.* Biblisch-theologische Studien 47. Neukirchen-Vluyn: Neukirchener.

———. 2007. "Zur Historizität der Evangelien: Ein Beitrag zur gegenwärtigen Diskussion um den historischen Jesus." Pages 104–46 in idem, *Von Jesus zum Neuen Testament: Studien zur urchristlichen Theologiegeschichte und zur Entstehung des neutestamentlichen Kanons.* WUNT 204. Tübingen: Mohr Siebeck.

Schürer, Emil. 1906. Review of Büchler 1906. *Theologische Literaturzeitung* 23:619–20.

———. 1907. *Die Geschichte des jüdischen Volkes im Zeitalter Jesu Christi.* Leipzig: Hinrichs.

Schüssler Fiorenza, Elisabeth. 1985. *In Memory of Her: A Feminist Theological Reconstruction of Christian Origins.* New York: Crossroad.

———. 1994. *Jesus: Miriam's Child, Sophia's Prophet.* London: SCM.

———. 2003. "Re-visioning Christian Origins: *In Memory of Her* Revisited." Pages 225–50 in *Christian Origins: Worship, Belief and Society.* Edited by Kieran J. O'Mahony. JSNTSup 241. Sheffield: Sheffield Academic Press.

Schwartz, Daniel R. 1992. *Studies in the Jewish Background of Christianity.* Tübingen: Mohr Siebeck.

Schweizer, Eduard. 1967. *The Lord's Supper according to the New Testament.* Philadelphia: Fortress.

Scobie, Charles H. H. 1973. "The Origins and Development of Samaritan Christianity." *NTS* 19:390–414.

Scott, Ernest Findlay. 1952. *The Crisis in the Life of Jesus: The Cleansing of the Temple and Its Significance.* New York: Charles Scribner's Sons.

Segal, Judah Benzion. 1963. *The Hebrew Passover from the Earliest Times to A.D. 70.* London: Oxford University Press.

Segbroeck, Franz van, et al., eds. 1992. *The Four Gospels 1992: Festschrift Frans Neirynck.* 2 vols. BETL 100A. Leuven: Leuven University Press; Peeters.

Selms, Adrianus van. 1950. "The Best Man and Bride: From Sumer to St. John." *Journal of Near Eastern Studies* 9:65–70.

Seneca, Lucius Annaeus. *Naturales Quaestiones.* 1971–72. Translated by Thomas H. Corcoran. LCL. Cambridge: Harvard University Press.

Senior, Donald. 1991. *The Passion of Jesus in the Gospel of John.* Collegeville, Minn.: Liturgical Press.

Shanks, Herschel. 2005. "The Siloam Pool in Jesus' Time." *BAR* 31.5:16–23.

Smalley, Stephen S. 1984. *1, 2, 3 John.* WBC 51. Waco, Tex.: Word.

Smith, D. Moody. 1984. *Johannine Christianity: Essays on Its Setting, Sources, and Theology.* Columbia: University of South Carolina Press.

———. 1992. *John among the Gospels: The Relationship in Twentieth-Century Research.* Minneapolis: Fortress.

———. 1993. "Historical Issues and the Problem of John and the Synoptics." Pages 252–67 in *From Jesus to John: Essays on Jesus and New Testament Christology in Honour of Marinus de Jonge.* Edited by M. C. de Boer. JSNTSup 84. Sheffield: Sheffield Academic Press.

———. 1996. "What Have I Learned about the Gospel of John?" Pages 217–235 in *What Is John? Readers and Readings of the Fourth Gospel.* Edited by Fernando F. Segovia. SBLSymS 3. Atlanta: Scholars Press.

———. 1999. *John*. Abingdon New Testament Commentaries. Nashville: Abingdon.

———. 2001. *John among the Gospels: The Relationship in Twentieth-Century Research*. 2nd ed. Columbia: University of South Carolina Press.

———. 2007. "The Problem of History in John." Pages 311–20 in *What We Have Heard from the Beginning: The Past, Present, and Future of Johannine Studies*. Edited by Tom Thatcher. Waco, Tex.: Baylor University Press.

Smith, Jonathan Z. 1997. "The Temple and the Magician." Pages 233–47 in Meeks and Jervell 1997.

Smith, T. C. 1959. *Jesus in the Gospel of John*. Nashville: Broadman.

Söding, Thomas. 2002a. "Erscheinung, Vergebung und Sendung: Joh 21 als Zeugnis entwickelten Osterglaubens." Pages 207–32 in *Resurrection in the New Testament: Festschrift J. Lambrecht*. Edited by Reimund Bieringer, Veronica Koperski, and Bianca Lataire. BETL 165. Leuven: Peeters.

———. 2002b. " 'Was kann aus Nazareth schon Gutes kommen?' (Joh 1.46): Die Bedeutung des Judeseins Jesu im Johannesevangelium." *NTS* 46:21–41.

Spiro, Abram. 1967. "Stephen's Samaritan Background." Pages 285–300 in *The Acts of the Apostles*. AB 31. Edited by J. Munck. Revised by W. F. Albright and C. S. Mann. Garden City, N.Y.: Doubleday.

Stanton, Graham N. 1997. "The Fourfold Gospel." *NTS* 43:317–46.

Stapfer, Edmond. 1885. *Palestine in the Time of Christ*. Translated by A. H. Holmden. New York: Armstrong & Son.

Stauffer, Ethelbert. 1960. *Jesus and His Story*. Translated by Richard and Clara Winston. New York: Knopf.

Stemberger, Günter. 1977. "Die sogenannte 'Synode von Jabne' und das frühe Christentum." *Kairos* 19:14–21.

Stephens, Susan A. 1994. "Who Read Ancient Novels?" Pages 405–18 in *The Search for the Ancient Novel*. Edited by James Tatum. Baltimore: Johns Hopkins University Press.

Sterling, Gregory E. 1997. "The Bond of Humanity: Friendship in Philo of Alexandria." Pages 203–23 in *Greco-Roman Perspectives on Friendship*. Edited by John T. Fitzgerald. SBLRBS 34. Atlanta: Scholars Press.

Stern, Ephraim, et al. 1993. *The New Encyclopedia of Archaeological Excavations in the Holy Land*. 5 vols. Jerusalem: The Israel Exploration Society.

Steward-Sykes, Alistair. 1998. *The Lamb's High Feast: Melito, Peri Pascha and the Quartodeciman Paschal Liturgy at Sardis*. Supplements to Vigiliae Christianae 42. Leiden: Brill.

Stibbe, Mark W. G. 1994. *John's Gospel*. New Testament Readings. London: Routledge.

Story, Cullen I. K. 1989. "The Bearing of Old Testament Terminology on the Johannine Chronology of the Final Passover of Jesus." *NovT* 31:316–24.

Strack, Hermann Leberecht, and Paul Billerbeck. 1922–61. *Kommentar zum Neuen Testament aus Talmud und Midrash*. 5 vols. Munich: Beck.

Strand, Kenneth A. 1965. "John as Quartodeciman: A Reappraisal." *JBL* 84:251–58.

Strawn, Brent A. 2000. "Psalm 22:16b: 'More Guessing.' " *JBL* 119:439–51.

Strickert, Fred. 1998. *Bethsaida: Home of the Apostles*. Collegeville, Minn.: Liturgical Press.

Sweet, J. P. M. 1991. "A House Not Made with Hands." Pages 368–90 in *Templum Amicitia: Essays on the Second Temple presented to Ernst Bammel*. Edited by William Horbury. JSNTSup 48. Sheffield: JSOT Press.

Swenson, Kristan M. 2004. "Psalm 22:17: Circling Around the Problem Again." *JBL* 123:637–48.

Swete, Henry Barclay. 1909. *The Gospel according to St. Mark.* 3rd ed. London: Macmillan.

Talbert, Charles H. 1978. "Oral and Independent or Literary and Interdependent? A Response to Albert B. Lord." Pages 93–102 in *The Relationships among the Gospels: An Interdisciplinary Dialogue.* Edited by William O. Walker. San Antonio, Tex.: Trinity University Press.

———. 1992. *Reading John: A Literary and Theological Commentary on the Fourth Gospel and the Johannine Epistles.* New York: Crossroad.

Tanghe, Vincent. 1984. "Abraham, son Fils et son Envoyé (Luc 16,19–31)." *RB* 91:557–77.

Tatum, W. Barnes. 1994. *John the Baptist and Jesus: A Report of the Jesus Seminar.* Sonoma, Calif.: Polebridge.

Taylor, Joan E. 1997. *The Immerser: John the Baptist within Second Temple Judaism.* Grand Rapids: Eerdmans.

Thatcher, Tom. 2005. *Why John Wrote a Gospel: Jesus—Memory—History.* Louisville: Westminster John Knox.

———. 2006. "The New Current through John: The Old 'New Look' and the New Critical Orthodoxy." Pages 1–26 in *New Currents through John: A Global Perspective.* Edited by Francisco Lozada Jr. and Tom Thatcher. SBLRBS 54. Atlanta: Society of Biblical Literature.

Theissen, Gerd. 1976. "Die Tempelweissagung Jesu: Prophetie im Spannungsfeld von Stadt und Land." *Theologische Zeitschrift* 32:144–58.

———. 1989. "Die Jesusbewegung als charismatische Werterevolution." *NTS* 35:343–60.

———. 1991. *The Gospels in Context.* Translated by Linda M. Maloney. Minneapolis: Fortress.

Theissen, Gerd, and Annette Merz. 1998. *The Historical Jesus: A Comprehensive Guide.* Minneapolis: Fortress.

Theissen, Gerd, and Dagmar Winter. 2002. *The Quest for the Plausible Jesus.* Louisville: Westminster John Knox.

Thiselton, Anthony C. 2000. *The First Epistle to the Corinthians.* NIGTC. Grand Rapids: Eerdmans; Carlisle: Paternoster.

Thomas, John Christopher. 1991. *Footwashing in John 13 and the Johannine Community.* JSNTSup 61. Sheffield: Sheffield Academic Press.

Thompson, Marianne Meye. 1988. *The Humanity of Jesus in the Fourth Gospel.* Philadelphia: Fortress.

———. 1996. "The Historical Jesus and the Johannine Christ." Pages 21–42 in *Exploring the Gospel of John: In Honor of D. Moody Smith.* Edited by R. Alan Culpepper and C. Clifton Black. Louisville: Westminster John Knox.

———. 2001. *The God of the Gospel of John.* Grand Rapids: Eerdmans.

Thyen, Hartwig. 2005. *Das Johannesevangelium.* Handbuch zum Neuen Testament 6. Tübingen: Mohr Siebeck.

Tomson, Peter J. 2001. *"If This Be from Heaven…": Jesus and the New Testament Authors in Their Relationship to Judaism.* Sheffield: Sheffield Academic Press.

Torrey, Charles C. 1931. "The Date of the Crucifixion according to the Fourth Gospel." *JBL* 50:227–41.

Tovey, Derek. 1997. *Narrative Art and Act in the Fourth Gospel.* JSNTSup 151. Sheffield: Sheffield Academic Press.

————. 2007. *Jesus, Story of God: John's Story of Jesus.* Adelaide: ATF Press.

Trumbower, Jeffrey A. 1994. "The Role of Malachi in the Career of John the Baptist." Pages 28–41 in *The Gospels and the Scriptures of Israel.* Edited by C. A. Evans and W. Richard Stegner. JSNTSup 104. SSEJC 3. Sheffield: Sheffield Academic Press.

Trumbull, H. Clay. 1894. *Studies in Oriental Social Life.* Philadelphia: The Sunday School Times.

Twelftree, Graham H. 1999. *Jesus: The Miracle Worker.* Downers Grove, Ill.: InterVarsity Press.

Tzaferis, Vassilios. 1970. "Jewish Tombs at and near Giv'at Ha-Mivtar, Jerusalem." *IEJ* 1:18–32.

————. 1985. "Crucifixion—The Archaeological Evidence." *BAR* 11.1:44–53.

Urman, Dan. 1993. "The House of Assembly and the House of Study: Are They One and the Same?" *JJS* 43:237–57.

Uro, Risto. 1993. "'Secondary Orality' in the Gospel of Thomas?" *Forum* 9:305–29.

Vall, Gregory. 1997. "Psalm 22:17b: The Old Guess." *JBL* 116:45–56.

Van Belle, Gilbert. 1998. "The Faith of the Galileans: The Parenthesis in Jn 4,44." *ETL* 74:27–44.

————. 2005. "Style Criticism and the Fourth Gospel." Pages 291–316 in *One Text, a Thousand Methods: Studies in Memory of Sjef van Tilborg.* Edited by P. Chatelion Counet and Ulrich Berges. BIS 71. Leiden: Brill.

Van Belle, Gilbert, Michael Labahn, and Petrus Maritz. 2009. *Repetitions and Variations in the Fourth Gospel: Style, Text, Interpretation.* BETL 223. Leuven: Peeters.

Van Belle, Gilbert, and Petrus Maritz. 2006. "The Imagery of Eating and Drinking in John 6:35." Pages 333–352 in *Imagery in the Gospel of John: Terms, Forms, Themes, and Theology of Johannine Figurative Language.* WUNT 200. Edited by Jörg Frey, Jan G. van der Watt, and Ruben Zimmermann. Tübingen: Mohr Siebeck.

VanderKam, James C. 1990. "John 10 and the Feast of Dedication." Pages 203–14 in *Of Scribes and Scrolls: Studies on the Hebrew Bible, Intertestamental Judaism, and Christian Origins.* Edited by Harold W. Attridge et al. Lanham, Md.: University Press of America.

————. 1998. *Calendars in the Dead Sea Scrolls.* London: Routledge.

————. 2004. *From Joshua to Caiaphas: High Priests after the Exile.* Minneapolis: Fortress; Assen: Van Gorcum.

Verhey, Allen. 1984. *The Great Reversal: Ethics and the New Testament.* Grand Rapids: Eerdmans.

Vermes, Geza. 1992. "Fragments: The 'Pierced Messiah' Text—An Interpretation Evaporates." *BAR* 18.4:80–82.

Vielhauer, Philipp. 1965. "Gottesreich und Menschensohn in der Verkündigung Jesu." Pages 51–79 in *Aufsätze zum Neuen Testament.* Theologische Bücherei 31. Munich: Kaiser.

Vööbus, Arthur. 1968. *Liturgical Traditions in the Didache.* Stockholm: Estonian Theological Society in Exile.

————. 1969. "Regarding the Background of the Liturgical Traditions in the Didache: The Question of Literary Relation between Didache IX,4 and the Fourth Gospel." *VC* 23:81–87.

Wahlde, Urban C. von. 2006. "Archaeology and John's Gospel." Pages 523–86 in Charlesworth 2006.

Watson, Wilfred G. E. 2000. "Hebrew Poetry." Pages 253–85 in *Text in Context*. Edited by A. D. H. Mayes. Oxford: Oxford University Press.

Watt, Jan G. van der. 2006. "Ethics Alive in Imagery." Pages 421–448 in *Imagery in the Gospel of John: Terms, Forms, Themes, and Theology of Johannine Figurative Language*. Edited by Jörg Frey, Jan G. van der Watt, and Ruben Zimmermann. WUNT 200. Tübingen: Mohr Siebeck.

Wenham, David. 1997. "The Enigma of the Fourth Gospel: Another Look." *TynBul* 48:149–78.

Werline, Rodney A. 2000. "The *Psalms of Solomon* and the Ideology of Rule." Pages 774–95 in *2000 Society of Biblical Literature Seminar Papers*. SBLSemPap 39. Atlanta: Society of Biblical Literature. Repr. as pages 69–88 in *Conflicted Boundaries in Wisdom and Apocalypticism*. Edited by Benjamin G. Wright and Lawrence Mitchell Wills. SBLSymS 35. Atlanta: Society of Biblical Literature, 2005.

Westcott, Brooke Foss. 1919. *The Gospel according to St. John*. 2 vols. London: Murray.

Wiarda, Timothy. 2000. *Peter in the Gospels: Pattern, Personality, and Relationship*. WUNT 2/127. Tübingen: Mohr Siebeck.

Wight, Fred Hartley. 1953. *Manners and Customs of Bible Lands*. Chicago: Moody Press.

Wilckens, Ulrich. 1998. *Das Evangelium nach Johannes*. Das Neue Testament Deutsch 4. Göttingen: Vandenhoeck & Ruprecht.

Wilken, Robert L. 1971. *Judaism and the Early Christian Mind: A Study of Cyril of Alexandria's Exegesis and Theology*. New Haven: Yale University Press.

Wilkinson, John. 1978. "The Pool of Siloam." *Levant* 10:116–25.

Williams, Catrin H. 2007. "Inspecting an Aerial Photograph of John's Engagement with Sources." Pages 83–85 in *What You Have Heard from the Beginning: The Past, Present, and Future of Johannine Studies*. Edited by Tom Thatcher. Waco, Tex.: Baylor University Press.

Wilson, Stephen G. 1995. *Related Strangers: Jews and Christians 70–170 C.E.* Minneapolis: Fortress.

Winter, Paul. 1974. *On the Trial of Jesus*. 2nd ed. Berlin: de Gruyter. 1st ed., 1961.

Witherington, Ben, III. 1984. *Women in the Ministry of Jesus*. SNTSMS 51. Cambridge: Cambridge University Press.

———. 1995a. *The Jesus Quest: The Third Search for the Jew of Nazareth*. Downers Grove, Ill: InterVarsity Press.

———. 1995b. *John's Wisdom: A Commentary on the Fourth Gospel*. Louisville: Westminster John Knox.

———. 2008. *The Lazarus Effect*. Eugene, Oreg.: Pickwick.

———. 2009. *Roman Numerals*. Eugene, Oreg.: Pickwick

———. 2009. *What's in the Word: Rethinking the Socio-rhetorical Character of the New Testament*. Waco, Tex.: Baylor University Press.

Wrede, Wilhelm. 1933. *Charakter und Tendenz des Johannesevangeliums*. 2nd ed. Sammlung gemeinverständlicher Vorträge und Schriften aus dem Gebiet der Theologie und Religionsgeschichte 37. Tübingen: Mohr Siebeck.

Wright, Benjamin G., III. 1997. "Jewish Ritual Baths—Interpreting the Digs and the Texts: Some Issues in the Social History of Second Temple Judaism." Pages 190–214 in *The Archaeology of Israel: Constructing the Past, Interpreting the Present*. Edited by Neil Asher Silberman and David Small. JSOTSup 237. Sheffield: Sheffield Academic Press.

Wright, N. T. 1996. *Jesus and the Victory of God*. London: SPCK.

Yamauchi, Edwin M. 1978. "Cultural Aspects of Marriage in the Ancient World." *Bibliotheca Sacra* 135:241–52.

Yee, Gale. 1988. *Jewish Feasts and the Gospel of John.* Wilmington, Del.: Glazier.

Young, Brad. 2005. "A Fresh Examination of the Cross, Jesus and the Jewish People." Pages 191–210 in *Jesus' Last Week: Jerusalem Studies in the Synoptic Gospel.* Vol. 1. Edited by R. Steven Notley, Marc Turnage, and Brian Becker. Jewish and Christian Perspectives 11. Leiden: Brill.

Young, Douglas, and Ernst Diehl, eds. 1971. *Theognis.* Leipzig: Teubner.

Young, Frances, and David F. Ford. 1987. *Meaning and Truth in 2 Corinthians.* London: SPCK.

Zahn, Theodor. 1983. *Das Evangelium des Johannes.* Wuppertal: Brockhaus. Reprint of 6th ed., 1921.

Zeitlin, Solomon. 1932. "The Date of the Crucifixion according to the Fourth Gospel." *JBL* 51:263–71.

Zias, Joe, and James H. Charlesworth. 1992. "Crucifixion: Archaeology, Jesus, and the Dead Sea Scrolls." Pages 273–89 in Charlesworth 1992.

Zimmermann, Johannes. 1998. *Messianische Texte aus Qumran: Königliche, priesterliche und prophetische Messiasvorstellungen in den Schriften aus Qumran.* WUNT 104. Tübingen: Mohr Siebeck.

Zumstein, Jean. 2004a. *Kreative Erinnerung: Relecture und Auslegung im Johannesevangelium.* 2nd ed. Abhandlungen zur Theologie des Alten und Neuen Testaments 84. Zürich: Theologischer Verlag.

———. 2004b. "Der Prozess der Relecture in der johanneischen Literatur." Pages 15–30 in Zumstein 2004a.

———. 2004c. "Sünde in der Verkündigung des historischen Jesus und im Johannesevangelium." Pages 83–103 in Zumstein 2004a.

———. 2004d. "Die Endredaktion des Johannesevangeliums (am Beispiel von Kapitel 21)." Pages 291–315 in Zumstein 2004a.

CONTRIBUTORS

Paul N. Anderson is Professor of Biblical and Quaker Studies at George Fox University, Newberg, Oregon. Author of *The Christology of the Fourth Gospel* (third printing with new introduction and outlines, 2009) and *The Fourth Gospel and the Quest for Jesus* (2006) and many Johannine and Jesus essays, his current projects include *The Riddles of the Fourth Gospel; An Introduction to John* (scheduled for 2010), and *Jesus in Johannine Perspective: A Fourth Quest for Jesus* (scheduled for 2011).

Mark Appold is pastor at St. Paul Lutheran Church and Associate Professor of Religious Studies in the Department of Philosophy and Religion at Truman State University in Kirksville, Missouri. He is the author of *The Oneness Motif in the Fourth Gospel* (1976) and three articles in the four-volume *Bethsaida* series (1995–2009).

Richard Bauckham is Professor Emeritus, University of St. Andrews, Scotland, and Senior Scholar at Ridley Hall, Cambridge, England. His recent publications include *Jesus and the Eyewitnesses: The Gospels as Eyewitness Testimony* (2006), *The Testimony of the Beloved Disciple: Narrative, History, and Theology in the Gospel of John* (2007), and *Jesus and the God of Israel* (2008). He is co-editor of *The Gospel of John and Christian Theology* (2008).

Helen K. Bond is Senior Lecturer in New Testament Language, Literature, and Theology at the University of Edinburgh, Scotland. She is the author of *Pontius Pilate in History and Interpretation* (1998) and *Caiaphas: Judge of Jesus and Friend of Rome?* (2004). She is interested in most aspects of first-century Judea and is currently writing books on both Herod the Great and the historical Jesus.

Richard A. Burridge is Dean of King's College London (U.K.), where he is also Professor of Biblical Interpretation. A classicist by training, he has recently updated his doctoral thesis on the genre of the Gospels, *What Are the Gospels? A Comparison with Graeco-Roman Biography* (2nd ed.; 2004) and *Four Gospels, One Jesus? A Symbolic Reading* (2nd ed.; 2005). His chapter here draws upon his more detailed project on New Testament ethics, *Imitating Jesus: An Inclusive Approach to New Testament Ethics* (2007).

James H. Charlesworth is the George L. Collord Professor of New Testament Language and Literature and Director and Editor of the PTS Dead Sea Scrolls Project at Princeton Theological Seminary, Princeton, New Jersey. He has written or edited over sixty books; his most recent books are *The Historical Jesus: An Essential Guide* (2008) and *The Good and Evil Serpent: How a Universal Symbol Became Christianized* (2010).

Jaime Clark-Soles is Associate Professor of New Testament at Perkins School of Theology, Southern Methodist University, Dallas, Texas. She is the author of *Death and Afterlife in the New Testament* (2006) and Scripture *Cannot Be Broken: The Social Function of the Use of Scripture in the Fourth Gospel* (2003). Her essay "'I Will Raise [Whom?] Up on the Last Day': Anthropology as a Feature of Johannine Eschatology" appeared in *New Currents through John: A Global Perspective* (2006). Currently she is completing *The Active Word: New Testament Studies and the Christian Believer* (2010). Her current Johannine research addresses the New Testament figure of Nicodemus.

Mary Coloe, P.B.V.M., is Associate Professor at the School of Theology of Australian Catholic University, Fitzroy, Victoria, Australia. She has published two books on the Gospel of John with Liturgical Press: *God Dwells with Us: Temple Symbolism in the Fourth Gospel* (2001) and *Dwelling in the Household of God: Johannine Ecclesiology and Spirituality* (2007). She is currently editing a volume on John and the Dead Sea Scrolls and collaborating with Sandra Schneiders on a book on the Johannine resurrection.

R. Alan Culpepper is Dean of the McAfee School of Theology, Mercer University, Atlanta, Georgia. He is the author of *The Johannine School* (1975), *Anatomy of the Fourth Gospel* (1983), *John, the Son of Zebedee: The Life of a Legend* (1994), *The Gospel and Letters of John* (1998), and commentaries on Luke (1995) and Mark (2007). His current projects include a revision of *Anatomy of the Fourth Gospel*, a commentary on Matthew (New Testament Library), and a 19-foot sailboat.

Craig A. Evans is Payzant Distinguished Professor of New Testament at the Divinity College of Acadia University, Wolfville, Nova Scotia, Canada. He has published several books, including *Word and Glory: On the Exegetical and Theological Background of John's Prologue* (1993), *Jesus and His Contemporaries: Comparative Studies* (1995), *Jesus and the Ossuaries* (2003), and, with N. T. Wright, *Jesus, the Final Days* (2009). Evans also serves on the editorial boards of *Dead Sea Discoveries* and *Bulletin for Biblical Research*.

Sean Freyne is Professor of Theology (Emeritus) and Fellow at Trinity College, Dublin in Ireland; he served as a visiting professor at the Harvard Divinity School in 2007–2008. He is the author of several books and many articles dealing with various aspects of early Christianity and its literature, mainly the Gospels. His special research interest has to do with Galilee in Hellenistic and Roman times, with a focus on the use of archaeology in reconstructing ancient history. His most recent book is *Jesus a Jewish Galilean* (2005), and he is currently working on a history of the development and expansion of early Christianity in both the Jewish matrix and the Greco-Roman world.

Jeffrey Paul García is a Ph.D. candidate at New York University and an adjunct instructor at Nyack College, Manhattan Campus, New York. His general research interests are in Second Temple Judaism and Christian origins, with specific interest in the Dead Sea Scrolls, postbiblical Jewish literature, the Synoptic Gospels, biblical interpretations and allusions in late antiquity, and early rabbinic literature.

Brian D. Johnson is Associate Professor of New Testament at Lincoln Christian University, Lincoln, Illinois. His essay " 'Salvation Is from the Jews': Judaism in the Gospel of John" appeared in *New Currents through John: A Global Perspective* (2006). He is currently working on a book focusing on Second Temple Judaism and the Gospel of John.

Peter J. Judge is Associate Professor and Chair of the Department of Philosophy and Religious Studies at Winthrop University, Rock Hill, South Carolina. His most recent publications are "John 20,24–29: More Than Doubt, Beyond Rebuke," in *The Death of Jesus in the Fourth Gospel* (2007), and "The Leuven Hypothesis in C/catholic Perspective," in *What We Have Heard from the Beginning* (2007). His research centers on redactional understandings of the Gospels, and he is currently working on the Documenta Q project with an international team of scholars.

Felix Just, S.J., is Director of Biblical Education at the Loyola Institute for Spirituality, Orange, California. Co-founder of the Johannine Literature listserve, he also manages the Johannine Literature website. He has written numerous reviews of Johannine books and is a co-founder of the John, Jesus, and History Project.

Craig S. Keener is Professor of New Testament at Palmer Seminary of Eastern University, Wynnewood, Pennsylvania. He has published numerous articles and fourteen books, most relevantly his two-volume, 1600-page commentary on John (2003); *A Commentary on the Gospel of Matthew* (1999); and *The Historical Jesus of the Gospels* (2009). His research focus is the Jewish and larger Greco-Roman context of early Christianity, and his commentary on John cites some 20,000 extrabiblical ancient references.

Edward W. Klink III is Assistant Professor of New Testament at Talbot School of Theology, Biola University in La Mirada, California. He is the author of *The Sheep* *of the Fold: The Audience and Origin of the Gospel of John* (2007), and he is editing and contributing to *The Audience of the Gospels: The Origin and Function of the Gospels in Early Christianity* (2010). His current research focuses on the relationship of history and theology in the Fourth Gospel.

Craig R. Koester is Professor of New Testament at Luther Seminary, St. Paul, Minnesota. His publications on John include *The Word of Life: A Theology of John's Gospel* (2008), *Symbolism in the Fourth Gospel* (2nd ed.; 2003), and numerous articles on the Gospel of John. He is co-editor of *The Resurrection of Jesus in the Gospel of John* (2008) and is currently completing a major commentary on Revelation for the Anchor Yale commentary series, having completed also the Anchor Bible commentary on Hebrews.

Michael Labahn is Privatdozent at the Martin-Luther-University of Halle-Wittenberg, Germany, and a Scientific Researcher on the postdoctoral level in a DFG (Deutsche Forschungsgemeinschaft) Project of the Kirchliche Hochschule, Wuppertal, Germany. He is the author and editor of numerous books and articles in German and English, including *Jesus als Lebensspender* (1999), *Offenbarung in Zeichen und Wort* (2000), *Heilstraditionen im Johannesevangelium: Festgabe für Johannes Beutler S.J.* (with Klaus Scholtissek and Angelika Strotmann, 2004), and *Repetitions and Variations in the Fourth Gospel* (with Gilbert Van Belle and Petrus Maritz, 2009). He currently serves as editor of the ESCO series and is a member of the LNTS series editorial board. His research focuses on the Fourth Gospel and the Sayings Gospel, and he is currently preparing a commentary on the Apocalypse of John.

Mark A. Matson is the Vice President for Academic Affairs and Dean and Associate Professor of Bible, at Milligan College, Elizabethton, Tennessee. His book *In Dialogue with Another Gospel?* (2001) reflects his academic interests in the Gospel of John, John and the Synoptics, Synoptic relationships, and narrative theory. His current research program involves a study of the Lord's Prayer and a comparative study of narrative time in the four Gospels.

James F. McGrath is Associate Professor of Religion at Butler University, Indianapolis, Indiana. James is the author of *John's Apologetic Christology* (2001) and *The Only True God* (2009), as well as numerous journal articles and book chapters. His current research focuses on, among other things, oral tradition in early Christianity.

Susan Miller is a Tutor in New Testament at the University of Aberdeen, Scotland. Her research interests include women in early Christianity, the Gospels, and the historical Jesus. She has published *Women in Mark's Gospel* (2004) and is currently writing a book examining the role of women in the Fourth Gospel.

Gail R. O'Day is Almar H. Shatford Professor of Preaching and New Testament and Senior Associate Dean of Faculty and Academic Affairs at Candler School of Theology, Emory University in Atlanta, Georgia. She is the author of numerous books and articles on the Gospel of John, including the John commentary in the *New Interpreter's Bible* (vol. 9), *Revelation in the Fourth Gospel* (1986), and *The Word Disclosed: Preaching the Gospel of John* (2002). In addition to the Gospel of John, her research and teaching interests include literary criticism and biblical studies, history of biblical interpretation, and biblical hermeneutics and preaching.

Tom Thatcher is Professor of Biblical Studies at Cincinnati Christian University, Cincinnati, Ohio. He is the author or editor of numerous books and articles, including *Jesus in Johannine Tradition* (2001), *Why John Wrote a Gospel* (2005), *What We Have Heard from the Beginning* (2007), and *Greater Than Caesar: Christology and Empire in the Fourth Gospel* (2009). His research interests focus on the Johannine literature, ancient media culture, and Jesus studies.

Derek M. H. Tovey is Lecturer in New Testament at the College of St. John the Evangelist and in the School of Theology, University of Auckland, Auckland, New Zealand. He is the author of *Narrative Art and Act in the Fourth Gospel* (1997) and *Jesus, Story of God: John's Story of Jesus* (2007).

Bas van Os received his Ph.D. from the University of Groningen (2007), where he has studied gnostic Christian literature. He has taught New Testament studies at the University of Utrecht, Netherlands, and is currently a research scholar associated with the Amsterdam Free University. His research topics include the study of early Christianity and the historical Jesus.

Urban C. von Wahlde is professor of New Testament at Loyola University of Chicago, Illinois. He is the author of two books and over forty articles on the Gospel of John. His three-volume commentary on the Gospel and Letters of John will appear in the Eerdmans Critical Commentary series in spring 2010. His recent work also includes a series of articles dealing with archaeology and the historical accuracy of sites mentioned in the Gospel of John.

Ben Witherington III is the Amos Professor of New Testament for Doctoral Studies at Asbury Theological Seminary in Wilmore, Kentucky, and he serves on the Doctoral Faculty of St. Andrews University in Scotland. He has written a commentary on every book of the New Testament and is currently finishing his two-volume work on New Testament theology and ethics, entitled *The Indelible Image* (2009). In addition, he has taken up writing archaeological thrillers, *The Lazarus Effect* (2008) and the *Roman Numerals* (2009). His essay in the present volume appears now in a somewhat different form in his *What's in the Word* (2009).

Index of Ancient Sources

Old Testament/Hebrew Bible

Genesis

1:26	21
5:1–2	21
18:4	259
18:5	228
19:2	259
21:14–21	56
24	57n
24:1–4	56
24:32	259
24:60	60
43:24	259

Exodus

3:14	111
6:7	23
7:5	23
12:6	332
12:10	308
12:46	125, 308
13:8–10	151
14:21–22	132
17:1–7	133
20:21	76
22:28	320n
28:21	135
30:17–21	259
32	24n
33	22, 24, 24n
33:14–17	24
33:15–16	24
33:18	24
33:18–19	24
33:18–34:7	21
33:19	24
33:20	24
33:23	24
34	22, 24, 24n
34:6	24
34:7	24
34:9–10	24
34:29–35	22
39:14	135
40:30–32	259

Leviticus

11:44–45	284
14:5–6	75
14:50–52	75
15:13	75
23:4–8	292n

Numbers

7:10–11	124
9:6	246
9:12	308
13:16–17	135
19:17	75
20:1–13	133
20:8–11	137
21	13, 64, 69, 72, 99, 100, 381
21:8	69
21:8–9	11, 64, 71
21:9	99, 137
28:16–17	292n
35:25	315

Deuteronomy

1:23	135
5:10	24
6:4–6	348
7:9	24

Deuteronomy (cont.)		7:38	259
13	182	8:63	124
13:1–5	320	17:3–5	132
14:1	75	18:31	132, 135
18:15	76, 80, 136	19:15–16	197n
18:15–18	76		
18:15–19	132	2 Kings	
18:15–22	112, 227, 229, 234n	1:8	132
18:18	136	2:8	132
18:19–20	78	2:14	132
18:20	320	5:10–14	132
21:22	327	8:13	75
21:22–23	300, 327	9:3	197n
27:4	132	9:6	197n
29:2–3	136	11:14–20	145
		17	74
Joshua		23:30	145
3:14–17	132		
4:2–23	132	2 Chronicles	
4:21–22	132	4:6	259
6:20	133		
8:27–29	327	Ezra	
		5:16	40n
Judges		6:16–17	124
2:10	23	6:19–21	145
14	57n	9:1	145
14–15	57n		
14:1–3	56	Nehemiah	
19:21	259	10:29	145
Ruth		Job	
4:11	60	42:11	228
1 Samuel		Psalms	
2:12	23	8:5	70
10:1	197n	22:16	328
16:1–13	197	22:18	308
17:43	75	23:5	228
25	259	34:20	308
25:41	264	69	36, 97
		69:21	308
2 Samuel		78:24	137
3:3	32	89:20	197n
		95:7	23
1 Kings		95:7b–11	133
1:39	197n	100:3	23
4:7	135	137:2	327

145:13–14	69	Daniel	
		7	123
Proverbs		8	123
8:2–3	320	11	123
9:3	320		
30:5–6	354	Hosea	
		1–2	55
Isaiah		2:20	23
1:2	75	5:4	23
6:1–8	21	6:3	23
6:9–10	21	8:2	23
11:15	132	11:1	75
14:29	71	11:11	79
19:21	23	13:4	23
25:6	77		
27:12–13	79	Micah	
30:27–28	134	5:2	229n
40:3	13, 50, 134		
40:11	23	Nahum	
43:16	132	1:3–6	327
44:3	137	2:12	327
45:18–19	320n	2:12–3:14	327
48:16	320n		
50:6	320n	Zechariah	
51:10	132	12:10	251, 308, 328, 331, 332, 333, 367
53	308, 329	14	36, 97, 122, 122n, 126, 128, 162
53:4–7	307	14:7	123
54:13	228	14:8	122
56	36, 97	14:16	122
61:1–2	135, 143	14:18	122
61:10	55	14:19	122
63:11	132		
		Malachi	
Jeremiah		2:14	56
2:2	55	2:16	134
7	36, 97	3:1	49, 134
22:16	23	3:2–3	134
24:7	23	3:5	134
26:11	143	4:1–2	134
31:34	23	4:4–5	98, 134
		4:6	47
Lamentations			
3:30	320n	DEUTEROCANONICAL BOOKS	
Ezekiel		Baruch	
16:8	56	3:29–32	19n
47:13	136	3:29–4:1	21

Baruch (cont.)

3:37	320

1 Maccabees

4:45–46	132
9:27	132
14:41	132

2 Maccabees

1:18	124
1:27	79
15:37	353
15:39	353

4 Maccabees

1:16–17	21n

Sirach

6:5–17	263
14:13	263
18:6	354
22:19–26	263
24	146
24:23	21
34:8	21
37:1–6	263
38:24–39:11	146
39:1	21
42:21	354
48:4	143
51:23	146

Wisdom of Solomon

6:14	320
6:16	320
7:22	22
7:24–27	21n
7:25–26	22
9:10	19n
9:15–16	19
9:17	19
18:15	19n

NEW TESTAMENT

Matthew

3:3	50

3:9	131
3:11	98
3:13–17	52
4:21	29
5:44	247, 348
6:12	345n
6:28–29	152n
7:6	75
7:7	247
7:28	152
8	91
8:5–13	12, 83, 101
8:7	88, 89, 89n, 90, 92
8:7–8	90
8:8	83, 90n
8:11	83, 152n
8:13	90
8:14–15	12
8:22	263
8:23–27	227
9:14–15	54
9:15	99
9:18–26	217
10:5	73, 100
10:16	72, 100
10:19–20	247
11:2–6	143
11:5	217, 241
11:7–9	49n
11:9–10	49n
11:10	49n
11:19	284, 346
11:21	28
12:40–41	152n
12:42	152n
13:37	87
14:15–21	227
14:22–33	227
15:22–24	89
15:26	89n
15:28	90
15:29–38	227
16:1–12	227
16:16	110, 227
18:23–30	345n
19:28	79, 136
20:29–34	193

21:12–13	35n	4–8	138
21:12–17	80	4:35–41	227
21:22	247	5:21–43	217
23–25	247	5:22	187, 190
23:37	143	5:22–43	241
24:2	35n	5:37	238
26:7	185	5:39	111
26:17	332	6	109, 110, 138
26:34	278n	6:2–3	152
26:52	185	6:4	87, 102
26:57	196n	6:7	132, 135
26:59–61	97	6:15	49
26:61	35n, 41	6:33–44	227
26:73	152	6:35–38	185
27:35	328	6:37	109
27:40	35n	6:39	109, 226
27:60	330	6:40	226
27:62–66	246	6:45–52	227
28:16	275	6:47–52	138n
		6:51–52	138n
Mark		7	14, 89, 90, 145
1	235n	7:1–2	149
1:2	49	7:3	169n
1:2–3	50	7:1–20	77
1:6	132	7:15	77
1:7	47, 98	7:19	74, 77
1:9–11	52	7:24	77
1:14	11	7:24–30	74, 101
1:15	346	7:25	190
1:22	152	7:26	74
1:23–28	10	7:27	74, 89n
1:24	110	7:29	90
1:27	152	7:29–30	90
1:29	238	7:30	91
1:30–31	12	8	109, 110, 138
1:44	208n	8:1–9	227
2:1–12	345n	8:11–21	227
2:5	345n	8:22–26	28
2:14	345n	8:28	49
2:15–17	345n	8:29	110, 227
2:17	345	9:1	239
2:18–20	54	9:2	238
2:19	99	9:11–13	49n, 132
3:14–17	135	9:29	193
3:14–19	132	9:38	239n
3:22	78, 149	10:6	152n
3:33–35	263	10:29–30	263

Mark (cont.)		14:57–59	39
10:38–39	228	14:58	13, 35n, 37, 41
10:39	239n	14:70	152
10:46	187	15:1	196
10:46–52	193	15:6	310
11	10	15:24	249, 328
11:1–6	195	15:25	308
11:12–14	192	15:29	13, 35n
11:15–17	35n	15:33	308
11:15–19	80, 192	15:42	246
11:18	194	16	10
11:20–21	192	16:7	275
11:24	247		
11:27–28	39	Luke	
12:1–12	136	1:1–4	205, 352, 373
12:9	136	1:2	236
12:26	111	2:42	118n
12:28–34	348	3:2	196n, 315, 316, 322
12:29–31	152n	3:4	50
13	247	3:8	131
13:2	35n	3:16	47, 98
13:3	238	4:17	150
13:10	77	4:20	150
13:11	247	4:22	152
14	206	4:24	87, 102
14:1	292	4:32	152
14:1–2	192, 198	4:34	110
14:1–11	192	4:36	152
14:2	309	5:1–11	341
14:3	185, 191, 192, 199	5:29	228
14:3–9	191, 192, 196	5:30–35	54
14:3–11	209	5:34–35	99
14:10–11	192, 198	6:16	188
14:12	246, 292, 332	6:20–22	346
14:14	292	6:22	182
14:22	76	6:27	247
14:25	76	6:35	247
14:26–27	278	7	91
14:33	238	7:1–10	12, 14, 83, 101
14:43–52	195	7:2	91
14:47	185, 195, 199	7:3	91
14:51–52	195	7:3–5	89n
14:53	196, 314	7:5	90
14:55–59	97	7:6	90n
14:57–59	39	7:7	83
14:62	319	7:9	86
14:55–64	314	7:10	90, 91

7:11–17	217	16:31	186n
7:18–23	143	17:11	14
7:22	217, 240, 241	17:11–19	73, 100
7:24–27	49n	17:16	14, 190
7:27	49n	18:9–19	345n
7:34	284, 346	18:35–43	193
7:36–50	185n, 260, 345n	19:1–10	345n
7:38	199	19:37	194n
7:44	260	19:41–46	39
8:3	187n	19:45–46	35n, 80
8:22–25	227	20–21	247
8:40–56	217	21:6	35n
8:41	187, 190	22	298n
8:35	190	22:7	246
9:12–17	227	22:8	238
9:20	110, 227	22:15	332
9:49	239n	22:17–20	298
9:51–56	73, 79, 80, 100	22:19	196n
10:13	28	22:24–30	265n
10:29–37	73, 100	22:27	278
10:38	189	22:30	79, 136
10:38–39	190	22:33–34	278n
10:38–42	185, 187, 189, 210, 214, 217	22:39	279n
10:39	189, 191	22:50	185
10:40	190	22:54	196n
10:42	191	22:59	152
11:9	247	22:66–71	314
11:13	247	23:2	314
11:30	152n	23:25	314
11:30–37	14	23:33	328n
11:31	152n	23:34	328
12:11–12	247	23:39	328n
13:28	152n	23:53	330
13:29	83	24	276, 373
13:34	143	24:36	332
14:26	263	24:36–43	332
15:4–7	345n	24:37	326
15:8–10	345n	24:39	325, 326, 332
15:11–32	345	24:43	326
15:13	345		
15:18	346	John	
15:18–19	346	1	4, 5, 9, 11, 12, 78, 92
15:19	346	1–4	4, 12, 102, 379
15:20	346	1–20	252, 338, 339, 340, 341, 342, 343,
15:21	346		344, 346
15:22	346	1:1–18	9, 19, 271, 320
16:19–31	186	1:1–3:36	61

John (cont.)

1:6   46, 58
1:6–7   61
1:6–8   96
1:7   46
1:10   23, 287
1:10–12   247
1:11   87
1:12   361
1:12–13   22, 234n
1:14   9, 15, 18, 24, 25, 45, 59, 94, 95,
        154, 285, 361, 392
1:14–18   20, 22n, 24
1:15   46, 47, 50, 52, 98
1:16   95
1:17   21, 24, 285
1:17–18   23
1:18   20, 22, 24, 59, 392
1:19   58
1:19–34   60
1:20   51n, 362
1:20–21   11, 50
1:20–22   142
1:21   48, 98
1:23   50, 58
1:25   51n
1:26   15, 23, 58, 153
1:26–27   58
1:27   47, 98
1:29   126, 307, 308, 321
1:29–30   58
1:29–34   51
1:30   52
1:31–34   58
1:32–34   51, 58
1:33   15
1:35–36   58
1:35–37   51
1:35–39   51
1:35–42   96
1:35–50   141
1:35–51   29, 60, 96
1:36   321
1:38–39   23n
1:39   58
1:40   29, 188
1:40–41   96

1:40–44   30
1:41   141, 154
1:42   51n
1:43   31, 360
1:43–46   188
1:43–51   110
1:44   95
1:44–45   141
1:45   93, 230
1:45–46   87, 392
1:45–50   141
1:45–51   288
1:46   142
1:47   154
1:49   142, 154
1:50–51   17
1:51   142
1:58   99
2   9, 92, 107, 117, 118, 119, 226, 235n
2:1–11   10, 59, 87, 92, 321
2:1–12   60, 110
2:6   10, 149, 230n
2:7–9   15
2:10   10, 235
2:11   10, 17, 25, 59, 69, 91, 117, 141
2:12   59
2:12–22   119
2:13   125, 307
2:13–22   35, 36, 41, 80, 97
2:13–23   10, 119, 226, 230n
2:13–25   60
2:16   59
2:18–20   194
2:18–21   92
2:19   13, 35n, 36n, 230n
2:19–21   76
2:19–22   321
2:20   13, 40
2:22   17, 91, 92, 93, 364
2:23   10, 69, 117, 226, 230n, 307, 327
2:23–25   87
2:24–25   226
2:25   154
3   9, 11, 13, 64, 65, 68, 69, 99, 137, 178
3:1   326
3:1–2   87
3:1–10   60, 288

3:1–15	319
3:1–21	60, 77
3:2	10, 69
3:3	91
3:3–5	60, 345
3:3–6	22
3:5	15
3:10	60n
3:10–15	93
3:11	361
3:11–13	19, 20
3:12	69
3:13–16	69
3:13–17	63, 65n
3:13–21	60
3:14	64, 64n, 65, 68, 71
3:14–15	11, 64, 65, 67, 68, 69, 70, 99, 100, 137
3:14–16	65, 71
3:15	60, 65
3:15–17	247
3:16	60, 285, 290, 392
3:17–21	319
3:18	392
3:19–21	21
3:22–24	60
3:22–26	96
3:22–30	99
3:23	15, 51
3:24	11
3:25	230n
3:25–30	54
3:25–36	60
3:27–30	51
3:28–30	96
3:29	52, 57, 58, 99
3:30	52, 60
3:32	240
3:32–33	359
4	9, 14, 78, 79, 80, 81, 85, 86, 100, 101, 108, 137, 235n, 345
4:1	78
4:1–54	110
4:2	48n, 267
4:2–3	226
4:4–42	73, 348
4:6	322
4:7	75
4:7–26	288
4:9	74, 75, 75n
4:10	15
4:11	75
4:12	74, 78
4:13–14	15
4:14	75
4:16–19	76
4:20–24	76
4:21	101
4:21–23	79
4:21–26	321
4:22	76
4:23	76
4:25–26	76
4:26	79
4:31–38	100
4:39–42	86
4:40	23n
4:41	29
4:41–42	88, 91
4:42	151
4:43	87
4:43–54	86
4:44	87, 102
4:45	10, 87, 91, 92, 117, 226
4:45–46	141
4:46	85
4:46–54	12, 14, 83, 86n, 91
4:47	83, 91, 226
4:48	86n, 89, 90, 91, 102
4:49	91
4:50	91
4:53	91, 92
4:54	226
5	3, 4, 10, 11, 107, 108, 111, 120, 178, 216, 226, 230n, 232, 235n, 321, 344, 345
5–10	384
5–12	109, 110, 111, 117, 225, 229, 379
5:1	117, 120, 120n, 230n
5:1–9	111
5:2	15, 231n
5:2–14	288
5:5–18	230n
5:9	117

John (cont.)

5:10	117
5:14	230n, 327, 344
5:16	117
5:16–18	94
5:17	111
5:18	24n, 111, 117, 226
5:31	361
5:31–47	69
5:35	52
5:37–38	22
5:41	87
5:42	348
5:46	108, 230
6	11, 107, 108, 109, 110, 112, 131, 138, 216, 225, 226, 227, 228, 235n, 271, 301, 321, 340, 385
6:1–71	110
6:2	108
6:4	117, 138n, 226, 301, 307, 327
6:5–7	31
6:5–8	185
6:7	109, 188
6:8	30
6:10	109, 226
6:11	340n
6:13	136
6:14	108, 136, 228
6:14–15	141, 142, 154, 226
6:15	128, 228
6:16–21	138n
6:20	111
6:25–65	321
6:27	137, 359
6:31	137
6:32	228
6:35	137
6:42	87
6:45	228
6:51	228, 301
6:51–58	131n, 339n
6:53–56	137
6:67	10, 79, 136
6:68	30, 151
6:69	23, 110
6:70	136
6:71	136, 267

7	4, 10, 11, 107, 108, 110, 122, 137, 139, 140, 141, 142, 143, 144, 146, 148, 149, 153, 154, 178, 182, 226, 229, 230n
7–8	118
7–10	321
7:1–10	108, 110
7:1–11	148
7:1–13	118n
7:2	117, 230n
7:3	87
7:9	326
7:10	326, 327
7:14	151, 230n
7:14–31	140
7:15	144, 145
7:15–16	140
7:19–20	140
7:21–24	230n
7:22	117
7:23	117
7:24	154
7:26	154
7:27	141, 154, 230
7:28	50, 151, 230n
7:31	142, 154, 234
7:32–52	140
7:35	151
7:37	50, 117, 151
7:37b–38	137
7:37–39	15, 77, 122, 140
7:38	75, 232
7:39	126, 127, 127n
7:40	142
7:40–41	154
7:41	142
7:41–42	87, 140, 141
7:42	142, 229
7:46	151
7:48	234
7:49	144, 145, 149
7:52	87, 123n, 140, 142, 154
7:53–8:11	204n
8	4, 10, 11, 78, 79, 107
8:3–11	288
8:7	327
8:12	52, 107, 123, 123n
8:12–59	78

8:13	78, 361
8:17	361
8:17–18	127
8:19	23
8:20	230n
8:22	78
8:28	68, 100
8:30–31	234
8:31	78
8:32	389
8:41–42	348
8:44	22
8:48	14, 73, 78, 80
8:51	78
8:53	78
8:56	20
8:58	78, 79, 111
8:59	300
9	3, 4, 10, 11, 107, 110, 111, 113, 173, 175, 177, 178, 182, 183, 188, 231, 232, 233, 235n, 344, 345
9:1–7	111
9:1–38	288
9:2	344
9:3	344
9:7	15, 113, 230n, 231
9:11	230n
9:13	327
9:14	117
9:14–16	230n
9:16	117, 344
9:18–34	94
9:22	111, 141, 175, 178, 181, 182, 183
9:24	344
9:25	327, 344
9:29	23
9:31	344
9:34	344
9:41	107, 344
10	4, 10, 11, 124, 226
10–12	321
10:1–2	135
10:1–9	107
10:1–18	342
10:1–21	124
10:3–4	23
10:8	124

10:10–18	107, 247
10:11	124, 343
10:14–15	23
10:22	117, 123, 226
10:22–39	323
10:23	230n
10:30	111
10:31	300
10:33	24n
10:42	234
11	4, 107, 111, 113, 185, 186, 189, 208, 209, 210, 212, 225, 226, 235, 242, 251, 315, 316n
11–12	235, 237
11–18	319
11–19	226
11:1	207
11:1–2	190n
11:1–16	108, 110
11:1–44	111, 177, 213, 214, 220, 288
11:1–54	195, 220n
11:1–12:8	188
11:2	217
11:3	114, 207, 212
11:4	17, 25, 220
11:5	190, 237, 238
11:7–10	220
11:13	216
11:14	111, 216
11:16	188
11:19	177, 190
11:20	190
11:20–27	216
11:21	190n
11:25	67, 220
11:25–26	107
11:32	189, 190n
11:33	220
11:36	237
11:36–47	208
11:37	216
11:38	220
11:39	190, 190n, 215, 216
11:40	25
11:43	50
11:44	220
11:45	234

John (cont.)

11:45–46	17
11:45–48	94
11:45–53	309
11:47	194
11:47–53	300, 318
11:49	318
11:49–50	194, 220n
11:50–51	319
11:51	315, 316
11:51–52	220n
11:55	117, 307
12 4, 107, 108, 113, 117, 178, 185, 189, 199n, 206, 208, 209, 226, 260	
12–19	117
12:1	117, 191, 192, 307
12:1–2	192
12:1–8	191, 266
12:1–11	209
12:2	189n, 190, 192
12:3	189n, 191, 199
12:7	191, 200n
12:7–8	200
12:9	194
12:10	200
12:11	177
12:12	307
12:12–19	125, 245
12:13	50, 125, 227
12:16	17, 25, 93, 154, 364
12:18	194n
12:20	307
12:20–21	12
12:20–22	30, 97
12:20–26	86
12:21–22	31, 33, 188
12:22	188
12:23–24	17, 25
12:23–33	107
12:24	288
12:25–26	288
12:32–33	343
12:32–34	68, 343
12:34	141
12:37–41	20
12:40	21
12:41	20, 25

12:42	111, 175, 178, 234
12:42–43	346
12:44	50
12:44–50	107
13 4, 5, 11, 30, 207, 208, 226, 228, 245, 255, 261, 262, 263, 265, 266, 267, 268, 269, 365, 371	
13–16	11, 276, 277
13–17 245, 271n, 272, 273, 274, 275, 276, 277, 279, 287, 371	
13–21 4, 5, 30, 245, 248, 281, 287, 365, 379	
13:1 117, 208, 246, 259, 278, 285, 292, 293, 332	
13:1–3	255
13:1–15	348
13:1–20	255, 272
13:2	267
13:4–5	255
13:5	15
13:5–14	261
13:6–10	256, 288
13:6–11	261n
13:8	261
13:10	261
13:10–11	230n, 256, 267
13:12	256
13:12–20	261n
13:13–17	246
13:14	278n
13:14–15	288
13:15–35	247
13:18–30	278
13:21–26	340
13:21–30	272
13:23	208, 246, 249, 304, 389
13:23–38	238
13:25	249
13:31	17, 278
13:31–32	25
13:31–38	343n
13:31–14:31	272
13:33	272
13:34	288
13:34–35	247, 348
13:36	248, 272
13:36–38	320

13:37	128, 343	16:1–4	280
13:37–38	278	16:2	111, 175, 177
13:38	343, 344	16:3	23
14	4, 11	16:5	248, 272
14–16	247	16:7–15	247
14–17	247	16:12	272
14:2–9	23	16:13	247
14:5	188, 272	16:13–15	20, 23
14:6	23, 67, 247, 276, 277	16:16	22n
14:7	22n	16:16–18	272n
14:7–9	22	16:16–33	272
14:8	188	16:23–24	247
14:8–9	24, 31	16:32–33	278
14:9	22n	16:33	247
14:13–14	247	17	4
14:15	348	17:1	17
14:16	247	17:1–25	272
14:16–26	247	17:4	276
14:17	17, 22n, 23, 23n	17:5	17
14:22	188	17:6–26	247
14:26	23	17:11	93
14:27	275	17:18	276
14:29	278	17:20–26	263
14:30–31	272, 278	17:24–25	17
14:31	248, 273	18	4, 11, 342, 344, 346, 365
15	4, 11	18:1	248, 272, 279n
15–17	235n, 248, 271, 385	18:2	267
15:1	247	18:3	248, 315
15:1–5	279n	18:4–5	269
15:1–16:15	272	18:5	87, 93, 269, 319, 392
15:3	230n	18:6	248, 269, 319
15:4–10	23n	18:7	87, 93, 392
15:7	247	18:8	269, 320
15:9–12	247	18:10	188, 199, 248
15:12	247, 288	18:10–11	185
15:12–13	288	18:13	248, 315, 319
15:13	247	18:13–14	196n
15:13–17	263	18:13–24	313, 369, 370
15:16	247	18:14	319
15:17	247	18:15	29, 208n, 317
15:18	280	18:15–16	208, 340
15:18–16:4	183n	18:15–17	343n
15:19	247	18:17	319, 339, 340, 344
15:20	280	18:18	249, 317, 340
15:26	23	18:19	319, 320
15:26–27	247	18:19–24	318
16	4, 11, 178, 272	18:20	108, 230n

John (cont.)

18:20–21	320
18:22	320
18:24	196n, 317, 318
18:25	319, 344n
18:25–27	339, 340, 343n
18:26	320, 344n
18:26–27	344
18:27	319, 344n
18:28	117, 246, 293, 307, 308, 317
18:28–19:16	143
18:33	128
18:33–37	124
18:33–38	323
18:37–38	154
18:39	117
18:40	50
19	11, 178, 209, 365
19–20	251, 252
19–21	206
19:6	50
19:7–11	323
19:12	50
19:13	249
19:14	117, 246, 293, 307, 308, 321, 322
19:15	50
19:17	249
19:19	87, 93, 245
19:20	249
19:23–37	245
19:24	249, 308, 328
19:25	339
19:26	209
19:26–27	249, 280n
19:27	208
19:28	308
19:29	125
19:30	276
19:31	117, 246
19:31–34	249
19:32	331
19:34	249, 331
19:34–35	15, 16, 25
19:35	2, 9, 249, 350, 362
19:36	125, 308
19:36–37	331
19:37	251

19:38	29
19:39	249
19:40	249
19:41	127n
19:42	246
20	11, 209, 212, 248, 251, 276, 277, 339, 359, 365, 367
20–21	245, 274, 277, 371
20:1	319
20:1–2	209
20:1–6	339
20:1–10	238
20:1–18	245
20:2	209
20:3–8	340
20:5–7	249
20:6–7	220
20:9	127n, 364
20:19	332
20:19–29	245
20:19–20	275
20:20–27	249
20:21	332
20:21–23	127, 359
20:24	79, 136
20:24–29	188, 325
20:25	326, 367
20:26	275, 295, 296, 332
20:26–29	359
20:27	332
20:28–29	277, 277n
20:29	22n
20:30	204, 211, 340, 360
20:30–31	109, 119n, 141, 207, 248, 339, 341, 351, 359
20:31	25, 216, 340, 350
21	4, 5, 10, 11, 29, 31, 209, 210, 235n, 248, 249, 252, 265, 271, 275, 335, 338, 339, 340, 341, 342, 344, 346, 349, 350, 359, 365, 373, 374, 385
21:1–14	245, 338, 339, 340n, 341, 342, 360
21:1–23	351
21:1–24	238
21:1–25	110, 141, 335
21:2	29, 96, 140, 188, 206, 209
21:3	29

21:7   169n, 206, 339, 342, 344, 389
21:9   340, 342
21:11   249
21:12–15   340
21:13   249, 340n
21:15   343
21:15–16   340
21:15–17   262, 343, 344, 345, 375,
21:15–19   335, 339, 340, 342, 343n, 346,
   347, 360, 374
21:15–22   288, 341, 346
21:15–25   338
21:16–17   342
21:17   340, 342
21:18–19   343, 344
21:18–23   239
21:18–25   245
21:19   343n, 360
21:20   246, 249, 304, 359
21:20–23   249, 360
21:20–24   210, 340, 389
21:23   350, 351
21:24   2, 5, 9, 15, 95, 114, 203, 246,
   249, 273, 340, 349, 350, 351, 354,
   359, 360, 361, 361n, 362, 363, 372
21:24–25   109, 252, 349, 350, 351, 352,
   353, 359, 360, 372
21:25   72, 204, 211, 248, 360, 386

Acts
1   276
1:1   283
1:3   274
1:8   73, 100
1:13   238
1:14   209, 238
1:15–26   10, 79
1:21–22   40n
2:23   328
2:33   68
2:42–47   228
3:1   238
3:3   238
3:4   238
3:11   238
3:22   228
4:1   238

4:1–31   230n
4:6   315, 316, 322
4:13   230n, 238
4:13–16   230
4:19   238, 240
4:19–20   12, 240
4:20   240
5:10   190
5:29   240
5:31   68
5:36   132
6:8–7:60   314
6:14   35n, 41, 80, 97
7   80
7:2–8   80
7:9–16   80
7:37   80, 228
7:47–48   80
7:54–8:1   80
8:1   73, 100
8:4–25   73
8:14   238
8:16   127n
8:17   238
8:25   238
9:43   33
10   75
10:25   190
11:17   240
12:2   206
13:25   47n
21:38   133
22:3   147, 190
22:15   240

Romans
1:16   75

1 Corinthians
3:17   37, 97
5   298
5:7   308n, 333
5:7–8   298
10:17   302n
11   298n, 310
11:17–22   228
11:23   323

1 Corinthians (cont.)

11:23–26	298		
11:23–34	228		
15:3–8	203		
15:3b–4	151		
15:6	273		

2 Corinthians

3:6–4:4	22
3:7	22
3:7–11	25
3:7–18	16n
3:18	19n, 22
4:4–6	22
4:7–12	22n
5:1–4	37, 97
6:8	182
11:2	55

Galatians

2:1–14	75
6:11	350, 355

Ephesians

5:27	55

Philippians

2:5–11	228

Colossians

1:15	21n, 22n
1:15–21	228
2:11	37n
2:14	326
2:16–3:3	19
3:1–2	19n
3:5–11	19n
4:18	350, 355

1 Thessalonians

2:3	182

2 Thessalonians

3:17	350, 355

1 Timothy

5:10	260

Philemon

19	350, 356

Hebrews

1:1–4	228
1:3	21n
2:3	133n
3:7–4:13	133n
3:19–20	134
3:23–24	134
4:11	133n
9:11	37

James

1:1	136

1 Peter

1:1	136

1 John

1:1–2	16n
1:1–3	9, 12, 240, 273
1:1–4	9, 361
1:4	361
1:5–10	361
1:3	240
2:1	361
2:2	312
2:7	361
2:8	361
2:18–25	234n
2:21	361
2:23	234n
2:26	361
2:28	22
3:2	18, 22
3:3	18, 22
3:6	18, 22
3:11	247
3:11–16	247
3:23	247
3:24–4:6	23
4:1–6	16n
4:2	22
4:2–3	93
4:7–12	247
4:20	18

5:13	361
5:16	361
5:18–20	361
2 John	
5	247
7	93
3 John	
1	361
2	361
3	361
4	361
9	361, 362
10	361, 362
12	361, 362
13	361
14	361
Revelation	
2:9–10	280n
2:13	280n
3:9	280n
3:10	280n
4:1–2	20
4:2	20
5:1–9	359n
5:5–6	20
5:9	51n
6:1–12	359n
7:2	359n
7:3–8	359n
8:1	359n
9:4	359n
10:4	359n
20:3	359n
22:10	359n

ANCIENT JEWISH TEXTS

'Abot de Rabbi Nathan	
31A	21n
42	21n
116B	21n
Apocalypse of Adam	
7:17	354

Babylonian Talmud	
Baba Batra	
16b–17a	21n
Berakot	
47b	146
'Erubin	
53a, b	152
Megillah	
24b	152
Sanhedrin	
11b	297
38ab	24n
43a	182n, 299
46b	327
Sukkah	
52b	333
2 Baruch	
4:3–3	21n
29:5–6	77
Dead Sea Scrolls	
1QM	
2:1–3	134n
11:15	23n
1QS	
4:22	23n
8:1	134n
10:12	23n
11:3	23n
1Q27	
1:7	23n
4Q159	
frgs. 2–4, lines 3–4	134n, 136n
4Q164	
4–6	134n
4Q285	
f7, 1–6	329
4Q521	143
4Q544	
10–12	21n
4Q547	
7	21n
4QpNah	
f3–4	327
7–8	327

Dead Sea Scrolls (cont.)
11Q19
   57:11–14 — 134n
11QT
   11–7 — 327

1 Enoch
   62:14 — 77
   90:35 — 22n
   90:38 — 51n
   108:4 — 354
   108:10 — 354
   108:15 — 354

3 Enoch
   16:2 — 24n

4 Ezra
   3:14 — 21n
   6:51 — 77
   7:98 — 22n

Genesis Rabbah
   17:5 — 21n
   31:5 — 21n
   44:17 — 21n

Jerusalem Talmud
  Šabbat
   13b. — 172
   16:8 — 146
   16:15d — 146
  Yebamot
   1.6 — 316n
   3.1 — 316n

Josephus
  Against Apion
   1.37–43 — 150
   2.178 — 146
  Jewish Antiquities
   4.202 — 327
   7.437–438 — 133
   8.87 — 259
   9.291 — 74, 79
   11.340–341 — 74
   11.341 — 79

13.296 — 146
13.379–80 — 327
17.295 — 330
18.2.1 §28 — 28
18:12–19 — 146
18.63–64 — 323n
18.64 — 323
18.85–89 — 76
20.97–98 — 132
20.118 — 79, 80, 133
20.181 — 148
20.188 — 133
20.198 — 316, 322
20.199–203 — 322
20.205 — 315
20.224–251 — 323n
21.323 — 125
Jewish War
1.110 — 146
2.8.5 §129 — 168
2.8.5 § 138 — 168
2.8.13 §161 — 168
2.162–166 — 146
2.229–230 — 150
2.261–263 — 133
2.305 — 330
2.308 — 331
2.441 — 315
2.95 — 33
3.41–43 — 144
3.57 — 33
4.317 — 330
5.145 — 166n
5.289 — 330
5.451 — 331
5.506 — 316
5.567 — 186n
6.300–311 — 143
6.7.2 — 171
7.439–442 — 134
7.150 — 150
Life
63 — 148
80 — 148
134 — 150
193 — 315
269 — 79, 80

280 150
424–425 133

Liber antiquitatum biblicarum
23:6 21n

Martyrdom and Ascension of Isaiah
11:43 353

Mishnah
Horayot
3:4 315
Miqva'ot
8:5 168n
9:1–4 168
9:5 168n
Parah
3:5 316n
8:9 165
Pesahim
5:3 332
5:5 332
Šabbat
6:10 330
Sanhedrin
4:5 24n
6:1 309n
6:4 327
7:1 328
Sotah
9:15 143
Sukkah
4:5 162
4:9–10 162
5:2–4 123

Pesiqta Rabbati
21:6 24n

Philo
On Dreams
1.171 19n
1.239 21n
2.45 21n, 22n
On Flight and Finding
101 21n
On Planting

18 21n, 22n
20 22n
22 22n
On Rewards and Punishment
39 19n
On Sobriety
133 21n
On the Change of Names
3–6 19n
On the Confusion of Tongues
92 19n
97 21n
146 19n
147 21n
On the Creation of the World
16 21n
36 21n
146 21n
On the Eternity of the World
15 21n
On the Life of Abraham
57 19n
80 19
On the Life of Moses
2.128 259
On the Special Laws
1.81 21n
Questions and Answers on Genesis
4.138 19n
Who Is the Heir?
230 21n

Pirqe 'Abot
2:5 145n

Psalms of Solomon
8:15–20 143
17:2–9 143
17:21–25 142
17:26 136
17:28 136

Sifre Deuteronomy
37.1.3 21n
329.1.1 24n
357.5.11 21n

Testament of Benjamin		6.4	17n
10:7	134n	7.17	17n
		Civil War	
Testament of Job		1.1	17n
53:1	354		
		Corneliusnepos 25	
Testament of Joseph		13.7	15n
19:8	51n	17.1	15n
Testament of Judah		Didache	
25:1–2	134n	9	301
		9:2	302
Testament of Solomon		9:4	302
26:8	354	10	301
Tosefta		Dionysius	
'Abodah Zarah		*On Thucydides*	
3:10	146	5	355
Sanhedrin		55	358
2.2	297	*Roman Antiquities*	
Yebamot		5.8	357
1:10	316n		
		Epictetus	
CLASSICAL AND ANCIENT CHRISTIAN		1.19.26	356
WORKS			
		Epistle of Barnabas	
Acts of Peter		5:13	328
36–71	343		
		Eunapius	
Arrian		*Lives*	
Alexander 4.14.3	16n	494	16
Aseneth		Eusebius	
13:15	264	*Historia ecclesiastica*	
		2.25.8	343
Book of Thomas the Contender		3.1.2	343
138.1–3	358	3.31	12
138.1–4	354	3.31.2	33
		3.39.3–7	205
Caesar		5.23.1	303
Gallic War		5.23–25	302
1.7	17n	5.24.1–8	303
2.1	17n	5.24.2–6	304
2.9	17n	5.24.11–18	303
3.28	17n	5.24.16	304
4.13	17n	6.14.7	45n, 281
5.9	17n	6.17	357

Gospel of Mary
  10.14–15   277

Gospel of Thomas
  71   13, 35n, 41

Ignatius
  To the Smyrnaeans
    1:1–2   328

Irenaeus
  Adversus haereses
    2.22.5   239

Lucian
  Verae historiae
    1.2–4   16n
    1.5–2.47   16n

Martyrdom of Polycarp
  22   357

Maximus of Tyre
  Origin
    1.5   19n
    9.6   22n
    10.3   22n
    11.11   18, 22n
    11.12   21
    21.7–8   18
    41.5   19n

Menander Rhetor
  2.9   19n
  414.21–23   19n

Nag Hammadi Codex III
  8.6   275n
  8.18–26   275n
  76.24–77.9   275n
  78.16   275n
  81.2–10   275n
  82.7–84.11   275n
  84.17–85.6   275n
  90.14–91.20   275
  91.20–24   275
  91.24–92.6   275

  93.8–12   275n
  93.24–94.4   276n
  94.10–14   275n
  95.19–21   276n
  96.14–18   276n
  96.19–97.16   275n
  97.19–24   275n
  98.9–13   276n
  98.21–22   275n
  100.16–21   276n
  101.9–15   275n
  103.22–104.5   276n
  105.3–10   276n
  105.13–19   275n
  106.5–9   275n
  106.9–15   276n
  107.11–108.15   275n
  107.13–108.1   276n
  108.5   276n
  108.16–23   276n
  114.14–119.8   276
  119.8–16   276

Papias
  Fragment 10:17   205

Philostratus
  Vitae sophistarum
    2.21.602   15n
    2.21.604   15n

Plato
  Laws
    12.953   356

Pliny the Elder
  5.15.71   28

Polybius
  29.21.8   15n, 17
  31.23.1–31.24.12   17n
  38.19.1   17n
  38.21.1   17n
  38.22.3   17n
  39.2.2   17n

Porphyry
  Ad Marcellam
    6.103–108   19n
    7.131–134   19n
    10.180–183   19n
    16.267–268   19n
    26.415–416   19n

Seneca
  Natural Questions
    5.18.16   356

Sibylline Oracles
    3:818–29   358
    3:827–829   353

Suetonius
  The Twelve Caesars
    100   66

Tertullian
  Scorpiace
    15.3   343

Thucydides
    1.1.1   17n
    1.22.2–3   15
    2.103.2   17n
    5.26.1   17n

Xenophon
  Anabasis
    2.5.41   17n
    3.1.4–6   17n

INDEX OF MODERN AUTHORS AND AUTHORITIES

Abegg, Martin G. 329
Achtemeier, Paul 138
Albright, William 232, 232 n. 6
Alexander, Philip 181, 234
Allison, Dale 134 n. 5, 136 n. 8
Anderson, Paul 1, 4, 5, 9, 14, 17, 36, 39, 40
n. 14, 63, 102, 107, 114, 131 n. 1, 136 n.
9, 191 n. 26, 225, 227, 228, 229, 229 n. 1,
234 n. 8, 236 n. 11, 239 n. 15, 240 n. 17,
241 n. 18, 245, 256 n. 1, 258, 260, 266 n.
12, 268, 271, 272, 273, 279, 280, 318 n.
6, 321, 335 n. 1, 366, 371, 379, 380, 382,
384, 385, 388, 389
Appold, Mark 12, 27, 95, 96, 380, 381,
382, 385
Arav, Rami 28, 32
Ashton, John 140, 141, 142, 154, 184, 229
n. 1
Asiedu-Peprah, Martin 120
Assmann, Aleida 337
Atkinson, Kenneth 136
Attridge, Harold 67 n. 8
Aune, David 176 n. 4, 354, 355
Barrett, C. K. 36 n. 4, 40 n. 14, 49, 73,
131 n. 1, 133, 189 n. 17, 199 n. 43, 264
n. 9, 306, 307, 313 n. 1
Bauckham, Richard 39 n. 12, 113, 114,
126, 185, 186 nn. 3 and 6, 187, 188, 196
n. 36, 199, 200 n. 44, 201 n. 48, 205 n. 2,
217, 218, 218 n. 8, 219, 221, 221 n. 13,
223, 235, 236, 237, 240 n. 16, 241, 252,
304 n. 20, 317 n. 5, 318 n. 7, 349, 351,
352, 360, 360 n. 5, 361, 362, 372, 381,
382, 383, 384, 385
Bauer, Walter 327
Baur, Ferdinand Christian 241

Beasley-Murray, George R. 68, 182, 186,
217, 264 n. 9
Becker, Jürgen 135 n. 6
Beckwith, Roger 297, 297 n. 10
Benoit, Pierre 317 n. 5
Berger, David 333
Bernard, John Henry 193
Berrin, Shani 327
Bickerman, Elias 357
Bieringer, Reimund 285, 287
Billerbeck, Paul 145, 145 n. 5
Blaskovic, Goran 341
Blinzler, Josef 296, 297, 297 n. 9, 309,
309 n. 24, 310
Bliss, Frederick Jones 157, 157 n. 2, 171
Blomberg, Craig 124 n. 15, 125, 192,
193 n. 29, 217, 293, 293 n. 4, 317, 317
n. 5
Blount, Brian 281, 286 n. 1, 287
Bock, Darrell 326
Boismard, Marie-Èmile 24 n. 40, 55, 58,
58 n. 27, 64 n. 3
Bond, Helen 251, 252, 313, 314, 316, 316
n. 3, 321 n. 11, 365, 367, 369, 370, 376,
380, 381, 382, 383, 384, 385
Borg, Marcus 149
Borgen, Peder 37 n. 8, 137
Bousset, Wilhelm 144 n. 3
Bowie, Ewen 16 n. 6
Boyarin, Daniel 176, 176 n. 3, 179, 180
n. 9, 233
Boyd, W. J. P. 273
Brandon, Samuel 313 n. 1
Broadhead, Edwin 197 n. 38
Brodie, Thomas 189 n. 14
Broer, Ingo 345

Brown, Raymond E.   38 n. 10, 45 n. 3,
    46 n. 5, 49 n. 14, 51, 51 n. 15, 52 nn.
    16–17, 73, 88 n. 5, 97, 99, 100, 110, 113,
    121, 123, 124, 131 n. 1, 140, 189 n. 17,
    192, 193 n. 30, 214, 234, 239 n. 15, 273,
    286, 286 n. 2, 291, 313 n. 2, 314, 315,
    316, 317, 319, 320 n. 9, 341, 361, 362,
    381
Browning, Robert   238
Bruce, F. F.   22 n. 34, 315, 317 n. 5
Büchler, Adolf   144, 145
Bull, Robert   76 n. 3
Bultmann, Rudolf   1, 28, 139, 229 n. 1,
    273, 339
Burge, Gary   317
Burns, Rita   68, 68 n. 10
Burridge, Richard   16 n. 7, 250, 253, 281,
    282, 365, 373, 374, 375, 381, 384
Byrne, Brendan   217, 222 n. 16
Byrskog, Samuel   217, 217 n. 7, 241, 341
Caragounis, Chrys   345
Carleton Paget, James   323 n. 13
Carlson, Stephen   358
Carroll, Kenneth   175 n. 2
Carson, D. A.   31, 192 n. 28, 317 n. 5, 321
Carter, Charles   283
Casey, Maurice   193, 221 n. 14, 284, 285
Catchpole, David   79, 86 n. 4, 313 n. 1
Chancey, Mark   147, 257 nn. 2–3, 258,
    259, 262, 264, 366
Charlesworth, James H.   13, 63, 63 n. 1,
    65 n. 5, 99, 100, 156 n. 1, 159, 232 n. 7,
    239, 240, 317, 327, 382
Chernus, Ira   19 n. 23
Clark, Kenneth   364
Clark-Soles, Jaime   5, 249, 250, 252, 365,
    366, 367, 368, 381, 382, 385
Claussen, Carsten   20 n. 24, 339, 342
Coakley, James   200 n. 45
Coggins, Richard   80
Collins, John   56, 56 n. 21, 57, 57 n. 24,
    80, 143
Coloe, Mary   5, 13, 45, 53 n. 19, 98, 99, 119
    n. 3, 262 n. 5, 380, 381, 382, 383, 390
Conway, Colleen   200
Corley, Kathleen   197
Cranfield, Charles   197

Crossan, John Dominic   37 n. 6, 266, 300
    n. 16, 318
Culpepper, R. Alan   2, 5, 178, 252, 253,
    339 n. 11, 349, 364 n. 8, 365, 372, 373,
    381, 385
Danby, Herbert   158 n. 3, 165, 165 n. 7, 168
Danker, Frederick William   327
Daube, David   75
Davies, W. D.   136 n. 8
Dawes, Gregory   222 n. 16
Deines, Roland   149
Dettwiler, Andreas   273, 273 n. 3
Dick, Karl   351 n. 2
Dickie, Archibald   157, 157 n. 2, 171
Dietzfelbinger, Christian   23 n. 38
Dillon, John   19 n. 15
Dodd, C. H.   36, 39, 140, 182, 191 n. 27,
    199 n. 43, 214, 313, 313 n. 1, 315, 316,
    317
Doudna, Gregory   327
Drummond, James   304 n. 21
Dunkerley, Roderic   214, 219 n. 10
Dunn, James   36, 39, 42 n. 17, 43 n. 19,
    132, 149, 151 n. 10, 285, 335 n. 1, 345
Ehrman, Bart   357
Eisenman, Robert   329
Elliot, J. Keith   197
Ellis, E. Earle   285
Engle, Anita   122, 123 n. 11
Epp, Eldon Jay   21 n. 29, 21 n. 30
Ernst, Josef   49 nn. 12–13
Escaffre, Bernadette   319
Esler, Philip   189 n. 16, 215, 215 n. 4, 216
    n. 5, 241,
Estes, Douglas Charles   353
Evans, Craig   36 n. 3, 112, 131, 132, 134,
    197 n. 38, 227, 228, 382, 384
Fitzmyer, Joseph   133, 326, 328
Flusser, David   23 n. 36
Ford, David F.   37 n. 6
Fortna, Robert   36, 191 n. 25
Fotheringam, J. K.   296 n. 8
Fowler, Francis George   364
Fowler, Henry Watson   364
France, Richard   197
Frankel, Eduard   358 n. 3
Fredriksen, Paula   108, 313, 313 n. 2

Freund, Richard 32
Freyne, Sean 112, 118, 139, 142, 146, 147, 148, 152, 228, 229, 229 n. 2, 230, 230 n. 3, 235, 237, 381, 382, 383, 384
Friedländer, Moriz 144 n. 3
Fuglseth, Kåre Sigvald 37 n. 6, 39
Funk, Robert 27, 35 n. 1, 256, 316
Fusillo, Massimo 352, 353
Gadamer, Hans Georg 337
Gagnon, Robert 90, 90 n. 9
Gamble, Harry 151
Garcia, Jeffrey Paul 251, 252, 325, 365, 367, 368, 370, 371, 381, 383, 384
Gardner-Smith, Percival 187 n. 8, 191 n. 27
Genette, Gérard 353
Gerhardsson, Birger 152
Giblin, Charles 91
Gibson, Shimon 158 n. 3, 167 n. 15
Gill, Dan 166 n. 12,
Glasson, T. Francis 22 n. 34
Gnilka, Joachim 127 n. 18, 135 n. 6
Goertz, Hans Jürgen 336
Goggin, Sr. Thomas Aquinas 72
Goldsmith, Dale 283
Goodblatt, David 316
Goodman, Martin 316
Graupner, Axel 132
Graves, Robert 66 n. 6
Gray, Rebecca 316
Green, Joel 326
Grenfell, Bernard 356
Guelich, Robert 352
Gutman, S. 150
Haas, Nicu 330
Haenchen, Ernst 68, 217, 307, 320
Hägerland, Tobias 181 n. 10,
Hagner, Donald 19 n. 15
Hahn, Ferdinand 49 n. 11
Hall, Stuart George 305
Hammer, J. 273
Hanson, Anthony 24 n. 40, 134 n. 4
Harrington, Hannah 168,
Harris, Murray 201 n. 47
Harrison, R. K. 71
Hartenstein, Judith 274, 274 n. 6
Harvey, A. E. 315
Hasitchka, Martin 340 n. 13

Hays, Richard 286 n. 1
Hayward, Robert 316
Hendricks, Obery 85 n. 2
Hendriksen, William 326
Hengel, Martin 31, 43, 70, 143 n. 2, 147, 152, 204, 205, 258, 304 n. 20, 326, 329 n. 4, 330, 331
Hezser, Catherine 150
Himmelfarb, Martha 19 n. 23
Hjelm, Ingrid 74
Hoffman, Paul 88, 89 nn. 6 and 8
Holland, Scott 118 n. 2
Holmén, Tom 345
Hoover, Roy W 27
Horbury, William 134 n. 5, 176 n. 3
Horsley, Richard 134, 134 n. 4, 197 n. 39
Horst, Peter van der 176 n. 4,
Ilan, Tal 186 n. 2, 186 n. 3,
Instone-Brewer, David 180, 180 nn. 8–9, 234
Isaacs, Marie 19 n. 15
Jackson, Howard 349, 349 n. 1, 350, 351, 352, 355, 360, 360–61 n. 5, 362, 372
Jaubert, Annie 294, 294 n. 6, 295, 296, 311
Jeremias, Joachim 56, 58, 89 n. 7, 135 n. 6, 296, 297 n. 9, 298 n. 12, 301, 309, 329
Johnson, Brian 111, 112, 117, 119, 119 n. 3, 124 n. 14, 225, 226, 227, 381, 382, 383, 384
Johnson, Steve 88, 89, 89 n. 6, 89 nn. 7–8, 90, 90 n. 9, 91
Jones, Henry Stuart 326
Jonge, Marinus de 141, 142
Jowett, Benjamin 356
Judge, Peter 14, 83, 88, 90, 101, 102, 384
Juel, Donald 37 n. 4, 314
Just, S.J., Felix 1, 4, 5, 14, 380, 387
Käsemann, Ernst 10, 49, 211
Kaltner, John 328
Katz, Steven T. 176 n. 3
Kazen, Thomas 149
Keener, Craig 12, 15, 16, 16 n. 7, 17, 17 n. 12, 18 n. 13, 20, 21 nn. 25 and 28–30, 22, 23, 23 nn. 36 and 38, 24 n. 40, 87, 94, 95, 120 n. 5, 123 n. 11, 125, 187, 200, 201 n. 47, 313 n. 2, 317, 356, 380, 384, 385

Kellum, L. Scott   273
Kerr, Alan   119 n. 3, 120 n. 6
Kimelman, Reuven   176, 176 n. 3, 179, 233, 234 n. 8
Kirk, Kenneth   19 n. 15, 19 n. 23
Klausner, Joseph   299 n. 15
Klawans, Jonathan   78 n. 4
Klein, Günter   135 n. 7
Klink, Edward   113, 175, 175 n. 1, 177, 177 n. 6, 179 n. 7, 183 n. 14, 232, 233, 234, 234 n. 9, 235, 381, 384
Kloppenborg, John   88, 89 n. 8, 147 n. 8
Koehler, Ludwig   327
Koester, Craig   4, 14, 91, 92, 93, 95, 96, 379, 380, 385
Koester, Helmut   28, 277, 293 n. 4, 300, 300 n. 16
Köstenberger, Andreas   199 n. 43, 317 n. 5
Kuhn, Heinz-Wolfgang   28
Kundsin, Karl   28, 95, 236 n. 12
Kvalbein, Hans   345
Kysar, Robert   286, 286 n. 3
Labahn, Michael   252, 253, 335, 335 n. 3, 339, 339 n. 10, 341, 341 n. 14, 348, 365, 374, 375, 376, 381, 382, 385
Lake, Kirsopp   303
Lamouille, Arnaud   64 n. 3
Lang, Manfred   335
Latourelle, René   191 n. 25, 193
Layton, Bentley   274, 358
Leal, Juan   59 n. 28
Lee, Dorothy   60 n. 32
Léon-Dufour, Xavier   64 n. 4, 288
Liddell, Henry George   326
Lietzmann, Hans   298 n. 11, 302 n. 19
Lieu, Judith   35, 39, 285
Lincoln, Andrew   73, 186, 190 n. 20, 199 n. 43, 206, 211, 217, 279, 284, 315, 339, 342, 343, 360, 361 n. 6, 363
Lindars, Barnabas   38 n. 9, 40 nn. 14–15, 75, 178, 189 nn. 14 and 17, 193 n. 30, 194, 214 n. 3, 222–23 n. 16, 309 n. 24
Lohse, Bernhard   22 n. 34, 304 n. 21
Lord, Albert   43 n. 19
Lorenz, Chris   336 n. 5
Lutz, Cora   19 n. 20
Magen, Yitzhaq   75 n. 2, 76 n. 3

Mahoney, Aidan   319 n. 8
Malina, Bruce   340 n. 13
Marchadour, Alain   191 n. 25
Marcus, Joel   77
Maritz, Petrus   335 n. 3, 340 n. 12
Marshall, I. Howard   326
Martin, James   215
Martyn, J. Louis   93, 110, 113, 140, 175, 175 n. 2, 176, 176 n. 3, 177, 177 n. 6, 178, 179, 180, 181, 181 n. 10, 182, 183, 183 n. 13, 184, 232, 233, 234, 234 n. 9, 286, 286 nn. 2–3, 381
Mason, Steve   316
Matera, Frank   281, 282, 286 n. 1
Matson, Mark   36, 36 n. 3, 191 n. 26, 250, 251, 252, 291, 298 n. 11, 332, 365, 367, 368, 369, 376, 381, 382, 383, 385
Mayo, Philip   176 n. 4
McGrath, James   12, 13, 35, 97, 98, 381, 383, 384
McKnight, Scot   134 n. 5
McLaren, James   315
Meeks, Wayne   73, 176 n. 3, 178, 179, 181, 234 n. 9, 281, 285, 320
Meier, John   42 n. 18, 46 n. 4, 47, 48, 48 nn. 8 and 10, 49 n. 12, 52, 53, 55, 55 n. 20, 74, 79, 85, 86, 86 n. 4, 135 n. 6, 191 n. 25, 213 n. 1, 214, 215, 217, 219 nn. 9–10, 222, 222 n. 16, 241, 256 n. 1, 268, 291 n. 1, 299 n. 15, 300 n. 16, 323 n. 13, 337 n. 7
Menken, Maarten   50, 51
Merkle, Stefan   16 n. 6
Merz, Annette   42 n. 18, 121 n. 7, 143, 230, 291 n. 1, 299 n. 15, 300 n. 16
Metzger, Bruce   49 n. 13, 75 n. 1, 189 n. 15
Meyer, Ben   36 n. 3, 135 n. 6
Meyer, Rudolf   145 n. 4, 147
Milavec, Aaron   301
Millar, Fergus   313 n. 1
Miller, Johnny   332
Miller, Susan   13, 14, 73, 100, 101, 382, 383
Mitchell, Margaret   203
Moloney, Francis   46 n. 4, 48 n. 9, 51, 52 n. 16, 53, 59 n. 29, 85, 85 n. 3, 87, 91, 92, 93, 100, 262 n. 5, 273, 286, 335, 335 nn. 1–2

Moore, Carey 357
Morris, Leon 190 n. 21
Motyer, Stephen 117, 126, 176 n. 3
Moulton, James 351 n. 2
Mowvley, Henry 24 n. 40
Moxter, Michael 337 n. 6
Mulder, Martin Jan 151 n. 11
Murphy, Catherine 46 n. 4, 47, 52
Murphy-O'Connor, Jerome 41 n. 16
Nautin, Pierre 305
Neagoe, Alexandru 197 n. 40, 314
Neale, D. 182, 234
Neirynck, Frans 88 n. 5, 92, 340, 340 n. 13, 341
Neusner, Jacob 146
Neyrey, Jerome 261, 261 n. 4, 262, 264, 267, 340, 343
Niederwimmer, Kurt 301
Nock, Arthur Darby 16
Nolland, Thomas 326
North, Wendy E. Sproston 215, 241
O'Collins, Gerald 326
O'Day, Gail 4, 242 n. 19, 252, 253, 262 n. 6, 365, 380, 384, 385
Oberweis, Michael 206
Oden, Robert 67 n. 8
Ong, Walter 252, 341
Oppenheimer, Aharon 145 n. 4, 145 n. 6, 146
Os, Bas van 250, 253, 271, 365, 371, 372, 381, 384, 385
Painter, John 14, 83, 84, 84 n. 1, 85, 91, 92, 363 n. 7
Parker, Richard Anthony 239, 239 n. 13, 239 n. 14, 296, 296 n. 8
Parsenios, George 273 n. 4
Perkins, Pheme 274
Piper, Ronald 189 n. 16, 215, 215 n. 4, 216 n. 5, 241
Plummer, Alfred 326
Pöhlmann, Wolfgang 345
Popp, Thomas 340 n. 12
Press, Jeremy 165 n. 10, 256, 256 n. 1, 257
Purvis, James 80
Reardon, Brian 353
Reed, Jonathan 147

Reich, Ronny 156, 156 n. 1, 158, 158 n. 3, 159, 160, 160 n. 5, 163, 164, 167, 167 n. 16, 171, 173, 173 n. 22
Reinhartz, Adele 121, 177, 233
Reiser, Marius 135 n. 6
Richardson, Cyril 304 n. 21, 305, 305 n. 22
Richardson, Robert 302 n. 19
Ricoeur, Paul 61, 61 n. 34, 152
Riesner, Rainer 152
Riggs, John 301 n. 17
Ringe, Sharon 21 n. 28, 262 n. 7, 263
Ritt, Hubert 348
Robinson, James M. 88, 89 n. 8, 91, 274, 296 n. 8, 354
Robinson, John A. T. 2, 40, 40 n. 15, 41, 41 n. 16, 49 n. 13, 118 n. 2, 195 n. 32, 285, 296, 296 n. 8
Rodda, Richard 364
Rohrbaugh, Richard L. 340 n. 13
Rousseau, John 28
Rouwhorst, Gerard 305, 306
Rubenstein, Jeffrey 121, 122, 122 n. 10, 125
Ruckstuhl, Eugen 294 n. 6
Rutherford, Ian 358
Sacchi, Paolo 332
Saldarini, Anthony 146 n. 7, 152
Sanders, E. P. 39, 39 n. 12, 40 n. 14, 79, 135, 135 n. 6, 147, 148, 149, 158 n. 3, 164 n. 6, 167 n. 15, 169, 258, 268, 316, 318
Satlow, Frank 56 n. 22, 58, 60 n. 33
Schäfer, Peter 176 n. 3
Schauss, Hayyim 125
Schenk, Wolfgang 349 n. 1
Schiffman, Lawrence 329
Schleiermacher, Friedrich 27
Schmidt, Carl 304, 305, 305 n. 22
Schnackenburg, Rudolf 131 n. 1, 217, 239 n. 13, 291 n. 2, 307, 308, 362
Schneemelcher, Wilhelm 274
Schneider, Johannes 319 n. 8
Schneiders, Sandra 45 n. 2, 215, 262 n. 5, 322
Schnelle, Udo 86 n. 4, 335, 337 n. 6, 342, 345, 348
Schoch, Karl 296 n. 8

Schoedel, William   205
Scholtissek, Klaus   273
Schrage, Wolfgang   286, 286 n. 1, 288
Schrijvers, P. H.   358, 358 n. 3
Schröter, Jens   336, 337, 338 n. 8
Schürer, Emil   144 n. 3, 145 n. 4
Schüssler Fiorenza, Elisabeth 197, 197 n. 39
Schwartz, Daniel   323
Schweizer, Eduard   298 n. 12
Scobie, Charles   73
Scott, Ernest Findlay   40 n. 13
Scott, Robert   326
Segal, Judah Benzion   125 n. 17
Segovia, Fernando   2, 273
Selms, Adrianus van   53 n. 19, 57, 57 n. 25
Seneca, Lucius Annaeus   356
Senior, Donald   313 n. 2
Shanks, Herschel   156 n. 1, 164
Shukron, Eli   156, 156 n. 1, 158, 159, 160,
    160 n. 5, 164, 167, 167 n. 16, 173, 173 n.
    22
Smalley, Stephen   362
Smith, D. Moody   5, 14, 16, 17 n. 12, 36, 36
    n. 2, 63, 64, 65, 84 n. 1, 88, 92, 97, 234 n.
    9, 286 n. 3, 291 n. 2, 313, 313 n. 2, 317,
    318 n. 6, 335 n. 1, 341 n. 14, 342, 347
Smith, Jonathan   143 n. 1
Smith, T. C.   175 n. 2
Söding, Thomas   154, 339
Spiro, Abram   80
Stanton, Graham   204
Stapfer, Edmond   56, 56 n. 21, 57, 58
Stauffer, Ethelbert   190 n. 19
Stemberger, Günter   176 n. 3
Stephens, Susan   16 n. 6
Sterling, Gregory   263, 263 n. 8
Steward-Sykes, Alistair   305
Stibbe, Mark   190 n. 19, 193 n. 29
Story, Cullen   293 n. 5
Strack, Hermann   145, 145 n. 5
Strand, Kenneth   304 n. 21
Strawn, Brent   328
Strickert, Fred   31
Sweet, J. P. M.   37 n. 6, 43 n. 19
Swenson, Kristan   328
Swete, Henry Barclay   195 n. 34
Talbert, Charles   43 n. 19, 342, 343

Tanghe, Vincent   186 n. 5,
Tatum, W. Barnes   52 n. 16
Taylor, Joan   47 n. 7, 53 n. 18
Thatcher, Tom   1, 4, 14, 97, 126, 209, 279,
    335, 364, 380, 390
Theissen, Gerd   42 n. 18, 121 n. 7, 143,
    143 n. 1, 152, 153, 195, 195 nn. 33–34,
    196, 230, 291 n. 1, 299 n. 15, 300 n. 16
Thiselton, Anthony   97
Thomas, John Christopher   200 n. 44, 259,
    260, 264
Thompson, Marianne Meye   93, 95, 283,
    285, 380
Thyen, Hartwig   335, 341
Tomson, Peter   286
Torrey, Charles   293 n. 4, 293 n. 5, 332
Tovey, Derek   114, 213, 214 n. 2, 222 n. 15,
    240, 241, 242, 381, 382, 384
Trumbower, Jeffrey   132
Trumbull, H. Clay   56, 56 n. 21, 57, 57 n.
    26, 59 n. 30
Twelftree, Graham   190 n. 19, 193
Tzaferis, Vassilios   330, 331
Urman, Dan   150
Vall, Gregory   328
Van Belle, Gilbert   87, 88 n. 5, 335 n. 3,
    340 n. 12
VanderKam, James C.   123, 124, 196, 295
    n. 7
Verhey, Allen   286 n. 1
Vermes, Geza   329
Vielhauer, Philipp   135 n. 6
Visotsky, Burton   121
Vööbus, Arthur   301, 302
Wahlde, Urban von   17, 63, 63 n. 1, 112,
    113, 155, 230, 231, 232, 232 nn. 6–7,
    381, 382, 383, 384
Watson, Wilfred   69 n. 12
Watt, Jan van der   343 n. 16
Wenham, David   182 n. 12
Werline, Rodney   136
Wescott, Brooke Foss   68
Wiarda, Timothy   190 n. 18
Wight, Fred Hartley   56, 57 n. 26, 58
Wilckens, Ulrich   344 n. 19
Wilken, Robert   179
Wilkinson, John   166 n. 13,

Williams, Cartin 341 n. 14
Wilson, Stephen 176, 176 n. 3, 176 n. 5, 233
Winter, Paul 291 n. 1, 329
Wise, Michael 329
Witherington, Ben, III 21 n. 28, 114, 189 n. 13, 190 n. 19, 193, 193 nn. 29–30, 194, 199 n. 42, 203, 211, 237, 238, 239, 240, 337, 381, 382, 383, 384, 385, 388, 389
Wolter, Michael 132
Wrede, Wilhelm 175 n. 2
Wright, Benjamin 158 n. 3

Wright, N. T. 323
Yamauchi, Edwin 57, 57 n. 24, 60 n. 33
Yee, Gale 123 n. 13
Young, Brad 328 n. 2
Young, Douglas 358
Young, Frances 37 n. 6
Zahn, Theodor 68
Zeitlin, Solomon 332
Zias, Joe 327
Zimmermann, Johannes 142
Zumstein, Jean 252, 338, 338 n. 9, 339, 343, 345, 347, 347 n. 21

CPSIA information can be obtained at www.ICGtesting.com
Printed in the USA
LVOW07s2105281015

459993LV00004B/168/P